EAST EUROPEAN MONOGRAPHS, NO. CXXII


Library of Congress Card Catalog Number 81-50886
ISBN - 0-930888-19-7

Printed in the United States of America

# East Central European Society and W
# in the Pre-Revolutionary Eighteenth Cent

Gunther E. Rothenberg,
Béla K. Király and Peter F. Sugar,
Editors

SOCIAL SCIENCE MONOGRAPHS, BOULDER
DISTRIBUTED BY COLUMBIA UNIVERSITY PRESS, NEW YORK

1982

ATLANTIC STUDIES

Brooklyn College Studies on Society in Change
No. 11
Editor-in-Chief Béla K. Király

*War and Society in East Central Europe*
*Vol. II*

## Contents

# Acknowledgement

Brooklyn College Program on Society in Change conducts research, organizes conferences and publishes scholarly books. The Program has been commissioned, encouraged and supported by Dr. Robert L. Hess, the President of Brooklyn College. The National Endowment for the Humanities awarded the Program a research grant for the year of 1978–1981, which was renewed for another three-year term (1981–1984). Without these substantial and much appreciated supports, the Program could not realize its goals, indeed could not exist. Additional financial contributions helped us in completing the research, holding conferences and covering the costs of preparation of the manuscript for publication. Among those institutions that aided our work are the Austrian Institute, The Center for European Studies (East European Section) Graduate School CUNY, The Center for Byzantine and Modern Greek Studies Queens College CUNY, The Institute on East Central Europe Columbia University, and The Kosciuszko Foundation.

The copy editing was done by Mr. Peter Beales, and the preparation of the manuscript for publication by Mrs. Dorothy Meyerson and Mr. Jonathan A. Chanis, both on the staff of Brooklyn College Program on Society in Change.

For all these institutions and personalities, I wish to express my most sincere appreciation and thanks.

Highland Lakes, New Jersey, October 23, 1981.

Béla K. Király
Professor of History
Editor-in-Chief

# Preface

The present volume is the second of a series which, when completed, hopes to present a comprehensive survey of the many aspects of War and Society in East Central Europe. The chapters of this, the previous, and forthcoming volumes are selected from papers presented at a series of international, interdisciplinary, scholarly conferences. Some were solicited for the sake of comprehension.

These volumes deal with the peoples whose homelands lie between the Germans to the west, the Russians to the east and north, and the Mediterranean and Adriatic seas to the south. They constitute a particular civilization, an integral part of Europe, yet substantially different from the West. Within the area there are intriguing variations in language, religion, and government; so, too, are there differences in concepts of national defense, of the characters of the armed forces, and of the ways of waging war. Study of this complex subject demands a multidisciplinary approach; therefore, we have involved scholars from several disciplines, from universities and other scholarly institutions of the USA, Canada, and Western Europe, as well as the East Central European socialist countries.

Our investigation focuses on a comparative survey of military behavior and organization in these various nations and ethnic groups to see what is peculiar to them, what has been socially and culturally determined, and what in their conduct of war was due to circumstance. Besides making a historical survey, we try to define different patterns of military behavior, including the decision-making processes, the attitudes and actions of diverse social classes, and the restraints or lack of them shown in war.

We endeavor to present considerable material on the effects of social, economic, political, and technological changes, and of changes in the sciences and in international relations on the development of doctrines of national defense and practices in military organization, command, strategy, and tactics. We shall also present data on the social origins and mobility of the officer corps and the rank and file, on the differences between the officer corps of the various services, and above all, on the civil-military relationship and the origins of the East Central European brand of militarism. These studies will, we hope, result in a better understanding of the societies, governments, and politics of East Central Europe, most of whose states are now members of the Warsaw Treaty Organization, although one is a member of NATO and two are neutral.

Our methodology takes into account that in the last three decades the study of war and national defense systems has moved away from narrow concern with battles, campaigns, and leaders and has come to concern itself with the evolution of the entire society. In fact, the interdependence of changes in society and changes in warfare, and the proposition that military institutions closely reflect the character of the society of which they are a part have come to be accepted by historians, political scientists, sociologists, philosophers, and other students of war and national defense. Recognition of this fact constitutes one of the keystones of our approach to the subject.

Works in Western languages adequately cover the diplomatic, political, intellectual, social, and economic histories of these peoples and this area. In contrast, few substantial studies of their national defense systems have yet appeared in Western languages. Similarly, though some substantial, comprehensive accounts of the nonmilitary aspects of the history of the whole region have been published in the West, nothing has yet appeared in any Western language about the national defense systems of the area as a whole. Nor is there any study of the mutual effects of the concepts and practices of national defense in East Central Europe. Thus, this comprehensive study on War and Society in East Central Europe is a pioneering work.

The eighteenth and nineteenth centuries, the first period our efforts concentrate upon, are crucial for all these nations, for they are the era of nation-building. Many of these peoples became nation-states during the period, a development in which their armed forces played critical roles. Even in the case of the Poles, whose state was partitioned in the eighteenth century and was not to be reestablished until after the nineteenth century, insurrectionary armies played an important role in consolidating national consciousness. The period this volume covers is the spring board of all these.

The Editors, of course, have the duty of assuring the comprehensive coverage, cohesion, internal balance, and scholarly standards of the series they have launched. They cheerfully accept this responsibility and intend this work to be neither a justification nor a condemnation of the policies, attitudes, or activities of any of the nations involved. At the same time, because so many different disciplines, languages, interpretations, and schools of thought are represented, their policy in this and in future volumes was and shall be not to interfere with the contributions of the various participants, but to present them as a sampling of the schools of thought and the standards of scholarship in the many countries to which the contributors belong.

The Editors.

# EAST CENTRAL EUROPE IN 1713

NOTES

① TO HABSBURGS IN 1718

② TO THE OTTOMAN EMPIRE IN 1739

# I

# War and Society in Western and East Central Europe

Béla K. Király

# War and Society in Western and East Central Europe in the Pre-Revolutionary Eighteenth Century

This volume is an integral part of a series on "War and Society in East Central Europe". This series in its own turn is the product of a six year research project. The contributors to this volume, like the participants in the six year research program, constitute a multidisciplinary, international group of scholars within which scholars of the area are prominently represented. The series when completed in 1984, will present a comprehensive study of the theme up to 1920, the consolidation of the post World War I states of East Central Europe and the completion of the building of their national defense forces.

In considering the relationship between war and society in the context of history of warfare, pre-revolutionary eighteenth century forms a watershed. That is the time when infantry firepower began really to affect tactics substantially.

The predominant Western European armed forces in the pre-revolutionary eighteenth century were the standing armies of absolute kings. In the words of J.F.C. Fuller: ". . . the army took the form of a disciplined body of long service troops, set apart from the civil population, and rigorously restricted as to its conduct in peace and war. . . ."[1] This definition shows the potential of and the limitations on eighteenth-century standing armies. Rigorous discipline, separation from the civilian population, and numerous other restrictions imposed on the soldiery made the standing army a tool of the monarch alone. Long terms of service assured a high degree of professionalism and efficiency. But the poverty of state treasuries and the low capacity of the preindustrial manufacturing system, drastically limited both the size and the range of action of such ar-

The author wishes to express his indebtedness to the John Simon Guggenheim Memorial Foundation for a fellowship grant which made the basic research possible, and to the National Endowment for the Humanities for a research grant which made it possible to complete the research of which this essay contains a part.

mies. Wars waged by these armies had to be, and were, limited in goals, scope, and final effects. These wars were, in fact, the only kind compatible with the balance of power, the prevailing system of international relations. "Restricted warfare," Ferrero comments, "was one of the loftiest achievements of the eighteenth century. It belongs to a class of hot-house plants which can only thrive in an aristocratic and qualitative civilization. We are no longer capable of it. It is one of the fine things we have lost as the result of the French Revolution."[2]

We ask now whether there is any difference between the Western and East Central European evolution of warfare, and what the differences may be? The full answer will be given only in the last volume of this series. For the time being, three samples of East Central European warfare will be presented to allow us to glance at its peculiarities and to see some similarities to and differences from their Western counterparts. These three samples describe certain features of East Central European standing armies; they show the revolutionary nature of warfare during the period and the predominance of war for liberation. Finally, they offer a short analysis of the Hungarian war of liberation, the Rákóczi Insurrection of 1703–1711 which, in various respects, embodied what might be considered characteristic East Central European forms of warfare.

## East Central European Professional Standing Armies

The only truly East Central European standing army at the turn of the century was the army of the Polish-Lithuanian Commonwealth. It entered the eighteenth century as a significant force, bearing the marks of the reforming zeal of John III Sobieski, the last native king of prepartition Poland (1674–96). The many reforms this soldier-king introduced into both the army of the *Korona* (Crown of Poland) and the army of the Grand Duchy of Lithuania included the transformation of infantry by increasing its fire power—through a 30 percent reduction of pikemen, with the concomitant increase of soldiers equipped with firearms. Sobieski also modernized training, improved discipline, increased tactical efficiency, and stressed cooperation in battle between the various branches of the army. Although the cavalry was still destined to launch the final blow, a massive charge against the enemy, already shaken by the infantry and artillery; nonetheless, typical, traditional Polish cavalry warfare, large scale, rapid mobile operations behind enemy lines, was not discontinued but rather encouraged. In such operations, the infantry support that the cavalry needed in actual combat was supplied by dragoons.

Reform continued even after Sobieski's death. In 1701 the flintlock musket, complete with bayonet, was introduced; these changes, combined with up-to-date tactical doctrines and good discipline, kept the Polish standing army abreast of Western development for a while. But the remarkable performance of the Polish army in relieving Vienna from the protracted Ottoman siege, in September 1683, was in fact the swan song of that kind of Polish armed force which was a factor that European powers could disregard only at their peril. The eighteenth century witnessed the rapid decline of this force, in direct relation to the decay of the Polish state. The army's retrogression in numbers, equipment, discipline, and training gradually made it an anachronism. Even the traditional Polish cavalry lost its former prominence. In prepartition Poland, financial, political, and other domestic difficulties caused the army to reduce its effectives even beyond the official budget estimates. The Kingdom of Poland, proper, was supposed to keep only a meagre force, 8,000 strong, but it maintained only 4,700 men in the army. The Grand Duchy of Lithuania was supposed to have an army of 2,300 strong, but only 1,500 effectives served under arms[3] before the first partition of Poland.

There is no need to drag Marshal de Saxe into East Central European military history, his desire and defeated effort to become the sovereign of the Duchy of Courland, notwithstanding.[4] But among his remarkable essays on war there is a study on Poland which makes exciting and informative reading on at least two counts: It vividly indicates the Polish war potential in mid-eighteenth century—in that respect it is indeed East Central European military history. Secondly, the Marshal presents a remarkably nonapologetic recipe for the conquest of Poland. The essay is a pragmatic, professional description of how a modern army should conquer a country whose economy, transportation, and system of defense are all underdeveloped and inadequate. From these pages, Marshal de Saxe, one of the foremost captains of the age, emerges completely enmeshed in his professional calling, scrupulously sticking to his own theme, the technique of military conquest; he remains totally unaware that he is advocating an act, ruthlessly aggressive politically and bloodily destructive of an innocent population.

Polanders [he writes] "make war in such a vague and irregular manner that if an enemy makes a point of pursuing them, he will thereby be presently rendered incapable of opposing their continual inroads. It is much more prudent, therefore, not to pursue them at all, but to possess himself of certain posts upon the rivers, to fortify them, to erect barracks for his troops, and to raise contributions throughout the provinces. . . ."[5] The Poles have no artillery worth mentioning, no siege tools nor ammunition enough to challenge the strong points an occupying force might erect. Poles have only cavalry. The Poles waged unconventional warfare with customs strange to Western armies. In 1716, Saxe claims, ". . . troops which surrendered on terms were massacred, but the eighty regular horsemen, who defended themselves at Jarislaw (sic), and marched 100 leagues to Warsaw could not be defeated by the Poles and reached the capital city with only sixteen men lost. . . ."[6] In other words, disciplined, cohesive, regular professional forces were, in Saxe's view, so superior that they could match irregulars many times over their own strength.

Polish cavalry was extremely light—it could ride thirty to forty miles a day in very large bodies and fall upon the enemy before proper reconnaissance could even be completed. Polish peasants and common people in the cities readily gave their cavalry compatriots intelligence. The only counter to such a cavalry army was a system of scattered infantry strongpoints. Therefore, de Saxe recommends conquest and fortification of the northern cities—Danzig (Gdańsk), Thorn (Toruń)—as bases of operation, supplied from the sea. From there, the conqueror could gradually advance inland, building more and more fortified places. "The whole country would be so effectually covered by this disposition, that it must infallibly be reduced to the necessity of submitting patiently to the yoke. . . ." All this, Saxe estimates, could be done by 48,000 infantry and 3,800 horses. The means of conquest should be earthworks rather than battles.[7]

Even the necessary artillery could be manufactured in the area. The Swedes would produce light pieces with carriages in great quantity and cheap; all of these could be shipped down the Vistula River to the forts. Controlling the country with the network of fortifications enables you ". . . to offer what terms of accommodation you please; [you] can impose your own laws, and see them carried into execution. . . ."[8]

Marshal de Saxe's recipe for the conquest of Poland is a blueprint for war against nonregular forces. Strong points at mutually supporting distances, located at waterways, through which they could be supplied, assures the conqueror that its "yoke" will be securely imposed. This indeed was what the British tried in America, during the Revolution, and during the Boer War. It is not too much to say that Saxe's blueprint was tried by the French in Southeast Asia as well as in Algeria, and failed. In the same way, Saxe's was the basic idea behind the American "pacification" efforts that miscarried in Vietnam. What de Saxe describes as the best method of conquest was studied and faced from the other side of the hill by twentieth-century "irregulars" like Mao Tse-tung, Ernesto Che Guevera, Vo Nguyen Giap, and others.

The destruction of Poland, however, was not achieved by the methods de Saxe recommended, but by massive conventional warfare of three great powers, against which the Poles were all but defenseless. Before the partitions, however, a remarkable revival occurred. The reforms after the first partition included the fundamental transformation and modernization of the army. The law of 1789 called for a modern force of 100,000 men. Political as well as financial difficulties, however, proved this a utopian expectation much beyond the realm of reality. The principle of voluntary enlistment, which the law envisaged, did not work; the projected effectives had to be reduced to 60,000 men. Even this number could not be secured. The Prussian type of cantonal system was therefore introduced. Every fifty farms owned by the crown and/or the clergy and every hundred farms owned by the nobility had to send one man to the new army. A modest improvement was achieved, yet the projected number of men could not be secured. Yet those who did join the army were very well trained, on the basis of up-to-date tactical doctrine. In short, the army organized after the first partition of Poland was made into a force of great combat value, albeit restricted size. This army became a nucleus, which could and indeed did expand rapidly in the initial stages of the Kościuszko Insurrection of 1794 into a force of 100,000.[9] This served as a rallying point for the more general uprising, a role quite similar to that of General Washington's Continental Army during the American Revolution, the subject of volume IV, of this series.

Another major East Central European standing army was the Hungarian portion of the Habsburg armed forces. Ever since the Ottoman onslaught in the sixteenth century, Hungary maintained a permanent military force in fortified areas which stretched from the Adriatic Sea to the Upper Tisza region.[10] These permanent forces were combined with the periodic call up of the Hungarian noble *levée* (*insurrectio*). Count Miklós Zrínyi (1620–64), prominent as a Hungarian commander and military theorist, strongly advocated a native standing army as the one sure means for liberating Hungary from Ottoman rule.[11] It was to no avail; the Habsburg dynasty prevented the creation of such force, lest an autonomous Hungarian standing army turn against the Habsburgs rather than the Turks. Hungary was liberated by standing armies in which Hungarians could and did serve as individuals, but not by a Hungarian national force.

During the War for Independence of Ferenc II Rákóczi (1703–1711), efforts were made to establish a permanent military force with an officers' school and a professional officer corps. But this war had only an indirect effect on future Hungarian military institutions. The war ended in the Compromise of Szatmár in 1711. The Hungarians acknowledged the Habsburg dynasty's hereditary rights in the male line. The dynasty, on the other hand, reestablished Hungary's constitutional self-government and acknowledged all the traditional privileges of the estates, including the tax-exempt status of the nobility. The dynasty's effort to tax the Hungarian nobility, as it taxed the nobility of the hereditary provinces, failed. Thus the substantial funds earmarked for military purposes which the taxation of the Hungarian nobles was expected to provide had to be supplemented from other sources. The solution was in concord with the Szatmár Compromise.

As in so many other compromises between the dynasty and the Hungarian estates, the serfs paid the bill. The dynasty persuaded the diet of 1715 to adopt a law which established the Hungarian standing army (*állandó hadsereg*). This army was to be an integral part of the Habsburg forces, maintained at Hungary's (that is, the serfs') expense. The law stated that the nobility were obliged to appear in arms, in defense of the country, and that, if necessary, the monarch would enforce the obligation. The law further stipulated that since this form of defense was insufficient, a Hungarian standing army, made up of both natives and foreigners, was to be established. Recruits and the tax (*contributio* or *subsidium*) needed to maintain them were to be voted by the estates assembled in the diet. The statute remained in force until the April laws of 1848 were promulgated. For a century and a half, this system represented three political and social realities prevailing in Hungary.

Only serfs served; the taxes needed for the upkeep of the army were paid by serfs and burghers alone. The nobility's contribution to national defense, the noble *levée,* was indeed summoned occasionally, and fought with considerable effect during the Seven Years War. During the French Revolutionary and Napoleonic wars, it was called up several times, but fought only once, at the Battle of Györ on June 24, 1809. The nobles' army was smashed by Napoleon's easternmost column. There was a prolonged debate on the causes of the debacle. Some called it a shameful cowardly affair, others depicted it as the last gallant stand of the noble *levée.* Whether individual nobles in this battle were heroic or cowardly was irrelevant. The *levée* was utterly obsolete; it could not stand against the modern equipment, training, and cohesion of the masses under Napoleon's command. Never again was the *levée* called to arms, as it will be exposed in volume IV.

The Hungarian army (*állandó hadsereg*), an integral part of the Habsburg standing army, was as modern as any other unit of that force, but like the rest, the Hungarian army was under the exclusive authority of the monarch; the Hungarian estates had no influence over its organization, command, and/or conduct. Hence the army was less a national defense force in Hungary's service than a means to further Habsburg power within the empire and internationally.

Because the diet had to vote war taxes and recruits, the nobility, the dominant factor in the diet, gained political leverage. The nobles could, and often did, refuse to vote taxes and/or recruits until the monarch accepted their views on other matters. The Hungarian standing army thus meant burdens for the nonprivileged, political bargaining power for the privileged, and a considerable asset for the dynasty.

The units of the standing army were housed in the serfs' dwellings because barrack construction, a general trend in the West, started late in Hungary and moved very slowly.

In the 1790–92 Hungarian revolt, feudal and protonationalist though it was, a grass-roots tendency began to incorporate the Hungarian standing army into the Hungarian body politic. There were stirrings in Hungarian units. Officers, commissioned and noncommissioned, signed petitions demanding a Hungarian supreme command, Hungarian as the language of command, and greater advancement for native officers and noncoms.[12] This movement failed, however, when another compromise between the estates and the dynasty was reached in 1792. The ever-increasing uproar of the French Revolution hastened the closing of ranks between the dynasty and the Hungarian estates.

At the southern flank of East Central Europe, in the Balkans, there were no typical native standing armies during the eighteenth century.[13] Nearest, were the mercenary forces of the Danubian princes which were abolished in 1711.

## East Central European Revolutionary Warfare: The Cycle of Wars for Liberation

The pivotal contrast between Western and East Central European warfare of the era studied was that, in the West, wars were limited in goal, in scope, and, concomitantly, in their results; in East Central Europe, on the other hand, wars were often ideological, more violent, with far less limited goals and more lasting results.

These tendencies, in turn, had roots in the previous centuries, when many of the wars waged in East Central Europe were between alien cultures, rather than between members of the same culture, as in the West. East Central Europe was the borderland where the Christian West fought its centuries-long struggle with the Islamic Ottoman power. Even when the Great Powers of the two opposite camps were at peace, a major portion of East Central Europe remained a zone of protracted, violent, unconventional small wars between people who belonged to different civilizations.

East Central Europeans fought their small wars alone and served as auxiliaries in the armies of the major powers—often on both sides—during major wars; even then, they generally carried on irregular warfare. The knowledge of, and skill in, this kind of warfare which East Central Europeans had amassed during the centuries was utilized for their own purposes first by the Ottomans, then by Habsburgs and Romanovs. Russia and Austria gradually incorporated East Central European contingents into their military establishments.

East Central Europeans in the service of the Great Powers remained most effective when they were permitted to retain their traditional command and organizational structure, their internal autonomy, and their unconventional tactics. As the two Great Powers tried first to regulate their military behavior, then to incorporate these units as the most cheaply sustained parts of their standing armies, their efficiency declined. Circumstances rather than internal strength kept the troops of the Habsburg Military Border in existence into the late nineteenth century and retained the Cossack military structure in Russia until the end of World War I.

At the opening of the period we are studying, East Central European military formations, their command structure and tactics, were quite alien to Western European military doctrine and practices. For example Lieutenant-General Feuquières (1648–1711) analyzed the Hungarian insurrection of the 1670s and 1680s. That insurrection was a response to the execution of the leaders of Wesselényi *Fronde* (April 30–December 1, 1671), the occupation of Hungary by German troops, and the suppression of the Hungarian constitutional government and its replacement on February 27, 1673, by a *gubernium*, an institution of absolute rule headed by the Grand Master of the Teutonic Order, Johann Ampringen. The rapidly spreading insurrection secured French cooperation; this brought into Hungary a French-Polish force, 2,000 strong, commissioned by Louis XIV. Hence the intimate French experience with this war. The insurrection raged to nearly the end of the century; its leader since November 1, 1678, was a leading Hungarian aristocrat, Count Imre Thököly.[14] The exposition of this war to be found in volume III of this series.

General Feuquières correctly recognized the precondition of this protracted insurrection as the precondition of any war of liberation: a high degree of motivation among a large number of warriors. That motivation grows out of sociopolitical doctrines, interests, and goals. Feuquières emphasized that the Hungarians were fighting for the constitutional prerogatives of their country which the Habsburg rulers tried to suppress by "Poison, Dagger, and Murder of the [Hungarian] Grandees. . . ."[15] He asserted that "the Hungarian cause was just," for the Habsburg rulers had violated their obligations as sovereigns. These obligations include, according to Feuquières, circumspect administration. General sedition is usually the sign of a policy which incenses large portions of the population. That is what the Habsburgs did in Hungary, Feuquieres claims, "if the Emperor, had not distressed the Protestants and the Grandees of Hungary . . . if he had not subverted the Privileges of the whole Nation . . . this Commotion would not have been so general as it proved. . . ."[16]

Feuquières' observations were not isolated. Guibert, as well as

Duteil, Wimpfen, and the ambitious and diligent translator and interpreter of late eighteenth-century, French military works, Lieutenant-Colonel John MacDonald, also wrote about the East Central European military experience. The French officers who participated in the late seventeenth-century Hungarian insurgent wars either as combatants or as military advisors were much impressed by the performance of Hungarian light horse, and brought several *huszárokat* (*hussars*, light cavalrymen) back to France. This inspired Marshal Luxembourg to raise in 1692 the first French hussar regiment (called *mortagni*).[17] Marshal Villars then created a second, and the Elector of Bavaria presented the King of France with a third complete light horse regiment. Marshal Brissac formed the first dragoon regiment on the same pattern. The French adaptation of the Hungarian military experience was then copied all over Europe, as was natural, for the French army was considered the foremost continental armed force, and its methods were often accepted by other European armies.

Guibert describes the Hungarian light horse as basically dragoon troops. They did wear neither boots nor spurs. They fought as infantry, their horses tied together two by two and left behind the firing line. Guibert explains that early in the eighteenth century the Hungarian estates had made their peace with the Habsburg dynasty.[18] Thus Maria Theresa was able to incorporate into her armed forces numerous Hungarian *huszár* regiments, which, like the Croat infantry, used irregular tactics. The first Hungarian troops fighting for the dynasty appeared in Flanders during the War of the Austrian Succession. The French invaders of Bohemia, Guibert claims, were defeated primarily by Croat and Hungarian light troops.[19]

Guibert warns that it would be absurd to counter these East Central European light troops and their irregular tactics with Western light troops attempting to carry on irregular warfare which needs a tradition and long experience. Only troops who had both—the East Central Europeans—could use such tactics. The West, which lacked both experience and tradition, could not employ them. Yet, both the French and Prussian armies increased their light troops during the Seven Years' War. But they did not achieve the expected success, for all their increased numbers. Guibert points out that light troops are useful in both irregular and conventional warfare. They do not depend on magazines and are extremely maneuverable, excelling in advance and as flank and rear guard as well as in reconnaissance duties. For lack of good light troops, Frederick had to employ his most trusted regular troops in such assignments.

Guibert was aware that light troops and unconventional warfare had sociopolitical prerequisites. For such warfare, he wrote, requires "a vigorous undaunted people superior to others in point of government and courage. . . ." Guibert, referring to the Hungarian example, summarizes the proper use of light troops: reconnaissance; harassing the enemy, especially during the night. But they must also know how to fight in regular tactics; they must be picked fighters, not deserters, whom Frederick the Great pressed into his light troops. Guibert warns that the major part of a modern army must consist of regular, not irregular troops. Light troops able to use irregular tactics should be only a small portion of the army, a force 1,000 to 1,200 strong would suffice—two-thirds of them should be hussars.[20]

Lieutenant-Colonel MacDonald claimed that the future belonged to the light cavalry, which would replace heavy cavalry and be the dominant mobile service in all armies.[21] The light horse system was introduced in Britain with the establishment of the first British dragoon regiment as early as 1681.[22] In sum, then, East Central European military patterns of warfare had a considerable influence on the West during the eighteenth century.

All these eighteenth-century military theorists were fascinated by the contrast between Western and East Central European warfare. Most of them restricted their remarks to the professional military aspects of the issue; others, like Guibert understood that political, social, and ideological factors lay at the foundation of the contrast. Indeed the typical soldiers in the standing armies of Western absolute kings had no vested interest in the war aims of their masters; hence they had small motivation to fight better. Only brutal discipline kept them in the ranks. A Western soldier could either fight the "enemy" and probably survive, or try to desert—and be killed if caught. Whether East Central Europeans fought the Ottomans or the neighboring Christian Great Powers, even when the struggle began as banditry, in the final stage, they fought for ideals. These mobilized a great portion of the population. East Central European wars were therefore more intense than balance-of-power wars in the West. In fact, a cycle of East Central European revolutionary wars commenced at the dawn of the period of our study and continued with ever-increasing intensity throughout the nineteenth century. For the eighteenth- and nineteenth-century history of East Central Europe is the history of wars for national independence.

A typical East Central European revolutionary war opened the century: the Hungarian War for Independence—the Insurrection of Ferenc II Rákóczi (1703–1711). Another similar conflict, the Polish War for Independence (the Kościuszko Insurrection) almost closed the century. The Rákóczi war lasted as long as the American Revolution, more than eight years, Kościuszko's struggle began March 24, 1794, and ended with the capitulation of Warsaw on November 5, seven and a half months later.

Both the Polish and the Hungarian wars for independence were diametrically opposite to contemporary warfare in Western Europe, in many respects, they resembled the American and French revolutions. The Kościuszko Insurrection will be one of the main themes of volume IV of our series. The Rákóczi Insurrection is one of the themes of volume III. Since however it is also an integral part of the theme of this volume, it seems necessary to present a short account of the Rákóczi Insurrection here.

## The Hungarian War for Independence of Ferenc II Rákóczi

The Rákóczi Insurrection bore a close relationship both to the War of the Spanish Succession (1701–1715) and the Great Northern War (1700–1721). Because of the former, the Habsburg dynasty had to pull out most of its troops from Hungary and transfer them to the Italian and Western European theaters. In Transylvania alone, a substantial Habsburg garrison was kept to face the Ottoman Empire. Only small garrisons were left in royal Hungary to guard certain key forts. This military vacuum gave the insurgents a chance to act. Peasant leaders, Albert Kis and Tamás Esze,[23] launched their first military action in 1697 before this evacuation and were promptly defeated. But as the Habsburg troops left the country, these same leaders felt that the time was ripe for another try. They convoked a meeting of peasant dissident leaders of the upper Tisza region. The vision of the assembled peasants was quite statesmanlike. They foresaw that achieving their goals was possible only by a nationwide armed struggle, and that required the cooperation of the nobility. For a national leader, they needed an aristocrat of the highest possible reputation and prestige. Thus, they turned to the exiled Prince

Ferenc Rákóczi.[24] The meeting between the representatives of the peasant insurgents and Rákóczi took place at Brzezan in Poland where he was living in exile. An agreement was struck between them, Rákóczi accepting the leadership. The Brzezan agreement fused two movements, the nobility's resistance to the unconstitutional tyrannical rule of the Habsburg dynasty and a popular (*kuruc*) grass-roots insurrection. For the first time in Hungarian history the traditions and experiences of resistance by the noble estate was joined with the popular struggle for social and economic improvement. The synthesis of the two gave the movement the broadest social foundations and was directed against Habsburg absolutism. Rákóczi's extraordinary social position, as a descendant of Transylvanian princes, Prince of the Holy Roman Empire, bearer of the Golden Fleece, the richest landlord of Hungary, tried to and indeed did bring the Hungarian struggle into the orbit of European foreign policy.[25]

A particular phenomenon supplied a sizable number of trained fighters to insurgent forces, in Hungary. A great many soldiers who had served in the extensive fortifications were discharged when Hungary was liberated from Ottoman conquest at the end of the seventeenth century. These discharged veterans formed gangs, and like many similar bands in the Balkans, often lived by brigandage. There were fewer in the Transdanubian regions, but in the Great Hungarian Plain, between the Danube and the Tisza rivers particularly, there were many such bands. Besides the discharged soldiers, serfs who escaped their masters' lands, outcasts, enthusiastic students, even priests and former officers could be found among them. Some of these former officers, notwithstanding their nobility, saw the growing numbers of the armed bands with alarm.[26] Just as in the nineteenth-century Balkan wars of liberation, armed bands were incorporated into national armies, so Rákóczi brought these Hungarian bands into his army. They contributed their warlike spirit, relentless, often cruel tactics, efficiency in using nonconventional methods—and also difficulty in imposing solid discipline.

In numbers, serfs dominated insurgent army of Rákóczi. The first fighters to join him at the northern slopes of the Carpathians in Poland were, as he himself remembered

> . . . armed with sticks and scythe . . . there were scarcely two hundred foot, equipped with poor peasant muskets, and with them fifty

> horsemen came. Their leader was Tamás Esze, a peasant, my serfs from Tarpa and Albert Kis, a thief and criminal sought for his crimes. . . . The people who gathered in camps elected their own leaders. They accepted the command of swine-herds, cowboys, hairdressers, tailors, depending on whose gallantry they estimated the highest. . . . It would have been dangerous, even impossible, to dismiss these officers, but there were none to replace them anyway.[27]

Such were the men from whom Rákóczi started to forge an army. It needed his personal attention to all details, including supplying them with their daily needs as well as introducing draconian regulations to establish discipline.The army swelled like a spring torrent and flooded central Hungary and Transylvania. The nobility escaped into forts and fortified towns, which stood like islands within an ocean of armed men. Nonetheless, very few Hungarian noblemen joined the Habsburg enemy; rather, they stayed neutral if they did not join the insurgents.

The problem with such broad mobilization of the masses was how to keep the serfs committed to the fight. From the beginning, Rákóczi did not promise to emancipate the serfs; the early eighteenth century was far from being ripe for such a fundamental reform. Emancipation would have alienated the Hungarian nobility and thrown them into the arms of the Habsburg dynasty, a sure way to lose the war. What Rákóczi did promise—and what even the Habsburg dynasty had to grant in the compromise that ended the war—was freedom for those who joined the army for the duration. In other words, not emancipation of the serfs, which would have changed the feudal structure, but rather rewarding fighters within the feudal system by putting them on the traditional road to advancement, winning privileges by virtue of combat.

Rákóczi ennobled a good many of the leading *kuruc* warriors, but ennoblement was less common than the granting of *hajdú* liberties. This kind of freedom was first accorded by István Bocskai (1557–1606), Prince of Transylvania and Lord of royal Hungary, who fought a successful war for liberation against the Habsburg dynasty between 1604 and 1606. The main strength of his insurgent army were the *hajdúk*, a host of martial individuals, partly cattlemen, partly marauders, who fought gallantly for Bocskai and his cause. Their struggle ended just as the Rákóczi Insurrection did, in one of the many compromises between the Habsburg dynasty and the Hungarian estates. This was embodied in the Treaty of Vienna of 1606 and codified by the diet of 1608.[28] The treaty guaranteed Hungary self-government, the privileges of the estates, freedom of religion, and other liberties. Bocskai repaid the services of the *hajdúk* by emancipating them from the jurisdiction of the lords, settled them on land grant cities and towns (*hajdú* towns), guaranteeing their right to landownership and personal freedom.

Precisely this Rákóczi promised to those of his soldiers who were not members of the estates, including naturally the discharged veterans. The response was great; there were enough volunteers, at least at the beginning. As the war dragged on, Rákóczi assigned quotas to the counties, a form of draft, which had to be utilized. Yet it was seldom necessary to force young men to join the flag. All these fighting men together constituted the "warrior estate"[29] (*vitézlö rend*), a new stratum in Hungarian feudal society. The warrior estate was a subterfuge for avoiding mass emancipation as well as a means of establishing a kind of citizen soldiery, the springboard of revolutionary warfare. The existence of this army was, in fact, not in the interest of the nobility. They wished the serfs to till the land rather than bear arms. Furthermore, a considerable armed force of nonnobles who entertained the traditional land hunger and desire for personal emancipation was a *de facto* threat to the *status quo*. This conflict required that Rákóczi be very tactful in order to keep the diverse elements of an insurgent army together.

Rákóczi, anticipating Washington's views, was convinced that fighting an enemy's professional forces required insurgents to organize standing armies of their own so that major battles could be fought even on the enemy's conditions.

Rákóczi's effort to build a regular standing army had a purely military purpose—ability to confront the Habsburg standing army and win decisive battles. As an East Central European prototype of the enlightened absolute monarch, Rákóczi also saw in that standing army-to-be the mainspring of his own government. He had immense obstacles to overcome, among them, the nobility's lack of professional military training, their eagerness to retain their political influence, and the absence of any effective means of financing the struggle.

Whereas Washington lost most of his pitched battles, Rákóczi lost them all. But he soon renewed his forces and was campaigning again. His recurring conclusion was the need for a disciplined regular army, as modern as circumstances permitted. As if we were reading one of Washington's repeated complaints to Congress, we see Rákóczi write, on January 24, 1710, after the loss of the Battle of Romhány: "I hope this battle persuaded our nation, that against the Germans we never will be able to prevail without a regular force. . . ."[30]

In developing his military theories, Rákóczi depended heavily on the work of the Hungarian military theorist Miklós Zrínyi,[31] whose *Az török áfium ellen való orvosság* appeared in 1705. Rákóczi accepted the Zrínyi thesis, that an army depends on internal discipline, good organization, purposeful leadership, a balanced proportion between the various services, and a centrally controlled logistical system, with quality stressed above quantitative growth.[32]

The organization of this standing army included varied means: many regulations were issued, some temporary, some permanent, all intended to establish order and uniformity. They dealt with defense, offense, and fortification, among other military problems. These regulations were codified by the Diet of Ónod in 1707 under the title *Regulamentum universale;*[33] this was promptly printed in Latin and Hungarian. It regulated the army's organization, the services, higher commands, logistics, pay, recruitment, the division of the state into military districts, etc. In addition Rákóczi issued edicts on morals, discipline, and the punishment of trespassers. A collection of these edicts was published in 1707.

One of Rákóczi's main concerns was the training and education of military leaders. He deplored the low level of the nobility's education. Gallantry and loyalty, he thought, were no substitute for knowledge. He created the Society of Noblemen (*Nemesi Társaság*) in order to gather young noblemen in his court where he could forge their morals, educate them, and train them to become the skilled officers he so badly needed, in order to form regular regiments. Until his own officers could be trained, like Washington, Rákóczi "imported" professional knowledge by inviting French, German and Polish officers.[34]

The *Regulamentum universale*, then, shows Rákóczi's own views on the army: its organization, leadership, and supply, and on other aspects of national defense. The long war made it possible for him to clarify and codify the doctrines and rules of his army for the warfare it was to wage. Yet one weakness of Rákóczi's army was the lack of an adequate number of well-trained officers. The most efficient generals in his army were the former Habsburg officers, Count Antal

Esterházy and Count Simon Forgách, the former a colonel and the latter, a general in the Habsburg army. Among the lesser nobles, the most professional was János Sréter, formerly an executive in mining enterprises—who, along with the Frenchman, La Motte, organized the artillery and was designated commandant of the Artillery Officers Academy. Bravest and most efficient in small warfare were Brigadiers János Bottyán[35] and László Ocskay.[36] The latter was the Hungarian Benedict Arnold; Arnold and Ocskay were identical in gallantry, professional know-how, superb tactical leadership, and treachery.

The regular troops were uniformed, paid, and equipped mostly at Rákóczi's own expense and only partially by the insurgent state. The majority of the soldiers were Hungarians, but large numbers of Ruthenians, Romanians, Slovaks, and Germans also served in the rank and file. The French and Polish experts, although a small group, contributed much to the professionalization of the regular troops. At the start of the insurrection, the total effectives amounted to approximately 70,000 men and officers. At the final stage, they decreased to 30,000. Among the twenty-six generals, eight were counts, seven barons, and ten lesser nobles. Among the brigadiers, two were nonnobles, Tamás Esze, a serf, and Orbán Czelder, a burgher. At the end of 1705, the regular army was organized into fifty-two *huszár* and thirty-one infantry regiments and six artillery companies. Most professional were the "court" regiments of Rákóczi. The first commander-in-chief of the regulars was General Simon Forgách, his successor was General Count Antal Esterházy, both former Habsburg officers. A general commissariat (*supremus bellicus commissariatus*) was responsible for the logistics; this office was headed by Count István Csáky. Health service was provided by the regimental medics. Rákóczi directed that the counties supply the army with food and fodder without payment. The main problem was transporting the collected food. Under control of the general commissariat, magazines and bakeries were built, and fortified places were established to protect the magazines. But because of the very backward transportation system, the logistics worked only if major troop concentrations did not garrison the same place long.

The main difficulty, of course, was supplying armament and ammunition. An intensive search was carried out to collect all the weapons available in the country, and to manufacture or to import arms. Major factories were founded in Besztercebánya, Kassa, and various locations in Gömör county. New iron works were built in Tiszolc. In concept and efforts, the system resembled the Reign of Terror's attempt to mobilize the preindustrial manufacturing system for the purposes of war. In France, however, an advanced mercantilist economy made it possible to produce most, if not all, the needs of the mass armies. Rákóczi, with a less developed economy, could not achieve this desired goal.

Importation was hampered by the utter lack of money. Efforts to barter cattle, wine, and copper for them did not work well. Yet some 10,000 muskets were imported during the war. Some cloth was imported from Silesia and Poland more or less on the basis of barter. The rest was produced at home or brought in by Balkan merchants, who accepted mostly copper in exchange. The troops were poorly uniformed, yet this branch of the logistic system came closest to fulfilling the army's need. It is not the low efficiency of logistic which catches one's eye, but the results Rákóczi achieved under the prevailing circumstances.[37]

Rákóczi seldom called out the *insurrectio* of the nobility (noble levy). Their frequent call up would not have been practical. It might have been an auxiliary of a standing army, as it was for the Habsburg army in the War of the Austrian Succession and, particularly, in the Seven Years' War, but as a main force it was obsolete. Instead of serving, the nobles were taxed to pay for mounted substitutes, their equipment and horses. The peasantry was obliged to produce infantrymen, equipped and armed. The basis was the *porta* system, a unit of taxation based on several serf families. A *porta* had to produce ten, later four, armed infantrymen. In the initial phases of the war, volunteers were abundant; as previously stated, the more prolonged the war the more often was this obligatory enlistment used.

The Hungarians in their unconventional tactics were superior to the slow-moving, typical standing armies of the dynasty; like Washington, Rákóczi made extreme efforts, as has been shown, to create a disciplined force able to wage conventional warfare in order to be prepared for the conventional final battle with the enemy. Most of the officers, however, including Rákóczi's own right-hand man, Chief General (Marshal) Miklós Bercsényi, believed that the Hungarian forces never would adopt the "German type" of conventional warfare. The army itself resisted such a change in discipline and tactics. Bercsényi wrote to Rákóczi, "The Hungarian inbued with volunteer spirit never will adjust his behavior to monthly payment and/or regulations . . . he either pursues or runs away . . . Hungarian gallantry needs self-confidence . . ."[38]

Rákóczi's main strategical concept was identical with Washington's. He, too, looked for decisive conventional battles, to wear down, and destroy the Habsburg standing army and thus to attain independence. He readily accepted and fought six large-scale battles, and lost them all.[39] Faulty leadership, lack of discipline, subordinates' failure to understand the tactical plan, ignorance of commanders of larger units, and Rákóczi's own lack of professional military training, were the main reasons for the defeats. Lack of discipline and training often caused defeat even when the *kuruc* troops had broken the Habsburg lines; they did not know how to conclude the battle.

There were successful campaigns, however, where the purpose was not fighting major battles, but securing the cumulative effect of small encounters, in which the *kuruc* troops were superior to their enemies. The most remarkable of such campaigns was the liberation of Transdanubia by General János Bottyán which started on November 4, 1705.

Except for some retaliatory raids on the easternmost Austrian provinces, the war was waged on Hungarian soil. The population gave the insurgents much aid and information about the enemy. But raids, scorched-earth tactics, and other effects of the war gradually wearied the Hungarian people of the long war. The initial enthusiasm burned away in the flames that destroyed their homes and property.

The *kuruc* troops were, of course, most successful in small combats, and the Habsburg troops suffered most when they had to conduct long marches on Hungarian terrain, as when the imperial forces marched to Transylvania in 1705 and marched back the following year. In both cases the Hungarians refused pitched battle, but made the life of the enemy miserable by raids and ambushes, capturing foraging units and supply trains, destroying bridges, and by other unconventional methods—like those of the American militia against General John Burgoyne in 1777.

The defeat of the *kuruc* troops in the battle of Trencsén on August 3, 1708 was decisive; they never fully recuperated from their losses. Parallel political and economic difficulties made the situation desperate. The income of the insurgent state fell; the army had to be entrusted with the collection of taxes. The base of the insurrection gradually shrank back to the northeastern zones of the country where it had started. The imperial administration gradually established its rule over northern Hungary (Slovakia); Transdanubia, too, was lost. In September 1710, the last major western base, the fort of Érsekújvár, had to capitulate. A devastating plague swept over the country during these years killing approximately 10 percent of the population.[40]

Rákóczi's perserverance was the basic force which kept the war going. More than ever he looked to foreign assistance. The ever weakening French aid seemed to be supplemented by Russian cooperation, particularly after the Battle of Poltava, July 9, 1709. Rákóczi had had a treaty with Peter the Great since September 1707. After Poltava, Rákóczi hoped to put this treaty into force. He wanted to make France change its traditional pro-Swedish policy into cooperation with Russia, but he failed. Instead, the French, in an effort to help the Swedes, recommended that the Porte declare war on Russia. Of course, the hope that the Russians could help Rákóczi against the Habsburgs was a utopian one, anyway.[41]

Rákóczi planned a strategic withdrawal and permanent defense in the northeastern corner of Hungary, based on fortresses and fortified towns. The strategy, as well as logistical preparation for a protracted area defense, started in 1710. His goal was securing time for diplomatic negotiations. The most reliable commanders were placed over the key defense establishments. The pivotal point of the area defense was the recently modernized fort of Munkács. Indeed, this bastion surrendered only two weeks after the Szatmár Compromise gave no chance for further resistance to the commandant, István Sennyey.

At this stage of the war, the situation has been disputed.[42] Some historians, Imre Lukinich among them, claim that the imperial forces faced so much hardship that a systematic offensive and sieges were beyond its potential. Field Marshal Count János Pálffy (1663–1751), the imperial commander-in-chief, was in no position to launch such an offensive. Yet, it would have been only a matter of time before the Habsburgs, after the conclusion of the War of the Spanish Succession, could have concentrated forces in Hungary and end the war by force. But that would require three or four more years of fighting.

The dynasty, however—wise for once—recognized that nobles ready for a compromise were in the majority in the *kuruc* camp. A speedy compromise seemed to offer more advantages than a protracted war, which might have alienated those nobles who were ready for a settlement in 1711. The cleverest move of the dynasty was including, as a key stipulation of the compromise, assurance of the privileges of the "warrior estate" (*vitézlö rend*). Thus, for these combatants, the backbone of Rákóczi's army, continuation of the war seemed unnecessary; they, too, were ready for compromise. So, the Treaty of Szatmár was signed on April 30, 1711, and was endorsed by the regent Empress Eleonora on behalf of her son, King Charles III, (Emperor Charles VI).

In strategy and overall military leadership, the determining factor was that Rákóczi, although an accomplished statesman and political leader, was not a professional soldier; he did not have even a rudimentary education or training in military affairs. The Habsburg court first had Rákóczi educated for the Church under the supervision of Cardinal Lipót Kollonich,[43] but when Rákóczi was adamant against being a priest, he was educated to become what he was born, a grandee. During the insurrection his main concern was international relations and domestic politics, the military being a poor third, among his concerns. Rákóczi went to war and learned military leadership "on the job."

As we have seen, the Hungarian war was initiated by popular forces. Its cause was massive discontent with Habsburg overtaxation, the rampages of German occupation troops, causing intolerable misery, and social and economic grievances. This popular force sought and won the leadership of Hungary's foremost exiled aristocrat, Ferenc II Rákóczi. He then persuaded a large segment of the lesser nobility and several aristocrats to join the conflict. As the struggle evolved national unity emerged of a degree unprecedented in Europe outside Revolutionary France. Political and economic considerations played a great role in the war, but the fight for national independence was the predominant factor after the nobility joined in.

The Hungarian war ended with the Treaty of Szatmár, April 30, 1711, a compromise between the Habsburg dynasty and the Hungarian estates. The compromise reestablished Hungary's self-government and the privileges of the estates; it assured freedom of conscience for Protestants; it emancipated even the non-privileged warriors who had fought for the cause and made them free men. The Hungarian estates in return acknowledged the hereditary rights of the Habsburg dynasty, in the male line, to the Hungarian crown.

The dual system, the main feature of Hungary's relationship to the hereditary provinces of the dynasty, was reinforced. Neither the compromise of 1867 nor the simultaneously established dual system was a new phenomenon in Hungarian-Habsburg relations; they were the quintessence of that relationship—to no small degree because the Hungarians again and again were willing to fight for their rights.

It was necessary to give this summary of the Hungarian War of Independence of Ferenc II Rákóczi, because this war virtually opened the epoch this volume deals with. Substantial elaboration on that war therefore should have opened this volume. However, our series of books on "War and Society in East Central Europe" is an integral study of the subject up to and including World War I and its effects. Since this is so, in other words since the individual volumes together intend to expose the entire picture, the detailed elaboration on the Rákóczi war seemed unnecessary because volume III of our series entitled, *From Hunyadi to Rákóczi: War and Society in Late Medieval and Early Modern Hungary*, does exactly that. This volume and the last part of volume III together present a comprehensive study of East Central European Society and War in Pre-Revolutionary Eighteenth Century. Volume III and IV are published simultaneously.

## Notes

1. Major-General J.F.C. Fuller, *The Conduct of War 1789–1961: A Study of the Impact of the French, Industrial, and Russian Revolutions on War and Its Conduct* (New Brunswick, N.J., 1961), 21.

2. Guglielmo Ferrero, *Peace and War* (New York, 1933), 63–64.

3. Jan Wimmer, "L'infanterie dans l'armée polonaise aux XV$^{e}$-XVIII$^{e}$ siècles," in Witold Biegański, *et al.*, *Histoire militaire de la Pologne, problèmes choisis* (Varsovie, 1970), 92–93.

4. Jon Manchip White, *Marshal of France: The Life and Times of Maurice, Comte de Saxe (1696–1750)* (Chicago, 1962), chap. IX.

5. Maurice, Count de Saxe Marshal-General of the Armies of France, *Reveries, or, Memoirs Concerning the Art of War* (Edinburgh, MDCCLIX), 134.

6. *Ibid.*, 135–36.

7. *Ibid.*, 142. De Saxe disregards the famous Polish "winged hussars," who were armored, heavy cavalry.

8. *Ibid.*, 146.

9. Wimmer, 93.

10. Detailed maps of this system may be found in Bálint Hóman and

Gyula Szekfü, *Magyar történet*, 5 vols. (Budapest, 1943), III: 256, 257, 288.

11. *Ne bántsd a magyart, Az török áfium ellen való orvosság avagy az töröknek magyarral való békessége ellen való antidótum*, written in 1660 or 1661, first published in 1705, and reprinted several times thereafter. References are to László Négyesy, ed., *Gróf Zrínyi Miklós válogatott munkái* (Budapest, n.d.), 293–320.

12. See Béla K. Király, *Hungary in the Late Eighteenth Century: The Decline of Enlightened Despotism* (New York, 1969), 173–95; see also, Árpád Markó, "Adalékok a magyar katonai nyelv fejlödéstörténetéhez," *Hadtörténelmi Közlemények* 7 (1959): 151–66. (Cited as *HK.*).

13. Colonel Georghe Romanescu, "Die Einstehung der nationalen Armee und ihre Entwicklung bis zum Unabhengigkeitskrieg," Colonel Dr. Al. HG. Savu, ed., *Aus der Geschichte der Rumänischen Armee* (Bucharest, 1978), 114–16.

14. Counte Imre Thököly (1657–1705), Prince of Transylvania and Upper Hungary. Allied with Turkey since 1682 and exiled there since 1699.

15. Lt. General (of the French Army) Antoine Manassés Pas, Marquis de Feuquières [the "Wizard"], *Memoirs Historical and Military*, 2 vols. (London, 1736), I: 225.

16. Feuquières, I: 224–25.

17. A. H. Jacques, Count de Guibert, *A General Essay on Tactics with an Introductory Discourse upon the Present State of Politics and the Military Science in Europe to which is Prefixed a Plan of a Work entitled The Political and Military System of France.* [Translated from the French of M. Guibert by an Officer] (London, 1781), 300–301.

18. He, of course, refers to the Szatmár Treaty of 1711.

19. Guibert, 303.

20. *Ibid.*, 309.

21. Introduction to Chevalier Dutel, *The Formation and Maneuvers of Infantry, Calculated for the Effectual Resistance of Cavalry and for Attacking them Successfully. On New Principles of Tactics.* [Translated from the French by John MacDonald] (London, 1810), I.

22. General of Division Francis Wimpfen (de Borneborg), *The Experienced Officer; or Instructions.* [Translated from the French by John MacDonald] (London, 1804), 98.

23. Tamás Esze (1666–1708) serf, a leader of the *kuruc* insurgents, brigadier in Rákóczi's army. Albert Kis (1664–1704), serf, colonel in Rákóczi's army. Kis had long experience as a junior officer in the Thököly insurgent army. For a few years he served in the Habsburg standing army but was discharged in 1694; thus he became one of the typical, unemployed military men, who played such an important role in Rákóczi's army.

24. Ferenc II Rákóczi of Borsi (1676–1735), Prince of Transylvania (1704–1711), ruling prince of Hungary (*vezérlö fejedelem*) (1705–1711), and

Prince of the Holy Roman Empire. When his mother, Ilona Zrínyi, after successfully defending the fort of Munkács against the Habsburg besiegers for three years, fell into captivity, Rákóczi was taken to Austria and raised there by his appointer foster father Cardinal Lipót Kollonich. The owner of 1,900,000 yokes of land, Rákóczi had been since 1694, perpetual High Sheriff (*föispán*) of Sáros county, in Northern Hungary. In 1797 he refused to lead a peasant insurrection organized by Tamás Esze and Albert Kis. But in 1700, because of the increasing tyranny of the Habsburg dynasty, he turned to Louis XIV and tried to enlist the king's support for a *fronde* rather than a general insurrection in Hungary. Betrayed, arrested, Rákóczi escaped and found refuge in Poland. At the renewed invitation of the same two insurgent leaders, he now accepted the leadership he had rejected in 1697, and entered Hungary with a small band of peasant insurgents on June 6, 1703.

25. Béla Köpeczi and Ágnes R. Vákonyi, *II. Rákóczi Ferenc*, 2d enlarged ed. (Budapest, 1976), 113–14. For a rich collection of contemporary sources see Köpeczi and Várkonyi, eds., *Rákóczi tükör, naplók, jelentések, emlékiratok a szabadságharcról*, 2 vols. (Budapest, 1973). See also Köpeczi, *A Rákóczi-szabadságharc és Franciaország* (Budapest, 1966).

26. For the origins of these "unemployed soldiers" see László Benczédi, "Katonarétegek helyzete a török elleni háborúkban," *HK* 12 (1966): 821–29. See also Imre Bánkuti, *Rákóczi hadserege 1703–1711* (Budapest, 1976), 9–10. A collection of documents, with concise essays on the various aspects of the Hungarian insurgent army.

27. *II. Rákóczi Ferenc emlékiratai* (Budapest, 1951), 38–39, 49, 48–49.

28. Béla K. Király, ed., *Tolerance and Movements of Religious Dissent in Eastern Europe* (Boulder, Col., 1975), 208, 210–12.

29. Ferenc Julier, *Magyar hadvezérek* (Budapest, n.d.), 283–316.

30. Letter to General Antal Esterházy. Kálmán Thaly, ed., *Archivum Rákóczianum* (Budapest, 1874), III: 10.

31. See note 11.

32. Bánkuti, 152.

33. *Regulamentum universale*, the general war regulation of the federated estates of the Kingdom of Hungary, for the military, as well as for the noble counties, the free royal towns, and all citizens. Published at Nagyszombat, 1707. Full text in Bánkuti, 181–219.

34. Bánkuti, 153.

35. János Bottyán (1643?–1709), a lesser nobleman, cavalry officer, colonel since 1692; in 1701, he commanded his regiment at the Rhine against the French. In 1703, he was sent against the *kurucok*, but joined Rákóczi in October 1704 and was promoted brigadier. He lost an eye earlier in fighting the Turks; his soldiers fondly called him "Bottyán the Blind."

36. László Ocskay (1680–1710), son of a gentry family, officer in a hussar regiment, joined Rákóczi in 1703, rose to brigadier, in 1708 he deserted to the Habsburg army and attained the rank of colonel, captured in 1710, court-martialed and executed for treason.

37. Bánkuti, 237–38.

38. Bercsényi to Rákóczi, September 18, 1704 in Thaly, III: 124. See also Imre Bánkuti, *A kurucok elsö dunántúli hadjárata (1704. január-április)* (Budapest, 1975); Gyula Erdélyi, *A magyarok hadiszervezete és hadvezetési müvészete ezer éven át* (Budapest, 1944), 174–208.

39. In 1704, two battles were fought at Koronco on June 13, and at Nagyszombat on December 26. In 1705, two more battles occurred at Pudmeric, August 11, and at Zsibó, November 11. In 1708 there was a battle at Trencsén on August 3; in 1710, one at Romhány on January 22. Except at Koronco Rákóczi himself commanded; on the other hand, in all but Romhány the imperial commander-in-chief directed the enemy troops. Bánkuti, 296.

40. *Ibid.*, 351.

41. B. K. Király and P. Pastor, "The Sublime Porte and Ferenc II Rákóczi's Hungary: An Episode in Islamic Christian Relations," in Abraham Ascher, Tibor Halasi-Kún, Béla Király, eds., *The Mutual Effects of the Islamic and Judeo-Christian Worlds: The East European Pattern* (New York, 1979), 129–48. See also Béla Köpeczi, ed., *A Rákóczi szabadságharc és Európa* (Budapest, 1970).

42. Mátyás Molnár, ed., *A Rákóczi-szabadságharc vitás kérdései. Tudományos emlékülés 1976 január 29–30* (Vaja-Nyíregyháza, 1976).

43. Count Lipót Kollonich (1631–1707), Archbishop of Esztergom, Cardinal. He started his career as a soldier, fought the Turks, and was one of the main advocates of a forceful neo-Counterreformation. As chairman of the Hungarian *kamara* (central financial authority), he was the main counselor of the dynasty on Hungarian affairs. As such, he elaborated the violent reestablishment of Habsburg absolutist rule over Hungary, including colonization of Hungary by non-Hungarians to suppress Hungarian nationality.

# II

# Reflections on the Causes of Eighteenth-Century Warfare in Europe

Robert A. Kann

# Reflections on the Causes of Eighteenth-Century Warfare in Europe

## Ideology and Warfare

It is widely assumed that a conspicuous change in the causes of warfare took place between the last phase of the Thirty Years' War, that is, the formation of the Franco-Swedish alliance against the Holy Roman Empire in 1635, and the outbreak of the First Coalition against the French revolutionary government in April 1792. Up to the alliance between the French Catholic and the Swedish Lutheran powers, initiated by a prince of the Roman Church, Cardinal Richelieu, ideological causes had dominated warfare; in the following century and a half usually more mundane reasons of aggrandizement, often contested successions (to wit, those of Spain, Poland, Austria, and Bavaria), led to armed collisions. With the rise of Jacobinism in France there came into being a new kind of ideological warfare which with the introduction of general conscription established the concept of the nation-in-arms. It meant at that time the revolution in its social and political aspects against reaction.[1] These assumptions, however, require reexamination and perhaps some modification.

It is true that the war of the Third Coalition of 1805 was another conflict against a monarchy, this time under Napoleon as emperor, and for the time being Jacobinism could be considered a bygone issue. Yet distinct social differences between the cause of France and that of its adversaries remained. More important, the reaction to the new French imperialism was a response in Prussia and Spain, and to a lesser degree also in Russia and Austria, which at least within the limits of national defense approximated that of the nation-in-arms under the French tricolor. The liberal expectations in the ranks of Napoleon's opponents, however, were sadly disappointed at the end of the war period in 1815 by the inauguration of the Restoration era. Nevertheless, even after the Congress of Vienna the reasons for war appeared markedly different from those of the one and a half centuries between 1635 and 1792. Nationalism, national unification, in general a patriotism independent of loyalty to a dynasty now became weighty factors as mainsprings of war. True, they were only partly of an ideological nature, and reasons for war that had nothing whatsoever to do with popular feelings by no means disappeared entirely. Even so, after 1815 war in its origins, logistics and strategy was never to be the same as it had been until the fourth decade of the seventeenth century.

Ideological warfare too has a tradition that goes back at least far into the Middle Ages. Ideologies change in the course of centuries, however, while issues of contested succession in monarchies, designs against the territories of neighboring countries and the wealth of their citizens, have remained stable causes of war throughout the centuries, whatever way they may be rationalized. In this sense it is legitimate to refer to nonideological war as traditional war, which at the same time usually means war of limited objectives.[2]

Issues of succession were the major professed causes of war between 1701 and 1778 (Wars of the Spanish, Polish, Austrian and Bavarian Succession); the French-initiated War of Devolution (1667–1668) and the War of the League of Augsburg (1689–1697) also fall into this category. In fact, wars over the issue of legitimate succession played an important role in even earlier modern and late medieval history as well. The Franco-English Hundred Years' War (1337–1453) was in part, and the long-drawn-out English civil War of the Roses (1455–1485) was fully, fought over the issue of succession. Should it then be concluded that prior to the fourth quarter of the seventeenth century the question of succession was one of several causes of war, all of them subordinated prior to the Reformation to the struggle between Christians and infidels, and after the Reformation to internecine war between Catholics and Protestants over the overriding question of the true faith? Should a line be drawn in mid seventeenth century strictly dividing the succession question as a genuine issue up till then and as a mere rationalization for imperialist warfare after that time?

### Etatism and Warfare

Obviously the problem is more complex than it appears at first glance. The same causes for warfare have existed for as long as the political associations that have organized warfare. The ability to wage war connotes the existence of fairly well-centralized states that are able to raise substantial armed forces. The birth of the centralized modern state in Western and somewhat later in Central continental

Europe is usually assumed to have occurred in the course of the sixteenth and the first half of the seventeenth century. Its corollary, the transition in the structure of warfare from mercenary to standing army, took place only in the latter part of that period. The reasons for this relatively late development are primarily that, unlike other, earlier activities of the centralized state, such as judicial and administrative functions and, above all, taxation, the establishment of a standing army presupposed a rather advanced state of economic development, which existed in France and in Spain somewhat earlier than in the Holy Roman Empire, and there sooner than in the Habsburg possessions outside the Empire.

In England, on the other hand, the evolution toward a centralized state took place already under the first two Tudor kings, that is, in the late fifteenth and early sixteenth century, thus even earlier than in France and Spain. Owing to its insular position and in part also to the skill of its rulers, the country managed to stay out of major European conflagrations from the end of the Hundred Years' War in mid fifteenth century to the war with Spain in the late sixteenth century. The issues of war before and after that time, however, differed in no way from those of continental wars in Western and Central Europe.[3]

What had gradually changed since the middle of the seventeenth century were not the origins of war but the evaluation of the individual factors that caused it. The religious issue, dominant but certainly not entirely separated from economic and political reasons in much of the sixteenth and early seventeenth century, by no means lost all its significance in the latter part of the seventeenth century. It was no minor impediment in the War of the Spanish Succession in the relationship between the Habsburgs and their allies, the Dutch republic and England, in such matters, for instance, as the Rákóczi uprisings in eastern Hungary and Transylvania from 1705 to the peace of Szatmár in 1711. Half a century later Empress Maria Theresa's anti-British sentiments were largely motivated by religious feelings and were no mean factor in cementing the economic alliance between Great Britain and Prussia during the Seven Years' War. On the other hand, the complete lack of ideological considerations was already obvious in the foreign policy of Francis I of France as early as 1536 in his underhand alliance with the infidel Ottoman power and in his support of Protestant princes against the Emperor. In France a century and a half later, on the other hand, Louis XIV showed strongly though not exclusively religious motivations in his domestic war against the Huguenots, as distinguished from his foreign policy where he operated more independently of religious affiliations, although Catholicism played a part in his policy toward Britain under the pro-Catholic Stuart king, Charles II, and his Catholic brother, James II. Thus while ideological issues undoubtedly follow a trend, they are so often mixed up with or replaced by other considerations that it is well nigh impossible to draw a sharp dividing line between ideology and tradition among causes of war.[4]

In this context another issue, to which Karl von Clausewitz has called attention, is of interest. The time of the rise of the standing army was the second half of the seventeenth century and the eighteenth century prior to the outbreak of the French revolution. The large standing army, though not yet an army based on general conscription, was in existence already prior to the revolutionary wars beginning in 1792. The nation-in-arms as a major social and political force may not be primarily and certainly not exclusively an offspring of ideology but of state power, which may likewise lead to rationalizations of ideological and traditional reasons of war.[5]

**Causes of War and Strategy**

Clausewitz has noted another factor of great significance that ought to be considered in this context. He and subsequently other outstanding military historians of war such as Hans Delbrück and Gerhard Ritter distinguish between a strategy focused on annihilation of the enemy[6] and a strategy of attrition. Inasmuch as war is a means and tool of politics the second type of strategy plays an increasingly important role in warfare that is not primarily governed by ideological reasons. Contrary to ideological warfare, always a war focused on completely uprooting a hostile ideology—if not the enemy himself, traditional war generally implies a strategy of limited objectives. This distinction is indeed a solid one as far as the religious factor goes. Where it dominated—in the crusades, in the religious wars of the sixteenth century, and the first, Bohemian phase of the Thirty Years' War—the strategy of annihilation was chosen, although dependent on the relative strength of the forces engaged in warfare on either side; in other words, destruction as far as feasible. Even during the crusades, in the Huguenot wars in France, the war of the Protestant Schmalkaldic League against Emperor Charles V in Germany, compromises were necessary simply because complete destruction of the enemy was out of reach.

Can it be said, on the other hand, that the type of warfare that deemphasizes ideological causes in favor of limited objectives always puts the strategy of attrition before that of destruction? If one fights the enemy for strictly traditional reasons, the argument goes, there would be none who speaks for his complete destruction. Much has been made by the admirers of Frederick II of Prussia of the fact, for instance, that he wisely conducted a strategy of attrition against his formidable adversaries in the Seven Years' War—France, the Habsburg Empire, and Russia, whereas Napoleon I less than half a century later tried to crush coalitions of his enemies completely. Whether Frederick or Napoleon was the greater commander may be open to question. In view of the limited size and the small population of Frederick's kingdom he was, however, so inferior to his opponents that he could never think of destroying them; whereas Napoleon, in direct or indirect control of most of Western and Central Europe, could count on the support of a full array of satellite countries. Such a possibility existed until 1809 and perhaps even 1812. Thus while it is true in general that devaluation of ideological factors, particularly in eighteenth-century warfare prior to the French Revolution of 1789, favored a strategy of attrition over one of destruction, one must add that lack of opportunity for the latter played an important part wherever the former was chosen.

This declining lack of opportunity was caused by several factors. First, owing to the rise of centralized state power, conflicts between near equals in war potential became more frequent in earlier modern times than they had been in late medieval times with their still feudal political structures. Linked to this rise of the centralized state, and in the case of Great Britain, France, and Spain the national state, was another newly emerging factor: the endeavors to maintain a balance of power in Europe, generally by means of coalitions against a power that threatened to achieve supremacy. All major wars of the seventeenth and eighteenth centuries were thus coalition wars, more often than not on both sides, which right from the start turned wars of annihilation into hopeless ventures. Even in wars such as the earlier ones of Louis XIV, where France had to face coalitions singlehanded, the country's complete annihilation, if feasible, would have upset the balance of European power completely. For that reason it would have appeared highly undesirable, as the partitions of Poland which took place contrary to these principles proved a century later.[7]

## War and Enlightened Philosophy

One argument that goes against overemphasizing distinctions among different types of warfare in the eighteenth century is the attitude of the French Enlightenment which debunked traditional diplomacy completely. Felix Gilbert in particular, in an essay "The—New—Diplomacy of the Eighteenth Century," has presented an array of highly significant views on the issue. To many if not most of the outstanding *philosophes* of the time, diplomacy was merely a kind of synonym for hypocrisy and mendacity. The balance-of-power concept, since it was based on the principle of armed defense, worked, according to these men, actually for war and not for peace.

Alliances were considered to be the preparatory step for war. Even if they were called defensive, they were actually supposed to be of a hidden offensive nature. This in turn meant that diplomats whose job it was to negotiate alliances were simply reprobates. Hence Denis Diderot referred to diplomacy as an "obscene art that hides itself in the folds of deceit."[8] Without identifying myself to the slightest degree with these well-meant but rather naïve views, I called attention several years ago, in an article "Alliances versus Ententes" published in *World Politics,* to an inherent weakness of alliance systems which in my opinion is still valid today. In an emergency situation that partners of a rigid alliance system will more often than not try to minimize their own obligations and maximize those of their allies, who naturally resent such efforts. The net result is that allies quite frequently will be at work to damage the covenant by sowing mutual distrust. In contrast to this, the far less rigid, far more flexible entente concept, in which obligations are not binding, challenges the parties to make agreements not less but more reliable since no compulsion to honor an obligation exists anyway. Accordingly, the entente has a built-in psychological apparatus working for the accentuation of common interests; the alliance, on the other hand, has a tendency to evade sworn commitments.[9]

Yet ententes or consultation pacts in the modern sense did not exist in the eighteenth century. In consequence all diplomacy almost without exception appeared superfluous and bad to the *philosphes.* Curiously enough, Jean-Jacques Rousseau, in some ways the most radical champion of the French Enlightenment, challenged that last proposition since to him diplomatic forms were the product of a natural historical development. But the prevailing views, those of Antoine de Condorcet, Diderot or Honoré de Mirabeau, were different. Diplomacy should be outlawed. These men strongly believed in a reason of state, and by nature of reason the interests of all states and nations were identical since all people were basically peace-loving.

Diplomacy was of course never practiced in accordance with these views, but they gained a certain influence in a completely distorted way that the *philosophes* could never have foreseen. The Silesian wars of Frederick II of Prussia or the partitions of Poland—to name only two examples—show that the enlightened undermining of the sacredness of alliances or political affiliations (Frederick II as prince of the Holy Roman Empire, Poland as a member of the community of Christian states) now exploded in the faces of the *philosophes.* Reason of state was evoked all right, but in the interests of each single state irrespective of those of others. Such were the views of Frederick II, Catherine II, Joseph II and after some hesitation even Maria Theresa, as well as of other rulers and statesmen of the time.

This in turn meant that the differences between conventional wars and ideological wars became more and more obscured and in the Napoleonic era practically meaningless. From this follows the perhaps most important contribution of the Enlightenment to the concept of war. Previously, distinctions had been made between *bellum justum* and *bellum injustum.* To the Enlightenment all wars were irrational and unjust. A major distinction between ideological and conventional warfare was thus abolished, at least in theory.

## War in the East

The situation was different with warfare in the East during the period in question. East in this context is to be understood more in a political than in a strictly geographical sense, meaning roughly five principal units: first and second, the lands of the Hungarian-Croatian and Bohemian crowns claimed as their domains by the German Habsburgs, then the Ottoman and the Russian Empires, and finally the Polish kingdom. How does war in these territories, several times larger than those of Western and Western Central Europe combined, relate to the issues of ideological conflict and legitimate succession?[10]

It is plain that the farther one moves east, the more conditions in these respects differ from the West. In the lands of the Bohemian, Hungarian and Polish crowns questions of legitimate succession of the ruling Jagiełło dynasties greatly influenced international relations in the area throughout the fifteenth and part of the sixteenth century.

Indirectly they became causes of major war to the extent that the mutual succession pacts between Habsburgs and Jagiełłos concluded in 1506 were contested in Hungary and Bohemia after King Louis II of Hungary fell in the battle of Mohács against the Turks in 1526. Ferdinand I, the Habsburg claimant to Louis's heritage, had to face war against a Hungarian nobility that did not recognize the succession pacts. In Bohemia the Habsburg succession was likewise challenged by the Estates.

Yet in Hungary as in Bohemia not the succession question but new brands of ideological warfare, though of different types, changed the course of history entirely. In Hungary where warfare over the issue of succession broke out between the new alien king, Ferdinand I, and the representative of the Estates, the Hungarian feudal lord John Zápolyai, the onslaught of the Ottoman Turks pushed the struggle over succession into the background. The Ottoman occupation of the best part of the country completely dominated Hungary's political and economic existence for the next one and a half centuries.

At the end of the period of Ottoman rule between the Peace of Karlowitz in 1699 and that of Passarowitz in 1718 the question of legitimate succession flared anew, but now as an issue of domestic politics and no longer as one of international relations. The issue itself, control of the country by a foreign dynasty, remained a major issue of Hungarian politics until as late a 1848/49.

The Habsburg succession in the lands of the Bohemian crown in 1526, challenged immediately by the Estates, remained a hot issue in Bohemian politics. It might well have led eventually to open conflict with the Emperor had it not, as in Hungary, been pushed into the background by an ideological issue, the Protestant Reformation. It became a decisive question of international politics later than the conflict between Ferdinand and John Zápolyai in Hungary, and the impact of the ideological struggle in the Bohemian lands likewise trailed the Ottoman occupation of Hungary as a cause of war. Yet the first, Bohemian phase of the Thirty Years' War had an even greater effect on European international relations than the Turkish warfare. There is another significant distinction between the Hungarian and the Bohemian situation. In Hungary the issue of royal succession as cause for revolt against the Habsburgs and civil war within the country was in origin unrelated to the Ottoman attack. In Bohemia the claims of the Catholic and basically also alien

Habsburg dynasty were the premise for the revolt of the Bohemian Estates in 1618 and their election of the Protestant Frederick V, the Winter King. Thus in Hungary ideological warfare replaced a type of traditional warfare, which, as in Bohemia, did not lack a strong element of nationalism. In the Bohemian lands traditional and ideological war fused. Yet, since the enemy of the Bohemian nobles, the Emperor and his forces, did not stand beyond the pale of Western civilization like the Turks, the impact of tradition was stronger in the Bohemian lands; the impact of ideology stronger in the Hungarian.[11]

In both countries the element of ideological warfare led to a strategy of annihilation. It was fully successful on the part of the Imperial forces against the Bohemian revolution. In Hungary, mainly owing to the Emperor's conflict with France in the West, ideological warfare in the East had to be suspended intermittently by armistices of many years' duration. Eventually the ideological issue in the wars against the Turks lapsed in the eighteenth century, as the second Ottoman war of Charles VI in the first half of the century and that of Joseph II and Catherine II in its second half clearly proved. Politics and no longer ideological ardor now ruled supreme, and quite openly at that. In both these wars a strategy of attrition—unsuccessful, as it turned out—was employed by the two Christian empires.

In the case of Poland, ruled by the Jagiełło dynasty until as late as the second half of the sixteenth century, conversion of the country to an elective monarchy by 1572 should logically have ruled out the possibility of war over the question of succession. Yet, as the irony of history will have it, a war over the issue of Polish succession was fought from 1733 to 1735.[12] Actually this war differed markedly from the other wars of succession since there was no question of claims of a national dynasty, but only of a national puppet king versus an alien satellite ruler, both in the service of foreign imperialism, French on the one side, Russian and Austrian on the other. Both sides intended to compromise the independence of the country; both met ineffective resistance within the country; but it is not too much to say that the causes of Polish wars in the eighteenth century, beginning with the seemingly insignificant one of 1733–1735, were focused on a specific brand of ideological issue which preceded those of revolutionary France beginning in 1792: the question of national survival. In the words of W. Konopczyński: "Poland lost the freedom of choosing her own king and became dependent on Russia. It was a gain that for the first time the bulk of the nation understood the meaning of political and constitutional independence at the very moment when they had lost it."[13] To be sure, such insight could not compensate for the loss of freedom of action for Poland since this conventional war was an important preliminary step toward elimination of the country from the political map of Europe.[14] This problem, wrapped in the trappings of other foreign and domestic issues, marks a specific type in international relations, namely, ideological war not over issues transcending national boundaries—like religion, social transformation, or constitutional government—but the specific concern of one country: its survival as a sovereign state against the threat of another sovereign state.

As to the Ottoman Empire, there is little doubt that the Turkish thrusts against Central Europe from the middle of the fifteenth century to the death of Sultan Süleyman II in 1566 were prompted by strong ideological as well as traditional imperialistic designs. Only the latter are discernible by the end of the seventeenth century and in the eighteenth century. After the Peace of Passarowitz in 1718 between the Ottoman Empire and the Habsburg power, the predominant Turkish motivation in warfare changed to the defensive objective of holding onto its own or, more correctly, to regaining its own as judged by Turkish interests and tradition.[15] In any case, by the end of the second siege of Vienna in 1683 and the liberation of Hungary by Imperial forces in 1688, war against the Turks both in motivation and in its major operations no longer differed markedly from the type of warfare conducted farther west. Only two differences need be noted. No permanent peace was concluded with the infidels; practically interminable armistices took their place. Second and more important, the stark barbarity of military conduct continued on both sides, even though the rules of war had been gradually humanized in late seventeenth and eighteenth century warfare in the West.[16]

Different again was the case of Russia. As a unitary state its political interrelationship with Western Europe which had gradually taken shape during the second half of the fifteenth century did not become really significant until the reign of Tsar Ivan IV, the Terrible, in the second half of the sixteenth century. Questions of contested succession of significance in international relations therefore could not arise prior to that time, nor did they affect foreign affairs after then. They were not a factor in Russia's wars with its neighbors—the

Muslim Ottomans, the Catholic rulers of Poland, or the Protestant kings of Sweden.

By contrast, the issue of succession was of major importance in Russian domestic affairs where it played a strange role in the seventeenth and eighteenth centuries. During the so-called Time of Troubles in the early seventeenth century the surface question was the contested rule of a false claimant to the throne, but the root problem was a conflict between the boyars and the lower strata of the population led by the Cossacks. Again, the surface issue in the great peasant revolt by the Don Cossacks under Stenka Razin in 1670 was a claim that the rebel leader was the genuine tsar. This phenomenon recurred in Yemilian Pugachev's peasant revolt in southeastern Russia in the 1770s during the reign of Catherine II, the Great, when it was again claimed that the leader of the revolt was the legitimate tsar ordained by God. In view of the almost divine status of the tsar, in all three cases a social revolt could be rationalized and justified only if it was meant not to overthrow but to install the true tsar.[17]

In considering armed conflicts between Russia and continental European countries, the primary focus of the present paper has to be on the eighteenth century, not on seventeenth-century brushes in disputed border regions against Turks and Poles. Owing to the strange and in many ways irresponsible personality of King Charles XII of Sweden, the Great Northern War (1700–1721) has to be seen as a conflict of mutual aggression on both sides, by Russia and its Polish ally as well as by Sweden, although Russian ambitions to expand had to be taken far more seriously than Swedish ones. In other eighteenth-century conflicts with the Ottoman Empire, Poland, and Prussia, Russian imperialist designs were hardly open to doubt, not so much because Russia was more aggressive than its adversaries, but because, owing to its late entry into the game of European power politics, it had no claims of legitimate succession based on marriage and succession pacts to invoke to justify war. Russia's strategy in all wars fought on its own soil was one of annihilation in the eighteenth century—and has been ever since; in regard to imperial conquests, however, it was a more cautious one of limited objectives. The first strategy was apparent in the Great Northern War, the second in the relatively minor political obstacle that eighteenth-century Poland represented. Here Catherine II preferred the safe method of joint partitions with other powers, although the risk to Russia of outright occupation of Poland alone might not have been excessive.[18]

At this point consider again the problem of distinctions between different types of warfare, and this time, unlike the issue of enlightened philosophy, on practical grounds and with special application to the East. In the long run the difference between ideological and nonideological warfare loses its meaning, as a few cases will illustrate.

Perhaps the most conspicuous example of a war fought over an essentially trivial issue of succession, strictly in the interest of three contending Great Powers—the empires of the Bourbons, the Habsburgs and the Romanovs—was the War of the Polish Succession, which has already been discussed.

There were also other cases of truly or supposedly limited warfare in the eighteenth century. The conflicts between the Habsburg and the Russian Empires on the one hand and the Ottoman Empire on the other offer striking examples. The first Turkish war of Emperor Charles VI was initiated as intervention against the Ottoman occupation of the Morea, the southern Greek peninsula in the possession of the republic of Venice. This could be called a preventive war of intervention with limited objectives against a barely conceivable Turkish threat to Habsburg territory. In the Peace of Passarowitz of 1718 the Habsburg Empire nevertheless secured very substantial territorial gains and reached its greatest territorial extent. The Turks were forced to cede a good part of northern Serbia, and Oltenia, but only a very small strip of northern Bosnian territory which was closer to the centers of Habsburg power. In Charles's second war with the Turks in 1736–1739 (surely one of limited objectives), the Habsburgs, bound by an outdated treaty of alliance, were forced to act more or less as Russian satellites. By the subsequent Treaty of Belgrade they lost most of what they had gained in the Peace of Passarowitz. In particular, the chance to incorporate Bosnia was missed, though not for good. The Russo-Austrian war against the Turks of 1787–1791, in which the Habsburg power again fought more or less as junior partner to Russia, offered a new possibility for the conquest of Bosnia. This time the Austrians gained a temporary foothold in Bosnia, but were forced to surrender it even before conclusion of the Peace of Sistova in 1791, which in essence confirmed the provisions of the Peace of Belgrade of 1739.

It appears possible, though by no means certain, that had Austria acquired Bosnia instead of fragments of more remote Serbian and Rumanian territories in the eighteenth century, there might have been an opportunity to solve the South Slav problem within the Habsburg boundaries, even to gain the Serbs' support for such a solution prior to their decisive early nineteenth-century risings against the Turks. The unsolved Bosnian question, from the dubious occupation of 1878 to the ill-fated annexation of 1908, was, so to speak, the cradle of the expanding world war crisis of July 1914. Surely here a chain can be perceived from relatively small causes to major consequences or, in other terms, from conventional origins to ideological results.[19]

And now finally a look at Russo-Ottoman relations. The causes of the Turkish-Russian war of 1768–1774 were limited ones in that they stemmed from Turkish demands that the Russians should evacuate southern Polish territory occupied by the Cossacks. This irruption certainly represented a kind of threat, albeit indirect. Anyway, it was a case of seemingly limited war. The victory of the Russians embodied in the Peace of Kuchuk-Kainarji of 1774 had no immediate shattering impact on Ottoman power but it contained at least two time bombs: the firm foothold Russia secured on the Black Sea coast and the recognition of Russian rights, though as yet only limited, to protect the interests of Orthodox Christians in the Ottoman Empire. The Peace of Jassy of 1792 after the new Turko-Russian war of 1787–1792 confirmed and expanded the gains of Kuchuk-Kainarji and strengthened the Russian prerogatives wrung there from the Turks. In particular the conquest of Ochakov and the territory around Odessa established firm Russian control of the Black Sea and threatened the principalities that were still under Turkish overlordship. These provisions helped to prepare the ground for the Crimean War of 1854, the ongoing hostility between the Russian and Habsburg powers, and the ever growing intimidation of Turkey. This in turn exacerbated the Balkan crisis and, even more directly than the Bosnian misadventures of the Habsburgs, contributed to the outbreak of World War I.[20]

## Public Opinion and Warfare

There are two additional factors that separate so to speak common imperialist war from ideological war, which at the same time indicate distinctions between warfare in the European West and East: popular war or, more correctly, war backed by large segments of public opinion, and the question of more or less predictable war.

Clearly both phenomena can be discussed only by approximation in the period under present consideration. In regard to the first, the question of popular war, the initiation of public-opinion research in the last decades has helped to make it possible to approach this issue with considerable assurance for contemporary history and through reasonable deduction even for the remote past.[21] On the question of predictability no similar progress has been made but here too at least educated guesses are possible for the past.

It stands to reason that ideological warfare could count on far wider support from broader strata of society than plain imperialistic warfare, particularly if the power-holders' economic acquisitiveness was not too conspicuous, and a ruler's claims in a question of contested succession were not strikingly alien to the inhabitants of the countries involved. On these premises no major war in Western and Central Europe after the Thirty Years' War and up to the war of the First Coalition against France in 1792 could be considered popular. Widespread reaction to such flagrant aggression as Louis XIV's invasion of the Netherlands or the second Ottoman siege of Vienna was to be expected. Attacks of this kind had a profound effect on a large part of public opinion, at least in Central Europe. Beyond such instances of aggression of international significance, the drive for national survival within national boundaries also came into play.[22]

In the East the situation was not the same. The effect of the religious issue on the first, Bohemian phase of the Thirty Years' War has already been noted, as has that of the Ottoman invasions of Hungary, at least roughly until the reconquest of Buda in 1686. Thereupon the impact of the Counter-Reformation, enforced by foreign soldiers, made people quickly forget the positive consequences of liberation from the Ottoman yoke. In general, however, the overall defensive character of the wars against the Turks—even up to the imperialist Peace of Passarowitz in 1718—was widely believed all over East Central Europe, and this kind of war presumably enjoyed wide public support.

Different again were circumstances in Russia. Here the wars against the Turks, which began seriously some two centuries later than Turkish warfare in East Central Europe, were almost from the start not defensive but offensive wars. They lacked the ideological core. The dream objective, to plant the Greek cross on the basilica of Santa Sophia in Constantinople, was never an issue of political necessity. The wars against Poland in the eighteenth century, on the other hand, were for the Poles struggles for survival and as such without question increasingly popular, in particular resistance to the third partition of the country in 1794–1795.

These distinctions lead to the question of predictability. Clearly it has always been easier to predict the eventual outbreak of ideological war than war over such causes as succession, whether rationalized or legitimate. The eighteenth century with its Diplomatic Revolution leading to the reversal of alliances, the surprise attacks of Prussia under Frederick II, and less spectacularly those of France and Spain earlier, is the classic age of unpredictable war. Sometimes it was not only unpredictable when such a war would occur but whether it would break out at all.

Here too a difference can be discerned between West and East. In the West political boundaries with many noncontiguous territories in the possession of Great Powers frequently left enclaves under the sway of potential enemies. The boundaries in Western and Central Europe in conjunction with the manifold dynastic relationships between ruling families just invited war at the opportune time. Since major ideological obstacles, including religious ones, rarely impeded and never prevented alliances in the eighteenth century, coalition partners could easily be found and generally identified in good time.

Russian territory on the other hand included no enclaves within the domains of Western powers whose political structure had originated in feudal times. Dynastic relationships to ruling houses farther west, although existing among the heirs of Peter the Great, were not nearly so intimate prior to the nineteenth century as those between the Habsburgs and Bourbons or the Hanovers and Hohenzollerns. Nonideological war in the East was therefore even more unpredictable than in the West. It was the tremendous and in a way equalizing impact of the French Revolution that accentuated the causes of war in East and West alike. Increased dangers of ever larger wars erased the differences between the Western and Eastern approach to war. The consequence was certain in either case. Whenever ideological warfare had led to larger armed forces, governments that turned to conventional warfare would accept these changes in military strength. One might speak henceforth of different causes of war, but not of larger or smaller armed forces according to the motivations of war. Politics, to be sure, determine the causes of war, but, regardless of its causes, war eventually determines its own conduct.

## Notes

1. M. S. Anderson, *Europe in the Eighteenth Century, 1713–1783* (London, 1968), pp. 152–170; Penfield Roberts, *The Quest of Security, 1715–1740* (New York, 1947), pp. 240–263; Walter L. Dorn, *Competition for Empire, 1740–1763* (New York, 1940), pp. 292–384; Leo Gershoy, *From Despotism to Revolution, 1763–1789* (New York, 1944), pp. 162–196; L. O. Lindsay (ed.), *The Old Regime, 1713–1763 (The New Cambridge Modern History*, Vol. VII [Cambridge, 1957]), esp. chaps, 8 and 9; Jacques Droz, *Histoire diplomatique de 1648 à 1919* (Paris, 1959), pp. 6–271.

2. Carl v. Clausewitz, *Vom Kriege* (Berlin, 1933), pp. 21, 23, 28 ff., 35, 308, 504, 517, 522, 609 ff., 621 ff., 633 ff., 648 f.; Hans Rothfels, "Clausewitz," in Edward M. Earle (ed.), *Makers of Modern Strategy* (Princeton, 1943), pp. 93–113.

3. Clausewitz, *Vom Kriege*, pp. 615, 621 ff.; Hans Delbrück, *Geschichte der Kriegskunst im Rahmen der politischen Geschichte*, IV: *Neuzeit* (Berlin, 1920), 297; Robert A. Kann, "The Law of Nations and the Conduct of War in the Early Times of the Standing Army," *Journal of Politics*, VI (1944), 77–105; M. Jähns, *Geschichte der Kriegswissenschaften vornehmlich in Deutschland* (Leipzig, 1889–91), Vols. II & III.

4. A. Lonsky, "International Relations," in J. S. Bromley (ed.), *The Rise of Great Britain and Russia, 1688–1725 (The New Cambridge Modern History*, Vol VI [Cambridge, 1970]), pp. 154–192.

5. Clausewitz, *Vom Kriege*, pp. 155, 189, 262, 308, 316 ff., 613 ff., 621 ff.; Delbrück, *Kriegskunst*, pp. 333–364, 497–530.

6. Clausewitz evidently had this in mind in writing of the concept of abstract war. *Vom Kriege*, pp. 23 ff.

7. Ludwig Dehio, *Gleichgewicht oder Hegemonie: Betrachtungen über ein Grundproblem der neueren Staatsgeschichte* (Krefeld, 1948), *passim;* Clausewitz, *Vom Kriege*, pp. 33 ff., 341–352, 504, 517, 609 ff., 621 ff., 633 ff.; Delbrück, *Kriegskunst*, pp. 489 f.; Gerhard Ritter, *Staatskunst und Kriegshandwerk: Das Problem des 'Militarismus' in Deutschland*, I: *Die altpreussische Tradition, 1740–1890* (2nd ed.; Munich, 1959), 41 ff.; Sir Charles Petrie, *Diplomatic History* (London, 1948), pp. 1–69; Robert R. Palmer, "Frederick the Great, Guibert, Bülow: From Dynastic to National War," in Earle, *Modern Strategy*, pp. 49–74; Jähns, *Kriegswissenschaften*, Vol. III.

8. Felix Gilbert, *History: Choice and Commitment* (Cambridge, Mass., 1977), pp. 328 ff. and 323–349 *passim*.

9. Robert A. Kann, "Alliances versus Ententes," *World Politics*, XXVIII (1976), 611–621.

10. Sir J.A.R. Marriott, *The Eastern Question* (Oxford, 1951), pp. 129–164; Bromley, *Great Britain and Russia*, chaps. 20/1, 20/2, 21; J[ohn] F. C. Fuller, *A Military History of the Western World*, II (New

York, 1955), 156–160.

11. László Makkai in Ervin Pamlényi (ed.), *Die Geschichte Ungarns* (Budapest, 1971), pp. 129–170; K. Richter in Karl v. Bosl (ed.), *Handbuch der Geschichte der böhmischen Länder,* II (Stuttgart, 1974), 99–125, 261–292; Robert A. Kann, *A History of the Habsburg Empire, 1526–1918* (Berkeley and Los Angeles, 1974), pp. 37–76.

12. The definitive peace treaty was signed in Vienna only in 1738.

13. Wł[adysław] Konopczyński in W[illiam] F. Reddaway *et al.* (eds.), *The Cambridge History of Poland* (Cambridge, 1950–51), II, 29.

14. Konopczyński, *ibid.*, chap. 2, 25–48; Reddaway, *ibid.*, chap. 5, 88–111; B. Dembiński, *ibid.*, chap. 6, 112–136; Reddaway, *ibid.*, chap. 7, 137–153; M[arian] Kukiel, *ibid.*, chap. 8, 154–186.

15. Issues over claims to succession on the Ottoman side, though not absent, would be considered by entirely different religious and social standards from those prevailing in Christian Europe. Discussion of them would be beyond the scope of the present essay.

16. Johann C. Allmayer-Beck and Erich Lessing, *Die kaiserlichen Kriegsvölker: Von Maximilian I. bis Prinz Eugen, 1479–1718* (Munich, 1978), pp. 165–248.

17. Strangely enough, the phenomenon of rationalizing social conflicts in dynastic terms recurs once more in European history: this time not in the east but in the west, in the Carlist wars of Spain.

18. George Vernadsky, *A History of Russia* (New Haven, 1930), pp. 67–105; Sir Bernard Pares, *A History of Russia* (London, 1949), pp. 159–197, 276–320; Reddaway *et al.*, *Cambridge History of Poland,* II, 88–176.

19. Kann, *Habsburg Empire,* pp. 68–70, 167–169; Karl A. Roider, Jr., *The Reluctant Ally: Austria's Policy in the Austro-Turkish War, 1737–1739* (Baton Rouge, 1972), pp. 32–53, 141–183.

20. Pares, *History of Russia,* pp. 299–319; Marriott, *Eastern Question,* pp. 129–164.

21. Cf. Robert A. Kann, "Public Opinion Research: A Contribution to Historical Method," *Political Science Quarterly,* LXXIII (1958), 374–396, and the literature quoted there; published also in Don K. Rowney and J. Graham (eds.), *Quantitative Analysis of Historical Data* (Homewood, Ill., 1929).

22. Clausewitz, *Vom Kriege,* pp. 139 f., 492–499, 646 f.

# III

# Habsburg Society and War

## A. Theories of War

Charles W. Ingrao

# Habsburg Strategy and Geopolitics during the Eighteenth Century

Historians have long acknowledged that the Habsburg monarchy owed both its military successes and its survival in the many wars it fought to the reassuring presence it provided its neighbors as a counterweight or buffer against foreign aggression. Whether the threat came from the Protestant heresy, the Turks, Louis XIV, Napoleon, or tsarist Russia, the house of Austria was the beneficiary of Europe's quest for security from the accession of Charles V to the death of Francis Joseph four centuries later.

What has tended to be overlooked, however, is that the Habsburgs themselves also looked to their frontiers for security, and frequently strove to maintain buffers of their own for added insurance against foreign aggression. Indeed, so much has been the preoccupation with the Byzantine turns of European diplomacy that sight has been lost of the existence of broader strategic issues in the formulation of Habsburg military and diplomatic priorities. The one exception has been awareness of the great dialogue between "easterners" and "westerners" as the Hofburg balanced its military options between war against the Turks and the French. This dualism is, however, applicable only to the sixteenth and seventeenth centuries and became increasingly outmoded and irrelevant after 1700.

In fact, a host of changing circumstances during the eighteenth century led the monarchy's statesmen to abandon for all time the traditional east-west dichotomy in favor of a new set of military and diplomatic priorities that took fuller account of its exposed position in East Central Europe. After 1700 Habsburg foreign policy and military strategy expressed concern for the maintenance of secure buffers in all four quarters contiguous to the monarchy's frontiers; the government in Vienna could no longer afford to concentrate principally on developments in the Empire and in the Balkans, but was also compelled to forestall the emergence of a foreign military presence in Italy and Poland. Moreover, even within Germany and the Balkans, Habsburg strategy focused on different regions and different neighbors than in past centuries.

Although the monarchy's geopolitical concerns were essentially quadrilateral in nature throughout the century, it would be erroneous to suggest that its statesmen consciously conceived of a comprehensive and well-coordinated program for dealing with this challenge. At best they made only occasional references to the monarchy's exposed position in the heart of the continent, and invariably concentrated on responding to individual crises as they arose in a particular theatre. Nevertheless throughout the century the course of Austrian foreign and military policy was generally dictated by these new geopolitical realities, even to the point of withstanding and overriding the individual prejudices of its rulers, whether they be the intense Francophobia of Joseph I, Charles VI's obsession with Spain, Maria Theresa's hatred of Frederick II, or Joseph II's quest for military glory.

By 1700 these new realities were already becoming evident. The monarchy's association and identification with the Holy Roman Empire had faded to the point where purely Austrian interests and security clearly superseded those of Germany. More important still, the Spanish dynastic tie of the past two centuries had snapped altogether. During that period the Spanish alliance had doubtless helped Austria to secure its frontiers in the Balkans, Italy and Germany, but had at the same time tied the monarchy to Spain's concerns in Western Europe, thereby committing it to conflicts that transcended its own strategic needs. With the extinction of the Spanish Habsburgs, Vienna could concentrate more fully on meeting the security needs of its Danubian possessions. Meanwhile, the military developments of the War of the Spanish Succession and the Great Northern War helped complete the catharsis by suddenly and simultaneously pushing all four of the monarchy's frontier regions to the fore as the Emperor and his ministers prepared their strategy.

No theatre of operations was more crucial to the Habsburgs than Italy. For the past two centuries their Spanish cousins had provided for the peninsula's defense against French or Ottoman invasion. Yet, with the imminent extinction of the Spanish branch of the dynasty, its retention became the principal goal of the Emperor's diplomacy. Indeed, Leopold I's abrupt rejection of the seemingly generous Second Partition Treaty (1700) culminated decades of negotiations in which Vienna steadfastly refused to offer France any compensation in Italy. Unless he secured his Italian glacis intact, the Emperor was bent on war, and once that conflict broke out, it was in and for Italy that he intended to fight.[1] Prince Eugene of Savoy's peninsular campaigns and the government's intense lobbying for Anglo-Dutch financial support reflected this commitment, as did the future Joseph I's successful attempt to force his brother Charles to cede Milan in perpetuity to the elder, Austrian branch of the family.[2] Eugene's decisive victory at Turin in 1706 did not alter the monarchy's Italian strategy, but merely enabled it to focus on securing Naples, which was widely regarded in Vienna as "a sword pointed at Hungary's side."[3] The subsequently negotiated French evacuation of northern Italy and Field Marshal Weyrich von Daun's march to the south did in fact complete the conquest of the peninsula, leaving the new Emperor Joseph I with no regrets, even though his Italian strategy had led directly to the failure of Eugene's Toulon offensive, Marshal Claude de Villars's occupation of Swabia, and his own brother's disastrous defeat at Almansa. Nor did Joseph stray from this determination at the Hague and Gertruydenberg peace conferences, where he steadfastly refused to yield an inch of Italian territory—including Sicily or Sardinia—to his enemies even though the dynasty could have secured the rest of the huge Spanish succession in exchange. Right up to his death in 1711 he remained true to the principle that "if a partition should be entered into, the Italian part is absolutely indispensable."[4]

If the Habsburgs wanted to secure Italy, they also attached great importance to Germany as a bastion in the West. Indeed, much has been made by historians of Joseph I's patriotic pronouncements on the Empire's behalf and of his two campaigns on the Rhine against the *Teufelsfranzosen.* Yet Joseph's personal proclivities did not prevent either him or his father from concentrating forces on other fronts along the monarchy's periphery, such as Italy. It was only in 1704, after Bavaria's desertion to the French had moved the western front from the Rhine to the Inn, thereby exposing the Austrian frontier and threatening the permanent loss of Habsburg dominion over the Empire, that Vienna attached top priority to military operations in Germany.[5] Moreover, once Blenheim had crushed the Bavarians and expelled the French, Austrian troops were diverted once again to Italy and other fronts for the war's duration. Even the taxes and troops raised by the Imperial military administration in occupied Bavaria were funneled to Italy by the determined Emperor Joseph.[6]

Just as Bavaria's desertion had unexpectedly forced the dynasty to fight for Germany's preservation, so the eight-year-long *kuruc* war of independence of Ferenc II Rákóczi suddenly opened up yet a third front perilously close to the Austrian and Bohemian hereditary provinces. Unlike the Austrian and even the Bohemian lands, Hungary had always been regarded somewhat as a foreign appendage and never viewed with the same concern by the Emperor and his ministers as a fully integrated or deserving part of the Habsburg commonwealth. Rather, since its acquisition in the sixteenth century it had been seen as an occasional source of revenue and, above all, as an indispensable buffer between the Turks and the hereditary provinces, the defense of which it was intended to serve.[7] The *kuruc* war deprived the Habsburgs of both of these advantages and once again exposed the hereditary lands to the ravages of battle. The crown could probably have negotiated a settlement with the "malcontents" after only three or four years had it been willing to concede their demands for the restoration of an independent Transylvania.[8] Yet Joseph I was determined to spare Hungary not only from partition but also from the numerous invasions that Transylvania had mounted against it and the hereditary provinces during the previous century. Hence he refused to negotiate and ultimately committed approximately 50,000 troops, or nearly half of the Austrian army, to the Hungarian front, concentrating much of his strength in Transylvania itself, partly in order to nullify Rákóczi there, and partly to discourage Ottoman intervention on behalf of the *kuruc* insurgents.[9]

While the War of the Spanish Succession had presented a serious challenge to the monarchy's security in Italy, Germany and Hungary, the Great Northern War presented it with a formidable military threat from Poland. Like the Italian peninsula, the Polish frontier had thitherto occasioned only minimal concern among the monarchy's military planners. Yet the royal republic's decline in the seventeenth century relative to its more politically and militarily sophisticated neighbors rendered inevitable both its collapse and yet another confrontation between Austria and its neighbors. The story of the Swedish conquest of Poland and occupation of Saxony does not need to be recounted here.[10] Suffice it to say that Emperor Joseph was compelled to balance carefully the expectations of Charles XII and Peter the Great in order to avoid becoming embroiled in a new war on his northeastern frontier.

Moreover, long after he had capitulated to Charles at Altranstädt

(1707), Joseph continued to take precautions against an outbreak of hostilities with either the Swedes or the Turks. Perhaps most significant was his fateful decision on the eve of the 1708 campaign to send Prince Eugene to command in Flanders rather than in Spain, where his presence could have prompted a stronger Anglo-Dutch military commitment and a reversal of the Archduke Charles's misfortunes. Eugene had to stay closer to home, however, because Joseph wanted him available to defend the monarchy against a sudden Swedish or Ottoman thrust.[11] As a further precaution the Emperor considered concluding a defensive alliance with the tsar, and did eventually move to establish the Neutrality League of German Princes designed to discourage a Swedish or Turkish advance into Poland and the Empire. Meanwhile, had he fallen into a war with either Sweden or the Ottoman Empire, there can be no question that Joseph would have accorded top priority to his exposed eastern frontier. As early as 1708, with Italy and Germany secure and Charles XII once again engaged in Russia, he had made it clear that, should the Turks invade Hungary, he would immediately sign a separate peace with the French (presumably sacrificing Spain) and march against them at the head of his troops.[12]

In view of these multiple concerns on his own frontiers, Joseph was ultimately forced to sacrifice virtually all of the dynasty's less tangible objectives in Flanders, Alsace, and Spain. Although he sent Eugene to command in Flanders, the total number of Imperial troops maintained on these three fronts never exceeded 20,000. Because of the lingering Swedish and Turkish threats to Poland and Hungary, the first fully supported Austrian contingents did not arrive in Spain until the end of 1711—that is, after the formation of the Neutrality League and the Peace of Szatmár had provided a measure of security on the monarchy's northern and southeastern frontiers.

The fruits of Joseph's grand strategy were embodied in the peace treaties of Utrecht, Rastatt and Baden, settlements that reflected the virtual abandonment of the Habsburgs' past imperial and Spanish dynastic policies and the emergence of an essentially quadrilateral, geopolitical approach to war and diplomacy that had given the hereditary provinces greater security on their periphery than had ever existed before. Moreover, in the years immediately following the peace, the wisdom of this more modest, intrinsically defensive strategy appeared to be even more apparent. The loss of Spain and death of Louis XIV led to an easing of the centuries-old antagonism between France and Austria. In addition, the monarchy's momentary isolation from the Maritime Powers now seemed to require a less broad and ambitious foreign policy that could be successfully carried out without the need for allies. Finally a new series of foreign threats were already beginning to emerge which, given their closer proximity to the monarchy, posed an ultimately greater threat to its security than had Louis XIV's France. More specifically, the emergence and expansion of three traditional allies in Russia, Prussia, and a resurgent, but now Bourbon, Spain required greater vigilance in each of those frontier regions so recently secured during the last war.

These new, largely regional challenges and the monarchy's attempts to neutralize them would, in fact, dictate the course of Austrian foreign policy and explain the monarchy's involvement in its remaining prerevolutionary conflicts. During this period the Emperors and their ministers continued to speak of maintaining a "balance of power," as did their counterparts in London, Versailles, and Berlin. But when an Austrian statesman did so, he was no longer speaking of a European-wide balance, as in the days of Louis XIV, but only of the regional balance of military power within a specific theater, such as the equation of Habsburg strength with Prussia in Germany, with Russia in the Balkans, and with Spain in Italy. Any broader implication was simply no longer intended or relevant.

In evaluating the foreign policy of Emperor Charles VI (1711–1740), it is not a matter of geopolitical considerations but rather of the obsession of the last male in direct Habsburg descent with Spain, the Pragmatic Sanction, and the creation of a maritime commercial empire. Yet, although he was never faced with the multiple threats that had confronted his predecessor, Charles also followed a course that favored the maintenance of secure buffer zones along the periphery of the hereditary lands. In the opening years of his reign, Charles's principal concerns and decisions did not involve the Rhine-Danube dilemma that had dominated his father's reign, nor even a resumption of the struggle with France over the Spanish succession which he still craved, but rather a choice between confronting simultaneous military advances by the Turks in the Balkans and by Spain in Italy. Far from seeking to extend its holdings in either peninsula, the Hofburg was motivated solely by the desire to neutralize these two threats lest "Your Majesty would no longer be secure in your own house."[13] Rather than resort to war Charles initially tried to forestall his adversaries by diplomacy, by offering to mediate a settlement in the Turko-Venetian war, and by seeking an Anglo-Dutch guarantee of his holdings in Italy. In addition, he carefully weighed the competing overtures made to him by both the Maritime Powers and by the French and, as Max Braubach has shown, was perfectly willing to ally with his old enemy if Versailles could guarantee his security in Italy and the Balkans.[14] In the end Charles concluded the Quadruple Alliance with all three powers—Austria's first alliance ever with France—though not before diplomacy had failed to end invasion in both theaters, or before he had been compelled to choose between Italy and Hungary as the site for the first Austrian military operations.[15]

His eventual decision to fight in the Balkans led to one of the many struggles between Prince Eugene and Charles's Spanish camarilla, which understandably gave a higher priority to retaining control over the former Spanish possessions in Italy. Yet, notwithstanding his own attachment to both his Spanish favorites and possessions, the Emperor reluctantly chose to act first in the Balkans because the Turks currently posed by far the greater threat to the monarchy's security.[16] Moreover, Eugene's subsequent campaigns were directed not at Bosnia, the annexation of which would have helped to consolidate the monarchy's territories, but at the Banat and Belgrade, which had long been recognized as a key fortress possession of which "would secure the entire kingdom of Hungary."[17]

At no point, however, did the Emperor and his ministers forget the Spanish advance in Italy. So once the Banat and Belgrade had been seized, they weighed the territorial advantages that might be won by further campaigns in the Balkans against concentrating their forces in Italy. Since there was general agreement that further Balkan conquests were superfluous to the monarchy's security, peace was concluded at once with the Turks.[18] Meanwhile, though Charles VI adhered to the Quadruple Alliance with some reluctance because of its explicit renunciation of the Habsburg succession in Spain, he did so nevertheless because, like his ministers, he judged that Sicily recently seized by the Spanish was indispensable to the defense of Italy.[19]

If geopolitical realities compelled Charles to sacrifice his Spanish fantasies in the first decade of his reign, they also forced him to jettison equally grandiose schemes in the second. His dreams of a lucrative Spanish match for Maria Theresa and of commercial expansion through the Ostend Company, as well as his illusions about leading a major alliance of Spain, Russia, Prussia and the Empire, were all disabused following the war scare of 1726–1728 during which a sober estimate of his enemies' military forces convinced Charles that a conflict would likely result in disastrous setbacks in Germany and Italy.[20] Nor was his immediate response to this reverse totally free of equally unfortunate illusions. In his subsequent retreat from his Spanish project, the Emperor resorted to the Old System—the traditional alliance with the Maritime Powers against the Bourbon powers. But the monarchy's new insularity and more localized security needs were no longer congenial to the interests of its allies, who remained concerned primarily with Western European and colonial affairs. The result was Charles's isolation in the War of the Polish Succession, a conflict that involved purely Austrian strategic needs.

As on the eve of his last Ottoman war, Charles's actions prior to the Polish conflict required assessing the security needs of two competing areas, in this case Poland and Italy. Since the Great Northern War the Hofburg had favored the retention of a weak, pro-Habsburg dynasty, such as the incumbent Wettins, on the Polish throne. Yet, when Prince Eugene urged a show of military strength in Silesia in support of the Wettin candidate during the 1733 election, Privy Council Secretary Johann von Bartenstein raised the specter of a descent on Italy by the Bourbon powers, whose Polish candidate was Stanislaus Leszczyński, Louis XV's father-in-law. While Eugene felt a French client in Poland posed a threat to Austrian security in the northeast, Bartenstein stressed that, though any Polish king would be a nonentity, Bourbon retaliation in Italy would seriously endanger the monarchy's frontier in the southwest.[21] Concern for Italy's security was indeed very keen, especially since Charles's resurrection of the Old System and repudiation of Spain. Just two years earlier the Emperor had labored mightily, if unsuccessfully, to prevent Spain from garrisoning Parma and Tuscany, and had even dispatched 11,000 troops to suppress a rebellion in Corsica, lest its Genoese overlords call in French troops instead.[22] In the end, however, Charles judged the Polish threat the more tangible with the result that, while Poland was secured easily by his Russian ally, the Bourbon powers declared war and overran the peninsula.

In the ensuing struggle the Emperor attached higher priority to the Italian theater, and sent the bulk of his forces there rather than to the far-off Rhenish front.[23] Once both Austrian armies had been defeated, however, he was faced once again with the need to assess his strategic needs. In the subsequent deliberations of the Privy Council both Eugene and Bartenstein argued for a quick peace that would still preserve the Habsburg position in both Italy and Germany, with Bartenstein stating explicitly that "it is theoretically justified [to expect] that any peace plan . . . be capable of providing for the future security of the hereditary provinces."[24] Since there was also reason to fear an opportunistic Ottoman assault on Hungary, the Privy Council was unanimous in its decision to hold its position in three of its frontier regions, especially now that it had protected its interests in Poland. In the Treaty of Vienna of 1738 the Emperor readily agreed to cede Naples and Sicily, and Lorraine to the Bourbons. He and his ministers tacitly accepted the French argument that neither the kingdom nor the duchy was essential for the monarchy's defense, and meanwhile welcomed the chance to come into possession of the far more strategically valuable Parma and Tuscany as compensation.[25] With the successful "election" of another Wettin king in Poland and the acquisition of the two northern Italian duchies, Austria's defeat in the War of the Polish Succession had proven a geopolitical triumph.

If the Treaty of Vienna had enhanced Austrian security in Italy and Poland, it was becoming increasingly apparent by the end of Charles's reign that the continuing evolution of the Prussian and Russian monarchies was compromising Habsburg hegemony in the Empire and the northern Balkans. In fact, Vienna was not only aware of this dual threat long before the appearance of Frederick and Catherine the Great, but was already taking precautions against their advance in Germany and the Balkans at the start of the eighteenth century.

The Habsburg monarchy's growing opposition to Prussian expansion after 1700 would surprise no student of Imperial politics. Past Emperors had always opposed the growth of those larger princes who threatened Austrian hegemony in Germany. Mühlberg, the White Mountain and, most recently, Blenheim stood as tombstones marking the end of previous challenges to Habsburg imperial authority. Prussia's prodigious territorial acquisitions and aspirations had already soured relations between Vienna and Berlin by the end of Leopold I's reign. By 1705 the Imperial court was in general agreement that the bestowal of the royal title on the Hohenzollerns had been a gross mistake because it had only heightened, rather than satiated, Prussian ambitions.[26] On the eve of the Blenheim campaign Leopold actually turned down Frederick I's offer of an additional 14,000 auxiliaries, and in the following year also blocked the formation of an autonomous 20,000-man Prussian corps in the Mosel Valley, out of fear that acquiesence in either instance would spawn further pretensions.[27] Following Leopold's death, Joseph I transformed his father's disillusionment into a comprehensive and well-coordinated policy of obstructing all Prussian territorial, financial, and political claims within the Empire, with the result that Frederick I not only broke off diplomatic relations but withdrew all his troops from the Imperial army.

Of course, what both Leopold and Joseph had done was to sacrifice the Empire's western frontier and the military effort against France in order to forestall a Prussian challenge to Austria within Germany. In justifying this policy, Joseph's prime minister, Prince Salm, bluntly—and prophetically—told the Prussian envoy:

> The House of Austria fears the power of the king of Prussia more than that of France, which is greater; that the king of France only gnaws at the edges of those countries that border on it, but that the king of Prussia proceeds directly to the heart.[28]

In fact, the Hofburg's conception of the "western front" was already shifting from the seventeenth-century notion of a struggle with France to defend the Empire's borders, to an eighteenth-century awareness of a contest with Prussia within Germany itself to protect the monarchy's own security.

Habsburg paranoia over the perceived Prussian military threat continued to grow under Charles VI. Once the Peace of the Prut and the formation of the Neutrality League had virtually eliminated the Swedish threat to Poland, the new Emperor adopted the view already prevalent among his brother's ministers that the monarchy had far more to lose from the growth of Prussia than it had to gain from the collapse of Sweden. He promptly arranged for Charles XII's return from exile at Bender and subsequently favored the territorial designs of the Danes, Saxons and Hanoverians in order to limit Prussian pretensions in northern Germany.[29] Indeed, right up to the close of his reign Charles VI continued to follow in his brother's footsteps by opposing the Hohenzollerns unquestionably legitimate succession in Jülich-Berg, and in his father's when in 1733 he declined Berlin's offer of 40,000 additional troops for service against the French lest it encourage Prussian claims to a special military position within the Empire.[30] Viewed in this light, Frederick II's seizure of Silesia on the morrow the the Emperor's death represented the only possible solution to the tension between Prussian expansionism and Habsburg geopolitics within the Empire.

Historians have long appreciated the degree to which Maria Theresa's moral outrage and hatred influenced her attitude toward "that evil man" Frederick II.[31] Yet, if she let her sense of morality and justice color her view of the Prussian "monster," the great Empress also appreciated the more rational judgment of Chancellor Wenzel von Kaunitz and was usually persuaded by his closely reasoned calculations, even when they went against her own deeply ingrained feelings. To Kaunitz Prussia was the monarchy's greatest enemy only because, by seizing Silesia and destroying Habsburg hegemony in the Empire, it now posed the most serious threat to its existence.[32] Frederick had, in fact, not only outflanked the monarchy's defensive bastions in Germany but, in seizing Silesia, had ravaged the very core of the monarchy that its buffers were designed to protect. Moreover, by acquiring the county of Glatz, he had exposed Bohemia to a similar fate. If feelings of revenge and retribution fortified Maria Theresa's spirit, it was the monarchy's security that guided her hand. Indeed when during the 1761 campaign victory over Prussia appeared to be at hand, she outlined her ultimate intentions to Field Marshal Leopold von Daun and spoke not of a Punic settlement but only of "the reduction of the house of Brandenburg to its former state as a rather secondary small power," indeed a power that would still be "comparable to the other lay electorates."[33]

Once the recovery of Silesia proved impossible, the monarchy resorted to the numerous, if ill-fated, Bavarian and Flemish exchange projects in order to regain at least its dominant position within the Empire. The idea of exchanging either territory was not a new one in the eighteenth century, given the monarchy's long-standing interest in consolidating its territories and rationalizing its frontiers. Yet, a closer examination of these various projects shows that the Habsburgs were determined to make an exchange only when their frontiers were threatened, and invariably temporized when streamlining was the only issue involved. Various Bavarian exchange projects in 1702, 1709, and 1718 that involved the retrocession of either Flanders or parts of Habsburg Italy were allowed to lapse by three successive Emperors.[34] After all, Flanders and the Italian territories were both far too wealthy and strategically situated at the edge of Austrian-dominated regions to justify their exchange for a territory whose location deep inside a militarily secure Empire gave it no strategic value whatsoever. By contrast the Hofburg desperately, if vainly, pressed Bavarian exchanges in 1703 following Bavarian Elector Max Emanuel's invasion of the hereditary provinces, in 1743 once Charles VII had cast his lot with Frederick, and after 1748 when Prussia's assimilation into the hereditary provinces was viewed as essential "in order to overcome Prussian power" and reestablish Habsburg hegemony in the Empire.[35]

Conversely Flanders was most seriously considered for barter only after the loss of Silesia had compelled the Habsburgs to abandon once and for all their forward position astride France in order to strengthen their security within the Empire. Maria Theresa offered parts of it to both France and Prussia during 1741 in exchange for the restitution of Silesia, and repeated her overtures to Versailles both in 1745 following the peace of Dresden, and again a decade later as part of Kaunitz's successful effort to wean France from its Prussian alliance.[36]

The monarchy's collapsing defensive perimeter in the west helps explain its final abandonment of the Old System. The Diplomatic Revolution was, indeed, not so much a "revolution" as a culmination of long-term trends dictated by Austria's changing strategic needs. If anything the realignment had come some decades too late. In a letter to Daun written shortly after Kaunitz's great coup, Maria Theresa still spoke bitterly of her disillusionment after her succession, when the British ignored her pleas for help at a time when she had already been attacked in Germany and Italy, and was expecting an Ottoman invasion as well.[37] Nor did she ever forget Whitehall's heroic efforts at the peace table to save Flanders—where she herself had committed only 2,000 troops—after it had forced her to give up strategic territories in western Lombardy, Parma, Silesia, and occupied Bavaria, where her largest armies had fought.[38]

Though Frederick now posed the most immediate threat to the Empire and merited the most attention, the monarchy was still compelled to protect its positions elsewhere along its periphery. In fact, by 1761 the future Joseph II was fretting to his mother that the monarchy was surrounded by potential enemies and therefore needed to strengthen its military position.[39] By then the Empress had already secured her position in Italy by achieving an entente with Spain and by launching her remarkably successful marriage diplomacy with the Italian princes. Nevertheless, Austrian security in both the Balkans and Poland was becoming compromised by the expansion of Russia.[40]

Like their perception of the Prussian threat in Germany, the Habsburgs' apprehension over Russian expansion can be traced back to the beginning of the century. As early as 1707 at the height of Joseph I's difficulties with Charles XII, his ministers cautioned him that incurring the wrath of Tsar Peter could have ruinous consequences for Hungary.[41] Four years later, during the short Russo-Ottoman war of 1710–1711, they went so far as to suggest that "if the tsar should be victorious [and] march into Ottoman territory on this side of the Danube . . . toward Constantinople, this also would . . . be not much less unfortunate" than a Turkish victory.[42] When Austria initiated hostilities with Turkey in 1716 the Emperor and his ministers even decided against seeking Peter's assistance, lest Russia's entry into the Balkans create a new military threat to the monarchy's southeast flank.[43]

Habsburg paranoia over the Russians continued to grow following the Peace of Passarowitz in 1718. This was partly because the Hofburg now recognized that the militarily weak Ottoman Empire was a far preferable neighbor to Russia, and wished to preserve the huge power vacuum that had rather fortuitously come into being in the Balkans. In addition, however, its definition of the monarchy's security needs had expanded to include those Ottoman territories adjacent to Hungary, such as the Danubian Principalities, which the Russians were beginning to threaten themselves. This was because, with Hungary's gradual if imperfect assimilation into the Habsburg state during the eighteenth century, Vienna ceased to view it merely as a buffer intended for the protection of the hereditary lands but as an integral part of the monarchy that now required a glacis of its own.

For the first time in its history the monarchy regarded the preservation of the Ottoman Empire as essential to its own security. Kaunitz certainly appreciated both the irony and the wisdom behind this policy when he wrote:

> To save our archenemy is rather extraordinary and such decisions can be justified only in truly critical situations, such as self-preservation.[44]

Indeed, for the rest of the century the Hofburg reacted to the outbreak of each Russo-Ottoman war with apprehension that Russia would attain a common border with Hungary.[45] It invariably tried to limit St. Petersburg's gains by various forms of mediation.[46] Once this approach had failed, Vienna would join Russia in the war, not to dismember the Ottoman Empire, but rather to limit its ally's acquisitions to areas far removed from the monarchy's frontiers, such as the eastern Black Sea shore or even Constantinople itself. Meanwhile, the Habsburgs were determined to keep Russia out of the Danubian Principalities and were prepared to annex them themselves, or at one point even to cede them to neutral Poland, if their retention by the sultan seemed impossible.[47] What territorial goals they contemplated therefore represented essentially preemptive moves to protect their strategic security. Indeed, even the bellicose Joseph II assumed an apologetic tone in explaining:

> Certainly I desire the preservation of Turkey . . . but if she destroys herself by her miserable condition, what else can be done?[48]

Joseph could also have said the same thing about Poland, which was threatened by both Prussia and Russia. As early as 1763 following the death of its last Wettin king, Kaunitz had warned "that the dismemberment of the Polish republic should be avoided."[49] Even more than in the Balkans he opposed any suggestion of partitioning Poland and could not hide his disgust when in 1772 Vienna's protracted efforts to frustrate Prusso-Russian designs on Poland "lasted so long that our modest original concern for a military cordon [in Galicia to protect Hungary] has been transformed against my humble counsel into a plan of conquest."[50] Maria Theresa shared Kaunitz's dismay at the prospect of seizing Galicia, though her concern was based more on moral than on Kaunitz's geopolitical considerations. Rather than besmirch her honor, she considered abstaining from the imminent Polish partition if Frederick would retrocede strategic Glatz to the monarch. As her envoy told the king, "Glatz is the key to Bohemia. . . . You do not need it for defensive purposes as much as we do."[51] Once this option had disappeared, however, the Empress and Kaunitz decided that they had no choice; though she did indeed weep sincere tears of sorrow both for the Poles and for "our honor, the monarchy's glory, and our good principles and piety," she and her chancellor took—and kept taking—Galician territory until they felt that their frontier was safe from Frederick and Catherine.[52]

Nor was Leopold II's concern for his Polish buffer any less intense. Just as Maria Theresa had confronted simultaneous threats to Turkey and Poland in 1769, Leopold was forced to juggle renewed foreign territorial ambitions in both areas, complicated by an ongoing Austro-Russo-Ottoman war in the Balkans and an imminent Prusso-Polish attack against the monarchy itself. Like Kaunitz he sought security through a stable, independent Poland. Toward this end he supported the Poles' drafting of a new constitution that stipulated a hereditary succession, with the sole proviso that it should not lead to a major improvement of their military position. As always Vienna wanted an independent neighbor, but not a strong one.[53] In fact, until the end of his brief reign Leopold remained far more anxious to secure a Russo-Prussian guarantee of Poland's neutrality and integrity than to become involved in the troubles then brewing in far-off France. His pursuit of a Prussian alliance in 1792 was, indeed, not designed to oppose France but to check Russian expansion on the monarchy's frontier.[54]

There is much evidence to suggest that the Habsburg monarchy continued to work for the creation and maintenance of secure and stable buffer zones on its periphery long after the disappearance of the *ancien régime*. Whatever role geopolitical considerations played after the eighteenth century, they were clearly a decisive factor in the formulation of Austrian policy during it. They not only determined its wars, which were fought in order to obtain, recover, or defend its position in these frontier regions, but also the virtual end of its expansion after 1718, for it became far too concerned with and distracted by events along its periphery to consider extensive conquests in any particular direction. To be sure, there seems to be no evidence that the Emperor and his ministers ever conceived or clearly elucidated a strategy for the maintenance of secure buffers beyond the monarchy's borders. Nor are there more than a few instances when they expressed an appreciation of the multiple strategic difficulties that were occasioned by Austria's exposed position in the heart of East Central Europe. The state and extent of their awareness, however, cannot confute the course of their actions, nor the compelling strategic structures that predetermined the path they chose. Rather like actors reading a new script for the first time, they simply stumbled through their lines without benefiting from the perspective that comes from familiarity with the plot. Such is often the lot of statesmen, whose concentration on meeting immediate needs rarely affords them the luxury of an overview. Historians, however, have no such excuse.

## Notes

1. Leopold Auer, "Zur Rolle Italiens in der österreichischen Politik um das spanische Erbe," *Mitteilungen des österreichischen Staatsarchivs,* XXXI (1978), 54, 57–59.

2. Charles W. Ingrao, *In Quest and Crisis: Emperor Joseph I and the Habsburg Monarchy* (West Lafayette, Ind., 1979), pp. 80–84, 91.

3. Postscript of Dolfin December 9, 1705, report, in Marcello Giudici, *I Dispacci di Germania dell'ambasciatore veneto Daniel Dolfin 30* (Venice, 1908), II, 128.

4. Wratislaw to Charles, January 26, 1706, Vienna, Haus- Hof- und Staatsarchiv (hereafter cited as HHSA), Familienarchiv, Korrespondenz A 18.

5. Resolution of April 12, 1704, Conference, *Feldzüge des Prinzen Eugen von Savoyen* (Vienna, 1876–1892), VI, 727–735; Max Braubach, *Prinz Eugen von Savoyen* (Vienna, 1963–1965), II, 43–44, 50–51.

6. Ingrao, *In Quest and Crisis,* pp. 44–48.

7. Stephen Fischer-Galaţi, *Ottoman Imperialism and German Protestantism, 1521–1555* (New York, 1972), p. 36; Gunther E. Rothenberg, *The Austrian Military Border in Croatia, 1522–1747* (Urbana, 1960), pp. 3–13; Robert A. Kann, *A History of the Habsburg Empire, 1526–1918* (Los Angeles, 1974), p. 36.

8. Ladislas Baron Hengelmüller, *Hungary's Fight for National Existence* (London, 1913), pp. 304–336.

9. Eugene to Joseph, May 18, 1705, *Feldzüge,* VII, Supp., 125–126, and IX, 307; Stepney to Harley, September 5, *Journal des Ministres Plénipoteniaires* . . . 21 September 1705, in Erno Simonyi, *Angol diplomáciai iratok: II. Rákóczi Ferencz korára* [English Diplomatic Papers: The Ferenc II Rákóczi Era] (Pest, 1871–1877), II, 202, 439–440; Joseph's notes of August 3, 1707, Conference, HHSA, Staatskanzlei, Vorträge 51.

10. Cf. Ragnhild M. Hatton, *Charles XII of Sweden* (London, 1968); Jaroslav Goll, *Der Vertrag von Alt-Ranstädt: Österreich und Schweden, 1706–1707* (Prague, 1881); Ernst Carlson, *Der Vertrag zwischen Karl XII. von Schweden und Kaiser Joseph I. zu Altranstädt, 1707* (Stockholm, 1907); Ingrao, *In Quest and Crisis,* pp. 54–69.

11. Joseph's notes of December 12, 1707, and February 7, 1708, Conferences, HHSA, Staatskanzlei, Vorträge 51.

12. Oswald Redlich, *Das Werden einer Grossmacht: Österreich von 1700 bis 1740* (4th ed.; Vienna, 1961), p. 156; Karl A. Roider, Jr., "Austria's Ottoman Question, 1700–1790," p. 41. The author would like to thank Professor Roider for making this soon-to-be-published manuscript available.

13. Eugene to Charles, January 23, 1715, *Feldzüge*, XVI, Supp. 14–15.

14. Max Braubach, *Versailles und Wien von Ludwig XIV. bis Kaunitz* (Bonn, 1952), pp. 89, 98, 103, 109–110, 116, 126, 132–133.

15. Redlich, *Grossmacht*, pp. 156–157.

16. Derek McKay, *Prince Eugene of Savoy* (London, 1977), pp. 173–175; Braubach, *Prinz Eugen*, III, 304–311.

17. Eugene to Leopold, January 31, 1697, *Feldzüge*, II, Supp. 6.

18. Roider, "Austria's Ottoman Question," pp. 179–180.

19. McKay, *Prince Eugene*, pp. 170–171; Braubach, *Prinz Eugen*, IV, 64.

20. Grete Mecenseffy, *Karls VI. Spanische Bündnispolitik, 1725–1729* (Innsbruck, 1934), pp. 135–136; McKay, *Prince Eugene*, p. 213.

21. Braubach, *Prinz Eugen*, IV, 240, 441.

22. G. R. Solari, *The House of Farnese* (Garden City, N.Y., 1968), pp. 284–292; Heinrich Benedikt, *Kaiseradler über dem Apennin* (Vienna, 1964); Redlich, *Grossmacht*, pp. 193–194.

23. Hugo Hantsch, *Die Geschichte Österreichs* (Vienna, 1962), II, 121; Braubach, *Prinz Eugen*, V, 268, 272. Prince Eugene would undoubtedly have served in Italy had he not declined to fight against the house of Savoy, which was allied with France and Spain.

24. Braubach, *Prinz Eugen*, V, 300, 315.

25. Braubach, *Versailles und Wien*, 241–242, 244, *Prinz Eugen*, V. 301.

26. Bartholdi November 12, 1705, *pro memoria*, and March 2, 1706, *relation*, in Arnold Berney, *König Friedrich I. und das Haus Habsburg (1701–1707)* (Berlin, 1927), pp. 255 ff., 264.

27. *Feldzüge*, VI, 95; Carl von Noorden, "Die preussische Politik im spanischen Erbfolgekriege," *Historische Zeitschrift*, XVIII (1867), 315; Berney, *Friedrich I.*, 126–127.

28. Bartholdi March 2, 1706, *relation*, in Berney, *Friedrich I.*, p. 265.

29. Hugo Hantsch, *Friedrich Karl Graf von Schönborn (1674–1746)* (Augsburg, 1929), pp. 219–220; Hatton, *Charles XII*, p. 383; McKay, *Prince Eugene*, p. 178.

30. Braubach, *Versailles und Wien*, pp. 319–321; Charles accepted only 10,000 of 50,000 troops offered, or Brandenburg's *Reichskontingent* quota. Hantsch, *Geschichte Österreichs*, II, 120.

31. Adam Wandruszka, *The House of Habsburg* (Garden City, N.Y., 1965), p. 122.

32. William J. McGill, "The Roots of Policy: Kaunitz in Vienna and Versailles, 1749–1753," *The Journal of Modern History*, XLIII (1971), 232; Hanns Leo Mikoletzky, *Österreich: Das grosse 18. Jahrhundert* (Vienna, 1967), p. 271; Braubach, *Versailles und Wien*, pp. 404–405; Hantsch, *Geschichte Österreichs*, p. 166.

33. Alfred von Arneth, *Die Geschichte Maria Theresias* (Vienna, 1863–1879), V, 279–281; Johannes Kunisch, "Der Ausgang des sieben-

jährigen Krieges," *Zeitschrift für Historische Forschung*, II (1975), 179–191.

34. Braubach, "Die Politik des Kurfürsten Max Emanuel von Bayern im Jahre 1702," *Historisches Jahrbuch*, XLIII (1923), 73–74; Redlich, *Grossmacht*, pp. 101–102.

35. Marcus Landau, *Rom, Wien, Neapel während des spanischen Erbfolgekrieges* (Leipzig, 1885), pp. 228–229; Paul Bernard, *Joseph II and Bavaria* (The Hague, 1965), pp. 9–10; Mikoletzky, *18. Jahrhundert*, p. 309.

36. Heinrich Benedikt, *Als Belgien österreichisch war* (Vienna, 1965), p. 92; Braubach, *Versailles und Wien*, pp. 350–351, 374–375, 397.

37. Maria Theresa to Daun, July 24, 1759, in Kunisch, "Der Ausgang," pp. 218–219.

38. Benedikt, *Belgien*, p. 92; Braubach, *Versailles und Wien*, pp. 370–371, 390; Richard Lodge, *Studies in Eighteenth Century Diplomacy* (London, 1930).

39. François Fejtö, *Un Habsbourg révolutionnaire: Joseph II* (Paris, 1953), p. 79.

40. Adam Wandruszka, *Österreich in Italien im 18. Jahrhundert* (Vienna, 1963), pp. 40–46, 229, 301.

41. February 13 & May 13, 1707 reports, HHSA, Staatenabteilung, Schweden 18a.

42. February 24 report of February 12/23, 1711, Conferences, HHSA, Staatskanzlei, Vorträge 16.

43. Roider, "Austria's Ottoman Question," pp. 124–125.

44. *Ibid.*, p. 215.

45. *Ibid.*, pp. 206–207, 210, 236; *idem*, *The Reluctant Ally* (Baton Rouge, 1972), pp. 59–60; Saul K. Padover, "Prince Kaunitz and the First Partition of Poland," *Slavonic and East European Review*, XIII (1934–1935), 392; Paul Bernard, *Joseph II* (New York, 1968), p. 77.

46. Roider, *Reluctant Ally*, pp. 59–60; *idem*, "Austria's Ottoman Question," p. 213.

47. Roider, "Austria's Ottoman Question," pp. 237, 239, 326, 332.

48. Padover, *The Revolutionary Emperor* (London, 1967), p. 251.

49. Herbert H. Kaplan, *The First Partition of Poland* (New York, 1962), p. 26.

50. Mikoletzky, *18. Jahrhundert*, p. 307; Padover, "Kaunitz," pp. 392–393.

51. Kaplan, *First Partition*, pp. 163–164.

52. Mikoletzky, *18. Jahrhundert*, pp. 307–308.

53. Kaunitz to Reuss, January 4, 1792, in Ernst Herrmann, "Die polnische Politik Kaiser Leopolds I.," *Forschungen zur Deutschen Geschichte*, IV (1864), 427–428.

54. Adam Wandruszka, *Leopold II.* (Vienna, 1965), II, 353–369; Robert H. Lord, *The Second Partition of Poland* (New York, 1969), pp. 218–219, 256.

Christopher Duffy

# The Seven Years' War as a Limited War

It is a familiar range of political, material and moral restraints that encourages a view of the eighteenth century as the era of limited warfare par excellence. However, just as modern strategists, in the light of the Vietnam experience, are questioning some of the easier assumptions that lay behind the limited-war theories of the 1950s and 1960s, so it would not be surprising if historians were to take a more critical look at the phenomenon of limited war as it existed two centuries ago. They might find something decidedly "unlimited" in the way the France of Louis XIV mobilized national resources in the last years of the War of the Spanish Succession, or they might point to the enthusiasm shown by the populations of the Habsburg Empire in the War of the Bavarian Succession in 1778–79—"the patriotic feeling was general, and no monarchs of the world could boast that they had better subjects, or were more loved, than Joseph and Maria Theresa."[1]

How far does the Seven Years' War measure up to the accepted standards of limited warfare? On the face of it, the objectives of the anti-Prussian alliance were pretty ambitious, involving the reclamation or seizure of Silesia and Glatz (for Austria), Halberstadt and Magdeburg (for Saxony), and Prussian Pomerania (for Sweden)—a violent territorial rearrangement that would have reduced Prussia to the status of a Württemberg or a Holstein.[2]

A Prussian veteran noted another striking feature of the war. "Never had there been a war in which so many battles were fought. No less remarkable was the great quantity of official declarations that were published during this period of general distress. The great monarchs were anxious to justify their extraordinary conduct in the eyes of all the world, being concerned to gain the good opinion even of such people whose approval they could easily have dispensed with. . . . Such was the victory of the Enlightenment which at that time was radiating its benevolent beams over Europe."[3] In addition to the voiceless people mentioned by Archenholtz, it is possible that the barrage of propaganda was aimed at such significant targets as

British public opinion (which helped so much to keep King Frederick II in the war), and as neutral bankers and contractors.

As Archenholtz indicates, the range and energy of the war were also worthy of note. In geographical extent it became a true world war (if only because of the conjunction of several disputes at the same time), and Bourbon France never recovered from the effort it put forth in the struggle. On the fields of Central Europe, Austria and Prussia met in a sequence of bloody battles in which the Austrians, even when they were beaten, usually inflicted more casualties on the Prussians than they sustained themselves.

Lastly it is possible to maintain that the Seven Years' War was a period of transition in the art of war. The nature of intensive and prolonged wars is to drive forward the military art at an almost geometric rate of progress, so that the struggle in the final years may share more in common with the next conflict, albeit lying decades in the future, than with the first campaigns of the war in question. These comments apply with particular force to the armed forces of the Seven Years' War.

More than in some other ages, armies in the eighteenth century needed the stimulus of actual warfare to spring into life. Hence the repeated appeals of commanders to their sovereigns to commit the troops to war, almost *any* war, in order to keep the forces *en haleine.* In peacetime the men were usually in poor physical condition, and schooled in tactics of little relevance to real combat. By the same token officers were devoid of the experience of moving large formations, and lacked the guidance of anything but regulations of the most routine kind. It was accepted that some of the most useful directions would come from commanders who drew up their own codes in the actual theater of war, like Philipp von Browne's *Verhaltungspuncte* of 1756, or Leopold von Daun's *Lagerordnung, Ordre de Bataille* and *General-Schlachtordnung* of May 24, 1757.

A wise military historian has written that "between 1748 and the outbreak of the Seven Years' War in 1756 we seem to step from one era to another. When we read of the operations of the latter war, we seem at last to be dealing with modern times, to be reading about officers who . . . are living in a world where the ideas which still affect us are beginning to germinate. The Industrial Revolution and *les droits de l'homme* are only just around the corner. The Age of Methodicism is passing. The Age of Reason is in its high summer."[4]

The war makes an impression of interesting advances in the expertise of the various belligerents. The British acquired a formidable amphibious striking power. On the continent the armies began to find out how to move on the battlefield in semi-independent formations, such as the ones adopted by the French at Bergen in 1759 and the Prussians at Burkersdorf in 1762. In the Austrian army Franz von Lacy was appointed quartermaster-general on February 20, 1758. He set to work immediately, assembling and training the personnel of his new staff corps, and already by October 14 of the same year the Austrians were able to carry out the successful night attack at Hochkirch in six main columns.

Do considerations like these negate the traditional view of the eighteenth century as an era of limited war? Probably not; they modify it, but leave the essential features intact. First of all the allies in the Seven Years' War never aimed to overset the regime in Prussia, let alone impose a new form of government or a new ideology. It was the trustworthy opinion of a veteran of that war, Field Marshal Aleksandr Suvorov, who insisted that the wars of the French Revolution were different in kind from anything that had preceded them. Earlier generations had encountered Muslim religious fanaticism, "but it has been left to us to witness another phenomenon, just as frightful, namely political fanaticism."[5]

Nor should the narrow and shaky foundations of the coalition be overlooked, or the apparent lack of single-mindedness with which the combatants pursued their "unlimited" goal. The news of the victory of Gross Jägersdorf on August 30, 1757 made the French doubt the wisdom of inviting Russian armies into Europe, and already by April 1758 Versailles was seeking to extricate France from the war.[6] Both Austria and France disliked the thought of Russia intervening in Central Europe as a full belligerent power. They were anxious lest the Russians should establish themselves permanently in East Prussia, and they successfully restrained the Russians from taking Danzig by force of arms—a venture that would have greatly alleviated the supply problems of the Russian army.

One of the relatively few occasions on which the Austrians and Russians worked together effectively was in their *coup de main* on Berlin in October 1760. Interestingly enough, when they now had the opportunity of inflicting a damaging blow on the machinery that sustained the Prussian war effort, they retired after a few days, leaving intact the state records, and establishments like the arsenal, the mint, the cloth factories, and the Splitgerber und Daum bronze foundary. The possible treason of the Russian commander, G. G. Totleben, may have had something to do with this misguided charity, but the episode as a whole scarcely corresponds to an image of the Austrians and Russians as protagonists of all-out war.

Civilian populations more than once took a lively part in the hostilities of the middle decades of the eighteenth century. This is a subject as yet scarcely touched by historians, and one that may reveal far wider popular involvement than generally indicated. All the same it is significant to find Baron Gideon von Laudon, in the crisis of 1758, writing of the populace of Moravia: "All the peasants are ready to take up arms and go out to fight the enemy. They demand only to be led. This could well bring on a peasant war, which is scarcely desirable, but we must do what we can to sustain these good people in their zeal."[7] King Frederick himself had to restrain the enthusiastic civilians of Borkum from putting up resistance to the French.

On the subject of all those bloody battles, it is worth mentioning that the sacrifice of life still had the power to shock the two ladies who created the alliance. The diaries of Khevenhüller-Metsch reveal that Maria Theresa was all too aware of what her policies entailed in terms of human suffering, and had many masses said for the souls of the dead soldiers. Elizabeth Petrovna had abolished the death penalty in criminal cases in Russia, and she was appalled by the contradiction between sparing rogues at home and offering so many innocent lives on the battlefield. She wrote a long and curious letter to the newly promoted Field Marshal Count Pyotr Saltykov after the great victory of Kunersdorf in 1759. She commented that Frederick might have been able to find excuses for the maulings the Prussians had received at Zorndorf and Paltzig, but the day of Kunersdorf must have shown him that he could not overthrow the Russian army even when he had significant advantages. Instead of following the argument through to what might be thought the natural conclusion, she suddenly drew back, and ended by telling Saltykov that he must avoid general actions as a matter of principle, because they were getting more costly and hard fought all the time.[8]

Here perhaps is the crux of the things that make the Seven Years' War such an arresting topic of study—the sense of movement and change restrained by an instinct for order and balance, in fact the suppressed excitement and the feeling of emotion under control found in the music of Mozart. The Seven Years' War remained a limited war, but one that had the capacity to spring all sorts of surprises on those who try to confine it within rigid categories.

Richard Pipes, an historian of old Russia, has written very sensibly about the dangers of wisdom after the event. "Nothing is easier to demonstrate than that whatever happened had to happen. It is also a very satisfactory exercise because it seems to confirm that all is always for the best, which cheers the common man and also suits his betters. However, the trouble with the concept of historical inevitability is that it works only retrospectively, i.e., for the writers of history, not for its makers."[9] The history of the Seven Years' War shows again and again that, if things had been only slightly different, Frederick would have undergone the doom prepared for him by the mighty alliance. However, the fact remains that Frederick did escape his just deserts, and it must be asked how far certain failings of Austrian strategy might have contributed to this sorry outcome.

There is space here to mention briefly only one aspect of the Austrian conduct of the war, namely, the apparent unwillingness of the Austrians to deal energetically with Old Fritz when they had him by the scruff of the neck. After his triple reverses of Kolín (1757), the Domstadtl ambush and the relief of Olmütz (1758), and Hochkirch (1758), Frederick was on each occasion suffered to break free, and wreak all kinds of havoc elsewhere, whether routing the French as Rossbach, fighting the Russians to a standstill at Zorndorf, or raising Count András Hadik's siege of Neisse. Most surprising of all was what Frederick termed "the miracle of the house of Brandenburg"—the failure of Field Marshal Count Leopold von Daun and his powerful and fresh army to exploit the opportunity offered them by Saltykov's Russians and Laudon's corps after they had virtually annihilated Frederick's army at Kunersdorf in 1759. Saltykov wailed, "We had it in our power to terminate the war, by imposing a peace or finishing the thing off in some other kind of way. The [Prussian] royal family sought refuge in Magdeburg, and Berlin was waiting from one day to the next to act as host to ourselves or the Austrians."[10]

Even Laudon, the hero of Kunersdorf, acted with some caution when he and Aleksandr Buturlin had Frederick penned up in a small corner of southern Silesia in the late summer of 1761.

In the last century von Arneth elucidated the role of the Court War Council *(Hofkriegsrat)* in the Seven Years' War, pretty convincingly acquitting it of the charge of strategic backseat driving, or putting undue restraints on the commanders in the field. However, another of the stock explanations of Austrian inactivity survives with greater credibility: the personal failings of some of the great men whom Maria Theresa and Francis I put in command of their armies. Prince Charles of Lorraine is universally admitted to have been a disaster, who retained his command only on account of his membership of the Imperial family. As for Daun, he owed his elevation not to a tigerish reputation in combat, but to his work for the reform of the Austrian army, and his wife's friendship with Maria Theresa. In both Russia and Austria the most aggressive spirits were to be found among the middle-ranking generals—people like Pyotr Rumyantsev, Zakhar Chernyshev, Hadik, Lacy and Laudon. Most unfortunately the distance that separated Maria Theresa, as a woman, from the management of her army prevented her from disciplining her generals in the way that was open in the Prussian army to Frederick. Thus the antagonisms between the factions of Lacy and Laudon were sharpened by the events of the day of Liegnitz (August 15, 1760), and they were going to split the army for the rest of the century.

One of the most difficult tasks facing the military historian is to identify the assumptions that eighteenth-century commanders carried around with them, and which they rarely bothered to set down on paper. The problem is accentuated with regard to Austria in the Seven Years' War by two things—the absence of any detailed history of the campaigns, and the seemingly almost total lack of memoirs and reminiscences from the pen of Austrian generals of the time. In the absence of any firm information, should it be concluded that nothing of importance was going on in a campaign when the activity did not relate directly to the fighting of a battle? Probably not. After all, this was a generation of high commanders who had grown up in the 1740s, when whole campaigns were decided by strategies of industrious advantages, concerning the denial of fodder, and other small-scale operations which could make a theater of war untenable for an enemy (Bohemia 1742 and 1744, northern Italy 1746).

In contrast there is much firm evidence to show that the Austrians had a very clear idea of the caliber of their Prussian opponents. What bad luck to be confronted by Frederick the Great at the height of his powers! This in itself must have given the most enterprising commander pause for thought. Writing of Daun's slow motions, a French officer commented: "There is such a narrow margin between a timorousness of this kind, and the prudence you must always show when you are facing the king of Prussia, that a naturally cautious man is inclined to confuse the two."[11]

There is perhaps no better evaluation of Frederick's military system than in the Austrian appraisals of the 1750s. Before the war Count Ernst Giannini was able to supply Vienna with a considerable amount of detail about Frederick's minor tactics and methods of training.[12] Then again, before Charles of Lorraine set out on campaign in 1757, he was furnished by his brother Emperor Francis with a laughably illiterate but very acute analysis of grand tactics *à la* Old Fritz, showing how Frederick ran his mercenary troops into the ground by his long marches, and how on the battlefield he liked to heap up his best forces on one flank, creating, perhaps, opportunities for an Austrian counterblow against the "refused" wing.[13] Finally in January 1759 the Austrian Major General Tillier presented to the Russians a most penetrating examination of what lay behind Frederick's apparently miraculous powers of survival—the high quality of the Prussian army, the military nature of the government, Frederick's personal talents, a central geographical position, and a network of fortresses and magazines, "all of which enables him to turn speedily against one after another of his enemies in succession, each time matching them with superior or at least equal force."[14]

It would seem plausible, last of all, that Daun had on his mind more than just the dangers of a reverse in the field. Using the words that Winston Churchill applied to Admiral John Jellicoe in 1916, he was a man who could lose the war for his country in an afternoon. Simply because Austria took the political and strategic offensive in the Seven Years' War, it is easy to forget how close the Habsburg body politic had come to dissolution as recently as 1741. While Maria Theresa began to piece her state together from 1748, the Prussians had been building on solid foundations since the time of the Great Elector, or in other words, for every year Maria Theresa had spent on consolidation the Prussians had been able to devote ten. Was it possible for Daun or any other responsible commander to be unaware of Hungarian separatism, of the absence of an identifiable military class, or the lack of a modern comprehensive fortress system? Was it not common prudence that made Daun consider that it was in the vital interests of the monarchy to maintain an army "in being," to revert to British naval comparisons? It was not defeatism that made Daun exclaim: "People talk about exterminating all and sundry, about attacking and fighting every day, about being everywhere at once and anticipating the enemy. Nobody desires this more than I do. . . . God knows that I am no coward, but I will never set my hand to anything which I judge impossible, or to the disadvantage of Your Majesty's service."[15]

## Notes

1. *Öesterreichischer Kriegs-Almanach* (Vienna, 1779), II, 153–154.
2. P. Paret, "The Relationship between the Revolutionary War and European Military Thought and Practice in the Second Half of the Eighteenth Century," in D. Higginbotham (ed.), *Reconsiderations on the Revolutionary War* (New York, 1978), pp. 146–148, 153–155.
3. J. W. Archenholtz *Geschichte des Siebenjährigen Krieges in Deutschland* (5th ed.; Berlin, 1840), I, 95–96.
4. P. Young, *History of the British Army,* (London, 1970), p. 49.
5. E. Fuchs, *Anekdoty knyazya italiiskago, grafa Suvorora,* [Anecdotes of Prince Italisky, Count Suvorov] (St. Petersburg, 1827), p. 36.
6. L. J. Oliva, *Missalliance: A Study of French Policy in Russia during the Seven Years' War* (New York, 1964), p. 93.
7. K. Buchberger, "Briefe Laudons," in *Archiv für österreichische Geschichte,* XLVIII (1872), 386.
8. A. Rambaud, *Russes et Prussiens: Guerre de Sept Ans* (Paris, 1895), p. 290.
9. *Russia under the Old Regime* (London, 1977), p. 59.
10. September 21, 1759, *Sbornik Imperatorskago Russkago Istoricheskago Obshchestva* [Journal of the Imperial Russian Historical Society] (St. Petersburg) IX (1872), 491.
11. Champeaux in R. Waddington, *La Guerre de Sept Ans* (Paris, 1899–1914), I, 334.
12. F. L. v. Thadden, *Feldmarschall Daun* (Vienna, 1967), pp. 192–200.
13. "Remarque sur ce que jay veut de pui tout ces ger avec le roy de Prusse," in A. v. Arneth, *Geschichte Maria Theresias* (Vienna, 1863–79), V, 171–172.
14. *Arkhiv Knyazya Vorontsova* [Archives of Prince Vorontsov] (Moscow, 1870–95), VI, 393–394.
15. Thadden, *Daun,* p. 374.

Manfried Rauchensteiner

# The Development of War Theories in Austria at the End of the Eighteenth Century

In 1777 Johann Thomas von Trattner, printer and publisher to the Austrian Imperial court in Vienna, published a book entitled *The School of War or the Theories of a Young Warrior for All Military Operations . . . Drafted and Compiled by an Imperial Captain of Infantry.*[1] The author, however, was not a simple anonymous captain, but *Feldmarschall-Leutnant* Count Philipp Georg von Browne, the son of the famous Ulysses von Browne.[2] The book itself was a compendium of 43 chapters on matters military that seemed significant to the author. It included such chapters as "How to Evaluate Terrain," "How to Lay Siege to a Place," "Battles and Encounters," as well as paragraphs in which the author discussed such problems as "How you should react to a Surprise Attack."

The book certainly deserves some attention, not because the author was famous, a neo-Austrian who tried to stay anonymous, but because it is representative of its time and place. The book generated no new ideas, it was merely a collection of excerpts from military writings ranging from Vegetius to Frederick II, from Antoine de Feuquières to Jean-Charles Folard and Marshal Jean-François Puységur.[3] For that matter it also was not a collection of doctrines then current in the Imperial Austrian Army. Only a few short passages taken from the works of Lazarus Schwendi, Hannss Friedrich von Fleming, Raimondo di Montecuccoli, and Giorgio Basta offer a sampling of specific Habsburg-Austrian operational thinking. And this despite the fact that in this era there had been hardly a decade in which the Austrian monarchy had not been involved in hostilities and that it was barely over the wars of Prince Eugene and Maria Theresa.

The publication was quite out of the ordinary. In Prussia, Saxony, the two Hesses, the Netherlands, and above all in France many competent and some not so competent spirits wrote countless books about war, and developed elaborate theories about the theory of war. They searched for universal rules and principles, and tried to classify and to create complex academic constructs to prove their theories. But not so in the Habsburg Empire. It fought wars almost continuously, certainly did not win all of them, but no one tried to theorize!

This lack of theoretical work, moreover, was not just typical of the eighteenth century; lack of theoretical military thinking was something Austria had to contend with for centuries. To this day, whenever the question of the great classics on war arises, Austria, somewhat diffidently, presents the Archduke Charles, though almost immediately it is argued that Charles cannot be considered the equal of Karl von Clausewitz or Antoine-Henri Jomini. Even lesser-known men like Decker, Willisen, and Georg Venturini are rather better. And recently there has been some evidence indicating that most of Charles's writings were adaptations from those of Rühle von Lilienstern and Venturini.[4] Indeed, it might be asked whether, considering that there is so little Austrian theorizing on war, any discussion of what appears to be mainly a compilation of plagiarisms is really worth the candle.

But the record is not all negative. To return once more to the book, it can be assumed that Count Philipp Georg von Browne's reason for remaining anonymous certainly was not only modesty, but that there were also other, more cogent reasons. It must be remembered that even Archduke Charles's writings were for the most part published anonymously and that by far the bulk of his work did not appear in print before 1860. Only then did it become evident how much he had written about warfare. In Archduke Charles's case it is plausible that it was modesty that induced him to remain anonymous. It certainly was not unusual for an archduke to be a writer, but for a professional soldier in Austria a certain sober reticence formed part of an unwritten code of the Habsburg Army. Formulation of elaborate theories or a continual preoccupation with military subjects would label an officer either an unworldly dreamer or one underoccupied by his assignment. Consequently, persons like this were somehow suspect. An this was an attitude that persisted into the second half of the nineteenth century. At the same time, officers with a literary bent were also suspect, and writing anything other than regulations, marching instructions, or topographical descriptions was not considered proper to their rank and station.

There were two additional factors that inhibited Austrian theoretical writing. One was the surprisingly low educational and intellectual level of most officers which provided little stimulus to work on theoretical questions of war. The other factor was the lack of incentive from the top to transform actual warfare into military theory. It is not necessary to read very much literature to ascertain this. The remarkable final paragraph of the *Generals Reglement*, published after lengthy preparation in 1769, makes the point. It admonished: "Generals will receive one copy of this manual from our Aulic War Council and must acknowledge receipt in writing. The generals will be held strictly accountable that no copy of this manual shall ever fall into the possession of a foreign officer or any other person. Should a copy of this book ever be missing or lost, a thorough inquiry will be conducted into whether the loss was due to failure and negligence and to order the severest penalties on those responsible."[5]

In sum, the failure to develop academic theories about warfare for centuries was rooted in the strict secrecy imposed, lack of education, and considerations of rank and status. These are basic reasons why discussion of Austrian theories of war cannot be based on the Austrian literature. When Prince Eugene of Savoy died, the army was in far from perfect condition, and when it went into the War of the Austrian Succession it had many lessons to relearn. The cure was seen in imitation of the Prussian military system. The number of regiments was increased, basic training was improved, and the excellent Prussian system of drill and maneuver, a sophisticated and geometric system of tactical movements and deployments of troops on the field of battle, was adopted. Finally, in the Seven Years' War, Austria sought victory by becoming more Prussian than the Prussians themselves.

These measures were partially successful. However, it must not be overlooked that all contemporary armies became so much alike in their tactics that victory or defeat was no longer primarily the result of the commanders' ability or the quality of the armies, but often a matter of pure chance.

It is interesting that in Austria it was not a professional military expert who recognized this somewhat anomalous situation, but a layman with great military ambitions, Emperor Joseph II. In a memorandum released in 1766, he made a survey of Austria's military situation and the problems to be encountered.[6] And he looked for the answers. The title of the memorandum was "*Si vis pacem para bellum,*" a well-known dictum of Vegetius. A conference held on March 7, 10, and 14, 1767, was the result of this memorandum, and produced a paper called "Organization of a Reliable Defensive Strategy" based on opinions expressed at a number of earlier meetings, written testimony by experts, and consultations. Its final draft was prepared by Field Marshal Count Franz von Lacy, State Minister Count Heinrich von Blümegen, and Count Johann von Starhemberg.[7]

The paper considered a number of questions, above all whether Austria would have to face a war on several fronts. While there was no simple answer to this, it was then held that only Prussia could be considered a real danger to the Empire because it alone was capable of launching a surprise attack. Austria's position in the Austrian Netherlands and Italy was considered secure. In addition, there was also the question of the Turks.

To deal with Prussia a standing force of 130,000 to 140,000 men was considered the requisite minimum, while against the Turks 40,000 to 50,000 men and a few additional detachments were thought adequate. A purely defensive strategy was deemed best against Prussia, and to bolster this strategy the paper recognized the need for the urgent construction of fortifications, should funds be available. So, the strategic concepts were forged and after 1780, as a result of the War of the Bavarian Succession in which it was proved again that two equal armies could totally exhaust themselves simply with futile maneuvering, they were actually realized. The fortifications constructed included Theresienstadt, Josefstadt, and Königgrätz. The mere presence of fortifications near the frontier was considered a guarantee of successful defense. Count Lacy was recognized as the father of the Austrian so-called cordon system, the forward deployment of protective forces. Fortifications fit well into this system. They were simply "forces in stone."

Scanning their horizons, Austrian strategies could easily discern the advantages of the linear system of defense. Of course, all armies of that time adopted the same philosophy and mastered the same strategy. All had studied Puységur's writings on "geometric warfare" and were obviously familiar with Henry Lloyd's *History of the Late War* and Hippolyte de Guibert's *Essai général de tactique.* As a result, in Western and Central Europe armies no longer were what they had been in the absolute monarchies just a few decades earlier.

On the other hand, the situation facing Austria in the south and east was different. The "Organization of a Reliable Defensive

Strategy" estimated that, while the Turks could field forces twice or three times as strong as Austria, the Ottoman army, because of its peculiar recruitment and adminstrative system, was not suitable for modern tactical employment. It was therefore believed that the Ottoman army would be no match for Austrian forces as long as the latter were able to utilize their tactical skills, that is, the same type of skills they would use against well-trained Western armies. The paramount tactical requirement in such a war would be the use of the proper formations on the march, in the attack and in camp. This, it was held, would keep the Ottoman hordes at bay.

There was a deep-seated belief in the Austrian army that the exact execution of linear tactics and the cordon system ensured superiority over the Turks. This belief was already evident in Joseph's memorandum from which the relevant paragraph was adopted for the *Generals Reglement.* Moreover, Austria always regarded a decisive war against the Turks as inevitable and desirable, and the Ottoman question became a foremost consideration in all strategic planning. In 1769, the year the *Generals Reglement* was issued, the Prince of Sachsen-Hildburghausen, the great reformer of the Military Border, and Field Marshals Count Reinhard Neipperg and Prince Károly József Batthyány analyzed such a war.[8] They concluded unanimously that it was certain to be won. It was therefore just a matter of time until the next war with the Ottoman Empire would break out. In fact, one wonders why this did not happen before 1788. The answer it that it was only then that the fortifications against Prussia had been completed and the danger from the north appeared checked.

Austrian strategic thinking favored a *defensive* strategy for which Lacy's cordon system was the theoretical underpinnings, but the basis of all considerations for war against Turkey was offensive warfare. Yet no one speculated on this discrepancy and there seemed to be no place and time for learned futurists. Jakob Bourscheid, for instance, who gained renown for his translation of the writings of the Byzantine Emperor Leo VI, tried a somewhat overblown military analysis of the War of the Bavarian Succession, but failed. The work, *Essay about All Sciences of War*, published in 1787 in Olmütz, is a curiosity at best, no more.[9] The writings of Karl Mack von Leiberich and Karl von Lindenau are useful only as tactical tractates.[10]

There appears to have been only one fundamental text on the theory of war written at this time. The work was never published, only the handwritten manuscript, anonymous again, was found in the papers of Major General Johann Baptist Freiherr von Burcell, a born Irishman.[11] It is not even sure whether Burcell was the actual author of this 610-page compendium.

The work starts out conservatively with such statements as, "The art of fighting wars is a discipline to fight wars well. The ultimate purpose is to struggle as best as possible. The main issue of the art of war is war itself. The best means to learn the art of war is the knowledge of geometry, and the proper application of available means." Other passages sound like sentences written by Jean Charles de Folard or Joaquin, Marqués de Santa Cruz. In the chapter "Of the Common Maxims and Rules of Warfare," the first paragraph states that "the basic maxim for successfully waging war is a prayer for divine help." This sounds very much like Montecuccoli. The author of the manuscript was also a staunch advocate of war of annihilation, something considered unusual and immoral at that time.

The author maintained that victory on the battlefield was inadequate for this objective. All food to which the enemy might have access should be destroyed; all his depots and resources should be scorched; fields and towns should be laid waste; mills should be demolished; wells poisoned; the people infected with contagious diseases, and discord sown between the people and the leadership. The author went on to recommend the total subjection of the enemy state, its pillage and devastation, the taking of hostages and, in short, everything that today is considered total war. He went so far as to say that in dealing with an enemy no distinction should be made between combatants and noncombatants. The only objective at all times was total conquest of the enemy.

At the same time, the author would not have been an Imperial Austrial officer had he not dealt with the question of how to fight the Turks. Once again he advanced unorthodox ideas. He recommended fighting a lengthy war of attrition because the Ottoman military system was not adapted to such conflict. He also recommended campaigning against the Ottoman Empire during winter, because, he maintained, it was not prepared for this season and because the Turks drank only water and shunned alcohol—then considered necessary to warm up soldiers in cold weather. It seems likely that the author was wrong on this last point.

For over ten years Austria's leading professional soldiers had considered a war against the Ottoman Empire would be more or less a cinch. It came as a rude shock, when war finally came in 1788, that such theories were shown to be just wishful thinking. The first year of the war brought numerous disasters, but even so the basic strategic and tactical assumptions on which the campaign had been undertaken were never seriously questioned. Instead it was believed that the setbacks were due to specific problems of this theater of war, especially the terrain. As Burcell's Maxim 19 stated: "the terrain is frequently of more value than gallantry." Then too, after Baron Gideon von Laudon took over command late in 1788 and achieved victory, the unfortunate events of the summer were never analyzed. This was a pity. If there had been an analysis of the early defeats in this war, it would have become clear that the rigid cordon system was ineffective even against the Ottoman Empire. Except for the capture of Belgrade, the Austrians were victorious only when the rigid system of careful maneuvering was abandoned. The "small war" tactics practiced by the borderers of the Military Frontier and by irregular troops had already proved their value against the Prussians, and worked just as well against the Turks.[12]

This kind of war, however, was difficult to wage on a large scale in an empire where society and sociological patterns favored the linear system on the established model. Only a few Austrian generals profited from the experience gained in the war against the Turks and for them this war was merely a passing incident, a strange adventure. Yet it should have given clear warning of things to come.

## Notes

1. The full German title is *Die Kriegsschule oder die Theorie eines junges Kriegsmannes in allen militärischen Unternehmungen aus den berühmtesten Kriegsbüchern gezogen und zusammengesetzt von einem kaiserlich-königlichen Hauptmann der Infanterie* (Vienna, 1777).

2. Count Philipp Georg von Browne (1727–1803) played a major role in the Seven Years' War. After the battle of Hochkirch he was made a knight of the Order of Maria Theresa and *Feldmarschall-Leutnant*.

3. The best survey of the theoretical work in Europe is still M. Jähns, *Geschichte der Kriegswissenschaften vornehmlich in Deutschland*, Vol. III (Munich, 1891).

4. M. Rauchensteiner, "Zum operativen Denken in Österreich, 1814–1914," Pt. 1, *Österreichische Militärische Zeitschrift*, No. 2, 1974, pp. 121–127.

5. "Die Generals werden ein gedrucktes Exemplar dieses Reglements von

Unserem Hof-Kriegsrath erhalten, und solches demselben quittiren, dagegen aber auch dafür zu stehen haben; wornebst schärfstens verboten wird, einem in fremden Diensten stehenden Officier, oder sonst jemanden ein derley Exemplar zu behändigen: und wenn eines hiervon abhanden kommen, oder verlohren gehen sollte, wird die strengste Untersuchung angestellt werden, um zu erörten, ob es aus Verschulden und Nachlässigkeit geschehen, um sohin nach Befinden die gemessenste Ahndung darüber zu verfügen."

6. Kriegsarchiv Wien, Mem. 2/20.

7. Cf. E. Kotasek, *Feldmarschall Graf Lacy: Ein Leben für Österreichs Heer* (Horn, 1956); Count Heinrich Cajetan Blümegen (1715–1788), from 1760 *Landeshauptmann* of Moravia and a member of the *Staatsrat*. Cf. Heribert Sturm (ed.), *Biographisches Lexikon zur Geschichte der böhmischen Länder* (Vienna, 1979); Count Johann Ludwig Adam Starhemberg (1717–1778). Cf. Konstant von Wurzbach, *Biographisches Lexikon des Kaiserthums Österreich*, Vol. XXXVII (Vienna, 1878).

8. All these studies are to be found in the Kriegsarchiv Wien, Mem. 1/7, 1/8 and 1/9.

9. Jähns, *Kriegswissenschaften*, pp. 2078 ff., 2116.

10. *Ibid.*, pp. 2116 (Mack), 2548 ff. (Lindenau).

11. "Anfangsgründe der Kriegskunst," Kriegsarchiv Wien, Mem. 6/48.

12. Oskar Criste, *Kriege unter Kaiser Josef II: Nach den Feldakten und anderen authentischen Quelle* (Vienna, 1904), pp. 159–181; F. Vaniček, *Spezialgeschichte der Militärgrenze*, Vol. III (Vienna, 1875).

William O. Shanahan

# Enlightenment and War: Austro-Prussian Military Practice, 1760–1790

Enlightenment and war—what can they have in common? How could the Enlightenment, which Immanuel Kant called "the departure of mankind from its self-inflicted immaturity," be concerned with war, except to condemn it? The world of enlightened discourse reverberated with efforts to assure peace and banish war. They ranged from Emmerich de Vattel's lawful order of states in a "universal society of the human race" to the Abbé Charles-Irénée de Saint Pierre's fanciful *Projet pour rendre la paix perpétuelle en Europe*. These reflections suggest that Enlightenment and war-making exist only in fierce opposition.

To make that admission would mean that enlightened thought had failed to relate individual satisfactions to society's interests. It would neglect Kant, whose attempts to establish this correspondence in moral duty crowned the edifice of enlightened thought. And it would neglect the Enlightenment's most important consequence: the radical secularization of life and thought. This consequence has enabled the state to embody the temporal order and become the arbiter of the most basic human issues. It was Jean-Jacques Rousseau, it should be recalled, who envisaged a state capable of delivering men from evil by providing them with perfect justice. To attain that level of civic tranquillity required actual forms of political power that could maintain and secure the public realm. The component of force—represented in Rousseau's day by the army—can never be more than an aspect of the power wielded by a well-ordered state.

Not every enlightened thinker understood the difference between force and power. Adam Smith and most German idealists could distinguish between them. Johann Fichte and Georg Hegel made the state the guardian of mankind's moral development, a view consistent with the effort of enlightened thought to make politics synonymous with morality. That effort made enlightened thinkers painfully aware of the darkness that encircled the light. One of them,

Edward Gibbon, who understood that power was an essential safeguard of the public realm, rendered an enlightened verdict on the martial spirit. His *Decline and Fall of the Roman Empire* opens this way: "The empire of Rome comprehended the fairest part of the earth, and the most civilized portion of mankind. The frontiers of that extensive monarchy were guarded by ancient renown and disciplined valor." Gibbon adds, "The Roman power, raised above the temptations of conquest, was actuated only by love of order and justice." And, "The terror of the Roman arms added weight and dignity to the moderation of the emperors."[1]

Gibbon's awe did not blind him to the gleaming double edge of the Roman sword—indeed, of every sword. Gibbon might have been writing Joseph II's epitaph: "The thirst of military glory will ever be the vice of the most exalted characters."[2] Gibbon spoke for his own age in acknowledging that the sword wielded by an exalted ruler could preserve the state and secure justice; in the hands of a tyrant, or an intemperate prince, the sword could impoverish the state—or worse, cause its downfall.

There was more to this than rhetoric. Eighteenth-century German rulers still held the Renaissance conviction that the prince's own talent and energy built and sustained the state. Frederick the Great's *Testaments* breathed this spirit, especially in dealing with foreign affairs and war. How the unexpected death of Prince Henry the Younger in 1767 shattered Frederick's hopes for Pussia's future is well known.[3]

Neither Frederick the Great nor his younger contemporary, Joseph II, understood that states had an organic quality, that they could exist and even thrive without the ruler's meticulous care. Each prince busied himself with the most minute details of government. Indeed, Joseph showed from the outset a veritable passion for military affairs. Foreign ambassadors reported that "the Kaiser thinks of nothing but his troops."[4] His initial memoranda to the State Council *(Staatsrat)* included an ambitious program to enlarge and improve the army. To Maria Theresa's horror, he not only admired but also expressed a wish to meet Frederick the Great, the House of Austria's archfoe. Joseph's military enthusiasm invariably betrayed something of the dilettante. This attribute persisted despite the zeal and intensity of his inspections, his drills, and his strenuous maneuvers in which he shared his troops' hardships. He drove himself inexorably to inspect the realm, often to decide from personal observation where new fortresses should be built. His habit of wearing his regiment's gray-green uniform at civil functions gave him an austere military countenance. He had accustomed himself to rough military life in camp and on the march; *but not to war itself.*[5] A single week of war in 1778 turned his stomach. This reaction could be ascribed to his moral sensitivity, or to his inability to endure the unforeseen, contingent event.

Joseph II had a more grievous fault: a consuming ambition to win military fame, to surpass Frederick the Great on the field of Mars. Joseph never overcame his fateful yearning for military glory; he considered war the prince's winged chariot. That folly brought his short reign to an end in the midst of a disastrous war that lacked a real political purpose. Joseph thereby failed an enlightened monarch's ultimate test. How he exercised his political responsibility had become the criterion of enlightened rule. Through self-discipline he had to show his agreement with the enlightened aversion to senseless wars. After 1763, in that age which Lord Acton called "the Repentance of Monarchy," power had not abdicated—it had to be put to better use.[6] The responsibility fell entirely upon the prince. This did not rule out a resort to war for a just cause or for reasons of state. Montesquieu had addressed that issue with his customary subtlety. He tried to distinguish between just and unjust wars, and like Niccolò Machiavelli, he pondered over the distinction between wars that served state interests and those originating in princely vanity or lust for conquest. Montesquieu eventually asserted that "the right . . . of war is derived from necessity and strict justice."[7] In that age, as in the present, war was a form of juridical action which became legitimate whenever it upheld a legal right or whenever it served a moral purpose. Conflicts over dynastic rights gave rise to many wars about monarchical succession, a form of legal contest submitted to the arbitrament of arms. Another legitimating factor arose from the readiness of enlightened opinion to follow the example of antiquity and assign a moral rank to the several forms of government.

Enlightened political theorists considered tyrannical and despotic governments more prone to wage aggressive war than either monarchies or republics. And since the makeup of armies had tended to acquire national characteristics, armies were generally believed to embody national virtues or vices. By various tests some nations could be considered enlightened; others were not. Strange peoples with unusual manners often seemed enlightened in proportion to their distance from Europe. Geographic remoteness alone qualified the Chinese, the Persians, and even the Iroquois.

Much closer to Prussia and Austria were cruel and barbarous peoples, made all the more terrible by their numbers and their mastery of modern arms. Europeans living in an age much given to studying Roman history drew an analogy between themselves and the Romans engaged in desperate struggles against barbarous foes. Frederick the Great did not consider either Russia or Turkey as European states. This did not cast them wholly into outer darkness, since at various times he considered them suitable allies. The Austrians were more explicit, at least about the Turks. In 1787 Austrian generals preparing for war against the Turks received this warning: "It cannot be denied that a Turkish attack on infantry drawn up in three ranks has a dreadful aspect because of the hideous sight of a mass of ten to twenty thousand or more screaming Turks hurling themselves forward."[8] This secret instruction also warned the Austrian generals to prepare their men for the Turks' shocking practice of beheading prisoners.

Other European observers spoke with awe about the Russian army's overwhelming numbers and savage brutality. Russian soldiers, said a Hessian officer, are at once servile and fanatical; fierce in attack and stubborn in defense; the prospect of loot goads the common soldiers who live miserably on onions and bread while their officers enjoy Asiatic luxuries. They know only the most barbaric style of war. Such armies, he said, require the raw brutality of an Aleksandr Suvarov to accomplish great deeds.[9]

Nonetheless, substantial amounts of force invariably command political respect. In the eighteenth century, the lack of military strength engendered contempt, unless tempered by wit and grace, as in Venice; or by money, as in the United Provinces. Poland's lack of arms invited a form of contempt that brought its political extinction. It was allowed to expire by degrees in keeping with the need for maintaining a highly competitive state system in equipoise.

Long before the partitions of Poland had begun, Poland's neighbors showed a persistent concern about its chronic weakness. Chancellor Mikhail Illarionovich Vorontsov told Tsar Peter III that Poland did not deserve to be called a European power as long as discord and disorder plagued its constitution. In this circumstance Frederick the Great's first *Testament* of 1752 showed princely restraint by proposing to gain Polish territory by diplomacy, not by war.[10] Frederick's reference to the metaphor used by Victor Amadeus of Savoy reveals the characteristic mores of an aristocratic age: that illustrious prince had proposed to devour the Milanese like an artichoke, leaf by leaf. The democratic era calls this piecemeal method "salami tactics."

An eighteenth century prince had to choose between nibbling and gulping. But he could expect to be judged by his manners. The moral responsibility for peace or war, for progress or stagnation fastened on the prince. Eventually the Jacobins made war a national responsibility; until then, the prince's character had to bear that awful burden. In Frederick's case, since he had loosed the bond between the Hohenzollern dynasty and the state, he began to infuse his character into his government. His sense of duty and his prudence bore witness to an enlightened statecraft based on the secular morality of his age.[11] His practices and his precepts gave rise to a military tradition that could sustain an enlightened understanding of war and statecraft. That outcome flowed directly from the Great King's intellectual initiatives. But it also shared in the intellectual quickening of contemporary German culture.

The Enlightenment loosed a rationalizing impulse that did not stay within the confines of morals, theology, philosophy or literature. It impressed itself on rulers by directing them to make their governments more effective in mobilizing their subjects and the national wealth for political purposes.[12] A nation that had become responsible to the prince's political will carried out the analogy between body and mind developed by enlightened thought. That the prince commands and the subjects obey paralleled the assumption that the mind should control the body. Joseph II's style of rule accepted that parallel without exercising the prudent limitations acknowledged by other enlightened rulers. He expected that his policies would become effective immediately, not merely because they had been decreed, but also because they emanated from a rational mind attuned to an enlightened age, an enthroned categorical imperative, as Heinrich Benedikt has commented.

A rational element entered into the military programs of the enlightened monarchs by bringing preparedness for war to bear on their over-all objectives. An international system that generated continuous state rivalries readily justified the propriety efforts to achieve the maximum rather than the optimum armament. But under enlightened influences the reasons of state had been broadened beyond interests to include the nation's general welfare. Frederick the Great's atttitude, expressed in his comment, "I am the first servant of the state," manifests the transformation of the state as an agency with narrow dynastic and power-political goals into a public instrument for raising the nation's moral and material wellbeing. Frederick's *Militärische Testament* of 1768 showed that his concept of reason of state went beyond Prussia's immediate political advantage to include the economic welfare, education, moral probity and even the happiness of his subjects.[13] These objectives had enveloped the traditional, narrowly political aims of reason of state, and although the basic political element persisted, it had to acknowledge and be coordinated with general welfare objectives. Frederick's practice and his European renown did much to fuse the directive elements in reason of state, the older ones inherited from dynastic politics, the others taken up boldly from the Enlightenment. The enlargement of the scope of reason of state had twofold consequences: it diminished suspicion of the monarchical state as an instrument of personal vainglory; and because it embraced the general welfare, the ruler could command the deepest loyalties of his soldiers and his subjects. He could now draw the sword with complete confidence.[14]

Frederick the Great, as an enlightened monarch, shared an ideal of justice and civil prosperity to be realized by an astute, rational statecraft that did not shun military necessity. His *Anti-Machiavel* (1740) represented more than a youthful prince's exuberance. It embodied the hope that mankind could realize its noblest goals, and even achieve universal happiness.[15] Only the state could assure that outcome, and to pursue it the state required power, that astute combination of military force, diplomacy, resolution and tenacity—the classic ingredients of political will. Maintaining that power laid an awful responsibility on the prince and his subjects; he bore the oppressive moral burden of calling forth its rawest ingredient, military force; the people bore its anguish with their labor, their sacrifices and their service under arms. The Prussian state's limited size, its lack of wealth, its scattered and hence vulnerable provinces necessitated a stern, highly disciplined mobilization of human and material resources. This taut system strained to the last bit of nervous energy did not serve the whim or caprice of an arbitrary despot. It was a political instrument that provided, at this stage of history, the best guarantee that humanity might realize the cultural program set forth by the Enlightenment. In the aftermath of the Seven Years' War the enlightened monarchs enhanced that prospect by their effort to avoid other protracted wars.[16]

After the Peace of Hubertusburg (1763) both Maria Theresa and Frederick the Great tried desperately to stave off another general war. They acknowledged that it would be protracted, exhausting and inconclusive. Frederick's foreign policy also recognized that a single state could not expect to make spectacular gains at the expense of another. And both Maria Theresa and Frederick concluded that the consolidation of the state could not be accomplished in one reign, no matter how prolonged. Frederick took great care to set down his observations and advice in his testaments, and also to provide, through his brother, Henry, some guidance for his nephew and successor. Maria Theresa prepared for the future by accustoming her eldest son, Joseph, to the weight of political responsibility from his twenty-fourth year (1765). He did not seem to share his mother's dread of another general war. He seemed convinced that war could overcome the tedious uncertainties of diplomacy. As a ruler, his impatient willfulness, which resented the slow pace of civil reform, brought impulsive interventions by decree that found a counterpart in rash decisions to go to war.

The terrible day of Kunersdorf (August 12, 1759), as well as all the other terrible days of battle, had left their mark on Frederick. His second *Testament* (1768) showed his hard-won political maturity by reaffirming his conviction that only a vital political need could justify a resort to war. Here also he acknowledged Prussia's precarious security in the state system since it could not be considered a Great Power. Prussia required allies; it foreign policy could succeed only by an adroit, opportunistic diplomacy. His correspondence with Prince Henry in 1775 showed a mounting dread of a general war over the Bavarian succession.[17]

After 1763 Maria Theresa seemed ready to preserve peace at any price. Previously, Minerva could not have been more exacting in her instructions to the army. The protracted wars had finally exhausted her astonishing zest for the martial arts. She lost the determination that had enabled her to say to Field Marshal Leopold von Daun, first director of the Wiener Neustadt military academy (1751), "Turn out sound officers for me!" Her changed mood expressed itself in her advice to Archduke Leopold in 1765: abandon all pretense of defending Tuscany by arms; keep only enough soldiers to suppress the brigands![18]

The military policy of Frederick the Great and the Queen of Hungary, save for their effort to avoid another general war, had little in common with the *philosophes'* characteristic demands. Neither monarch considered effective disarmament; each continued to stretch the state's resources thin in order to maintain a large force under arms. Frederick bequeathed his successor an army that had reached it maximum peacetime strength; when Archduke Joseph became coregent in 1765 he immediately proposed to expand the Austrian army. By the end of the Old Regime all armies had stabilized at the extreme limit of the state's financial and material resources.[19]

Despite their emphasis on vast armaments, monarchical governments in the last decades of the Old Regime gradually turned warfare into a calculable instrument of state policy. It did not make war any less brutal, nor did it become more humane. The actual clash of arms raged with its customary savagery. Nonetheless, coordinating the resort to war with policy objectives did strengthen the hand of military restraint. The preparation for war stressed the advantages gained by mastering technical details; the operational conduct of war emphasized a patterned geometry based on secure positions. The rational moment in strategic doctrines invariably brought a strong preference for fortifications[20] and defensive postures, an emphasis that combined with the military restraint being shown by the principal rulers to appear to make the military system amenable to the transformation being advocated by the *philosophes*.

The militia represented a form of military service approved by the enlightened literati, as well as by English colonists and Corsican patriots. Justus Möser, the historian and publicist, pleaded with the German princes to establish militias—all to no avail. Neither the Prussian nor the Austrian rulers proposed to transform the standing army with its component of conscripted native subjects into a militia.

Not every Habsburg disdained the militia. Grand Duke Leopold I of Tuscany outlined a plan in 1777 for disbanding his mercenary army and replacing it with a militia made up of his subjects. He was convinced that it would be less expensive, less damaging to the economy, and in the long run more reliable than a force of foreign mercenaries. In 1778 he advised Joseph II to follow the same course. By 1781 Leopold made Tuscany's defense and internal security depend solely on militia companies. But his successor, Ferdinand III, facing the stress of the French Revolutionary wars, dissolved the Tuscan militia and reestablished a mercenary army.[21]

Elsewhere the House of Austria stood fast in its suspicion of popular or feudal armed forces. Although Hungary had been given a regular standing army in 1715, the historic *insurrectio* had survived. The Hungarian *insurrectio* was not a militia. It was a traditional feudal levy which had survived because it provided a basis for the Hungarian nobility's tax exemption. Maria Theresa had summoned it once during the initial military crisis of her reign. And at a few critical moments between 1800–1809 it was also called upon to provide a last-ditch defense. Vienna always feared the political threat posed by military units not immediately beholden to the sovereign, and with good reason, since the Hungarian feudal revolt of 1790 brought forth an illegal county militia, the *banderium*, modeled on the *insurrectio*. Once the regular Austrian army had overawed the restless political elements in Hungary, Leopold II promptly dissolved the various companies that made up the *banderium* (November 18, 1790).[22]

Frederick William I's dissolution of the Prussian militia in 1713 had paved the way for the canton system of compulsory recruitment adopted in 1733. Frederick the Great identified Prussia's disproportionate military strength with that system. To safeguard the cantons, he had dismantled the militia hastily assembled in East Prussia and other provinces east of the Elbe during the Seven Years' War. During that war, Frederick tried to avoid making excessive demands on the native manpower supplied by the canton system. Nonetheless, the army and the Prussian population's staggering losses—about 400,000 lives—did bring the canton system perilously close to ruin. Peace brought no respite from the strenuous demands that Frederick continued to make on the cantons' manpower. Anticipating a war with Russia, he even considered establishing a navy to support a projected Baltic offensive by the army.[23]

A rearmament fever raged with particular intensity in Vienna, where in 1765 Joseph as coregent, had assumed responsibility for military affairs. He found a diligent if uninspired collaborator in Field Marshal Count Franz von Lacy, who proved more capable in administration than he had in battle. He gave the Austrian army its first uniform tactical regulations; started three massive fortresses in Bohemia and one in Hungary; and won Joseph's approval late in 1765 for a systematic conscription modeled on the Prussian cantons. Political opposition barred Lacy's conscription program from Hungary and the Tyrol until the 1780s; remoteness barred Lombardy and the Netherlands altogether. Elsewhere in the realm conscription lists had been compiled and private dwellings had been numbered by 1772.[24] Foreign travelers invariably commented on Austria's painted house numbers, a practice known in Paris but generally unknown in the rest of Europe.

These numbers became symbols of oppression during the 1780s when Joseph II and Count Lacy tried to apply conscription to lands previously exempt. Joseph inspected the Bukovina himself and joined its military administration with Galicia's. There, local resentment combined with poverty to preserve the old-style frontier guard. Not so in Transylvania and Wallachia where armed force finally compelled the peasants to leave the militia and enroll in standing regiments. Pleas and threats of force could not compel the Tyrolese to yield. Able-bodied youths fled into the ecclesiastical principalities of Trent and Brixen; resentful Tyrolese peasants threw dung at the numbers that had been painted on their houses. Hungary's nobility announced its stand on conscription by preparing to rebel.[25] Formal attempts to apply conscription in Hungary ended in 1785, but not the unrest, which persisted amid the misfortunes of the Ottoman war that erupted in February 1788.[26] In that misguided effort Joseph II contracted the fatal illness that forced him to cancel his projected civil reform.

It should not be imagined that the Prussian army had succeeded in overcoming the inertia that seized it after the Seven Years' War. The concerted effort to make a rapid military recovery hardened all the established methods. Heavy losses among the officers, including many of high rank, could not easily be made up. All the severities and constraints built into the Prussian military system, not the least among them Frederick's own military conservatism, barred an effective adaptation to the lessons of a prolonged war. Frederick's austere character, his style of personal command, and his reliance on Junker officers all worked toward the perpetuation of the existing military system[27]

The Prussian army's dependence on conscripted native recruits linked it to the feudal manorial basis of Prussian agriculture. Despite criticism from highly placed civil servants, and even Frederick's apprehension of the flaws inherent in the agrarian-military linkage, the cantonal element anchored in a servile agricultural population survived bureaucratic criticism and cameralist reform alike. Its survival blocked the adaptation of Prussian agriculture to the improved methods of husbandry being applied in other countries. And although cantonal recruitment tended to militarize some aspects of manorial relations, it had other effects that worked to the army's disadvantage. It allowed an influential group of officers to perpetuate outmoded and unproductive agriculture on their estates. They were thereby encouraged to remain aloof from the enlightened current flowing into all spheres of activity, including their own profession.[28]

Frederick the Great's energies turned increasingly toward safeguarding the realm for his successor. But his meticulous instructions went for naught: the vagaries of dynastic succession put a mediocrity on the throne. Frederick William II soon dashed the hope that he might begin a serious military reform. Before disaster overwhelmed Prussian arms in 1806, Frederick William II had encourged the idea of military reform without sanctioning much of it.

It is evident that neither Austria nor Prussia could consistently sustain an enlightened military policy. Their persistent attempt to make a maximum military effort and their sufferance of catastrophic losses during the Seven Years' War testify to an over-zealous respect for reason of state. Both powers strove essentially to increase their military capabilities along technical and organizational lines. Even in that respect Joseph II's efforts to broaden the base of recruitment ran afoul of provincial traditions and regional animosities. A far more serious trial lay ahead because the military system put together by the Duke of Marlborough, Prince Eugene of Savoy and Frederick the Great had run its course.[29] Whether the monarchical armies could imitate the French Revolutionary and Napoleonic methods would depend in large measure on the strength and vitality of their own enlightened military cadres.

In Prussia after 1789 there was a notable quickening of civil and military reform energy. Although it left the army little changed, it did develop an awareness of the military crisis among Prussian military intellectuals. Flaws in the theoretical studies made by such officers as Christian von Massenbach, Karl von Phull, Georg Venturini as well as by Gerhard von Scharnhorst, should not obscure the intensity of their effort to decode the meaning of the French war-making. In their zeal some officers overstepped the bounds of permissible speculation. Georg von Berenhorst loosed a discussion about the continued merit of Frederick the Great's methods; Heinrich von Bülow moved from a refined geographical schema to a perception that the levy en masse could release the pent-up energy of political enthusiasm.[30]

This literary and speculative activity provided some of the momentum that carried over into the effort to regenerate the Prussian state and army after 1806. Before the disasters of that year the learned officers had joined the higher civil servants in consolidating the nation's intelligentsia with the cause of the state.[31] Their collaboration made possible Prussia's eventual reestablishment as a political power in the European community. In this coordinated civil and military reform effort lay Prussia's advantage vis-à-vis its great Germanic rival. Frederick the Great's example had much to do with the intelligentsia's readiness to serve the state. The Soldier King had sustained their confidence in Prussia as the political emodiment of rational and moral purpose in the world. The late Professor Rudolf Stadelmann observed that the nineteenth-century Prussian concept of an officer had originated among the learned officers of the late eighteenth century. He concluded that Frederick the Great's example enabled Prussia to sustain the moral cost and accept the political risk of a massive army while assimilating the old monarchical tradition to the new enlightenment.[32]

For this task Prussia had succeeded in marshaling an impressive number of German military intellectuals. Phull and Massenbach were Swabians; Karl von Lindenau a Saxon; and Scharnhorst a Hanoverian. Prussia had become a magnet that attracted learned and innovative soldiers. More than that, some effort went into soliciting their services. The Duke of Brunswick tried to persuade Scharnhorst to enter Prussian service in 1795. Repeated requests were made until 1801 when Scharnhorst accepted a Prussian commission because it offered a better prospect for advancement as a staff officer. But enlightened officers, especially the foreign born, did not move easily up the ladder of command. Most *Stockpreussen* still looked askance at these bookish "foreigners." For every General Möllendorf, who lacked intellect but remained tolerant as befitted a grand military seigneur, there was a General Blücher, whose undisciplined temperament and mad excesses as a leader of hussars personified the officer schooled only in his regiment. Time was running out for that school. Very soon Prussia's military disasters would give military learning the advantage over the outlook that preferred the camp to the classroom.

Military schools for officers had been sharply differentiated between cadet institutes for young noblemen, and technical schools for middle-class youths being trained for the artillery and engineering services. Neither form developed the whole officer nor provided insights into the relations between war and society. By the 1770s German military education began to acquire more scope by providing technical training in all arms along with the broad learning appropriate for professional officers. One center emerged in Duke Karl Eugen's *Militärakademie* established near Stuttgart in 1773.[33] Another appeared in Göttingen where the mathematician, Albrecht L. F. Meister, bombarded the Hanoverian government with proposals for a wide-ranging military curriculum. His effort influenced Scharnhorst's subsequent plea (1788) for the university to provide military instruction. Joseph II's pragmatic attitude toward all education beyond the primary level ruled out such arrangements in Austria. After closing the *Theresianum*, an elite academy for noble youths, he assigned its quarters to a school for military engineers. There from 1784–1797 the *k.-k. Ingenieurakademie* trained its fledgling scholar-cadets.[34] Most rulers preferred to separate military and civilian education, an outlook shared by Colonel Ferdinand Friedrich von Nicolai, an able artillerist as well as a military theorist, who directed the Stuttgart *Militärakademie*. His instruction combined field exercises with an intense formal training that did not neglect the celebrated French military theorists, Marshal Jean-François Puységur, Hippolyte de Guibert and Jean-Charles Folard. Military education, Nicolai said, should deal with every aspect of war.[35]

Through Scharnhorst's efforts the new form of military education came to Prussia. He had experienced its breadth as a cadet at the Wilhelmsteiner military school founded by Count Wilhelm zu Schaumburg-Lippe. There he had received a solid mathematical and scientific training in the technical arms as well as a deep sense of the urgent need for uniting the army with the people. That schooling had also awakened his lifelong enthusiasm for humane learning. Prussian service gave that enthusiasm ample scope. Only a few months after his arrival in Berlin, Scharnhorst had been appointed (September 5,

1801) head of a modest institute for training young infantry and cavalry officers. Within three years Scharnhorst had transformed it into a model *Akademie für Offiziere* that bore the stamp of his concern for giving military education a broad intellectual content. Karl von Clausewitz, one of forty young officers enrolled in the academy, became Scharnhorst's close friend as well as the principal legatee of his intellectual effort to relate war to statecraft.[36]

Scharnhorst's educational innovations also brought him into the circle of reform-minded persons, both civilian and military. He selected two officers trained in Duke Karl Eugen's school, Phull and Massenbach, to lecture at the academy. And in these years Scharnhorst began to reflect on the means to transform the army's staff function into a school of advanced military learning in order to insure the continuity of talented leadership in the highest echelons. Scharnhorst's reforming zeal could not be confined even though it stirred some critics to speak out about his boldness. His initial proposals of 1801–1802 dealt only with military technicalities, but at length, in his memoir of April 1806 he boldly asserted that the emerging bond between state and nation required an army based on universal military service.[37]

Breadth of view combined with an objective outlook characterized Scharnhorst's contribution to military journalism, a form of discourse that supplemented formal military education. Military journals had begun to flourish in Germany after the Seven Years' War and Scharnhorst first gained notice as a military editor and writer.[38] His journalistic ventures which strove to harmonize military theory and practice merged with his military education program. Scharnhorst's first journal, the *Militair-Bibliothek* (1782–1784), defended a general academic education for officers because ignorance debased and dishonored their profession, and, Scharnhorst added, their ignorance could bring ruin to the state.[39]

By their informed writing about military topics and issues, Scharnhorst and other Prussian officers who took pen in hand maintained the surge of German interest in military professionalism. By and large, the Austrian military establishment held aloof from the new style of military education and showed only a casual interest in the flood of military journals. The Austrian officers' indifference to theoretical and comparative studies had lasting consequences. It reinforced the army's anti-intellectual attitude toward military education and limited efforts to overcome the army's staff weakness, if it did not obscure that weakness altogether. In the long run, the Austrian failure to combine military education with the training of staff officers delayed the development of a general-staff system of command.[40]

The German military journals did not neglect topics or issues that affected strategic decisions, or even basic political principles. They published articles on critical aspects of civil and military relations as well as the significance of military strength for foreign policy. Their conclusions persistently upheld the state as the best means for attaining the prospect for humanity held out by the Enlightenment. In one way or another these journals insisted that the wellbeing and prosperity of the state depended on an alert, well-trained army. The kind of war it would wage depended on the form of government and its policy. Montesquieu had popularized the association between aggressive war and large monarchical states, and defensive war and small, republican states. Both forms of government, the military intellectuals argued, required effective armies appropriate to their nature. Correspondence between the army and political purpose would preserve the "health of the state," either by preventing territorial loss or by making territorial conquests. In this way the military journalists associated the army with an overarching civil and cultural purpose.[41]

Scharnhorst shared the hope that an enlightened age had invested in the state. If the kings of Prussia, he said, had not been obliged to make themselves formidable against their neighbors, they might not have been able to harness all their realm's energies and strength. In that case, they might not have attained their present wellbeing, nor would they have advanced culture, enlightenment and happiness. For, he concluded, war is, in a certain sense, a means for promoting good fortune.[42]

As an active military journalist, Scharnhorst extolled the beneficial effects of military writing on the army. He often overstated the case since the pragmatic value of theoretical military knowledge had not yet been fully acknowledged in any contemporary army. He argued that an extensive use of written instructions had developed the precision and uniformity that made the Prussian army so formidable. He observed the same consequences on a restricted scale in the French army. Its artillery, he said, had gained distinction because that service had produced significant military authors. The Danish and Saxon artillery had also been improved because noteworthy instructional books had been prepared for its officers. This did not mean, he added, that any army without military writers is necessarily in a poor condition. But he was certain that an army could overcome its shortcomings only when correct measures had been introduced by means of well-written books. An army that lacked its own original military writers could act purposefully by seeking out and compiling information about new principles and methods being applied in other armies. Good military writers, Scharnhorst said, could awaken a sound military understanding so that army officers who took to the pen were rendering their sovereign an honorable service.[43]

Scharnhorst has in some measure been overshadowed by Clausewitz, his pupil. The master's talent showed to best advantage in the Prussian military reforms undertaken after 1806. Their objective, Scharnhorst said, was to renew and invigorate the spirit of the army and unite it with the nation to serve a common destiny. His ideals had grandeur as well as intellectual content, so that Clausewitz's historical stature is not diminished if he is understood in relation to the continuity of Prussian military intellectualism.[44]

The Austrian military tradition failed to maintain an equivalent intellectual current. Its intermittent energy glowed from time to time without sustaining any degree of continuity. This weakness at the highest levels of military policy-making and military education contrasts sharply with the prolongation of Josefinism—the rationalizing impulse in the civil bureaucracy—which had a continuing influence on public affairs and on the liberalism of the *Vormärz* era. Why did Josefinism continue to influence basic aspects of civil policy while Austrian military policy veered now in this direction, now in that? Did the international makeup of the eighteenth-century Austrian officer corps contribute to that outcome?

The Habsburgs drew their officers from all the distant reaches of their realm: from the Netherlands, Lorraine, Lombardy, Hungary and even Protestant lands in the Empire. The prestige conferred by Austrian service lured many talented officers away from promising careers in rival armies. But the international elements in the officer corps appear to have ruled out the solidarity achieved among officers in the British and the Prussian armies that provided the basis for their gradual professionalization.[45] Nor should sight be lost of the effect of the affluence enjoyed by many Austrian commanding generals on their subordinates' concern for sharpening their professional skills. An aristocratic scorn for military professionalism kept the old aulic nobility away from the Wiener Neustadt academy and even from their own cadet school in Vienna, at least in the period of the Old Regime. An anti-intellectual attitude spread among field officers who took their social cues from the higher levels of command. And in the Austrian army, as in other European armies, the existence of proprietary regiments made the colonels indifferent and even hostile to the academic form of military professionalism.[46]

It is striking that in contrast to Prussia, and even Saxony, the Austrian officers did not contribute substantially to the torrent of military literature that spilled over Europe after the Seven Years' War. There were exceptions such as Charles, Prince de Ligne (1735–1814), a friend and counsellor of Joseph II, who had served with distinction in the Seven Years' War and was present at the siege of Belgrade in his sovereign's last war. The prince's output was prodigious, but apart from the evidence that he belonged to the school of Guibert, his persistent lighthearted style has made him memorable for witticisms rather than serious military instruction. At the outset of the Congress of Vienna, the Prince de Ligne commented perceptively, "Here pleasure secures peace."[47]

The fitful quality of intellectual currents in the Austrian army contrasts unfavorably with the persistent Josefinist current. Josefinism is usually identified with the Habsburg effort that began in the 1760s to carry out a state-directed reform of the Roman Catholic Church in Austria. It proposed to transform the church into an enlightened instrument, largely free of papal and episcopal control, that could assist the state in raising the popular levels of spiritual and material wellbeing.[48] This program had begun in Maria Theresa's reign, but Joseph II's stern Jansenist morality and his readiness to extend control over the liturgy, the religious orders, clerical education, and even to determine the number and location of parishes, gave Josefinism its most characteristic contours. Beyond this customary meaning, the term is applicable to all the political, economic and cultural efforts of Austrian enlightened monarchical rule, especially its goal of realizing a unified public realm with predominantly German features. In this larger sense, Josefinism had a long life as a deeply respected set of governmental methods and objectives.[49]

Josefinism spoke for an enlightened outlook that made the state responsible for both the measure and the satisfaction of the most basic human needs. Confidence that an authoritarian state could confer and extend the general well-being remained a Josefinist hallmark. It required a well-trained, conscientious bureaucracy acting uniformly under central direction. Its respect for bureaucracy, embodied in the traditional Austrian belief that "if it is written down it will happen," emphasized civil at the expense of military affairs. It drew nourishment from the Catholic Enlightenment as well as Jansenist morality. Its civil objectives made Josefinism a formative element in the development of the "old Austrian liberalism." But for want of military attributes, Josefinism could not sustain either "the Austrian" or "the German idea."[50]

Sustaining and promoting either of those ideologies required an effective army. But apart from its stress on bureaucratic efficiency, Josefinism contributed little to military effectiveness per se. The great vehicle of civil enlightenment in Austria made little use of military routes.

The mastery shown by Austrian cameralists, educators and jurisconsults, as well as the zeal shown in building a *Staatskirchentum*, had no counterpart in a rational military effort. In other European armies the educated officers had begun to propagate their views. They could not as yet make a deep impression on a military system still beset by the uncertain quality of aristocratic leadership, by colonels preoccupied with their regimental economies, and not least by recruiting methods that filled the ranks with foreign and domestic outcasts.[51] Everywhere the realities of army life raised formidable obstacles to the ideas and programs being advanced by the military intelligentsia. In this circumstance only the example set by an intellectual monarch with an illustrious record of command could sustain an illuminating school of military theory in the face of dismal regimental reality.

Joseph II's persistent and conscientious efforts to strengthen the Austrian army did not succeed in infusing it with a serious respect for intellectual military interests.[52] His lack of battlefield honors was partly to blame. Some part of it also stemmed from his choice of a principal collaborator, Count Franz Moritz von Lacy (1725–1801), an able administrator who paid scrupulous attention to detail without being able to distinguish between basic and trivial matters. Field Marshal Leopold von Daun had recommended that Count Lacy succeed him as president of the Court War Council *(Hofkriegsrat)*, the central institution of military administration.[53] Many high-ranking aristocratic officers resented his appointment (February 15, 1766) so that the court made haste to quiet them by freely distributing marshal's batons, additional military honors and lucrative assignments. Even so, the old military nobility never overcame its initial annoyance and continued to treat Lacy coolly.[54] His rise as Joseph's military counsellor steadily eclipsed Field Marshal Baron Gideon von Laudon's influence in the army. That proved to be a serious loss since Laudon had displayed high qualities of leadership during the Seven Years' War. Joseph became increasingly dependent on Lacy, even for operational plans which Lacy weighed down with his customary caution.[55]

Lacy's operational style epitomized the Austrian generals' preference for the defensive and for cautious movements preceded by elaborate logistical preparations. Lacy also neglected general instructions about the strategic conduct of war; no broad statements about the principles of war reached the field commands. Lacy's field service regulations concentrated on the minutiae of regimental housekeeping, forming the camp, the order of the march, and so forth. Under these circumstances the staff controls, which were poorly developed in every European army, remained very informal.[56] Lacy did achieve some positive results. He overcame the marked deficiency in military engineering;[57] he maintained the field artillery's excellence; the disciplinary treatment of the men became more humane; and the wholesale corruption in regimental economies came to an end. The Austrian army also maintained the high quality of its intelligence-gathering which had provided accurate information about the Prussian army on the eve of the Seven Years' War.[58] These technical and organizational accomplishments should not be dismissed lightly; they kept the Austrian army abreast of the other armies that accepted the conventional military methods. The Austrian army remained flawed, nonetheless, because it lacked both institutional means and the intellectual cadres that could adapt it to the dynamics of the national and industrial era.

Joseph II and Lacy's military administration showed to good effect during the brief War of the Bavarian Succession (1778–1779), although it did not test the Austrian troops in a large-scale battle. A serious test began in the war against the Turks that opened ominously in December 1787 with the failure of a surprise attack on the fortress of Belgrade.[59] In the campaign that followed the Austrian army had moments of glory as well as deep humiliation. Throughout the army's trials, Joseph II suffered the agonies of his last campaign with soldierly fortitude. On February 14, 1790, six days before his death, his general orders reiterated his deep personal attachment to military life.[60]

Emperor Leopold II, Joseph's successor, had to agree to terms of peace at Reichenbach on July 27, 1790. Army reductions followed as an immediate consequence and a newly appointed commission began to investigate the army's shortcomings. In all this, Lacy retained a certain ceremonial and diplomatic importance, although he had to submit to a curt investigation by the followers of Field Marshal Laudon who had never been active in military administration. The episode revealed the persistence of serious discontinuities in the formal direction of the armed forces; it also showed the dearth of creative military reformers.[61] Only the fortuitous appearance of Archduke Charles (1771–1847) enabled Austria to realize its military capability.[62]

In 1796 Archduke Charles's brilliant riposte in the German theater showed that a resourceful commander could employ the Austrian army as a supple striking force.[63] Thereafter, Archduke Charles energetically advanced the cause of military reorganization and reform. For some time he made headway against resistance from traditional elements within the army; to some extent he overcame the inertia that makes all large-scale organizations resist change. He brought to his task the laurels of brilliant generalship, and, as the third son of the Emperor Leopold II (d. 1792), the prestige of the Imperial archducal household. None of these assets availed Archduke Charles after his defeat by Napoleon at Wagram (1809). He fell victim to the fateful discontinuity that had repeatedly overturned Austrian military leadership. After Wagram, the archduke languished in the anterooms of Austrian public life.

It was Austria's misfortune that the army's most capable leader and reformer should have been dishonored by the loss of a decisive battle. The Prussian military disasters in 1806–1807 had the contrary effect, at least temporarily, of humiliating the military traditionalists. Defeat cleared the way for far-reaching civil as well as military reforms. It gave Scharnhorst the opportunity for which he had been prepared by his scholarly military vocation. At the outset, his capable and inspired leadership enabled the work of military reform to draw sustenance from the prospect of a profound transformation of the government and civil society. Change on that scale did not occur and the military reforms also fell short of their idealized goals. Yet Scharnhorst's and his associates' zealous effort enabled a reorganized Prussian army to take the field again. It also gained an embryonic general staff and a nucleus of administrative functions that eventually became a war ministry (1814). And the reformers implanted the concept that military leadership should be selected in terms of excellence in the mastery of the theory as well as in the practice of military science.[64] That the study of war had an empirical-historical basis became established in Prussia through Scharnhorst's own efforts as a military writer and educator. And as a military thinker Scharnhorst renewed the Frederician inquiry into the rational employment of war in the service of the state. Through Clausewitz that inquiry came into full maturity.

Archduke Charles's legacy did not go unheeded in Austria since his military writing did set certain guidelines for subsequent courses of Austrian military policy. Whether those guidelines marked the real course of events remains a moot point. For Archduke Charles's theoretical account of war-making compared unfavorably with his own vigorous conduct of operations. His literary record of those events upheld the methodical school of military strategy with its defensive cordons and massive fortresses.

General Count Josef Radetzky as the legatee of the Austrian military tradition became that school's natural exponent.[65] His prominence in the post-Napoleonic Austrian army epitomized the short-lived influence of the rationalizing aspect of the Enlightenment on Austrian military thought and practice. Radetzky did not neglect the higher echelons of military learning but his main efforts invariably concerned the practical details of military life. Steadiness in the ranks was always his basic concern. From his officers he demanded resolution; from his soldiers, courage. And courage, said *Vater* Radetzky, comes more easily on a full stomach: "*Der Soldat, der nix z'essen hat, kann keine Courage haben.*"[66]

However admirable, Radetzky's soldierly paternalism does not compare favorably with the intellectual style that characterized Clausewitz and Moltke. Scharnhorst's enduring influence had insured their careers in Prussia. In turn, they gave Prussia a first-rate army; and that army enabled Otto von Bismarck to turn his gambit into a master game.

## Notes

1. Edward Gibbon, *The History of the Decline & Fall of the Roman Empire* (New York, 1946), I, 1, 6–7.
2. *Ibid.*, I, 4.

3. Prince Henry, the king's most cherished nephew, died unexpectedly following regimental exercises in the spring of 1767. Frederick poured his grief into a euology read to the Berlin Academy on Dec. 30, 1767. Its text is in Walter Elze, *Friedrich der Grosse: Geistige Welt, Schicksal, Taten* (3rd ed.; Berlin, 1942), pp. 264–275.

4. "The Emperor thinks of nothing else than his troops," the French Ambassador Breteuil reported to Vergennes, the French foreign minister, on Oct. 30, 1779. Carl August Rauscher, "Die Aussenpolitik Kaiser Josephs II. (1780–1790) und ihre internationalen Zusammenhänge im Spiegel der französischen Botschafter Berichte" (Univ. of Vienna diss., 1951), p. vii.

5. Pavel Mitrofanov, *Joseph II: Seine politische und kulturelle Tätigkeit* (Vienna and Leipzig, 1910), p. 347. This biography, translated from the Russian, remains one of the best. Mitrofanov (pp. 347–349) observed Joseph's paradoxical combination of military zeal and squeamishness about the bloody horror of battle.

6. Lord Acton, *Lectures on Modern History* (New York, 1961), p. 285.

7. Montesquieu, *The Spirit of the Laws* (London, 1902), Book X, "Of Laws in the Relation They Bear to Offensive Force," p. 144. Montesquieu forsook the general intellectual attack on the army in order to deal realistically with its relation to the state and nation. Cf. Émile G. Léonard, *L'armée et ses problèmes au XVIIIe siècle* (Paris, 1958), pp. 143–144, 146–147, 149–150.

8. Oskar Criste, *Kriege unter Kaiser Josef II: Nach den Feldakten und anderen authentischen Quelle* (Vienna, 1904), p. 293.

9. *Neue Bellona*, VII (1804), 315 ff.

10. Friedrich Meinecke made the classic analysis of Frederick's *Testaments* and other political reflections. Meinecke held that Frederick acknowledged the state's dual task of advancing humanitarian ideals while maintaining its own power. And that in the later stages of his reign the humanitarian aspect grew more pronounced without, however, being able to dispense with the state's fundamental basis in power. Cf. *Machiavellism: The Doctrine of Raison d'Etat and Its Place in Modern History* (New York, 1965), pp. 272 ff., particularly pp. 282–283.

11. Recent studies have borne out the continuity of Frederick's response to the ethos of enlightened monarchical rule. Consult Walther Hubatsch, *Frederick the Great of Prussia: Absolutism and Administration* (London, 1975), Chap. V, "The Second Rétablissement," pp. 148 ff.; and Hubert C. Johnson, *Frederick the Great and His Officials* (New Haven and London, 1975), Chap. VII, "Rétablissement," pp. 188 ff.

12. Henri Brunschwig's pioneering study, *Enlightenment and Romanticism in Eighteenth-Century Prussia* (Chicago and London, 1974), acknowledged the Prussian state's receptivity to the rational mode of inquiry generated by the Enlightenment. But he believed that the army and the economy had not been stirred by it. About 1780, a new generation frustrated by private as well as public existence, turned from enlightened to romantic

models. Cf. Brunschwig's account pp. 81–82, 96–98, 146 ff. and 160 ff.

13. Meinecke, *Machiavellism*, pp. 280–282, 305–306.

14. The importance that rulers attached to the public goals of enlightened statecraft should not obscure their persistent view that their subjects benefited from increases in the territorial scope of the state. That view permitted a casuistic attitude about territory that could be gained at the expense of less powerful states. And in a governmental system that matched place with royal favor, ministers did not always recommend ideal policies. They often held on determinedly to rash projects, or they devised policies solely to redeem previous failures. Kaunitz longed to obtain revenge or compensation for the loss of Silesia. In France, Choiseul burned with eagerness to reverse the outcome of the Seven Years' War.

15. Article LXXVII of the Prussian General Civil Code promulgated in 1794 made that objective explicit. Cited in R. R. Palmer, *The Age of the Democratic Revolution* (Princeton, N.J., 1959), I, 510.

16. Gerhard Ritter, *Frederick the Great: A Historical Profile* (Berkeley, Calif., 1974), pp. 68–72. Oscillations in the historical judgment of Frederick the Great are surveyed in Walter Bussmann, "Friedrich der Grosse im Wandel des europäischen Urteils," in Werner Conze (ed.), *Deutschland und Europa: Festschrift für Hans Rothfels* (Düsseldorf, 1951), pp. 375–408. Bussmann's assessment of Meinecke, pp. 399–400; and of Ritter, pp. 402–403.

17. Gerhard Ritter, *The Sword and the Scepter: The Problems of Militarism in Germany*, Vol. I: *The Prussian Tradition, 1740–1890* (Coral Gables, Fla., 1969), pp. 30–33, 35 ff., 38–39.

18. Cf. *Maria Theresa in ihren Briefen und Staatsschriften*, pp. 15 *et seq.* Maria Theresa appeared to be free of the "Wallenstein Complex" that disturbed relations between many Austrian rulers and their successful generals. Her successors were often suspicious of military success, even when attained by a member of the archducal household. It gave rise to discontinuities in military leadership that plagued Austrian efforts to correlate military power and foreign policy. Cf. Gordon Craig, "Command and Staff Problems in the Austrian Army, 1740–1866," *War, Politics and Diplomacy: Selected Essays* (London, 1966), pp. 4–7.

19. The Prussian army had 158,000 men in 1756; 219,000 men at the end of the Seven Years' War; and 195,000 men when Frederick the Great died in 1786. By that date the Austrian army had risen to 297,000 men, the largest peacetime establishment in Europe. The Russian army had 224,000 men. See Christopher Duffy, *The Army of Frederick the Great* (New York, 1974), pp. 205–206; and Hubatsch, *Frederick the Great*, pp. 130, 133.

20. Although eighteenth-century military operations emphasized and often exaggerated the role of fortresses, the Austrian army had inadequate engineering services. Prince Eugene's bitter complaint to Emperor Charles VI that the army lacked engineers brought the *Technische Militärakademie* into

being (Dec. 17, 1717). It had an uneasy existence, suffering several changes of name, and its graduates, who were not numerous, had a modest role before the nineteenth century. Moritz von Brunner and Hugo Kerchnawe, *225 Jahre Technische Militärakademie 1717 bis 1942* (Vienna, 1942), pp. 13, 15 ff., 31 ff. and 36–39.

21. Details in Adam Wandruszka, *Leopold II. Erzherzog von Österreich, Grossherzog von Toskana, König von Ungarn und Böhmen, Römischer Kaiser* (Vienna, 1965).

22. Béla K. Király, *Hungary in the Late Eighteenth Century: The Decline of Enlightened Despotism* (New York and London, 1969), pp. 183–186, 189–190.

23. Hubatsch's general account of Prussian military administration suggests some aspects of its wartime (1756–1763) breakdown, difficulties which Johnson describes specifically, especially the uneven service of provincial officials, civil-military rivalry, and the ad hoc measures that often put the central administration on a day-to-day basis. Hubatsch, *Frederick the Great*, pp. 113–137; Johnson, *Frederick the Great and His Officials*, pp. 156–187.

24. Edith Kotasek, *Feldmarschall Graf Lacy: Ein Leben für Österreichs Heer* (Horn, 1956), pp. 101 ff., 115 ff. and 126 ff.

25. On recruitment, Mitrofanov, *Joseph II*, pp. 358–365, 376–377, 387–389.

26. A popular protest (made possible by the lifting of censorsip) mounted against the Ottoman war. A detailed, accurate account of Turkish warmaking by a Prussian, but published in Vienna in 1788, did not calm the public by its methodical account of the initial intensity of a Turkish attack. Nonetheless, the author said (p. IX) that he intended to disprove the "legend" of Turkish cruelty. J. C. G. Hayne, *Abhandlung über die Kriegskunst der Türken von ihren Märchen, Lägern, Schlachten und Belagerungen, usw.* (Vienna, 1788).

27. Although Prussia drew heavily on its native aristocracy, the *Junker*, for officer material, the Prussian officer corps also had a large foreign contingent. Between 1740–1763 about one-sixth of the Prussian generals were foreign born. Duffy, *Army of Frederick the Great*, p. 30, and pp. 199 ff. on the Prussian army after the Seven Years' War.

28. Otto Büsch, *Militärsystem und Sozialleben im alten Preussen, 1713–1807* (Berlin, 1962), pp. 71–73, 142–143, 161–166 and 167–170. Büsch develops a severely critical account of the "social militarization" brought about in Prussia by combining the system of cantonal recruitment (1733 ff.) with dependence on Junker landowning officers. It brought the officer-soldier disciplinary relationship of the army into the manorial economy making it rigid and unproductive. The outcome, Büsch concludes, set the military tone of all phases of Prussian public life. But various reviewers have pointed out that the scale of his study did not warrant such broad conclu-

sions. See Horst Stuke's review, *Historische Zeitschrift*, CIIC (1964), 389–393.

29. The conventions of that military system provided the basis for Frederick the Great's voluminous military analysis and comment. For an excellent compilation with informative notes, see Jay Luvaas (ed.), *Frederick the Great on the Art of War* (New York, 1966).

30. Georg Heinrich von Berenhorst, *Betrachtungen über die Kriegskunst* (Leipzig, 1798–1799); Heinrich Dietrich von Bülow, *Der Geist des neueren Kriegssystems* (Hamburg, 1799). Being a military innovator had its perils: Massenbach's and Bülow's careers ended in public disgrace. Cf. Carl Hans Hermann, *Deutsche Militärgeschichte: Eine Einführung* (Frankfurt am Main, 1968), pp. 136–138.

31. On this continuity see Ritter, *Sword and Scepter*, I, 42, ff, and 270, n. 15.

32. Rudolph Stadelmann, *Moltke und der Staat* (Krefeld, 1950), p. 76.

33. The original *Hohe Karlsschule*, established in 1770, trained both civil servants and military officers. Friedrich Schiller was the *Akademie's* most celebrated graduate. His brief military career as a regimental surgeon, 1780–1782, ended in his flight to Mannheim, where *Die Räuber*, which he had written at age nineteen, received its first performance (1782). Franz Miller, *Reine Taktik der Infanterie, Cavallerie und Artillerie* (Stuttgart, 1787), I, 79–100, surveyed German schools and academies that provided officer training. Miller argued that tactics had to be learned in theory as well as practice because a spirit of pettiness made an officer a poor tactician. *Ibid.*, I, 8–9 ff.

34. Brunner and Kerchnawe, *Technische Militärakademie*, pp. 39 ff.

35. Rudolf Stadelmann, *Scharnhorst: Schicksal und geistige Welt* (Wiesbaden, 1952), pp. 146–148.

36. *Ibid.*, pp. 38–39; Peter Paret, *Clausewitz and the State* (New York, 1976), pp. 60–61, 67–74.

37. Stadelmann, *Scharnhorst*, pp. 58–74; the April 1806 *Denkschrift*, pp. 72–74.

38. On the German military journalism, see Willian O. Shanahan, *The Prussian Military Reforms, 1786–1813* (New York, 1945), pp. 61–63.

39. *Militair-Bibliothek*, I (1782), 5. The progressive educational thrust of the military journals is developed in "Der Einfluss der Wissenschaften auf die Kriegskunst," *Militärische Monatschrift*, IV (1787), 457–483 (published by A. L. von Massenbach in Berlin). Study was said to form the officers' spirit in the same way that drill and field exercises strengthened the men (p. 476). And military affairs embraced a true science appropriate for study in schools, not only to impart technical knowledge but to fortify civic virtues. Another article, "Einige Bemerkungen über das österreichische Militär," *ibid.*, IV (1786), 351–363, reported unfavorably on Austrian military usage, especially the woeful lack of staff services.

40. Craig, "Command and Staff Problems," p. 12.

41. Inevitably, some military writers inflated the army's importance. All categories of art and science, one author said, are beholden to the art of war because it is the primary basis of the state's wellbeing. Theologians show the way to eternal bliss, doctors heal us, mathematicians measure things, and physicists peer into nature, but the welfare of all depends on the soldier, for his estate is ready to sacrifice itself for the peace, freedom and happiness of all the rest. And if the army is to do this, it must be renewed by banishing mechanical drills along with all the absurd toiletries that now afflict soldiering. Military honor must be restored by stiffening the army's moral fiber. *Bellona: Ein militärisches Journal,* I (1781), 3–4, 6–7.

42. *Neues militärisches Journal,* II (1789), 43. Comments from Scharnhorst's long review (pp. 31–94) of Mirabeau's *De la monarchie prussienne sous Frédéric le Grand* (1788), which he found "interesting and authentic" although incorrect in its main emphasis.

43. "Woraus kann man den Fortgang, den eine Armee in diesem oder jenem Zweige der Kriegskunst macht, am sichersten abnehmen?" *Neues militärisches Journal,* V (1792), 182–188. Another article, "Ueber die Ursachen des französischen Kriegsglücks," *Neue Bellona,* II (1802), 142–143 (published in Leipzig), denied that the "cruelties" of the French government could be ascribed to the Enlightenment. Military writers were reluctant to make that indictment since their pleas for military reform drew heavily on enlightened rationalism.

44. Duffy concedes that the Prussian officer corps achieved a remarkable degree of cohesion, and despite its often rough and bawdy tone an intellectual element persisted in it. *Army of Frederick the Great,* pp. 47–50. Stadelmann pointed out that the tension between the "learned officers" and the "line officers" persisted in the Prussian army as it did in every other one. But the Frederician army had developed a core of respect for *Intelligenz* that enabled the Prussian army to assimilate the continually expanding spheres of civil and technical learning. Stadelmann, *Moltke,* pp. 9–15.

45. Christopher Duffy, *The Army of Maria Theresa: The Armed Forces of Imperial Austria, 1740–1780* (New York, 1977), pp. 43–46.

46. An anti-intellectual attitude invariably begets military pedantry. The Austrian army had no monopoly. The Prussian army could provide the example of Maj.-Gen. Friedrich von Saldern who preferred a march tempo of seventy-five paces per minute over seventy-six paces. Nonetheless, the Austrian army regulated minutiae left to individual discretion in other armies. The *Exerzierreglement* of 1749 specified the soldier's proper physical stance for prayer. It also set forth the precise manner for tightening drumheads.

47. Ligne's comment cited in Constantin de Grunwald, *Metternich* (London, 1953), p. 120. Prior to Ligne, notable military studies had been made by

Count Ludwig Andreas von Khevenhüller (1683–1744), an Austrian officer who had served with distinction in all the major wars from 1701–1740s. He provided instructions for his own dragoon regiment as well as a manual of infantry tactics (1737), and, posthumously, a general account of war, *Kurzer Begriff aller militärischen Operationen sowohl im Felde als in Festungen* (Vienna, 1756).

48. Eduard Winter concentrated on the ecclesiastical aspects of Josefinism: *Der Josefinismus und seine Geschichte: Beiträge zur Geistesgeschichte Oesterreichs, 1740–1848* (Brno, Munich and Vienna, 1943), p. 126. In this sphere Joseph II did not neglect the new forms of education. On Mar. 30, 1783 he decreed the formation of General Seminars enrolling both secular and regular candidates for the priesthood in a six-year course of study. All other clerical education in dioceses and cloisters would cease so that the Austrian clergy might attain a uniform moral and theological outlook. The General Seminar aroused enthusiasm in circles committed to the Catholic Enlightenment, but constant objections from bishops and prelates forced Leopold II to abandon the entire scheme in 1790. *Ibid.*, pp. 184–194, 211–214.

49. The broad usage is characteristic of Georg Franz, *Liberalismus: Die deutschliberale Bewegung in der Habsburgischen Monarchie* (Munich, 1956), pp. 12–13; and Fritz Valjavec, *Geschichte der abendländischen Aufklärung* (Vienna, 1961), pp. 180 ff. The Theresan Enlightenment distinguished between its religious and political elements although it entailed a state-directed ecclesiastical reform that sought to enroll the church in the service of the state. Maria Theresa's outlook remained half worldly, half spiritual; she believed that rulership had a sacral quality. Joseph II endorsed the secular rational thrust of enlightened rule which made religion an instrumental adjunct of political affairs. Cf. Angela Lampen, "Maria Theresia und die Aufklärung" (Vienna University diss., 1945), pp. ii-iii, 56, 60–64, 137 ff.

50. Cf. Fritz Valjavec, *Der Josefinismus: Zur geistigen Entwicklung Österreichs im 18. und 19. Jahrhundert* (Munich, 1945), pp. 82–83, 85.

51. Hermann, *Deutsche Militärgeschichte*, pp. 110–126 describes the Old Regime's military system in all its bleakness.

52. Cf. Oscar Teuber, *Die österreichische Armee von 1700 bis 1867* (Vienna, 1895), "Kaiser Josef II. u. sein Heer," pp. 187 ff.

53. The *Hofkriegsrat*, like so many aspects of monarchical administration, had developed gradually in response to political and military requirement. By the 1760s it had absorbed the domestic *Hofkriegsrat* at Graz and it had taken over details of recruitment and provisioning formerly left to the regional diets. Daun replaced its civilian with military personnel in the hope that officers could lend weight to its efforts. But monarchical government in the Old Regime rested on many contractual agreements and customary usages so that the *Hofkriegsrat's* effectiveness was diminished. It did bring

order into a widely dispersed military establishment and it had an honorable role in Maria Theresa's creation of the "Austrian state army." Cf. Oskar Regele, *Der osterreichische Hofkriegsrat, 1556–1848* (Vienna, 1949), pp. 21–24, 32, 40, 43, 47.

54. Kotasek, *Graf Lacy*, pp. 68–71.

55. Criste, *Kriege unter Kaiser Josef II*, pp. 223–224, and p. 133 on Lacy's predominant influence during the War of the Bavarian Succession. Lacy favored the career of Karl Frhr. Mack von Leiberich, a major and ADC to Joseph II in the Turkish War, 1788–90. As General Mack he capitulated to Napoleon at Ulm on Oct. 20, 1805.

56. Duffy, *Army of Maria Theresa*, pp. 141–144. Mitrofanov lays the blame for the army's sluggishness on Joseph, whose caution had become apparent to the army, even to the men in ranks. But Joseph did not lack courage; he lacked resolution. *Joseph II*, pp. 367–368.

57. The articles of war did not allow the flaws of existing fortresses to excuse a commander who surrendered his *Platz* to the enemy. General Nikolaus Doxat was sentenced to death for surrendering the fortress of Nisch to the Turks in 1737. Robert Doxat, "Ein kaiserlicher General und Ingenieur des XVIII. Jahrhunderts" (University of Vienna diss., 1954), pp. 38 ff.

58. Austrian intelligence reports *(Observationspunkte)* compiled for the guidance of field commanders at the start of a campaign contained a great deal of practical information about their foe, his organization, strength and manner of fighting. But this excellent practice, started in 1757, could not compensate for the lack of staff channels whereby this intelligence could be used to overcome the army's persistent operational sluggishness. The report issued in 1787 on the Ottoman army is provided in Criste, *Kriege unter Kaiser Josef II*, App. VII, pp. 283–296.

59. *Ibid.*, pp. 149–155.

60. Viktor Bibl, *Kaiser Josef II: Ein Vorkämpfer der Grossdeutschen Idee* (Vienna and Leipzig, 1943), p. 290.

61. Kotasek, *Graf Lacy*, pp. 186–188.

62. The Archduke Charles's military education followed a routine customary for princes. He became a colonel at age nine in order to perpetuate the ruling house's command of the Regiment of Lorraine *(Infanterie-Regiment Nr. 3)*. His father, Grand Duke Leopold of Tuscany, did little to advance his military knowledge. But from 1790–1791 in Vienna the archduke received some instruction in military engineering. In the Austrian Netherlands (Oct. 1791 ff.) the archduke was able to immerse himself in *Truppendienst*. He also received instruction from a former Prussian officer, Col. Karl Friedrich von Lindenau, who had entered Austrian service because his book, *Ueber die höhere preussische Taktik* (Leipzig, 1790), had criticized some aspects of Prussian military training. Cf. Viktor Bibl, *Erzherzog Karl* (n.p., n.d.), pp. 15 *passim*.

63. E. H. Carl, *Grundsätze der Strategie erläutert durch die Darstellung des Feldzuges 1796 in Deutschland* (Vienna, 1862), provides a detailed analysis together with many fine maps.

64. Details in Shanahan, *Prussian Military Reforms*, pp. 127 ff. and pp. 179 ff.

65. Consult Gunther E. Rothenberg, "The Austrian Army in the Age of Metternich," *Journal of Modern History*, XL (1968), 155–165.

66. Oskar Regele, *Feldmarschall Radetzky: Leben, Leistung, Erbe* (Vienna and Munich, 1957), p. 427; on the importance Radetzky attached to fortresses, pp. 415–416; his educational program, pp. 416–420; on discipline, pp. 422–423.

# III

## Habsburg Society and War

### B. Military Institutions and Society

Johann Christoph Allmayer-Beck

# The Establishment of the Theresan Military Academy in Wiener Neustadt

Austria celebrated the bicentennial of the death of the great Empress Maria Theresa in 1980 with numerous exhibitions and publications. It is only fitting that this sovereign should also be remembered here. Her impact, especially in military affairs, has already been given due appreciation in Christopher Duffy's essay, "The Seven Years' War as a Limited War." The focus now will be on a single feature of her military reforms, a feature that was a turning point in eighteenth-century Austrian military history and has remained important to the present day—the founding of the Theresan Military Academy *(Theresianische Militärakademie)* in Wiener Neustadt.

The academy is located in an historic castle some 45 miles from Vienna, and officers are still being trained there for the Austrian army today. It is one of the few institutions of the present military establishment that can look back on an almost uninterrupted tradition of over 200 years. Founded in 1752, the academy is the oldest military school in continuous existence on the European continent. But it is not just age that makes this school remarkable, it is the role it has played for over two and a quarter centuries. The circumstances of its establishment, in particular throw light on the changes in the nature and role of the officer corps of the Imperial army in the eighteenth century.

The actual decree founding the academy was issued in the second half of the year 1751, and while the circumstances of its establishment still remain obscure, it is clear that it was not the result of a sudden impulse of the Empress, such as a wish to find a suitable use for this ancient castle of the Babenbergs dating back to the twelfth century and untenanted for some time. The decision appears to have been the outcome of intense and lengthy deliberations. As early as 1747 Count Friedrich von Haugwitz, one of the Empress's chief counsellors, advised her that as part of her great reforms Austria—

just like its enemy Prussia—should establish a noble cadet corps which, centrally located in the castle at Wiener Neustadt, would draw its cadet entrants from a preparatory school *(Pflanzschule)* in Vienna. It was neither the first nor the last time that the unpopular Prussians were taken as exemplars. Yet precedents had already been set within the country. Since the last quarter of the seventeenth century, both individuals and the provincial Estates had followed the custom of the time by founding academies of knighthood and schools for gentlemen commanders. The difference was that Prussia was concerned with preparing officer replacements, while Austria's schools sought to turn out polished gentlemen and courtiers. The Empress was well aware of these facts and it is worth noting how she originally proposed to deal with the situation. But first it has to be asked what made the sovereign interested in a matter that, apart from the engineering schools that already existed in Vienna and Brussels, had been left to private initiative till then. There was good reason.

To understand the reason requires a brief look back at the changing functions and conceptions of officers over the last few centuries before the Theresan period, in fact back to the fifteenth and sixteenth centuries. The end of the Middle Ages was a major turning point. Innovations in weapons technology, the development of artillery under Emperor Maximilian, and even more important, changing infantry tactics demanded a totally new type of combat leader—the modern officer. What distinguished these new leaders from medieval captains and knightly champions was that they were no longer primarily concerned with individual prowess in combat but instead, by deliberately diminishing their previously preeminent role as individual fighters, now concentrated their efforts on maintaining the combat effectiveness and mobility of the units under their command. Personal success in combat was no longer paramount; the new objective was to lead a mass of foot soldiers by discipline and personal example. Thus from the very first the criterion of the modern military professional officer has been the same. The one who can score the most bull's-eyes with an assault rifle or who can throw a grenade farthest is not necessarily the best qualified for command; the best professional officer is the one who can provide what even then was called "leadership."

During the sixteenth century another factor was added to this prerequisite—commercial enterprise. A figure who originally existed only on a fairly modest scale flourished during the seventeenth century, especially in the period of the Thirty Years' War: this was the military entrepreneur. The proprietors of the Imperial regiments as well as those of the free *Fähnlein* and independent companies represented a type of officer for whom campaigning not only was an opportunity to command but in a very real sense of the word also constituted a commercial enterprise in which he participated with his capital according to the principles of risk and profit. It is no surprise that at least from the early baroque on, the military entrepreneurs as well as those in higher command were primarily drawn from the nobility, mainly because the nobles possessed what was necessary to fill major military command positions—the required capital, above all in the form of land.

To be the colonel and proprietor of a regiment was essentially a noble occupation, though it was only one part of the far-ranging functions of the nobility in those days. In civilian life the counterpart to the colonel proprietor was the lord of the manor who combined economic, administrative, and judicial functions in his person. A noble became an officer not because he considered it a lifetime's profession in the sense of a calling, but because it gave him an opportunity to pursue an occupation proper for a member of his class. Courage, bravery, daring decisions, but also "fortune" and social rank—these were the major qualities expected of an officer. How he succeeded and acquired the necessary professional experience and knowledge was left up to him and was of no real interest to anyone else, just as today no one is interested whether a poet or a painter, provided he has talent, has attended a certain school or not. The question of formal professional training was entirely secondary to the fulfillment of the noble function.

This worked well enough as long as the conduct of war corresponded to this social order and made no further demands. Even Raimondo Montecuccoli still had a low opinion of book learning. He and his successors in command regarded the camps of the Imperial army as the best classrooms for learning the science of war.[1] This situation changed in the first half of the eighteenth century. The ever more complicated requirements of warfare conducted in a fortress environment soon made the need for specialists apparent. Prince Eugene of Savoy's complaint in 1710 about the catastrophic situation of engineering in the Imperial army and the lack of trained engineer officers made its mark. It led to the establishment of the engineering academies mentioned above.[2] At best, however, this merely palliated the general situation. For a man like Count Leopold von Daun, one of the military advisors closest to the young Maria Theresa, it was clear from the outset that not only members of the technical troops but above all also the officers of the main combat arms, that is the infantry and the cavalry, needed a uniform and professional education. As he expressed it himself: "The rank and file requires a courageous fist and a well-trained body, but for command in war an able head is more necessary than a strong arm. Mere experience alone is not enough to acquire a systematic knowledge of the art of war."[3]

The professional requirements were a major consideration in establishing the state-controlled military schools, but there were others too. The catastrophic condition of the Austrian army during the War of the Austrian Succession had convinced Maria Theresa that only a complete reform of the military system could improve matters for Austria. The new, more specialized style of warfare made demands that could be met only by new methods and new leadership, and this required curtailing the system of noble colonel proprietors. The army had to become an instrument of the state, and this demanded assertion of the crown's overriding authority, and increased centralization and control in all areas. A basic prerequisite for this was to bring under closer control the class that until then had provided the support for the old system, that is the nobility. Education appeared to be one way to help achieve this goal.

To tackle the problem a two-pronged approach was taken. First was the creation of the cadet school in Wiener Neustadt together with its preparatory school in Vienna, decreed in December 1751 and established the following year.[4] These schools admitted sons of impoverished nobles who did not have the means for their education, sons of officials with 20 years of meritorious service in the civil and financial agencies, and children of officers who had served the Imperial house loyally and well in war. This orientation and the social origins of the pupils had long-range consequences for the history of the school and for the composition of the Austrian officer corps. As Nikolaus von Preradovich has shown rather convincingly, neither the old, and even less the high, nobility then or later appeared in the rolls of the Neustadt academy in proportion to what their earlier military role might lead one to expect.[5]

To draw these elements into the army and at the same time bring them under a certain degree of control, yet another military school, patterned after the old academies of knighthood, was to be set up. About two years after founding the academy in Wiener Neustadt, the Empress created a Noble Military Academy in Vienna, *(Adelige Militär Akademie)* to be headed by the principal of the preparatory school for Wiener Neustadt, who thus acquired a double function.[6] Both the new academy's curriculum and the life style of its pupils operated on a freer and more grandiose plane than Wiener Neustadt, yet even so, the Noble Military Academy proved a failure. It was probably to this school and not the Wiener Neustadt academy that the Empress was referring when she wrote in deep disappointment in 1755: "It is truly incredible that no one wishes to profit from this benefaction."[7] Evidently the high nobility was not prepared to sacrifice its old preferential position in the army for the paltry benefits of training in a state-financed school. On the contrary, the nobility continued to cherish the old principle of "leadership based on class origins," and rejected new principles of selection on the basis of professional competence. If it entered military service at all, it persisted in exercising the right of regimental proprietors to appoint officers.

A decisive turning point had nevertheless been reached. The Noble Military Academy in Vienna, originally designed for the high nobility, closed its doors in 1769. There remained the noble cadet corps in Wiener Neustadt with its new educational orientation. There the aim was not to turn out young gentlemen instructed in military science, but to train "competent officers" and "upright men." It is not important whether these were the expressions Empress Maria Theresa actually used in her directives to General Count Leopold von Daun, the first director of the Theresan Academy, or whether they were attributed to her later. The fact is that they were the perfect formulation of her intent. After the failure of the Noble Military Academy, Maria Theresa's concept of "competent officers" became men no longer tied to old aristocratic ideas of a noble occupation, but who followed the new principle of enlightened performance, which at just this time came to correspond to the even more recent bourgeois ideal of "competence." This is underlined by the fact that she did not require her eponymous academy to train "lordlings" or "cavaliers." This was to have been done in Vienna; Wiener Neustadt simply trained "upright men" who could combine the concepts of an enlightened humanistic ideal with the demands of a contemporary professional education.

In time there developed a clear dichotomy between the graduates of Wiener Neustadt and of the other military academies and the remainder of the officer corps. Indirect evidence of this comes from the pen of *Feldmarschal leutnant* Leopold Unterberger, commander of the Order of Maria Theresa, who in 1802 felt obliged to issue a training program for infantry officers, because, he claimed, only a few of his officers had graduated from a military academy, and the rest did not know very much. Just how great was their ignorance is shown by Unterberger's inclusion of basic arithmetic—addition and subtraction as well as division—in his syllabus.[8]

It was not just a matter of military professionalism that distinguished Wiener Neustadt graduates from other officers. More important perhaps was their wider general education, which indicates that the heritage of the unsuccessful Noble Military Academy was not entirely lost. In future, graduation from the Neustadt academy was to be not necessarily an essential condition but certainly a very important condition for a successful military career. Some figures collected by *Feldmarschal leutnant* J. Lustig-Prean after World War I illustrate this. Out of a total of 10,475 cadets who either graduated or at least completed over half the course from the academy's inception to August 17, 1918, a total of 1,024 (that is 10 percent) had attained general grade by the end of 1918. This figure included two admirals, 20 intendant generals, and nine court or ministerial counsellors. Of these thousand-odd general officers 579 reached the rank of *Feldmarschal leutnant*, 173 that of full general of infantry or cavalry or chief of ordnance, 16 that of *Generaloberst*, and four that of field marshal.[9]

In other words, establishment of the Theresan Academy in Wiener Neustadt gave the Austrian army an educational institution which on the one hand trained a considerable proportion of the senior officers of the Imperial army and on the other hand provided a significant degree of access for the bourgeoisie and minor nobility to command positions until then restricted to the high nobility.

## Notes

1. Kriegsarchiv Wien (hereafter cited as KA) (ed.), *Ausgewählte Schriften des Raimund Fürsten Montecuccoli*, II (Vienna-Leipzig, 1899), 482.
2. KA, Feldakten 1710–8–52, p. 25.
3. Quoted in Friedrich Walter, *Männer um Maria Theresia* (Vienna, 1951), p. 106.

4. For the history of the Theresan Military Academy see Johann Svobida, *Die Theresianische Militärakademie zu Wiener Neustadt und ihre Zöglinge von der Gründung der Anstalt bis auf unsere Tage* (Vienna, 1804–1897); Johann Jobst, *Die Neustädter Burg und die k.u.k. Theresianische Militärakademie* (Vienna-Leipzig, 1908), n. 5.

5. *Die Führungsschichten in Österreich und Preussen, 1804–1918, mit einem Ausblick zum Jahre 1945* (Wiesbaden, 1955), pp. 6–8 *et passim*.

6. Information about the Noble Military Academy is unfortunately rare. See Eduard R. V. Zambaur, "Über die Gründung der Theresianischen Militär-Akademie in Wiener Neustadt," in *Jahres-Bericht der k. und k. Theresianischen Militär-Akademie in Wiener Neustadt für das Schuljahr 1911/12* (Wiener Neustadt, 1912), p. 12. Cf. Th. Jg. Leitner v. Leitnertreu, *Ausführliche Geschichte der Wiener Neustadter Militär-Akademie* (Hermannstadt [Sibiu], 1852), pp. 73, 115.

7. Eugen Guglia, *Maria Theresia*, II (Munich-Berlin, 1917), 22–23.

8. KA, Memoirs, VII, 49. The plan was actually printed as *Nöthige Anfangsgründe der Rechenkunst zum Gebrauch der Infanterie- und Cavallerie-Officiere der k.k. oesterreichischen Armee* (Vienna, 1870).

9. J. Lustig Prean, "Zur Geschichte der Neustädter, 1752–1918" (Lecture to the Club Alt-Neustadt [1926], MS in KA Library, I 47843).

Thomas M. Barker

# Military Nobility: The Daun Family and the Evolution of the Austrian Officer Corps

To the social-scientific-minded historian of early modern Europe and to people in allied disciplines working on the same epoch, the process of societal change seems an excellent, overall framework for scholarly effort. What has generally come to be known as comparative modernization, particularly since the appearance in 1966 of a ground-breaking study by Barrington Moore, Jr., is clearly also well suited to serve as a comprehensive rubric for the military historian who concentrates upon examining the manifold and intricate linkages of war and society. Among Moore's particular theses that of the "reactionary coalition" should perhaps be kept in mind. Traditional landed elements often ally with a weak, modernizing bourgeoisie; occasionally there can even be a "revolution from above."[1]

These concepts reflect the ultimate complexities of group life. Its beginnings, however, are simple enough. The most basic social unit is the family, whether of the nuclear or extended variety. Its central role continued undiminished as Europe's tribal societies evolved into the initial forms of the bureaucratic state. It follows that, in order to understand change and its military connotations on the higher levels of social stratification, the histories of individual, biologically more tenacious noble dynasties are of some interest.

The Dauns make an unusually good case study. First, they were a clan that managed to endure for much longer than the average, which is possibly no more than three generations.[2] One can trace their collective fate from the mid fifteenth century until their extinction in 1904.[3] Second, their involvement in warfare from the late 1640s onward was more frequent and more prominent than that of

I wish to thank Margaret W. Dow, Christopher Duffy, Raimondo Luraghi, John Monfasani, Gunther E. Rothenberg, Géza Perjés and Peter Sugar for genuinely useful criticisms. I am grateful to the American Philosophical Society in the International Research and Exchanges Board for financing various stays in East Central Europe.

the great majority of their fellow Habsburg grandees. Last, in the person of Count Leopold (1705–1766), the family name is associated, in a pioneering sense, with several of the most salient aspects of modernization—the alteration of the character of military institutions and the enhanced systematization of violence. Empress Maria Theresa's paladin was a chief protagonist in a broad effort to overhaul and strengthen the Austrian army—an essential feature and the *raison d'être* of the larger Habsburg reform movement. He may thus be seen as a symbol of the accelerating development of the profession of arms and of an incipient transformation in civil-military relations—phenomena that are a hallmark of the eighteenth century altogether.[4]

This essay's title refers to the Dauns as "military nobility." While the choice of words is deliberate, it involves semantic peril. Among other things, the layman is likely to be confused because with his Round-Table stereotype he will think first of the early medieval circumstances when martial skills were usually a prime quality of nobility. One way of dispelling the conceptual haziness is to draw a chronological distinction. Prior to the modernizing trends ascertainable in all of Europe's standing armies and navies, albeit at varying rates, military nobility probably corresponds more or less to Fritz Redlich's "military entrepreneurship."[5] The titled warrior practices the trade of a soldier, a term, after all, synonymous with pay. As a mercenary he may be said to be exercising an occupation.[6] At this earlier juncture in time profession can mean only that a fighting man's career absorbed most of his energies, permitting him little other employment, and that a special sense of corporate identity, while present, was probably not so complex or sophisticated as with professional groups in urban industrial society. The individual in question sprang in most instances from the lower strata—in a legal sense from the knightly order—of the relatively broad seignorial or ruling class, as well as from the cadet lines of magnate dynasties, which themselves, at least in certain instances, had come into being as the consequence of particularly successful military entrepreneurship.[7]

Another way to approach "military nobility" in its earliest context is from the vantage of civil-military relations, one of the chief susidiary foci of current interdisciplinary research. Following Alfred Vagts and Morris Janowitz, one may speak of the "heroic" or "feudal-aristocratic" model, even if these adjectives send shivers down the spines of historians versed in medieval studies and political theory, not to mention those who object to anything that smacks even remotely of Marxian categories.[8] Janowitz for his part refers to situations in which "civilian and military elites are socially and functionally integrated," adding that the relatively restricted "base of recruitment for both elites" and a less articulated "power structure provide the civilian elite with a method of 'subjective control' of the military."[9]

If one is to apply Janowitz's definition to Austrian circumstances, the object of attention must be the court nobility *(Hofadel)*, the members of the most powerful septs, those at the aulic pyramid of the ruling class. This uppermost elite, paired with the Emperor, formed one part of a dyarchy.[10] It participated on an equal basis in ruling the Austrian state to the extent that there was central government, and in a wider diffusion of power it was also influential on the provincial and local planes. This element, especially where there was a family tradition of soldiering, sent its lesser scions into the army. Thereby they were not only provided for materially, but the interests of the dominant social group were simultaneously (if unwittingly) secured also. Clearly, the top stratum could not provide all the officers required. It was not that large, and a soldier's life was not every lordling's cup of tea.

The lower levels of the nobility were the main source of aspirants for the officer corps. Those who may be loosely called the gentry and middle baronage constituted the major replenishment pool. To be sure, such men joined the colors as relatively humble clients. Moreover, their chances of advancement on merit progressively declined in the earlier eighteenth century owing to the relative monopoly over the higher military offices enjoyed by the progeny of the Establishment and its counterparts from outside the Habsburg domains proper.[11]

The second meaning that may be ascribed to "military nobility" is closely tied to the equally elusive concept of "service nobility" *(Dienstadel)*.[12] While service to a lord, both in antiquity and in the early Middle Ages, was probably always the prerequisite of upward social mobility, it was only at the end of the early modern period, after the reception of Roman law and with the consolidation of the initial forms of the bureaucratic state, that conditions favored the growth of a genuine *Dienstadel*. One can find vague intimations of it from the fifteenth century onward, but its real flowering, in the

Austrian lands at any rate, came only after 1740. By this time soldiering too could no longer be a mere occupation. The military entrepreneur, although able to retain certain of his prerogatives for more than a century, was an anachronism. Technology and economic advance spelled doom for the old system of fighting. The era of professionalization was at hand. "Military nobility" thus begins to assume new connotations. In time the services that men-at-arms render come to resemble those of their civilian bureaucratic colleagues. Ennoblement reflects achievement only. Officers are rewarded not with lands and lordship but with prestige, guaranteed employment and old-age security. They develop a special, novel kind of corporate consciousness. This process characterizes the history of all higher cultures, something that again brings to mind how fundamental the relationship between war and society actually is.

There are periods in history when military institutions seem more firmly rooted in society at large than other times. Redlich believes that during the epoch of military entrepreneurship such relationships were tenuous; only with the advent of mass armies drawn from all sectors of the populace did "reintegration" occur.[13] The importance of war in the lives of noble dynasties also varies. Some clans are bellicose for the whole of their existence. Others have pacific enough origins, turn only later to socially legitimized violence, and end up by reverting to the civilian ways of their progenitors. The Dauns represent the latter pattern.

Though the social psychology of Baroque Austria's aulic nobles caused the Dauns to dig around for documentary proof that they sprang from the feudal high, free lords of Duna in the forested lake and hill country of the Eifel, the evidence is flimsy. What is certain is that from about 1400 they controlled the castle town of Daun as tenants of both Electoral Trier and the county of Manderscheid. Their first shred of prosperity began when Burgrave Dietrich, a dwarf-like rustic ("Dunegin" or "Däunchen"), acquired as his wife's dowry a tiny, long-vanished, local fief, a farm in a nearby village.[14]

Ascent to the level of well-to-do gentry was the achievement of the burgrave's heir, Peter, who served the Electors of Trier as a senior estate manager and magistrate of the Eifel towns of Daun and Nürburg a few miles north. In 1543 he was enfeoffed with a more substantial, nearby manor—Kallenborn. His son, Wilhelm, also magistrate of Daun and Nürburg, had 16 offspring, endangering the clan's collective welfare, but by now landed families were beginning to realize that the Salic principle of property division among all male heirs was self-defeating. In the case of Catholic lines the church was the most obvious way out. Five of the nine young Daun males became ecclesiastics; one was a Knight of Malta. Another remained a bachelor, the last died young. Two sisters were stuck into convents, and the third was married off. The two remaining brothers and one of the clerics attended to the family's fortunes. Dietrich Nicolas resigned his canonry in 1572, espoused the sister of the youngest brother's wife, and thus cemented an alliance with an older, free Imperial knightly line, the Groschlags, who hailed from the putatively wealthier Rhine-Main town of Dieburg. Property succession was judiciously worked out. Carl, a magistrate in Baden who had married into the Luxembourg seigniories of Sassenheim (Sanem), Hollenfells and Brandeville, ultimately inherited everything. It certainly helped that his wife was the Elector of Trier's sister.[15]

Once again fertility proved more burden than blessing. Five of Carl's male issue had to take holy orders. One became a Knight of Malta, another a Teutonic Knight, affirming a shift from *Dienstadel* to *Militäradel.* Three sisters were married, two to Groschlags; two others suffered the then hard fate of maiden ladies. Two remaining brothers were free to marry. One Philipp Ernst (d. 1671), Leopold Daun's great grandfather, also wed a Groschlag. Chief magistrate of Trarbach, a military entrepreneur, and nonproprietary colonel in the Spanish and German Habsburg armies toward the end of the Thirty Years' War, he seems to have laid the foundations for his family's rise to real aristocratic affluence. Three of his brothers fell in battle.

Although Philipp's documentary legacy is negligible,[16] circumstances imply that he acted hand in glove with his gifted clerical brother, Johann Jakob (d. 1660). The latter was not only commendator of the Teutonic Order's Austrian province but also privy councillor and equerry to Archduke Leopold Wilhelm (1614–1662). Emperor Ferdinand III's brother was a most puissant patron. Bishop of five different sees, Grand Master of the Teutonic Order, a competent if not particularly victorious commander, and governor of the Spanish Netherlands (1647–1655), he had tremendous resources and influence. Johann Jakob became an Imperial count in 1643 and Philipp was one of the beneficiaries of the famous 1655 bonanza of Imperial countships. The money somehow accumulated during the dreary final years of the Thirty Years' War, together with what may have been a Groschlag legacy, enabled Philipp to purchase another domain (Immerath) on much better land just south of Daun, plus smaller holdings in Lower Austria, where in 1657 along with his son he received the *indigenat*. He later obtained the *incolat* in Bohemia and Hungary, implying the purchase of lands there as well. All this, together with the marriage of Philipp's children to members of the Althann and Breuner families, suggests that the Dauns were now on the fringes of Austria's aulic Establishment. Still, their wealth both in the old *Reich* (as they themselves put it) and on Habsburg soil hardly approximated that of magnates like the Dietrichsteins, Liechtensteins or Schwarzenbergs.[17]

Perhaps it was this relatively modest base, plus his father Philipp's example, that led Wilhelm Johann Anton (1621–1706) to carry on soldiering. In all events, he struck permanent roots in Austria. In the earlier part of his career, before Philipp died and during the life of Wilhelm's first wife, who sprang from a Protestant Styrian line of military entrepreneurs (the Regalls of Kranischsfeld), Ladendorf in the lush wine country of northern Lower Austria came into the hands of the family. Nearby Kirchstetten was added in 1675. (Among the Dauns' Trier revenues was also a Mosel Valley wine tithe.) Deputy commander of the Vienna City Guard, a hero of the 1683 siege of Vienna, Imperial chamberlain, privy and war councillor, owner of the Alt-Daun (1691), commandant of Prague, and field marshal in 1694, Wilhelm enjoyed both access to Leopold I and his confidence. Among other things the sovereign entrusted him with delicate diplomatic missions. Wilhelm was also an astute manager of his various business interests, including the regiment, with one of whose captains he had a public dispute over the now pervasive *Kompaniewirtschaft*, a late manifestation of military entrepreneurship.[18]

Both Philipp and Wilhelm sought to avoid dissipating their patrimony through division among heirs, even though they somehow failed to win a grant of *Fideicommissio* from the Emperor, as many other Establishment figures were able to do. Wilhelm's four brothers and sisters were either bought off or appropriately betrothed. He himself fathered eight descendants. Luckily, in view of the family's martial skills, the times remained violent. The wars of Louis XIV and various conflicts in Hungary provided plenty of opportunity, buttressed by excellent *Protektion*. All four sons took up arms; the girls were married to other aulics, the Starhembergs and Portias.

The last born, Heinrich Dietrich Joseph (1678–1761), field marshal and owner of the Jung-Daun Regiment of foot (1711), achieved little distinction as a military leader but was eminently successful as a suitor and money manager. He married Baroness Maria Leopolda Jansková z Vlašime, heiress to vast lands in the delightful Moravian countryside near Bítov (west of Znojmo), a complex of estates to which he himself was able to add. He thus secured the wellbeing of the Dauns' cadet Austro-Moravian line, the branch of the family that endured into the twentieth century.[19]

The third born of the old warhorse's brood, Heinrich Reichard Lorenz (1673–1724), resigned his canonical livings in 1697, married a Countess Sporck and, just before his father's death, had himself appointed a colonel-commandant. He later attained the common, often honorary rank of major general. Founder of the junior Main line of the family, he had a son, Benedict, who like his cousin, Leopold, was one of Maria Theresa's more reliable, second-string generals. The line itself died out in Bavaria in the early nineteenth century.[20]

The second-born son, Wilhelm Eustachius, fell in battle in Hungary as a young man. His fate has some historical relevance. While close links with the Imperial house might result in an officer's commission without the fuss and bother of having to demonstrate talent, the profession still entailed risk to life and limb. The case of Wilhelm Eustachius and many others implies that the chivalric ethos continued to inspire men in combat.

Wilhelm Johann Anton's eldest son, Field Marshal Weyrich Philipp Lorenz (1668–1741), established the Daun senior Main line. Prince Eugene of Savoy's comrade-in-arms, hero of the French assault on Turin in 1706, titular prince of Tiano (1710), viceroy and captain-general of Naples and Sicily (1713), grandee of Spain, Knight of the Golden Fleece, owner of the Alt-Daun Foot (1699), and commandant of Vienna, Weyrich may be characterized as a grand seigneur whose income was not up to the lifestyle that his high social station demanded. It was for him that Lukas von Hildebrandt built Vienna's Daun Palace (now the Kinsky Palace). However laudable the esthetic consequences may seem to posterity, the fiscal strain was impossible to bear. In time both the magnificient city residence and Ladendorf had to be sold.[21]

Three other circumstances may have affected this relative material decline. Firstly, records in Bratislava indicate that Heinrich Dietrich and Heinrich Reichard shared in the revenues from the Austrian portion of the patrimony. Secondly, hostilities damaged Weyrich's German frontier properties, some of which were sold in 1716. Finally, in

1734 Weyrich fell into Emperor Charles VI's disfavor, at least temporarily, for his dubious performance as the defender of Austria's Milanese redoubt. The prince's sole advantage was that he had fewer children to provide for than his forebears. Only two seem to have survived to adulthood and married: Ferdinand, who with three of his own children predeceased his father in 1739, and Leopold. Weyrich's most exalted moments may well have been in 1722, the year the palace was completed and the date of Ferdinand's marriage to a countess Herberstein in the presence of Vienna's social *crème de la crème*—the Starhembergs, Windischrätzes, Khevenhüllers, Dietrichsteins, Trautsons, Schönborns, Harrachs, Sinzendorffs and Althanns.[22]

A really satisfactory biography of Field Marshal Count Leopold Joseph von Daun has yet to be written.[23] At least for his formative years the task will not be easy and may even be impossible because of the paucity of documentation. For present purposes, however, it is what is known about Daun's later life that is crucial. A figure whose own family history affords so vivid a paradigm of military nobility in its pristine stage of development fostered changes that would lead to the formation of a new Austrian officer corps, a group of men ennobled solely for meritorious service, not because of kinship ties and resources based on landed wealth. Remarkably, an old-style military noble provided much of the impetus for the initial spurt of professionalization in Austria.

If little is known about Daun's first three and a half decades of existence, two recorded facts do deserve attention. Firstly, a younger son, he was committed at a tender age to a military career, both as a Knight of Malta and as a cadet in his father's regiment. This contrasts with the plans for Ferdinand, cast in the role of country gentleman and courtier. The arrangement corresponded to that of many aulic dynasties. Secondly, after the disgrace of his father, Leopold was wounded while displaying great courage in a battle of the ill-fated Austro-Ottoman War of 1737–1739.[24] He thus caught the eye of the Imperial family. The shedding of blue blood still made an impression at court, the effete environment notwithstanding.

A survey of Daun's achievements and failures after his rise to a position of influence in Vienna (greatly facilitated by marriage to the daughter of Maria Theresa's governess, Countess Katharina Fuchs (*"die Füchsin"* [vixen]), would be superfluous, for Christopher Duffy has provided scholars a well-balanced, deftly composed account of the fighting career of the *Feldherr* and his confreres.[25] In reviewing the seminal institutional changes of the age one may commence, as does Duffy, with an assessment of the state of the Habsburg host in 1740, that is, just after humiliating campaign setbacks and just before events that count among the monarchy's greatest hours of peril, the War of the Austrian Succession. Since the professionalization of the mid eighteenth century was still embryonic and as the existing structure of the army endured in many essential respects, the analysis must go into some detail. The stirrings of reform and Daun's role as a prime mover will receive only summary treatment.

There seems no reason to dispute traditional explanations for the army's poor performance. They center on two shortcomings—tactics and personalities aside. The first, the army's financial straits, can be attributed in the final analysis only to the existing dyarchic system of government and were the price of it. In practice the system depended on the various seignorial elites who tended to look out mainly for their own interests. The second cause, so the argument runs, was the junior officers' deficient motivation. Their numbers were also insufficient, especially in comparison with the superfluity of generals. Lieutenants, captains, majors, lieutenant colonels and even colonels who did not own regiments themselves were drawn overwhelmingly from impoverished minor noble lines and from the burghers. They lacked capital and were frozen in rank with little chance of advance on merit, even in wartime. The great families monopolized the top echelons.[26]

Be this as it may, an important question remains. Did the officer corps, more particularly the generals, who are often depicted as a highly variegated group from an ethnic, linguistic and political viewpoint, possess no real sociopsychological cohesion? Did they have only a "feeble" awareness, as Duffy puts it, of corporate responsibility? Were they more or less devoid of group pride and communal purpose? Were they too cosmopolitan, representing too broad a spectrum of the seignorial class, as opposed to the more homogeneous Junkers from whom the Prussian officer corps was recruited?[27] Perhaps there is a danger of overstressing diversity. After all, the Austrian army surmounted the mortal crisis of the early 1740s. Was there in fact some more primitive bonding element?

There are two possible answers. The first is the residual power of the vassal relationship, that is, consciousness of a personal tie to the monarch both as an authority figure and as a potential source of material benefit. The second relates to a basic tenet of cultural anthropology. Most European nobles of the eighteenth century, regardless of the stratum to which they belonged, shared a supranational class culture.[28] If they happened to owe allegiance to the same suzerain, they had even more in common. A survey of some 200 prominent generals of Maria Theresa's and Joseph II's reigns would seem to substantiate both arguments.[29] The men in question derived overwhelmingly from lands that were directly controlled by the Habsburgs, or had only recently come under their rule, or were geographically adjacent to their territory and hence under their influence, or had long family traditions of semifeudal service.

It is instructive to investigate the social structure and inner workings of the contemporary corps of generals, whose numbers are quite manageable statistically. The Austrian army high command consisted of four distinct elements. First, there were the younger sons of the Austrian Establishment, the coruling aulic dynasties. Because of many supernumerary and honorary appointments, they were disproportionately represented. As Daun himself noted weighing his leadership assets in 1756: "Of course there are far too many other generals, unfortunately individuals of little utility."[30] Even when one considers the tactical need for a large headquarters staff and for a swarm of senior line officers, the ratio of one general to 1,750 men seems excessive.[31] Admittedly, not all of these commanders came from the dominant aristocracy.

The second component was drawn from a congeries of other older families, for which a century or so of documentable gentility and a noble title may serve as rough yardsticks. The adjective middle, if a bit vague, may be used to describe this stratum. Then there was a smattering of persons who had emerged from the bottom of the noble heap, poor gentry, whether of ancient lineage or only recently raised to the knightly estate. Commoners were the least significant constituent.[32]

The geographic origins of the army's upper echelons are equally revealing. The nucleus was Austro-Alpine and Bohemo-Silesian, corresponding largely, though not entirely, to the aulic Establishment. No matter how cosmopolitan their family roots, by 1740 these men were relatively uniform economically and culturally, as indicated by their preference for communicating in German. The dynastic roll call (not synonymous with the full roster of court clans) reads as follows: Abensberg-Traun, Althann, Colloredo, Czernin,

Daun, Fürstenberg, Harrach, Herberstein, Hohenembs, Kaunitz, Kinsky, Königsegg, Kolowrat, Khevenhüller, Leslie, Liechtenstein, Lobkowitz, Löwenstein, Podstatsky, Salburg, Starhemberg, St.-Julien-Wallsee, Taaffe, Thürheim, Trautson, Trauttmannsdorf, Wallis, and Wurmbrand-Stuppach. The core in the hereditary lands and the kingdom of St. Wenceslas did include a few lesser families, such as the German Bohemian Leveneurs and the Czech Malovci and Příchovští z Příchovic. The name Hradecký z Hradec also comes to mind. It may be inferred that there was some interest in military careers among the Bohemian gentry in the latter half of the eighteenth century.

Aristocratic patronymics raise another issue, subsidiary but still significant. It would be false to assume that, even though the historic compromise between the monarchy and nobility dating from the Thirty Years' War had become governmentally impractical, the sons of the great families in the army were merely an array of fops. There are not only Daun's own example and that of the public-spirited Prince Wenzel Liechtenstein, father of Austria's professional artillery corps, but the names of such other sturdy, steady men as Otto Abensberg-Traun, Joseph Colloredo, Andreas Khevenhüller and Winulph Starhemberg should also be recalled.[33] Notwithstanding the treachery of most of the Bohemian nobility during the Bavarian occupation (there were seditious mutterings among the Viennese populace as well), the ruling elite was certainly neither degenerate nor incapable of response to challenge. The generals who assisted Daun and the Empress in the reform period belonged to the highest social category. So, too, did the civilians Kaunitz and Haugwitz. Although there was grumbling at court and a tendency to view advocates of change as class renegades, what occurred was after all a conservative-sponsored shake-up. Finally, the foundations then laid were so firm that a supposedly ramshackle state was able, whatever the *Reich* German role, to withstand more than four years of twentieth-century warfare.

About the Hungarians two conclusions can be drawn. The first and more certain is that the court aristocracy contained a small but solid kernel of Hungarians, members of dynasties that had remained at least relatively loyal to their kings for upwards of two centuries—the Batthyánys, the Erdődys, the Esterházys, the Pálffys, the Serényis, and the Széchényis. There were also a few lesser clans like the Kohárys. These families lived relatively near Vienna, in northern and western Hungary in the Little Alföld and today's Slovakia, where they had suffered less from the Ottoman occupation of Pannonia than many of their compatriots had. Their early rise to high status was linked to their frequent performance of military functions. The second interesting feature about Hungary is that the establishment of a political *modus vivendi* with the Habsburgs in the second quarter of the eighteenth century caused an influx of Hungarians and Slavs into the Imperial army. The Hungarians' forte was their highly useful, special military skills—the hussar and Croat regiments, for instance. It might be supposed that in such light cavalry units the chances for parvenus would be especially good. There were those who rose from humble origins, such as András Hadik of Czech descent and the Banat-born József Siskovics, but a check of regimental proprietors' names shows that most families who furnished soldiers for the crown were fairly old and had been politically prominent since the late Middle Ages.[34]

Hungary regularly supplied a number of reliable military leaders to the Habsburgs and thus contributed modestly to the creation of an *esprit de corps*, but the role of Lorraine and the adjacent southern Netherlands was more important. (The French-speakers in the Habsburg army at this time derived almost entirely from there.) That the Lorrainers, Luxemburgers (French and German), Walloons and Flemings were so conspicuous is not hard to understand in the light of the ruling dynasty's own venerable political and marital links with their home provinces. The ties with Nancy stretched back to the Thirty Years' War and those with the Low Countries to the days of Maximilian I (1493–1519), primordial architect of Austria's military might. In the time of Maria Theresa and Joseph II the names that stood out were Arenberg, Aspremont-Lyndon, d'Ayassasa, Clerfayt, Croÿ, Dombasle, Henricourt de Grünne, Jacquemin, de Ligne, Mercy d'Argenteau, Mérode d'Aysne, St. Ignon and Sincère.[35] Among their ranks there seems to have been more room for the socially mobile gentleman, the officer of fortune.

Help provided by northern Italy also contributed to the monarchy's survival. The high quality of Italian warriors was already legendary. Both they and their Spanish brethren deserve credit for having saved the German Habsburgs at the outset of the Thirty Years' War, even though later Ottavio Piccolomini I, Raimondo Montecuccoli and others were to complain bitterly about the anti-Italian prejudices of their Teutonic and Czech comrades. The Italians lent powerful support to Maria Theresa and her son too. There is some symbolism in the fact that one of Daun's best commanders in 1756 was Ottavio Piccolomini II. The list of family names contains a high proportion of venerable *condottiere* lineages; conversely, the ratio of newcomers appears low.[36]

The *Reich* German constituents of the Austrian army require circumspect treatment. The most difficult question is that of the territorial princes. By the Theresan-Josephian era their importance had apparently much declined. The troops of Germany's local rulers, whether middling or petty, were in fact hirelings, no matter how fine their training and equipment. Redlich has thoroughly probed eighteenth-century princely military entrepreneurship. Its heyday in Austria was Charles VI's reign. No mercenary regiments served in the War of the Austrian Succession, and only seven between 1756 and 1763.[37] Whether geographical and political circumstances had caused the shift, whether Vienna could no longer afford such units, or whether their fundamental unassimilability was deemed disadvantageous is not clear. In all events, it was only under Maria Theresa that the Habsburg host began to develop a really strong autonomous sense of identity. To be sure, even then Austria did not entirely eschew the employment of princely *Feldherren.* She was served well and loyally by such stalwarts as Sachsen-Teschen, Sachsen-Hildburghausen, Wied and Zweibrücken-Birkenfeld.

The lesser *Reich* German members of the Habsburgs' general officer corps fall into three groups. The first included men of middling Catholic, south German and Rhenish families. Some of them, like Johan Berlichingen, were of proud, primeval, Imperial knightly stock. Others, like Reinhard Neipperg, a hardy aulic perennial who possessed several smaller seigniories west of Heilbronn, were not so venerable. The same was true of the commander of the left wing of the cavalry at Kolín, Philipp Gottfried Wöllwarth, whose fascinating *Nachlass* lies in Bratislava awaiting scholarly scrutiny.[38] The second and third groups, Protestant Saxons and cadet Junkers from Mecklenburg, Brandenburg and Pomerania, were not only significant in numbers but also included particularly proficient soldiers.[39]

Perhaps the Protestants, whose acculturation was presumably facilitated by the Empress's commonsense lenience in matters of religion, should be considered "foreigners." The problem arises with those from other regions of Europe as well, indeed to an even greater degree since a more alien political background might go hand in hand with well-developed ethnic consciousness.

The French, statistically insignificant among the panoply of Austrian generals, require no comment. The Spanish, though few in numbers, were prominent, in part because of the achievements of Field Marshal Caspar Conde de Córdoba and Lieutenant General Antonio Puebla, Conde de Portugallo. Of course, as time passed, the vestiges of Charles VI's Iberian retinue were gradually naturalized, especially within the aulic milieu. The Helvetian contingent, operating in the twilight of a trade and tradition half a millenium old, apparently consisted of five persons. The Bernese Rupert Lentulus does not seem to have been discouraged by the unfortunate recent example of his fellow townsman General Nikolaus Doxat de Morez.[40] In all events the Swiss did fairly well, at least for themselves.

The most exotic foreign element was Celtic, chiefly Irish. Some families, like the Wallises and the Taaffes, were either already long Austrianized or well on the way to assimilation. It is hard to do justice to the Irish: the phenomenon of the "Wild Geese" is unique in European history. For Austria the copious quantities of Irish blood may have been more on the order of a lifesaving transfusion: Schmidhofer claims that the monarchy was saved from destruction by its Irish champions.[41] Certainly no other ethnic group provided so many distinguished newcomers. Of two stellar personalities (apart from Daun himself), one, Field Marshal Count Franz Moritz von Lacy, may be considered a son of the Emerald Isle, albeit born in Russia. The other, Baron Gideon Ernst von Laudon, descended from Baltic German squires, was not Celtic but did concoct a Scots pedigree for himself.[42] The reason was probably a similarity of family names, but perhaps he also sought to benefit from the charismatic nimbus that hovered about his many colleagues from the British Isles.

The preceding sketch of the Habsburg general officer corps is problematic in one respect. Although it is a cross section of five decades (with the stress upon the twenty-five years prior to Daun's death), it does not reflect the effects of personnel changes that occurred between the Second and Third Silesian Wars (1745–1756), or of reforms carried out after the Peace of Hubertusburg (1763). The span of time needed for them to be felt was unduly short. To be sure, the names collated do include those of numerous warriors whom the exigencies of a struggle for survival called to center stage. The mid eighteenth century, which saw two worldwide conflicts, was clearly an era of sustained combat and enhanced career mobility.

Attention may now be directed to the first period of reforms, conceived and instituted by Daun, the Empress, her sometimes too quickly denigrated Lorraine consort Francis, his brother Charles, Haugwitz, and a few other forward-looking military representatives of the old order like Khevenhüller and József Esterházy. In the present context it will suffice to touch upon only three aspects of their work: finance, military schools, and a novel psychological reward system.[43]

Gunther E. Rothenberg has pinpointed the pragmatic rather than theoretical basis of innovation. The key issue was to assure a flow of income that would cover the accelerating costs of the incipient technological revolution. Consequently, the first move (1744) was to curb certain of the military entrepreneurs' fiscal perquisites, a problem already recognized but left unresolved by Prince Eugene. While the process of curtailment dragged on for the rest of the reign and was not actually completed until 1868, at least the reformers had begun to attack the root evil. (Rothenberg correctly emphasizes that the proprietors of the seventeenth and earlier eighteenth centuries "on the whole—had served well.") They also perceived that their own social stratum could not shape the future on its own. The state would never have enough money to attract most members of the magnate class; there was no hope of staffing the whole officer corps from it.[44] It apparently took the Empress a while to accept this unpalatable judgment. Either she felt that the aulics had a collective obligation or that martial instincts ought to be a hallmark of aristocracy. Haugwitz, however, saw from the start that the government could recruit effectively only among the middle nobility and minor gentry. (His reflections were not devoid of some moralizing.)[45] It shortly became apparent that even these strata could not furnish a sufficient number of officer candidates, and so there was increasing recourse to solid burgher stock.[46]

A wide-ranging, social and scientifically conceived study of the Viennese military preparatory school and the Wiener Neustadt academy (both founded in 1752), and the engineers' college (set up in 1717 and reorganized in 1747) would be a welcome addition to scholarly literature.[47] One can only speculate that the initial decision to segregate nobles (even gentry) and commoners reflected the Empress's wish or belief that integration of the social classes would cause problems.

The apparent hesitation notwithstanding, status elevation as the incentive for improved professional performance was an idea whose time had come. The year before the academy opened, it was announced that all officers could be admitted to court in uniform, a reversal of custom that, it seems, stuck in the craw of many a snobbish aristocrat. The prospect of having to associate with rough-and-ready frontier types and the rawer sort of eastern nobles now serving in hussar regiments must have been particularly galling. While Maria Theresa often indulged the aulics (her unwillingness to sack antiquated generals of high birth is well known), reasons of state occasionally induced her to beard them. Yet, by not challenging the courtiers' value system too radically, as her successor did, she was acting pragmatically.

The policy of upgrading the officers' self-image and the attitude of society toward them was pursued fairly consistently. At first men were ennobled individually in a rather perfunctory way, but in time ennoblement became automatic, based on years of service. Even more important, the Empress's most brilliant sociopsychological stroke, was the establishment, immediately after Kolín, of the Military Order of Maria Theresa.[48] With the introduction of what was in effect a carefully graduated, hierarchically ordered system of decoration for valor, *esprit de corps* was coming of age. The state was pursuing monopolization of the means of violence by institutionalizing the concept of honor. Granted, honor is not easy to define, especially from a social scientific viewpoint. Redlich, for example, speaks of a reliable behavior pattern based upon internalized sanctions that operate within a specific setting (peer group).[49]

Also of great sociopsychological moment was the personal military charisma of Maria Theresa, the beloved *mater castrorum*, the damsel in distress, for whom, *pro rege* (!) *nostro*, Hungarian cavaliers were ready, at least theoretically, to sacrifice *vitam et sanguinem*. Is it really true, as Duffy avers, that the unifying power of a male authority figure like Frederick was stronger than the maternal image?[50]

Study of incipient military professionalism in Austria should likewise encompass domestication or internal pacification, that is, the effective disciplining of officers' private lives.[51] As the state now had to invest its own money, it could not tolerate the internecine waste of dueling. Maria Theresa's reign witnessed a fairly effective repression of this antediluvian manifestation of male competitiveness. The Empress's efforts to regulate sexual mores and the state's involvement in decisions to marry are equally significant.

The changes outlined here did not lead rapidly to a full-blown professional officer corps, especially in the case of the high command. There is cogent evidence of an aristocratic resurgence in the mid nineteenth century, and high nobles served in top posts even during World War One.[52] Nevertheless, Friedrich Walter probably goes too far when he bewails the "dark shadows and grievous weaknesses of an only recently matured princely absolutism, for which family and descent meant so much, indeed were so pervasive that towering ability and outstanding successes could be recognized but rarely, only after overcoming major opposition and when fortified by an excellent position in aristocratic society."[53] The era of Maria Theresa and Joseph II did in fact see the rise of an impressive phalanx of *novi homines.* Indeed, all the glory-shrouded names, aside from Daun's and Liechtenstein's, are of men who started out as unknowns: Philipp Beck; Laudon; the Irishmen Maximilian Ulysses von Browne, Lacy, John Sigismund MacQuire of Inniskillin and Carl Claudius O'Donnell; Hadik, Siskovics and the masterful artilleryman, Anton Feuerstein. They had the backing of a handful of prescient blueblooded generals, but the fame is chiefly theirs.

The secret lay, let it be reiterated, in the ability of enlightened representatives of the Habsburg *ancien régime* to conquer class prejudice and insist on precedence for talent. Of all the dignitaries involved, Daun himself seems to have been most conscious of the true scope of the steps that were being taken. He stated bluntly that "the art of war is not a craft organized like a guild" and that "experience by itself is inadequate for cultivating a systematic knowledge or science of things military." He declared that, "in order to carry out wartime assignments efficiently, it is first essential to grasp theory." Only then, he believed, was the martial estate genuinely honorable, deserving of the sovereign's backing for "all its rights, prerogatives and suitable privileges."[54]

Perhaps Daun was thinking of himself. The compensation he received for his own services was of the new, professional, not of the old seignorial kind. As has been noted, his father left the family's fortunes in disarray. While there was talk of helping the son to repurchase Ladendorf, his main material reward turned out to be a cash grant— a 250,000-florin trust fund, set up in 1758. If Leopold was able to repair the fortunes of his own line (which became extinct in 1851),[55] it was because he resorted to the device so successfully employed by most of his forebears, namely, espousal to an heiress, a marriage of convenience that made sense both financially and politically. It was with Fuchs money that he bought the Lower Austrian manor of Wallsee in 1755.

A final consideration in surveying the Dauns' family history in the context of evolving military leadership is Leopold's importance as a field commander. Scholars agree in portraying him as a deliberate, even lethargic cunctator, a genius at castramentation who, while not personally pusillanimous, was reluctant to seek the decisive engagement. Both he and his colleague and successor, Lacy, are seen as a sort of counterpoint to the killer instincts of Frederick II.[56] (Laudon, however, was known for his dash.) Does this guarded approach have anything to say about the Austrian attitude toward the management of violence, toward humanity and civilization? While Daun was firm-minded about the army's internal autonomy (thus symbolizing the maturation of professional identity),[57] perhaps the Austrian variety of civil-military relations was not as venomous, at least not until 1914, as that of the polity whose aggression initiated the process of reform in the Habsburg realms:

*In Öst'reichs schönem Heere*
*Da ist ein Regiment*
*Das Windischgrätz-Dragoner*
*Mit edlem Stolz sich nennt*
*Denn seiner Reiter Pallasch,*
*Ihr sich'rer Heldenblick*
*Blieb stets treu der Devise*
*"Qui s'y frotte s'y pique!"*

## Notes

1. Barrington Moore, Jr., *The Social Origins of Dictatorship and Democracy: Lord and Peasant in the Making of the Modern World* (Boston, 1966). For an evaluation of the impact of this study, see Jonathon M. Wiener, "The Barrington Moore Thesis and Its Critics." *Theory and Society,* II (1975), 301–330. Of special relevance for social-military historians is Moore's broader view that the progress that humanity has made toward rationality and freedom has been the consequence of an increasing resort to violence, especially in revolutionary contexts.

2. This is the opinion of Joseph Polišenský and Fred Snider who have closely studied Bohemian noble families. See Polišenský, *War and Society in Europe, 1618–1648* (Cambridge, 1978), pp. 202–216, esp. 212–213.

3. Státní Archiv v Brně, *Průvodce po archivních fondech* [Guide to Archival Collections] III (Prague, 1966), 17.

4. In the socially more advanced, western maritime states the process was under way already in the seventeenth century, above all in the navies. See Gerke Teitler, *De woording van de professionele officierscorps* [Genesis of the Professional Officer Corps] (Rotterdam, 1974); the English translation (Beverly Hills, Cal., 1977) is poor.

5. Fritz Redlich, *The German Military Enterpriser and His Work Force* (Wiesbaden, 1965), Beihefte 47, 48, "Vierteljahresschrift für Sozial- und Wirtschaftsgeschichte." Redlich regards the period 1350–1600 as "embryonic." However, there is increasing evidence of organized mercenary forces further back in the Middle Ages. See John Beeler, *Warfare in Feudal Europe, 730–1200* (Ithaca, 1971).

6. The distinction between occupation and institution (profession) may be regarded as fundamental to sociological analysis.

7. Thomas M. Barker, "Military Entrepreneurship and Absolutism: Habsburg Models," *Journal of European Studies,* IV (1974), 19–42; and "Armed Forces and Nobility in the Holy Roman Empire: General Aspects and Habsburg Particulars," *Armed Forces and Society,* IV (1977–78), 449–500.

8. Alfred Vagts, *A History of Militarism, Civilian and Military* (rev. ed.; New York, 1959); Morris Janowitz, *Military Conflict: Essays in the Institutional Analysis of War and Peace* (Beverly Hills, Cal., 1975). (Methodologically speaking, Vagts was a pioneer; many of his views now seem simplistic, e.g., generalizations about the military qualities of nobility in early modern Europe. Redlich has superseded him.)

9. Janowitz, *Military Conflict,* p. 58.

10. Jean Berenger, *Finances et absolutisme autrichien dans la seconde moitié du 17e siècle* (Paris, 1975).

11. Johann Christoph Allmayer-Beck, "Wandlungen im Heerwesen zur Zeit Maria Theresias," *Schriften des heeresgeschichtlichen Museums in Wien,* III (1967), 7–24.

12. "Military" and "service nobility" are concepts that arose in the latter eighteenth century. André Corvisier, "La Noblesse militaire: Aspects militaires de la noblesse française du XVe et XVIIIe siècles," *Histoire Sociale/Social History,* XI (1978), 336–355. Corvisier's perspicuous, semantically oriented exposé, which examines the shifting relationships between the profession of arms and the nobility as a whole, confronts critical questions; by defining the situation in France it underlines the need for comparative study.

13. Redlich, *Military Enterpriser,* II, 148.

14. This account is based on a genealogical table drawn up in 1725 for Weyrich Daun supported by substantial documentation, some of it medieval; both the chart and the records are catalogued as "Klassen I, II and III" of the Daunovská časť [Daun Section] of the "Rodový archív Pálffy-Daun" [Pálffy-Daun Family Archives] in the Slovak State Central Archives in Bratislava; see Štátny Slovensky Ústredný Archív v Bratislave, *Sprievodca po archívnych fondoch,* [Guide to Archival Collections] I, *Oddelenie feudalizmu* [Department of Feudalism] (Bratislava, 1964), pp. 125–130. (The documents in each "Klasse" are individually numbered, but they cannot be indicated here.)

15. "Daunovská časť", "Klassen VIII, XIV, XVII; Johann Heinrich Zedler, *Grosses, vollständiges Universal-Lexicon,* Vol. 7 (Halle-Leipzig, 1734), p. 275.

16. This is puzzling since there is more material for the periods before and after his time.

17. Daunovská časť", XVI; Ernst Kneschke, *Neues allgemeines deutsches Adels-Lexicon,* II (Leipzig, 1860), 427; František Rieger, *Slovník naučny,* II (Prague, 1862), 72.

18. Daunovská časť", XXIX, XXX.

19. *Průvodce po archivních fondech,* 15–16.

20. Kneschke, *Adels-Lexicon,* II, 42; Constant von Wurzbach, *Biographisches Lexikon des österreichischen Kaiserthums,* III (Vienna, 1858), 171; Daunovská časť", XXXI.

21. Franz-Lorenz von Thadden, *Feldmarschall Daun: Maria Theresias grösster Feldherr* (Vienna, 1967), p. 21. (Thadden errs in stating that Weyrich acquired Ladendorf).

22. Daunovská časť", Klassen IV, XXV and XXXII. The materials for both Wilhelm and Weyrich are especially rich.

23. Thadden's study, if helpful, is not exhaustively researched and contains a lot of "filler". (There is relatively little material in Bratislava on Leopold.)

24. Thadden, *Daun,* pp. 33 ff.

25. Christopher Duffy, *The Army of Maria Theresa: the Armed Forces of Imperial Austria, 1740–1780* (New York, 1977).

26. Cf. Gustav-Adolph Auffenberg-Komarów, "Das Zeitalter Maria Theresias," *Unser Heer* (Vienna, 1963), pp. 117–118.

27. Duffy, *The Army of Maria Theresa,* pp. 45–6. Duffy has pointed out to this writer that, in respect to diversity of personnel, the Austrian officer corps closely resembled Russia's.

28. Robert T. Anderson, *Modern Europe: An Anthropological Perspective* (Pacific Palisades, Cal., 1973).

29. The figure is approximately 70%. I have compiled the list from stan-

dard accounts and from Alphons Wrede, *Geschichte der K.u.K. Wehrmacht* (Vienna, 1898–1901). Biographical details have been culled from a variety of sources, including Kneschke, Rieger, Otto *(Slovník naučny)*, Zedler and Wurzbach. The 70% could be weighted upward since I have not counted more than one or two figures from each of the aulic clans (which seem to have had an average of about four sons in service) and since the stubbornly loyal Irish have been classified in the 30% "foreign" contingent.

30. Thadden, *Daun*, p. 209.

31. There were forty generals for 70,000 effectives in one of Daun's armies in 1756. *Ibid.*, pp. 208–209. As for the military establishment as a whole, Vehse counted "no less than 367 generals at the end of Maria Theresa's reign." There was also a handful of "Imperial" *(Reich)* field marshals, "Imperial" cavalry and infantry generals. Eduard Vehse, *Geschichte des österreichischen Hofs und Adels und der österreichischen Diplomatie*, Part 7 (Hamburg, 1852), pp. 83–84.

32. Rough distinctions between high and middle nobility can be made by comparing titles. Ideally, this would be supplemented by property statistics, but in most instances data are too sparse and heterogeneous. As for nonnobles I find the term "bourgeoisie," diffuse even for the nineteenth and twentieth centuries, misleading; of course the earlier "burgher" class or "burgessdom" was hardly uniform either.

33. The role of generals from aulic clans during the crucial War of the Austrian Succession is noteworthy. To some extent they compensated for Charles of Lorraine's incompetence. (Just how bad Neipperg, who remained loyal, and Seckendorff, who did not, actually were is an open question.) Certainly their discipline contrasts with the opportunism of the Bohemian nobility—which may say something about military corporate spirit.

34. I am grateful to Géza Perjés for debating these conclusions with me and for linguistic assistance (Hungarian) in checking family histories. We have used Bálint Hóman and Gyula Szekfü, *Magyar Történet* (Budapest, 1941–1943); and the Slovak state archival guidebooks which contain useful résumés of the histories of some Hungarian families. Perhaps one should also point to the problem of cultural Germanization among the Hungarian aristocracy after the Rákóczi insurrection. Cf. Vehse, *Geschichte*, VII, 167 ff. Presumably the many military jobs had something to do with this. The roots of the phenomenon clearly go back to the seventeenth century and to the family histories of "loyalist" dynasties (especially the Pálffys and the Kohárys).

35. Jacquemin and Sincère could be considered *arrivés;* there were others like Ruttant.

36. See the chart following n. 57.

37. Redlich, *Military Enterpriser*, II, 92. Redlich's picture of the Austrian officers' corps' social structure (p. 114) requires some modification.

38. *Sprievodca*, p. 272.

39. I have counted 9 north Germans: Buccow was the most outstanding.

40. Kneschke, *Adels-Lexicon*, V (1864), 465–466.

41. Ernst Schmidhofer, "Das irische, schottische und englische Element im kaiserlichen Heer" (Doctoral dissertation, University of Vienna, 1971), p. 3.

42. Johannes Kunisch, *Feldmarschall Laudon: Jugend und erste Kriegsjahre* (Vienna, 1971), *passim*.

43. Auffenberg-Komarów, "Das Zeitalter . . . ," pp. 137–144 (for all aspects of the reform).

44. Gunther E. Rothenberg, "Nobility and Military Careers: the Habsburg Officer Corps, 1740–1914," *Military Affairs*, XL (1976), 182.

45. Duffy, *The Army of Maria Theresa*, pp. 29–30; Auffenberg-Korarów, "Das Zeitalter . . . ," p. 137.

46. *Ibid.*, p. 138. The question also arises whether the demographic basis of the nobility was too narrow.

47. Cf. Johann Allmayer-Beck's contribution to the present volume (pp. 127–135).

48. Rothenberg, "Nobility . . . ," p. 182; Auffenberg-Komarów, "Das Zeitalter . . . ," pp. 147–148.

49. Redlich, *Military Enterpriser*, II, 145.

50. Duffy, *The Army of Maria Theresa*, p. 46. Duffy's rejoinder (to this author) is that the Empress could not be a Joan of Arc, i.e., personally inspire and discipline troops in the thick of battle; this was what really counted.

51. Redlich, *Military Enterpriser*, II, 148 ff.

52. Rothenberg, "Nobility . . . ," pp. 183–185.

53. Friedrich Walter, "Feldmarschall Leopold Graf Daun und Feldmarschall Gideon Ernst Freiherr von Laudon," in *Gestalter der Geschicke Österreichs* (Innsbruck, 1962), p. 263.

54. Thadden, *Daun*, p. 144. The juxtaposition of "craft" and "estate" (social order) is semantically intriguing; Cf. Corvisier, "La Noblesse militaire," p. 341.

55. *Ibid.*, pp. 111 ff., 377, 461; *Sprievodca*, pp. 125–126. The line died out with the field marshal's grandson, Joseph Albin Franz, a canon of Salzburg and capitulary of Passau. The clergyman willed the *fideicommissio* to the Pálffys of Stupava who thereby became quite wealthy. This was a sequel to the marriage of Leopold's daughter, Theresa, to Field Marshal Leopold Pálffy (1739–1799).

56. Duffy, *The Army of Maria Theresa*, pp. 143–144.

57. Walter, *Daun und Laudon*, p. 274.

*The Italian Ethnic Element among the Generals of the Imperial-Royal Army 1740–1790*

| *Family Name* | *Region* | *Social Stratum* |
|---|---|---|
| Bettoni | Lombardy | burgher |
| Botta d'Adorno | Genoa | high noble |
| Brentano-Cimaroli | Como | burgher |
| Campitelli | Piedmont (Cuneo) | middle noble, *condottiere* |
| Caramelli | Piedmont | middle noble |
| Caraffa | Naples | high noble |
| Clerici | Lombardy | high noble |
| Doria (Caravaggio) | Genoa | high noble |
| Guasco (Quasco) | Piedmont | middle noble |
| Lanthieri | Friuli-Carniola | high noble |
| Lucchesi d'Abarra | Sicily-Aragon | high noble |
| Lužan (Luciano?) | Aragon-Milan (?) | burgher (?) |
| Modena | Modena | princely (ruling) |
| Novati | north Italy | middle noble |
| Pallavicini | Genoa | high noble, *condottiere* |
| Pellegrini | Verona | middle noble |
| Pestalozzi | Milan | burgher |
| Piccolomini | Siena | high noble, *condottiere* |
| Porporati | north Italy (?) | middle noble |
| Radicati di Passerano | Piedmont | middle noble, *condottiere* |
| Serbelloni | Lombardy | high noble, *condottiere* |
| Spada | Papal State, Turin | high noble, *condottiere* |
| Stampa | Lombardy | high noble |
| Voghera | Naples | high noble |

Note: In northern Italy's case, because of a long and unique history of urban development, the distinction between burghers and low to middle nobles is especially hard to draw.

Sources: *Enciclopedia biografica e bibliografica italiana,* serii XIX, XX ("Condottieri") (Rome, 1936, 1943); Kneschke, Wrede, and Zedler.

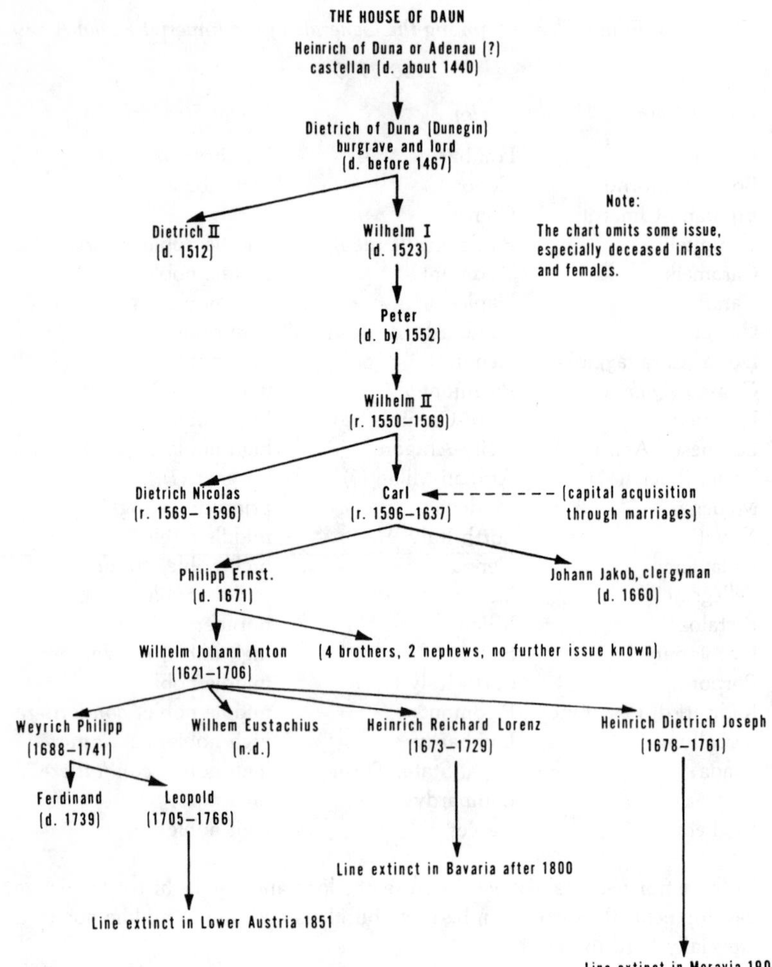
THE HOUSE OF DAUN
Heinrich of Duna or Adenau (?)
castellan (d. about 1440)
Dietrich of Duna (Dunegin)
burgrave and lord
(d. before 1467)
Dietrich II
(d. 1512)
Wilhelm I
(d. 1523)
Note:
The chart omits some issue, especially deceased infants and females.
Peter
(d. by 1552)
Wilhelm II
(r. 1550–1569)
Dietrich Nicolas
(r. 1569– 1596)
Carl
(r. 1596–1637)
(capital acquisition
through marriages)
Philipp Ernst.
(d. 1671)
Johann Jakob, clergyman
(d. 1660)
Wilhelm Johann Anton
(1621–1706)
(4 brothers, 2 nephews, no further issue known)
Weyrich Philipp
(1688–1741)
Wilhem Eustachius
(n.d.)
Heinrich Reichard Lorenz
(1673–1729)
Heinrich Dietrich Joseph
(1678–1761)
Ferdinand
(d. 1739)
Leopold
(1705–1766)
Line extinct in Bavaria after 1800
Line extinct in Lower Austria 1851
Line extinct in Moravia 1904

Karl A. Roider, Jr.

# No More Infidels: Enlisting Popular Support For a Turkish War in the Age of Enlightenment

The Austro-Ottoman war of 1788–1791 was perhaps the most unpopular war in the history of the Habsburg Monarchy. And it occurred at a time when that unpopularity could be vigorously expressed. The easing of censorship by Emperor Joseph II in 1781 gave rise to the *Broschürenflut,* that outpouring of pamphlets, broadsides, books, and journals that became such an integral part of the Josephian era in Habsburg history. The flood of literature in turn inspired "a veritable urge to read" among the Austrian and especially the Viennese public.[1] As a result, there emerged an informed public that was appealed to by writers of all opinions and which in turn eagerly debated the major and minor issues of the age. As one pamphleteer noted, "In every Viennese coffeehouse the fate of Europe is decided every day at least three times."[2] The Josephian government was well aware of this public opinion and sought support from it for its various policies. Not only did the regime pay writers to persuade the people to its point of view, but pamphleteers often competed with one another in endorsing government policies in the hope that an effective argument or an impressive work would lead to a permanent position for the author in the state bureaucracy.

The easing of censorship and Joseph's enlightened measures—especially the anticlerical ones—made the Emperor and his government quite popular among the pamphleteers in the early 1780s. But as the decade wore on and the coldly rationalistic side of the reforms seemed to predominate over the humanistic side, the popular writers criticized the Emperor more and more. In 1787 came his most unpopular decision: he agreed to join Catherine of Russia in a war against the Ottoman Turks.

From its beginning, the war evoked protests. To many there seemed to be no justification for an Austrian declaration of war on the Turks, and plenty of reasons for the monarchy to remain at peace. The Ottoman Empire appeared to most people in the late

1780s as a temperate power that posed no danger to the Austrian state. For the past fifty years the Sublime Porte had shown itself not only peaceful toward the Habsburgs but at critical times actually considerate, especially during the War of the Austrian Succession and the Seven Years' War, when a Turkish assault on Hungary could have seriously damaged the monarchy. As thanks for those years of peace, Joseph now seemed intent on joining the aggressive and arrogant Catherine to destroy a power that was becoming one of Austria's friends. The reason for this ingratitude, many pamphleteers argued, was the Emperor's *Eroberungs schwindel,* his lust for conquest, which bordered on the irrational, a lust masterfully exploited by the wily Catherine.[3] Some brochures condemned Joseph's uncontrolled desire for new lands in thunderous terms. "The Kaiser has no right to attack the Turks," one author wrote. "His policy is worthy of a Machiavelli [a pejorative term in those days], and his invasion of Turkey an example of the crassest injustice and the blackest ingratitude."[4]

Scholars who have studied the last years of Joseph's reign have focused much attention on the pamphleteers who criticized the Emperor and his Ottoman policy. They have cited their writings as evidence of the widespread unrest that led to revolution in some provinces and the revocation of many of Joseph's reforms. But what about the popular defenders of the war? After all, not all writers opposed the struggle, and the government was too experienced in the art of pamphleteering to fail to promote its own cause through popular tracts. Besides, some writers believed as much out of conviction as because of subsidies that Joseph's decision to enter the war was the correct one.

The most important of the prowar pamphleteers was Johann Michael Schweighofer. Born and educated in Graz, Schweighofer first came to Vienna to study law. After completing his studies, he found employment in the united Hungarian and Transylvanian Chancellery and later served on the staff of Duke Albert of Saxe-Teschen. His opinions regarding the Turkish war were respected among the Viennese, for prior to 1787 he had emerged as a popular authority on the Ottoman Empire. His initial contribution to enlightened literature in Vienna, a book entitled *Grösse der Handlung unter Joseph II nebst meinen Gedanken von der neuen Handlung auf dem Schwarzen Meere* (Vienna, 1782), encouraged Viennese merchants to take advantage of certain new rights of Austrians to transport goods through the Ottoman Empire to the Black Sea and then to the Russian port of Cherson. Following this offering, Schweighofer wrote regularly for the Austrian public, mostly on commercial and political topics and frequently on matters relating to the Turks. His information on the Ottoman state was secondhand, gleaned from books and travel literature, and some of it sadly out of date. Nonetheless, when the war broke out, he was the one writer who could present the government's policies to the public with authority and persuasiveness.[5]

Prior to and throughout the first year of the war, Schweighofer published an editorial magazine entitled *Der politische Zuschauer, eine Fortsetzung des Freundes angenehmer und nützlicher Kenntnisse,* in which he discussed various aspects of the war and, more importantly, tried to answer public criticisms of it and muster support for it. As befits a writer of the late eighteenth century, Schweighofer presented his views in a rational and straightforward manner. The reasonableness of his arguments suggests that the audience to which he appealed was intelligent, rather prosperous, and educated. When he appealed to his readers, he did so in measured terms, suggesting to them that his position was worthy of their support because reason indicated that it was the correct one. Throughout his work, however, there emerged a pronounced devotion to Joseph II, a devotion that seemed to go beyond the call of duty. He was obviously convinced that Joseph was badly misunderstood by his subjects and appreciated far less than he deserved. Moreover, Schweighofer revealed a strong sense of patriotism for Austria in general and for Vienna in particular. One gets the impression that the criticisms of his Emperor and his country that he tried to rebut affected him far more deeply than his reasoned replies indicated, and that he suffered considerably when the Emperor and the army failed to live up to his and his countrymen's expectations.

At the outset of the war, Schweighofer regarded his first task to respond to the criticism that Joseph's decision to fight was a manifestation of *Eroberungsschwindel.* In an issue of the *Zuschauer* entitled "Why has the Emperor Gone to War and Is His Decision a Correct One?" Schweighofer argued that Joseph had no uncontrolled lust for conquest but was obligated to defend his ally, Catherine of Russia. The sultan, not the Emperor or the tsarina, had declared war first, and the treaties that Austria had with Russia obliged Joseph to come to his ally's side. It was the sultan who broke the peace; the

Emperor was only trying to reestablish it. The decision to enter the conflict, Schweighofer maintained, was not only understandable but right. "No war is more justified than that which one fights to restore peace."[6]

Schweighofer undoubtedly realized that one could argue that all wars are fought to restore peace, and he also knew that many objected to Joseph's *Eroberungsschwindel* not because they opposed his winning some worthwhile territory but because in this war there seemed nothing of value for Austria to win. These critics argued that Joseph was simply a tool of the tsarina, helping her to annex vital territories along the Black Sea while he had to content himself with at best depopulated lands on his own border that would require substantial investment to defend and would yield little in return. The sacrifices in this war would be Austria's, the gains Russia's. Schweighofer answered that Austria would likely win Serbia and Bosnia, provinces that many writers regarded as worthless only because they knew nothing about them. "Not every acquisition of land is advantageous for a state," he conceded. "With Serbia," however, "this is fortunately not the case." Serbia possessed rich lands, capable of growing much grain and feeding many cattle, mines that produced silver and copper, and a population that could provide 40,000 soldiers and a yearly revenue of 1,000,000 gulden. It would cost 10,000,000 gulden to take Serbia, Schweighofer admitted, but that would be made up in ten short years.[7] Bosnia would be an equally valuable acquisition. After extolling its human and natural resources, Schweighofer added that it was strategically important as well, making protection of the Austrian and Croatian lands substantially easier for the Austrian army. "No land would better serve the Germans than Bosnia, when after the natural course of political events it should come under the rule of the Germans."[8] For those who still ridiculed the insignificance of such gains, Schweighofer reminded his readers that in 1739 Austria had lost lands to the Turks and must seek to recover them. In a statement full of meaning for the Habsburg state in its last decades, he wrote, "An empire that always loses and never regains must of itself come to an end, and its own preservation is always the first law of a monarchy."[9]

Those still skeptical of the reasons for Austria's going to war and those who still belittled the gains likely to come of it Schweighofer tried to assure that victory would be swift and certain, and the people's sacrifices minimal. The Turks were no match for the Austrian army alone, much less for the Austrians and Russians together. And here Schweighofer at least indirectly argued that the military reforms introduced by Joseph, especially the conscription law which had elicited such widespread public protest, would prove their worth. The army was now much better than it had been in previous years and could be moved in substantial numbers to the Turkish front with remarkable speed and efficiency. "The quick, general mobilization of the imperial-royal army shows that the whole machine of state defense is splendidly organized, and is led by a vigorous and decisive spirit." In fact, organization by itself would give the Austrians a definite advantage at the outset. "The first victory that the allies have achieved over the Turks is undoubtedly the victory in state and military affairs." Not only was the army superior, but the common Habsburg soldier was better than his Ottoman counterpart. The Austrian conscript was not only more enlightened, well bred, and disciplined, but also full of courage and enthusiasm. Waxing eloquent, Schweighofer praised the ranks as composed of "spirited and brave Austrians, fiery and courageous Hungarians, steady Bohemians, steadfast Moravians, brave and purposeful Styrians, obliging Poles, daring Croats, boisterous Italians, and belligerent Netherlanders."[10]

In contrast, the Turks had no such organization and no such men. Their soldiers, Schweighofer argued, went into battle against their will and thus would not stand up to the disciplined and well-organized Habsburg forces. Besides, their first defeat would likely inspire revolution in the Ottoman capital and threaten the sultan and his government with deposition and death. The war would not last long, proclaimed Schweighofer. "As soon as the Turks are defeated in battle, they will gladly make peace and abandon whole provinces willingly."[11] The war would be short and victorious, and the sacrifices that it would demand from the people would be easy to bear.

Schweighofer's optimism was sadly misplaced. The Austrian army did not live up to the expectations of Schweighofer and most of Europe. Instead of launching a major assault on the fortress of Belgrade (as everyone expected the Austrians to do) and then supporting it with pincer movements through Moldavia and Bosnia, the high command established a long cordon from the Adriatic Sea to the Bukovina and undertook only minor action along it. To the

Viennese, such a strategy seemed to be nothing but inaction, and and inaction meant a prolongation of the war and its hardships. Increasingly strident criticisms of the Emperor and his officers began to appear in pamphlets and coffehouse conversations.

Schweighofer, in his role of publicist for the government and now more and more in that of apologist, came forth to answer the complaints. They stemmed not from any careful consideration of military affairs, he explained, but from impatience and a faulty understanding of strategy. "Everyone finds a lot to complain about, because everyone compares the achievements of a commander to his own opinion and comprehension of things. Consequently, there are many who are unhappy with the government, or do not approve of the commanders, or complain about the decisions themselves." After listing and trying to refute the most common complaints—those generally condemning the army's inaction, Schweighofer remarked that the problem was not what the army had or had not achieved, but what people had expected it to achieve. The war had begun with great promise, and the promise was not fulfilled as speedily as most believed it should have been. "Everyone had great expectations for the Austrian undertakings; everyone believed that the monarch would achieve great victories quickly, indeed very quickly."[12] Of course, Schweighofer himself had been confident of swift success at the outset and had passed on this confidence to his readers. In fact, his efforts to justify Austrian inaction ring hollow, as if he were trying to persuade himself as much as others.

By the summer of 1788 the Viennese people were criticizing not only the Austrian high command. The war tax caused significant grumbling especially among the burghers and the civil servants, and the requisitions of the army caused food shortages for everyone. The army's practice of paying for food and fodder in scrip *(Garantiescheine)* instead of cash encouraged peasants and food dealers to horde their stores, which only made the shortages more severe and drove prices higher. On the last day of June 1788 Viennese crowds plundered food shops, convinced that the owners were holding back their wares until price controls were lifted altogether.

Schweighofer was deeply moved by this and other outbursts, and was distressed that such events could occur in his beloved Vienna. At one time he had cynically welcomed the war tax, remarking that it would turn some critics into patriots. "Earlier many cherished the hardhearted wish that the Turks would win and the Emperor lose.

. . . Now they remember the all-encompassing war tax that the fatherland imposes even upon them, and discover that they have wished misfortune to befall themselves."[13] With the uprising of June, Schweighofer realized that the dissatisfaction among the people ran deeper than he had anticipated. He apparently, however, thought that it stemmed more from rumors, uncertainty, and pessimism about the war than from any deeper economic, political, or social concerns. Two parties existed in Vienna, he informed his readers, one being "the honorable and well-intentioned citizens who want, hope, and cherish the thought that everything good for Austria will be the result of this war." The other party consisted of those "who wish misery to befall us. . . . They spread news of lost battles; they predict famine and pestilence. . . . What terrible minds and hearts such people have, who can trample the state and their fellow citizens, who can find so much pleasure in doing so especially since the misfortunes have not happened, who can devise them in order to take delight in telling them so that they can torment their fellow citizens with fear."[14]

The discontent with the war grew increasingly bitter in the late summer when the Turks broke through the cordon east of Belgrade, ravaged the banate of Timişoara (Temesvár), and then fell back across the Danube. This setback, which followed the inaction of the spring and early summer, prompted increased criticism of the war effort, this time directed largely against Joseph himself and his apparent incapacity as a military commander. This criticism touched Schweighofer particularly, but he was hard-pressed to respond to it since he knew that most of it was justified. What pained him most were the assaults on the Emperor's character, especially the complaints that he cared not at all for his men, that he did not appreciate their hardships, and that he did not know of their sufferings. In reply Schweighofer extolled particularly the Emperor's concern for the common soldier. While in the field he afforded himself few luxuries; he slept on the ground "like his warriors," dressed simply, and liked nothing better than being with his men, none of whom he would sacrifice needlessly. Here Schweighofer suggested that the Austrian army's inaction might in fact be a virtue, for he described Joseph as reluctant to undertake any plan that might result in unnecessarily high casualties. While sparing his men, however, Schweighofer emphasized that the Emperor did not spare himself. He slept little but worked much, either planning the war effort, reading reports from and dispatching orders to Vienna, or being with his men. Above all, his virtue rested in his humanity. His humanity demanded caution, and caution might be misinterpreted as inaction. "Joseph II is not so lucky as Joseph I, not so ambitious as Louis XIV, and not so daring as Frederick II, but more careful and more humane than all these heroes."[15]

By the end of the campaign of 1788, the unpopularity of Joseph and his war had deepened dramatically. A new war tax, a call for more conscripts, and the disappointments of the campaign added to the discontent. In his last issue of 1788 Schweighofer tried to prove that things were not as bad as they seemed. He composed what he called *"Die grosse Rechnung,"* a balance sheet that he knew would appeal to every businessman's heart. "When a year ends, the intelligent burgher draws up a balance sheet, and when a campaign is finished kings make up a balance sheet for their expenses; but do so to compare gains and losses." In his *grosse Rechnung* Schweighofer did not play down the Austrian losses, nor did he proclaim that Austria had enjoyed great but hidden successes. He admitted that the people suffered, that the losses in men and resources were significant, and that the gains were minimal. But he tried to point out that the Turks had suffered even more and that with a determined effort—and, he admitted, with a new commander in chief—Austria and Russia would emerge victorious the next year.[16]

Only one *Zuschauer* appeared in 1789, and it lacked the sensitivity of those of 1788. A straightforward assessment of Austria's chances for victory, it did not answer the concerns of the Viennese and did not contain the exhortations to them that had characterized the earlier editions.[17] Perhaps the government had decided that the dissatisfaction of the people could be better resolved with action and censorship, and that subsidies to writers like Schweighofer were no longer necessary, or perhaps Schweighofer had begun to believe that the war was becoming so unpopular that no effort on his part could rouse the people to support it. He may have become convinced that the war was causing such massive unrest that it should be brought to an end. In any case, as the campaign of 1789 opened, the *Zuschauer* closed.

Schweighofer's effort to muster support for Austria's last Ottoman war failed. The reasons are not difficult to find. To the people the sacrifices were considerable and the advantages minimal. Moreover, the Emperor had slowly but surely lost the popularity that he had enjoyed at the beginning of his reign, and Schweighofer could not prevent the war from depriving him of what little popularity remained. But for those who have studied the Ottoman wars of the seventeenth and eighteenth centuries and the popular appeals and enthusiasm that accompanied them, the striking fact of this struggle is the absence of appeals to the people to defend Christianity. From this war came no pieces like *"Auf, Auf ihr Christen,"* which appeared in the great war of 1683–1699, or *"Prinz Eugen, der edle Ritter,"* composed in the war of 1716–1718, works that called for and rejoiced in victories over the infidel. The absence of such writings is easily explained. Vienna was an enlightened city in the 1780s. Irreligion was the fashion in many circles and had been encouraged in part by the reforms of Joseph II. In such circles there could be no infidels, for in times of religious toleration such a word described no one and hence raised no ire among the reading population. Schweighofer belonged to that society and addressed his appeals to it. In doing so, he carefully avoided reference to the Turks as enemies of Christendom. He did on occasion refer to the savagery with which the Turks often treated Austrian prisoners, but he did not suggest that it came from religious hatred, preferring instead to describe it as a quaint practice that one would have expected a hundred years ago but certainly not in the late eighteenth century.

What Schweighofer was admitting—and what was evident among both the promoters and critics of the war—was that Austria had lost its traditional reason for fighting the Turks. The protection of Christendom from the infidel had been the foremost purpose in the popular mind, but by the 1780s that purpose had vanished. Sacrifices no longer seemed necessary; exhortations to defend the faith were out of place. What then could replace religion as the motivation for the people to support war? Schweighofer could not think of a good one beyond cooly explaining reasons of state. And that was obviously insufficient. Religious toleration robbed the Habsburgs of their primary war cry to call their people to arms against the unbeliever. The appeals in 1788 were reasonable, moderate, passionless, and ineffective. At one point Schweighofer even lamented that the best reason for fighting the Turks could no longer be used. "Half Germany favors the Turks," he sighed. "Italy is pro-Turkish, France pro-Turkish; consequently, the majority of Christians are for the enemy of Christendom, for unbelievers. What kind of patriotism is that?"[18] By 1788 patriotism in Austria was no longer associated with religion; hence enlisting popular support for war with the Turks (and others) required a new appeal. In the nineteenth century, two rallying cries emerged to challenge one another among the people: loyalty to the Emperor and loyalty to the nation. Unfortunately for the monarchy, loyalty to the nation would be the victor.

## Notes

1. Paul P. Bernard, *Jesuits and Jacobins: Enlightenment and Enlightened Despotism in Austria* (Urbana, 1971), p. 6.
2. Johann Willibald Nagl, Jakob Ziedler, and Eduard Castle, *Deutschösterreichische Literaturgeschichte* (Vienna and Leipzig, n.d.), II, 291.
3. Ernst Wangermann, *From Joseph II to the Jacobin Trials* (2nd ed.; Oxford, 1969), p. 28.
4. Paul Mitrofanov, *Joseph II: Seine politische und kulturelle Tätigkeit* (Vienna and Leipzig, 1910), p. 213.
5. For biographical information see Constantin Wurzbach, *Biographisches Lexikon des Kaiserthums Oesterreich*, XXXII, 360–361; and *Allgemeine Deutsche Biographie*, XXXIII, 357.
6. Johann Michael Schweighofer, *Betrachtungen über die Ursachen und Folgen des gegenwärtigen Tuerkenkriegs* (Frankfurt and Vienna, 1788), p. 10. Each issue of *Der politische Zuschauer* has its own title but no volume number.
7. *Idem*, *Gedanken und Bermerkungen des politischen Zuschauers bei dem Türkenkrieg* (Frankfurt and Vienna, 1788), pp. 70–74.
8. *Idem*, *Von dem gegenwaertigen Krieg der beiden Kaiserhöfe wieder die ottomanische Pforte* (Frankfurt and Vienna, 1788), p. 56.
9. *Idem*, *Betrachtungen über die Ursachen und Folgen*, p. 8.
10. *Idem*, *Von dem gegenwaertigen Krieg*, p. 7.
11. *Ibid.*, p. 45.
12. *Idem*, *Bemerkungen über die gegenwärtigen Staats- und Kriegsangelegenheiten* (Vienna, 1788), pp. 31–32.
13. *Idem*, *Beobachtungen über die Kriegsoperationen der Oesterreicher, Russen, Schweden, und Türken im Jahre 1788* (Vienna, 1788), pp. 195–196.
14. *Idem*, *Von den gegenwärtigen Kriegsvorfällen* (Frankfurt and Vienna, 1788), pp. 55–56.
15. *Idem*, *Beobachtungen über die Kriegsoperationen*, p. 177.
16. *Ibid.*, pp. 119–123.
17. *Idem*, *Gedanken bei den dermaligen Aussichten zum zweiten Feldzug der Kaisermächte wider die Türken* (Vienna, 1789).
18. *Idem*, *Beobachtungen über die Kriegsoperationen*, p. 190.

Gunther E. Rothenberg

# Conclusions

The seven essays on "Habsburg Society and War" represent a wide variety of methodological approaches—institutional, narrative, intellectual, as well as the "new history." They are, however, united by a common assumption and address themselves to the problem of war and society in the framework of the Clausewitzian concept that war is the application of force toward political ends. Then too, reflecting the primacy of this development during the eighteenth century, all stress the emerging central institutions of the monarchy. Finally, there is an uncommon degree of consensus in interpretation, most apparent in the four essays dealing with strategic thought and concepts of war, but also evident in the three essays dealing with the officer corps and the attempt to influence public opinion. In particular, if the first four essays illustrate a rather restrained approach to the uses of military power, the second group explains some of the peculiar difficulties and requirements confronting the Austrian state, and throw light on the background of the incomplete and always far from uniform structure of the Habsburg military establishment. In this connection it is perhaps useful to remember that, in Central and Eastern Europe at least, the successes and failures of the Habsburg Monarchy should be judged not in comparison with France or Prussia, even though Shanahan's essay provides some useful insights, but with the Russian, Polish, or Ottoman models. The complexities and restraints of the Habsburg realm were already recognized at the end of the historical period under discussion. In 1791 a promising young staff officer, Colonel Baron Karl von Mack Leiberich, wrote that "lack of unity, conflicting jurisdictions, and large distances make the Austrian military system far more complex and difficult to manage than the Prussian."[1]

In point of time, the essays cover the period from the repulse of the Turks before Vienna and their eviction from Hungary, signaling the decline of the Ottoman Empire as a major military threat, followed by the emergence of Austria during the War of the Spanish Succession as one of the Great Powers of Europe, to the new threat, albeit at first dimly perceived, of the French Revolution. The first development sets the stage for Ingrao's discussion of the geopolitical position of the monarchy, perhaps less precarious than before, but still requiring a strategic glacis, political barriers provided through political expansion. The doctrine was not entirely new. It dated back to the sixteenth century when, in order to defend their possessions, the Austrian Habsburgs in cooperation with the still powerful provincial Estates began to develop such a glacis in northwestern Hungary and Croatia. To be sure, after the relief of Vienna in 1683, and following Prince Eugene of Savoy's victories in Hungary, this glacis was no longer required against the Turks. Austrian attention then returned to Italy and the Rhine, but here France, a much stronger power than the Ottoman Empire, as well as emerging Prussia came into conflict with Austria's objectives. Around the middle of the eighteenth century, Austrian expansion came to an end and strategic thinking, as Rauchensteiner points out, turned towards finding security by means of a powerful standing army, the cordon system, and fortifications. This "stagnation" in military thinking, as Rauchensteiner describes it, was in part based on the Austrian experience during the lengthy conflict with Prussia, culminating in the Seven Years' War. As Duffy's contribution explains, having, in the face of considerable difficulties, managed to put a very respectable army together, neither the Austrian monarch nor the field commanders wished to hazard it unnecessarily. To keep an "army in being" became a constant preoccupation in Austrian military calculations, and the desire to preserve the army, the very real and in many ways the only guarantor of the Habsburg dynasty, played a major role in the strategic decisions made by Archduke Charles during the wars of the French Revolution and Napoleon. There were, of course, other considerations as well. Everywhere the evolution of linear tactics, depending on highly trained and expensive soldiers, together with the restraints exercised by absolutism, mercantilism, and the thinking of the Enlightenment, tended to make the conduct of war more formal and limited. Even the Prussians during the War of the Bavarian Succession were content with a maneuver and cordon strategy.

In many ways Joseph II, so often regarded as a truly enlightened monarch, acted out of a desire for military aggrandizement and glory. While he agreed with the assessment that the monarchy's military stance toward Western Europe should be defensive, he hoped to exploit the patent weakness of the declining Ottoman Empire for a war of conquest. Its failure, due to faulty strategy and the collapse of the supply system, confirmed most Austrian generals in the wisdom of a defensive strategy. Yet there was more. In Austria, high society never found its fulfillment in military careers, hence the difficulties in recruiting an officer corps from the nobility, described in the paper by Allmayer-Beck, and the need to look to specific families, perhaps even "new men," discussed by Baker. Perhaps only in Austria could the major military figure of the age of the French Revolution and Napoleon, Archduke Charles have prefaced his most basic work on the fundamentals of warfare with the sentiment that "war is the greatest evil a state or nation can experience."[2] To be sure, his great contemporary, the Prussian Karl von Clausewitz, also warned against entering conflict lightly, but he regarded war as part of the natural order, the continuation of policy by other means, while Charles regarded it as a violent interruption of the natural order. The implication derived from Clausewitz is that a state must be prepared to respond to all kinds of military challenges both intellectually and organizationally, while Charles's sentiments suggest an eighteenth-century dichotomy between military policy and the state. If so, this arose in large part out of the archduke's recognition of the special character of the Habsburg monarchy, its multinational framework, and its numerous and diverse political institutions. As toward the end of the eighteenth century Europe moved closer to the nation state and to the concept of the nation-in-arms, this situation was a substantial weakness. Still, as Albert Sorel once wrote, Austria "always was one idea and one army behind, but it always had an idea and always had an army."[3]

Even before the inception of the nation-in-arms, the major European states maintained very sizable military establishments, especially after 1763. In Austria the army increased from 100,000 at the start of the period discussed to 300,000 by 1792. Such establishments were supported by a vast bureaucratic structure. And while the state bureaucracy in Austria was by no means as pervasive as in Prussia or in France, it was enough to arouse internal opposition. In the Austrian hereditary lands Maria Theresa had overcome resistance by the Estates, and for the first time had assured her army replacements and constant financial support. In Hungary, however, it was a different matter. With memories of the Ferenc II Rákóczi insurrection, still fresh, the Empress did not enforce military reforms and the diet retained control over recruitment and supply. And during the Prussian wars, despite protestations of loyalty and devotion, Hungary had provided little support. In the end, Maria Theresa decided to leave well enough alone. "In the Kindgdom of Hungary," she wrote in her so-called *Political Testament*, "I think it better not to introduce any changes." When Joseph II tried to introduce centralized administration, the Hungarian nobles revolted and had to be pacified by Leopold II with a mixture of threats and concessions. These events, of course, are discussed at some length and from different aspects in Volume III of this series, but their effects on the central administration must be remembered here.

Moreover, despite its relative remoteness from the currents of Western European thought, there emerged during the Josephian era a substantial outpouring of printed matter which, at least on one occasion, the government tried to enlist to gain support for an unpopular war against the Turks. Roider describes this attempt in the last paper in this section. Already the question of the individual nationalities and their respective attitudes toward military service had to be considered. Indeed, only four years later, in 1792, a junior officer asked whether an army of "Hungarians, Croats, Transylvanians, Italians, Bohemians, Moravians, Poles, Vlachs, Slavonians, Austrians, Styrians, Tyroleans, Carniolans, and Gypsies could march under one flag and fight for a cause it knows nothing about."[4] It is a truism that the war of the lieutenants differs greatly from the war of the generals, but by 1804 these sentiments were echoed by Baron Mack, meanwhile promoted to lieutenant general. In submitting his thoughts on a new infantry manual, the general noted that "no other army in Europe faces the problem of a rank and file differing totally not only in language but also in customs and attitudes from its officers."[5] He recommended an increased number of officers and noncommissioned officers, but this was at best a partial solution to a problem that would haunt the Habsburg army to the very end in 1918.

In these, as in many other things, the evolution of the military establishment and society in the eighteenth century foreshadowed the shape of things to come. And to the degree that these problems could not be resolved within the society and the body politic of the Habsburg monarchy, they also could not be resolved in the army.

## Notes

1. "Betrachtungen über die österreichische Kriegsverfassung," cited in M. v. Angeli, "Die Heere des Kaisers und der französischen Revolution im Beginn des Jahres 1792," *Mitteilungen des k.u.k. Kriegsarchivs*, New Ser., IV (1889), 24.

2. *Grundsätze der höheren Kriegskunst für die Generäle der österreichischen Armee* (Vienna, 1806), p. 1.

3. A. Sorel, *L'Europe et la Révolution Française* (Paris, 1885), I, 455.

4. A. Ellrich (ed.), *Humoristische und historische Skizzen aus den Jahren der Revolutionskriege: Aus den Papieren eines verstorbenen Soldaten* (Meissen, 1844), pp. 251–252.

5. "Suggestions for Foot Drill and Maneuvers," Kriegsarchiv Wien, Nachlass Mack, B/573–9.

# IV

# Polish Society and War

Emanuel Rostworowski

# War and Society in the Noble Republic of Poland-Lithuania in the Eighteenth Century

## A Republic Surrounded by Monarchies

The causes of the partitions of Poland constitute one of the main dilemmas of the nation's history. Without going into the details of this very complex problem, suffice it to say that the ultimate reason for the downfall of Poland was its military weakness. Strength and weakness are relative terms. Poland was surrounded by three of the greatest military powers of contemporary Europe. It is doubtful whether even a very well-armed Poland could have resisted the combined powers of its neighbors. However, the collusion of those neighbors against Poland was not predetermined by fate, but was the result of a complicated political game, which arosegfrom Poland's relative weakness.

In the eighteenth century, a ratio of one soldier to about one hundred subjects was fairly normal. The Great Powers whose populations were in the range of 20 million, such as France, the Habsburg Monarchy and Russia, thus kept permanent armies of about 200,000 soldiers. The only exception was the huge army of tiny Prussia, where there were three to four soldiers for every 100 people. Poland's western neighbor was a perfect match, from the military point of view, for the Russian and Austrian giants—and so the three Great Powers that surrounded the Polish Republic kept peacetime armies totaling half a million men. In contrast, Poland, which before the First Partition had been the second largest country in Europe with 282,000 square miles of territory and a population of about 10 million, similar to that of the British Isles or Spain, in the years 1717-1789 maintained a standing army of only 14,000 to 18,000 a ratio of one soldier to 500-600 subjects.

In a Europe containing numerous small states, there were many armies of not more than 10,000 or 20,000 soldiers; but they were the armies of the principalities of the German *Reich* or of Italy, where the ratio of soldiers was about one to every 100 subjects. An analogy with Poland could be found only in Great Britain in the era of the Whig supremacy, when this world power kept an army of 12,000 to 18,000 during peacetime, in addition to the Irish establishment of about 12,000. But the same number also served in the navy. Had Britain not been an island, the British military establishment could not have withstood a confrontation with the French armies, 200,000 strong.

In the second half of the eighteenth century, many Polish thinkers of the Enlightenment considered Great Britain and Poland to be similar. They usually divided European countries into monarchies and republics. In the latter category they included Venice, Genoa, Switzerland and the United Provinces, as well as parliamentary monarchies such as England, Sweden in the "liberty era" after the reign of Charles XII, and Poland. Later on this republican family was joined by the United States of America. The Poles considered the Anglo-Saxon political patterns to be especially familiar and worthy of imitation.[1] On May 3, 1791, Stanisław Małachowski, marshal of the Polish Diet, when presenting a draft of a new constitution, spoke about the "two most famous republican governments in our times, that is, the English government and the American one, the latter being an improved version of the former." He assured his listeners that the Polish draft "combines whatever is best and most suitable for us in both of these systems".[2]

Obviously any further analogies between Great Britain, which at that time was economically and intellectually the most advanced country in the whole of Europe, and Poland, which was both poor and backward, are quite illusory. However, in the political sphere (if not in social structure) and in constitutional thought these analogies are not without significance.

The Poles thought that, in contrast to militant and aggressive monarchies, republics by the nature of things were peaceful and mostly concerned with the preservation of their freedoms. Furthermore, these freedoms were threatened not only by outside enemies but perhaps even more also by the despotism of rulers supported by military power. In the view of the Polish nobility, it was inevitable that a large standing army must become the basis either for monarchial absolutism or for the despotism of hetmans.[3] This opinion was also shared by the philosophers of the Polish Enlightenment. In 1787, in the face of a mortal threat to Polish sovereignty, Stanisłlaw Staszic proposed the establishment of an army of 100,000 men; he presented the case most dramatically: "The day when the Polish Republic has a regular army of 100,000 men will mark both the presence of Poland in Europe, and the beginning of a march toward autocracy. The creation of political power to control the army may either accelerate or delay this process, but there is no way of averting it."[4] This statement points to one strong similarity between Britain and Poland which is in no way accidental, for in England, following the experiences of the seventeenth century, there was a deep-rooted fear of a standing army as a menace to civil liberties. Yet this "burdensome and useless army at home," as the English referred to theirs,[5] was absolutely indispensable in Poland, for Poland was not an island.

The absolute monarchies were the most effective in constructing military forces, for under absolutism even a country with a very backward social and economic structure was capable of organizing a huge, modern army, as clearly exemplified by Russia during the reign of Peter I. But this kind of regime was quite impossible in the social and political framework of Poland's Noble Republic. What is worse, after the disastrous Great Northern War, the republican system in Poland slowly disintegrated. The country was plunged into half a century of anarchy fanned by the neighboring monarchies, for which Poland's weakness was opportune. Finally, when Stanisław August Poniatowski ascended the throne in 1764, the commonwealth came completely under Russia's political domination. Attempts to cast off this domination, to modernize the country and put together a strong army, not in the spirit of enlightened absolutism but by introducing reforms passed by the Diet, formed perhaps the most interesting political experiment in East Central Europe of that day. This experiment was brutally terminated by the last war with Russia in 1792 and by the suppression of the Kościuszko insurrection in 1794.

## Society and Military Service

The background to the dramatically changing political scene was provided by a durable social structure, considered here on the basis of approximate calculations for the year 1790, that is, for Poland after the First Partition.[6] The population of the commonwealth was about nine million, of whom 45 percent were Poles, 40 percent Ukrainians, Belorussians and Lithuanians, 10 percent Jews, 2-3 percent Germans and 2-3 percent Armenians, Tatars, Russians and others. Poles comprised practically the whole of the ruling class of the nobility. Half of the nobles were of Lithuanian or Ruthenian descent, but by the turn of the seventeenth century the process of Polonization, combined with conversion to Roman Catholicism, was virtually complete.

The nobility in Poland was variously referred to either as the "knightly estate" (*stan rycerski*), which the French translated as *ordre équestre*, or as the "nation." It was a very solid community (7.5 percent of the population), uniform in respect to its official civil rights, but differing widely in social composition.

At the top there were twenty to thirty families of magnates, which, thanks to their wealth, relations and connections, really held sway in the commonwealth. This, however, was not a formal aristocracy; the Polish magnates were not peers but millionaires. As a rule they held supreme military command in the commonwealth, although many of them were more or less titular generals. A special prerogative of the magnates, and a unique anarchronism in Europe by then, was the maintenance of private armies which were still kept by many of them, mainly in the eastern provinces. The biggest regular private army, of several thousand men, including dragoons, infantry, artillery and cadets, was kept by the Radziwiłł family in Lithuania. The great Ukrainian lords usually kept a few hundred Cossack guards at their courts. The size of these private armies is difficult to establish. The numbers quoted by contemporaries—30,000 to 50,000—have to be recognized as grossly exaggerated. However, it is probable that all the private armies in the middle of the eighteenth century were equal in size to the army of the Noble Republic.

The magnates' armies were no use for the defense of the country, and their fighting ability was slight. Except for parades, guard and hunting duties, they were used for settling personal and political disputes, and for controlling the peasantry. A lot of the minor nobility served in these regiments as well as at the magnates' courts. This was an important aspect of the dependence of the poorer nobles on the great lords. A large army raised by the Czartoryski and Poniatowski families played an important part in the struggle for the throne in the years 1763-1764, but when this faction came to power, a bill of the Diet of 1764 forbade private persons to keep more than 300 soldiers at court. The magnates' militias still played an important role in the Confederation of Bar, but later on they gradually disappeared.[7] Having lost their oriental splendor and their ambitions reminiscent of German princelings, the life-style of the Polish magnates increasingly resembled that of the West European aristocracy.

Below the magnates came the *szlachta zamożna* (the nobles of means), although the demarcation line was very indistinct. They were about 200,000 strong (2 percent of the population), and included landed nobles and leaseholders. They were, to some extent, equivalent to the English gentry—a group holding all the local offices, appearing alongside the magnates in the Senate, and filling almost the whole of the House of Deputies in the Diet.

Next came the Polish oddity, about 500,000 petty nobles, who were either in service or who cultivated small farms. Many of their holdings were leased to them by magnates—a further source of dependence.

The higher ranks of the officer corps were recruited from among the wealthier nobility, but the posts of captains of horse and cavalry companions were often honorary. Active, professional army officers were drawn from among the less wealthy nobles. The fact that all military commissions could be purchased was a further element in the parallel pattern between social status and the military hierarchy. Petty nobility filled the ranks of the cavalry but also served in other formations. A small but militarily significant group derived from the Muslim Tatars who lived in eastern Lithuania. Because of the growth in numbers of the nobility and the fact that they could no longer find posts at magnates' courts, the second half of the eighteenth century saw public opinion openly demanding the employment of Poland's nobles in an expanded army. It was felt that if taxes had to be paid, they should at least go for troops of "their own kind," and that an army consisting of the nobility would best protect the commonwealth's liberties.[8]

The whole of the "knightly order" was formally obliged to serve in the so-called noble levy (*pospolite ruszenie*), and this "blood tribute" was the theoretical justification for the privileges enjoyed by the nobility. The law affirming the obligation of the gentry (*popisy, okazowania*) to report for the noble levy and to participate in periodic maneuvers was renewed in 1764 and was never repealed. From the second half of the seventeenth century, however, this medieval institution was practically defunct. All that remained of it was the myth that in its hour of danger the Noble Republic could muster 150,000 sabers in its own defense.

Another relic of medieval knight-service was the organization of the permanent cavalry troops. No wonder the proponents of modernizing the army scathingly described the cavalry as a "noble levy within the army." The system was that a squire could join the army either as an "active companion" (*towarzysz przytomvy*) possessing his own equipment, mounts and orderly (*pocztowy*), or else as an "affluent companion" (*towarzysz sowity*), in which case he could remain at home, provided that he supplied two of his "retinue" (*poczet sowity*) to the army. The difference between the companion's and the substitute private soldiers' pay went into the pockets of the "affluent companions" so that it provided a definite source of income. Besides, their title carried a measure of social prestige. "Affluent companions" were often even small children and senile old men. A companion was something between a soldier and an officer. He took part in the political life of the army—the so-called banner circles—and in the provincial dietines (*sejmiki*). Right to the very end of the commonwealth there was a law that a companion could at any time change his status from active to affluent companion, or vice versa. Because a companion's equipment differed from that of a soldier, as did the regulations they each had to obey, this flexible, half-military and half-civilian system made it extremely difficult to turn the noble cavalry into any kind of regular army force.

In Europe, as well as in Poland itself, there was a widespread conviction that a Polish noble was a born cavalryman. Maybe it was true. At one time noble cavalry had been successful in wars against Tatars, Turks and Muscovites, in the oriental type of warfare, where it was confronted by an army of the same kind. Polish cavalrymen fought well in foreign armies. Trained in the Napoleonic army at the beginning of the nineteenth century, they again raised the prestige of the Polish cavalry. But in the eighteenth century the organization of this cavalry had become deeply anachronistic.[9]

The number of burghers in Poland at this time can be estimated at around one million, half of whom were Christian, the other half Jewish. The Jews were a separate estate of people who were not included in the "municipal order." They also remained beyond the range of military service. They contributed to the city militia in Warsaw, but only in 1794, during the Kościuszko insurrection, was a Jewish volunteer regiment formed, headed by Berek Joselewicz.[10] The 500,000 Christian burghers were subject to the draft into formations other than the noble cavalry—that is, dragoons, infantry, artillery, or engineers. In the towns recruitment was allowed only "by the drum." Except for Warsaw, whose population at the end of the eighteenth century had reached 100,000 and ten other towns with populations ranging from 10,000 to 20,000, the majority of burghers lived in small towns similar in character to rural settlements. It was from these that most soldiers were recruited. Half of the Christian townspeople were Polish Roman Catholics; in the west there were many Germans among them; in the east the majority were Ukrainians and Belorussians. Germans were willingly accepted into the army as officers, noncommissioned officers, and men, whereas Ruthenians rarely entered the ranks. In towns not only the residents but also all kinds of wandering seasonal laborers were drafted. Not only volunteer recruitment was used but so, too, was forcible enlistment. The press-gang would often resort to all sorts of tricks and devices to enlist so-called volunteers by force. A soldier's life in the non noble regiments was anything but attractive. Desertion was rife.[11] The problems were the same as those in the rest of Europe where the volunteer system was becoming outdated. Yet it may seem odd that these problems should have occurred in Poland, considering the small size of its army. However, it should be remembered that under Polish law only nobles, Christian burghers, and vagrants were accepted into the army, so that an army of less than twenty thousand had to be raised from between one and two million people. In this way, the "normal" ratio of one soldier to every 100 subjects was maintained.

Finally, there was the main bulk of the population: 6.5 million peasants (72 percent), not quite half of whom were Polish, the rest being Ukrainian, Belorussian, and Lithuanian. "The peasant order" had been formally excluded from the standing army of the Noble Republic before 1790, although it had not always been so. In the seventeenth century, by virtue of the substitution of the noble levy for the personal knight-service of the nobles, peasants came to be admitted into the infantry.[12] Later this practice was stopped. The lords, however, could, if they wished, form their own peasants into improvised provincial militia. The conscription of peasants into the army also occurred during the confederations, but these were exceptional situations from the point of view of state law. The confederates of Bar put a lot of emphasis on enlistment.[13] In addition, the magnates recruited the majority of their private troops from among their own serfs. Before these private armies finally disappeared, the numerous Cossacks in armed service at magnates' courts on the eastern fringe of Poland frequently posed real danger to their masters. In 1768, a Cossack officer in Palatine Franciszek Salezy Potocki's militia, Ivan Gonta, became the leader of a great peasant uprising.[14] So when peasant recruitment was eventually resumed, special precautions were taken over the Ukrainians.

Before 1790 a peasant from a nobleman's estate could only enter the Noble Republic's army either as a private supplied to the cavalry by his master or as a fugitive serf. The serfdom laws, however, were much laxer in villages belonging to the crown (*starostwa*) and to the church, which encompassed about 30 percent of all the peasants. Many projects were put forward to allow recruitment not only in the towns but also in church and crown villages, and to form permanent peasant militia forces on the crown lands.[15] The recruitment of peasants from church and crown lands was the easier to approve. Meanwhile the lands belonging to the nobility and inhabited by four and half million peasants—half the population of the commonwealth—remained resolutely closed to recruitment. The enlistment of peasants was seen not only as a loss of manpower on the land but also as a significant threat to the principle of serfdom.

## The Army of the Noble Republic

The army that grew out of this society was divided into two: the "Polish Contingent" (*polski autorament*), a noble cavalry force that dated back to medieval knight-service, and the "Foreign Contingent" (*cudzoziemski autorament*). The latter did not consist of foreigners, although a number of foreign officers and noncommissioned officers served in it, but its regiments were organized and trained according to foreign models—in the eighteenth century mainly Saxon and Prussian. The problem of modernization of the commonwealth's army is best expressed in the mutual relationship of these two contingents and in the relative proportions of cavalrymen and infantrymen. In the major eighteenth-century European armies, cavalry constituted about 20-25 percent of the entire force. In Poland the situation was different.

Although the Diet of 1717 established a budget for an army of 24,000 men, the size of this army was a fiction right from the start. The system of pay provided soldiers' pay, but officers' salaries had also to be found from this general sum. It was assumed that the latter would consume a third of the entire budget. According to this fictional reckoning, the cavalry of the Polish Contingent was to receive 34 percent of the privates' pay allotment, while the whole of the cavalry together with the dragoons would take 57 percent of it. The reinforcement of the dragoons in the Foreign Contingent was a step toward its modernization, but it continued to have one serious weakness—far too many money-oriented officers. As the saying went: "Four officers to five grenadiers." Soon, officers' salaries devoured half the budget of the dragoon and infantry regiments, so that the Polish Contingent with its lighter load of officers came to constitute half of the army, and the infantry and artillery, only one-third.[16]

At the beginning of Stanislas Augustus's reign a number of army reforms were begun. The king set up a good cadet's school[17]—Tadeusz Kościuszko was one of its pupils—and an important cannon foundry. From then on Polish artillery and military engineering were on a high level.[18] In 1768 a new set of regulations was issued for the Polish Contingent. This order was so unpopular in the army and among the nobles that in Warsaw it was thought at first that the new reforms had caused the outbreak of the Confederation of Bar.[19] The new regulations were rescinded, though this did not end the confederation, the causes of which were far more serious. The confederates had an army varying in size from 10,000 to 20,000 men, 90 percent of whom were cavalry.[20] A number of Polish Contingent units (*chorągwie*) joined the confederation. The regiments of the Foreign Contingent mainly remained loyal to the king. The resulting four-year guerrilla (1768-1772) with Russia, combined with civil war, threw the Noble Republic's army into total confusion.[21]

After the defeat of the confederation and the First Partition of Poland, the army was thoroughly reorganized. The problem of officers' and soldiers' pay was finally resolved. The regiments were small, but the relatively large number of officers could be explained by the "cadre" nature of the army and the constant hope of expanding it. A number of noble units were turned into dragoon regiments, but according to a 1776 edict the Polish Contingent, the units of which were now called the National Cavalry and the Vanguard (*Straż przednia*), still constituted one-third of the whole, and the cavalry nearly one-half.[22] In the years 1776-1786 the king tried in vain to reform the National Cavalry. These attempts failed because of opposition in the Diet headed by Hetman Ksawery Branicki, who used this means to court the companions.[23] Another blow struck by the opposition and aimed at the king's attempts to modernize the army was a 1786 bill that denied officers' commissions to foreigners and burghers.[24]

While the struggle over the character of the "cadre" army was in full swing, there occurred the Diet of 1788 that cast off Russian political domination. With patriotic enthusiasm it envisaged an army of 100,000 men.[25] According to a new bill it adopted, no new regiments were to be formed, but the existing ones were to be expanded. Cavalry was to constitute a third of the army's strength. Again however, thanks to Branicki's party, the dragoon regiments, except for the guards, were converted into the Polish Vanguard, so that the cavalry (whose numbers were to be four times greater than before) was almost entirely based on the old companion system.[26] This system had just one advantage: it was quite easy to carry out a fast, voluntary enlistment. Soon the commonwealth had 25,000 cavalrymen, although things went much more slowly with the infantry, because of scarce finances and the imperfect system of recruitment. Impressment of "vagrants" did not produce ihe required result, and finally at a meeting of the Diet in December 1789 it was decided that peasants were to be conscripted into the infantry in a ratio of one soldier per 50 households on crown and church lands, and one soldier per 100 households on noble estates. This could bring in 18,000 new recruits.[27] Accordingly, the overall size of the army was reduced from 100,000 to 60,000 men, though the state of affairs in the cavalry was accepted as a *fait accompli*.[28]

The Four-Year Diet thus sei up an army of 60,000 men, half of whom were noble cavalry, but it failed to implement any significant reforms within this formation. During this Diet, which ran the country from 1788 to 1792 through a number of select commissions, the nobles managed to rid themselves of their old fears of military despotism. The enlarged army was popular, and enjoyed considerable social prestige, probably due to the large number of nobles who served in its ranks.

The reorganization of the army took a new turn in May 1792 when war with Russia broke out once more. The plan was modern and well prepared. According to a new bill, cavalry was to comprise a quarter of the army's strength, and the companion system was to be greatly reformed.[29] Although the reform remained solely on paper, it served as an argument for the opponents of the Constitution of May 3, who claimed to be defending "the prerogatives of the National Cavalry companions." The same point was included in the manifesto of the Confederation of Targowica, which served as a tool of Russia's policy toward the commonwealth. However, Hetman Branicki and his supporters overreached themselves by thinking that the cavalry would join hands with them.[30] The cavalry, which constituted more than a half of the 40,000 men sent to the front against 100,000 Russians, did not fight very effectively, but there were only a few isolated instances of treason.[31]

After defeat and the Second Partition, the Noble Republic still retained a force of 15,000 cavalry and 21,000 infantry with artillery.[32] In 1794 this force was to be cut in half, the other half destined for incorporation into the Russian army. However, there were rebellious groups within the army, the most active of which were the officers of the National Cavalry. Insurrection broke out, and General Antoni Madaliński and his cavalry brigade marched off to join forces with Kościuszko in Kraków.[33]

## The Nation under Arms

Kościuszko's American experiences are frequently emphasized in connection with his military ideas, which were based on the cooperation of the regular army with militia forces and a general levy of the whole nation, to which the term *pospolite ruszenie* was again applied. No doubt the latter were not without significance, but it should be remembered that, in addition to the standing army and the magnates' troops, Poland had a long tradition of general levies for improvised confederate units and of provincial militias that could be called on whenever required. An article in the Constitution of May 3 entitled "The National Military Force" gave the word "army" a very broad meaning: "The nation itself is responsible for defense against invasion of its borders and for guarding its own integrity. Therefore, all citizens shall defend this integrity as well as the national liberties. The army is but a defense force drawn from the total strength of the nation."[34]

Projects for the creation of militia forces were often put forward in political journals and during Diet debates, and were based both on a combination of national traditions and on examples taken from Switzerland, Sweden, and later, America. These ideas were supported by several foreign observers of Polish affairs, such as Jean-Jacques Rousseau, Gabriel Bonnot de Mably or Luigi Antonio Caraccioli, who praised "la Pologne guerrière" and its "constitution militaire," and acclaimed the "petite guerre" of nobles and confederates.[35] Even Voltaire, who had no sympathy for "Sarmatians," had good words for the Polish general levy.[36] A whole body of European opinion was emphatically opposed to the costly, "despotic," and "servile" nature of huge standing armies. The robot-soldier of the barracks was contrasted with the citizen-soldier, who, while working for the good of his country, could take up arms when need arose, and defend his home and land. The morale of professional soldiers was often put on the level of the well-drilled "slave-soldier" accustomed to the corporal's baton. This way of thinking was very familiar to the Poles.

The National Education Commission introduced military exercises into its schools, but the schools were mainly for the nobility.[37] Nonetheless, the need to provide military training for peasants inspired various bold projects for agrarian reform. As a typical suggestion contained in the contemporary political press, there were the words of journalist Piotr Świtkowski (1789): "Tell your peasants that they are free, and you will get a host of defenders of universal freedom, against whom the troops of all foreign invaders will be unable to achieve anything."[38]

Apart from general agrarian reform, as a way of encouraging peasants into military service various inducements were proposed, such as granting them freedom or even raising them to the nobility. There were a few utopian nobles who predicted a gradual ennoblement of the whole nation[39]—but maybe it was not a utopian idea after all, considering that in Poland nobility meant nothing more than full citizen's rights.

During the Four-Year Diet the main efforts were directed toward the construction of a standing army. At the critical moment, however, a municipal militia was organized in Warsaw, while in the spring of 1792, in face of the prospect of war, various citizens' foreaiions were set up. Insufficient effort in this direction was later cited as one of the causes of defeat. Those responsible answered that, because of the attitude of Austria and Prussia, they did not want to create the impression that in Poland there was revolutionary activity similar to that of the French Revolution.[40] However, it was not only the neighboring monarchs who could be apprehensive about the social consequences of a people's war. The peasants formed the fundamental body of the nation, and how was it possible to combine the patriotic enthusiasm of soldier-citizens with the social philosophy of serfdom?

By taking up the desperate life-and-death struggle in 1794 Poland embarked on a course that in East Central Europe was considered revolutionary.[41] Only the military matters are of concern here, however. In a country occupied by the Russians, and whose territory had shrunk to 82,000 square miles with a population of only four million, it was decided that the size of the standing army should be raised from 35,000 to 100,000 men in accordance with the 1792 bill. In order to do this, the insurgents decided to launch an intensive recruitment campaign on the ratio of one infantryman for every five households, and one cavalryman for every 50 households. Moreover, all men between the ages of 18 and 40 were summoned to take part in the general levy. Provincial militia units, which were to join in army operations, were formed from recruits who were not incorporated into the army and from part of the general levy. The rest of the levy were to take part in military exercises and protect their own area.[42] Owing to the shortage of guns, the weapons of the levy and the peasant militia consisted mainly of spears and scythes mounted on staves.[43] In order to encourage them to fight, the peasants were granted personal freedom and their corvée was reduced by 25-50 percent;[44] especially deserving cases were to be rewarded with grants of state land. The improvised peasant troops were to be headed by local nobles.

This is how things were to be in theory and in accordance with the bills passed by the authorities of the insurrection. In practice, however, the main burden of the war lay on the standing army whose size at its peak approached 70,000 men. This time the proportion between cavalry and infantry was right. The Warsaw municipal militia—some 20,000 men—fought in defense of the besieged capital.[45] A 2,000-strong unit of peasant militia gained fame at the battle of Racławice by launching a heroic scythe charge against Russian cannon. However, the peasant militia forces went outside their local areas only reluctantly, acted erratically, and frequently dispersed. The general levy proved to have no military value whatsoever. A number of noblemen suppressed the insurrection appeals, preferring their peasants to do the harvesting rather than take part in military drills. In the final stage of the insurrection the general levy was abandoned and a new recruitment drive was put into effect. It should be remembered that the insurrection lasted only a few months over a small, constantly shrinking territory, while the radical change of agrarian conditions was supposed to be implemented by the nobles themselves as the decisive gesture of the insurgent administration. Finally, under the traditional system of compulsory labor, the village and manor formed a compact unit, breakup of which was bound to have an immediate impact on food supply.

The insurrection was suppressed but the legend of its popular character survived. The heroes of this legend were Tadeusz Kościuszko, commander in chief, dressed in his russet peasant coat and attended by Wojciech Bartosz Głowacki, a hero of the battle of Racławice who was promoted from a peasant militiaman to officer rank,[46] by the shoemaker Jan Kiliński, who became a colonel in the Warsaw municipal militia,[47] and by the Jewish patriot, Berek Joselewicz.[48] The man who promoted this ideology was Jósef Pawlikowski, Kościuszko's secretary, who in 1800 published in Paris a very popular booklet entitled "Can the Poles Fight Their Way to Independence?"[49] His answer was that, if all the peasants, freed by agrarian reform, had armed themselves with scythes, the resultant force would have been invincible. By engaging in guerrilla war they would undoubtedly have been able to defeat the joint forces of Russia, Austria, and Prussia, and plant the seeds of revolution in those countries as well. This visionary brochure became the cornerstone of thought in the nineteenth century, inspiring whole generations of Polish emigrants, conspirators, insurrectionaries, and revolutionaries, who were in any case largely of noble origin. It contained a strong belief in the contentions first that the cause of Polish independence was inextricably bound up with agrarian revolution, and second that an improvised partisan war launched not against the peoples but against the governments of the partitioning powers under the slogan "For our freedom and yours" would be victorious.

In the nineteenth century, the military ideology of the risings grew out of the earlier traditions of the levy en masse and the confederations. The outlook is admirably summed up by Adam Mickiewicz in Book VI of *Pan Tadeusz.* On hearing of the approach of Napoleon's army, a provincial nobleman and magistrate, in a parochial plot with a monk and the Jewish taverner, Jankiel, tells of his readiness to lead the rising:

What is your view, sir? But enough of this. Shall the genesis
Of action start at once? Some musketeers
Can be easily found. Through the years,
I've collected power, and the parish priest
Keeps a few small cannon oiled and greased;
Jankiel has told me that he does indeed
Possess some lances, which are mine in case of need.
There'll be no lack of sabers.
So, when the gentlemen mount their chargers,
With me and my nephew at their head,
Somehow, we'll pull it off—have no dread![50]

## Notes

1. Emanuel Rostworowski, "Republikanizm polski i anglosaski w XVIII wieku" [Polish and Anglo-Saxon Republicanism in the 18th Century], *Miesięcznik Literacki* [Literary Monthly], August, 1976, pp. 94–103.
2. *Dzień Trzeciego Maja 1791* [May 3, 1791] (Warsaw, 1791), p. 63.
3. Emanuel Rostworowski, "Stanislas Leszczyński et l'idée de la paix générale," in *La Lorraine dans l'Europe des Lumières* (Nancy, 1968).
4. Stanisław Staszic, *Uwagi nad życiem Jana Zamoyskiego* [Notes on the Life of Jan Zamoyski] (Wrocław, 1952), p. 214.
5. Basil Williams, *The Whig Supremacy, 1714*–1760 (Oxford, 1942), p. 203.
6. The basic source on this is still Tadeusz Korzon, *Wewnętrzne dzieje Polski za panowania Stanisława Augusta* [Domestic History of Poland during the Reign of Stanislaus Augustus], I (Warsaw, 1897). I have reduced Korzon's estimates of the well-to-do nobility from 318,000 to 200,000.
7. Emanuel Rostworowski, *Sprawa aukcji wojska na tle sytuacji politycznej przed Sejmem Czteroletnim* [The Question of Army Reinforcement against the Background of the Situation before the Four-Year Diet] (Warsaw, 1957), pp. 29–34.
8. *Ibid.*, pp. 109–116.
9. Konstanty Górski, *Historia jazdy polskiej* [History of the Polish Cavalry] (Kraków, 1893); Emanuel Rostworowski, "Z dziejów genezy Targowicy: Sprawa Kawalerii narodowej w dobie Sejmu Czteroletniego" [From the History of the Origins of Targowica: The Question of the National Cavalry at the Time of the Four-Year Diet], *Przegląd Historyczny* [Historical Review], Vol. XLV (1954).
10. Andrzej Zahorski, *Warszawa w Powstaniu Kościuszkowskim* [Warsaw in the Kościuszko Insurrection] (Warsaw, 1967), pp. 170–173.
11. Rostworowski, *Sprawa aukcji wojska*, pp. 65–73.

12. Jan Wimmer, *Historia piechoty polskiej do r. 1863* [History of the Polish Infantry to 1863] (Warsaw, 1978), pp. 225 ff.

13. *Zarys dziejów wojskowości polskiej do r. 1864* [Outline History of the Polish Military System to 1864], II (Warsaw, 1966), 189–190.

14. Władysław Serczyk, *Hajdamaczyna* [The Hajdamak (Cossack) Uprising] (Kraków, 1972).

15. Rostworowski, *Sprawa aukcji wojska*, pp. 97–108.

16. Michał Nycz, *Geneza reform skarbowych Sejmu Niemego: Studium z dziejów skarbowo-wojskowych z lat 1697–1717* [Origin of the Financial Reforms of the Silent Diet: A Study of Financial-Military History for the Years 1697–1717] (Poznań, 1938), Władysław Konopczyński, *Polska w dobie wojny siedmioletniej* [Poland in the Time of the Seven Years' War], I (Kraków, 1909), 334–337.

17. Kamila Mrozowska, *Szkoła Rycerska Stanisława Augusta Poniatowskiego (1765–1795)* [Stanislaus Augustus Poniatowski's Knights' School (1765–1794)] (Wrocław, 1961).

18. Konstanty Górski, *Historia artylerii polskiej* [History of the Polish Artillery] (Warsaw, 1902); Jan Giergielewicz, *Zarys historii korpusu inżynierów w epoce Stanisława Augusta* [Outline History of the Corps of Engineers in the Time of Stanislaus Augustus](Warsaw, 1933).

19. Emanuel Rostworowski, "Z dziejów genezy konfederacji barskiej: Związek wojskowy Pułaskiego a dworski projekt reformy kawalerii" [From the History of the Origins of the Confederation of Bar: Pułaski's Military Association and the Court's Plan for Reform of the Cavalry], in *Z dziejów wojny i polityki* [From the History of War and Politics] (Warsaw, 1964), pp. 147–157.

20. Władysław Konopczyński, *Konfederacja barska* [The Confederation of Bar] (Warsaw, 1936–1938).

21. Bronisław Pawłowski, "Wojsko koronne i Komisja Wojskowa w dobie konfederacji barskiej" [The Crown Army and the Military Commission during the Confederation of Bar), in *Od konfederacji barskiej do powstania styczniowego* [From the Confederation of Bar to the January Insurrection] (Warsaw, 1962), pp. 11–54.

22. Rostworowski, *Sprawa aukcji wojska*, pp. 138–140.

23. *Ibid.*, pp., 151–157.

24. *Ibid.*, p. 223.

25. The basic accounts of the Four-Year Diet are still Walery Kalinka, *Sejm Czteroletni* [The Four-Year Diet] (Kraków, 1895–1896), also translated into German: *Der vierjährige polnische Reichstag, 1788–1791* (Berlin, 1896–1898); and Władysław Smoleński, *Ostatni rok Sejmu Wielkiego* [The Last Year of the Great Diet] (Kraków, 1897).

26. Act of 8 X 1789. Leonard Ratajczyk, *Wojsko i obronność Rzeczypospolitej 1788–1792* [The Army and the Defense of the Commonwealth,

1788–1792] (Warsaw, 1975), pp. 77–78.

27. Wimmer, *Historia Piechoty*, pp. 343–344.

28. Act of 22 I 1790. Ratajczyk, *Wojsko i. obronność*, pp. 81–84.

29. "Etat wojska Rzeczypospolitej Obojga Narodów dnia 22 maja 1792 w Stanach Sejmujących uchwalony" [The Standing Army of the Commonwealth of Both Nations As Resolved by the Diet of the Estates on May 22, 1792]. This law, published as a comtemporary flysheet, was not printed in the *Volumina Legum* and has remained little known in the history of the subject. Cf. Rostworowski, *Z dziejów genezy Targowicy*, pp. 29–31.

30. *Ibid.*, pp. 31–32.

31. Adam Wolański, *Wojna polsko-rosyjska 1792 r.* [The Polish-Russian War of 1792] (Poznań, 1922–1924).

32. Korzon, *Wewnętrzne dzieje*, V, 281–282.

33. Wacław Tokarz, "Marsz Madalińskiego" [Madaliński's March], in *Dozprawy i szkice* [Discussions and Sketches], II (Warsaw, 1959).

34. *Volumina Legum*, IX (Kraków, 1889), 225.

35. Rostworowski, *Sprawa aukcji wojska*, pp. 82–86.

36. Emanuel Rostworowski, "Voltaire et la Pologne," *Studies on Voltaire and the Eighteenth Century*, LXII (1968), 107.

37. Ambroise Jobert, *La Commission d'Education Nationale en Pologne* (Paris, 1941), pp. 442–444.

38. *Pamiętnik Historyczno-Polityczny, 1789* [Historical-Political Diary, 1789], IV, 1000.

39. Emanuel Rostworowski, "Kwestia społeczna Polski Kościuszkowskiej" [The Social Issue in Kościuszko's Poland], *Studia Historyczne* [Historical Studies], XI (1968), 480.

40. Emanuel Rostworowski, "Sprawa milicji mieszczańskich w ostatnim roku Sejmu Czteroletniego" [The Question of Bourgeois Militia in the Last Year of the Four-Year Diet], *Przegląd Historyczny* [Historical Review], XLVI (1955), 561–584.

41. Bogusław Leśnodorski, *Les jacobins polonais* (Paris, 1965).

42. Jerzy Kowecki, *Pospolite ruszenie w Insurekcji 1794* [The General Levy in the 1794 Insurrection] (Warsaw, 1963).

43. Andrzej Zahorski, *Uzbrojenie i przemysł zbrojeniowy w powstaniu kościuszkowskim* [Armament and the Munitions Industry in the Kościuszko Insurrection] (Warsaw, 1957).

44. Jerzy Kowecki, *Uniwersał połaniecki i sprawa jego realizacji* [The Połaniec Manifesto and the Question of Its Implementation] (Warsaw, 1957).

45. Zahorski, *Warszawa w powstaniu*, pp. 96–98.

46. *Polski Słownik Biograficzny* [The Polish Biographical Dictionary], Vol. VIII (Warsaw, 1959–1960), *s. v.* Głowacki, Wojciech (życiorys i legenda) [Life and Legend].

47. *Ibid.*, Vol. XII (1966–1967), *s.v.* Kiliński, Jan.

48. *Ibid.*, Vol. I (1935), *s.v.* Berek Joselewicz.

49. *Ibid.*, Vol. XXV (1980), *s.v.* Pawlikowski, Józef. The latest edition of his booklet is Emanuel Halicz (ed.), *Czy Polacy wybić się mogą na niepodległość?* (Warsaw, 1967).

50. Amended from *Pan Tadeusz*, trans. Watson Kirkconnell (Toronto, 1962), VI, ll. 249–258.

Marian Zgórniak

# The Financial Problems of the Polish Military System During the Saxon Period

The connection between the economic situation of a country and its military potential is undeniable. From time immemorial, arms and supplies for the army have consumed a large percentage of the national budget of every country, and with the development of new technologies and weaponry, military expenditures have increased considerably. There have been isolated cases of poor and badly equipped armies defeating much better-equipped adversaries, but usually the opposite is true. In the era of mercenary armies, European countries did not as a rule keep large permanent armies. It was only during preparations for a campaign that their size was increased. In the second half of the sixteenth century and in the seventeenth century in peacetime Poland also kept a rather small standing force—the so-called quarter army, financed from a quarter (in practice a fifth) of the revenues from all the crown land leased out for life to the nobility. In case of war, this force of a mere 4,000 men was supplemented, if necessary, by hired mercenaries or by the noble levy (*pospolite ruszenie*), troops composed of the entire nobility mobilized for the defense of the state. In the wars of the seventeenth century, these troops were not very useful, and so the size of the regular army had to be increased by hiring more mercenaries. Because of the limited financial resources of the Polish state, changing the size of the army required the Diet to introduce a new system of taxation. According to the 1652 constitution, introduced by the Diet in response to Bohdan Khmiel'nytskyi's Cossack uprising in the Ukraine, the payment of a new army, the so-called *komput*, was to be financed from taxes collected from different counties and provinces.[1] The army thus received its first territorial organization. The bill was an expression of the increasing decentralization of the state.

In the long-lasting wars of the second half of the seventeenth century Poland was more than once capable of mustering an army tens of thousands strong that did not differ very much from the armies of the contemporary major European powers.[2] For example, during the worst moments of the war with the Ottoman Empire in 1676, Poland raised an army of 50,000 from the Polish crown lands alone, and a further 16,000 from Lithuania, not to mention many private armies and magnates' retinues.[3] For the relief of Vienna, King John III Sobieski led an army of 27,000 men, while those of the Emperor and the *Reich*, hurrying to succor the capital besieged by the Turks, jointly numbered only some 47,000 men.[4] Before the military reform introduced by Peter the Great, Russia could, in the event of war, mobilize up to 160,000 men; Sweden between 35,000 and 45,000. France, which was very well populated, after the reforms of Louis XIV could alone field an army of several hundred thousand.[5]

From 1648 to 1716 Poland was devastated by wars with Cossacks, Russia, Sweden and the Ottoman Empire. In those 62 years, there were only seven years of peace. The population of Poland decreased by about one-third. Many towns were completely destroyed, agriculture and the crafts suffered severely, the conditions of the peasants worsened. Among the nobility, the power of the magnates grew, further increasing the dependence of the gentry and petty nobility.[6] The change of European trade routes, the decreased opportunities for selling Polish grain on foreign markets, and above all, the backward social and economic structure of the country made the process of the restoration of Poland all the more difficult. While in the majority of European countries there was a tendency toward strengthening the power of the state, which was backed by powerful economies and armies, in Poland there was a general decline of both the latter as well as an ever growing trend toward restricting the central power of the state. The nobility, greatly attached to its liberties and privileges, was afraid that a powerful treasury and army might enable the king to increase his power and slowly move toward absolutism, which was a characteristic feature of many European countries.

Already in the last two decades of the seventeenth century, with increased taxes and expenditures caused by the continual war, the Polish treasury was unable to raise more revenue than it had done during the reign of King Stefan (István) Báthory in the second half of the previous century.[7] Polish national income in the 1690s was more or less on the same level as that of Prussia in the last years of Elector Frederick Wilhelm's reign. In the year 1687–88 Prussia's national income was reported to be 2,500,000 thalers,[8] which equaled approximately 7,500,000 Polish zlotys. Yet it has to be remembered that, although the population of Poland had decreased from about 10 million in the middle of the seventeenth century to 6 or 7 million, it was still four times greater than that of the Hohenzollern lands. In the eighteenth century the disparity between Poland's financial resources and armed forces in comparison with the growing fiscal and military might of its neighbors became even more marked. The political and military reforms of Peter I had turned Russia into a great power which began to play an increasingly important role in Europe, exerting an ever greater influence over Poland. During the last years of Tsar Peter's reign, the income of his country of 25 million souls grew from 3.5 to 8.5 million rubles.[9] Russia had the most powerful fleet on the Baltic Sea as well as an army of 200,000 men of whom 130,000 were regulars.[10] During the reign of Emperor Charles VI, the Habsburg monarchy with a population of around 20 million had a yearly income of 33 million thalers and a 135,000-strong army; in 1756 these figures had grown to 36.9 million thalers and an army of 200,000.[11] The income of the Prussian state with a population in 1740 of 2.5 million equaled 7 million thalers, and during the Seven Years' War with the population grown to 3.7 million, 24.8 million thalers a year. On coming to the throne in 1740, Frederick the Great inherited an army of 82,000 men, and in the course of the Seven Years' War managed to expand it to 200,000. Toward the end of this war Russia and the newly elected Empress Catherine II had a treasury with a yearly revenue of 19.4 million rubles and an army of 350,000 soldiers.[12]

The weakened Poland of the eighteenth century could no longer remain on an equal footing with these neighbors growing in might. During the Great Northern War (1700–1721), which for many years devastated a considerable part of its territory, Poland was still capable of mobilizing an army of almost 48,000 men in 1703. In 1705, 36,000 men were mustered in the Polish crown lands and 12,000 in the grand duchy of Lithuania.[13] However, after the defeat of Charles XII of Sweden and his supporter Stanisław Leszczyński, the Polish nobility, worried by Augustus II's drive toward absolutism, proclaimed the Confederation of Tarnogrod aimed against his Saxon army garrisoned in Poland.[14] The conflict between the confederates and Augustus II ended in arbitration by Peter the Great, followed by the arrival of the Russian army under whose pressure the confederates reached an accommodation with the king. This agreement was ratified without protest by the so-called Silent

Diet of February 1, 1717, in Grodno. The acts passed by the Silent Diet specified the size of the army, which was not to exceed 18,000 soldiers in the Polish Kingdom and 6,000 in Lithuania. They also defined the financial principles of the state for the next several decades. Despite the continuous devaluation of Polish currency in the period 1717–1764,[15] the income of the Polish state was set at a mere 5,655,704 zlotys in the kingdom and 1,907,627 zlotys in the grand duchy.[16] These sums were mostly made up of revenues from the "quarter" (the leased-out crown lands) and from taxes, mainly the poll tax. Officially, the nobles were liable to this capitation, but in practice the entire sum came from individual estates and was split equally among the peasants and burghers. The peasants on the crown lands had also to pay a wintering tax (*hiberna*) to aquit themselves of the obligation to provide the upkeep of the soldiers garrisoned on these estates during winter. The peasants living on ecclesiastical lands were forced to pay a "charitable donation" (*subsidium charitativum*) as well as to fulfill certain other customary obligations going back to the Middle Ages.[17] A tiny part of the state revenues was derived from a tax paid by burghers for the right to manufacture and sell alcoholic beverages.[18] The budget introduced in 1717 proved inadequate to maintain even a modest army of 24,000 men. For purely financial reasons, the size of the Polish and Lithuanian armies for many decades had to be smaller than established by the Silent Diet. In 1745 their numbers amounted to 12,600 officers and men in the Polish Kingdom and 4,000 in Lithuania.[19] The structure of these small armies was old-fashioned, especially as a result of the excessive strength of the cavalry in comparison with the infantry and artillery.[20]

Although some modernization of the infantry and to a certain extent of the artillery[21] was introduced during the reign of Augustus II, modernization of the cavalry to adapt it to the changes taking place in the art of war in the eighteenth century occurred much later, when the Polish kingdom was already in decline. During the whole period of the Wettin dynasty in Poland, no reform of fiscal policy was achieved, so nothing could be done about expanding the size of an army that remained out of all proportion to the size of the state. Contemporary political journalism showed there were quite realistic possibilities to expand the size of the army despite the economic backwardness and antiquated social and economic structure of the country. National income could have been increased several times over had the land been taken away from the magnates and the crown and leased to subjects, not to mention introducing taxation of the nobility and clergy.[22] As it was, however, the state's financial resources were not much bigger than those of individual aristocratic families.[23] Yet the country was already seriously threatened by its mighty neighbors. The reforms undertaken in the 1760s came to nothing, partly because of foreign intervention. The neighboring Great Powers did not wish the Polish state to be strengthened, and the Httempts to introduce reforms and counteract outside intervention brought on the First Partition of Poland. The various reforms introduced by the Four-Year Diet, aimed at increasing the strength of the army and adopting a new fiscal policy, were also frustrated by foreign interference. Poland was punished by further partition and ultimately the total annihilation of the Noble Republic.

## Notes

1. Marian Kukiel, *Zarys historii wojskowości w Polsce* [Outline Histpry of the Army in Poland] (5th ed.; London, 1949), p. 87.

2. In the years 1660–1661 the Polish kingdom's army numbered 32,000 men. Jan Wimmer, "Materiały do zagadnienia organizacji i liczebności armii koronnej w l. 1660–1661" [Data on the Question of the Organization and Strength of the Crown Army in the Years 1660–1661], in *Studia i materiały do historii wojskowości* [Studies and Data in Military History], VI, Pt. 1 (Warsaw, 1960), 213–249.

3. Kukiel, *Zarys historii,* p. 94; Jan Wimmer, *Historia piechoty polskiej do roku 1864* [History of the Polish Infantry to 1864] (Warsaw, 1978), pp. 246–249; *idem, Wojsko polskie w drugiej połowie XVII wieku* [The Polish Army in the Second Half of the 17th Century] (Warsaw, 1965), pp. 203–205.

4. Jan Wimmer, *Wyprawa wiedeńska* [The Vienna Expedition] (Warsaw, 1957).

5. Janusz Sikorski, *Zarys historii wojskowości powszechnej do końca XIX wieku* [Outline History of General Military Systems to the End of the 19th Century] (Warsaw, 1972), pp. 376–378.

6. J. Rutkowski, *Historia gospodarcza Polski (do 1864)* [Polish Economic History (to 1864)] (Warsaw, 1953), pp. 187–194.

7. A Pawiński, *Skarbowość w Polsce i jej dzieje za Stefana Batorego* [Finance in Poland and Its History under István Báthory] (Warsaw, 1981), *passim.*

8. A. F. Riedel, *Der brandenburgisch-preussische Staatshaushalt in den beiden letzten Jahrhunderten* (1866), p. 32.

9. R. Rybarski, *Skarb i pieniądz za Jana Kazimierza, Michała Korybuta i*

*Jana III* [Finance and Money under John Casimir, Michael Korybut and John III] (Warsaw, 1939), p. 503.

10. Emanuel Rostworowski, *Historia powszechna: Wiek XVIII* [General History: The 18th Century] (Warsaw, 1977), pp. 377, 379.

11. F. Bujak, *Siły gospodarcze: Przyczyny upadku Polski* [Economic Forces: The Causes of Poland's Downfall] (Kraków, 1918), pp. 104–105.

12. *Ibid.*

13. Tadeusz Nowak and Jan Wimmer, *Dzieje oręzia polskiego do roku 1793* [History of Polish Arms to 1793] (Warsaw, 1968), p. 337.

14. Józef Gierowski, *Traktat przyjaźni Polski z Francją w 1714 roku* [Poland's Treaty of Friendship with France of 1714] (Warsaw, 1965), pp. 230–247; *idem, Historia Polski 1505–1864* [History of Poland, 1505–1864], I (Warsaw, 1978), 377–378.

15. In 1500 one ducat containing 3.5 grams of fine gold was worth 30 grosz and was equivalent to 1 Polish zloty. In 1601 its value had risen to 60.5 grosz, in 1699, to 420 grosz, and in 1786, to 540 grosz, that is 18 Polish zloty. E. Tomaszewski, *Ceny w Krakowie w latach 1601–1765* [Prices in Kraków in the Years 1601–1765] (Lvov, 1932), Table I.

16. M. Nycz, *Geneza reform skarbowych Sejmu Niemego: Studium z dziejów skarbowo-wojskowych z lat 1697–1717* [The Genesis of the Silent Diet's Financial Reforms: A Study in Military Financial History in the Years 1697–1717] (Poznań, 1938), Table II.

17. Marian Zgórniak, *Relikty średniowiecznych powinności skarbowych na wsi małopolskiej XVI-XVIII w.* [Relics of Medieval Fiscal Dues in a Little-Poland Village of the 16th-18th Centuries] (Warsaw, 1959), pp. 96–102.

18. Nycz, *Geneza reform*, Table II.

19. Nowak and Wimmer, *Dzieji oręzia*, p. 343.

20. T. Korzón, *Dzieje wojen i wojskowości w Polsce* [History of Wars and Military Affairs in Poland], III (Kraków, 1912), 107–116.

21. Wimmer, *Historia gospodarcza*, pp. 288–330.

22. Rutkowski, *Historia gospodarcza*, p. 200.

23. The yearly income from the lands of Prince Karol Radziwiłł amounted to 5,000,000 Polish zloty. The joint incomes of 12 members of the Potocki family around 1750 was estimated at some 8,300,000 zloty. Bujak, *Siły gospodarcze*, p. 97.

Jerzy Kowecki

# The General Levy in Eighteenth-Century Poland

From medieval times to the fifteenth century the noble levy (*pospolite ruszenie*) was the main organizational form of military force in Poland. Its basic structure was established in the first half of the twelth century. From the fifteenth century onwards, the main role in warfare was borne by the standing army. The noble levy was called out only in moments of great danger, or for local defense when an enemy was in the immediate vicinity.

The noble levy began to lose its fighting value in the fifteenth century, both because of its character and its social composition. The core of it at first were the feudal knights, and then, with the development of social estates (*stany*) the nobility and gentry (*szlachta*). With the passage of time the latter evolved from fighting knights into shrewd owners of manors (*folwarki*) primarily concerned with their own wellbeing. Changes in weaponry and in the principles and methods of warfare (strategy and tactics) now demanded a trained standing army. The required level of training was difficult to attain to campaign with militiamen. They were recruited from the *szlachta*, and trained only on short exercises known as reviews. Members of this privileged estate would turn out for these reviews with increasing reluctance, being more concerned for their properties.[1] As a result the noble levy was called out rarely, and its importance declined.

Tadeusz Kościuszko's decision to revert to the tradition of the *pospolite ruszenie* in the uprising of 1794 resulted from the necessity of putting the whole nation under arms to struggle against Poland's invaders, especially Russia. The decision was made possible by a new conception of the noble levy.[2] The requirement for a war that embraced the whole nation was a natural consequence of the political and military situation of the *Rzeczpospolita* (Polish-Lithuanian Commonwealth) and its social relations.

Poland, wholly deprived of sovereignty even in that small area of land left after the partitions of 1772 (Russia, Prussia, Austria) and 1793 (Russia and Prussia), had too small an army to count on success in war against even one of its invaders. Yet in their plans the insurrectionary leaders had to take into account the need to fight simultaneously with Russia and Prussia, maybe even with Austria. Kościuszko therefore wrote in December 1793 in his instructions for the uprising: "We cannot rise with a small number of men, but with a force more than half that of the enemy . . .; we must start with a hundred thousand . . . and increase it gradually to two hundred thousand."[3]

It was impossible to create such a large regular army on an *ad hoc* basis, especially under foreign occupation or in a consequent state of insurrection. The sole possibility was to supplement the regular army with improvised formations; the call to all levels of the population including the wide mass of the peasants, was thus inevitable. In any case it coincided with the political and social program of the uprising. It was to bring not only independence to the state but also social freedom to the peasant masses and the liquidation of serfdom and corvée.[4] According to a chronicler, Kościuszko summed up the program in September 1793 in the brief but significant sentence: "I will not fight for the *szlachta* alone; I want freedom for the whole nation and only for this will I lay down my life."[5] This whole situation was explained to the revolutionary authorities of France before the uprising by Franciszek Barss, the insurrectionaries' representative in Paris, in a memorial of February 19, 1794. He wrote that the *szlachta* could not fight alone, "without calling for help from the masses, to whom it will be forced to reinstate their ancient rights. Only under this condition will the masses join the *szlachta*."[6]

Putting into practice the idea of the *pospolite ruszenie* in its new form, Kościuszko creatively exploited native Polish and foreign models and experiences. Among native examples he delved back to the old traditions of the campaigns of the nobles, which were supplemented by the participation of the peasants. These traditions appealed to the *szlachta*, without whom it would have been impossible to organize the uprising. The greatest contribution to preinsurrectionary thinking about the organization of the armed forces of the uprising came from critical analysis of the experiences gained while preparing the defense of the country during the Four-Year Diet (1788–1792). Inspiration was also drawn from the many publications on the subject that appeared at the time, and from experience in the war with Russia of 1792 in defense of the Constitution of May 2. During the latter no appeal had been made to the peasants and as a result it had not been possible to field an adequate army against the Russians.

Under the influence of the Enlightenment, in Poland, as in France and America, political and military thinkers were convinced of the superiority of the soldier-patriot, fighting with belief in the righteousness of the cause he was defending and with personal involvement in the victory of that cause, over the "serf" soldier. Contemporary ideologists were reinforced in this conviction by the achievements of France and the United States. Kościuszko had personal experience of both those revolutions, and exploited it in forming his concept of Poland's insurrectionary armed forces. In America he had learned both the advantages and disadvantages of its militia. In Year II of the revolution he had been in France, where on August 23, 1793, a national draft had been decreed. Kościuszko in America had lived through times of drama connected with the system of short-term recruitment and the disbandment of units before the creation of new ones.[7] He also saw how local militia organizations sometimes saved situations where other formations failed. Though the militia could not replace an army, the supreme commander of the insurrection decided to make use of it in Poland. The value of the experiences of the British colonial struggle in America was also not lost on other insurrectionary leaders of 1794, even if they knew them only from reports in the Warsaw newspapers that publicized them.[8]

Above all, revolutionary France offered the perfect example of the total mobilization of a country and people for the needs of war, even if, because of a different situation, both military and especially social, French methods could not be copied in Poland. Recruitment in France had encountered difficulties. The levy en masse passed by a resolution of the Convention of August 23, 1793, which in effect meant the conscription of all Frenchmen, was not feasible in practice. Instead there was a return to the wholesale recruitment of bachelors between the ages of 18 and 25, which was realized with greater success.[9]

Ultimately, the core of the armed forces of the Kościuszko insurrection was the regular army. At the outset it was 30,000 strong, and increased during the course of the war to 100,000 by means of the old Polish practice of drafting the peasant conscript (*rekrut dymowy*). For every ten foot soldiers one peasant was recruited; in the cavalry the proportion was one peasant for every 50 cavalrymen. In consequence, the social composition of the regular army changed, as did the relationship of the infantry to the cavalry (traditionally made up of the *szlachta*) to the advantage of the former.

Equally important in the eyes of the insurrectionary planners, the regular army was to be supplemented by various improvised military formations. Among these the leading role fell to the *pospolite ruszenie,* next to the city, palatine and provincial militias and to volunteer units. In preparing the country for the uprising already in the conspiratorial pre-insurrectionary period Kościuszko appointed commanders of palatinates and districts, who were given the rank of territorial major generals. Their main task, as Kościuszko told them, was to lay the foundations for the military organization of the country. They were also to command various improvised units when the rising began.

In insurrectionary planning and in the orders of the conspiratorial period as well as in practice, the *pospolite ruszenie* of 1794 differed most notably from its *szlachta* predecessors in the principle of universality. In the course of the insurrection there was a return to the traditions of the old *pospolite ruszenie,*[10] but this was only a tactical maneuver to convince the nobility and gentry of the necessity to accept the new institution. The source of inspiration for the new general levy lay in the experiences of revolutionary France. Hugo Kołłątaj, one of the leading creators of the program of the uprising and a keen observer of developments in Paris, thus wrote towards the end of 1793: "The levy en masse makes the French unbreakable, so that even the most intelligent and brave armies of the united enemy are unable to break through, let alone annihilate them."[11] It is neither here nor there that the French levy en masse did not correspond to the Polish *pospolite ruszenie,* for it made Frenchmen continuously subject to recruitment into the army until the enemy was forced out of France. The Polish formation was more like the *insurrection générale* demanded by the Jacobins.[12]

March 24, 1794, saw the publication of the act of insurrection, the swearing of Kościuszko's famous oath in Kraków market place, and the first decree ordering "universal self-armament." This decree enjoined all citizens without distinction among the estates to ready their arms for the supreme commander's call.[13] Universal armament was the basis of the new general levy. The following day Kościuszko began to issue orders prescribing the principles of this armament, military exercises in towns and villages, and the organization and conditions for calling out the *pospolite ruszenie.* Formations of the general levy began to be set up rapidly where the need was greatest.

Eventually, a declaration of June 6 standardized the norms for the levy for the whole country.[14] It codified a number of decrees in accordance with Kościuszko's orders. The preamble described the purpose of the levy: "To arm all the citizens of the Polish land, to turn the whole nation into soldiers, and to count on them for fast and strong support for the army whenever the need arises." All men between 18 and 40 years of age were obliged to take up arms. Equipment was to consist of "the arms available" to militiamen, "that is, rifles, shotguns, pikes, straight scythes, and cutlasses." In each village and town military drill was obligatory for these armed masses every Sunday. The *pospolite ruszenie* was to act to meet the needs of the "palatinate, district or the whole province." A general of the regular army was responsible for calling out any particular formation, which would be headed by the local squire. The minor nobility and gentry were required to join up in person.

In accordance with Kościuszko's recommendations, the levy was to cooperate with field forces, not to act independently, because of its lower fighting quality due to its less professional leadership and poorer training and equipment—mainly pikes and scythes. Tragic experiences of militiamen annihilated by enemy forces made them stand by these regulations.

The implementation of such a universal mobilization of the population and its call-up to active duty entailed various difficulties. Economic shortages and the still feudal social structure of the Noble Republic presented considerable obstacles. The greatest problem was the resistance of a significant part of the *szlachta* partly out of fear of arming the peasants but mainly for economic reasons. The majority of the manors of the *szlachta* were reliant on the serfs' labor dues. Yet Kościuszko had been limiting the amount of these dues since the beginning of the uprising. Calling up the peasants further reduced the size of the work force on the manors. The low level of national consciousness among the peasants was also a problem. The reforms that had been proclaimed could not be carried out everywhere, and were not enough of an incentive to induce the peasants to join the rising of their own accord. Ultimately their attitude depended mainly on local conditions, the introduction of reforms, and the actions of the *szlachta*, clergy, local authorities and army commanders.

At all levels of insurrectionary authority, perforce composed mainly of the *szlachta*, conservatives were often in the majority.

Though spurred by patriotism, they made no contribution to implementing the reforms to be carried out by the regulation commissions, who were the insurrectionary authorities on the palatinate and district level. In extreme cases they sabotaged the levy. The conservative nobility and gentry could not reconcile themselves to the democratization of society. There were cases where they refused to take part in campaigns together with the peasants. Also a large number of front-line officers, trained in the old schools and military traditions, were incapable of cooperating with improvised units. The lack of adequate officer cadres for the *pospolite ruszenie* was keenly felt.

In consequence advantage could not be taken of more than a small part of the theoretical possibilities afforded by the general levy. It should be remembered, however, that the improvised forces were not to take part in major independent actions but only in support of the regular army and under its cover. Their main purpose was local or district defense against smaller enemy units.

In the event, the part played by the *pospolite ruszenie* in major battles was small. Properly commanded and under the cover of fire from regular units, however, it could decide the outcome of a battle at a critical juncture. Kościuszko led his scythemen thus at Racławice on April 4, 1794. On June 6 at Szczekociny peasant units withstood a cavalry charge, and then bravely carried out nightly attacks from besieged Warsaw. Ineptly led, on the other hand, the militiamen could not long withstand enemy fire.

There are no sources available to give a precise figure for the strength of the *pospolite ruszenie,* but it is generally accepted that some 150,000 went through its ranks. This was no small figure. The levy was effective above all because of its size, and thus had meaning in shows of strength. The armed demonstration of the Kraków area levy in the second half of April, for instance, paralyzed the endeavors of the Prussians to attack the city and helped Kościuszko to survive a difficult situation. In May the movement of militiamen from the Chełm and Lublin areas stopped Russian attempts to cross the river Bug. There were other similar examples.

The levy also played a role in clearing neighboring territories of enemy outposts, covering its own districts, tying down small enemy forces, capturing minor command posts, cutting communications and signals, making intelligence difficult, and fighting off patrols and forays. Such were its activities during the insurrection.

On September 18 on Kościuszko's instructions the Supreme National Council suspended summoning the *pospolite ruszenie* and order a new call-up of recruits. From then on the militia was to be mustered only in the "greatest need" and with the agreement of the supreme commander.[15] This decision was not taken for military reasons alone. Economic reasons were more important. The uprising was threatened by famine. The reduction of corvée and especially the removal of large numbers of peasants from agricultural work and their recruitment to active duty had disorganized agricultural production. This was especially menacing because of wartime destruction and requisitioning by the enemy armies. News of harvest delays and lack of labor came from all parts of the country. Giving up the general levy thus became a necessity for the survival of the insurrection.

The impact of the September 18 order can be seen clearly in the reactions of various commanders. Many demanded to keep the militia, and even to halt new campaigns because without its help they could not hold their positions. As a result the levy was still active in October in the last month of the insurrection.

The significance of the *pospolite ruszenie* was greater than just its military role. Universal armament, the training of large masses of people, preparing them for service in other formations, such as the militia, volunteer units, and the regular army, mobilized the whole country, made it spiritually prepared, and created the climate for the struggle. It had a great influence on the peasantry, on their minds, and on raising their national consciousness. It established a tradition of peasant participation in the struggle for independence. This tradition already bore fruit in one of the first plans for another rising in the nineteenth century. In their joint work, *Can the Poles Win Independence?* the Jacobin Józef Pawlikowski and Kośiuszko were able to write in 1800, "Our peasants are experienced, they have been under fire, and in the districts where they did not take an active part they know that their brothers fought and captured cannon with scythes. The spirit of freedom has spread through the populace of Poland."[16]

## Notes

1. Cf. Marian Kukiel, *Zarys historii wojskowości w Polsce* [Outline History of the Army in Poland] (5th ed.; London, 1949), pp. 11, 22; Janusz Sikorski (ed.), *Zarys dziejów wojskowości polskiej do roku 1864* [Outline

History of the Polish Army to 1864], I (Warsaw, 1965), 23–24, 108–110, 256–257, 296–299. Both contain extensive bibliographies on the subject.

2. For greater detail see Jerzy Kowecki, *Pospolite ruszenie w insurekcji 1794 r.* [The General Levy in the Insurrection of 1794] (Warsaw, 1963), which lists sources and literature on the subject.

3. Tadeusz Kościuszko, *Pisma Tadeusza Kościuszki* [The Letters of Tadeusz Kościuszko], ed. Henryk Mościcki (Warsaw, 1947), pp. 75–76.

4. See Jerzy Kowecki, *Uniwersał połaniecki i sprawa jego realizacji* [The Połaniec Manifesto and the Matter of Its Realization] (Warsaw, 1957), esp. pp. 21–39.

5. Józef Pawlikowski, "Pamiętnik o przygotowaniach do insurekcji Kościuszkowskiej" [Memoir on the Preparations for the Kościuszko Insurrection], *Przegląd Polski* [Polish Review], X, No. 7, 1876, 86.

6. Aleksander Kraushar, *Barss palestrant warszawski, jego misja polityczna we Francji 1793–1800* [Barss, the Warsaw Advocate, His Political Mission in France, 1793-1800] (Lvov, 1903), p. 57.

7. Douglas S. Freeman, *George Washington: A Biography*, IV: *Leader of the Revolution* (New York, 1951), 128, 146–148, 180–183, etc., and V: *Victory with the Help of France* (New York, 1952), 146, 186, 195, etc.; Max Savelle, *A Short History of American Civilization* (New York, 1957) pp. 170 ff.; Christopher Ward, *The War of the Revolution* (New York, 1952), I, 111 ff.

8. Zofia Libiszowska, *Opinia polska wobec rewolucji amerykańskiej w XVIII wieku* [Polish Opinion about the American Revolution in the 18th Century] (Łódź, 1962), pp. 53–54.

9. Cf. Antoine Picq, *La Législation militaire de l'époque révolutionnaire* (Paris, 1931); Marcel Reinhard, *Le Grand Carnot* (Paris, 1950), I, 133, 170, 216–217, 223, and II, 10–12 *et seq.*; *idem*, "Observations sur le rôle révolutionnaire de l'armée dans la Révolution française," *Annales historiques de la Révolution Française*, XXXIV (1962), No. 168, pp. 171, 178 ff.; Jacques Godechot, *Les commissaires aux armées sous le Directoire: Contribution à l'étude de rapports entre les pouvoirs civils et militaires* (Paris, 1937), I, 21–22

10. For example, the proclamation of the Commission for Order of Kraków Palatinate of April 19, 1794 (Jagiellonian Library, Kraków, ref. 222410/III, position 50); proclamation of the Supreme National Council of July 7, 1794, in Szymon Askenazy and Włodzimierz Dzwonkowski (eds.), *Akty powstania Kościuszki* [Acts of the Kościuszko Insurrection], I (Kraków, 1918), 412–413.

11. Lucjan Siemieński (ed.), *Listy Hugona Kołłątaja pisane z emigracji w r. 1792, 1793, i 1794* [Hugo Kołłątaj's Letters Written from Exile in 1792, 1793 and 1794] (Poznań, 1872), II, 161.

12. Picq, *La législation militaire*, pp. 82, 103–105; Reinhard, *Le Grand Carnot*, II, 71.

13. Resolution of the Citizens of Kraków Palatinate of March 24, 1791 (Jagiellonian Library, Kraków, ref. 222410/III, position 8).

14. Askenazy and Dzwonkowski, *Akty powstania Kościuszki*, I, 267–269.

15. *Ibid.*, II, 171–173.

16. *Czy Polaci mogą się wybić na niepodległość?* [Can the Poles Win Independence?] (2nd ed.; Warsaw, 1831), p. 26.

Leonard Ratajczyk

# Changes in the Polish Officer Corps in the Eighteenth Century

The eigtheenth century saw fundamental changes in the nature of European armies and their place in society. The absolutist states did away with costly mercenary troops and conscripted in their place large standing forces armed with flintlocks and bayonets. To enhance their military effectiveness, these armies perfected the linear order of battle, which demanded precise maneuvering and relatively high firepower. In order to function, such armies required professional cadres of commissioned and noncommissioned officers whose chief task was to train the troops in linear tactics and to maintain the rigid discipline necessary to perform complicated movements under fire. Soldiers were expected neither to act nor think on their own; commonly they were considered cannon fodder. In the perhaps apocryphal words of Frederick II of Prussia, the common soldier was to fear his corporal more than the enemy. To this end, discipline was harsh and usually enforced by corporal punishment.

These new standing armies reflected the feudal social order. The rank and file consisted of compulsorily enlisted, unlettered serfs and homeless vagrants. The noncommissioned officers were recruited among the burghers, impoverished nobility and gentry, and a few richer peasants. Cavalry and infantry officers were drawn from the nobility, while artillery and engineer officers belonged to the educated bourgeoisie. Noncommissioned officers signed up for long terms; enlisted men served for life or until disabled. As C. Wright Mills observed, "The balance of forces within the ruling strata has been reflected within the standing army. And finally, there developed in this standing army, or in many of them, certain gratifications which even men of violence often want: the security of a job, but more, the calculable glory of living according to a rigid code of honor."[1]

The most socially homogeneous officer corps and the remotest from the men of the ranks was that of the Prussian army from which King Frederick William I (1713–1740) had expelled all cavalry and infantry officers not of noble descent. He and his son, Frederick II, the Great (1740–1786), believed that only noblemen could make good officers and provide reliable support for the throne. To ensure enough officers, the sons of the nobility and gentry had to enter the army, and only after completing their military service were they allowed to pursue other careers. In the Habsburg Empire and France the restrictions were less stringent: a burgher of distinction might receive a commission. Even there, however, the higher ranks were reserved for the nobility, while general officers almost invariably came from the high aristocracy.

Because the new organization and tactics required standardization, officer training schools were set up in some countries. In others, officer cadets learned their profession in elite guards regiments. The need for training tended to diminish the practice of purchasing commissions, and, though not entirely eliminated, it gradually gave place to promotion through seniority.[2]

For the feudal ruling strata the main attraction of service as an officer was that it accorded with their class interests. The officer corps thus became the mainstays of the concepts of dynastic allegiance, loyalty to the colors, and a special military code of honor. Moreover, the officer corps enjoyed privileges that separated them from the noncommissioned officers and other ranks whom they regarded as a feudal labor force. Under such circumstances, despite the emphasis on military education, dilettantism was widespread among officers. Excessively large, the officer corps often had no real duties. In most armies, the daily task of training and supervising the rank and file was handled by the noncommissioned officers. Idleness contributed to a low level of morale among the commissioned.[3]

By contrast, noncommissioned officers, separated by a considerable social gap from officers, had few more rights than other ranks. While noncommissioned officers' duties kept them apart from the rank and file, their lowly social origins closed further opportunities for promotion in the army. In time, their resentment against the privileges extended to commissioned gentry and nobility led them to look toward the common soldiers for support. In the end, it was only the revolutionary transformations begun by the French Revolution that relieved the noncommissioned officers' ambiguous position.

The Polish-Lithuanian Commonwealth established its standing army in 1717, based on voluntary recruitment, not conscription, into the infantry, and "companion" recruitment into the cavalry.[4] Its strength, however, was quite inadequate for the defense of the commonwealth's vast territories as well as small in comparison with the armies of neighboring Russia, Austria, and Prussia. This was due to the reluctance of the Polish nobility expressed both in the Diet (*Sejm*) and in the local dietines, to bear the burden of taxation necessary to maintain a larger standing force. In 1717 the paper strength of the army was only around 16,000 men, including some 1,600 officers and noncommissioned officers. The Noble Republic, one of the major European powers of the age, had the weakest standing army of any.

At the head of the military hierarchy stood four hetmans each with an annual pay of 400,000 zlotys, or as much as the total pay of 2,000 infantry soldiers or 66 major generals. The hetmans, representatives of the richest magnate families, were appointed by the king for life and in time became practically independent. In the eighteenth century they were frequently in opposition to the crown and used their troops for separatist and personal aims. The monarchs in turn tried to curb the hetmans' power by removing them from their positions.

Within the Polish crown (or royal) army of 12,000 and the Lithuanian army of 4,000, the hetmans exercised command through appointed officers who numbers, because of pressure from status-hungry noblemen, increased well beyond the needs of the service. Following late-seventeenth-century reform of the forces and introduction of contingents organized on foreign models, both the commissioned and the noncommissioned officers were more diversified in professional and class terms than was the case in other European armies.

In the mounted units of the Polish Contingent the officers came exclusively from the minor nobility and gentry, while the noncommissioned officers were "companions" of gentle origin.[5] The peasants serving as orderlies together with these "companions" formed the rank and file. The units of the Foreign Contingent, including dragoons, infantry, artillery, and engineers, were organized along Western European lines. Their officers were generally of foreign origin but appointed by the king.[6] According to Jan Wimmer, "These foreigners rarely proved loyal and devoted citizens of the state that paid their high salaries and assured their careers. For the most part they were men of no scruple who toadied to the king in pursuit of their private aims while robbing their subordinates, growing rich at the expense of the common soldier. These officers were rarely of noble descent, but even so felt no ties with the Polish soldier of peasant or burgher origin."[7]

During this period commissions could be purchased by any who could afford to do so, normally costing between one and four years' pay. There were neither educational nor practical prerequisites. Officers usually neglected their duties and often stayed away from their units, caring more for their social life and landed interests than military service

As in other armies, the noncommissioned officers were primarily selected from the rank and file with the right to appoint them vested in the regimental commanders. When proposing a soldier for promotion, company commanders had to certify his blameless services as well as his ability to read and write.[8] Noncommissioned officers had a poor reputation as being dissolute and maltreating the lower ranks.[9]

The small army of the Noble Republic in the first half of the eighteenth century was thus poorly organized and commanded. It did not constitute a force evoking respect from the neighboring absolutist states—a situation that was welcome to the dominant minor nobility and gentry. A weak army could not enforce the power of the state, and because the state itself was weak, it was believed that it would have no external enemies. In this conviction the antimilitarism of the Polish nobility reached its peak in the first half of the eighteenth century.[10]

Much-needed reform and reorganization of the Polish armed forces were not implemented until the reign of the last Polish king, Stanislaus II Augustus Poniatowski (1764–1795), when the country was faced with the danger of losing its independence and being partitioned. Four major phases can be distinguished over this relatively brief period of 30 years. In the first stage there were changes in the command system, and improvements in the organization and training of the officer corps, followed by the destruction of the military forces of the Confederation of Bar and the events connected with the First Polish Partition. The second stage, from 1775 to 1788, saw efforts by the Military Department of the Permanent Council to improve organization and raise the strength of the army. The third stage, only four years long, saw the military reforms of the Four-Year Diet cut short by the confederation of Targowica and the

Polish-Russian war of 1792. Finally, the fourth stage witnessed the desperate attempt to save the remnants of the state and the army during Tadeusz Kościuszko's insurrection of 1794, the collapse of which resulted in the temporary liquidation of all Polish armed forces in the final partition of Poland in 1795.

On his accession, Poniatowski clearly recognized the risks of military dilettantism and the dangers of leaving the armed forces in the control of the hetmans and their subordinates.[11] Reform of the archaic military leadership he considered his first priority. In 1764 the Polish Crown and the Lithuanian military commissions were set up. Both were composed of Diet deputies and senators and presided over by hetmans with one vote for each. Thus although much later than in other states, the nucleus of the future ministry of defense was created on the principle of collective administration by representatives of what was still a "nation of gentry."[12]

Among the first actions of these commissions was to reduce the number of officers and to recommend increasing the number of soldiers. In the cavalry, the "companions" of gentle birth, who were treated like officers, were prohibited from absenting themselves from their units and taking extra posts elsewhere. In 1765 the king founded the first "Knights' School" to educate sons of the petty nobility and gentry for military and civil service. Among its graduates were some of Poland's most illustrious officers and statemen, all imbued with the spirit of patriotism.[13] To raise the combat effectiveness of the army, the king commissioned Saxon and Prussian officers who, together with a handpicked group of Polish magnates and officers, began to restructure the army along more modern lines.[14]

Further reforms were checked by the Confederation of Bar of 1768–1772. The act of confederation abolished the two military commissions and restored the power of the hetmans. At the same time the confederation, under the influence of the gentry who feared the reforms and under pressure from the Russian ambassador, began a struggle for supremacy in the state. The confederates hoped to raise an army of over 200,000 by voluntary enlistment of the gentry and conscription of peasants and burghers, but its strength never exceeded 20,000 poorly disciplined cavalry from the minor nobility and gentry. French officers brought in by the confederates proved of little value. Senior commanders were elected by the confederate assemblies, while commissioned and noncommissioned officers were appointed. Organized along obsolete lines, lacking a central command and a qualified officer corps, without financial resources or assured supplies, the confederate army was an ineffective force, and ultimately disbanded. At the same time, however, the civil war weakened and disorganized the standing army which had remained loyal to the king.

The next round of military reforms did not begin until after the Second Partition when the Diet created the Permanent Council, presided over by the king, to administer the affairs of state. Within this council the former commissions were replaced by a Military Department, which still included the hetmans who were to preside over it in turn. Thus once again the hetmans' authority over the military establishment was limited, a fact to which they never became reconciled but which did not prevent them from collecting their high salaries. The Diet also fixed stipends for the ancient high military officers of state, now mere figureheads, such as the Field Clerk, the Camp Commandant and others. By resolution, the Diet abolished the old system of soldier "rations" and replaced it by a set scale of pay provided by the Treasury Department.[15] The reorganization of the army into territorial divisions conferred greater stability by quartering its scattered units in permanent garrisons, generally small towns where the officers would take up residence.

Finally the Diet abolished the obsolete division of the army into Polish and Foreign Contingents. All officers were to be commissioned by the king who, "taking into consideration the abilities, merits, and years of service, was to make a choice from among candidates proposed by their superiors."[16] Candidates for the ranks of general and colonel were proposed by the Military Department. Only in the National Cavalry recruited from the nobility was the prerogative of making promotions left to the captains, with the king only granting commissions. All noncommissioned officers, normally craftsmen, journeymen, and other urban workers, but occasionally also impoverished noblemen, were selected according to their abilities and had to be able to read and write.

As before, the officer corps was drawn primarily from the nobility, except in the technical branches, artillery and engineers, where entry was open to educated burghers and foreigners. In these latter branches there existed a degree of social mobility. As Konstanty Górski has pointed out, "The Polish artillery enjoyed a privilege which, to their detriment, other branches of the service did not enjoy, namely, that of promotion to commissioned rank without distinction as to estate, so that every gunner who had the zeal and made progress in his education could become an officer."[17] However, this did not mean, as J. Jedlicki believes, that social diffusion "had already before the Four-Year Diet led to the obliteration of divisions among the estates."[18] This view is not borne out by recent research. For the most part, the officer corps continued to reflect the feudal structure of society.

And for this very reason, there were considerable differences in career expectations even for the nobles in the army. The most privileged were the magnates, their protégés and those with connections at court or with generals, regimental commanders, and so forth. They had great influence on promotions by granting or selling military ranks.[19] Nor were military careers the sole source of income for the richer nobles who often derived considerable revenue from their estates.[20] It goes without saying that in such a hierarchical structure the distance between commissioned officers on the one hand and noncommissioned officers and common soldiers on the other was as great as that between the nobility and the commonalty in civilian life.

Such social distinctions did not contribute to cohesiveness in the expanding military establishment. On the contrary, they weakened combat effectiveness, impaired discipline, spurred desertions, and caused other negative phenomena. Progressive officers such as Austrian Lieutenant General F. Kiński or General of Crown Artillery F. Brühl were well aware of this. Brühl asserted: "Birth is of no significance for soldiering; in war the blood of a plowboy is as valuable as that of the son of the first lord." And: "Subordination is not attached to a person but to the office or to seniority in the service."[21] Although such ideas were offensive to the minor nobility and gentry, and destructive of their privileges, they paved the way for new relationships consistent with the spirit of the Enlightenment in the more progressive feudal armies.

The next step in resolving the problem of defense by strengthening the armed forces and regulating their cadres was taken when the Four-Year Diet convened in 1788. The Diet, the supreme legislative body, exerised executive authority through commissions. It reformed the high command and resolved to raise the strength of the army from 18,000 to 100,000. The Permanent Council and its Military Department were abolished and replaced by the Military

Commission of the Diet. The hetmans continued to preside over this body in turn, but were responsible to the Diet. Meanwhile the king's influence in military matters was also reduced.

Assigning military authority to the Diet and its commission was a phenomenon peculiar to Poland on the European scene, as was the equality of privilege of the nobility and gentry of the commonwealth. The lack of strong royal authority, the obsolescence of the institution of hetman, and the failure to develop alternative forms of command could not yield effective one-man leadership, the most efficient for an army. Only when faced by war with the confederates and Russia, and in defense of the May 3 Constitition, did the Diet hand over authority to the king and dissolve itself. It was the right course, but too late. The king was unprepared for such a role and the war was too brief for him to be able to establish a capable system of command. Even so, he did make improvements. A War Council was established as a consultative body at the national level, while autonomous commands were established in the various theaters of operations—in Podolia, Volhynia, the Ukraine, and Lithuania. The early end of hostilities, however, did not permit an adequate test of these new institutions.

Another nettle grasped by the Four-Year Diet was the military cadres, still burdened by the unfavorable heritage of the mercenary period and the decline of the Polish military establishment in the first half of the century. In spite of the gravity of the situation, the Diet, excessively influenced by the particularist interests of the nobility, was unable to find a progressive solution for the cadres of the army, now 65,000 strong. Noble domination of the state was reflected in the nobility's preponderance among the commissioned and noncommissioned cadres and prevented the Diet from implementing reforms both in the number and proficiency of the cadres. In 1788 the number of officers fluctuated between 1,000 and 2,700 at most 4.5 percent of the total establishment; by 1792 there were some 4,300 non-commissioned officers, about 7 percent of the establishment.

Within its very limited possibilities, including its brief period of activity, the Diet and its military leadership either eliminated or at least weakened a number of ancient abuses in the cadres. Promotions were made more equitable, and favoritism was curtailed. Minimum qualifications were required for the purchase of rank, and this had a positive influence on the entire army. These developments influenced the noncommissioned officers, though this body still requires additional research. During this period the noncommissioned officers of the Polish Commonwealth improved their position, in contrast to the royal French army where, according to J. Brun, the noncommissioned officers were poised on the brink of disaster.[22] While in France there was an unbridgeable gap between noncommissioned officers and the rank and file on the one hand and commissioned officers on the other, in Poland the noncommissioned officers, recruited among the poorest nobles as well as talented burghers, formed a link between the various groups, an avenue of promotion from private to commissioned ranks. This was an important factor for the development of the cadre, despite the continuation of nepotism.

The present author's research, published in his book on the military establishment at the time of the Four-Year Diet[23] and on the state of the military cadre in the Polish Commonwealth, has confirmed to a considerable degree the findings of S. Herbst that in these years "the former sinecurists, laymen, ignoramuses or at best goldbricks, with the hetmans first and foremost, were in almost complete retreat. They were replaced above all by young officers, products of the cadet corps and the new school system. They excelled in education, ability, and patriotism. In the tense political struggles of the Four-Year Diet they became mature citizens."[24]

The achievements of the Four-Year Diet were shattered by the victory of the Confederation of Targowica, which was opposed to progressive reform, and by the intervention of the neighboring powers. The army, improved with such great difficulty, was reduced. A substantial proportion of the officers, nobles, and burghers, however, would not accept this.[25] To save the remnants of the Polish state there arose the first national insurrection led by Lieutenant General Tadeusz Kościuszko who declared: "I shall not fight for the gentry alone."

This sentiment determined the character and objectives of the insurrection and its improvised armed forces. Military leadership was entrusted to progressive officers headed by Kościuszko and made full use of the cadres shaped during the Four-Year Diet. In addition, the insurrection enriched the cadre with new elements. These were the officers of the irregular troops—the militia, the general levy, and the various volunteer formations. Although here too the gentry dominated, a few craftsmen and peasants rose to officer rank. In Warsaw Jan Kiliński, a cobbler, was promoted to the rank of colonel and appointed commander of the Twentieth Infantry Regiment in recognition of his services. Wojciech (Bartosz) Głowacki, a scytheman from Rzedowice who distinguished himself in battle, was made a cornet in the Kraków Grenadiers. But these were isolated instances. The gentry was reluctant to introduce popular elements into the officer corps. The conservative stance of the gentry and clergy prevented the insurrection from becoming truly national and appealing to all burghers and peasants, and this was one of the main reasons for its collapse. It was followed by the Third (and last) Partition and the disappearance of the Polish state.

The steadily improving, patriotic and more radical cadre of the Polish army had to seek refuge in exile. At home many were drafted into the armies of the partitioning powers. Many pressed the struggle for Polish independence at every opportunity. It was they who formed the Polish Legions in Italy in 1797 and first sang "Poland has not yet perished as long as we are alive," a song that encouraged successive generations to fight for independence and that has become the national anthem of a reborn Poland.

The attitude of the Polish army cadres in the eighteenth century toward the issues of defense and preservation of the sovereignty of the state was a function of the nobility's level of political awareness. This, as shown, underwent considerable changes. Attitudes during the Saxon period in the first half of the century were different from those prevailing during the reign of Stanislaus II.

According to T. Łepkowski, Polish society sank to its lowest poitical level in the period around 1730–1750.[26] The army at that time was neither tied to the nation nor an instrument of defense for the weak and disorganized state.[27] Both native and foreign officers considered military service as a personal career unrelated to the question of defending the country. Little was said or written about defense. One exception was the exiled King Stanislaus Leszczyński who advocated strengthening Poland's defense in a pamphlet entitled *A Free Voice to Secure Freedom*, published in 1733 in France. It is unknown whether his ideas ever reached the Polish army cadres, however.

Under the influence of the progressive ideas of the Enlightenment in the second half of the century awareness of the need for defense was promoted by the Czartoryski party, aided by the king, the Diet and the "Knights' School." Awareness was also fostered by such ideologists of the Polish Enlightenment as Stanisław Staszic and

Hugo Kołłątaj. National defense was strengthened by the Four-Year Diet and was a major concern of the military cadre both during the war of 1792 and the Kościuszko insurrection.

The "Knights' School" paid particular attention to the moral education of its cadets. The aim was to shape a progressive citizen-patriot, a defender of the homeland. According to its commandant, Prince Adam Czartoryski, a cadet "should love his motherland and hold its good above all, and be prepared to sacrifice himself in its service."[28] These principles were disseminated by various means throughout the officer corps.[29] Moreover, through the Commission for National Education, considered the first Polish ministry of education, patriotic precepts were introduced even in elementary schools where, when possible, they were taught by commissioned and noncommissioned officers.

Celebrations of national days, dedications of colors, and swearing-in ceremonies were all used as occasions for patriotic indoctrination, reminding both soldiers and civilians of their duty to defend the homeland. Finally, a proper patriotic attitude toward the defense of the nation was encouraged among the military by regulations issued in particularly large numbers during the Four-Year Diet. These the officers and noncommissioned officers not only had to know but had also to transmit to the rank and file.[30]

As a result, during the armed confrontations of 1792 and 1794 the Polish army displayed greater fighting spirit and patriotism than the enemy. The army's morale and political attitudes, shaped by the officer corps, won the highest acclaim throughout society. Łepkowski concluded: "In the course of six or seven years, the national army had become an important factor in the life of the disintegrating state and in the consciousness of a considerable number of citizens. . . . In Poland's situation the national army had become the most important defender of the state and the nation."[31] This remained an element of significance all through the period of Poland's struggle for national liberation.

The commissioned and noncommissioned officer corps of the Polish army in the eighteenth century, though only slightly changed in class composition, underwent a profound transformation in professional, political and moral terms when the country found itself in mortal danger. From an almost alien element, indifferent to the fate of the state, demoralized and pursuing its own interest, the cadre of the Polish army together with the mass of its soldiers by the end of the century had become the most valuable part of society and the mainstay of the struggle for Poland's independence.

## Notes

1. C. Wright Mills, *The Power Elite* (New York, 1955), p. 173.

2. Jan Wimmer, *Historia piechoty polskiej do roku 1864* [History of the Polish Infantry to 1864] (Warsaw, 1978), pp. 293–294.

3. During the Seven Years' War (1756–1763) in France, "the proud and arrogant officer corps, with few exceptions, showed in combat its professional incompetence and moral decadence." J. Brun, *Narodziny armii narodowej 1789–1794* [The Birth of a National Army, 1789–1794] (Warsaw, 1956), p. 19.

4. For further detail see Leonard Ratajczyk, "Przyczynek do sprawy werbunku i poboru rekrutów na ziemiach polskich w XVIII wieku" [A Contribution to the Question of Recruitment and Conscription on Polish Territory in the 18th Century], in *Studia i materiały do historii wojskowości* [Studies and Materials in Military History], XV, Pt. 1 (Warsaw, 1969), 61–72.

5. "Companion" is derived from the term "companion recruitment," that is, voluntary enlistment in the army by the gentry together with serf attendants on the principle of the gentry's free choice of the company in which it would serve.

6. The Polish kings in the first half of the 18th century were themselves of foreign descent: Augustus II (1694–1733) and Augustus III (1734–1763) were both of the Wettin dynasty of Saxony. This is why there were many Saxon officers in the commonwealth army.

7. Jan Wimmer, *Wojsko Rzeczypospolitej w dobie wojny północnej 1700*–1717 [The Army of the Commonwealth in the Time of the (Great) Northern War, 1700–1717] (Warsaw, 1956). pp. 441–442.

8. *Ibid.*, p. 445.

9. Wimmer, *Historia piechoty*, pp. 321, 323, 325.

10. Cf. H. Krawczak, "Sprawa aukcji wojska na sejmach za panowania Augusta III" [The Army Reinforcement Question in the Diet during the Reign of Augustus III], in *Studia i materiały do historii wojskowości*, VII, Pt. 2 (Warsaw, 1961), 40–41.

11. Regretting his lack of military experience, the king in his memoirs, written before 1775, made an observation that has not lost its significance to this day: "Whoever, having been called on to rule a state, does not know war himself is like a man deprived of one of his five senses. If during his lifetime he is forced to wage a war, long or short, he conducts it through his generals and through them alone, and they, realizing that he must not only act through their arms but also see through their eyes, will take advantage of

their superiority. The army's attachment is then only to the commanders who lead it, and it obeys the soveriegn only to the extent that they allow." *Pamiętniki Stanisława Augusta Poniatowskiego* [Memoirs of Stanislaus Augustus Poniatowski] (Dresden, 1870), p. 7.

12. In 18th-century Poland the gentry and nobility regarded themselves alone as the "nation," even though, as Władysław Smoleński noted, they numbered only some 300,000 men, women and children out of a total population of 7.4 million. Enjoying numerous privileges, the nobility and gentry "held whole masses in serfdom; they were for the nation as a whole what the crowned despots were in the neighboring states." Smoleński, "Szlachta w świetle opinii wieku XVIII" [The Nobility and Gentry in the Light of 18th-Century Opinion], in *Pisma historyczne* [Historical Writings], I (Kraków, 1901), 45.

13. The most extensive monograph on the school and its graduates is Kamila Mrozowska, *Szkoła Rycerska Stanisława Augusta Poniatowskiego 1765–1794* [The Knights' School of Stanislaus Augustus Poniatowski, 1765–1794] (Wrocław-Warsaw-Kraków, 1961).

14. Emanuel Rostworowski, *Sprawa aukcji wojska na tle sytuacji politycznej przed Sejmem Czteroletnim* [The Question of Army Reinforcement against the Background of the Situation before the Four-Year Diet)] (Warsaw, 1957), p.. 51.

15. *Zarys dziejów wojskowości polskiej do roku 1864* [Outline of Polish Military History to 1864], II: *1648–1864* (Warsaw, 1966), 202; "Awans w wojsku oboyga narodów" [Promotion in the Army of the Two Nations] (pamphlet of the 18th century, National Library, Warsaw, Special Collection, No. 33237). This improved the army's financial situation, but did not eliminate all problems. Regiments and companies still received their pay irregularly, a subject of frequent complaints in reports to the Military Department. Cf. Gen. J. Morawski's note, October 8, 1784 (Central State Historical Archives, Vilnius (Lithuanian SSR), 18278), pp. 62–63.

16. *Zarys dziejów wojskowości*, II, 205. In the records of the Military Department for the years 1775–1786 there are memoranda to the effect that the king, in accordance with regulations, was unwilling to promote more generals than established, to grant supernumerary commissions, etc. The king, on the other hand, did order a review of all officers' complaints about promotion, and ordered publication of lists of regimental cadres and a promotion roster so that everyone knew what to expect and would have no grounds for complaint. Central Archives for Historical Documents, Warsaw, Militaria of Jabłonna, Vol. XXXVII.

17. *Historia artylerii polskiej* [History of the Polish Artillery] (Warsaw, 1902), pp. 172–173.

18. *Klejnot i bariery społeczne: Przeobrażenia szlachectwa polskiego w schyłkowym okresie feudalizmu* [The Armorial Crest and Social Barriers:

Changes in the Polish Nobility in the Declining Years of Feudalism] (Warsaw, 1968), p. 59.

19. This is evident in documents about favoritism in promotions in the State Archives in the Wawel, Kraków, Młynów Archives of the Chodkiewicz Family, Militaria, Military Chancery Files (1776–1785), Nos. 15–17. Inequities in the granting of promotion are also apparent in numerous officers' complaints in Polish archives and libraries, and in the discussion published under the tital "Rozprawa między kilku wojskowymi komu się najsprawiedliwiej awanse należa" [A Dispute among Several Soldiers about Who Most Rightly Deserves Promotion] in *Polak Patryota* [The Patriot Pole] (Warsaw, 1785), III, 831-848.

20. For example, the purchase of land by Maj. Gen. Stanisław Łuba, commander of the Great-Poland Brigade of the National Cavalry, and his brother Col. Samuel Łuba, or the leasing of a village in the Kalisz district for 3,000 zlotys a year by Col. Ignacy Hoffman in 1788. Provincial State Archives, Poznań, Kalisz Gr. (municipal records) 473, k. 203–204, 411: 475, k. 210. Leaflets distributed in 1789 contended: "Officers' pay has seemed to prove so far that only a wealthy person can be an officer." National Library, Warsaw, Special Collection, XVIII, 1.1362, p. 160.

21. *Elementarz służby wojskowej tłum. z dzieła grafa F. Kińskiego . . . z niektórymi przydatkami przez A.F.B. G.A.K. oficera polskiego* [The Elements of Military Service Translated from the Work of Count F. Kiński . . . with Some Additions by A.F.B. G.A.K., a Polish Officer] (Warsaw, 1787), pp. 70–71.

22. Brun, *Narodziny,* p. 20.

23. Ratajczyk, *Wojsko i obronność Rzeczypospolitej 1788–1792* [The Army and the Defense of the Commonwealth, 1788–1792] (Warsaw, 1975), pp. 193–269. This is the most thorough study to date of the 18th-century Polish officer corps.

24. S. Herbst, *Demokratyczne tradycje Wojska Polskiego: Sesja naukowa poświęcona wojnie wyzwoleńczej narodu polskiego 1939–1945* [The Democratic Traditions of the Polish Army: (Proceedings of a) Scholarly Session on the Polish National Liberation War, 1939–1945] (Warsaw, 1959), p. 130.

25. Their moral and political dedication to the cause of defending progress under the May 3 Constitution, their love for the homeland betrayed by the magnates, and their repudiation of that treachery were shown by the protest resignations of their commissions by Gens. J. Poniatowski (the king's nephew and commander in chief of the Crown Army), T. Kościuszko, A. Gorzeński and M. Zabiełło and some 200 other officers. Leonard Ratajczyk, "Rola wojska w kształtowaniu polskiej świadomości narodowej w okresie walk wyzwoleńczych w XVIII i XIX w." [The Army's Role in Shaping Polish National Consciousness during the Struggle for Liberation in the 18th and

19th Centuries], in *Armia, Wychowanie, Polityka: XX lat WAP* [Army, Education, Politics: The Twentieth Anniversary of the M(ilitary) P(olitical) A(cademy)] (Warsaw, 1971), pp. 65–66.

26. T. Łepkowski, *Polska—narodziny nowoczesnego narodu 1764–1870* [Poland—Birth of a Modern Nation, 1764–1870] (Warsaw, 1967), p. 12.

27. *Ibid.*, p. 250.

28. J. Karwin *et al.*, *Z dziejów wychowania wojskowego w Polsce od początku państwa polskiego do roku 1939* [On the History of Military Education in Poland from the Foundation of the Polish State to 1939] (Warsaw, 1965), p. 355. This book discusses these problems in detail.

29. Education at the "Knights' School" had very favorable results for the nation. Graduates of the school were among the most progressive deputies in the Diet; in office they were carriers of political culture of a high caliber; and in the army they formed the most progressive element in the officer corps. Among the school's graduates were Gen. Tadeusz Kościuszko; Gen. Jakub Jasiński, organizer of the Kościuszko insurrection in Lithuania, Jacobin poet, and model of patriotism and heroic dedication to his homeland; Kazimierz Nestor Sapieha, deputy to the Diet in 1778, 1784, 1786 and 1788, general of the Lithuanian artillery, chief of the corps of engineers, marshal of the Lithuanian Confederation at the Four-Year Diet, and participant in the Kościuszko insurrection; Gen. Michał Sokolnicki, distinguished military engineer, active participant in the Kościuszko insurrection, coorganizer of the Polish Legions in Italy in 1797, general of the army of the Duchy of Warsaw, wartime governor of Kraków (1807–1812), after 1812 aide-de-camp to Napoleon I; Stanisław Woyczyński, member of the Society of Friends of the May 3 Constitution, deputy in the Four-Year Diet, major general of the Rawa provincial militia, coorganizer of the Polish Legions in Italy, general in the army of the Duchy of Warsaw (1807–1813), and member of the Paris Military Committee in 1814 who helped Polish soldiers to return home after Napoleon's abdication.

30. These instructions, regulations and patriotic ceremonies are examined in detail in Ratajczyk, *Wojsko i obronność*, pp. 327–349.

31. Łepkowski, *Polska*, pp. 252–253.

Józef Andrzej Gierowski

# The Polish-Lithuanian Armies in the Confederations and Insurrections of the Eighteenth Century

Of the many experiments that the Polish-Lithuanian Commonwealth initiated in the eighteenth century, the act of unilateral disarmament proved to be particularly disastrous. Apart perhaps from a few similar events in tiny Italian states, it had no parallel in contemporary Europe. Nor is it easy to ascertain the reasons for it. The increasing threat from Poland's neighbors, territorial annexations, and wars waged on its territory for almost 70 years (from 1648 till 1718 the country enjoyed only some 10 years of peace) resulted neither in the creation of a strong standing army nor in the transformation of the Noble Republic into a military state. The exhaustion of a country ruined by military operations played some part, but the political doctrines of the nobility were of equal importance. While proclaiming their readiness to defend the country "with their own breasts," the nobles ignored the need to develop their armed forces.

Only after disarmament had become a fact did foreign meddling in the affairs of the commonwealth make the nobles realize their country's true plight. Their mentality began to change slowly, and the need to improve the state began to dawn on them. In the era of the Enlightenment the army, formerly a marginal group, became a symbol of independence. Once a disintegrating factor, the army grew into one of the most important components of the process of integration.

The changes that were taking place can be seen through the resolutions of regional dietines (*sejmiki*), debates of the Diet, and political writings that focused on military questions. The phenomenon that succinctly but most pointedly characterized the attitude to the army of the nobility as a whole however, was the confederations. These spontaneous associations of the nobility were connected with crucial moments in the struggle for the nature of the state and for its independence. Their influence on noble attitudes was particularly deep. Sensations caused by the confederations were short-lived but of great intensity and highly dramatic, and thus counterbalanced other, lasting and systematic influences. They left permanent marks on the psyche of the nobility. While the importance of research into long-term influences should not be belittled, analysis of the place given to army problems in the confederations is sufficient. It reflects summarily the whole attitude of the nobility to the army, and the attitude of the army to the other members of society.

From the middle of the seventeenth century the army of the commonwealth entered a period of crisis which culminated in the middle of the eighteenth century. Poland and Lithuania were unable to keep pace with European powers that were increasing their military manpower. This was mainly the result of weak central government, particularly the Diet. Frequent adjournments interrupted the Diets' fiscal efforts and made it impossible to secure regular pay for the forces. Fixed taxes did not apply to noble estates and sufficed to maintain only a very modest army that could not cope with the needs of a vast country.

Had the commonwealth not been at war, its fiscal revenue might conceivably have covered the most unavoidable expenses. According to diet resolutions of 1667 and 1678, the standing army in peacetime was to number 18,000, which required a budget of some 3.7 million zlotys, that is, less than a million thalers. Most of such a sum could be raised from fixed taxes. In time of war, however, the number of soldiers had to be doubled, sometimes even trebled. Yet only on rare occasions (for example, between 1673 and 1678) were Diet resolutions passed regularly enough to raise adequate sums for the enlarged army. Even then the tax burden was noticeably low in comparison with other European countries. Usually arrears were incurred which were not beyond the country's solvency (in 1699 the debts to the Polish crown army amounted to 33 million zlotys—about 4 million thalers), but which, during times when the Diets and regional councils were paralyzed, became a deadweight that would frustrate any rational policy in army matters for years. Although the nobility, pressed by unpaid soldiery, managed occasionally to pay the arrears, the lack of systematic tax resolutions made it impossible to maintain an adequate army (it was the Diet that set the military budget) or to ensure discipline. What then proliferated were the military associations *(związki wojskowie)* which would collect their own dues, usually occupying crown and church lands until they had settled accounts with committees of noblemen. There were numerous cases of soldiers deserting for not being paid.[1]

After the disastrous experience of the early eigtheenth century, when even the estates of the nobility did not escape plunder by unpaid domestic soldiers, fixed direct taxes were introduced in 1717 which also applied to the properties of the nobility and gentry. At the same time appropriations were made for an establishment of 24,000 men. As no adequate provison was made for officers' pay, however, officers could be paid only by commuting these appropriations for men of the line. This immediately reduced the actual army's strength to approximately 18,000 men. In the course of time the number of officers increased, while the number of soldiers decreased. The situation was not changed by the formation in 1726 of an infantry regiment consisting of peasants from crown lands (*wybrancy*). Although the establishment was raised to 30,000 in 1775, army manpower did not change considerably until the Four-Year Diet of 1788–1792. So for more than fifty years the Noble Republic numbered among the states without armies able to defend them.

This did not mean that the commonwealth possessed fewer than 20,000 troops *in toto*. Some towns, like Gdańsk, were obliged to keep troops, as were the indivisible entailed latifundia (*ordynacje*) like those of the Zamoyskis or Ostrogskis. Particular districts or provinces could recruit troops for their own purposes (so-called *powiatowe* or *łanowe* regiments). Such recruitment, which often replaced the general levy, consisted of raising one soldier for a specified number of acres or homesteads from every kind of property. The ratio was generally smaller from crown or church lands, and on towns only rarely were taxes levied for the recruitment of soldiers. In the eighteenth century the Cossacks, who had strengthened the army so effectively in the first half of the previous century, were no longer in the service of the commonwealth. Many of them, however, still served in the private armies of magnates. The manpower of these private forces is difficult to establish; it varied according to needs. It is assumed that their numbers ranged from under 20,000 up to 30,000. Their main task was the defense of the latifundia, and their military quality was uneven, though it was not necessarily lower than that of the standing army.

The composition and organization of the army had not changed significantly since the reform of King Ladislas IV in the 1630s, when its division into Polish and Foreign Contingents (*autorament*) was introduced. The former consisted of the traditional cavalry units of the Polish and Lithuanian forces. The "foreign" troops consisted of infantry trained according to Western models and of cavalry units capable of reinforcing infantry or even of fighting on foot as reiters or dragoons. The proportion of cavalry to infantry was traditionally one to one, which differed from the European average, but which was dictated by the character of the enemy and by the vast territory over which the army operated. The army's weapons were slightly outdated by comparison with Western Europe, but in the early eighteenth century the infantry was equipped with the rapid-firing flintlock and bayonet. Artillery was good until the Great Northern War. Thereafter there were plenty of guns in the commonwealth, but they were more suited to firing a salute than to battle. A weak point of the army was its undeveloped engineering units.

The Polish-Lithuanian army was based primarily on the local soldier. This does not mean, however, that this soldier was only either Polish or Lithuanian. The commonwalth was a multinational state, so the ethnic composition of the army was varied, and as well as Germans, Ukrainians and Belorussians it included a considerable number of Tatars. The number of foreigners decreased steadily in the seventeenth century. Their number was lowest at the time of Sobieski. Similarly, few foreigners served in the eighteenth century, other than the Royal Guards of the Saxon kings. It was more common for citizens of the commonwealth to find service in the Saxon, Prussian, Austrian or even Russian armies. The nobility formed an increasingly smaller part of the army, comprising only 20 percent of its strength in the late seventeenth century. This was true not only of the Foreign Contingent but even of the Polish cavalry establishment, including the hussars, where service was both prestigious and expensive. The officer cadre, however, consisted almost entirely of nobles; for a commoner an officer's career was exceptional, though not impossible. The highest functions and honors were given as a rule to the magnates or to the well-to-do minor nobility and gentry (*srednia szlachta*).

The decline of military *esprit de corps*, increasingly serious from the late seventeenth century, became disastrous. Its sources can be found in the long series of failures that the army experienced after the relief of Vienna, in difficulties over pay, and in political indecision. At the time of the Great Northern War (1700–1721), the army and the nobility remained unconvinced of the rightness of the cause for which they happened to be fighting, whether they were on the side of Augustus II or of Stanisław Leszczyński. Whole units changed sides without much scruple, and gave more thought to plundering the estates of their adversaries than to fighting the enemy. A reform of 1717 made the situation still worse. To avoid the concentration of income in the hands of the treasury, that is, the king, the nobility introduced the system of so-called military repartitions, which consisted of allotting fixed taxes from specified estates or districts to particular military units. This system changed solderiers into tax collectors. Time-consuming military requisition resulted in a considerable part of the army being absent from their units for months on end, frequently busy with the administration of estates. Although special treasury tribunals, consisting mainly of commissioners chosen from among the nobility by regional councils, were supposed to look after the systematic distribution of pay and decide matters of controversy, they functioned fecklessly and did not fulfill their task.

In such circumstances the commonwealth soldier was turning into a parade soldier, required to take part in state, church or family ceremonies. Hence, the chronicler Jędrzej Kitowicz called him a "funeral soldier."[2] The Polish Contingent became particularly suitable for special occasions, as its men looked splendid and put more emphasis on fine horses, gem-studded caparisons, and magnificent uniforms than on military training. Only the troops of the Contingent and the guards were of some fighting value. This situation continued throughout the Saxon era.

The condition of the army matched the general internal circumstances of the Noble Republic. The political system is not easy to classify, and calls to mind the words of Samuel Pufendorf about the German *Reich* that it was "a shapeless body, similar to a monster." Historical opinion in Poland today holds that the commonwealth in the second half of the seventeenth century and the first half of the eighteenth was a state of magnates where the government of the country was run by an aristocratic oligarchy, split internally in a struggle for supremacy. The continuous equilibrium among the aristocratic factions was the reason why all attempts to strengthen the central government failed and the commonwealth found itself on the brink of a catastrophe that could not be averted by belated attempts at reconstruction. The petty nobility and gentry, which once had striven for leadership of the country's political life, now cooperated with the magnates in keeping the *status quo ante*. In any case, the whole Establishment unanimously believed the basis of the political system to be almost perfect, though it did not always applaud the practice of the moment.

Political writers and Western historians, especially French and English, have frequently described the situation of the Noble Republic after the late seventeenth century as "anarchy." They have usually understood it as a state of random chaos, inertia, social and political confusion, where everything depended on the license of strength. It would be difficult to deny that such phenomena were quite common, yet it seems that they were rather subsidiary manifestations of a more general process. It can be argued whether it was not a matter of anarchy as a specific form of social organization. The society of the nobility, certainly, comprised a privileged group that lived at the expense of the serfs and the subjugated middle class. This had little in common with the later, nineteenth-century notion of anarchy. Worship of the rights and liberties of the nobility led to doubting the need for efficient functioning of the instruments of state power, especially of the central power, that might impair this Golden Freedom.

Meditating in the early eighteenth century on ways of improving the commonwealth, Stanisław Dunin Karwicki inculpated the "antiquated politicians," the defenders of the status quo: "They do not allow discussion of the necessary improvement, having taken it into their heads that Poland lives by nongovernment and will die by nongovernment. More, they have changed it into a subtler conceit, persuading us that nongovernment is inextricably connected with Poland. As the salamander lives by the fire that devours all things, so Poland preserves itself by the nongovernment by which other states fall. For it, in contrast, all government is adverse and harmful."[3] The Polish word "nongovernment" (*nierząd*) in this interpretation is equivalent to "anarchy." A eulogist of the political system of the Noble Republic, Jan Dębiński, claimed soon afterwards that the commonwealth existed "not in some foreign fashion . . . but in our own Polish way, which is not human, but divine."[4] It would be difficult to imagine more utopian pretensions.

At its roots there were a number of myths—common origin, equality, unanimity, the "power of noble breasts." The first of these assumed the alleged common descent of the whole nobility from the ancient Sarmatians, and imputed to them a uniform style of life and thought. The second claimed that there was no difference between a great magnate and a poor, petty nobleman, for both enjoyed the same rights and liberties. The myth of unanimity was based on the assumption of the nobility's complete uniformity; the resulting *liberum veto* was supposed to safeguard the right of each individual to save liberty when it was endangered. Finally, the "power of noble breasts," as expressed in the noble levy *(pospolite ruszenie)*, was seen as the strongest shield of the Noble Republic, defended by the bodies of its citizens.

For a society endowed with such ideas, efficient instruments of central power were superfluous. The king was sufficient to uphold the authority of the commonwealth in relations with other states, yet his power had to be limited lest it threaten the Poles' Golden Freedom. The *liberum veto* effectively paralyzed the Diet. The institutions that counted most were those in which the whole nobility could take part: regional dietines, confederations, elections of the king.

In practice these assumptions led to serious deformities, to the great advantage of the magnates, who exploited the weakness of state organization for their private ends. They resulted in increasing internal chaos and in the debility of the commonwealth abroad. That it had not fallen victim to its neighbors' expansiveness much earlier was most probably due to the protective shield that had been raised around it in the early eighteenth century, partly by the efficient Saxon Electorate, and partly by Russia which, by supporting anarchy in the commonwealth, was able to establish its protectorate there quite firmly in the reign of Augustus III.

The weakness of the Polish-Lithuanian army was thus not caused by mischance, the devastation of the country, or fiscal distress. It was the result of the general conservative concept of the state, which ensured that neither the king nor any faction became dominant. The reason the standing army was not dispensed with altogether was that it became an important factor in maintaining the balance between the contending aristocratic factions. This was so already in the 1660s during the rebellion of Jerzy Lubomirski, when the victorious magnate had failed to overthrow the king by humiliating him. Then began the fruitless struggles for domination of the commonwealth, struggles in which only the actors changed.

The crown hetmans, the commanders in chief of the Noble Republic's army, might be expected to have had the chance to create a strong power center, which might have initiated the reconstruction of the state. A few hetmans, beginning with Lubomirski, tried to make use of these opportunities, and Jan Sobieski owed the crown to his military office. There were effective checks on the organization of the high command, however, to prevent these possibilities. State dualism enabled the Lithuanian hetman to offset the crown hetman, as even Sobieski experienced, and the field hetman at the side of the grand hetman acted in a similar capacity. Still, the defenders of Golden Freedom were alarmed by the opportunities of the hetman's office, and in 1717 the Diet limited his authority. The hetman's power remained sufficiently strong to thwart despotic tendencies of the monarch, yet too weak for the hetman to reach for the throne. Besides, there were neither statesmen nor genuine leaders among the hetmans at this time.

As for the army, its defensive functions became increasingly limited. At the time of the Holy League, formed against the Ottoman Empire in 1684, the army of the commonwealth could still play an independent part important for the whole of military operations. Later, its participation in the wars on Polish-Lithuanian territory or in its immediate vicinity was of secondary importance, or confined to monitoring the passage of foreign troops. Only a few military events did not follow this pattern. The armed forces tried to secure order in peacetime in the borderlands, particularly in the southeast, but not always effectively. The struggle against Cossack rebels (*hajdamacy*) was their most significant military responsibility after the accession of Augustus III in 1735. Both the army and private troops protected the nobles and magnates, so that they could enjoy their properties in peace. Peasant rebellions were comparatively rare and ineffectual. The restricted activity of the army met the needs of noble society, as did its ceremonial activities, for the troops constituted one of the necessary components of the panoply of noble life.

The army of the commonwealth contributed considerably to the wakening of central power and to the intensification of domestic chaos. The nobles who served in the army had long enjoyed the privileges common to their class, and these "companions" transferred to the army the customs of the regional councils. They held meetings of "circles" (*koła*), where assembled units debated public matters, for the army believed it had a right to have a say in the country's future. They sent deputations to the Diet and dietines, and took part in confederations or formed them themselves. These military associations usually combined financial claims with political demands. The example of the Sacred Association (*Związek Święcony*), which proclaimed in 1661 that it would fight for the rights and liberties of the nobility and which threw out reform at the Diet of 1662, was eagerly followed. Although the nobles made up only part of the soldiery, they were the most politically active element, demanding the rights of almost a separate estate. In the disintegration of central power this attitude of the army played a significant role.

Contrary to the interests of the nobility, the army committed countless acts of violence and plunder, and now spared no kind of property. It became a serious threat to the country's economy. While the normal exploitation by a landowner was moderated by his own interest, which prevented him from ruining his serfs, the soldier had no such scruples. He had no thought for the need to preserve an estate for further production, heeding only the necessity of the moment. This military economy, which the commonwealth had already experienced with distress in the seventeenth century, came into full flower during the Great Northern War. Court documents and letters of the time abound with complaints, protests and grievances against army violence which was precipitating the ruin of the manorial economy.

Plundering serfs was disguised as "recovering arrears of pay." It was ruthless. Contemporary pamphlets contain detailed descriptions of noble units' dealings with serfs, and other sources corroborate their reliability. "There were men in the Polish divisions who, after dragging poor people naked through heavy frost, would poor salt water over them and give them to the cattle to lick, until they said where they had money hidden. . . . There were those who would hang them by their feet in the chimney and smoke them with straw until they took away everything."[5] The reform of 1717 did not put a decisive stop to such violence. Complaints against the ruthlessness of the army recurred continually. The more the army abounded with gentlemen officers, the fewer soldiers it had, and the more tax collection resembled the sharing of feudal rent.

The influence of the army on the internal affairs of the commonwealth in the second half of the seventeenth century and the first half of the eighteenth was both pernicious and centrifugal. The army, which under other circumstances might have provided important support for the monarch's power, contributed to the commonwealth's weakness and to the establishment of the system of anarchy. It could not have been otherwise if the model for the army's attitudes and behavior was the nobility. In this sense it was truly a "gentlemen's army."

There were times when the coincidence of the attitudes of the nobility and of the army was particularly apparent. These occurred during the confederations.

Since the death of the last Jagiellonian king in 1572, confederations had become an increasingly frequent form of political life, especially in times of emergency. They were occasioned either by a threat to the existing system of privileges and dominance of the nobility, usually connected with a crisis of central power, or by a threat from abroad to the state's existence which could not be dealt with effectively by the normal apparatus of state. There was a clear correlation between the increasing inertia of the instruments of state, the Diet in particular, and the increasing significance of confederations. Consequently in the early eighteenth century Augustus II tried to retain the authorities introduced by the Confederation of Sandomierz, and under Stanislaus II the form of confederation accounted for the relatively efficient functioning of the most important Diets. This does not mean, however, that the confederations themselves did not contain disruptive elements, or that they were not used to maintain the existing system of anarchy and to check modernization of the state. The functioning of the confederations has thus aroused controversial opinions among historians, including entirely negative ones. The predominant ideology of the nobility, however, makes the role of confederations in the eighteenth century easier to understand.

There were several kinds of confederation in the Polish-Lithuanian commonwealth. Apart from general confederations embracing the whole country, there were provincial ones, embracing particular districts (*ziemie*) or provinces (*województwa*), or rarely entire regions. Among general confederations there was a separate group of confederations formed during an interregnum to secure peace and order by creating a new source of power and law until the royal election. Military confederations, the so-called associations (*związki*), which have already been mentioned, involved only the army or a part of it. Yet other confederations embraced, or could embrace, the whole nobility and royal cities as well. Confederations were dominated by the well-to-do nobility and magnates. These groups usually accumulated confederate power in their hands, although in some circumstances, for instance when the nobles assembled en masse, they could be pressed hard by the poorer nobles.

General confederations are of particular interest. They usually organized armed forces of their own, or took over command of the commonwealth army or part of it. They commonly had a two-tier system of power. The confederate General Council was the authority for the whole country. It consisted of separate marshals for the Polish kingdom and for Lithuania; of councillors appointed by districts and provinces who formed a permanent council; then of secretaries, and sometimes of army marshals if the army had entered into the bond of association. The General Council, summoned by the marshal and acting as an equivalent to the Diet, met rather infrequently. Sometimes high judicial authorities and special committees were appointed, such as those dealing with the treasury or the army. The confederation also set up lower-grade authorities in districts and provinces. They were made up of confederate district or provincial marshals, councillors, commanders of general levies or confederate militia, and sometimes special deputations. Local judiciary and administration were created as well. A confederation could begin with the formation of provincial confederations first and then the General Council, or vice versa.

The function of the marshal general was particularly responsible. Although he was supposed to follow the councillors' advice, much depended on his authority and personality. A talented marshal could subordinate the administration, diplomacy and treasury to himself, and summon meetings and regional councils. Army affairs, recruitment, billeting and strategic decisions also came under him.

Having accomplished its tasks, a confederation was dissolved, usually at a pacification Diet. In the eighteenth century some confederations did not achieve their objectives and wound up only slowly and informally.

Military matters thus played a vital part in confederations. This part increased when a confederation claimed to be defending or upholding the independence of the state. In the eighteenth century formation of a confederation was practically the only feasible way of dragging the commonwealth army out of its inertia. Four confederations were particularly important: the Confederation of Sandomierz (1704–1715), the Confederation of Tarnogród (1715–1717), the Confederation of Dzików (1734–1736) and the Confederation of Bar

(1768–1772).[6] All these confederations were stimulated by foreign aggression or incursions onto Polish-Lithuanian territory, and were formed in defense of the country and the existing order. The Confederations of Sandomierz and Dzików were both confronted by rival confederations, the Confederation of Warsaw (1704–1709) and a second confederation of the same name (1733–1736). The former relied on the Swedish army, the latter on the Russian and Saxon armies, for both were instruments of foreign powers. The enemies of the four general confederations varied. The Confederation of Sandomierz was formed to defend the legal accession of Augustus II against the Swedes,. The Confederation of Tarnogród was aimed against the presence of Saxon troops in the commonwealth, thus indirectly against Augustus II. The Confederation of Dzików defended the legal election of Stanisław Leszczyński against Augustus III and Saxon and Russian troops, whilst the Confederation of Bar opposed Russian interference in the Noble Repulic's affairs. Each of these confederations had dependent armed forces, apart from the general levy which was never risked on the battlefield in the eighteenth century.

There was no uniform pattern of solving military problems in these confederations. Much depended on political circumstances, on the system of power, on the capacity of the enemy, and on possible allies. The personal abilities of confederate leaders were not without significance either. To look separately at the military effort of each confederation and at the position secured in each by the army is impossible in a short paper, so attention will be limited here to a comparative presentation of such matters as authority and command in the confederate armies, manpower and methods of recruitment, the quality of troops, strategy and tactics, and finally the attitudes of society.

The degree of dependence of the military on civil authorities during confederations was reflected in the methods used to secure control over the army. There were not only differences between particular confederations, but vital changes could take place in the course of the same confederation. It was especially important whether the hetman (or the provisional commander in chief) or his deputy (*regimentarz*) joined the confederation and could keep the troops in hand. In such a case the control of the army and its leader by the confederate council was largely illusory and limited to cooperation in deciding strategy. A typical example was the confederation of Sandomierz after the treaty of Altranstädt of 1706. In this confederation, the Polish crown army at first formed an association (*związek*) with a chosen marshal of its own, since the crown hetman, Hieronim Lubomirski, had joined the rival Confederation of Warsaw. When in due course Lubomirski submitted to Augustus II, the association proved unnecessary. After Lubormirski's death, command of the crown army passed to Adam Sieniawski. Hetman and owner of a huge estate, Sieniawski soon began to dominate the Confederation of Sandomierz. His influence on the organization, manpower and activities of the confederate army was certainly much stronger than that of the marshal of the confederation, Stanisław Denhoff. He accumulated in his hands not only the command of the army but control of the treasury and the diplomatic service as well. Sieniawski also secured a strong influence over the Lithuanian army, particularly when its grand hetman, Michał Wiśniowiecki, joined Leszczyński's party and the remnants of his army, standing by the Confederation of Sandomierz, passed under the command of the Lithuanian field hetman, Grzegorz Ogiński, and his deputy, Ludwik Pociej. The excessive growth of the hetman's power that took place during the Confederation of Sandomierz became one of the most difficult internal problems of the commonwealth after the restoration of Augustus II in 1709.

The firm animosity felt by the nobility for the hetmans became manifest in the Confederation of Tarnogród, although this confederation was primarily aimed against the presence of Saxon troops and against Augustus II's flouting of the laws of the Noble Republic. The general and provincial confederations were preceded by an association of Polish crown troops at Gorzyce which overthrew the hetmans. After the formation of the general confederation in Tarnogród its marshal, Stanisław Ledóchowski, secured decisive influence in military matters. This was facilitated by an internal crisis in the military association when its marshal, Władysław Gorzeński, was charged with treason and dismissed, and his successor, Józef Branicki, became Ledóchowski's subordinate. In Lithuania, after forming a confederation in Wilno, the troops were at first under the command of Ludwik Pociej, now grand hetman. He did not enjoy the confidence of the nobility, however, and all his orders had to be countersigned by the marshal of the Lithuanian confederation, Krzysztof Sulistrowski. After the merger of the Polish and Lithuanian armies, Pociej was stripped of command because of his intrigues with the Saxons, and the Lithuanian troops formed their own association under Marshal Stanilsław Potocki. Pursued by the confederates, Pociej barely escaped with his life to the Saxon camp. Meanwhile the crown grand hetman, Sieniawski, was kept in custody by the confederates who intended to bring him to trial for treason against the commonwealth. Only the intervention of Tsar Peter I saved him. In practice now the command of the confederate troops was in the hands of Ledóchowski and the councillors. Ledóchowski also appointed the commanders of the units sent against the Saxons, although the subordination of, say, Chryzostom Gniazdowski, who operated far away in Great Poland, was largely ficticious and extended only to general policy.

Relations between the confederate council and the army at the time of the War of the Polish Succession in 1734–1735 were different. The hetmanships were then vacant, and Leszczyński nominated Aleksander Pociej in the grand duchy and Józef Potocki in the Polish kingdom to command the army as deputies. The former was subordinated to the Lithuanian general confederation, set up in Wilno already on April 5, 1734, under Marshal Marcjan Ogiński, and shared command with him in military actions. Potocki, however, was offended when the confederation of Dzików, formed in November 1734, decided to divide command of the army between him and the marshal of the confederation, Adam Tarło. The deputy was to command the regular troops in the field, while the marshal took over the fortresses and the troops recruited from the provinces. Strategic decisions were to be shared. Eventually Potocki refused to take the confederate oath, and went over to the camp of Augustus III together with the majority of the army. Then the General Council of Dzików nominated a new deputy, Jan Tarło, and commanders from the crown troops which were still loyal. This meant that the army in fact became subordinate to Marshal Adam Tarło whose political and military experience was scant.

In the Confederation of Bar the question of the army command occasioned repeated crises. At first, a military association was formed quite separate from the confederation of the nobility, and Józef Pułaski was nominated deputy. He managed to secure authority over only a part of the crown army. After the fall of Bar he took refuge in the Ottoman Empire and his function was taken over by Joackim Potocki. Pułaski's authority became entirely nominal, since he was kept in custody by the Turks. As a result, each unit of troops and provincial confederation that had formed in the country had its own nominated authorities, which made cooperation impossible. The situation was changed only by the creation of a General Council in the autumn of 1769. When the nominated commander in chief, Adam Szaniawski, became a prisoner of war in Russian hands, the General Council at first tried to act as a collective. It not only reserved the right to nominate to senior military posts but also to approve plans for military campaigns and to give tactical instructions to the deputies. Finally, a special authority, the Army Council, was formed to direct military matters under the supervision of the General Council. In fact it mainly carried out the recommendations of two French advisors, Colonel Charles Dumouriez and Lieutenent General Viomenil.

Provincial confederations that either preceded or followed the general confederation nominated their own military leaders who commanded either the local general levy (*pospolite ruszenie*) as colonels, the troops recruited by a province as captains, (*rotmistrze*) or all the troops in the territory as deputies (*regimentarze*). The General Council of the Confederation of Bar at first attempted to subordinate these to itself. Sometimes however, the autonomous confederate authorities in the provinces worked more efficiently than the General Council itself. Such was the case in Great Poland in 1769 and 1770. Decisions in military matters were usually in the hands of amateurs, for it was by no means a rule that the General Council would nominate professionals. Anyway, the tendency to subordinate the troops to the civil authorities of the confederation was strong, and it usually had negative consequences for the effectiveness of the fiscal and military effort.

The results of this effort as reflected in the manpower of the confederate armies were not very momentous. The Confederation of Sandomierz hardly approached the establishment of 48,000 planned by the Diet of Lublin in 1703 and by the confederate council in Grodno in 1705. After the treaty of Altranstädt, through the efforts of Hetman Sieniawski, the recruitment of infantry and dragoons, and the development of light cavalry, this target was probably reached, although numbers varied as a result of desertions to the enemy camp. Similarly, in the Confederation of Tarnogród Ledóchowski and Branicki developed the crown troops to the establishment of 35,834 of which 19,070 were infantry and dragoons. The manpower of the Lithuanian army is harder to ascertain, but it can be assumed that it numbered at least 12,000. Thus the confederates of Tarnogród probably had twice as many men under arms as the standing army of the commonwealth set up by the Diet of 1717. In the struggles with the Saxons a very signal contribution was made by informal units to which the peasants and burghers as well as the nobility flocked. The same provinces that had been unable formerly to raise money for the army, now voluntarily levied taxes and recruited regiments. The enthusiasm abated in the course of time, and this demonstation of military spirit was exceptional for the Saxon period.

The military effort at the time of the Confederation of Dzików was more modest. Although the details are not known, it can be taken that the Confederation of Wilno rallied approximately 8,000 to 10,000 soldiers in 1734, and the Confederation of Dzików about 18,000 in 1735. It is more difficult to estimate the military effort of the Confederation of Bar. Manpower varied considerably. In the initial period of fighting in May 1768 it numbered approximately 5,000 men. The confederates reached their maximum strength in 1769 with about 20,000 men under arms. Yet early in the next year that number fell by half, and stabilized later around 12,000. These figures are not impressive. Yet it must be remembered that the regular troops of the commonwealth for the most part remained outside the confederation. Moreover, in the four years of fighting many more soldiers passed through the confederate ranks than these figures may imply. However, the 200,000 target of which the founders of the confederation dreamed must never have come near.

Contrary to a persistent opinion of historians, the part played by the *pospolite ruszenie* in confederate armies was entirely secondary. The nobility rallied in varying degrees to confederate regional councils or assemblies. The confederate marshal general usually had the right to summon the general levy in case of need, and many provincial confederations summoned the noble community to the general levy. Yet this does not mean that the efficacy of the nobles' military institution was taken seriously. Even at the time of the Confederation of Tarnogród, when even those "who had given up fighting for more than ten years"[7] were flocking to the colors, the provinces could not press the whole of the nobility into the general levy. So instead of enlisting in the person the nobles of the Ruthenian Palatinate were asked to contribute 300 zlotys each for the hire of a soldier in their place. Finally, some units of the general levy did accompany confederate troops fighting the Saxons, particularly in the early period. Yet in winter they generally went home. So they were replaced by draftees (*łanowy*) or their obligation was commuted for a payment adequate for the recruitment of volunteers. The situation was similar at the time of the Confederation of Dzików. The province of Volhynia, which was the first to confederate on November 7, 1733, decided to raise 1,200 cavalry, appropriating 400,000 zlotys from taxes. The province of Sandomierz voted soon afterwards to recruit soldiers in ratio to the acreage of all landed property. These recruits plus volunteers from the general levy were the basis of the army of the Confederation of Dzików. The Confederation of Bar began its activities by proclaiming conscription, requiring one infantryman for every 10 serfs on the estates of the nobility and one for five on crown and church lands, and one cavalryman for every 10 homesteads on the former and one for every 42 acres of plowland (3 *łany*) on the latter. The soldiers were to be provided with uniform, arms, and mess for six months. The cities were also to raise infantry and cavalry in proportion to the number of their inhabitants and their prosperity. These proposals proved to be unrealistic and later provincial confederations moderated the requirments, usually demanding only one cavalryman from 20 homesteads or per 70 plowed acres (5 *łany*). Following the tradition of general levies, numerous nobles volunteered for confederate units. Such volunteers supplied the first line of picked troops, the "Knights of the Holy Cross," who pledged to fight to the last.

Neither noble volunteers nor recruits were properly trained or uniformly armed. They usually acquired experience on the battlefield. Professional soldiers who happened to be in the confederate troops were therefore specially valuable. When the confederates managed to win over part of the Noble Republic's standing army (*wojsko komputowe*), this became the core of their troops. Such was the case in the Confederations of Sandomierz and Tarnogród, and it was not without influence on their military capacity. The Confederation of Dzików was less successful in this respect, and the Confederation of Bar least of all. In the latter, regular troops joined the movement reluctantly and often deserted the confederate ranks. The Polish and Lithuanian military committees, which ran the army and remained loyal to the king, tried to keep their units far from the battlefield. The case of Michał Ogiński, the Lithuanian grand hetman, who joined the confederation with 2,500 men, was exceptional. It was the Lithuanians who scored the only serious victory in the field over Russian troops at Bezdzież, but soon afterwards they were defeated by General Aleksandr Suvorov.

Professional soldiers were also supplied from the private armies of the magnates. There are too few data to establish what proportion they represented of the confederate troops, but it seems to have increased during the Confederations of Dzików and Bar. At the time of the Great Northern War they were rather in the troops of Stanisław Leszczyński's party, that is, in the Confederation of Warsaw, than in that of Sandomierz. The quality of the private units varied, and Cossacks units appeared quite frequently. They could not be properly used, however, since they were closely subordinated to the private interests of the magnates. A typical case was the abortive attempt in 1768 to incorporate the 4,000-strong, well-equipped army of Karol Radziwiłł into the troops of the Confederation of Bar. This frightened magnates into surrendering to the Russians. In the same year, Franciszek Sułkowski, an ex-Russian general, led his brother's private units into the field. They amount to 240 soldiers, "good-looking, well-equipped and armed, well-trained and well-disciplined."[8] Sułkowski added to them his own enlisted units, but at the crucial moment this private militia, apparently insufficiently informed about their leader's designs, refused orders and deserted as one.

In view of the inadequate military training of local soldiers and of the poor officer cadre, securing officers from abroad was very important for the confederate armies. Several foreigners served in the armies of the Confederations of Tarnogród and Dzików, headed by General Stenflycht of Sweden. In the Confederation of Bar French officers became instructors. They inspired the formation of a legion of foreigners, mostly deserters from the Russian and Prussian armies.

Of the four confederations only those of Sandomierz and Bar had enough time to train new recruits. While the confederates of Sandomierz operated over a vast territory not threatened directly by the enemy, however, each group of the confederates of Bar was exposed to rapid attacks by Russian troops on its assembly area. Still, after the creation of the General Council and the seizure of fortresses on the southwestern border of Little Poland, better conditions for training were achieved. The most important centers were the fortress of Częstochowa and the assembly area at Muszyna on the frontier of

Upper Hungary (today's Slovakia). Unfortunately, neither center became Poland's Valley Forge.

In the earlier confederations, the pattern of formations differed little from the usual composition of the standing army, but in the Confederations of Dzików and particularly Bar, a clear preponderance of cavalry over infantry was apparent. In the Confederation of Bar the infantry probably did not exceed 2,000 men at most. The cavalry, apart from regular units, especially dragoons, included a comparatively large number of irregulars, modeled on the light horse of the Polish Contingent. The artillery strength of the confederate troops varied considerably, but even the Confederation of Bar had some. By October 1769 Russian troops had captured about 300 guns from the confederates. Till then there had been no battle in which the confederates did not field some ten or twenty guns. The supply of cannon in the country was sizable, but skilled gunners were lacking. The confederate authorities, particularly those of Dzików and Bar, had serious trouble supplying their units with small arms. Supplying uniforms was equally difficult, and some units of the Confederation of Bar finished the campaign barefoot and in rags. Nevertheless, some very well-armed and equipped units did take the field from time to time.

Inadequate training and equipment was made more serious by the indiscipline and insurbordination of the confederate troops. In this respect the army did not differ from the whole noble community. It proved impossible to keep a tight rein on the armies of the Confederations of Sandomierz and Tarnogród. Although they were fairly efficiently organized and under one command, the situation in the forces of the Confederations of Dzików and Bar was still worse. The approach of the confederate army of Dzików toward the Saxon frontier ended in the pell-mell scattering of the majority of the troops after the victory at Kargowa. Such an outcome was typical of the attitude of the period, when a soldier would criticize almost every order, refuse to fight without pay, take to his heels, after a defeat, and went home with his loot after a victory. Even with the enemy to hand, there was drinking, merrymaking, and firing into the air. The situation was similar in the Confederation of Bar, although military regulations tried to enforce discipline by prescribing heavy penalties.

*Esprit de corps* was not common in such an army. The confederates of Tarnogród were capable of a brave and stubborn fight.

Half a century was to pass before real soldiers and leaders reappeared in the Confederation of Bar, ready to suffer and make sacrifices, tough enough to withstand the hardships of war, and convinced that their cause would triumph. Yet they comprised only a part of the confederate army, and their will to fight could not outweigh the lack of military training of the rest of the troops.

The quantity and quality of soldiers clearly influenced the strategy and tactics of the confederate armies. Even in cases of numerical superiority, pitched battles in the field with the regular Swedish, Saxon or Russian troops were generally avoided. On occasion, however, whole armies executed withdrawals that positively influenced the result of an entire campaign. This tactical maneuver, commanded by Hetman Sieniawski in 1709, frustrated the attempt by Leszczyński's Swedes to break through toward Poltava to render assistance to Charles XII. Equally consequential too, in the winter of 1715–1716, was the retreat of the confederates of Tarnogród, who fell back before Saxon Field Marshal Jakob Heinrich Flemming's offensive and secured the survival of the army in the fortresses of Volhynia. Another tactic used to good effect was the dispatch of strong confederate raiding parties to the enemy's rear. Such were the actions of Z. Rybiński in 1708 and 1709, and Gniazdowski's sortie in 1716 that culminated in the capture of Poznań. Meanwhile the main confederate force would try to engage the foe along the front. This device was revived to good purpose in the operations of the confederates of Bar in 1770–1772, while Dumouriez's offensive, based on a chain of fortresses, ended in failure.

Confederate tactics were based on attack in limited force on small, dispersed enemy units. These guerrilla methods had been practiced since the time of Stefan Czarniecki in the 1650s and would eventually wear away the enemy. They produced telling results in the struggle with the Saxons in 1716, and were used on a large scale by the confederates of Bar. Yet the successes were too rare for this course of action to influence the final result of the campaign. The confederates of Bar attempted coordinated actions by adjacent units, sometimes even of units operating far away from each other. In spite of the difficulties of such actions in conditions of primitive communication and poor discipline, they could be successful, as was Kazimierz Pułaski's defense of Częstochowa in the winter of 1770–1771. This was facilitated by the diversionary operations of confederate units toward Poznań and Kraków. On the other hand, attempts to field large forces by the Confederations of both Dzików and Bar invariably came to grief.

Hit-and-run guerrilla warfare often resulted in the dispersal of units; then the essential became to regroup them rapidly. In the Confederation of Bar, a system of "dispersals" was introduced and successfully employed by Zaremba, who commanded troops in Great Poland. Faced with a strong enemy, he used to break up his forces into smaller groups for them to reassemble elsewhere. The operations of the confederate armies demonstrate that their leaders learned to adjust strategy and tactics to the skills of the improvised troops.

Relations between the army and the population were spoiled by the devastation of the countryside, by taxes levied to support the army, and by the reprisals of the Swedes, Saxons or Russians against any who had been helping confederate units. The social composition of the confederate troops was probably not much different from that of the standing army of the commonwealth. Given Władysław Konopczyński data[9] that of the prisoners of war sent into exile in Siberia from among the former confederates of Bar the nobility made up only one-third or even one-quarter, it can be taken that the nobles' participation in the confederate forces was only slightly higher than in the standing army. The forms of draft also suggest that burghers and peasants were in the majority among the troops. Cities were known to join confederations, as did Kraków in 1735 and 1768; in the latter case the burghers' valiant defense of their city cost them dear. The burghers in Great Poland were particularly active in the Confederation of Bar. Less frequently, confederate leaders appealed to peasants to join the stuggle. The 1716 manifesto of the marshal of the confederation of Kraków province (*województwo krakowskie*) was rather exceptional just because he appealed to the peasants: "Hit the Saxons as hard as you can . . . and you shall have our gratitude and reward."[10] This occurred even before the peasants, driven to the wall by Saxon requisitioning, joined the struggle spontaneously. The confederates of Bar were unable or unwilling to make use of the potentialities of peasantry, although a few leaders did form peasant units.

At all events, peasants could not be expected to make sacrifices in defense of the Noble Republic if they were not promised some improvement in their unbearable lot. They were ready to fight any kind of troops, however, to preserve their scant property. The same peasants of the Kurpie region, some 60 miles north of Warsaw in the *starostwo* of Ostrołęka, who fought so bravely against the Swedes in 1708 and against the Russians in 1735, had in 1707 with equal ferocity attacked a unit of the Confederation of Sandomierz that was collecting taxes.[11] Requisitions by confederate troops invariably caused resentment, and were often difficult to avoid. Kraków, at first well disposed towards the confederates of Dzików, sighed with relief when their units left, for contributions and duties had been very hard on the city. How much harder they must have been on the smaller towns and villages!

The attitude of the nobility to the confederate armies was also highly controversial. When initial enthusiasm waned and successes came slowly or not at all, reluctance to make any fiscal or military effort would return. The nobility eagerly deluded themselves that the protection of mighty neighbors was the best shield of all their liberties. Even at the time of the Confederation of Bar, when the subjection of the commonwealth to Russia and Prussia had become commonly recognized, only a small part of the nobility could honestly repeat the words of a contemporary song: "I stand in the field by God's order. I forsake rank for an opening in Heaven. I die for liberty in concord with my faith. This is the risk I run."[12]

The ineffectiveness of the confederate armies, particularly those of Dzików and Bar, has led military historians to neglect their military experience. Yet it is difficult to ignore the continuity between these attempts to improve an army in a society that had voluntarily disarmed itself and the insurgent armies of the following century created by a nation disarmed by the partitioning powers. Certainly, without the military reforms of the Four-Year Diet and without the example of the American and French revolutions, a rising in the style of 1794 would haver been impossible. Kościuszko discarded confederate traditions and appealed to the whole nation, not only to the "nation of the nobility." He created a truly national army, in which units of peasant scythemen and city milita were of peculiar importance. Nonetheless, analysis of the methods used in the Kościuszko insurrection to draft soldiers and form the so-called mobile militia and volunteer units or examination of its art of war reveals definite parallels to the solutions adopted by the confederate armies.

The confederate armies of the eighteenth century reflected the ideas of the nobility about the character and function of the military. Hastily organized and subject to the control of the nobles, the army was to be an instrument for achieving the limited defensive objectives at which the confederations aimed. This concept, however, was borne out neither by experience in the Great Northern War, when the standing army in association with the confederations became the core of the confederate armies, nor by experience in the Confederations of Dzików and Bar, when the employment of untrained soldiers, even when they fought bravely, proved disastrous. It was on the ruins of this military doctrine of the nobility that there grew the realization of the need to develop the standing army and to recognize it as the symbol of independence.

## Notes

1. Jan Wimmer, *Wojsko polskie w drugiej połowie XVII w.* [The Polish Army in the Second Half of the 17th Century] (Warsaw, 1965).
2. Kitowicz, *Opis obyczajów za panowania Augusta III* [A Description of Customs during the Reign of Augustus III], ed. R. Pollak (Wrocław, 1950), p. 304.
3. Dunin Karwicki, "Egzorbitancyje we wszytkich trzeck stanach Rzeczypospolitej" [Exorbitance in All Three Estates of the Commonwealth] (MS 5393 in National Library, Warsaw).
4. Henryk Olszewski, *Doktryny prawno-ustrojowo czasów waskich, 1697–1740* [Legal-Constitutional Doctrines in the Time of the Vasas, 1697–1740] (Warsaw, 1961), p. 175.
5. "Krzywda nad wszystkie krzywdy, niesprawiedliwość nad wszystkie niesprawiedliwośći, zgorszenie nad wszystkie zgorszenia—hiberna w Polsce" [Injustice above Every Injustice, Iniquity above Every Iniquity, Outrage above Every Outrage—the Wintering Tax in Poland], 1712.
6. The most important military histories of these confederations are Jan Wimmer, *Wojski Rzeczypospolitej w dobie wojny północnej* [The Army of the Commonwealth during the Great Northern War] (Warsaw, 1956); S. Truchim, *Konfederacja dzikowska* [The Confederation of Dzików] (Poznań, 1921); Władysław Konopczyński, *Konfederacja barska* [The Confederation of Bar] (Warsaw, 1936–1938).
7. Józef A. Gierowski, *Między saskim absolutyzmem a złotą wolnością: Z dziejów wewnętrznych Rzeczypospolitej w latach 1712–1715* [Between Saxon Absolutism and Golden Freedom: From the Domestic History of the Commonwealth in the Years 1712–1715] (Wrocław, 1953), p. 315.
8. Wojciech Szczygielski, *Konfederacja barska w Wielkopolsce, 1768–1770* [The Confederation of Bar in Great Poland, 1768–1770] (Warsaw, 1970), p. 98.
9. Konopczyński, *Konfederacja barska*, II, 375–376.
10. Jerzy Gierowski (ed.), *Rzeczpospolita w dobie upadku 1700–1740*

[The Commonwealth in the Period of Its Decline, 1700–1740] (Wrocław, 1955), p. 233.

11. W. Herbowski to A. Sieniawski, January 3, 1707 (MS 5831 in the Czartoryski Museum, Kraków), cited in J. Ronikier's dissertation on the Polish crown army's commanders in the early 18th century (in preparation).

12. Jarosław Maciejewski (ed.), *Literatura barska* [The Literature of (The Confederation of) Bar] (Wrocław, 1976), p. 316.

Daniel Stone

# Commoners in the Polish Officer Corps in 1790

In November and December 1790, the Polish Diet ennobled more than 400 soldiers, bankers, merchants, lawyers, professors and other distinguished commoners. The act generated controversy that has persisted into modern times. Some viewed ennoblement as a bribe intended to defuse the burgeoning third estate; others saw in it a just recognition of valuable service to state and society. Holding the general question in abeyance, the legislative acts of ennoblement reveal the number of commoners serving in the Polish officer corps. The present purpose is to assess the number of commoners and their distribution throughout the ranks and branches of service. Full study of the role of commoners in the Polish army cannot be attempted here and would have to include questions of social attitude, promotion, training, and many other issues.

In ennobling officers of plebeian origin, Poland followed a common European practice. Russia's Table of Ranks went furthest in automatically ennobling any commoner reaching the rank of major in the army or its naval equivalent.[1] Prussia also ennobled most of the few commoners who reached officer rank and other German states practiced similar policies.[2] England allocated commissions through purchase, which left burghers free to achieve officer rank. Only France after 1781 allowed no scope for commoners' ambitions by requiring four quarters of nobility for an officer's commission.[3] Many commoners found their way into the officer corps of different armies because nobles simply could not fill all the positions needed in long-drawn-out wars. Another reason for commoners becoming officers was the development of technical services like artillery and engineering which put a premium on a type of education that nobles disliked, at least until late in the eighteenth century, and those services became havens for non-noble officers. In addition, traditional rivalries between kings and nobles sometimes led rulers to search for commoners whom they could trust, particularly in the seventeenth century.

Nevertheless, the nobility provided the bulk of the officer corps across Europe. In peacetime 90 percent of the Prussian officer corps was noble; other German states allowed commoners somewhat easier access. The Swedish army contained 25 percent commoner officers in 1780 while the number swelled to 34 percent in 1790 as a result of war with Russia. One-third of French officers came from non-noble families in mid century.[4]

State policy generally favored the nobility for military service. Prussia went furthest in identifying the interests of the state with the nobility. Frederick II purged his army of non-noble officers after the Seven Years' War and called the nomination of such officers "the first step leading towards the collapse of the state."[5] France passed a series of laws that restricted and finally abolished the right of commoners to seek commissions or, if already serving, to gain promotion. Non-noble officers serving in these and other armies generally filled junior posts. The higher the rank, the more nobles appeared, except, perhaps, in the technical services which remained peculiarly open to commoners.[6]

While studies of Europe's officer corps have nowhere been extensive, the social background of Poland's officers is virtually unknown. Two studies on the seventeenth century have shown that commoners could serve and even, on occasion, rise to positions of authority both in the army's so-called National Contingent and its modernized Foreign Contingent, established in the mid seventeenth century. The latter regiments were originally officered in large part by foreigners who were quickly Polonized and whose children continued to serve in Poland. Many officers came from plebeian backgrounds but achieved noble status in Poland.[7]

While the seventeenth-century Polish army could boast of military triumphs against the Swedes, Russians, Cossacks, and above all against the Turks at Vienna in 1683, the eighteenth-century Polish army declined into insignificance. Limited in size by the Diet of 1717 and again by the 1775 treaties with Russia, Prussia and Austria, the Polish army of 1776–1788 barely numbered 18,500 men and could scarcely defend the commonwealth's borders against its numerous and well-armed neighbors. Nonetheless, the energetic work of deputies from the Diet and especially the head of the Royal Military Chancellery, General Jan Komarzewski, accelerated the modernization of training and organization. Komarzewski himself provides a curious example of just how fluid social lines could be in the late eighteenth century. He was secretly ennobled in 1781 by King

Stanislaus II Augustus Poniatowski, a fact that has only recently come to light.[8] Komarzewski's patent of nobility stated that he had been born a noble and was commonly considered to be one but that documentary proof had been lost. The accuracy of the statement is open to question, however. On the one hand, destruction of private and official documents often occurred, and Komarzewski's early life fits the typical pattern of a poor noble seeking a career. On the other hand, political opponents accused Komarzewski publicly of non-noble origins even if they failed to challenge his seating as a deputy to the Diet.

This professionalization of the army antagonized many Polish nobles who sought traditional employment on easy terms. Royal attempts to negotiate a military alliance with Russia in 1787 and 1788 in order to gain subsidies that would permit some increase in the size of the army played into the hands of antiroyalist factions. In 1788 these groups captured the Diet, renounced Russian "protection," restructured the government, and decided to increase the army to 100,000 men. The diet lacked the financial resources to create so large an army at once, but new taxes enabled its strength to reach 46,000 by mid 1789, 56,000 in 1790, and 65,000 in May 1792.[9] Although half the army consisted of undisciplined National Cavalry, it fought the Russians on equal terms in several engagements during the wars of 1792 and 1794, before superior Russian numbers took their toll, forcing the Poles to retreat and eventually surrender.

The social composition of the eighteenth-century officer corps in Poland has not been studied. Legally, the officer corps was open to candidates from all estates until 1767, when new articles of war restricted officer posts to the nobility except in the artillery corps.[10] Apparently the administration failed to enforce this regulation, so antiroyalists in the Diet of 1786 passed a law limiting all new officer appointments to native Polish nobles. In its political context, the measure seemed directed more against foreigners than Polish commoners, and its aims were as much political (against the king) as military.[11] The presence of non-noble officers is evidenced by a series of ennoblements: in 1764, the diet ennobled six serving officers; in 1768, thirty-one; in 1775, seventeen; in 1790, one hundred and nineteen; and in 1794, nineteen.[12]

Newly ennobled officers were warmly greeted by all political camps. Conservatives saw in ennoblement a reaffirmation of the feudal-estate model of social organization; they considered their estate to be a military elite and willingly accepted warriors into their ranks. An anonymous pamphleteer typically defended the ennoblement of the "unbroken soldier whose breast stands as a wall to protect his brothers from the enemy, or the warrior leader who dies on the field of battle for the freedom of his fellow countrymen." This romantic patriot complained, however, that the Diet had failed to distinguish between exceptional service and time-serving.[13] Even the reactionary Confederation of Targowica of 1792–1794, which annulled most achievements of the Four-Year Diet and might have been expected to oppose dilution of aristocratic privilege, confirmed the ennoblements of 1790 and added a few more. Furthermore, the confederate leaders directed the Military Commission to recommend deserving commoners for ennoblement.[14]

More progressive nobles also accepted the idea of ennoblement but gave it a more systematic character and extended it beyond the military to prominent civilians. King Stanislaus II and, above all, Hugo Kołłątaj built up political systems based in part on burgher support; Kołłątaj had originally advocated creation of a House of Burgesses in the Diet before turning to ennoblement of prominent commoners as more practical.[15] The progressive wing of the Diet which predominated in 1790 and 1791 enacted an urban reform bill which provided for automatic ennoblement of certain categories of burghers, including all officers reaching the rank of captain; the Targowica confederates abolished the provision along with the other urban reforms.[16]

A few radical publicists attacked the ennoblements on the grounds that they would weaken internal bourgeois cohesion which had been demonstrated in the "Black Procession" of 1789, when representatives of 141 cities had submitted a petition to the king and the Diet. Urban delegates also signed a "Union of Cities" and requested urban reforms. A few deputies from Volhynia and the Kiev district suggested that restriction on promotion of burghers to high positions in secular and clerical life should be ended.[17]

As the foregoing implies, contemporaries assumed that all ennobled commoners came from the bourgeoisie; the possibility that peasants might rise through the ranks of the army into the officer corps or enter more traditionally bourgeois occupations was never mentioned. Publicists discussed ennoblement in the context of the "urban question" or, translating literally from the Polish, the "burgher question" (*sprawa mieszczańska*). The 1790 acts of ennoblement placed army officers among undoubted burghers such as bankers, merchants, and lawyers. An urban bill, which passed the Diet in April 1790 and passed without change into the Constitution of May 3, 1791, provided for automatic ennoblement of certain categories of burghers, including all officers reaching the rank of captain.[18] The preponderance of non-Slavic names among the 1790 ennoblements (62 percent) gives further credence to this supposition in view of the non-Polish origins of so many Polish burghers.[19] Despite the similarity to Russian policy established by the Table of Ranks, there is no indication of any Russian influence. Undoubtedly the overwhelming majority of officers ennobled in 1790 came from the bourgeoisie, although the presence of some peasants in their midst is at least possible.

Even though ennoblement of officers was popular and gave rise to systematic policies, the mass ennoblement of November and December 1790 occurred in an unpremeditated, haphazard manner. While awaiting the arrival of newly elected deputies from the provinces, the currently sitting members decided to reward worthy citizens for their services to Poland. Financial reward appeared beyond the slender means of the treasury so the deputies adopted ennoblement instead. As names were put forward, deputies seemed to compete to name the largest number of bankers, manufacturers, teachers, lawyers, and army officers. Marshal of the Diet Stanisław Małachowski refused to pass on the merits of individual nominations, and the Diet requested the Military, Treasury, and Education Commissions to submit lists of candidates, which it subsequently approved.[20]

The acts passed by the Diet list each individual by name. The officer's rank is generally given while the service details also appear frequently. Sometimes the regiment is listed or the branch of service. In many cases the officer is identified as belonging either to the crown (Polish) army or to the Lithuanian army. There is no indication of social origin. Other persons, chiefly retired officers, are listed in the acts. No information appears about such factors as their social origin or age.

The universal character[21] of the ennoblements permits comparison with the army list, that is, the number of officers of each rank and each branch of service authorized by the Diet. From this can be discovered the percentage of persons in each rank and branch of service who were ennobled by the Diet of 1790, and hence the minimum percentage of commoners serving in each category. The current account considers only actively serving officers. The 1790 ennoblement acts list some retired officers as well as those on active service; a few officers from the Marshal's Guard or from the treasury service appear as well. These have been eliminated from analysis.

To begin, Table I lists the total group of ennobled soldiers during the reign of Poniatowski, a period in which the Diet returned to activity without interruption by the *liberum veto*. Table I shows that ennoblements occurred throughout the reign but the heaviest concentration by far came in 1790 when 63 percent of the total were ennobled. The category "other" included noncommissioned officers and individuals whose rank was not specified.

*TABLE I*

*ENNOBLEMENTS BY RANK 1764–1794**

| *RANK* | *1764* | *1768* | *1775* | *1790* | *1794* | *Total* |
|---|---|---|---|---|---|---|
| General | — | — | 1 | 1 | — | 2 |
| Brigadier | — | — | — | — | — | — |
| Colonel | 1 | 7 | — | 2 | 1 | 11 |
| Vice-brigadier | — | — | — | — | — | — |
| Lieutenant colonel | — | 1 | 1 | 4 | — | 6 |
| Major | 1 | 2 | 3 | 11 | 3 | 20 |
| Cavalry captain | — | 2 | — | 3 | — | 5 |
| Captain | 3 | 9 | 5 | 37 | 8 | 62 |
| Ensign (National Cavalry) | — | — | — | 1 | 1 | 2 |
| Lieutenant | 1 | 8 | 3 | 38 | 3 | 53 |
| Second lieutenant | — | — | — | 12 | — | 12 |
| Ensign | — | 2 | — | 9 | 3 | 14 |
| Warrant officer | — | — | — | 1 | — | 1 |
| Other | 1 | 1 | 5 | 17 | 3 | 27 |
| TOTAL | 7 | 32 | 18 | 136 | 22 | 215 |

*Source: *Volumina Legum*, VII, 377, 801–804; VIII, 301–304; IX, 189–209; X, 338–341.

These figures are further refined in Table II which examines the ennobled officers of 1790 in comparison with the estimated number of officers actually serving in mid 1790 at about the time of the ennoblement.[22] Table II shows that commoners were particularly well represented in the rank of captain where 32.5 percent of the estimated actual number of captains serving in 1790 received ennoblement. Significant figures are also found for major (15.3 percent), lieutenant (13.1 percent) and lieutenant colonel (11.4 percent). Overall, however, only 6.5 percent of Polish officers in 1790 came from plebeian backgrounds.

These figures represent a minimal figure that further research might increase. The 1793 Diet of Grodno reaffirmed the ennoblements of 1790 and added a few more "deserving" officers to the list. These additions may represent officers overlooked in the scramble to prepare the acts of 1790, as a 1791 proposal to open the door for further ennoblements implies. It is unlikely that they represent new commissions since they fall chiefly in the middle officer ranks, although they may reflect transfers from foreign armies. If the assumption that they were overlooked in 1790 is correct, the total commoners in the officer corps would be 8.0 percent instead of 6.5

*TABLE II*

*COMMONERS AS A PERCENTAGE BY RANK IN 1790*

| *RANK* | *No. of serving officers* | *Percentage ennobled* |
|---|---|---|
| General | 19 | 5.3 |
| Brigadier | 7 | — |
| Colonel | 30 | 6.7 |
| Vice-brigadier | 7 | — |
| Lieutenant colonel | 35 | 11.4 |
| Major | 72 | 15.3 |
| Cavalry captain | 147 | 2.0 |
| Captain | 114 | 32.5 |
| Ensign (National Cavalry) | 113 | 0.9 |
| Lieutenant | 289 | 13.1 |
| Second lieutenant | 238 | 5.0 |
| Ensign | 123 | 7.3 |
| Warrant officer | 598 | 0.2 |
| TOTAL | 1822 | 6.5 |

percent; the percentage of captains would increase to 39.5; and majors would increase to 19.4. Included in addition should also be those officers ennobled in 1764, 1768, and 1775 who remained in service in 1790; their numbers cannot be calculated but some must still have been serving.

While the middle officer ranks included numerous commoners, the higher and lower ranks contained relatively few. The figures for general and colonel imply that obstacles stood in the way of the commoner aspiring to high rank; contemporary reports show that the highest ranks were clearly reserved for great nobles. The sharp decline in the number of commoners below the rank of captain is harder to understand. Free commoner access to the lower officer ranks would produce larger concentrations of commoners in the ranks of lieutenant, second lieutenant and, probably, ensign than in the rank of captain, while the reverse in fact occurred. Probably the 1786 law forbidding non-nobles to gain commissions prevented commoners from launching their careers and kept them from junior officer positions between 1786 and 1790. Presumably, the 1790 law on automatic ennoblement of captains obviated restrictions on the junior ranks as well.

The National Cavalry was particularly free of commoner influence in keeping with its swashbuckling noble traditions. Fewer than one percent of the officers in the junior ranks of warrant officer (*namiestnik*) and chief warrant officer (*chorąży*) were ennobled and none in the ranks of brigadier and vice-brigadier. Curiously, two percent of the company commanders, whose rank was that of cavalry captain (*rotmistrz*), came from common backgrounds. Perhaps the larger figure represents a search for greater training and education although the absence of ennoblements from the higher ranks of brigadier and vice-brigadier works against that assumption. In any event, the percentage of commoners in the modernized Foreign Contingent can be calculated by eliminating the National Cavalry and the similar Vanguard (*straż przednia*), which were anachronistic in the late eighteenth century; the professional leaders of the army failed to reduce their numbers only because of their political defenders. If these are dropped from consideration, what is left is shown in Table III. Removal of the ranks of brigadier, vice-brigadier, *rotmistrz, chorąży* and *namiestnik* doubles the percentage of ennobled officers. Obviously, the National Cavalry remained a stronghold of the nobility which commoners could not penetrate.

*TABLE III*

*COMMONERS IN THE POLISH ARMY 1790*

| | *Estimated actual officers* | *Percentage ennobled* |
|---|---|---|
| Total | 1822 | 6.5 |
| National Cavalry | 872 | 0.06 |
| Foreign Contingent | 950 | 12.0 |

The 1790 ennoblements reveal the presence of commoners in the branches of service as well as by rank (Table IV). Unfortunately, the number of omissions from the acts is greater by branch than by rank, so the data are less secure. In 1764, 1768, and 1775, branch of service is reported so infrequently as to make analysis pointless.

The general profile by rank is roughly similar among the three branches and resembles the general pattern in the army as shown in Table I. The preponderance occurs in the middle officer ranks.

More significant is a comparison with the total number of serving officers by branch of service shown in Table V. It shows that Poland's closely resembled other European armies by including a large percentage of commoners in the technical services of artillery and engineering, and virtually excluding them from service in the cavalry, even if the Foreign Contingent is considered alone. A moderate percentage found their way into infantry service.

The acts of ennoblement also permit analysis of distribution between the Polish crown provinces and the grand duchy of Lithuania. The army of the Polish crown provinces contained 68 percent of the ennobled officers identified by location of service while the remaining 32 percent served in the Lithuanian army. The crown army as a whole outnumbered the Lithuanian army by three to one. The difference is not significant; both the crown and Lithuanian armies provided equal opportunities for commoners.

In summary, analysis of the 1790 ennoblements reveals that commoners occupied a noticeable place in the Polish officer corps. At a total strength of 6.5 percent, non-noble officers did not quite reach the number allowed by Prussia, the most exclusive major state in eighteenth-century Europe (at least before the French legislation of 1781). Yet if the National Cavalry and Vanguard formations are ignored, the number rises to 12 percent, a figure well within the mainstream of social patterns for European armies, and might rise

*TABLE IV*

*COMMONERS BY RANK AND BRANCH OF SERVICE 1790*

| *RANK* | *Cavalry* | *Infantry* | *Technical* |
|---|---|---|---|
| General | — | — | 1 |
| Colonel | — | 2 | — |
| Lieutenant colonel | 1 | 3 | — |
| Major | — | 7 | 1 |
| Cavalry captain | 3 | — | — |
| Captain | 5 | 19 | 5 |
| Cavalry warrant officer | 1 | — | — |
| Lieutenant | 2 | 13 | 5 |
| Second lieutenant | 1 | 5 | 5 |
| Ensign | — | 5 | 1 |
| Unspecified | 1 | 1 | 1 |
| TOTAL | 14 | 55 | 19 |

*TABLE V*

*COMMONERS BY BRANCH OF SERVICE 1790*

| *BRANCH* | *Number ennobled* | *Percentage of estimated serving officers* |
|---|---|---|
| Cavalry | 14 | 0.07 |
| Infantry | 55 | 6.8 |
| Technical | 19 | 19 |

still further by including certain categories whose number cannot be determined at present. As in other European armies, commoners occupied a particularly prominent place in the middle officer ranks, especially captain, and gravitated towards the technical services. Despite its noble traditions and aristocratic constitution, Poland's social patterns resemble the social patterns of absolutist and economically better-developed states in Central and Western Europe.

## Notes

1. Basil Dmytryshyn (ed.), *Imperial Russia: A Source Book, 1700–1917* (New York, 1967), pp. 19–21.

2. André Corvisier, *Armies and Societies in Europe, 1494–1789* (Bloomington, Ind., 1979), p. 87.

3. *Ibid.*, pp. 155–156; Louis Tuetey, *Les officiers sous l'Ancien Régime* (Paris, 1908), pp. 179–180.

4. Corvisier, *Armies and Societies*, pp. 155–170; Karl Kemeter, *The German Officer Corps in Society and State, 1650–1945* (New York, 1974), p. 8; Christopher Duffy, *The Army of Frederick the Great* (London, 1974), pp. 24–28; Manfred Messerschmidt *et al.* (eds.), *Handbuch zur deutschen Militärgeschichte 1648–1939* (Frankfurt, 1964), II, 128–130.

5. Karol Korányi, "Burżuazja a armia" [The Bourgeoisie and the Army], *Państwo i Prawo* [State and Law], V (1950), No. 2, 7.

6. Corvisier, *Armies and Societies*, pp. 97–104; Tuetey, *Les officiers*, pp. 255–280.

7. Bohdan Baranowski, "Skład społeczny wojska polskiego w połowie XVII wieku" [The Social Composition of the Polish Army in the Middle of the 18th Century], in *Bellona* (Łódź, 1945), pp. 807–880; Marian Kukiel, "Skład narodowy i społeczny wojsk koronnych za Sobieskiego" [The National and Social Composition of the Crown Armies under Sobieski], in *Studia historyczne ku czci Stanisława Kutrzeby* [Historical Studies in Honor of Stanisław Kutrzeba] (Kraków, 1938), II, 431–441.

8. Księgi kanclerski [Chancery Records] 50, f. 59, in the Central Archives for Ancient Documents, Warsaw. Komarzewski's secret ennoblement has remained unknown to Polish genealogists and historians, including the author of the recent entry in the Polish Biographical Dictionary who reported that an early biographer thought Komarzewski's mother was a poor noble; resumably his father was not. *Polski Słownik Biograficzny* [Polish Biographical Dictionary], XIII (Warsaw, 1968), 380, *s.v.* Komarzewski, Jan.

9. Leonard Ratajczyk, *Wojsko i obronność Rzeczypospolitej 1788–1792* [The Army and the Defense of the Commonwealth, 1788–1792] (Warsaw, 1975), pp. 116, 135.

10. Konstanty Górski, *Historia artylerii polskiej* [History of the Polish Artillery] (Warsaw, 1902), pp. 169–173.

11. *Volumina legum*, IX (Kraków, 1889), 35; Emanuel Rostworowski, *Sprawa aukcji wojska na tle sytuacji politycznej przed Sejmem Czteroletnim* [The Question of Army Reinforcement against the Background of the Situation before the Four-Year Diet] (Warsaw, 1957), pp. 157–161.

12. *Volumina legum*, VII, 377, 801–804; VIII, 301–304; IX, 189–209; X, 338–341.

13. *Materiały do dziejów Sejmu Czteroletniego* [Materials on the History of the Four-Year Diet] (Wrocław, 1960), III, 459, 464.

14. *Volumina legum*, X (Poznań, 1952), 209.

15. Emanuel Rostworowski, *Legendy i fakty XVIII wieku* [Myths and

Realities of the 18th Century] (Warsaw, 1963), p. 419; Krystyna Zienkowska, *Sławetni i urodzeni* [Famed and Well-born] (Warsaw, 1976), pp. 138, 318 f. n. 155.

16. *Volumina legum*, IX, 215–219; X, 209.

17. *Materiały do dziejów*, III, 403, 426–432, 557.

18. *Volumina legum*, IX, 215–219.

19. Władysław Smoleński, *Mieszczaństwo warszawskie* [The Burghers of Warsaw] (Warsaw, 1976), pp. 331-332.

20. Archiwum Sejmu Czteroletniego [Archives of the Four-Year Diet], X, November–December 1790, in the Central Archives for Ancient Documents, Warsaw.

21. *Materiały do dziejów*, III, 420–421, 463–464, provides contemporary assertions that the Diet ennobled all officers.

22. Ratajczyk, *Wojsko i obronność*, p. 228, gives the established manpower and estimates that one-third of the officer posts had not been filled by March 1790. Presumably the figures were not drastically different in the fall when the ennoblements took place.

Norman Davies

# Conclusions

Since the two keynote papers of Professors Rostworowski and Gierowski amply survey the main themes of the present symposium, and since my own reflections have already been published in an earlier volume of the series,* I must confine myself to one or two general observations.

To date, Polish military historians of the eighteenth century have largely concentrated their efforts on similar topics to those of their colleagues elsewhere. While in no way concealing the shortcomings of Polish military organization in this period, it is only natural that Polish scholars should wish to show that Poland-Lithuania was at least beginning to develop in the same direction as other countries. Hence existing literature tends to emphasize two features—first, the attempts to create a strong, state standing army, as in neighboring Prussia or Russia, and second, the growth of the concept of the "nation-in-arms," as in revolutionary France.

In contrast, the present symposium attempts to underline some of the more particular aspects of Polish military and social history. Emanuel Rostworowski outlines the military consequences of Poland-Lithuania's unique social structures, whilst Józef Gierowski explores the implications of those archetypal Polish institutions, the confederation and the insurrection. Daniel Stone examines one of the countercurrents of Polish society—the ennoblement of bourgeois officers, while Leonard Ratajczyk and Jerzy Kowecki present two different commentaries on the terminal crisis of Poland-Lithuania in 1788–1794. Marian Zgórniak adds data on the financial problems facing the Polish military establishment.

In different circumstances, the organizers would have wished to see this approach extended to several other neglected topics. For example, it had been hoped to include a study of the magnates' private wars which did so much to paralyze the internal life of the com-

*"The Military Traditions of the Polish *Szlachta* 1700–1864," in *War and Society in East Central Europe*, I (New York, 1979), 37–46.

monwealth. Although Polish noblemen had never been averse to settling their disputes by the sword, the growth of magnates' armies led to a series of protracted civil wars, such as that between the Radziwiłłs and the Sapiehas in Lithuania, which totally preoccupied whole provinces for decades at a time. Any detailed examination of these events, all too often dismissed as mere parochial brawls, would throw much light on the workings of political patronage, on the interrelationship of the magnates and the petty nobility, and on the penetration of foreign interests into internal conflicts—in short, on the central social and political themes of the age.

A documented study of the office of hetman in the later eighteenth century would also have proved rewarding. As commanders in chief of the armies of the commonwealth, the hetmans obviously held a position of prime importance; but the fact that their office fell into the hands of men who were at once opponents of domestic reform and in the pay of St. Petersburg reveals much about Poland-Lithuania's subservience to foreign interests. At the same time, the ability of the ultraconservative hetmans to control and manipulate the reform movement almost to the end of the Noble Republic's existence says a great deal about the sclerotic and passive nature of Polish society.

Finally, it would have been worthwhile to include a study of Polish noblemen in foreign service. From marshals of the highest caliber, such as Maurice de Saxe, down to lowly troopers in the Prussian or Imperial cavalry, Poland supplied a constant stream of military recruits for the armies of Europe. It would seem, in effect, that the émigré tradition was well established long before the loss of national independence, and it is clear that research into the careers both of individual soldiers and of typical social groups, especially the petty "mercenary" nobility, would prove very fruitful.

These omissions, and others, remain to be filled, and the foregoing modest contributions cannot claim in any way to form an exhaustive review of the problems of "War and Society" in eighteenth-century Poland-Lithuania. However, drawbacks notwithstanding, it is confidently hoped that the contributors have succeeded in their aim of advancing knowledge of the subject and making the products of Polish scholarship better known in the world at large.

# V

# Balkan Society and War

Peter F. Sugar

# Unity and Diversity in the Lands of Southeastern Europe in the Eighteenth Century

For the purpose of this volume Southeastern Europe is defined as that part of the continent that was under direct or indirect Ottoman rule during the eighteenth century. The various chapters dealing with this region are devoted to specific topics which, taken by themselves, lack description of the context in which occurred the events and developments to which they are devoted. Without placing these historical occurrences and changes in their proper setting, their full significance cannot be grasped, a difficulty enhanced by the great diversity of the events analyzed by the authors. The following pages will attempt to present a broad picture of the situation and life in Southeastern Europe in the eighteenth century, supplying the framework within which the important developments presented in the subsequent chapters took place, and thus give them the contextual unity that otherwise they would lack. The most convenient way to highlight the most important of the almost endless forces that shaped the history of the people of Southeastern Europe during the century under review is to stress the common and the peculiar features that shaped their behavior and action.

For all those who lived under Ottoman domination, the eighteenth was the worst century. Following the partial revival of Ottoman fortunes during the years of the Köprülü grand viziers, the Ottoman state entered a long period of rapid and drastic decline that went on unbroken until 1826 when Sultan Mahmud II succeeded in destroying the janissary corps.[1] Irrespective of what is considered the beginning of this period of decline, weakness, and even chaos, whether the Ottoman defeat under the walls of Vienna in 1683 or the Peace of Karlowitz of 1699, it mainly encompasses the eighteenth century. During these years the Ottoman Empire was constantly on the defensive, and always in search of additional human and material resources to maintain its very existence and to reestablish the authority of the central government in the provinces and dependencies.[2] This task was difficult, and nowhere more arduous than in Southeastern Europe where two of the empire's neighbors independently gained strength to practically the same degree as that to which the Ottomans' had declined. Furthermore, the Habsburg and Romanov states pursued, as did all great dynasties and states in the eighteenth century, a policy based on the principles of balance of power and compensation, which, given their geographic location, meant an imperialist policy aimed at producing a contemporary version of the "Eastern Question." This alteration in relative strengths and the resultant aggressiveness of Austria and Russia led to seven wars, all of them of several years' duration, within an eighty-year time span (1710–1792).[3] The Ottoman Empire had fought that many wars in previous centuries too, but this time all these confrontations took place on Ottoman territory in Southeastern Europe. Given the directions from which the attacks came, north and northwest, the Rumanian and Slav lands suffered more from these conflicts than did the Greek regions, although no corner of the empire in Europe escaped the ravages of war.

These wars not only imposed a heavy burden on the population in the form of the requisitions of the invading armies, which lived off the land, but also produced large-scale destruction of property, damage to the land severe enough to prevent replanting for years, rape and other abuses, and recurrent, tragically widespread and severe epidemics. This connection between war and society is so obvious that it needs no further elaboration. Other developments also established a direct relationship between military action and societal change. The Ottoman Empire's constant search for the means to defend itself also affected Southeastern Europe, although the Christian inhabitants of the region were only very seldom used for military service. They were, however, used, as were the Muslim inhabitants, for auxiliary services which often involved heavy and extended physical labor under circumstances that caused frequent illness and high mortality. Most onerous for the people were the forced deliveries of products, mainly agricultural, to supply the sultan's forces, and the constantly increasing taxes to pay for war. Practically every one of the following chapters deals with this problem, often in great detail. Old taxes were increased, new ones were introduced, their collection was more strictly enforced, and the number of tax-exempt individuals, communities, and professional groups was drastically reduced. Thus the actions of the Ottoman authorities and of hostile armies combined to create a physically unhealthy and insecure environment in which the economic well-being of the population declined steadily and significantly all through the century. Avdo Sućeska's contribution clearly shows that not even the Muslim inhabitants of Southeastern Europe were protected from these numerous ills and tribulations in spite of the fact that they had always enjoyed a privileged position. They had paid for this position through the additional burden of rendering military service. It is important to realize, when the relationship between war and society is studied, that in a state in full decline numerous problems arise and have an impact on the life of even the most modest and insignificant individual, but that most of the difficulties that the European subjects of the sultan faced resulted from the needs and actions of invading and defending armies.

The various wars fought in Southeastern Europe during the eighteenth century lasted for a total of twenty-two years. If this century is defined as lasting from the Peace of Karlowitz to the beginning of the Serb revolution in 1804, roughly twenty percent of this time the Ottomans spent fighting wars in their European possessions. This is an appreciable percentage, but it fails to tell the full story. International conflicts are not the only armed actions that can and do affect populations. Uprisings, large-scale banditry, the depredations of local satraps, regional conflicts, and the high-handed action of corrupt officials and discontented soldiers also involve the use of force and produce the same results—requisitioning, property damage, numerous personal abuses, and epidemics—as formal wars. There was not a single year during the century under review when several regions of Southeastern Europe were not suffering from local armed conflict. With the Ottoman authorities unable to maintain even minimal law and order, total chaos reigned in the provinces, producing an endemic and widespread *bellum omnia contra omnes* that afflicted the local population whether it stood by passively or was deeply involved. This situation has been discussed in detail elsewhere; all that can be given here is a short summary.[4]

Power vacuums must be filled. People whose position, wealth, and even life are in danger must try to find means to restore the security that the authorities are no longer able to guarantee; individuals whose livelihood has disappeared must attempt to find other ways to sustain themselves and their families; the great masses suffering from the legal, or most often illegal, actions by which the preceding groups try to achieve their aims must defend themselves or sink into organized or *de facto* slavery. For all these sectors of the population strife is inevitable in their search for security, survival, and possibly for the establishment of a new power structure that would introduce some kind of stability. In the century-long struggle for survival every individual, from the highest-ranking Ottoman functionary to the lowest and poorest peasant, and every institution from the merchant and trade guilds to the churches and from the military to the civil service was involved.

While every member of Southeast European society tried to protect himself from the actions of all others, for a study of war and society only the elements that bore arms and affected the life of large numbers of people are important. Basically these were those who wielded power, those who tried to gain power, and those who resisted the efforts of the former two groups. The wielder of power could be practically anybody who, in a given location at a given moment, was able to impose his will on those around him. Some of these strong men could base their claim to supremacy on legally achieved positions, be they pashas appointed by the sultan, the ruling princes of the Rumanian lands, or hereditary dignitaries (including Christians) whose special positions had been recognized and often utilized for centuries by the Ottoman authorities. Others rose to prominence through ruthless action, or by exploiting the chaotic situation in which they lived in the lead of men who had similar ambitions. The *âyans*, of whom Osman Pasvanoğlu of Vidin and Ali Pasha of Ioannina are the best known but by no means the only ones, are a good example of men who achieved power and prominence by carving out states within the state for themselves, while the leaders of marauding bands who constantly appeared and disappeared represent the latter group. They each organized their own armed forces for a longer or shorter period in the strength needed to establish and maintain their power. The two types, those who had some legal claim to supremacy and those who had none, were interchangeable. A strong local potentate, like Pasvanoğlu, could force the central government into giving him an official title, while others stayed in their position even after the official appointment on which it rested was terminated.

None of these men were consciously rebels or modernizers; they were simply interested in their own wellbeing, yet their actions were both revolutionary and, at least in a limited sense, modernizing. The revolutionary aspect is easy to understand, for it follows from the very nature of their existence: they were power centers operating independently and outside of the recognized, legal institutions of the state. The modernizing nature of their activities, both in the Rumanian Principalities and in the Balkans proper, was a consequence of their efforts to maximize their power—legal or illegal, for their own good or for that of the Porte—by increasing their armed might and revenue. This led to broadening the popular base for recruitment into the armies that they maintained, and included the arming of Christians in Serbia and in the lands dominated by Ali Pasha of Ioannina. Numerous were those who used the military training gained in this manner for the purposes of the liberation movements of their people. Equally important was the elimination of numerous privileges that certain occupations and regions enjoyed previously, and the elimination of men, for example the Rumanian boyars, whose power previously stood between the central authority and the population at large. The result was a marked centralization and hence modernization of governmental structures in those regions where these measures were taken. That these changes often had to be enforced by armed might or that the local satraps constantly fought either to extend their realms or simply to keep their soldiers occupied must be self-evident. All these activities added up to the constant warfare that deeply affected the society of Southeastern Europe.

Intolerable as these power wielders might have been in the eyes of the great, mainly rural, masses, they at least tried to protect the regions over which they "ruled" from the depredations of others. Much worse were those who were trying for power, especially when they believed that it was legally and rightfully theirs to begin with. The most numerous in this group and the most hated by the inhabitants of Southeastern Europe were the janissaries.

By the eighteenth century the janissaries had nothing in common with the men, mainly of Slav origin, who used to be forcibly recruited and converted; they had long ceased to be the reliable core of the Ottoman army. The system of the *devşirme* hardly even crossed the minds of these men who were the sons and grandsons of janissaries. The janissary corps' compostition had drastically changed. Originally they were all young men brought to Constantinople by the *devşirme* system and found unsuited for more important functions in the state administration. The system began to be diluted as early as 1582 when Sultan Murad III (1574–1595) rewarded some entertainers who had performed at the circumcision of his son by enrolling them among the janissaries. During the next century, the janissaries first gained the right to marry and then forced the Sublime Porte to limit membership in their corps to their direct descendants. The result was a rapid increase in the corps' membership. Coupled with their decreasing value as soldiers and the inability of a financially straitened state to pay them, this transformed this branch of the military into a practically uncontrollable mob. To lessen the chance of the janissaries' creating trouble in Constantinople, more and more of them were stationed in the provinces, mainly in Southeastern Europe, where they soon set up organizations of their own. Claiming that the state was not fulfilling its obligations toward them (this was true) and that they had to fend for themselves if they wanted to avoid starvation (equally true), they tried to take over entire regions and establish themselves as masters there. They were opposed by the legal and illegal power wielders as well as by the local population everywhere, becoming "legal outlaws" who fought constantly everywhere "for their legal rights and privileges" in the most ruthless, inhumane and illegal manner. Nobody was more responsible for the perpetuation of the *bellum omnia contra omnes* and therefore more universally feared and detested than were the janissaries. The fact that they occasionally found "employment" with one of the *âyan*s and thus, for a while, became units of a "regular army" does not alter this general evaluation of their behavior, role, and reputation.

Finally, the third type of men who contributed to the constant armed strife in Southeastern Europe, the ones described earlier as those who fought all the other forces, must be mentioned. These men, the heroes of many folk songs and legends, existed for many centuries, as Bistra Cvetkova's chapter shows, and were known under a great variety of names, including haiduk, klepht, uskok, morlach, *armatole,* and a few others.[5] Their origin as a fighting force differed very little from one region of Southeastern Europe to another, and therefore the picture painted for the Bulgarian lands by Professor Cvetkova can be accepted as valid generally. That the chaos that reigned in Southeastern Europe in the eighteenth century increased the need for this kind of armed popular resistance to the steadily increasing legal and illegal demands made on people is obvious. At the same time, the absence of well-organized and disciplined security forces made the activities of these fighting units easier.

There can be no doubt that their numbers and activities increased considerably during the period under review, and while the population backed and supported them, they too represented strife, they had to be supported with the produce and other goods of the people, and their actions often elicited bloody retaliation that hurt those who supported them more than it affected them.

There is no question that these popular forces were composed of "freedom fighters," and that a great many military leaders of the wars of independence of the next century emerged from their ranks. The crucial issues are for what and for whose freedom did these men fight? What was the framework of their self-identification? To what extent did events of the eighteenth century change the nature of haiduk action?

A great variety of answers have been offered to these questions. We have been told that these popular forces fought for freedom from excessive taxes and other impositions, that they fought for freedom of worship, that they fought for freedom from alien rule, or that they fought for freedom from any authority except those they traditionally recognized. We have been told that they fought for the freedom of their village or clan only, that they fought for larger but traditionally united geopolitical entities, or that they fought simply for themselves. We have been told that their self-identification was with peasants, with Christians, or indeed with Serbs, Greeks, Bulgars, etc. Apart from the fact that documentary evidence that one explanation is correct and others are erroneous is hard to find at best, the reason for the great variety of answers is that all of them contain grains of truth. Undoubtedly, the armed popular resistance movements started independently of each other in various locations as a result of specific socioeconomic abuses. With the deterioration of effective Ottoman rule, the number and gravity of these abuses increased and the growth of armed resistance was commensurate. The larger the movement became, the easier it was for the various armed bands to learn of each other's existence, to establish contact, and to begin to cooperate. In this respect the eighteenth century was crucial. The interrelatedness of lawlessness, arbitrary action by "authorities," in short, all the developments already briefly referred to, including the growth of the haiduk movement, becomes clear to anybody who studies the history of Southeastern Europe in the eighteenth century. Haiduk action became a massive and widespread form of self-defense and even self-assertion.

One question remains unanswered: what was the self-identification and goal of the eighteenth-century haiduk? It is understandable that folk literature, originating mainly in the eighteenth century, made "national heroes" of these brave men, and it is equally understandable that historians have seen in them the first "freedom fighters," the harbingers of the national wars of liberation. Documents dating from much earlier periods already prove that these fighters referred to themselves as Bulgarians, Greeks, Serbs, etc. This too is understandable. The memory of pre-Ottoman days was still alive, and everybody knew at least that he was speaking a certain language. The real issue is to what extent was this self-identification "national" in today's sense of the word. It is almost universally accepted that the contemporary concept of nation and the subsequent motive force of nationalism developed during the Enlightenment and the years of the French Revolution and the Napoleonic wars. The present author has repeatedly argued that the transmission of ideas and concepts that developed in Western Europe during the eighteenth century was extremely slow, and that they penetrated into Southeastern Europe only with considerable delay.[6] If the above consensus and this author's interpretations of events are accepted, it becomes almost impossible to argue that the various haiduk forces or the popular military units in the Rumanian Principalities fought for "nationalistic causes." Yet there can be no doubt that the various revolts that broke out in Southeastern Europe soon after the close of the eighteenth century, beginning with that in Serbia in 1804, were genuine national liberation movements. It would be absurd to contend that large-scale revolts of this nature resulted from some sudden and massive popular understanding of forces operating in far parts of the continent. What one confronts is an interesting phenomenon that has not yet been studied. During the endemic armed conflicts in which the popular forces were involved during the period under review, those who made up these "peoples' armies" gradually evolved a new variety of their self-image, practically without any knowledge of western developments, which was indeed nationalism in the sense the term is used today. This development proves again the ability of the people living in Southeastern Europe to generate meaningful and long-lasting changes on their own, and also clearly indicates how important the eighteenth century was in their historical development.

The generalizations made so far are valid, although not to an equal degree, for all the regions and people of Southeastern Europe. To complete the broad background picture that these pages are intended to provide, regional variations must also be presented and explained.

Among the numerous reasons that explain regional differences the historical and geographic ones are the most important. The effects of these determining factors coincide to a considerable degree with rough ethnic boundaries, a fact that explains both the conditions under which the major ethnic groups lived at the beginning of the eighteenth century and the unfolding of their history during these hundred years. While no nationality's situation can be considered to have been "good" in 1699 and none of them "lived well" between then and 1804, there are nevertheless significant differences in both the level of "oppression" to which they were subjected, and the means and possibilities at their disposal to fight back.

In the opinion of this author, the situation of the areas inhabited mainly by Greeks was the least intolerable. The direct link between war and society offers the first argument to support this contention. Of the seven international wars of the century only one, the Venetian-Ottoman war of 1715–1718, was fought in these regions, and only one other war, the Russo-Ottoman war of 1768–1774, produced a "sideshow" that affected them, the Russians' naval expedition under the command of Count Aleksey Orlov. While it is perfectly true that the Greek territories suffered heavily from the depredations of those who created the steady, locally motivated "civil wars," the Greek regions were less plagued by them than were the Slav-inhabited lands north of them. Furthermore, not only did Ali Pasha's strong rule, for a while at least, protect some Greek regions from the worst, but there were also more Greek areas under the "traditional leadership" of local Christians better equipped to fight back than in any other Christian-inhabited part of Southeastern Europe. Finally, the important Greek-inhabited islands of the Aegean, while certainly not immune to the chaos of the eighteenth century, suffered less from the general turmoil, owing to their protection, than did the Balkan mainland.

The Greeks enjoyed two further advantages in comparison with others who lived under Ottoman rule, and both are of great importance. In the Orthodox church, which they dominated, they had a very significant, almost national institution that made it possible for them to safeguard their considerable cultural heritage and language.

As traders and mariners, the Greeks were not only able to develop a small, true urban middle class, but, more importantly, also remained in constant contact with the world outside the Ottoman Empire. Thus all major cultural and intellectual movements, from the Renaissance to the Enlightenment, found a rapid echo among the members of this small but significant commercial elite, who were the only exception to the slow penetration of western ideas into Southeastern Europe.

The political-economic role of the Phanariots and the drastic overall economic changes that occurred in the region during the century to which this volume is devoted enhanced these considerable advantages further. Under these circumstances the emergence among the Greeks of men like Eugenios Voulgaris, about whom Pachalis Kitromilides's chapter gives ample information, and an entire school of modern thinkers (in the eighteenth-century sense) is understandable. The resulting cultural revival was significant and by the end of the century had reached down to a considerable proportion of the lowlier segments of the population.

Turning from the southernmost part of Southeastern Europe to the most northerly region, the Rumanian Principalities, an interesting comparison presents itself. The Greek lands were, with the exception of those regions in which the Ottomans decided to rule through locally established authorities, under direct rule by the Sublime Porte, while the Rumanians retained basic self-government as a result of the agreements concluded with the Ottomans by Prince Basarab-Laiotă of Wallachia in 1476 and Prince Bogdan III of Moldavia in 1512.[7] As long as the Ottoman regime was strong and the agreements were honestly kept, the Rumanians' obligations remained light in comparison with those shouldered by those under direct Ottoman rule, and furthermore they retained their own social structure and institutions. The advantages of this arrangement are obvious. Even after corruption became prevalent, both in Constantinople and the principalities, the Rumanians remained the political masters of their lands. Not even the establishment of Phanariot rule altered this relationship much, because the hospodars, appointed by the Sublime Porte and representing its interests, had to collaborate with established local forces if they were to perform their duties. The emergence of "popular fighting units" in time of war, mentioned in the subsequent chapters dealing with the Rumanian lands, is a clear indication of traditional forces asserting themselves under Phanariot rule.

In contrast to their political advantage over the Greeks, the Rumanians were worse off when economic activities, the church, and contact with the world outside the Ottoman realm are compared. While the Rumanians traded across their borders, often in spite of Ottoman regulations forbidding it, those with whom they came in contact were not the Western European states, so the import of ideas, together with trade goods, was much more limited than it was in Greek-inhabited territories. The Habsburg lands and Poland in the eighteenth century were not territories from which advanced ideas could penetrate to the east or south respectively. While new, modern ideas entered the principalities more slowly and affected a much smaller segment of the population than they did in Greece, the Rumanians were not hermetically sealed off from the trends of advanced contemporary thought, and by the middle of the century these began to have their Rumanian echoes.[8] The ecclesiastical institutions of the principalities, dominated by Greek prelates and abbots, were not "a national institution," and represented a heavy drain on the finances of these lands. Thus in spite of their politically privileged position, the developmental base for the Rumanians' national growth at the beginning of the eighteenth century was less favorable than that in the Greek-inhabited southern regions of Southeastern Europe. A further handicap for the Rumanians was that, with the exception of the war with Venice, every other Ottoman conflict of the century affected their territory. This disadvantage was offset by the fact that, except for some minor incidents, the Rumanians did not have to deal with the janissaries and their "legal banditry."

At the bottom of hell, in the ninth circle solidly frozen in ice, dwelt the Southern Slavs. This Dantesque image is used on purpose because the life, and more importantly the chances for development, of these people had indeed been frozen into immobility by the Ottoman system. Once again, geography and history explain their situation. Living in the central regions of Southeastern Europe, the Southern Slavs were easier to isolate from "outside" influences than were either Greeks or the Rumanians. While Dubrovnik and the Dalmatian coast were contiguous to the lands they inhabited and no language barrier separated the former from the areas under Ottoman domination, the littoral did not serve as an important transmission belt between the West and the Southern Slavs. There were two reasons for this. First of all, the trade between the Adriatic region and the interior was mainly in the hands either of Greeks or of Slavs who lived by the sea. They traveled inland; those living in the Ottoman-controlled interior hardly ever got to the coast. The other reason was religious and cultural. Deeply attached to their only remaining native institution, the church, the Orthodox Slavs (mainly Serbs and Bulgarians) would often refuse cooperation with their Catholic brothers (mainly Croats) of the coast. While the population was mostly illiterate, the use of different alphabets in the Catholic and Orthodox Slav regions was also a barrier to cultural exchange.

While resolutely loyal to their church, the Slavs, unlike the Greeks, could not consider it a "national institution" because the church was run by a Greek hierarchy and its valuable literature was written in an alphabet different from both the Latin and the Cyrillic. From the "folk religion" of the humbler levels of the Southern Slavs, no cultural revival struck root before the very end of the eighteenth century. The Southern Slavs were unable either to retain their old leadership (as the Rumanians had in their boyars) or to develop a new one (as the Greeks did in their commercial and maritime circles). The leadership that did take shape was entirely local and served mainly as the point of contact between the local population and the Ottoman authorities.

To these many considerations must be added another that relates very closely to the present topic: war and society. The main military highway to the west used by the Ottomans followed the line Constantinople-Edirne-Polvdiv-Sofia-Niš-Belgrade; the secondary route was the Danube. Consequently the cities along the highway and the major Danubian ports were always heavily garrisoned and kept under strict control and supervision, and their environs served as the principal supply bases for the upkeep of the soldiers and the important military routes. The population of these lands was therefore tied much more closely to Ottoman institutions, above all the army, and so was much more closely watched and policed than those farther south or north. While this close connection between the Slav regions and the Ottomans might have offered certain relative advantages to the inhabitants while the Ottoman system was functioning well (the peasants of these regions, for example, owed fewer dues and services than did those in the Romanian lands), these advantages rapidly became liabilities when the system broke down. Nowhere was the eighteenth century more chaotic and nowhere did the janissaries behave worse than in the Slavic heartland of Southeastern Europe. Not surprisingly, haiduk activity was most prevalent in these parts of the Ottoman domain. Constant armed action was the rule in the Slav territories all through the eighteenth century.

While this gloomy picture was equally true of all Slavs at the beginning of the century, it changed considerably during the hundred years to which this volume is devoted. The Serbs moved ahead faster than did the Bulgarians because of factors closely tied to military events.

The first and more important of two events occurred just before the eighteenth century began and resulted from the Habsburg-Ottoman war that ended in the Peace of Karlowitz. The steady advance of the Habsburg forces, following the second attack on Vienna, brought the Imperial armies into lands that were very sparsely inhabited and that the victors had to repopulate to make productive. The series of defeats suffered by the Ottomans greatly encouraged the Serbs who attacked the Ottoman garrisons stationed among them. When it became obvious that Serbia proper would, in all probability, remain under Ottoman rule at the end of the hostilities, giving Constantinople a chance to "punish its Serb traitors," the interests of the Serbs and Vienna became identical. The Serbs needed a haven and the Habsburgs needed cultivators for the lands of southern Hungary (mainly today's Vojvodina). Emperor Leopold I (1657–1705) issued his letters of guarantee to the Serbs on August 21, 1690, and August 21, 1691, promising them virtual self-government, and under the leadership of the Metropolitan Bishop of Peć, Arsenije III Crnojević, roughly 200,000 Serbs moved across the Danube and Sava rivers. The ecclesiastical and cultural institutions that developed around the new archbishopric of Sremski Karlovci provided the Serbs with a source of information and education that responded to their needs and inspired various movements in the Ottoman-occupied lands too.

The second development tied to military action followed the Peace of Passarowitz of 1718, when Austrian forces occupied important Serb-inhabited territories until 1729. During these years they tried to organize the Christian population, supposedly friendly to them, into effective administrative and economic units by expanding already existing, traditional and effective organizations of self-rule into larger, more effective, and interrelated institutions. A significant example was the introduction of the rank and office of *oberknez* (roughly, chief headman). The holder of this office had to work with several of the traditional *knez*es before he could act as the spokesman of a considerably enlarged demographic-geographic unit. Contact with the outside and better internal organization accelerated the thaw and moved the Serbs out of the ice of the ninth circle of hell.

The Bulgarians were less fortunate. Once again, geography and history give the needed explanation. Not only were the Bulgarian lands closest to Constantinople and so the easiest to control, but this proximity also served to link the economies of the capital city and Bulgaria rather intimately. Therefore the potential Bulgarian leadership element, the *çorbacıs* had selfish economic reasons to maintain both their mastery over their countrymen and the structure of the Ottoman Empire. Nowhere did Bulgarian-inhabited regions with important cultural centers border on the Bulgarian lands proper to be able to play the role that the Serb-inhabited regions of Hungary farther to the west played for the Serbs. The Bulgarian lands were thus those most affected by all the problems that the eighteenth century presented to the inhabitants of Southeastern Europe.

The Bulgarians date the revival of their national self-consciousness from the appearance of the *History of the Slav-Bulgarians* of Father Paisiy (1722–1798). This work was finished in 1762 but was not printed, and its dissemination and effect took a long time to develop. The true awakening of the Bulgarians occurred only at the very end of the eighteenth and mostly in the first decades of the nineteenth centuries. The reason for this development is clearly explained by these sentences:

> The development of trade and crafts, as well as the troubles in the last years of the eighteenth century, led to fundamental demographic changes in the towns. . . . The towns, which had so far been quite deprived of their Bulgarian elements, began to be filled with a Bulgarian population and in the early nineteenth century the Bulgarian element was predominant in trade and the crafts.[9]

As a result of wars and constant armed conflicts on the local level, people sought out the safest places, the towns and cities, and settled in them. This was true all through Southeastern Europe, but the trend to move from rural to urban areas was strongest in the most troubled region of all, the Bulgarian lands. Only after this shift had occurred and only after the new urban element became economically secure could a new leadership element develop that would point its countrymen in a different direction. While the roots of this change are in the eighteenth century, it became truly important only in the next.

Albania has not been discussed because this chapter was designed to serve as an introduction to those that follow it and none of these is devoted to it. This omission is due to this alone and does not mean that developments in Albania were not important in the eighteenth century. While very different in detail from those to which these few pages have been devoted, Albanian events could easily have been fitted into the double framework presented here—common features of Ottoman-dominated Southeastern Europe and regional differences within this area. The general picture would not have changed substantially or significantly. The eighteenth century would still have emerged from this short summary as the most unpleasant and burdensome period for those who lived under Ottoman rule for many centuries.

## Notes

1. The first Köprülü grand vizier, Mehmed, was appointed in 1656, and the last, Numan, lost office in 1710. The so-called Köprülü period effectively ends with the Ottoman defeat at Vienna in 1683 and the subsequent execution of the grand vizier, Kara Mustafa.

2. The crisis of the empire is not negated by the fact that during the years under consideration it lost amazingly little additional territory in Southeast Europe while bringing considerably more land under its dominion. Disregarding the regions north and east of the Dniester, which fall outside Southeast Europe proper, the only major territorial loss incurred by the Ottomans involved those lands north of the Danube that they still retained after 1699. The Peace of Passarowitz cost them a quadrangle of territory between the cities of Szeged, Belgrade, Orşova and the middle reach of the Timiş River. Meanwhile, the Ottomans captured the island of Tinos in 1715, reconquered from Venice all of the Peloponnese, the city of Corinth and the islands of Limnos and Tenedos (Bozca Ada) in 1718, and regained Belgrade in 1739 when peace was concluded in that city.

3. The seven wars include only those in Southeast Europe, not all the

campaigns of the Ottoman Empire, and were the following: 1) War with Russia, 1710–1711; 2) with Venice, 1714–1718; 3) with Russia, 1716–1718; 4) with Russia and Austria, 1736–1739; 5) with Russia, 1768–1774; 6) with Russia, 1787–1792; 7) with Austria, 1788–1791.

4. Peter F. Sugar, *Southeastern Europe under Ottoman Rule, 1354–1804* ("A History of East Central Europe," Vol. V [Seattle, 1977]), pp. 235–247.

5. For a more extensive treatment of the subject see Bistra Cvetkova, *Haydutstvoto v bulgarskite zemi prez 15-18 vek* [The Haiduk Movement in Bulgarian Lands during the 15th–18th Centuries] (Sofia, 1971).

6. See Peter F. Sugar, "The Enlightenment in the Balkans: Some Basic Considerations," *East European Quarterly*, IX, No. 4 (Winter 1975), 499–507, and *idem*, "Some Thoughts on the Preconditions of Modernization and their Applicability to the European Provinces of the Ottoman Empire," in Nikolai Todorov *et al.* (eds.), *La Révolution Industrielle dans le sud-est européen—XIX^e siècle* (Sofia, 1977), pp. 76–102.

7. The agreements signed by the Rumanians with the Ottomans are usually described as vassalage agreements. Strictly speaking, this is a misuse of the term vassalage, which refers to a very specific Western European feudal institution unknown to the Ottomans. The Turkish term used for agreements of this nature was *ahdname*, which can be translated variously as oath, promissory document, letter of injunction, or simply as treaty. While the *ahdname*s in question had some features resembling a Western European feudal contract, they were less strict and left the Rumanian princes much greater latitude of action than that granted by a Western lord to his vassals.

8. See Vlad Georgescu, *Ideile Politice și Iluminismul în Principatele Române, 1750–1831* [Political Ideas and the Enlightenment in the Rumanian Principalities, 1750–1831] (Bucharest, 1972).

9. Nikolai Todorov *et al.*, *Bulgaria: Historical and Geographical Outline* (Sofia, 1968), p. 100.

Wayne S. Vucinich

# Prince-Bishop Danilo and His Place in Montenegro's History

The thirty-eight years (1697–1735) of Bishop (*Vladika*) Danilo's episcopate marked a turning point in Montenegro's struggle for freedom. The bishop's many activities left a lasting imprint on the history of church and society in Montenegro, and had deep repercussions throughout the Serbian world. He focused his entire attention on achievement of national independence. In pursuance of this goal he undertook to strengthen the almost nonexistent ecclesiastical organization of the metropolitanate of Montenegro, end intertribal strife, eliminate the Montenegrins of Muslim faith (*poturicas*), bring about cooperation among the tribes of Montenegro, Brda, and Herzegovina, and secure support from a trusted foreign power.

The election of Bishop Danilo in 1697 proved no easy task for the Montenegrins because of foreign interference and domestic feuds. Patriarch Kalinik I of Peć (1691–1710) urged that a cleric who shared his pro-Turkish position should be selected as Montenegrin bishop. The Catholic hierarchy in Boka Kotorska maneuvered to place a Catholic over the Montenegrin see.[1] But the Montenegrins insisted on following their traditional practice of choosing a bishop by election. Their leaders assembled in Cetinje in 1697 and elected Danilo Šćepčev as the head of the church. The twenty-five-year-old ordained monk (*jeromonah*) from Cetinje Monastery was the son of Šćepan Kaludjerović, a merchant from a prominent Njeguši tribe. From then on all the bishops with one exception came from the house of Petrović Njegoš, in which the office passed from uncle to nephew till 1851, when another Danilo proclaimed himself a secular prince (*gospodar*). Thenceforth the princes of Montenegro came from the house of Petrović-Njegoš and the bishops were once again elected from different families as of old.

Danilo's consecration as bishop presented another problem. Patriarch Kalinik, who often visited Montenegro, insisted that he should officiate at the ceremony, but Danilo wished to be consecrated by the exiled Patriarch Arsenije III Crnojević, who had been forced to flee to Hungary in 1691 with thousands of his fellow Serbs, and whom he considered the only legal patriarch of Peć.[2] In 1700 Arsenije III, who attached great importance to the metropolitanate of Cetinje,[3] consecrated Danilo during a meeting of the church synod in Hungary at Pécs (Pečuj). On the occasion the patriarch issued a diploma (*sindjelija*) to Bishop Danilo, listing the areas under the jurisdiction of the metropolitanate of Cetinje—an essential in view of the increasing difficulties of the bishops of Cetinje in maintaining contact with the Orthodox communities on Venetian and Ottoman territory. The areas under the metropolitans' authority, according to the diploma, included Montenegro, Zeta, Kuči, Bratonožići, Piperi, Bjelopavlići, Grbalj, Paštrovići, Krtole, Luštica, and the Ottoman-ruled towns of Bar, Scutari, Ulcinj, Podgorica, and Žabljak.

The previous relatively stable relations between the Montenegrin metropolitanate and the Ottoman state had undergone an alteration during the seventeenth century, especially after the Candian War (1645–1669). The bishops of Cetinje began to identify with the popular resistance to Ottoman rule and to connive with foreign powers against the sultan.[4] The church assumed the leadership of this struggle with the backing of the Montenegrin general assembly (*zbor*), representing the whole of Montenegro. The contest with the Turks acquired the character of a religious struggle, a conflict between the Cross and the Crescent.[5] The bishop of Montenegro was the sole authority who could speak on behalf of the entire Orthodox population inhabiting the territory of what was once medieval Zeta. The church was the only institution that, albeit weakly, linked the divided tribes and districts (*knežina*s) of Montenegro, Brda, and certain adjoining areas under Ottoman and Venetian rule.[6]

It was of no small significance, particularly at a later date, that the monastery in Cetinje was a common shrine for all Montenegrins and their neighbors, and a center of whatever meager cultural and educational activity went on within the world of the metropolitanate. The tribes of the Brda (which rarely cooperated even among themselves) and Herzegovina began to cooperate with the Montenegrins for the first time in major undertakings against the Turks. The monasteries at Morača (Brda) and Cetinje (Montenegro) played an important role in bringing about this tribal cooperation.[7] All this enhanced the prestige of the bishops of Cetinje and contributed to their increasing responsiveness to political life. To legitimize their political ambitions they sought historical justification, claiming that political authority had been transferred to them by Ivan Beg Crnojević in the fifteenth century.[8]

It was under Bishop Danilo that the monastery of Cetinje became the real guiding force in the struggle of the Montenegrin and neighboring tribes against the Ottomans,[9] marking a new period in Montenegro's history. When he thought the policies of the patriarchate of Peć were wrong, Danilo was outspoken about it. He refused, for instance, to recognize Kalinik as the new patriarch until after Arsenije III's death in Hungary. His relations with his successor, Patriarch Mojsije (1712–1726), however, were unusually cordial for a time. On the occasion of a visit to Montenegro, Mojsije consecrated Bishop Danilo's nephew Sava a bishop. On the other hand, Bishop Danilo reproached patriarch Arsenije IV when the latter visited Montenegro in 1726 with an escort of twenty-five mounted men, bridling at the extravagant fanfare that accompanied the visit and at the inclusion of Turks in the Patriarch's escort. His censure incensed the new patriarch who retaliated with statements intended to belittle and discredit Danilo.[10]

Roman Catholic proselytizing and Venetian measures against the Orthodox religion weighed heavily on Bishop Danilo. The Catholic bishop of Kotor tried in various ways to bring the Orthodox parishes in Boka Kotorska and Paštrovići into union with the Roman church. This was in line with Venetian policy since 1690 when the archbishop of Philadelphia accepted union with Rome. During his canonical visits to Boka Kotorska, Bishop Danilo spoke in defense of Orthodoxy and tried to persuade the Catholics to accept the eastern rite. The Venetians responded by denying the bishop permission to visit Orthodox parishes on Venetian territory, and on January 18, 1708, outlawed the Orthodox religion on their territory altogether. Bishop Danilo protested against the Venetian policy.[11] The essence of the controversy between the Venetians and the bishops of Cetinje concerned the latter's jurisdiction over the Orthodox community in Boka Kotorska. The Venetian authorities conceded only that a part of their Orthodox population was under the spiritual jurisdiction of Bishop Danilo, but this jurisdiction needed to be defined.[12]

Spokesmen for the Roman church attached great importance to Boka Kotorska as a Catholic frontier. Particularly aggressive in this connection was Vincenzo Zmajević, archbishop of Bar (later archbishop of Zadar), who was believed to have been a prime mover of the Venetian legislation against the Orthodox religion.[13] Archbishop Zmajević sought to discredit Bishop Danilo, hoping this would lead to his removal from the see of Cetinje. What had particularly disturbed Zmajević and other Catholic prelates was the influx of a large number of Orthodox refugees (about 3,000–4,000) into the Boka region from Herzegovina during the latest war with the Turks. The majority of the refugees settled in Budva, and for a time were not allowed to build a church of their own.[14] The Orthodox community around Boka Kotorska survived discriminatory measures through the years, and Bishop Danilo never relented in his determination to uphold the cause of Orthodoxy, but in the meantime, of more immediate concern was tribal anarchy at home. The bishop worked strenuously to reconcile the feuding factions.

A charismatic and determined leader, Bishop Danilo was widely respected by his coreligionists in Montenegro and neighboring districts. This, coupled with the economic strength of Cetinje Monastery, whose properties[15] were under the protection of the *zbor*, enabled the bishop to win greater esteem among the tribes and clans than any of his predecessors. The monastery was where the general assembly of the nation's leaders held its annual meetings[16] on St. Peter's Day, a holiday traditionally celebrated there. Taking advantage of his stature, Bishop Danilo sought to settle differences among them and to subject their actions to some form of control. He used the dignity of his religious office, with sermons and anathemas, to curb internecine conflict and persuade the tribes to work toward the common good. To this end Bishop Danilo traveled among the people, participated in communal assemblies, and pleaded with local leaders to seek reconciliation. A number of individuals and groups heeded the bishop and buried old hatchets.[17]

In 1717 Bishop Danilo went so far as to propose the creation of an intercommunal court made up of clan representatives whose purpose would be to promote and keep peace among the feuding sectors of Montenegrin society. This was an instrument to preserve the tribal system and did not imply an attempt to found centralized state authority. During the thirty-eight years of his episcopate (1697–1735), Bishop Danilo did more than any of his predecessors to bring tribal peace and cooperation, but the tribes continued to cling stubbornly to their independence and tribal traditions until the middle of the nineteenth century.[18]

Just what role the Montenegrin tribes played in the coalescence of the Montenegrin nation and state still awaits full investigation and assessment. Beset by divisiveness, the tribes nonetheless contributed greatly toward national and political integration. Among other things, the tribes were preservers of historical tradition and a reservoir of military power that could be abused as well as employed for the common good. To be sure, the primary occupation of the tribes was war and banditry (*četovanje*).[19] Martial existence was the way of life in Montenegro, whose people lived "under arms and by arms." This type of existence was the product of geography and prevailing social and political conditions, in which banditry, always present, came to be regarded as a form of struggle for survival and freedom.[20]

Banditry was consequently viewed as an honorable pursuit. It was a form of "revenge" (*osveta*) against the Turks and other enemies, and when driven by hunger, the bands attacked and plundered one another. It was important for the members of bands to demonstrate personal and group bravery (*junaštvo*), an attribute deeply cherished in the Montenegrin "military democracy" and more highly valued than material possessions.[21]

After 1699 the Ottoman Empire found itself in serious economic and political straits. The empire had lost substantial territory as a result of military reversals suffered in wars with Christian states between 1683 and 1699. Its financial resources were drained. All of this aggravated existing internal instability, and the Ottoman feudal state system fell still deeper into crisis. The Christian wars against the Turks and the weakened condition of the Ottoman Empire inspired the Serbian rayah to rise against Ottoman rule. In Montenegro this took the form of an increase in armed banditry, and in the number and size of the bands. In Bishop Danilo's time banditry expanded markedly as more and more Montenegrins refused to pay tribute—a symbol of submission—to the Turks. The Montenegrins were within the Ottoman political and social system but refused to recognize the sovereignty of the Ottoman sultan. Groups of individuals, members of particular clans and tribes, banded together, and attacked and robbed the Turks. The Turks in turn employed force to exact their tribute from the Montenegrins, seizing and confiscating the Christians' animals and property, burning their villages, and taking hostages, both simple peasants and village headmen, to be ransomed for money and military supplies. To contain the bands, the Turks built a chain of fortresses (Spuž, Nikšić, Trebinje, etc.) at strategic points and tried unsuccessfully to transplant the more recalcitrant tribes. Every attempt by the pashas of Scutari and Herzegovina, and others, to collect tribute by force met stiffer Montenegrin resistance.[22] The armed bands continued attacking caravans, seizing animals, and murdering people.[23]

Bishop Danilo undertook to give the bands direction and a semblance of organization. He defended them and apologized for them. But the bands operated on their own, plundering not only Ottoman regions but also Dubrovnik and Venetian territory, attacking and robbing Muslims and Christians alike. The Montenegrins attacked Dubrovnik in reprisal for the latter's cooperation with the Turks. On Venetian territory the bands attacked out of vendetta and for economic gain; they particularly singled out for attack the merchants of Risan who traded with the Turks in Trebinje. Interestingly, the Montenegrin epics record only the attacks on Muslims, for only these were worthy of praise.[24] The activities of the armed bands during Bishop Danilo's tenure began to acquire the character of a national resistance.

With the accession of Bishop Danilo there began a long, bitter and costly conflict with the Turks. The Montenegrins found themselves "neither at war nor at peace."[25] Their country became "a besieged fortress," struggling for survival, as Petar II Petrović-Njegoš put it in verse. The bishop and the Montenegrin general assembly increasingly assumed the posture of an independent state. By the middle of the eighteenth century many contemporaries began to consider Montenegro a "free" land,[26] but the Turks never ceased claiming it as their province, and throughout the eighteenth century the neighboring pashas continued to use force to exact tribute from the Montenegrins. The Turks initially viewed their armed encounters with the Montenegrins as punitive expeditions, but for the Montenegrins every encounter with the Turks was a war, even though some Turkish armed forays against them were not ordered by the sultan but were the work of unruly local chiefs (*derebeyis*). The Montenegrins claim to have fought a total of forty "wars" with the Turks in the eighteenth and nineteenth centuries—an average of one "war" every five years.[27]

How did the Montenegrins arm themselves and what kinds of weapons did they employ? Weapons, powder, and lead were never plentiful because the martial existence of the Montenegrins created an almost continuous demand. They either purchased weapons and military supplies, or captured them from the enemy, or received them as military aid from Venice, Russia, and Austria. The Montenegrins gained valuable military experience from tribal warfare and banditry. They were particularly adept at fighting in the mountainous terrain and were masters of surprise attack. They excelled in guerrilla combat. Montenegro lacked a regular military establishment. In major encounters with the Turks the Montenegrins brought together a popular force made up of tribal, clan, district (nahie), and village units, each under its own leader (*knez*, sirdar, and voivode). Every man was responsible for his own food and dress. The arms usually borne by a fighter were a long musket (*kremenjača* or *kapislara*), a pistol (*kubura* or *ledenica*), and a saber (*handžar*, from Turkish *hancer*).[28]

**The Question of the Renegades—the Poturicas**

Over the centuries, for various reasons, individuals and groups of Montenegrins had become converts to Islam.[29] Bishop Danilo believed that eradication (*istraga*) of these Muslim Montenegrins (*poturica* or *poturčenjak*, literally, Turkified) was necessary because they were in the service of the Ottoman government and impeded the struggle for liberation. In any confrontation with the Turks, the Montenegrin Muslims took the Ottoman side and came to constitute what in today's terms would be called a "fifth column." From the end of the seventeenth century on, the subversive activities of the *poturicas* within the tribes of Montenegro and Brda reached dangerous proportions. They connived with the Turks and threatened groups and individuals, including the bishop himself. The Christian Montenegrins saw them as Ottoman lackeys (*izmećari*). Bishop Danilo deliberately incited hatred of them and organized a movement for their liquidation.[30]

Up to the seventeenth century there had been no major conflict between the Montenegrins of Christian and Islamic faiths. The family, clan and tribal ties between them seemed stronger than the religious differences. As the Montenegrin struggle against the Turks intensified in the seventeenth century, so did attacks begin on the *poturicas*. Bishop Danilo rejected the traditional view that tribal membership was more important than religious affiliation, and introduced the notion that religious affiliation was the mark of national identity.[31] In other words, one could not be a Montenegrin Serb unless he was Orthodox.

Animosity toward the *poturica*s grew so strong that only a pretext was needed for a bloody accounting. A Serbian village in Zeta, on Ottoman territory, had built a church, and was granted permission by the pasha of Scutari to invite Bishop Danilo to consecrate it. The bishop was guaranteed safe conduct to Zeta, but once he arrived, he was seized, shackled, taken to Podgorica, and tortured. A group of Montenegrin leaders, however, managed to raise the money to ransom him. The *poturica*s were blamed for the incident, and once freed, Bishop Danilo decided to destroy them. At a meeting with the leaders, Bishop Danilo railed against the *poturica*s and urged their extermination.[32]

From a statement written either by Bishop Danilo or another contemporary, it appears that the prime instigator of the attack on the *poturica*s was the bishop himself. The document describes how the bishop organized the attack on them, and offered them a choice of accepting Christianity or of being driven from the country or destroyed. After some difficulty Bishop Danilo finally found a group of Montenegrins from Cetinje and Ćeklići who agreed to carry out the ugly deed. The so-called Montenegrin Vespers probably took place on Christmas Eve 1709. Not all the *poturica*s were liquidated; some remained in Montenegro until the end of the eighteenth century.[33] The property of the murdered Muslims and of those who fled the country was appropriated by Christians, although some runaway Muslim agas managed to retain legal ownership of the land they left behind. In Bishop Sava's time some agas still had estates (*odžakluk*s, from Turkish *ocaklık*) in Cetinje, Ulcinj, Spič, and elsewhere in Montenegro, and collected annual rent from them.[34]

Many Montenegrin historians have considered the annihilation of the *poturica*s an event of momentous importance and one that inaugurated Montenegro's struggle for national liberation. Yet most of what is known about it is based on popular tradition that cannot always be trusted. The liquidation of the Muslim converts has been celebrated in Montenegrin tradition and in an epic poem about Christmas Eve, which appears to have been written by Bishop Petar I (1782–1830). The poem was later refined by Sima Milutinović and by Bishop Petar II Petrović-Njegoš in his celebrated work *Gorski vijenac* (Mountain Wreath). Apart from the poetry of the two bishops and a written statement erroneously attributed to Bishop Danilo, there are no other sources on the Muslims' annihilation. Even the precise date of the bloody affair is not certain, but most historians have accepted 1709 as the year of the assault.[35]

The first to investigate the drive against the *poturicas* critically was the historian Ilarion Ruvarac, who dated the event to the period of the Morean War (1684–1699).[36] On the basis of Venetian documents, Jovan Tomić put the assault in the time of Bishop Danilo.[37] Another prominent historian, Vladimir Ćorović, could not establish whether the attack occurred in 1707 or in 1709.[38] Historians have been bemused by popular tradition and particularly by Njegoš's *Gorski vijenac* which gives prominence to the campaign against Montenegro's Muslims and has been taken at face value by many writers. Njegoš himself did not know exactly when the annihilation of the Muslims took place. Gligor Stanojević is sure that the drive against the *poturicas* took place in the time of Bishop Danilo and that he inspired it—not overnight, but over a period of time.[39] The archives of Kotor make no mention of the episode.[40] The fact remains, however, that the name of Bishop Danilo is linked with the *poturica* affair in Montenegrin historical works and popular tradition, and this has made of him a national hero.[41]

**Uprising against the Turks**

In December 1710 Russia and the Ottoman Empire were once again at war, which aroused great hopes in the Balkans that liberation was imminent.[42] On March 3, 1711, Tsar Peter I issued an appeal (*gramota*) to the Balkan Christians, both Orthodox and Catholic, to rise against the Turks.[43] The influence and prestige of Russia in the Balkans had increased greatly since the accession of Peter the Great (1689–1725). His victory over the Turks at Azov opened bright prospects for the future of Russia as well as the Balkan Christians.[44] Although contacts between the Serbs and Russians had existed since the Middle Ages, it is doubtful that the Russians knew much about the Montenegrin Serbs until the time of Peter the Great. Petr Tolstoy, whom Peter sent to Europe to study military science and tactics, included Dalmatia and Boka Kotorska in his itinerary. He discovered and wrote about a "free people" called the Montenegrins, who were of the same religion as the Russians and spoke a Slav language, and added that sometimes they fought the

Turks and sometimes the Venetians.[45] At this time several Serbs from Herzegovina and Montenegro were in the service of Russia, and they probably pressed for the establishment of Russo-Montenegrin contacts. The tsar's predecessor had made many appeals to the Balkan Orthodox Christians[46] for aid against both the Ottoman and Austrian Empires. Peter had come to appreciate the potential value of the Balkan peoples as allies against the Turks, and the Balkan peoples had begun to look to Russia for their liberation. Although they pursued different objectives, the anti-Ottoman interests of Montenegro and Russia coincided.

Between 1704 and 1711 at least four Serbs had been in Russia to plead for aid or to offer their service to the tsar.[47] One of these men was Sava Vladislavić (Raguzinskiy), by origin from Foča. He was a talented man who had many connections and rendered important services to the tsar. In 1702 he had been invited to Russia by Peter the Great, who sent him on a mission to Turkey three years later.[48] It is generally believed that Peter's appeal to the Balkan Christians of 1711 was written by Vladislavić or under his influence.

On Vladislavić's advice the tsar sent two officers of Serbian origin, Colonel Mihajlo Miloradović and Captain Ivan Lukačević, as emissaries to Serbia, Montenegro, and Albania to persuade the Balkan Christians to rise against the Ottomans and to distribute copies of his March 3 appeal.[49] In the appeal the tsar portrayed himself as the Christians' liberator; identifying them by geographical regions, he asked them to join Russia in a struggle for their freedom. The tsar alluded to Alexander of Macedonia and Skanderbeg, the Balkan heroes of old, in the hope that their Balkan descendants would seek to emulate them.[50]

The Montenegrin tribal leaders responded enthusiastically to the tsar's appeal and were particularly pleased with the offer of Russian aid. The tsar's appeal was reproduced and copies sent to all the Montenegrin tribes. Miloradović reported to Moscow on conditions in Montenegro and the Montenegrins' decision to rise against the Turks.[51] The Montenegrins sent word that they had attacked the Turks on June 15, and requested arms and financial aid. In return the tsar ordered 500 ducats (*chervonnykh*) sent to Miloradović for distribution among the Montenegrin leaders.[52] Miloradović and Lukačević joined Bishop Danilo in organizing the uprising, so that the abortive attempt of 1688 to liberate Montenegro, Brda, and Herzegovina with Venetian support was now resumed with the backing of Russia. For the first time a direct political connection was established between Russia and Montenegro, and for the first time Montenegro was the recipient of Russian aid. From this time on the contacts between Russia and the Serbs in general increased steadily.[53]

The Montenegrin tribes drove the Turks into the strongholds of Gacko, Grahovo, Nikšić, Spuž and Trebinje. The Grbljani, Paštrovići, Brdjani and tribes from Herzegovina joined the insurgents. Better armed and superior in numbers, the Turks were able to withstand the Montenegrin attacks. After five days of fighting at Nikšić, the Montenegrins were forced to raise their siege. The uprising did not spread as had been expected and remained limited to parts of Montenegro and Herzegovina. Venice agitated against the uprising, largely because it was apprehensive of Russia's presence in the region and had come to consider Brda, Montenegro and Herzegovina as its own sphere of influence. On two occasions in the seventeenth century Venice had attempted to extend its sway over these territories.[54] Venice preferred to have borders with Turkey rather than "Moscow," and took a number of steps to prevent its Orthodox subjects from aiding or joining the Montenegrins. At the same time the Ottomans, who suspected all Christians, accused Venice and Dubrovnik of aiding the insurgents.[55] Archbishop Zmajević of Bar believed that an Orthodox victory over the Muslims would be detrimental to the Catholic cause.[56] The Montenegrins complained to the Russians about the isolation in which they found themselves.[57] To relieve the pressure on the Montenegrins, Miloradović tried to incite the Serbs of Boka Kotorska to come to their support, and Bishop Danilo urged Bishop Savatije of Herzegovina to help by calling on his congregations to take up arms against the Turks.

The Montenegrins did not yet know that the Turks had defeated the Russians at Stănileşti on the River Prut on July 22, 1711. News of Russia's defeat was slow to reach Montenegro. The Montenegrin elders wrote to the tsar for financial aid, and on September 27, 1711, the bishop turned to the proveditor general of Kotor for military support. Neither initiative produced results.[58] By October the Montenegrins came to realize that a Russo-Ottoman peace had been concluded. A letter from the tsar advised the bishop to withdraw into the mountains and continue fighting.[59] To discuss future plans, the Bishop called a meeting at Cetinje attended by representatives from Brda, Zeta, and Grbalj as well as the Montenegrin leaders. A minority of the participants favored continuation of the war, but the majority preferred postponement of the fighting until spring. As a result an armistice was concluded with the Turks to last from October to April 1712.[60] Bishop Danilo informed the Russian state chancellor, Count Gavriil I. Golovkin, about the truce.[61]

The Montenegrin bands resumed the fight the following spring, confident that aid from Russia would be forthcoming.[62] Their activities, however, no longer had the organized cohesion that Bishop Danilo and Miloradović had given them the previous year. Regardless of protests from the authorities of Venice and Dubrovnik, Bishop Danilo made no attempt to restrain them. Montenegro was in a precarious situation; it was under Venetian blockade, and could not purchase lead or powder either from the Venetians in Boka Kotorska or from Dubrovnik.[63] The bishop wanted to go to Russia in quest of help, but the elders would not allow him.[64] In mid-December 1712, Miloradović sent his brother Gabrilo to Russia with a letter to the tsar and Vladislavić[65] describing the plight of Montenegro and requesting financial aid.[66]

In June 1712 a Captain Pavel Arkulei unexpectedly arrived in Cetinje, presenting himself as a Russian secret diplomatic agent who had come for discussions and to deliver a gift of 500 ducats from the tsar to the Montenegrins. Who Captain Arkulei was and what he wished to accomplish have not been established. In any case, Captain Arkulei told the bishop that the tsar wanted the Montenegrins to stay at war because he planned to renew hostilities with the Ottoman Empire and had authorized Miloradović to conclude a treaty with Montenegro. A treaty was drafted, recognizing Russia's suzerainty over Montenegro.[67]

## The Ottoman Invasions of 1712 and 1714

Arkulei's appearance coincided with the Sublime Porte's decision to send a punitive expedition against Montenegro.[68] The sultan's firman ordered tough retribution against the Montenegrin and Brda rebels, destruction of Cetinje Monastery, the capture of Bishop Danilo and Colonel Miloradović, punishment of all Montenegrins who resisted the Turks, and the taking of hostages from those who submitted to the Turks.[69] The expedition was justified on the grounds of the Montenegrins' attacks on the Turks and their neighbors, and dealings with Russia. The vali of Bosnia, Ahmed Pasha, was put in command of an Ottoman army of some 20,000 men recruited from Bosnia, Serbia, Macedonia and Albania.[70] Bishop Danilo called an assembly of leaders to decide on a plan of defense, and together with Colonel Miloradović organized a Montenegrin force of about 8,000 men.[71] To demonstrate neutrality, the Venetian governor at Boka Kotorska prohibited his subjects from aiding the Montenegrins.

After failing to persuade the Montenegrins to surrender and to turn Danilo and Miloradović over to him, Ahmed Pasha launched an attack on July 29 and entered Cetinje on August 8, 1712. One group of Montenegrins surrended, paid tribute, and supplied hostages. The Ottomans destroyed the monastery, recently rebuilt by Bishop Danilo, and other episcopal buildings as well as many homes.[72] Meanwhile Tahir Pasha of Scutari also forced several tribes into submission.[73]

Although victorious, the Turks were not satisfied with the outcome of the expedition. They had not destroyed the Montenegrin will to resist, and neither Montenegro nor Herzegovina was pacified. Bishop Danilo and Colonel Miloradović had escaped with about 500 men, and continued to resist.[74] Despite heavy Venetian patrols many Montenegrins succeeded in crossing into the territory of Venice or Dubrovnik. The Ottomans withdrew from Cetinje later in August but without establishing a stronghold or stationing troops there. Ahmed Pasha and Tahir Pasha had failed to capture either Bishop Danilo or Colonel Miloradović, so Sultan Ahmed III had them replaced.[75]

The Venetians finally persuaded the Grbljani and the bishop to submit to the Turks and to give them hostages. The bishop was given full amnesty, permission to return to Cetinje, and the right to exercise his religious offices.[76] Although the Montenegrins had unmistakably suffered a serious military setback, popular legend speaks not of defeat but of a great Montenegrin victory at Carev Laz.[77] Few topics in Montenegrin historiography have been so controversial as this one. There is no agreement among historians when the Battle of Carev Laz was fought or who was the victor. Some historians doubt if it ever took place.[78]

After a winter of quiescence Montenegrin armed bands resumed action again in the spring of 1713, and as in the past they made incursions into Ottoman districts of Herzegovina and into neighboring

Christian Boka Kotorska and Dubrovnik. Bishop Danilo hastened to prepare for a confrontation with the Turks.[79] In November 1713 Hajji Mehmet Pasha of Scutari began negotiations with a delegation of Montenegrins and Bishop Danilo's emissary. He demanded tribute and hostages, promising in return to repair damaged churches and the monastery.[80] The assembly of Montenegrin leaders met on November 5 and agreed to pay tribute, but refused to provide hostages.[81] Placing strong hopes in Russia, Bishop Danilo urged his people to rise against the Turks and asked those at the assembly to shout "Long live the Russian tsar."[82]

In November 1713 Bishop Danilo sought Tsar Peter's guidance, reminding him that the Montenegrins had not yet concluded a peace with the Turks.[83] The bishop's emissary, Archdeacon Maksim, waited for the imperial reply until the end of 1714, and was then informed that, because of war with Sweden and treaty commitments to the Ottoman Empire, Russia would not be able to aid the Montenegrins in any substantial way.[84] The archdeacon was told, however, that the "boyars and voivodes" could settle in Russia if they wished, and that they would be given land. A similar invitation was extended to the monks whose monasteries had been destroyed by the Turks, offering them the opportunity to settle in Russia and live in Russian monasteries.

Colonel Miloradović had gone to Russia himself, and on his return urged Bishop Danilo to continue fighting the Turks and to maintain contact with the Brdjani and the Herzegovinians. Dubrovnik and Venice complained about the Montenegrin bands, as did Patriarch Mojsije of Peć, who urged the Montenegrins to stop their "evil work" and submit the sultan.[85] In June 1714 the sultan ordered the new vali of Bosnia, Numan Pasha, to launch the strongest possible offensive against Montenegro and force it into full submission.[86] By mid September 1714, the armed forces of seven sanjaks, under as many pashas, were put under Numan Pasha's command.[87] The pasha invited Montenegro's leaders to negotiations, promising them safe conduct. A group of them accepted the invitation against Bishop Danilo's wishes. On arrival they were ordered seized and decapitated. Finally, in September, after long preparation, the Turks attacked Montenegro.

At a general assembly that met in August 1714 the majority of Montenegrins favored submission to the Turks. The Katunjani were the sole exception.[88] For this reason Numan Pasha's main objective was the nahie of Katun. His troops had little difficulty in taking Cetinje, Ozrinići and Njeguši.[89] Bishop Danilo and many others escaped to Boka Kotorska, while several hundred men, led by Vukota Vukašinović of Ozrinići, withdrew into the mountains. One by one, the Montenegrin tribes surrendered to the Turks. Numan Pasha told the tribal leaders that, in accordance with the sultan's firman, the most recalcitrant Montenegrin tribes, which he listed by name, would be removed to some other region, but this threat was not carried out.[90] The pasha did leave a unit of troops in Spuž to control Katun nahie and to prevent the people from returning to their homes. As he withdrew from Montenegro, Numan Pasha plundered the countryside and took a large number of captives. In the Montenegrin popular mind Numan's expedition brought great misfortune to Montenegro. In a statement written in 1714 Bishop Danilo described Ottoman brutalities and the large Montenegrin human and material losses. A goodly number of Montenegrins found refuge on Venetian soil despite the Ottoman demand to Venice not to accept refugees or aid the Montenegrins. Both the Venetians and the senate of Dubrovnik had in fact closed their borders to Montenegro, and had announced that they would not supply the Montenegrins with either food or ammunition. The Venetians were simply unable to stop the flow of refugees; the Turks even pursued some of them over their borders.[91]

Numan Pasha punished the Montenegrins, but he failed to fulfill all the instructions in the sultan's firman. He captured neither Danilo nor any other important Montenegrin leader, nor did he succeed in removing the population of Katun nahie. Only one small group of Montenegrins was successfully removed to Glasinac in Bosnia.[92] Thus the Turks won the two major "frontal" encounters with the Montenegrins, but the fighting was to continue with varying degrees of intensity for the next two centuries. Montenegrin bands would continue to make incursions into Ottoman territory as far as Mostar and deep into the sanjak of Novi Pazar, and they would continue to plunder and murder neighboring fellow Christians despite the repeated protests of Dubrovnik and Venice.

## Prince-Bishop Danilo in Russia

Numan Pasha's invasion forced Bishop Danilo to flee to Boka Kotorska. There he secured a passage by ship to Rijeka, and then by way of Vienna, where he met with representatives of the government, he continued to Russia, arriving at the end of 1714. He was the first Montenegrin bishop and national leader to visit Russia and establish direct contact between Montenegro and Russia.[93] Tsar Peter gave Bishop Danilo a cordial welcome, during which the bishop described the devastating results of Numan Pasha's invasion of Montenegro. The initial Russian response was the issue of an imperial ukaz in January 1715 offering Serbs who entered Russian military service land in the provinces of Azov and Kiev and financial aid corresponding to their ranks.[94]

Russia was not able to do much for the Montenegrins at this moment. The tsar advised them to live in peace with the Turks, but said that when Russia returned to war with the Ottoman Empire he expected the Montenegrins, people of the "same faith and the same race as the Russians," to join Russia.[95] As Bishop Danilo was leaving Russia in July 1717, the tsar told him that Russia's assistance to Montenegro would have to be small because Russia was still committed to war with the "heretical" king of Sweden, Charles XII. The tsar presented the bishop with a letter dated July 9, 1715, in which he acknowledged the Montenegrin contributions to the fight against the Turks, and promised substantial aid once the war with Sweden was over.[96] The bishop received 2,700 ducats and 13,400 rubles for the repair of churches and monasteries and for aid to those who had suffered most from the enemy. He was also given episcopal vestments, church books and furnishings,[97] and two charters (*gramota*). One charter bound Montenegro to alliance with Russia in any war with the Ottoman Empire, and the other pledged an annual grant of 500 rubles to the monastery in Cetinje.[98] On his way home, Bishop Danilo again stopped in Vienna to establish firmer political contacts with Austria. This time he spoke with a number of prominent Austrian leaders, including Prince Eugene of Savoy, and offered them Montenegro's military cooperation against the Turks.[99] But it was on Russia that Montenegro pinned its hopes and aspirations.

Russia became Montenegro's principal benefactor until the demise of Montenegro in the First World War. Four out of the five Montenegrin bishops of the eighteenth century, including Bishop Danilo, made journeys to Russia in quest of aid and protection. Bishop Sava traveled to Russia in 1743.[100] Bishop Vasilije (1750–1766) visited Russia no less than three times (1752, 1758, 1765), and died there on his last visit.[101] Bishop Peter I (1782–1830) studied in Russia from 1762 to 1766, and visited Russia in 1777 and again in 1785–1786. On his second visit he was given a cold reception and expelled from the country under false accusations.[102] All the Montenegrin bishops who visited Russia returned disappointed in one way or another. Yet the Montenegrins and their bishops, with the possible exception of Sava, continued to put their faith in Russia. There emerged a cult of Russia in Montenegro, a blind trust in the goodness of Russia and the conviction that with Russia's aid the Serbs would be liberated from Ottoman rule. But Russia's aid was not always available, and on occasion the Montenegrins were still forced to seek help from Venice.

### Montenegro and Venice

The place of Venice in the history of Montenegro remains a subject of polemics in Montenegrin historiography.[103] Until the eighteenth century the Montenegrins relied primarily on Venice for support against the Turks, and on a number of occasions they joined Venice in wars against them. The Montenegrins participated on the Venetian side in such major confrontations as the Cypriot War (1570–1573),[104] the Candian War (1645–1669),[105] and the Morean War (1684–1699).[106] So close were relations between Montenegro and Venice during the Candian War that the Montenegrin general assembly that met in Cetinje in 1648 expressed readiness to place Montenegro under the protection of Venice on condition that the latter recognize the autonomy that the Montenegrins possessed in the Ottoman Empire.[107] Again in 1688, during the Morean War, the Montenegrins voluntarily placed themselves under Venetian protection, and asked Venice to station troops in Cetinje. This decision was accompanied by a Montenegrin uprising, precipitated by increased Ottoman taxes, Turkish attempts to collect tribute by force,[108] and anti-Turkish agitation by Venice and the Catholic church. Bishop Visarion (1685–1692), in particular was committed to an uprising against Ottoman rule. Venetian "sovereignty" over Montenegro was shortlived; it ended in 1696.[109]

The Turks accepted the Peace treaty of Karlowitz in 1699 grudgingly and never ceased plotting for revenge against Venice. The opportune moment came in December 1714 and the Sublime Porte declared war on Venice.[110] Not prepared either on land or sea, Venice was anxious to win the tribes of Montenegro, Brda, and

Herzegovina to its side.[111] The Venetians did not fare well in the war. The Ottoman advance into Dalmatia was against Austria's strategic interests, compelling the latter, an ally of Venice, to embark on a preventive war against the Ottoman Empire in 1716.

When Bishop Danilo got back to Montenegro in April 1716, he found it still suffering from Numan Pasha's ravages, and the situation further aggravated by tribal conflicts and the Venetian-Ottoman war on Montenegro's borders. Realizing that little tangible help could come from Russia, Bishop Danilo entered into discussions with Austria, which had assigned a prominent role in Prince Eugene's strategic plans to the Balkan Christians. In July 1716 the bishop sent a Montenegrin emissary, Nikola Rajić (a one-time captain in Russian service), to Prince Eugene with a proposal that, if Austria dispatched 40,000 troops to Montenegro, the Montenegrins would join them against the Turks, provided Austria confirmed the "old privileges" of the Montenegrins.[112] Nothing came of the bishop's proposal. This and later discussions between the Bishop and Vienna gave Venice ample reason for concern. Venice abandoned a plan to enlist the neighboring Serbian tribes in war against the Ottoman Empire.[113] It suspected the bishop of having made political commitments to both Austria and Russia, and decided to put him out of action. In September 1716 the Venetian State Inquisitors ordered Bishop Danilo poisoned to death.[114]

During Bishop Danilo's absence from Montenegro the leaders of Katun nahie had sent Venice a delegation to seek a Venetian protectorate over Montenegro. The Venetian senate on February 23, 1717, approved the petition, and on March 7 the doge issued a ducal decree defining Montenegrin rights and obligations.[115] This idea for a Venetian protectorate came from the leaders of Katun, which stood in the forefront of the liberation struggle and assumed the right to speak for all the Montenegrin nahies. In their petition to Venice the leaders of Katun nahie stressed self-government, and proposed appointment of a governor (*guvernadur*) who would represent Venice in Montenegro and function as a kind of civil administrator. This proposal coincided with the Venetian aim to establish control over the bishop and the Montenegrin tribes. Venice sent to Cetinje a *guvernadur* who was to help Bishop Danilo manage the civil affairs of Montenegro and organize resistance against the Turks. The first *guvernadur* was a Venetian citizen, who was replaced four months later by a native, Vukadin Vukotić. Henceforth the office of *guver-*

*nadur* remained in the house of Vukotić (from the Čevljani or Čevo tribe) until 1750. That year the last member of the Vukotić clan relinquished the title of *guvernadur* to Stanko Radonjić, the leader of the Njeguši, in exchange for the office of sirdar and 100 sequins.[116]

The appointment of a governor followed the earlier practice of electing a spahi as the head of Montenegro.[117] M. Bolizza's description of the sanjak of Scutari, published in 1614, shows that in the seventeenth century Montenegro was headed by a spahi. Bolizza describes the bishop of Cetinje as spiritual head and the spahi as the leader of the country (*capo di Monte Negro*). In the course of the seventeenth century the spahi was often identified as *vojvoda* or *colonnello* of Montenegro. His position was hereditary and much like that of the *guvernadur.*

The Montenegrins were slow in accepting the foreign term *guvernadur* or *guverner.* It was for this reason that Vukotić as late as 1723 still bore the title of *knez* rather than *guvernadur;* he employed the title *guvernadur* for the first time in 1730 in signing an agreement with Kotor. The Turks insisted on calling him voivode and captain.

That the office of the secular leader of Montenegro should be resuscitated in Bishop Danilo's time was not without significance. Bishop Danilo rightly perceived the appointment of a *guvernadur* as a move against him, especially since he was not even mentioned in the agreement between Venice and the Katunjani. His argument was that Montenegro could have no other protector than the Russian tsar.[118] As it turned out, the establishment of the office of *guvernadur* did little more than create rivalry between him and the bishop, and between their respective supporters, rivalry that was to last until the accession of Peter II Petrović-Njegoš (1830–1851).

## The Turkish Reprisal

During the Venetian-Austrian war with the Turks, the Montenegrins could not remain on the sidelines. To secure the assistance of the Montenegrins, the Venetians offered them provisions and war supplies, opened their markets to them, and bribed some Montenegrin elders with money.[119] The bishop called an assembly of tribal leaders on February 23, 1717, to decide whether or not to join Venice. Despite threats and warnings from the Ottoman authorities of Scutari and Nikšić, a decision was made to enter into an alliance with Venice.[120] Armed by the Venetians, Montenegrin irregulars took over the role once played by the haiduks, who had been inactive since the Morean War. The Montenegrin irregulars made forays into Ottoman-occupied Herzegovina and into Dubrovnik. Their leaders were paid by Venice, but the ordinary fighters lived from brigandage. (This was the time when Vuk Mićunović, celebrated in popular poetry for his exploits against the Turks, perished during an attack on heavily fortified Trebinje.)[121]

Not ready to break the agreement that the Katunjani had concluded with Venice, Bishop Danilo decided to endorse it. This action, he believed, would enable him to secure undisputed leadership over the Montenegrins. In any case, since no substantial help could be expected either from Russia or Austria, Bishop Danilo had no choice but to turn to Venice. In September 1717, accompanied by 50 Montenegrin leaders, Bishop Danilo met in Herceg Novi with the proveditor general of Kotor and reached an agreement on Montenegrin-Venetian military cooperation against the Turks. The Brdjani welcomed Bishop Danilo's decision to cooperate with Venice, and took up arms against the Turks. In October 1717 a combined Montenegrin-Venetian force attacked Bar but failed to take it.[122] The proveditor sent a letter to the Venetian senate in which he praised the Montenegrins for their aid and bravery at Bar.[123] The Venetian senate awarded Bishop Danilo 1,000 ducats for his help and personal gallantry.[124] The Montenegrins and Bishop Danilo did indeed prove to be superb fighters.

The Herzegovinian tribes this time showed little inclination to join Venice in war against the Turks, and only a few tribes from Brda (the Kuči, for example) responded favorably to the Venetian call. The commune of Grbalj went to war against the Turks only after Venice had reaffirmed the privileges that Grbalj had been enjoying since 1647. Once the Montenegrins and Grbalj had joined Venice, the Sublime Porte ordered Durmiš Pasha Čengić to seize Cetinje and to stop the Montenegrins from escaping with the Venetians. Durmiš Pasha invaded Cuce, and at the village Trnine engaged the Montenegrins in battle. This time the Montenegrins emerged victorious, capturing a number of prominent Turks, who were executed as reprisal for recent Turkish execution of Montenegrin captives.[125] As in many other instances, the bards have exaggerated the importance of the victory and some have identified it with the much discussed Battle of Carev Laz.[126] Late in 1717 Bishop Danilo appealed to Venice for financial assistance to erect a system of defense against the Turks, but his appeal was turned down. After 1717 the fighting between the Turks and Montenegrins subsided for several years, though it never stopped completely. The bloodiest encounters recorded are those at Nikšić (1719), Podgorica and Spuž (1721), and near Žabljak (1725). The Turks preferred peace, but the Montenegrins and armed bands from Brda continued attacking and robbing them.[127]

Bishop Danilo never lost sight of his ultimate objectives. He was the first Montenegrin leader to give serious consideration to the idea of Montenegrin independence,[128] and the first who understood the importance to Montenegro of access to Lake Scutari. In April 1718 Bishop Danilo went to Venice to seek support for several plans and to define the religious rights of the Montenegrin metropolitanate in Venetian territory. He was accompanied by representatives of Riječka and Crmnička nahies, which had not been included in the agreement previously concluded between Venice and the leaders of Katun. The Venetian governor of Split refused to allow the bishop to continue the trip to Venice, but he permitted the representatives of the two nahies to go on. On the bishop's recommendation, the Venetian government admitted Riječka and Crmnička under its protection, and confirmed this decision by a ducal decree of May 7, 1718.[129]

The same decree also recognized the jurisdiction of Bishop Danilo in communities that Venice had acquired in its current war with the Ottoman Empire, the freedom of their inhabitants to practice their Orthodox rites, and the right to repair old and build new churches in all places under the bishop's jurisdiction.[130] The bishop was not satisfied with these terms and sent another memorandum to Venice. Venice issued a new decree on June 4, 1718, which extended the bishop's jurisdiction to other communities in Boka Kotorska on condition that no new churches or monasteries were to be built there. The bishop would be allowed to visit parishes in Boka Kotorska at the discretion of the governor general. Thus the jurisdiction of the bishop of Cetinje was confirmed in the regions where the metropolitanate had already been exercising it (Grbalj, Maine, Pribori), and under certain conditions over additional Orthodox communities in Boka Kotorska. Dispute did not end here, however, and Bishop Danilo still found it necessary to protest against continued Venetian infringement on Cetinje's jurisdiction and against various restraints imposed on the Orthodox clergy and believers.[131]

## The Treaty of Passarowitz (Požarevac)

Venice had no outstanding victories in the latest war with the Turks. On the other hand, the Austrian army, ably led by Eugene of Savoy, captured Belgrade on August 18, 1717, and advanced deep into Serbia. The war was ended by the Treaty of Passarowitz, signed on July 21, 1718. In one last effort, two days after the treaty had been signed, a combined Venetian-Montenegrin force made an unsuccessful attempt to seize Ulcinj.[132] Under the terms of the treaty, Venice retained all the territories it had won during the war in Dalmatia and Boka Kotorska.[133] It thus acquired Grbalj, Maine, Pobore, and Brajići, which until then had been considered Montenegro's fifth nahie. (The other four were Katunska, Riječka, Lješanska, and Crmnička.) Venice also obtained Krivošije, Ubli, and Ledenice north of Risan. The Montenegrins, by contrast, not only failed to gain anything from the war, but also lost lands they had long considered their own to their Venetian ally. By losing Grbalj, Montenegro was cut off from the sea. Worse yet, the people of Grbalj in time lost some of their Montenegrin consciousness, although the same was not true in Maine, Pobori, and Brajići. In fact, Stanjevići Monastery in Maine was no less the see of the Montenegrin metropolitans than Cetinje Monastery.

Bishop Danilo was particularly disappointed that the war had not brought liberation to Montenegro. His relations with the Venetians were aggravated by his agitation against Venetian rule in the Serene Republic's new acquisitions. Under the Treaty of Passarowitz the juridical status of Montenegro remained unchanged: Montenegro was still a part of the Ottoman Empire, although neither governed nor controlled by it. Venice and the other European states continued to treat Montenegro as an Ottoman province. But despite the disappointments of the treaty, participation in war against the Turks had strengthened the Montenegrins' will to resist and their independence from the Turks. The treaty also marked the end of two centuries of Montenegrin dependence on and cooperation with Venice in the struggle against the Ottomans.

* * *

Under Bishop Danilo's dynamic leadership the struggle against the Turks in defense of Montenegrin autonomy and traditional rights was superseded by a struggle for national independence. The tribes became more conscious of their common interests, and the international position of Montenegro was enhanced as Austria, Russia, and Venice vied for influence over it. Bishop Danilo freed his country from dependence on Venice, and tied its destiny to Russia.

Neither a theologian nor a pious man, Bishop Danilo was an uncompromising defender of Serbian Orthodoxy, fully aware of its interdependence with Serbian national indentity. He gave the metropolitanate of Cetinje a political mission, improved its ecclesiastical administration, and affirmed its jurisdiction over the coastal region, then under Venetian rule. Bishop Danilo fought against Catholic proselytism and maintained close relations with the metropolitanate of Sremski Karlovci and the synod of the Russian church. He did not accomplish much of what he set out to do, but he charted the course that his successors followed successfully toward national liberation and Montenegro's transformation from a tribal to a state system.

## Notes

1. J. Radonić, *Rimska kurija i južnoslovenske zemlje od XVI do XIX veka* [The Roman Curia and the South Slav Lands from the 16th to the 19th Centuries] (Belgrade, 1950), p. 432.
2. G. Vitković, *Budimski spomenici* [Monuments of Buda], I (Belgrade, 1873), 5–8; Jagoš Jovanivić, *Stvaranje crnogorske države i razvoj crnogorske nacionalnosti* [The Creation of the Montenegrin State and the Development of Montenegrin Nationality] (Cetinje, 1948), p. 91.
3. *Ibid.*
4. Gligor Stanojević, *Crna Gora u doba Vladike Danila* [Montenegro in Vladika Danilo's Time] (Cetinje, 1955), pp. 204–205.
5. *Istorija naroda Jugoslavije* [History of the Nation of Yugoslavia] II (Belgrade, 1960) [hereafter cited as *INJ*], 160–163, 169.
6. Branko Pavićević, *Stvaranje crnogorske države* [The Creation of the Montenegrin State] (Belgrade, 1955), p. 27; *Starine* [Antiquities], XII, 169.
7. *INJ*, II, 162–163.
8. S. Milutinović, *Istorija Crne Gore* [History of Montenegro] (Belgrade, 1935), p. 23; Radonić, *Rimska kurija*, p. 613; J. Milović, *Zbornik dokumenata iz istorije Crne Gore* [Collection of Documents from the History of Montenegro] (Cetinje, 1956), p. 191; *Istorija Crne Gore*, III:1 (Titograd, 1975) [hereafter cited as *ICG*], 33.
9. Jovanović, *Stvaranje i razvoj*, p. 90.
10. Stanojević, *Crna Gora*, pp. 208, 215; R. Grujić, "Problemi istorije karlovačke mitropolije" [Problems of the History of the Metropolitanate of

Sremski Karlovci], *Glasnik istoriskog društva* [History Society Herald] (Novi Sad), II, 62.

11. Stanojević, *Crna Gora*, pp. 209–211; Radonić, *Rimska kurija*, pp. 432–433.

12. Gligor Stanojević, "Crna Gora u doba kandiskog rata (1645–1649)" [Montenegro at the Time of Candian War (1645–1649)] 32; *idem, Crna Gora*, pp. 212–213.

13. *ICG*, III:1, 274–275; N. Milaš, *Pravoslavna Dalmacija* [Orthodox Dalmatia] (Novi Sad, 1901), p. 332.

14. *ICG*, III:1, 275.

15. The monastic properties included pastureland in Lovćen, vineyards in Rijeka Crnojevića, fishing rights in Lake Scutari, salterns and olive groves.

16. *INJ*, II, 1183–1184.

17. Jovanović, *Stvaranje i razvoj*, pp. 91–92, 114.

18. Stanojević, *Crna Gora*, p. 180.

19. Pavićević, *Stvaranje*, p. 39; Gligor Stanojević, "Iz istorije Crne Gore u XVI i XVII vijeku" [From the History of Montenegro in the 17th and 18th Centuries], *Istoriski zapisi* [Historical Records], XV (1959), No. 2, 413; Milenko Filipović, "Pleme" [Tribe], in *Enciklopedija Jugoslavije* [The Encyclopedia of Yugoslavia] (Zagreb), VI (1965), 512.

20. *INJ*, II, 1175–1176.

21. Gligor Stanojević, *Mitropolit Vasilije i njegovo doba, 1740–1766* [Metropolitan Vasilije and His Time, 1740–1766] (Belgrade, 1979), pp. 49–52; *ICG*, III:1, 318, 322–323; Vladislav Skarić, "Trebinje u XV vijeku" [Trebinje in the 15th Century], *Glasnik Zemaljskog Muzeja* [The Regional Museum Herald] (Sarajevo), XLV (1933), 64.

22. F. Ongania, *Il Montenegro da relazione dei proveditori veneti (1687–1735)* (Rome, 1896), pp. 116–121; Stanojević, *Mitropolit Vasilije*, pp. 49–52.

23. Stanojević, *Crna Gora*, pp. 51–52.

24. Gligor Stanojević, *Mitropolit Vasilije Petrović i njegovo doba, 1740–1766* (Belgrade, 1978), p. 52; *ICG*, III:1, 314.

25. *Ibid.*, 26; J. Tomić, "Turski pohod na Crnu Goru, 1712" [The Turkish Assault on Montenegro, 1712], *Glas SAN* [News of the S(erbian) A(cademy of) S(ciences)], XCVI (1920), 268; *idem, Pitanje Careva Laza* [The Question of Carev Laz (Emperor's Glade)] (Belgrade, 1934); Stanojević, *Crna Gora*, pp. 81–96.

26. According to Jovan Stefanov Balović, quoted in Marko Dragović, *Mitropolit Vasilije Petrović* [Metropolitan Vasilije Petrović] (Cetinje, 1884), pp. 122–123.

27. Trifun Djukić, *Pregled književnog rada Crne Gore* [Survey of the Literary Work of Montenegro] (Cetinje, 1951), p. 3.

28. *Enciklopedija Jugoslavije*, II (1966), 426.

29. Jovanović, *Stvaranje i razvoj*, p. 63.

30. *Ibid.*, pp. 67–68; *ICG*, III:1, 247.

31. *Ibid.*, 247–249.

32. Jovanović, *Stvaranje i razvoj*, p. 93.

33. *INJ*, II, 1170–1171.

34. H. Hadžibegić, "Turski dokumenti u Državnom muzeju na Cetinju" [Turkish Documents in the State Museum in Cetinje], *Istoriski zapisi*, XI (1955), No. 1–2, 115–130; *ICG*, III:1, 247.

35. N. Banašević, "Pesnička legenda o Badnjem večeru" [The Poetic Legend of Christmas Eve], *Prilozi* [Addenda], Nov. 1–2, 1957, pp. 13, 21; *ICG*, III:1, 244.

36. Ilarion Ruvarac, *Montenegrina: Prilošci istorije Crne Gore* [Montenegrina: Supplements to the History of Montenegro] (Zemun, 1899), p. 173.

37. Jovan N. Tomić, *Dve rasprave iz istorije Crne Gore* [Two Essays from the History of Montenegro] (Zemun, 1901), pp. 51–57; *idem*, *Pitanje Careva Laza*, pp. 148–149.

38. V. Ćorović, "Odnošaji izmedju Crnogoraca i Albanije u početku XVIII veka" [Relations between the Montenegrins and Albania at the Beginning of the 18th Century], *Arhiv za albansku starinu, jezik i etnologiju* [Archives for the Albanian Past, Language and Ethnology] (Belgrade), I (1923), No. 1–2, 52–53; *idem*, "Odnošaji Crne Gore sa Dubrovnikom od Karlovačkog do Požarevačkog mira" [Relations between Montenegro and Dubrovnik from the Peace of Karlowitz to the Peace of Passarowitz], *Glas SKA* [News of the S(erbian) R(oyal) A(cademy)], CLXXXVII (1923), 23–24; Stanojević, *Crna Gora*, pp. 31–44, 54–55.

39. *Ibid.*, pp. 39, 44.

40. *Ibid.*, pp. 41–42.

41. *Ibid.*, p. 44; Jovanović, *Stvaranje i razvoj*, pp. 114–115.

42. Radonić, *Rimska kurija*, p. 529.

43. Benedict H. Sumner, *Peter the Great and the Ottoman Empire* (Oxford, 1949), p. 46.

44. *Ibid.*, pp. 34–35.

45. Radovan Lalić, "O tradicionalnim vezama izmedju Crne Gore i Rusije" [On the Traditional Ties between Montenegro and Russia], *Istoriski zapisi*, No. 7, 1951, p. 251.

46. Sumner, *Peter the Great*, p. 33.

47. S. M. Solov'ev, *Istoriya Rossii s drevneyskikh vremen* [History of Russia from the Earliest Times], VIII (Moscow, 1962), 377–378; S. Bogoyavlenskiy, "Iz russko-serbskikh otnoshenii pri Petre pervom" [On Russo-Serbian Relations under Peter I], *Voprosy istorii* [Problems of History], VIII–IX (1946), 25; Sumner, *Peter the Great*, p. 45.

48. Solov'ev, *Istoriya*, VIII, 413–415.

49. Bogoyavlenskiy, "Iz russko-serbskikh otnoshenii," pp. 21, 31; Stanojević, *Crna Gora*, pp. 60–61.

50. Solov'ev, *Istoriya*, VIII, 377–379.

51. *Ibid.*

52. *Ibid.*, 414.

53. Sumner, *Peter the Great*, p. 41.

54. *ICG*, III:1, 254.

55. Stanojević, *Crna Gora*, pp. 65–67.

56. A. Theiner, *Vetera monumenta Slavorum meridionalium*, II, 241; *ICG*, III:1, 254.

57. *Ibid.*, 225.

58. Stanojević, *Crna Gora*, p. 69.

59. Jovanović, *Stvaranje i razvoj*, p. 68.

60. Stanojević, *Crna Gora*, p. 68.

61. Bogoyavlenskiy, "Iz russko-serbskikh otnoshenii," p. 35; *ICG*, III:1, 264.

62. *Ibid.*, 255.

63. J. Radonić, *Dubrovačka akta i povelja* [Acts and Charters of Dubrovnik], V (Belgrade, 1952), 81–82; Stanojević, *Crna Gora*, pp. 74–75.

64. *Ibid.*, pp. 75–76.

65. *Ibid.*, p. 73.

66. On Montenegrin financial difficulties, see *ibid.*, pp. 75–76.

67. Sumner, *Peter the Great*, p. 48; Bogoyavlenskiy, "Iz russko-serbskikh otnoshenii," p. 36.

68. Stanojević, *Crna Gora*, p. 79; St. Dimitrijević, "Gradja za srpsku istoriju" [Materials for Serbian History], *Spomenik* [Memorial], LIII, 56–57; *ICG*, III:1, 255–256.

69. Tomić, "Turski pohod," pp. 171–172; *ICG*, III:1, 81–82.

70. Stanojević, *Crna Gora*, pp. 81–82.

71. Jovanović, *Stvaranje i razvoj*, p. 100.

72. Tomić, "Turski pohod," pp. 181–182; Stanojević, *Crna Gora*, p. 83.

73. Tomić, "Turski pohod," p. 179.

74. *ICG*, III:1, 256.

75. Jovanović, *Stvaranje i razvoj*, pp. 100–101.

76. Tomić, "Turski pohod," p. 194; Stanojević, *Crna Gora*, p. 98.

77. The legend has been challenged in Tomić, "Turski pohod," pp. 171–172; *idem*, *Pitanje Careva Laza*, p. 108; *ICG*, III:1, 256–257; Milutinović, *Istorija Crne Gore*, p. 72.

78. Dj. Lazarević, *O boju na Carevu Lazu* [On the Battle of Carev Laz] (Belgrade, 1934); S. Mijušković, "Dogadjaji u Crnoj Gori od pojave Miloradovića do Numanpašinog pohoda (1711–1714)" [Events in Montenegro from the Appearance of Miloradović to Numan Pasha's Assault (1711–1714)], *Istoriski zapisi*, XI (1955), 198–199; J. Vuletić, "Boj na Carevu

Lazu" [The Battle of Carev Laz], *Spomenik SAN* (Belgrade), CVI (1956), 79; V. Ćorović, "Odnošaji Crne Gore sa Dubrovnikom od karlovačkog do požarevačkog mira" [Relations between Montenegro and Dubrovnik from the Peace of Karlowitz to the Peace of Passarowitz], *Glas SAN*, CLXXXVII (1941), 232. See also n. 25.

79. Stanojević, *Crna Gora*, p. 100.

80. *Ibid.*; Ongania, *Il Montenegro*, p. 128.

81. Tomić, "Turski pohod," pp. 60–61.

82. Mijušković, "Dogadjaji u Crnoj Gori," p. 205; *ICG*, III:1, 263.

83. Solov'ev, *Istoriya*, VIII, 414.

84. *Ibid.*

85. Tomić, "Turski pohod," p. 75; Stanojević, *Crna Gora*, p. 104.

86. J. Tomić, "Pohod Numan-paše Ćuprilića na Crnu Goru u 1714" [Numan Pasha Ćuprilić's Attack on Montenegro in 1714], *Glas*, CXLVII (1932), 52; *ICG*; III:1, 263; Jovanović, *Stvaranje i razvoj*, p. 102.

87. *Ibid.*, p. 103.

88. Tomić, "Turski pohod," pp. 77, 81–85.

89. *Ibid.*, pp. 87–90.

90. Stanojević, *Crna Gora*, pp. 104–105.

91. Tomić, "Turski pohod," pp. 81–96.

92. Jovanović, *Stvaranje i razvoj*, p. 92.

93. Stanojević, *Crna Gora*, pp. 59–80. Contacts between the Serbs and the Russians had existed since medieval times, but this time the Montenegrins established political ties with Russia on a more regular basis. *Enciklopedija Jugoslavije*, II, 1180–1181.

94. Bogoyavlenskiy, "Iz russko-serbskikh otnoshenii," p. 38.

95. Jovanović, *Stvaranje i razvoj*, pp. 106–107.

96. Solov'ev, *Istoriya*, VIII, 415, 598–599.

97. Jovanović, *Stvaranje i razvoj*, p. 106. Cf. Solov'ev, *Istoriya*, VIII, 415; M. Dragović, "Materijal za istoriju Crne Gore" [Material for the History of Montenegro], *Spomenik*, XXV, 2.

98. *Ibid.*; Bogoyavlenskiy, "Iz russko-serbskikh otnoshenii," p. 38; Milutinović, *Istorija Crne Gore*, pp. 65–67; *ICG*, III:1, 269; Stanojević, *Crna Gora*, p. 116. For details on how the money was spent and what books, gifts and charters Danilo brought with him, see Lj. Stojanović, *Stari srpski zapisi i natpisi* [Old Serbian Records and Inscriptions], Vol. II (Belgrade, 1903), Nos. 2289, 2296.

99. *ICG*, III:1, 268, 289; Milutinović, *Istorija Crne Gore*, pp. 65–67.

100. B. Pavićević, "Vladika Sava Petrović u Rusiji 1743–1744 godine" [Prince-Bishop Sava Petrović in Russia, 1743–1744], *Istoriski časopis* [History Magazine], XIV–XV (1963–1965), 93–109.

101. Stanojević, *Crna Gora*, pp. 101–191.

102. On Peter I's visit to Russia, Austrian and Russian policy and rivalry

over Montenegro, financial and military aid to Montenegro, the Austrian and Russian missions, and Catherine the Great's appeal to Christians to join in war against the Ottoman Empire, see *ICG*, III:1, 395–418; Vladan Djordjević, *Ispisi iz bečkih državnih arhiva* [Transcriptions from the Vienna State Archives] (Belgrade, 1931); *idem*, *Crna Gora i Rusija (1784–1814)* [Montenegro and Russia (1784–1814)] (Belgrade, 1914); *idem*, *Crna Gora i Austrija u XVIII veku* [Montenegro and Austria in the 18th Century] (Belgrade, 1912); V. Čubrilović, "Crna Gora i rusko-austrijski ugovor o podeli Turske 1782 godine" [Montenegro and the 1782 Russo-Austrian Agreement on the Partition of Turkey], *Glas*, CCL (1961), 171–196.

103. *Jugoslovenski istoriski časopis* [Yugoslav Historical Magazine], No. 1–2, pp. 132–134. On Montenegrin-Venetian relations in 1714–1718, see Stanojević, *Crna Gora*, pp. 111–146.

104. *Enciklopedija Jugoslavije*, II (1956), 419; Milović, *Zbornik dokumenata*, p. 251. J. N. Tomić asserts that the Montenegrins took no part in the Cypriot War but merely supplied the Venetians in Kotor with food. Tomić, "Politički odnos Crne Gore prema Turskoj, 1528–1684" [Montenegro's Political Relationship with Turkey, 1528–1684], *Glas*, LXVI (1903), 17 n. 27.

105. Stanojević, "Crna Gora u doba kandiskog rata," pp. 3–53.

106. J. Tomić, *Crna Gora za morejskog rata (1684–1699)* [Montenegro during the Morean War (1684–1699)] (Belgrade, 1907).

107. Stanojević, "Iz istorije Crne Gore," pp. 378–385.

108. Tomić, *Crna Gora za morejskog rata*, p. 277; *idem*, *O crnogorskom ustanku u početku morejskog rata (1684–1685)* [On the Montenegrin Uprising at the Beginning of the Morean War (1684–1685)] (Novi Sad, 1903); Pavićević, *Stvaranje*, pp. 17, 33–34; Djurdjev, *Turska vlast* On Venetian agitation among the Montenegrins, and Bishop Ruvim's decision to join the Venetians, see Tomić, *Crna Gora za morejskog rata*, p. 12.

109. Ongania, *Il Montenegro*, pp. 31–33; Pavićević, *Stvaranje*, p. 36.

110. *ICG*, III:1, 266–267; Amy A. Bernardy, *L'ultima guerra turco-veneziana (1714–1718)* (Florence, 1902), pp. 21–22.

111. Jovanović, *Stvaranje i razvoj*, p. 108.

112. *ICG*, III:1, 270; Luigi Matuschka, *Campagne del principe Eugenio di Savoia*, VII (Turin, 1900), 25–26.

113. *ICG*, III:1, 268.

114. *Ibid.*, 270. For details of the Inquisitors' proceedings and decision see Stanojević, *Crna Gora*, pp. 121–124.

115. For the text of the 12-point petition submitted by Vukadin Vukotić in the name of the Montenegrins, and of a 5-point petition submitted the same day by Voivode Radonja Petrović on behalf of the Kuči, see Stanojević, *Crna Gora*, pp. 126–129; Ongania, *Il Montenegro*, pp. 132–137; *ICG*, III:1, 271.

116. Stanojević, *Crna Gora*, pp. 196-197.

117. The spahi (Serbocroat, *spahija;* Turkish, *sipahi*) was designated by an imperial berat which defined his prerogatives. He served as intermediary between the Ottoman authorities and the Montenegrins, and had the right to collect certain taxes. *INJ*, II, 510. Contrary to the opinion of many historians who have contended that the Venetians introduced "dualism" in Montenegro, the practice had existed there for two centuries. Stanojević, *Crna Gora*, pp. 129-130. Its reintroduction at this time served only to obstruct the struggle for liberation.

118. *Ibid.*, p. 131; *ICG*, III:1, 271-272.

119. Jovanović, *Stvaranje i razvoj*, p. 110.

120. *ICG*, III:1, 266-267; Stanojević, *Crna Gora*, pp. 113-114.

121. *Ibid.*, pp. 114-115; Vuk St. Karadžić, *Srpske narodne pesme* [Serbian Folk Poems], IV (Belgrade, 1896), 8.

122. Stanojević, *Crna Gora*, pp. 136–137; *ICG*, III:1, 272.

123. Jovanović, *Stvaranje i razvoj*, pp. 112–113.

124. M. Milošević, "Oko pokušaja osvajanja Bara i Ulcinja 1717 i 1718 godine" [On the Attempt to Seize Bar and Ulcinj in 1717 and 1718], *Istoriski zapisi*, XVII (1961), 788–795; Stanojević, *Crna Gora*, pp. 138–139.

125. Jovanović, *Stvaranje i razvoj*, pp. 111–112.

126. Tomić, *Pitanje Careva Laza*, p. 108; Milutinović, *Istorija Crne Gore*, p. 72.

127. Jovanović, *Stvaranje i razvoj*, p. 113.

128. *ICG*, III:1, 273–274.

129. For details see Stanojević, *Crna Gora*, pp. 143-144; Ongania, *Il Montenegro*, pp. 144–145.

130. Stanojević, "Crna Gora u doba kandiskog rata," p. 32; *idem*, *Crna Gora*, pp. 212–213.

131. *Ibid.*, pp. 214–215.

132. *ICG*, III:1, 277-278.

133. Bianchi Vendramino, *Istorica relazione della pace di Pasarovitz* (Padua, 1719), pp. 191-205; *ICG*, III:1, 276. The Venetian-Ottoman boundary commission began its work in December 1718 and completed it in June 1721.

Bistra Cvetkova

# The Bulgarian Haiduk Movement in the 15th–18th Centuries

The haiduk movement was the longest-lasting resistance to Ottoman rule in the Bulgarian lands. An indomitable popular movement that grew steadily in scope and strength, it was through the centuries a spontaneous expression of the antifeudal opposition of the populace—the so-called rayah—to the order and institutions of the Ottoman feudal system. At the same time, the haiduks were a symbol of the national spirit of the Bulgarians and their implacable hostility to the rule of alien conquerors of a different faith.

Until recently historians have had very scanty sources on the haiduks, and the sources have been very alike in character and quality—haiduk epics, a few references in the narratives of foreign travelers, occasional glosses. Haiduk epic songs give a distorted and often very inaccurate picture of events, persons and facts, and their dating is very imprecise. Their use as source material therefore requires the application of complicated and often not very reliable methods to eliminate the poetic elements and extract a credible historical reality. The majority of travel notes are superficial, and all too frequently contain information obtained from the hostile Ottoman authorities in the places through which the travelers passed. The very few Bulgarian observations mostly take the form of passing references and oblique asides. The scattered, sporadic actions of the haiduks could not be encompassed in their entirety in the works of the few Bulgarian men of letters and chroniclers of the time, who led secluded lives dispersed all over the country, suffering the spiritual and intellectual deprivation of a Bulgarian society shorn of its leaders by conquest and humiliated to the extreme nationally, politically and culturally.

Over the last twenty years the search for written evidence and the publication of rich and extensive material, mainly from Ottoman Turkish sources,[1] have opened possibilities for new historical inquiry. They have made it possible to give a documented exposition of the real dimensions and character of the haiduk movement and its significance for the fate of the Bulgarian nation.

The origin of these new sources implies per se one-sided historical data because they were produced by the institutions and representatives of foreign rule that subjected the Balkan nations for centuries to slavish dependence, and to religious and national discrimination against non-Muslims.[2] The Ottoman Turkish sources reflect the interests and attitudes of the ruling class. Its view inevitably misrepresents the real condition of the subordinate class, the rayah, who included ordinary Turkish Muslim working people who were no less exposed to feudal exploitation than Christians. This fact has to be constantly borne in mind when analyzing Ottoman Turkish documents to study the haiduk movement. The element that pervades these sources is the age-old, undying hatred felt by the Ottoman rulers for all those who violated the order they had imposed on the conquered Balkan lands, or who dared to rise against the burdens of this order. Social prejudice and to a certain extent also the national and religious intolerance of Ottoman rule were why the haiduk movement is portrayed in Ottoman official documents and chronicles with all the features of common banditry.

All the negative connotations of "bandits" are applied in these sources to the haiduks, who are treated with contempt and whose deeds are dismissed as outlawry. The Ottoman administration ascribed to the haiduks all the crimes of common brigandage: assaults on travelers, attacks on property, murder, plunder and robbery. When working with such sources every care has to be taken to distinguish the two essential motives of the haiduks' actions—the social and the national. This is especially necessary when it is realized that banditry too is born out of the inconsistencies and injustices of a social system. Research based on Ottoman sources has therefore to proceed along two lines. First, it must seek the social origin of those always typified as "bandits, haiduks and brigands," and the social significance of their targets. And secondly, it must look for the national element in the haiduk movement and for signs of national consciousness. These are what gives the movement its anti-Ottoman character.[3]

Existing literature on the haiduk movement is of variable quality. Much of it is based on popular epics, local legends and vivid folk memory. It tends to trace the story chronologically up to the eighteenth century with little attempt at scientific verification of the data preserved in folklore. The result is the propagation of romantic and inaccurate historical notions that reduce the haiduk movement to the deeds of a few brave men inspired by personal revenge or heroism.

The publication of more detailed and variegated source materials during the last two decades has led contemporary researchers to seek documentary support for the older accounts. Though not numerous, these modern studies have yielded a clearer and historically more authentic outline of the haiduk movement. Some of these studies have continued to treat the haiduk movement in isolation from other efforts at resistance and liberation, making it difficult to arrive at a correct evaluation of the movement's character and dynamics. Not all of them have established criteria to distinguish the deeds of the haiduks from the violence of common banditry, and too little attention has often been paid to the national elements in the actions of the haiduks and their connection with liberation movements.

The present purpose, then, is to limn the fundamental characteristics of the haiduk movement, its dynamics and its specific features during the various stages of the Bulgarians' history, and its significance to their development.

* * *

Armed resistance began immediately after the Bulgarian lands fell under Ottoman dominion. From the meager historical evidence the haiduk movement in the first decades of the fifteenth century seems to have had the features of a liberation struggle. The memory of an independent Bulgarian state was still alive in people's minds. A group, mainly members of the previous ruling class, around the two representatives of the former royal dynasty, Prince Fruzhin, son of the last tsar, Ivan Shishman, and his cousin Prince Konstantin, made an attempt to restore Bulgarian freedom even before the end of the fourteenth century. Legends, backed by a few shreds of evidence, have it that they led the defense of part of the Bulgarian lands against the Ottoman onslaught and continued to fight after the conquest.[4] Hard-burdened by the Ottoman socioeconomic structure,[5] deprived of social and political leadership, disarmed by the intensity of the religious and national discrimination against them, feudal dependents almost to a man, the Bulgarians continued to struggle against their new social oppressors, the Ottoman feudal lords, not only foreigners but of another faith to boot. Spontaneously and without organization, singly at first or in small bands, the local people fought on. The oldest written records, preserved in fifteenth-century Ottoman land registers (*tahrir defterleri*), mention haiduk hideouts in a number of places in the Bulgarian lands.[6] The area around Surnevo, a village near present-day Cherven is described as a dangerous "haiduk lair" in the statute of the village recorded in a detailed Ottoman land register now in the Turkish archives in Sofia.[7] There is similar evidence that from the very beginning of Ottoman occupation haiduks were active near the bridge over the River Erkene outside Uzunköprü (in eastern Thrace),[8] and in the vicinity of some deserted farmlands (*mezra*) near the River Ketenlik in the southwest.[9] In many cases these lands were the vestiges of abandoned or demolished settlements.[10] Their frequent mention as haiduk hideouts suggests that the haiduks wandering these lands may well have been former inhabitants of the ravaged communities. It would not then be surprising if the most irreconcilable warriors against the Ottoman regime were from among those who had suffered most under foreign domination.

From as early as the first half of the fifteenth century foreign travelers in their journals mentioned places they had visited where haiduks were known to be active.[11] It is only to be expected that many of them referred to the haiduks as "bandits and scoundrels," for their information came from biased sources, the Ottoman officials who escorted them. In 1433 the Burgundian Knight Bertrandon de la Broquière reported that the heights above Ikhtiman were a refuge for haiduks.[12] As early as this the Turks had organized the *derbentci*, special guards of mountain passes and strategic locations, as a measure to bring the haiduk threat under control. According to Broquière, the Ottoman authorities had established the *derbentci* villages of Vetren and Klisura in the mountains above Ikhtiman. They also tried the same method against the haiduks in the Voynitsa area near Vidin. The area was officially designated a *derbent* (mountain pass) and twenty households with *derbentci* status were settled there. Elsewhere the Ottoman authorities tried other approaches: they would bring in Muslim settlers (the safest defense against haiduks) or set up Muslim religious centers in haiduk areas to attract a constant influx of Muslim faithful. Sultan Murad II had a mosque and an imaret built in the haiduk region near the bridge over the River Erkene; little by little the predominantly Muslim town of

Erkene came into being there. To keep the peace in the Razgrad district, Tutrakan, the local prefect (*subaşi*), endowed a house of dervishes (*tekke*) there, turning the town into a place of Muslim pilgrimage protected by these selfsame crowds of religious visitors. This was also how the now vanished village of Surnevo was established.

Armed Bulgarians, probably haiduks, acted in support of the crusader army that King Ladislaus II Jagiełło and János Hunyadi led into the Balkans in 1443. According to the insufficiently studied *Gazavât-i Sultan Murad,* after the battle of Niš on November 3, 1443, the crusaders encountered a detachment of mounted Bulgarians on the way from Pirot to Sofia.[13] In all likelihood these were not ordinary Bulgarians but men used to bearing arms and possessing some military skills, for Hunyadi organized them as a vanguard for the crusader army. They had therefore to be either haiduks or one of those segments of the population who acted in some capacity or other as auxiliaries of the Ottoman army or in frontier defense, such as the *voynuks* or martolos.[14]

Examples of spontaneous national resistance continued through the second half of the fifteenth century, always arising at some moment in the grim political situation that sparked hopes of liberation among the oppressed populace. A gloss in the margin of a 1454 document makes vague reference to a liberation attempt near Sofia and the capture of the Bulgarian Voivode Radich, presumably a haiduk leader, by Sultan Mehmed II himself.[15] The brief information does not even hint at the historical circumstances of Radich's capture, but it is possible that he led a struggle of some importance since it involved the Grand Turk in person.

The incident was almost certainly a product of the confusion and unrest that swept the Balkan peoples in the wake of the fall of Constantinople in 1453. Only one year after this catastrophe for the Balkans Mehmed the Conqueror set out on his campaign against Serbia. It is possible that the Bulgarians in Sofia wanted to take advantage of the sultan's involvement to the northwest to begin a struggle in his rear on the road his army had followed. It was not simple chance that these events were centered on Sofia, where Broquière, who was there in 1433, reported that there existed a shrewd, freedom-loving population with a clear sense of national consciousness longing for liberation.

Once Ottoman rule had been consolidated over Southeast Europe by the end of the fifteenth century, the burdens of that rule began to weigh ever more heavily on the population. The Bulgarian lands were now a central province of Ottoman Rumelia through which Turkish troops frequently passed on their marches toward Central Europe, and were a major source of provisions for the capital. These circumstances were fertile soil for the development of antifeudal sentiment, the growth of armed resistance, and haiduk actions. This can be safely concluded from an order of Sultan Süleyman I, the Magnificent, of 1528, copies of which have been preserved in Paris and Cairo.[16] The order appears to have been a circular sent to the Ottoman authorities in all the provinces of the empire when matters of major importance were at issue. The order admits that haiduks and rebels had appeared in the sanjaks of Kyustendil, Vulchitrun, Prizren and Alaca Hisar and in the cazas of Sofia and Skopje. It said a special inspector was to be sent out from the capital to check the situation in these areas with the help of the local authorities and then to launch a drive to round up the haiduks' supporters (*yataks*). The order instructs the beys of other sanjaks to be on the alert lest the haiduks withdraw into their territories. The date and the places mentioned permit certain assumptions. The order was issued not long after the decisive Hungarian defeat at Mohács in 1526. The continuing Ottoman expansion in the northwest was absorbing the Turks' forces, easing the pressure against national resistance. Nor is it accidental that the areas of unrest were precisely those western Bulgarian lands that were later to become famous for the vigor of the haiduk movement. They were far from the Ottoman heartlands, the terrain is mountainous, yet they were close to major highways where damage could be inflicted on Süleyman the Magnificent's forces when they passed through. These may well have been the same considerations that concerned the sultan when he ordered the measures to bring order and peace along the main roads behind his troops, as they pressed for new conquests in Central Europe. At any rate, his order implies that haiduk actions were causing disturbances in the areas mentioned serious enough for the sultan to alert his officials in so many sanjaks and to appoint a special inspector to look into the situation. Widespread social support for the haiduks can be deduced from the fact that the sultan's order mentions the *yataks* with the same virulence as the haiduks themselves.

Even if the haiduk movement was not yet a major preoccupation of the Ottoman authorities, by a few decades later it had become a palpable threat. The noticeable changes in the intensity and scope of the haiduk movement in the latter half of the sixteenth century were associated with alterations in the socioeconomic structure of the Ottoman state, the Turks' first military and political failures,[17] and an increase in all forms of popular resistance and the preparation of the ground for liberation movements.[18]

Changes in the military-fief system and in the entire administrative order together with the development of monetary-commodity relations in the towns and villages were at the root of a twofold process that determined the evolution of Bulgarian society during this period. The disintegration of old institutions, a product of the natural dynamics of the evolution of feudal relations and of the tendency of feudal immunity to increase and the power of the central authorities to decrease, set the conditions for the constant expansion of feudal exploitation, the growth of arbitrariness, and the aggravation of religious and national discrimination.

The growth and increasing immediacy of the links of both the rural and urban sectors of Bulgarian society with the gradually expanding market prepared the way for the emergence of Bulgarian property owners whose social standing became more important with the passage of time. These parallel processes explain the simultaneous occurrence of two apparently contrary but in fact concomitant and complementary phenomena in the evolution of the Bulgarian people: a steady worsening of feudal oppression and increasing evidence of social action, national awareness, and readiness to resist foreign domination.[19]

Of the Bulgarians whose national consciousness was becoming increasingly evident, those who must above all be singled out are the merchants and craftsmen, mostly in the towns, and the wealthier government meat and produce dealers (*celeps*). In addition to them, certain other special sectors of society also demonstrated greater social activity and national consciousness: these were the men who served in the military auxiliary corps or had other military obligations to the Ottoman government. Over the centuries their hereditary special status contributed to their differentiation from other sectors of Bulgarian society and to the development of their own traditions, peculiarities, mentality, and attitudes toward the Ottoman authorities.[20] The greater independence of these groups from local feudal rulers, their favorable fiscal situation, the right of the military auxiliaries to bear and use arms, and their awareness that the Ottomans could not do without their special services aroused in them a spirit of greater independence, desire for freedom, and unalloyed national self-confidence. This is why these special categories of people began to react more readily and more sharply than other members of the rayah against encroachments on the more privileged but still certainly not enviable status they had acquired during the course of the fifteenth and sixteenth centuries. They turned their arms against the regime they were obliged to serve, demonstrating their solidarity with the defenders of the people and helping them in their struggle against the injustices of the oppressors' rule.[21]

A major role in fostering national consciousness and in determining people's attitude and behavior toward foreign rule was played by the Orthodox Bulgarian clergy through the parish churches, monasteries and church schools.[22]

In the villages, where the most heavily burdened segment of the population lived, the surviving remnants of communal organization served, often spontaneously, as a rallying and uniting force. They enabled villagers to show solidarity in the face of social and political oppression, bolstered by traditions passed down in folkways and folklore.[23]

The Roman church's increased proselytizing efforts in the seventeenth century contributed to the emergence of a Catholic intelligentsia which, with the support of local Bulgarian Catholic notables, not only became the vehicle of a vivid sense of national consciousness but also strove to guide Bulgarian society toward better-defined ideals and more purposeful actions for political liberation. Though they were representatives of the Western church, which was seeking to establish the supremacy of the church and the pope in Southeast Europe and to facilitate the Habsburg dynasty's plans for conquest, the Bulgarian Catholic missionaries acted first as patriotic pastors, deeply concerned with the people's cultural progress and liberation.[24]

To grasp its essential details correctly, the haiduk movement has to be considered against the background of these developments in Bulgarian society and the national concerns of the more distinguishable elements in it.[25]

These elements demonstrated a greater or lesser degree of unrest during the latter half of the sixteenth century. Through their representatives or by spontaneous actions of their own, they joined the growing antifeudal resistance to encroachments on the nation's interests, aiding the struggle against foreign domination.

The rayah worst affected by the changes[26] taking place in the Ottoman feudal regime, those who bore the brunt of their rulers' outrages, filled the prisons, fell victims to the spreading lawlessness, even losing their homes and belongings, and became the source of the most irreconcilable rebels against the hardships of their living conditions. They became part of the steadily spreading national resistance which found its clearest expression in the haiduk movement. The grimness of conditions in the late sixteenth and seventeenth centuries gave a decisive fillip to the expansion of this popular movement. It acquired particular momentum during the frequent wars the Ottoman Empire waged, generally unsuccessfully, against its many enemies. This trend cannot be ascribed solely to haiduk awareness that conditions of continual warfare favored their cause. The fact is that the haiduks' objectives were fairly limited and only incidentally somewhat social and national in character. Given the mutual isolation of Bulgarian villages and the primitive means of communication in those days, the peasants from whom most of the haiduks were drawn would hardly have been well informed about the military and diplomatic failures of the Ottoman administration. Because the pressures of war increased the feudal burdens on the rayah of official arbitrariness and military exactions, the war years raised tensions and spurred on the disintegration of the state. Besides, in war years all the spahis and even local garrison troops were sent to the front. Settlements and fortresses were left almost undefended, encouraging the haiduks to act more freely. From the end of the sixteenth century, moreover, wars promoted the struggle against oppression. Every Ottoman defeat raised hopes of freedom among better-informed Bulgarian circles where national consciousness was highest. Such hopes gave impetus to liberation attempts and actions. More than one Bulgarian uprising broke out precisely in conjunction with a war, undoubtedly giving a boost to the haiduk movement at the same time.

Growing unrest became evident in certain areas as early as the latter half of the sixteenth century, especially in Macedonia. Haiduks appeared in many places, and clashes with the Ottoman authorities ensued. In 1564, for instance, five peasants from the Prilep region (Dimitriy Stale of Satoka, Father Dimitri of Gradešnica, Mate Nikola of Bešište, and Stoyan Peyov and Father Yako of Stravina) led a revolt against the excesses of the voivode who managed the vizier's khass of which the villages formed part. The Ottoman authorities searched for the five men in vain: they had joined the haiduks and disappeared. Popular discontent in the Prilep-Mariovo area flared into open rebellion in 1565.[27] The rebels' aims were not purely social; their rising was a reaction to the torment of Bulgarians by Muslim mob fanaticism. The presence of three priests among the rebels' leaders lends credence to self-preservation being one of the rebels' motives.

As living conditions became harder in the last years of the sixteenth century and the changed international situation made the fate of Southeast Europe an international issue once more, the will to fight for liberation grew. After the Holy League's rout of the Ottoman fleet at Lepanto in 1570, a rash of insurgence swept through the Balkans.[28]

The upsurge of haiduk actions and other resistance in Macedonia in the 1570s was in line with the general agitation throughout the Balkans, and especially in Greece, following Lepanto. It was hardly a coincidence that in the early days of 1572 Sultan Selim II sent a special order to the cadi of Bitola to seize the weapons of all the rayah in the town. The cadi was to report back what kinds of weapons were found, how many, and where the rayah had obtained them.[29] The authorities' urgency to have this operation carried out expeditiously implies that they already had wind of arms in the hands of the populace and were in a hurry to nip any attempt at rebellion in the bud.

The growth in the number of haiduks added to the tension in Macedonia. In 1573, for instance, a haiduk unit had been formed in the Bitola-Prilep region from villagers from Pusta Reka, Arilovo, Kruševo and Belošin near Prilep; the most renowned and valiant among them was Voivode Tole, probably the leader of the unit.[30] In spite of all the authorities' efforts, haiduk activity was commonplace in the area. In 1578 some seventy to eighty haiduks were active there.[31] Pusta Reka and Divjaci near Bitola teemed with Haiduks who harried the Muslims not only of Bitola but also of Prilep and Kičevo. The haiduks had many *yataks* in the villages, which made their capture all the harder; some of those the Ottoman authorities did manage to catch were executed. Many punitive raids were made, and dealt particularly ferociously with Divjaci, which the Ottomans considered a nest of rebels and brigands (*harami*). In the 1570s, too, some of the privileged groups of the population rose in revolt, the *voynuks* first of all.[32]

The general climate of turbulence encouraged the rayah to resist their feudal obligations. During several years of commotion in Ohrid sanjak, the villagers refused to pay the non-Muslim poll tax (*cizye*) and rose against the local rulers. Things became so bad that the authorities put the spahis of the sanjak on alert to crush the revolt.[33]

Haiduk activity cropped up in many parts of the Bulgarian lands. Foreign envoys' reports and travelers' journals are full of sensational accounts of the activities of haiduks, those brave and awesome Bulgarians lurking along mountain roads who would suddenly appear in large bands and equally unexpectedly disappear. Pierre Lescalopier saw such a group near Edirne in 1574 getting ready to attack the convoy in which he was traveling and the Turkish escorts guarding it. The Frenchman reported that the Ottoman authorities pursued the rebels relentlessly, offering very high rewards for their capture and destruction.[34]

The haiduks caused the Ottoman authorities many problems in some areas in the 1580s. Turkish documents from the cadiliks of Skopje, Tetovo, Strumica, Tikveš, Vranje and Priština all testify to official concern at the extent of haiduk actions. The Ottoman government therefore insisted that local authorities should make concerted and determined efforts to end the menace.[35]

A group of some 500 to 600 haiduks operated in the Kačanik Gorge where their murder of a cadi aroused particular consternation. To curb them, the Sublime Porte ordered the construction of a fortress in the gorge in 1586. The bey of Skopje was instructed to have the fortress built with the compulsory labor of local craftsmen and to mobilize the minor spahis of the area who were not involved in military campaigning elsewhere.[36] The situation was considered grave enough for Sultan Murad III to threaten the bey with the most serious consequences if the construction work was not completed promptly.

In the 1580s haiduks became active even outside Macedonia. The Venetian ambassador to Constantinople, Paolo Contarini, recorded in his travel diary in 1580 that haiduks were said to infest the Troyan Pass through the Balkan Mountains where, because of the favorable terrain, they were supposed to have been hiding out for years.[37] Melchior Besolt reported that in 1584 haiduks had made the Maritsa Valley road through the Rhodope Mountains unsafe in the vicinity of Kharmanli.[38] Jacob Bongars and his companions were frightened in 1585 by tales of hundreds of haiduks roaming the mountainous areas around Vize in Thrace.[39]

The vigor of this resistance encouraged certain circles to consider organizing liberation movements with the help of one of the Ottoman Empire's European enemies. Information about the haiduks became more plentiful during the Austro-Ottoman war of 1593–1606, during the course of which the Serbs of the Banat organized a liberation movement and the vassal principalities of Transylvania, Moldavia and Wallachia sought to repudiate Ottoman suzerainty. The emissaries of Turkey's European enemies, who wanted to foment uprisings in the Balkans, and the leaders of the political struggle in the Bulgarian lands constantly repeated that the Bulgarians were capable of putting up armed resistance, and there is no doubt that the most experienced fighters were the haiduks. Yet Western references to haiduk activity are not conclusive evidence that the Bulgarian haiduks participated *en masse* in the military operations against the Ottoman state. It is more likely that the ever more frequent mention of haiduks referred to the haiduks of the Hungarian borderlands, special units of Balkan émigré irregulars who saw much service in the Habsburg army and the forces of Michael the Brave.[40]

Some documents that can be accepted at face value, however, do give evidence of the intensification of Bulgarian haiduk activity in the propitious climate created by military action and the insurgencies on the periphery of the empire. Groups of what the Ottoman documents branded "evildoers" formed in the sanjak of Skopje in 1595, for instance. Haiduks or revolutionaries, they gained the ascendancy in Skopje.[41] Folk tradition also has it that this was the time when the legendary Voivode Chavdar with his uncle Lalush and 300 brave men came down out of Mount Kozjak onto the Macedonian plain to punish the oppressor and then disappeared back into their fastness.[42] This ferment in Macedonia was certainly not unconnected with the political activities of Patriarch Atanasije of Ohrid and the insurrectionary movements in the western Balkans.[43]

When Michael the Brave, the hospodar of Wallachia, invaded northern Bulgaria in 1595 and almost yearly thereafter, the Bulgarian population's longing for liberation was made clear by those of them who contacted the prince.[44] One Western source reported that in this connection a group of 2,000 haiduks and *"Rasci"* invaded Sofia, sacked it and put it to the torch.[45] They would undoubtedly have had the support of all the anti-Ottoman circles who looked to drive out the Ottoman garrisons and officials.

The Bulgarian emissaries to Michael the Brave pledged the Bulgarians' support and undertook to block the passes through the Balkan Mountains to interdict Ottoman access to the Danube.[46] The offer cannot have been empty; the emissaries must have been counting on the guerrilla experience of the haiduk bands scattered though the area as well as the help of the *voynuks* and martolos. According to other sources, after a series of successful engagements in which Wallachians, Moldavians and Bulgarians fought side by side, Michael the Brave's troops reached the very outskirts of Edirne in 1595.[47] Bulgarians, probably haiduks, also fought in the units led by the Bulgarian Baba Novak and the Dalmatian Deli Marko.[48] Haiduk activity, barely reflected in the sources, encouraged the organizers of the first Turnovo uprising in 1598. The Dubrovnik merchant Pavel Djordjić, one of the leaders of the uprising, praised the militant readiness, inspired by the haiduks, and the rebellious spirit of the Bulgarians who took up arms against the Turks.[49] Their resistance did not pass unnoticed by contemporaries, for foreign official records specify that during Michael the Brave's invasion in 1598 "many Orthodox subjects of the sultan rose in support of Michael, above all many Bulgarians."[50]

The growing haiduk menace combined with the power struggle in the Danubian principalities and the war with Austria led to the inclusion in the sixteenth-century Vidin code of a decree against the haiduks. The decree specifically concedes that their activities dated back a long time.

Epicenters of haiduk activity in the first two decades of the seventeenth century were the East Morava valley, the vicinity of Sofia, and Macedonia. Lefèvre, the secretary of the French ambassador to the Sublime Porte, A. de Sancy, wrote of the existence of a band of 250 to 300 haiduks on the mountainous road to Niš in 1611.[51] In 1616 a party traveling from Prague to Constantinople did not dare fall asleep and kept fires burning all night long near the village of Vetren lest they were "attacked suddenly from the forest by Bulgarians [haiduks], as this had befallen Turks several times near that village."[52]

The court records of Sofia for 1618 contain an account of the deeds of a local haiduk unit led by one Burzak,[53] and of another group near Pasarel under Voivode Petko Ilyov.[54] The same source shows that Peyo Ivanov of Kremikovtsi was suspected of being involved in haiduk activities.[55] That same year, too, the Ottoman authorities were trying to prevent the spread of haiduk activities around Kriva Palanka.[56] The monks of the Macedonian monasteries of Lesnovo, Kriva Reka and Turnovo lent the haiduks every sort of assistance and took a part in their activities.[57] Some haiduk bands were bold enough to attack Ottoman officials in the center of the towns where the authorities' greatest strength lay.[58]

The unsettled conditions in Bitola, Lerin, Prilep, Veles, Sarugyol, Cuma Pazar and Kostur in the 1620s and 1630s led Kenan Pasha, beylerbey of Rumelia, to press the local authorities to take energetic steps to stamp out the haiduks. It was at this time that Petre Dundar of Berantsi became known as a haiduk leader in the troubled Lerin area.[59] Haiduk activities during the 1630s and 1640s took on more and more the form of antifeudal resistance as whole villages refused to fulfill their obligations; the Ottoman records report that many communities "were in constant agitation and often did not obey Holy Law."[60]

Such a climate could not have been more propitious for the haiduks, who made frequent raids on Ottoman settlements and strongholds. One group operating in western Macedonia in 1637 had the temerity to make its attacks with colors flying and trumpets blaring.[61] The upswing in haiduk activity in the villages of Brod, Cer and Magarevo and the *derbentci* settlement of Gyavato so alarmed the Ottoman notables of nearby Bitola that in 1640 they petitioned the sultan for help.[62] As a result a detailed survey of the Bitola-Lerin area was made under the instructions of a specially appointed official,[63] and 131 villages were required to make a mutual commitment not to offer shelter to the haiduks.[64] The number of communities on which this obligation was imposed is an indication how widespread sympathy for the haiduks had become. Five years later the Ottoman authorities had to admit officially that haiduks still existed in all the villages of the Bitola region,[65] where Voivode Loshan, one of the haiduk leaders, had become a local hero. Loshan had originally been a member of Petre Dundar's group, but when it appeared that the latter had reached an accommodation with the authorities in 1640, Loshan joined the martolos.[66] During periods of unrest, the Ottomans would call on the martolos, Christians who enjoyed certain tax concessions and the right to bear arms in return for services as military auxiliaries. As time went by, however, the martolos were as likely to join forces with the haiduks and popular warriors.

In the mid 1640s the Ottomans made persistent and methodical efforts to bring the haiduk problem in the Prilep-Bitola-Lerin area under control.[67] Yet on July 14, 1646, a group of haiduks under Tane of Čairli raided the main bazaar in Bitola and carried off the goods of the wealthy merchants as well as 120,000 aspers just left for safekeeping in the *Celepkeşan*'s strongbox by Ahmed Ağa, the tax collector. The prolonged hearings that followed, some of which brought entire villages before the cadi, still failed to produce the desired result: haiduk actions continued. Five years later Tane was captured and sent to his death.[68]

The Candian War of 1645–1666 and the Morean War of 1684–1699, in which the Ottoman Empire suffered severe defeats by the Venetians, brought new inspiration to the subject Balkan nations to resist the feudal system that oppressed them.[69] From the frequent haiduk raids and more ambitious Bulgarian plans for liberation the will to fight affected a broader spectrum of the Bulgarian people. The rejection of alien rule and the system it had imposed began to play a more definite role in motivating the haiduks, touching the lowliest of them and their *yataks* just as the eminent Bulgarian Catholics, Petur Bogdan and Petur Parchevich, were pressing their case for political liberation and resurrection of "the once flourishing Bulgarian kingdom." Both of them saw Bulgarian ethnic unity stretching from the mouth of the Danube through the Morava region to today's Albania and Greece.[70] Parchevich must have had in mind the growing spirit of insurgency inspired by the spread of antifeudal and liberation sentiment in the Bulgarian lands when he told the Venetian Senate that "the sultan more wanted peace than a hare hunted by hounds, in view of the great agitation in his realm."[71]

The southwestern Bulgarian lands were full of haiduks. It was probably fear of their depredations, especially in Aegean Macedonia, the area nearest the Cretan theater of war, that prompted the Ottomans to bring in forces all the way from Anatolia to strengthen their Aegean defenses.

Traveling through the southwest in the 1660s, Evliya Çelebi came across many haiduk hideouts. The haiduks, he said, were discussed everywhere, and the heads of several were impaled on spears on the towers of the fortress of Niš. He also noted that Kriva Palanka was still one of their strongholds.[72] The French traveler Quicklet reported in 1658 that haiduks might be met at any moment between Niš and Pirot.[73]

The haiduks were so strong and well organized around Bitola, Lerin, Kostur and Kajljari that they amounted to a formidable armed popular force that the local Ottoman officials stood in awe of. Voivode Bayo, who headed some 500 men armed with pistols, sabers and spears, controlled the whole area, permitting no exorbitant tax collections from the rayah, and punishing injustices. Not long after Bayo had led a raid on the bazaar in Bitola and made off with a rich booty in 1661, Evliya Çelebi himself fell into his men's hands. It was Çelebi's task to collect the area's back taxes, especially the *zehire beha,* the cash in lieu of compulsory food deliveries, for the Ottoman troops in Hungary, so he headed for Bayo's camp in the mountains to seek his permission and cooperation.[74] After threading their way through the dense forestlands, Çelebi and his Ottoman companions were met by the first haiduk guards, who escorted them to a military camp of several hundred haiduks bearing a short spear, two or three pistols, and a sharp saber apiece. Çelebi reported seeing tailors cutting and stitching clothing, and cooks roasting meat. In spite of the hyperbole that characterizes the Ottoman's narrative, his description of his visit to Bayo's camp gives an indication of the haiduks' power and strength.

For protection against them, tall towers with iron gates were built in the little town of Kratovo below the Osogovska Mountains in Macedonia. A few miles south, in Kočani, the rayah consorted openly with the haiduks; south and east again, in and around Petrich haiduks were everywhere to be seen. In another effort to stamp them out, the Ottoman authorities dispatched pursuit groups. Some 40 or 50 haiduks were rounded up and hanged in Petrich, Kyustendil, Dupnitsa, Samokov and Sofia.[75]

Captured haiduks were often brought before the court in Bitola which showed them no mercy.[76] Despite the executions, the struggle continued. Order after order came down to the local authorities for massive manhunts and draconian punishment of those caught—to no avail. The haiduks would enter towns and villages with more and more impunity, carrying banners and wreaking revenge on their conquerors and persecutors. They became active all over Aegean Macedonia. Ottoman sources refer to the support given them by the populace from Skopje to Lerin: "Besides the bandit haiduks moving from vilayet to vilayet with colors flying, groups of Christians gather with swords, guns and other weapons, and carrying banners they hide by day and attack by night . . . causing great trouble and commotion." In 1672 four companies (*bölüks*) of haiduks, some mounted, some on foot, were formed, each under its own colors, and began operating around Lerin, Bitola, Prespa, Prilep, Veles, Mariovo, Neselič, Skopje and Cuma Pazar, to the grave concern of the Ottoman authorities.[77]

Haiduk activities were no less audacious during this period in the Balkan Mountains above Gabrovo. While crossing the Shipka Pass, Evliya Çelebi and his companions were twice attacked by bands of haiduks, one of which assailed them with clubs and sticks for lack of other weapons. Of Gabrovo itself, a *derbentci* community, Çelebi exclaimed: "Forgive me, Allah! The village is a nest of rebels and no one should be there overnight."[78] Many travelers noted that large haiduk bands were also operating (still) in the Troyan Pass.[79] At a loss to come up with an effective recourse against the haiduks, Sultan Mehmed IV on January 14, 1683, issued a solemn order to the entire population of Rumelia to stamp them out.[80]

International events, however, were to contribute to the expansion of the haiduk movement and to reduce Ottoman rule to a state of continual warfare with the haiduks in the empire's European provinces. For 1683 was the beginning of the empire's multi-front war with the Austrian Empire, Venice, Poland, and Russia, a war that would culminate in the humiliating Treaty of Karlowitz in 1699. In an effort to secure the main military artery between Constantinople and Belgrade, the sultan issued a series of decrees in 1683 to purge it of the haiduk menace. The decrees specifically mention the presence of haiduks in certain regions between Belgrade and Ikhtiman and in the Momin Pass, south of Ikhtiman.[81]

The Austrian army's successes in Hungary were a new inspiration for the haiduks of Macedonia. As early as 1686, four or five haiduk bands of 100 to 200 men apiece were in action around Kostur, Voden and Hrupišta. Armed groups were also operating in the vicinity of Kriva Palanka, Bitola, Lerin, Radoviš, Veles, Demir Hisar, Nevrokop, and Razlog.[82] In 1689 an experienced haiduk leader named Karposh launched a popular uprising in Kriva Palanka, one of the cradles of haiduk resistance.[83] In the second half of the year the Ottoman authorities in turn stepped up their countermeasures.[84] Numerous orders went out to the leaders of the martolos, summoning them to help crush the haiduks. The haiduk units responded by becoming more aggressive, causing particular problems in the Kriva valley. A general decree then ordered the cadis of Kyustendil, Skopje, Salonika, and Trikkala to block all passes, and rid the villages and mountains of haiduks. As an extreme measure because of the shortage of Ottoman troops in the provinces owing to the war, the Ottoman authorities ordered the destruction of the forests that gave the haiduks cover along the line between the cadiliks of Veles and Prilep, where the roads were in the Bulgarians' hands. Popular resistance simply increased, and in September 1689 broke into open revolt.

At the end of 1688 Sayyid Mehmed, the cadi of Bitola, had passed on to the Sublime Porte information from Mehmed, the khass voivode of Prilep caza, that haiduks in Mariovo were preaching rebellion to the khass rayah. Concerned for their safety, the local officials sought the support of the central authorities, who ordered the cadi of Prilep to seize the rebels. The ineffectuality of this order is made obvious by a new decree issued in September 1689 to the cadis, the vilayet *âyans*, and the officials of Prilep, reiterating the earlier order. It is the new decree that records the fact that the peasants of Mariovo nahie had risen up, formed haiduk groups, and fallen on the Muslims of the local towns and villages.

This rebellion in the rear of the Ottoman army came at a critical juncture before the Austrian capture of Niš. The rebels had wide popular support, and violence broke out in Štip, Radoviš, Veles, Dojran, Seres, Demir Hisar, Nevrokop, and Razlog. The Ottoman authorities turned in vain to the local martolos, but all too often they were in the forefront of the rebels. Ive, a Bulgarian who served the Ottoman officials of Štip as a guard, for instance, was sent to watch the local passes at the head of 50 or 60 martolos. Soon afterwards he converted to Islam, and was then ordered to lead several thousand Bulgarian auxiliaries to the Ottoman army in Sofia. When news reached him that Niš had fallen to the Austrians, instead of marching on to Sofia, he took ten companies of the Bulgarians and led an assault on Skopje and Kyustendil. Around Niš the haiduk peril grew apace, as it did between Breznik and Pirot, and in Leskovac and Vranje. Haiduk bands gathered openly, terrifying the local Muslims, who began to flee for safety. The authorities ordered the mobilization of the whole population of Kyustendil sanjak. The defenses of the Vranje defile were to be strengthened, and the local spahis were to form a camp between Kyustendil and Kriva Palanka to protect local Muslim families. The purpose of the general mobilization was to paralyze the haiduks by depriving them of their main support, the local peasantry. Hoping for help from the Austrian troops, haiduks, and *voynuks* rose in arms in the area between Plovdiv and Pazardzhik.[85] The whole of Macedonia was in a ferment, ready to take up arms against the Ottomans, inspired by the haiduks and spurred on by the Turks' defeats. Karposh united the disparate resistance of the haiduks and the insurgent populace.

According to the Ottoman chronicler Silâhdar, Strahil, a haiduk leader from Yeniköy village in Pazardzhik nahie, remembered in the haiduk epics, organized bold attacks by his band of 200 men. Frightened by these events, which were creating widespread unrest in the insecure areas behind the Ottoman army, the authorities ordered the recruitment of volunteer units in the Plovdiv and Pazardzhik region. Commanders were appointed and two special detachments of bostanjis were organized to capture the haiduks. In the face of this threat, the rebels took refuge with their families and cattle in Austrian-occupied Niš, beyond reach of their pursuers.[86]

Silâhdar's information throws light on events alluded to in other documents, but which have not yet been treated in their proper historical context. These refer to haiduk activity in the Pazardzhik area in 1689 under a police auxiliary (*seğban*), Balcho. His men sheltered in the villages of Otlukköy, Mechka, Poibrene, and Avretalan in the Balkan Mountains.[87] Elsewhere there is evidence of unrest among the *voynuks* in the Rhodope above Pazardzhik and Plovdiv, who were helping the haiduks.[88] These sources are describing different elements of a widespread insurgency in which Strahil's actions played a focal role. It amounted to a general liberation movement, for soon afterwards, Silâhdar reports, Strahil was fighting alongside 4,000 Austrians, Hungarians and haiduks in an assault on Kyustendil. Exploiting the cumbersomeness of Ottoman reaction, they rushed into the city itself, killing many Muslims, taking captives, and inflicting heavy damage to Turkish property. Strahil's haiduks then withdrew with the Austrians and Hungarians.

Recovering from their surprise, the Ottomans sent the local garrison, aided by police auxiliaries (*seğban* or *seğmen*) and surviving Turkish townsmen, in pursuit. There followed a battle in which Turks and, according to Silâhdar, 200 Austrians and Hungarians fell. Soon thereafter Strahil and his men joined the Austrian army at Niš, but then fell out with the Austrian command.[89]

The haiduks flourished in the late 1680s and 1690s in northern and northwestern Bulgaria, where the proximity of the Danubian Principalities was not only an encouragement but also afforded a refuge for the haiduks after forays on Bulgarian territory. Ottoman alarm is evident in an order of 1694 from the provincial governor (vali) to the cadi of Nikopol, the cadis of all sanjaks, and the *âyan*s of the vilayet, requiring all men capable of military service to stand by. All the governor's lieutenants (*mütesellim*) were to scour the sanjaks for haiduks and bandits, and act jointly to eliminate them.[90]

The Ottomans had solid ground for their alarm. In 1690 a band of 100 haiduks was operating in the northwest, led by the priest of Cherna Reka in Vidin sanjak, and reinforced by haiduks from villages around Lom and Vidin. They were pursued in vain by Receb *Mubassir* (superintendent) whose attempts to capture them they evaded by crossing the Danube. Sultan Süleyman II insisted that the voivode of Wallachia should round them up and surrender them to the Ottoman authorities.[91] Further evidence of the extent of haiduk activity along the Danube is contained in a report of April 29, 1698, from Hassan, commandant of Vidin, to the Sublime Porte about incursions into the sanjak from across the river during the year. "With the help of Allah," the men of the Vidin garrison were reported to have destroyed two such groups in the "Simanili krayina" of Vidin nahie; they had decapitated the leaders, Milko and Kurtuli, and sent one captive haiduk to the seraglio. Bands of haiduks had also appeared elsewhere and been scattered by pursuing troops.[92]

Another instance was an order of March 8, 1698, from the deputy (*kethüda*) of Mehmed Pasha, admiral (*kapudan*) of the Danube, to the cadis of Turnovo, Tuzluk, Sevlievo, Lovech, Etropole, Pleven, Vratsa, Nikopol, Oryakhovo, Svishtov, Ruse, Razgrad, Shumen, Ala Klisse, and Eski Cuma, and to the *âyan*s and officials of these districts. Because of the appearance of "bandits" near Vidin, Oryakhovo, Polomie and elsewhere, they were to recruit 600 local armed and mounted men to put a stop to their activities.[93]

During the campaigning before Karlowitz, haiduk operations had reached the pitch where they were impeding the movement of the Ottoman armies from the war zone. The authorities bent every effort to bring the situation under control and prevent the haiduks from using Wallachia as a sanctuary.[94] To the very end of the war, the haiduks cooperated with the empire's Central European enemies, for a document of 1700 records the capture of several Hungarians among 45 haiduks taken in the Turnovo district.[95] The presence of Hungarians in the area so late can probably be explained either by the Hungarians joining the Bulgarians in an effort to escape to safety in the Balkan Mountains, or by a possible attempt to rekindle rebellion in an area that had risen up in 1686 and where the forces of resistance were not yet spent.

The haiduk ferment south of the Danube prompted Şerban Cantacuzino, the voivode of Wallachia (1678–1688), to assert in a petition to Ivan V and Peter I (the Great), Russia's co-tsars, that, "when the Russian army approached Akerman, the voivode [Şerban] would go to the tsars' army, where all the Serbians, Bulgarians and Moldavians would join them, and there would be no obstacle all the way to Constantinople."[96]

In these last years of war haiduk activities were not confined to the Danubian north. In Aegean Macedonia there were haiduk attacks on Ottoman officials.[97] They staged daring raids in 1694 on the heights of Ümir between Niš and Aleksinac to the north.[98]

The haiduk movement gradually became more entrenched during the opening decades of the eighteenth century, fed in part by growing opposition to the *çiftliks*, properties under the new system of landholding that had slowly been taking shape and increasingly burdening the rayah.[99] In addition to the inspiration the haiduks took from the Ottomans' defeats by their European foes, they were further encouraged by Tsar Peter the Great's Balkan policy and plans for joint action with the Russians against the Ottomans. The abundant reports of haiduk actions in the northwest throughout the eighteenth century are not only a reflection of the closeness of the war zone between the Ottomans and their northern adversaries but also of Russia's growing political influence in the Balkans.

A decree of 1702 reminds the cadis of Vidin, Svrljig, Soko Banja, Timok, and Aleksinac that the approaching spring will green the forests again, giving cover to the haiduks, and to make the customary forays to find them and bring them to account before that happens.[100] Haiduks appeared in 1704 and 1705 near the Danube fords by Oryakhovo, attacking Ottoman river shipping.[101] In 1705 a band of haiduks, some mounted, some on foot, under one, Chokan, plagued the Vidin area.[102] Edicts of 1707 and 1708 commanded the local authorities to stamp out haiduks operating near Lom and Timok and in the vicinity of Svrljig and Soko Banja.[103] In 1709 the authorities captured Nedelya Damyanov of Banya village,

Velcho, Yancho and Miho of Bukovo, Petre of Chepintsi, and Sile of Kalkandzhi, who had been active near Sofia.[104]

In an effort to curb the lawlessness, which was fostered by the support of the rayah, the Sublime Porte forced communities to make a binding commitment before the courts to brook no haiduk activities. Sultan Ahmed III's orders to the villages warned that any losses suffered by travelers at the hands of haiduks would have to be made good by the local peasantry.[105]

Barely had the war with Russia of 1710–1711 ended in Constantinople's favor than Sultan Ahmed renewed hostilities with Venice in the Peloponnesus in 1715. A year later the empire was also at war with Austria again. Heartened by Prince Eugene of Savoy's successes, the predominantly Bulgarian population of Vidin rose in revolt once more.[106] This was the official justification for a new crackdown on the haiduks in Vidin sanjak, which was described as populated exclusively by "infidels" and too close to the "Hungarian haiduks."[107]

In Macedonia, too, the haiduks were active, though they were hampered at this time by the rampages of gangs of Turkish and Albanian bandits. The Ottoman authorities concentrated on ridding the area of Albanian martolos and replacing them with local guards such as the *seğbans*.[108] To try to pacify the region, several amnesties were offered to active haiduks who would return peacefully to their home villages.[109] The haiduk leaders Balcho and Alagyoz achieved notoriety during these years for their exploits around Štip and Kyustendil.[110]

Farther east, the activities of haiduks around Khaskovo, Mahmud Pasha, Lozengrad, and Bunar Hisar in 1701 caused the appointment of a special commander of the imperial bodyguard (*bostancıbaşı*) to direct operations against them.[111] In 1713 official alarm was expressed over peasants uprooted from the Kičevo area who had formed small groups of 10 or 15 haiduks whose persistent actions were causing unrest around Skopje, Tetovo, Štip, Tikveš, Bitola, Prilep, Lerin, and Ohrid.[112] Another special official was appointed in 1714 to crush a large group of haiduks led by a priest's son named Papazoğlu, but ten days before the delegate's arrival in Oryakhovo, they crossed the Danube into Wallachia beyond his reach. The authorities conceded that bands of haiduks were now regularly crossing into Bulgarian territory every spring and returning to Wallachia in the fall.[113] The number of haiduks around Skopje,

Kosovo, Vulchitrun, and Priština was reported in 1717 to have increased, but every effort to crush them was to no effect. The Holy Roman Empire's ambassador to the Sublime Porte, G. K. von der Driesch, traveling in 1718, reported haiduks active in the heights above Ikhtiman. The janissaries escorting his party warned them not to stray from the road because haiduks were swarming everywhere.[114] It was in the 1720s that a Bulgarian, Chavdakhan, was leading a band of 20 to 30 haiduks in the Sofia area. They would periodically disappear by working as shepherds for rich Turks or going into hiding.[115] About 1722 haiduks began operating along the road from Sofia to Gömürcina.[116]

The persistence of the haiduk menace led to the issue of yet another decree in 1731 ordering its eradication from around Sofia, Pirot, Breznik, Znepole, Radomir, and Sirishnik. Probably referring to the continual unrest in this area about the highway from Constantinople to Belgrade since the latter years of the seventeenth century, the edict claimed that the haiduks here had already risen against Ottoman rule twice.[117] Nor were the Ottoman authorities' anxieties made any easier by the fact that the villages were ungarrisoned because of a new outbreak of war with Austria.

As had happened under similar circumstances in the past, the war of 1735–1738 sparked a major Bulgarian uprising, which gave added heart to the haiduks. When the Treaty of Belgrade brought an end to the war, the Ottoman authorities turned their gaze anew to the question of crushing the haiduks. Orders went to all the powers in Rumelia to stamp out the haiduk threat.[118] In 1742 the cadis and officials of Ruse and other towns in the northeast were reminded in an order (*buyurultu*) that a number of decrees had been issued against the haiduks in the empire. Owing to the negligence of the constabulary (*zabita*), *âyans* and village headmen (*kocabaşı*), however, "bandits" had appeared in the cazas addressed, and they had to be captured. The local authorities were to follow the instructions issued by the vali of Vidin.[119] This implies that measures were having to be taken in that area, too, to curb the haiduks' nationwide deeds.

The folk tales collected by the poet Petko Slaveykov have preserved the memory of the exploits of Voivode Tseko in Strumica, Radoviš and Kočani. In the 1730s and 1740s Voivode Ivan was operating in the Seres area, and Voivodes Vulchan and Stoyan were carrying out bold raids on the road to Constantinople in the Istranca Mountains in Thrace.[120] Later documents mention haiduk actions around Sofia, Voden and Ber. A Captain Makri led a band of 30 to 40 men, including the haiduks Tseno, Petre and Kone, in the Voden area in 1757.[121] Another haiduk group led by a certain Proycho was found in the nearby village of Breshor. They were being pursued on the vali's instructions. During a fair being held in the village, the haiduks tried to enter the community unnoticed in the crowds. Recognized by their pursuers, they gave battle. The Turks caught the haiduks Besho and Khristo; two others were killed and their heads sent to the divan of Rumelia. A few Turks were also killed.[122] The Dubrovnik humanist R. J. Bosković and the Frenchman Jean-Claude Flachat reported that haiduks infested the Shumen area and the more inaccessible parts of the Balkan Mountains.[123]

An order of 1772 to the aga and other officials of Vidin demands the suppression of haiduk activities in that area.[124] It is known from other sources that there was an unsuccessful attempt at an uprising in the Vidin region during the Russo-Ottoman war of 1768–1774.[125]

Haiduks were still roaming the Vidin area years after the war, and the Ottoman authorities would sporadically invest money in their pursuit. The accounts of Vidin for the years 1777–1778 show that a considerable sum was granted the aga to hunt for haiduks in the area, a sum that was promptly recuperated by collecting extra taxes from the rayah.[126] A haiduk band under a certain Captain Kokino began operating in the caza of Grebenesh around 1781. The cadi reported to his superiors that they had been engaged in battle. The voivode and Dimo, a haiduk, had been killed, and the rest of the band driven from the area.[127] About this time the authorities in Sofia revived the custom of hiring mounted guards against the haiduks to serve from St. George's Day (May 6) to St. Demetrius's Day (October 26) for a salary of 5 or 6 groş.[128] The French traveler Lusignan reported the presence of many haiduks in the Dragoman Pass on the Niš-Sofia road and around Vakarel in the 1770s.[129] Popular epics and folk tales remember the heroic deeds of many Bulgarian men and women haiduks during these years, but reliable documentary corroboration is still lacking.

The sources that are available, however, demonstrate the pronounced antifeudal character of the haiduk movement.[130] Most of them show the haiduks were predominantly peasant. It is known that the rural communities bore the heaviest burden of the Ottoman feudal system. For oppressed working peasants, who were forbidden by their conquerors to carry arms, the haiduk movement was the only escape, a spontaneous protest against feudal exploitation, and the only worthy form of revenge for their suffering and plight.

The haiduk movement was most vigorous and tenacious in the northwest and Macedonia, where *çiftlik* ownership was most widespread and pauperization of the peasantry by the landlords' exactions was most extensive. The movement's concentration in these areas is indicative of its antifeudal spirit. Moreover, the mountainous nature of the terrain and its remoteness from the centers of administration made possible the survival of national awareness. Its proximity to the Ottomans' actives foes, Austria and Venice, helped to inspire the peasants' combativeness and resistance. The official Ottoman sources reveal the social roots of the haiduks' actions by noting the solidarity of the local populace. So numerous were the haiduks' *yatak*s in certain localities that the Ottoman authorities would declare whole villages and regions to be haiduk centers. Yet it is highly unlikely that all the communities in a given area were simply engaged in brigandage for its own sake; they had to be motivated by other causes and goals. Apart from peasants, the haiduks' ranks were also filled with people from special categories of the population—*voynuk*s, martolos, *derbentci*s—all to a greater or lesser extent involved in provincial armed defense.

Other evidence of the antifeudal character of the haiduk movement in Ottoman documents derives from data on the social standing of those against whom the haiduks directed their operations. The social hatred for those who had grown rich from the labor of others was expressed by robbing them of their money and property.[131] There were many documented cases, especially in Macedonia, of haiduks attacking *çiftlik*s, firing the buildings, stealing food and goods, and killing the occupants.[132] There were also attacks on spahiliks, and above all the khasses of the sultan and grand vizier.[133]

More than once prosperous Bulgarians were the object of haiduk assault. According to a document of 1669, for instance, haiduks and peasants (so-called *çiftçi*) attacked the home of Yano in Borešnica, near Bitola, making off with all his food and property and 5,000 akçes.[134] Other favorite objects of attacks were convoys of merchants, the treasure trains of the sultan and vizier, markets, and rich bazaars. Hard guerrilla war fought by disparate groups of haiduks in uncoordinated actions required a way to be found to feed and arm the warriors, and the most obvious source was those thought to be wealthy. In Ottoman society wealth was usually associated with power and class privilege, so that expropriation of this wealth by force could be justified as seizing riches acquired through feudal exploitation.

Another aspect of the antifeudal character of the haiduk movement, illustrated in Ottoman documents, was the many cases of haiduks protecting the rayah against constant overtaxation and directing their actions against tax collectors. In 1669, for example, haiduks in southern Macedonia set upon the collector of *avariz* and *nuzul* (special levies) on his way to Salonika and took the money he had just collected from the peasantry.[135] In 1676 the haiduks Yovo, Nikola and Niko from Gorno Virovo, near Bitola, attacked and killed Mehmed, the collector of *haraç, nuzul* and *celep,* and took his money.[136] Three years later a poll-tax collector (*cizyedar*) was assailed in Tikveš caza. The Ottoman sources make it clear that the haiduks' activities curbed the increase of feudal exploitation to some degree.

Evliya Çelebi, for instance, comments that the strength of Bayo's haiduks around Bitola, Lerin, Kostur, and Kajljari prevented the imposition of a heavy military tribute on the local population.[137] Official documents disclose that the rayah, encouraged by the presence of the haiduks, more and more openly evaded their feudal obligations and opposed their feudal masters. Summoned to court for arrears of land tax (*ispence*), the inhabitants of Malovište, near Bitola, told the suing spahi: "We shall not go to court; we shall stone you to death and escape to the mountains."[138] Whole villages are recorded as taking up arms to resist feudal rule by haiduk actions. In the face of local concern at haiduk activities in Miratovac, near Vranje, in 1749, for instance, Sultan Mahmud I ordered the village burned to render it uninhabitable and the capture of the haiduk-villagers, clear evidence of mass popular discontent with the Ottoman regime.[139] Ottoman data make it clear that the haiduks represented the boldest, most intelligent and freedom-loving elements of the population, those aware of the need to fight against their oppressors' institutions and system. As early as 1636 it was a haiduk, Nikle, from Capari, near Bitola, who was among those who refused to pay their taxes to the local landholder (*zaim*).[140] Another document of 1669 speaks of the haiduk Marko from Bojšta, near Bitola, who incited the local rayah by refusing to pay his land and poll taxes, and held up the collection of taxes for 1668 and 1669. Yakub Aga, the *nuzul* collector, complained specifically that Marko had caused the delay.[141]

Despite their unmitigated denigration of the haiduks, Ottoman sources cannot disguise their broad social support; they leave no doubt that the non-Muslim rayah sympathized with them and protected them. When called by the court of Bitola in 1622 to identify those who robbed Mehmed Effendi's *çiftlik,* the villagers of Mogila refused mettlesomely in order to protect the assailants: "We will not go to court," they replied.[142] Under orders to defend vulnerable points against haiduk penetration, the rayah along the Danube from Ruse to Belgrade at the beginning of the eighteenth century did their best to obstruct the authorities.[143] Dozens of documents bespeak the Ottoman authorities' powerlessness in the face of the solidarity and determination of the haiduks' *yataks* in the villages. In some cases the Muslim rayah also showed sympathy for the haiduks, seeing them as fighters against oppression. The Muslim Bendo Ali, for instance, who was well known in Bitola, raided the prison there in 1639, killed three guards, and released the inmates, who included several tax debtors. Mehmed, the prison warden, told the cadi that the Ottoman officials were frightened and that he had not dared to complain to the court because the haiduks had threatened to break his back if he did so.[144] A seventeenth-century source reported that the poor Muslims of Bitola had refused to take part in the town's defense, so that the mufti had had to invoke the faith and the law to persuade them.[145] Islam's fanatic intolerance of other faiths, however, severely limited the number of instances of Muslims demonstrating solidarity with the haiduks.

The scope and intensity of the haiduks' opposition to feudalism are underscored by the Ottoman authorities' constant efforts to suppress them, particularly their attempts to impose a legal obligation on whole communities to bar haiduk activities in their vicinity. It is also clear that the haiduk movement and the spontaneous outbursts of the rayah were a manifestation of the subjugated Bulgarians' national self-awareness as well as their implacable opposition to the system their oppressors had installed. Even in the scant information in official documents, the distinctiveness the Bulgarians felt comes through in the references to their clothing and appearance, both provocative to the Turks. As one element of Ottoman religious and national discrimination, the non-Muslim rayah was forbidden to wear bright or striking garments; flouting this convention would be seen as rebelliousness. Thus the Turks testifying against the haiduk, Voivode Chavdar of Sopotnica, near Bitola, did not fail to mention that he wore a red cloak and feathers in his cap.[146] The contention that the haiduk movement was a demonstration of national distinctiveness is lent weight by the fact that the vast majority of the haiduks were Bulgarians. Other indications of national self-consciousness appear in an Ottoman document of 1627. When captured haiduks from Gramatikovo, near Ostrovo, had to appear before the cadi of Ber, Emanuil Khristov of Ber called together the local people and, forcing his way into the court, demanded: "Why are you judging them by the law of your faith, when you know we do not recognize its sanctions?"[147] And so, too, in 1669 Marko of Bojšta, who had been a haiduk for fifteen ears, was quoted as saying: "You destroy our churches, we shall destroy your mosques. Our priests are better than yours."[148] The frequent mention in Ottoman sources that there were many priests and monks in the haiduk movement from the beginning of the sixteenth century should also be considered in the light of national awareness.

This helps to explain why the haiduk movement took on strength when the Ottoman Empire was at war with its European foes from the 1670s on. Many Turkish sources confirm that haiduk bands several hundred strong were operating in many areas, especially those close to the theater of war, or where it would be easiest to establish contact with European countries hostile to the Sublime Porte. Some of these bands attacked important strong points, such as the fortresses of provincial garrisons. In 1638 a mufti even issued a fetwa that the struggle against the haiduks was a holy duty of every Muslim.[149] This declaration of a domestic jihad against all infidel rebels was directed against the whole Bulgarian population.

The tendency of the haiduk movement to acquire national features is evident in Ottoman documents that testify to the growth of the movement during the empire's war with the Holy League (1683–1699). At the very outset of the war a decree of the sultan noted that "many haiduks, brigands and bandits have appeared in Rumelia this year."[150] Both in Macedonia and along the Danube haiduks directed their operations more and more against fortresses and the Ottoman army on the march, actions aimed increasingly intentionally against the foundations of the regime and hence with a national political purpose.[151]

Ottoman evidence of mass haiduk collaboration with hostile troops who had penetrated Bulgarian territory and of associated popular revolts clearly indicates that even in the seventeenth and eighteenth centuries the haiduk movement was aspiring to higher goals keyed to national liberation.

Ottoman documents may be scattered and prejudiced, but they give the lie to any claim that the haiduk and similar movements in Ottoman Europe had no national content or intent, but rather were symptoms of the decay of the old military-fief system in Rumelia and Anatolia. It can no longer be believed that the haiduk movement was a spontaneous and unconscious struggle of individuals or small groups out for revenge. The significance the Ottoman authorities attached to it and its potential for undermining the system from within are suggested by the numerous ways the Ottomans sought to combat it.

There were their fruitless attempts to bind the local population of affected areas to keeping haiduks away and seizing those whom they found. There were their equally disappointing appointments of *derbentci*s, martolos, pandours, galley men and others to guard roads, passes, fords, and other strategic locations. The Ottomans reinforced their fortresses, built new ones, put up palisaded earthworks, and increased the strength of garrisons, concentrating them in the larger settlements as a protection against the haiduks. Maintenance of these troops often fell on the local population. The janissaries stationed in the provinces also had to search for haiduks. Towns were fortified, night watchmen and martolos guarded them, Muslim volunteer corps and posses were mobilized.

The Sublime Porte appointed special officials, generally from the court hierarchy, to organize the struggle against the haiduks. As the centralized Ottoman feudal system gradually decayed, the burden of this struggle was shifted more and more onto the local authorities, more especially the *âyan*s.

Harsh discipline, including forced labor and even capital penalties, was introduced in the Ottoman navy and the state shipyards in Constantinople. When supplies of slaves ran short, the supreme command would send reminders to the officials in the Danube region to deliver more oarsmen, who were usually captured haiduks.[152]

Despite the Ottoman ruling class's almost universal detestation for the haiduks, there were documented cases of large feudal landlords giving them refuge as laborers on their *çiftliks* and fiefs. Some even resisted the authorities' searches for hiding haiduks on the ground that their property was immune (*serbest*).[153]

The haiduk movement was for several centuries a serious and continuous popular counterforce within the Ottoman feudal system. The haiduks' actions, though uncoordinated, put the authorities in a state of permanent war against the masses. However limited in scope, the haiduks' operations made the entire Ottoman feudal class perpetually insecure. Their attacks on fiefs and *çiftlik*s and their incitement of the rayah to defiance of their overlords reduced the income of Ottoman officials and feudatories alike. The growth in the number of haiduks thinned the ranks of farm labor and left the properties of many spahis unworked and barren. This was why some landholders—*çiftlikçi,* the managers of khasses and wakfs, and others—would take in haiduks on the run, using their labor to boost their income.

The cost of measures taken to control the haiduks was one of the factors that contributed to the eventual bankruptcy of the Ottoman treasury. As military pressure increased on many fronts, the haiduks became a growing concern for the Ottomans. At critical junctures, especially after the seventeenth century, the Ottoman state was compelled to commit some of its military forces to a permanent and exhausting struggle with an unremitting internal enemy on a multiplicity of fronts.

The haiduk movement, it has been seen, sapped the very foundations of the Ottoman feudal system, and hence of foreign rule over the Bulgarian lands. At the same time, it was a movement of immense significance for the struggle of the Bulgarian people during one of the most painful episodes in its history. Just by its existence, even in the form of isolated actions by haiduk groups or individuals, it gave strength to the oppressed Bulgarians' spirit of militancy and inspired their faith that their national suffering would not go unavenged. It gave the defenseless rayah the courage to resist intensifying feudal domination and to add to the numbers of those who assailed the regime's strongholds. This, in turn, prepared the ground for the organization of liberation movements. Erupting as scattered acts of resistance to feudal lawlessness and the violence of local officials, it gradually grew in scope and intensity. Isolated incidents became better coordinated as the haiduks' struggle evolved into a fight for higher goals of greater significance, and the longing for national liberation infused it. This development was typified by the haiduks who joined forces with Michael the Brave and the followers of Karposh who became the mainspring of the national uprising in northeast Macedonia in 1689. When Voivode Strahil sought the support of Austria's troops, he was obviously prompted by something other than narrow, local desires for revenge against some individual. More than one Bulgarian insurrection drew strength from the haiduk movement, and haiduks with experience of armed resistance were always among the first to join an insurrection. The haiduk movement laid the foundations for militant solidarity with other Balkan peoples groaning under the burdens of the Ottoman feudal system and, like the Bulgarians, expressing their opposition in the actions of clephts, Uskoks, and others.

When all is said and done, though, the haiduk movement remained in essence a form of resistance of a preeminently spontaneous character and with limited objectives. By the end of the eighteenth century there still existed no social circle capable of organizing and directing this extemporaneous form of armed resistance into a mass liberation movement. Widespread haiduk actions, even when combined with Balkan political movements, were not yet enough to throw off the yoke of a still-powerful Ottoman Empire.

## Notes

1. D. Shopova, *Makedonija vo XVI i XVII vek: Dokumenti od Tsarigradskite arkhivi (1557–1645)* (Skopje, 1955); I. Vasdravellē, *Historika archeia Makedonias*, Vol. I: *Archeion Thessalonikēs, 1695–1912* (Salonika, 1952), and Vol. II: *Archeion Veroias kai Naousēs, 1598–1886* (Salonika, 1954); A. Matkovski, *Turski izvori za istorijata na ajdutstvoto i aramistvoto vo Makedonija* (Skopje, 1961–1979); B. Cvetkova, "Novi arkhivni istochnitsi za vŭorŭzhenata sŭprotiva v bŭlgarskite zemi sreshtu turskiya feodalen rezhim prez XVI–XVIII v.," *Izvestiya na Dŭrzhavnite arkhivi*, VIII (1964), 208–243; B. Cvetkova, *Khaydutstvoto v bŭlgarskite zemi prez 15–18 v.* (Sofia, 1971).

2. For greater detail, see B. Cvetkova, "O religiozno-natsional'noy diskriminatsii v Bolgarii vo vremya turetskogo vladychestva," *Sovetskoe vostokovedenie*, No. 2, pp. 78–88.

3. B. Cvetkova, "Les sources osmano-turques concernant le mouvement des haydouks du XVe au XVIIIe siècles," in *Vostochnye istochniki po istorii narodov Yugo-Vostochnoy i Tsentral'noy Evropy*, Vol. V (Budapest, 1980).

4. Cf. B. Karakanovski, "Prevzimaneto na grad Lovech ot Turtsite v 1474 g.," in *Sbornik Lovech i Lovchansko*, II (Sofia, 1930), 96–100.

5. Cf. B. Cvetkova, "Typical Features of the Ottoman Social and Economic Structure in South-Eastern Europe during the 14th to the 16th Centuries," in *Études historiques*, IX (Sofia, 1979), 129–149; *idem*, *Institutions ottomanes en Europe* (Wiesbaden, 1978).

6. Cyril and Methodius National Library (hereafter cited as C&MNL),

Orientalski otdel (hereafter cited as OrO), OAK 265/27, fol. 1V.

7. *Ibid.*, OAK 217/8, fol. 28V–29V.

8. M. T. Gökbilgin, *XV–XVI asırlarda Edirne ve Paşa livâsı vakıflar-mülkler-mukataalar* (Istanbul, 1952), p. 216.

9. C&MNL, OrO, OAK 52/59, fol. 17V.

10. B. Cvetkova, *Pametna bitka na narodite (Evropeyskiyat Yugoiztok i osmanskoto zavoevanie kraya na XIV i pŭrvata polovina na XV v.)* (Varna, 1979), p. 153.

11. For greater detail, see Cvetkova, *Khaydutstvoto v bŭlgarskite zemi.*

12. *Le voyage d'outremer de Bertrandon de la Broquière* ("Recueil de voyages et documents pour servir à l'histoire de géographie," Vol. XII) (Paris, 1892), p. 201.

13. H. Inalcık and M. Oğuz, *Gazavât-i Sultan Murad ve Mehemmed hân: Izladi ve Varna Savaşları (1443–1444) üzerinde Anonim Gazavâtnâme* (Ankara, 1978), pp. 16–17.

14. See Cvetkova, *Pametna bitka*, p. 208, and the literature cited there; M. Vasić, *Martolosi u jugoslovenskim zemljama pod turskom vladavinom* (Sarajevo, 1967).

15. Lj. Stojanović, "Srpski rodoslovi i letopisi," *Glasnik srpskog učenog društva* (Belgrade), LIII (1883), 90.

16. Bibliothèque Nationale de Paris, Fonds turc 81, fol. 66v–67v.

17. See Cvetkova, *Institutions ottomanes*, pp. 78 ff. and the literature cited there.

18. B. Cvetkova, "Mouvements antiféodaux dans les terres bulgares sous la domination ottomane du XVe au XVIIIe siècle," in *Études historiques*, II (Sofia, 1965), 150–168.

19. B. Cvetkova, "Problems of the Bulgarian Nationality and the National Consciousness in the XV–XVIII Centuries," in *Études historiques*, VI (Sofia, 1973), 58–80; *idem*, "Problèmes de la nationalité bulgare pendant les XVe–XVIIe siècles," *Palaeobulgarica*, III (1979), No. 4, 13–25.

20. B. Cvetkova (ed.), *Izvori za bŭlgarskata istoriya*, Vol. XX (Sofia, 1974).

21. Cvetkova, "Mouvements antiféodaux," pp. 149 ff.; *idem*, "Iz istoriyata na sŭprotivitelnite i osvoboditelnite dvizheniya v bŭlgarskite zemi pre 80-te i 90-te godini ot XVII v.," *Voenno-istoricheski sbornik*, 1979, pp. 109 ff.

22. Cf. Khr. Gandev, "Bŭlgarskata narodnost prez XV v. (Sofia, 1972), pp. 269 ff.; *idem*, *Faktori na bŭlgarskoto vŭzrazhdane* (Sofia, 1943); B. Cvetkova, "Problems of the Bulgarian Nationality," pp. 70–71.

23. B. Cvetkova, "Conditions et facteurs intérieurs et extérieurs des processus avant la Renaissance nationale bulgare," *Bulgarian Historical Review*, 1973, No. 4, pp. 60–61; E. Grozdanova, "Fiskal'nye funktsii obyazannosti bolgarskikh knezov, stareyshinykh i kodzhabashiev (XV–XVIII v.)," *Bulgarian Historical Review*, 1973, No. 3, pp. 42–60.

24. N. Milev, *Katolishkata propaganda v Bŭlgariya* (Sofia, 1914); Iv. Duychev, *Politicheskata deynost na Petŭr Parchevich za osvobozhdenie ot tursko vladichestvo*, Vol. I: *Bŭlgaro-rumŭnski vrŭzki i otnosheniya prez vekovete* (Sofia, 1965), 157–193; B. Cvetkova, "Novi dokumenti za istoriyata na osvoboditelnite dvizheniya v Bŭlgarskite zemi prez XVII v.," *Izvestiya na Instituta za istoriya*, XIX (1967), 243–262.

25. Cf. V. N. Zlatarski, "Bŭlgarski vŭstaniya do sredata na XIX v.," in *Sbornik Bŭlgariya 1000 godini* (Sofia, 1930), pp. 715–717; N. Milev, "Edin neizdaden dokument za bŭlgarskata istoriya, 1597," *Izvestiya na Istoricheskoto druzhestvo* (Sofia), IV (1915), 89–99; *idem*, "Okhridskiyat patriarkh Atanasiy i skitaniyata mu v chuzhbina (1597–1615)," *Izvestiya na Istoricheskoto druzhestvo*, V (1922), 113–128; A. Tamborra, *Gli Stati italiani, l'Europa e il problema turco dopo Lepanto* (Florence, 1961); M. Yonov, "Politikata na Avstriya i politicheskite dvizheniya v Bŭlgariya ot kraya na XVI do kraya na XVII vek," *Godishnik na Sofiyskiya universitet, filosofsko-istoricheski fakultet*, II (1958), No. 2. 253–331; B. Cvetkova, "Les Bulgares et la situation politique internationale au XVIIe siècle," *Bulgarian Historical Review*, 1978, No. 2, 25–46.

26. For the effect of the changes on the situation of the people, see B. Cvetkova, "Changements intervenus dans la condition de la population des terres bulgares (depuis la fin du XVIe jusqu'au milieu du XVIIIe siècle)," in *Études historiques*, V (Sofia, 1970), 291–318.

27. Shopova, *Makedonija vo XVI i XVII vek*, Nos. 6–8.

28. On the international situation and the liberation movements in the Balkans in the last decades of the 16th century, see in particular *Vsemirnaya istoriya* (Moscow), IV (1958), fol. 259, 373 ff.; E. Lavisse and A. Rambaud, *Histoire générale du IVe siècle à nos jours* (Paris), V², 81 ff.; F. Braudel, *La Méditerranée et le monde méditerranéen à l'époque de Philippe II*, II (Paris, 1966), 279 ff., 370 ff., 495 ff.; L. von Pastor, *Geschichte der Päpste* (8th ed.; Freiburg im Breisgau, 1927), Vol. VII; J. Radonić, *Rimska kurija i južnoslovenske zemlje od XVI do XIX veka* (Belgrade, 1950); O. Redlich, *Geschichte Österreichs*, VI (Gotha, 1921), 217; E. Alberi, *Le relazioni degli ambasciatori veneti al Senato*, 3rd ser. (Florence), Vols. II (1844) and III (1855); N. Tommaseo, *Relations des ambassadeurs vénitiens sur les affaires de France au XVIe siècle*, Vol. II (Paris, 1938); J. Tomić, *Pećki patriarh Jovan i pokret hrišćana na balkanskom poluostrovu, 1592–1614* (Zemun, 1903); N. Iorga, "La France dans le Sud-Est de l'Europe," Pt. 3: "La croisade à la fin du XVI siècle," *Revue historique du Sud-Est européen* (Bucharest), XIII (1936), No. 406, 111–112; W. Leitsch, "Rudolph II und Südeuropa, 1593–1606," *East European Quarterly*, Vol. VI (1972); Al. Ciorănescu, *Documente privitoare la istoria Romănilor culese din arhivele din Simancas* (Bucharest, 1940); M. Yonov, "Politikata na Avstriya i politicheskite dvizheniya v Bŭlgariya"; B. Cvetkova, "La situation internationale et le peuple bulgare à la fin du XVI et au début du XVII siècle," *Bulletin de l'AIESEE* (Paris), IX

(1971), No. 1–2, 57–72; A. Pipidi, *Les pays danubiens et Lépante,* Vol. II: *Mediterraneo nella seconda metà del'500 alla luce di Lepanto* (Florence, 1974), pp. 289–323; L. Chasiōtē, *Oi Hellēnes stis paramones tēs navmachias tēs Navpaktou* (Salonika, 1970); *idem,* "O archiepiskopos Achridos Iōakeim kai oi synōmotikes kinēseis stē Voreio Epeiro (1572–1576)," *Makedonikes Spoudes* (Salonika), CCIII (1964), 237–255; *idem,* "O epanastasē tōn Chimariōtōn sta 1570 kai ē alōsētou Sopotou," *Epeirōtikē Estia* (Iōannina), XVII (1968), 265–276.

29. Shopova, *Makedonija vo XVI i XVII vek,* No. 19.

30. *Ibid.*, No. 24.

31. *Ibid.*, No. 38.

32. A. Refik, *Türk idaresinde Bulgaristan (973–1259)* (Istanbul, 1933), No. 28.

33. Shopova, *Makedonija vo XVI i XVII vek,* No. 31–32.

34. Pierre Lescalopier, "Voyage fait par Moi Pierre Lescalopier l'an 1574 de Venise à Constantinople par mer jusqu'à Raguse et le reste par terre et le retour par Thrace, Bulgarie, Walech, Transylvanie ou Dace, Hongrie, Allemagne, Frioul et March Trevisane jusqu'à Venise" (MS in the library of Montpellier University). The section on the Bulgarian lands is translated into Bulgarian in B. Cvetkova, "Edin frenski pŭtepis ot XVI v. za Bŭlgarskite zemi (Pier Leskalopie—1574)," *Izvestiya na Istoricheskoto druzhestvo,* XXIV (1968), 254–255, 261.

35. Shopova, *Makedonija vo XVI i XVII vek,* No. 44.

36. *Ibid.*, No. 49.

37. Paolo Contarini, *Diario del viaggio da Venezia a Constantinopoli di M. Paolo Contarini che andava a bailo per la repubblica veneta alla porta ottomana nel 1580* (Venice, 1856), p. 29.

38. P. Matković, "Putovanja po balkanskom poluotoku u XVI vjeku," *Rad jugoslovenske akademije znanosti i umjetnosti,* CXXIX (1896), 73.

39. *Rad,* CXXX (1897), 107.

40. István Rácz, *A hajdúk a XVII. században* (Debrecen, 1969).

41. Shopova, *Makedonija vo XVI i XVII vek,* No. 58.

42. P. R. Slaveykov, "Belezhki za nyakoi stari voyvodi," *Sbornik za narodni umotvoreniya,* II, 318–320; B. Angelov and Khr. Vakarelski, *Trem na bŭlgarskata narodna istoricheska epika* (Sofia, 1940), pp. 279–285.

43. Milev, "Okhridskiyat patriarkh Atanasiy."

44. K. Veliki, "Pokhodite na Mikhay Vityazul na yug ot Dunav," *Istoricheski pregled,* 1973, No. 1, pp. 67 ff.

45. L. Hulsius, *Chronologia hoc est brevis descriptio rerum memorabilium in provinciis, hac adiuncta tabula topographica* (Nuremberg, 1597), pp. 58–59.

46. E. Hurmuzaki, *Documente privitoare la istoria Românilor,* III, Bk. 1 (Bucharest, n.d.), 236.

47. *Ibid.*, XII (Bucharest, 1903), 39.

48. P. Panaitescu, *Documente privitoare la istoria lui Mihai Viteazul* (Bucharest, 1936).
49. Milev, "Edin neizdaden dokument," pp. 97–98.
50. Hurmuzaki, *Documente privitoare,* XII, 415–416.
51. Ministère des Affaires Etrangères, Paris, Turquie, Mémoires et documents, VI (1611–1619), fol. 22v–23v.
52. A. Wenner, *Ein gantz neu Reysebuch von Prag biss gen Constantinopel . . .* (Nuremberg, 1622), p. 103.
53. C&MNL, OrO, Sofiyski kadiyski registŭr 1-bis, f. 38v, IV.
54. *Ibid.*, f. 131v, III
55. *Ibid.*, f. 131v, V.
56. Shopova, *Makedonija vo XVI i XVII vek,* No. 68.
57. *Ibid.*
58. A. Matkovski, "Khaydutite v Makedoniya prez pŭrvata polovina na XVII v.," *Izvestiya na Instituta za istoriya,* XIV–XV (1964), 198.
59. Matkovski, *Turski izvori,* I (Skopje, 1961), Nos. 26, 29, 35, 36, 39; *idem,* "Podatotsi za nekoi ajduti od Zapadna Makedonija (1622–1650)," *Glasnik na Institutot za natsionalna istorija,* V (Skopje, 1961), No. 1, 103–105.
60. Cf. Matkovski, *Turski izvori,* I, Nos. 2, 55 *et seq.*
61. *Ibid.*, No. 40.
62. *Ibid.*, I–II.
63. *Ibid.*, I, Nos., 49, 64.
64. Iv. Katardzhiev, *Ajdutskoto dvizhenie i Karposhovoto vostanie vo XVII v.* (Skopje, 1958), p. 18.
65. Matkovski, *Turski izvori,* I, Nos. 90, 104, 107.
66. *Ibid.*, Nos. 29, 39, 54, 62, 82.
67. *Ibid.*, Nos. 104, 107, 109.
68. *Ibid.*, Nos. 94–97; A. Matkovski, "Khaydutite v Makedoniya prez pŭrvata polovina na XVII v.," *Izvestiya na Instituta za istoriya,* XIV–XV (1964), 202–206.
69. Gl. Stanojević, *Jugoslovenske zemlje u mletačko-turskim ratovima 16–18 vijeka* (Belgrade, 1970); Iv. Dujčev, *Avvisi di Ragusa: Documenti sull'-imperro turco nel sec. XVII e sulla guerra di Candia* (Rome, 1935).
70. For details see E. Fermendẓin (ed.), *Acta Bulgariae ecclesiastica* (Zagreb, 1887), pp. 17, 25, 29–30, 33–35, 41–42, 136–137; J. Pejacsevich, "Peter Freiherr von Parchevich," *Archiv für slawische Philologie,* LIX (Vienna, 1880), 499, 501–502; Iv. Duychev, "Proyavi na narodnostno sŭznanie u nas prez XVII v.," *Makedonski pregled,* XII, No. 2, 26–52.
71. Pejacsevich, "Peter Freiherr von Parchevich," pp. 501–502.
72. Evliya Çelebi, *Siyahatnamesi,* V (Dersaadet, 1315), 363.
73. M. Quicklet, *Les voyages de M. Quicklet à Constantinople par terre, enrichis d'annotations par le sieur P. M. L.* (Paris, 1664), p. 134.
74. Çelebi, *Siyahatnamesi,* V, 565, 574–578.

75. *Ibid.*, VI (1318), 123; VIII (1928), 759–760.

76. Matkovski, *Turski izvori,* I–II.

77. *Ibid.*, II, Nos. 64–66, 71, 76, 78, 80, 85–86, 89, 98, 100–102.

78. Çelebi, *Siyahatnamesi,* VI, 161.

79. E.g., P. Ricaut, *Histoire de l'état présent de l'empire ottoman* (Paris, 1670), p. 648; Quicklet, *Les voyages,* p. 139.

80. Matkovski, *Turski izvori,* II, No. 102.

81. J. Grzegorzewski, *Z sydzyllatów rumelijskich epoki wyprawy wiedeńskiej* (Lwów, 1912), Nos. 6, 10.

82. Matkovski, *Turski izvori,* II, Nos. 110, 112–113, 120.

83. Cvetkova, "Iz istoriyata na sŭprotivitelnite i osvoboditelnite dvizheniya," pp. 108–120 *et seq.*

84. Data on the haiduks on the eve of the Karposh uprising and during it are taken from Katardzhiev, *Ajdutskoto dvizhenie;* A. Matkovski, "Ushte edna moriovska buna," *Glasnik na Institutot za natsionalna istorija,* XIV, No. 1, 95–96; *idem,* "Turski dokumenti od vremeto na avstro-turskata vojna i neposredno pred Karposhovoto vostanie," *Glasnik na Institutot za natsionalna istorija,* XV, No. 1, 165–181.

85. For details see Cvetkova, "Iz istoriyata na sŭprotivitelnite i osvoboditelnite dvizheniya," pp. 108 ff.

86. *Silâhdar tahiri,* 2 (Istanbul, 1928), p. 498.

87. Refik, *Türk idaresinde Bulgaristan,* No. 52; cf. *Dokumenti za bŭlgarskata istoriya,* III (Sofia, 1950), No. 56.

88. Refik, *Türk idaresinde Bulgaristan,* No. 54; *Dokumenti za bŭlgarskata istoriya,* III, No. 58.

89. *Silâhdar tahiri,* pp. 506, 519.

90. C&MNL, OrO, Rusenski kadiyski registŭr R/2, f. 78, I.

91. Refik, *Türk idaresinde Bulgaristan,* No. 59.

92. C&MNL, OrO, OAK 2/7.

93. *Ibid.*, Rusenski kadiyski registŭr R/2, f. 55v, III.

94. *Ibid.*, f. 20r, II.

95. Refik, *Türk idaresinde Bulgaristan,* No. 70; *Dokumenti za bŭlgarskata istoriya,* III, No. 72.

96. P. Cernovodeanu, "Bucarest: Important centre politique du Sud-Est européen à la fin du XVIIe siècle et au commencement du XVIII siècle," *Revue des études sud-est européennes,* IV (1966), No. 1–2, 150–160.

97. Matkovski, *Turski izvori,* II, Nos. 125–127.

98. M. Cesar, *Osmanlı tahirinde levendler* (Istanbul, 1965), p. 403, No. 20.

99. Khr, Gandev, *Zarazhdane na kapitalisticheski otnosheniya v chiflishkoto stopanstvo na Severozapadna Bŭlgariya prez XVIII v.* (Sofia, 1962); Khr. Khristov, *Agrarnite otnosheniya v Makedoniya prez XIX i nachaloto na XX v.* (Sofia, 1964).

100. C&MNL, OrO, Vidinski kadiyski registŭr 38, f. 89 r, I; f. 15 v, II; f. 121 v, I; f. 122 r, II; f. 44 v, I; f. 60 r, II; f. 61 r, I.

101. *Ibid.*

102. *Ibid.*

103. *Ibid.*

104. *Ibid.*, Sofiyski kadiyski registŭr 4, f. 6 v, I.

105. *Ibid.*, Vidinski kadiyski registŭr 38, f. 44 v, I; 61 r, I.

106. B. Cvetkova, "Un document turc inédit concernant un mouvement de résistance en Bulgarie du nord-ouest au XVIIIe siècle," *Rocznik orientalistyczny*, XXXVIII, 93–100.

107. C&MNL, OrO, Vidinski kadiyski registŭr 305, f. 10 r, I.

108. Cvetkova, *Khaydutstvoto v bŭlgarskite zemi*, No. 226.

109. C&MNL, OrO, fond 148, No. 1.

110. *Ibid.*, Vidinski kadiyski registŭr 38, f. 57 r, II.

111. Cvetkova, *Khaydutstvoto v bŭlgarskite zemi*, No. 225.

112. Matkovski, *Turski izvori*, III, Nos. 145, 112.

113. Refik, *Türk idaresinde Bulgaristan*, No. 75; *Dokumenti za bŭlgarskata istoriya*, III, No. 79.

114. *Historische Nachricht von der Röm. Kayserl. Gross-Botschaft nach Constantinopel v. G. C. von den Driesch* (Nuremberg, 1723), p. 110.

115. C&MNL, OrO, Sofiyski kadiyski registŭr 312/1, f. 22 v, II; f. 29 r, II.

116. *Ibid.*

117. *Ibid.*, 309 bis, f. 8 v, III; Rusenski kadiyski registŭr R/6, f. 44 r, I.

118. *Ibid.*, Vidinski kadiyski registŭr 18, f. 3 v, I.

119. *Ibid.*, R/38, f. 80 r, II.

120. Slaveykov, "Belezhki za nyakoi stari voyvodi," p. 325; D. P. Nikolov, *Odrinska Trakiya* (Sofia, 1919), pp. 47–48; Angelov and Vakarelski, *Trem na bŭlgarskata narodna istoricheska epika*, pp. 408–413.

121. C&MNL, OrO, Mk 24/17.

122. *Ibid.*, fond 14, No. 84.

123. J. Boscowich, *Journal d'un voyage de Constantinople en Pologne fait à la suite de Son Excellence Mr. Jaq. Porter* (Lausanne, 1772).

124. C&MNL, OrO, Vidinski kadiyski registŭr 159 a, f. 41 r, II.

125. Khr. Gandev, "Edin opit za vŭstanie vŭv Vidin i Vidinsko po vreme na rusko-turskata voyna ot 1768–1774 g.," *Istoricheski pregled*, X, No. 6, 39–52.

126. C&MNL, OrO, Vidinski kadiyski registŭr 310, f. 12 v, II.

127. *Ibid.*, OAK 85/14.

128. *Ibid.*, Sofiyski kadiyski registŭr 26, f. 15 r, II.

129. Iv. D. Shishmanov, "Stari pŭtuvaniya prez Bŭlgariya v posoka na rimskiya voenen pŭt ot Belgrad za Tsarigrad," *Sbornik za narodni umotvoreniya*, IV, 469–470.

130. Cf. Matkovski, *Turski izvori*, I, No. 119; Refik, *Türk idaresinde Bulgaristan*, No. 52 *et al.*

131. Cvetkova, *Khaydutstvoto v bülgarskite zemi*, p. 66 and the documents cited there.

132. *Ibid.*

133. *Ibid.*, p. 67.

134. Matkovski, *Turski izvori*, II, No. 55.

135. *Ibid.*, No. 62.

136. *Ibid.*, Nos. 87, 74.

137. Çelebi, *Siyahatnamesi*, V, 574–578.

138. Matkovski, *Turski izvori*, I. No. 1.

139. C&MNL, OrO, Sofiyski kadiyski registür, 311/1, f. 15 r, II.

140. Matkovski, *Turski izvori*, I, No. 28.

141. *Ibid.*, No. 52.

142. *Ibid.*, No. 2.

143. C&MNL, OrO, Vidinski kadiyski registür 38, f. 117 r, I.

144. Matkovski, *Turski izvori*, I, No. 52.

145. *Ibid.*, No. 61.

146. *Ibid.*, No. 34.

147. Vasdravellē, *Historika archeia Makedonias*, II, 12–13, No. 16.

148. Matkovski, *Turski izvori*, II, No. 52.

149. *Ibid.*, I, No. 61.

150. *Ibid.*, II, No. 103.

151. Cvetkova, *Khaydutstvoto v bülgarskite zemi*, p. 69.

152. C&MNL OrO, Vidinski kadiyski registür 46, f. 36 v.

153. Matkovski, *Turski izvori*, I, Nos. 18, 19, 76, 110; II, Nos. 88, 89.

Avdo Sućeska

# The Eighteenth-Century Austro-Ottoman Wars' Economic Impact on the Population of Bosnia

Throughout the period of Ottoman rule, Bosnia and Herzegovina were distinguished by certain peculiarities of their own, due in no small measure to their position on the frontier (*serhad*) of the empire.[1] One area where these were manifest was in the feudal obligations of the Bosnian populace to the spahis and to the Ottoman state. In principle, its obligations to the spahis were not unlike those in other provinces of the empire, with the Muslim rayah bearing a somewhat lighter burden than their non-Muslim peers. The Christian peasantry, whose number in relation to the Muslims was considerably lower by the end of the seventeenth century than it had been earlier, owed the spahis a tithe (*üşür*), a change-of-residence tax (*salariye, priselica*), a land-use fee (*ispence*), and three days' unpaid labor (*kulluk*) a year. To the state the Christians owed a poll tax (*cizye* or *haraç*) and the child levy (*devşirme*). The Muslim rayah owed the spahis a rent in kind, corvée, and personal taxes (*resmi raiyyet*). The land-rent (*resmi çift*) part of the Muslims' personal taxes was comparatively low in Bosnia, and often only the other two Muslim personal taxes were collected: *benak*, the tax paid by a married man, and *mücerred*, the tax paid for each unmarried male member of a household. The tax differences between Muslims and non-Muslims were part of Ottoman policy to encourage conversion to Islam.[2]

In addition to their obligations to the spahis, the rayah of the whole Ottoman Empire were liable for various services, supplies, and monetary tributes to the state. These special exactions comprised the levies known as *avariz-i divaniye* and *tekâlif-i örfiye*.[3] For a long time in Bosnia these had been levied only exceptionally, because the majority of the populace was exempt (*muaf*) from them. For in Bosnia not only the spahis, who, as a social estate, were everywhere free from the obligations owed by the rayah[4] and from taxes due to the state, but also the whole Muslim urban population enjoyed exemption (*muafiyet*) from the state's special levies. The prime example of this freedom were the inhabitants of Sarajevo.[5] Aside from this privileged urban element, the sultans had very early granted exemption to Bosnia's Muslim peasants,[6] and ever since the conquest of Bosnia to many Christians in return for special services they rendered to the state. These immune non-Muslims included the cattle breeders (*eflak*s—the Vlachs),[7] the miners (*madenci*s),[8] the guards of passes and strategic sites (*derbentci*s), the oarsmen (*kürekçi*s), and the military auxiliaries (martolos).[9] The leaders (*primiçur*s, *knezes*, *tekliče*s) of these special groups enjoyed the additional privilege of the freehold (*serbest*) of a fief (*timar, baština*). Some also received a cash emolument. Finally, beginning in the latter half of the sixteenth century, exemption from state tribute was extended to Jews, who were starting to settle in some Bosnian towns, particularly Sarajevo.[10]

This situation had become firmly established during the course of the sixteenth century, but from early in the seventeenth century certain changes were occurring in agrarian society[11] and special levies began to be imposed on nearly the entire population, exempt or not. Provincial governors levied tribute known as *tekâlif-i şakka.*[12] At the same time the central Ottoman authorities also imposed on certain of the rayah occasional taxes called *avariz* and *bedel-i nezl,* abridging former exemptions.[13] The Sublime Porte's new levies were probably to help pay part of the cost of maintaining new mercenary troops—*seğmen*s, pandours, *levend*s among others.[14]

The turning point in the Bosnians' tax situation came with the alteration of the eyalet's circumstances in the wake of the Treaty of Karlowitz of 1699, which ended the empire's sixteen-year war with the Holy League (the Austrian Empire, Poland, Russia and Venice), the so-called Great War. Bosnia's people and territory had suffered grievously from the Ottoman reverses in the Great War.[15] Ottoman assessments of conditions in Bosnia describe the province as in the process of disintegrating.[16] There can be no quarrel with the evaluation. An enormous number of Bosnians had been killed, many hundreds displaced, numerous towns plundered and burnt, and the survivors themselves had come through economically and physically exhausted. Under Karlowitz, most of Bosnia's border was now in direct contact with the Austrian Empire, Venice, and Montenegro, all of them hostile toward the Ottoman state.[17] This fact combined with the destruction and disruption occasioned by the Great War wrought a substantial change in Bosnia's circumstances and social relations during the course of the eighteenth century. This change affected the rayah's dues in two ways.

Agrarian relationships were undergoing major alterations, all of them to the disadvantage of the rayah. The transformation of rayah land intc holdings of certain privileged sectors of Ottoman society (the *çiftlikçi*s), a process that had already been going on for some time, picked up in pace. In frontier areas of Bosnia, the commanders and men (agas and *nefer*s) of the border garrisons appropriated land abandoned during the hostilities as their own holdings (*çiftlik*s), while in the interior the spahis and local officials (cadis, *âyan*s, voivodes) were turning their fiefs into private holdings, and were seizing deserted land, and even buying land from the peasants in some places, for their own *çiftlik*s.[18] This hurt the rayah because they now had to pay their new type of master a far greater rent than before. Meanwhile, those sectors of the Bosnian rayah, especially the cattle breeders, who used to pay their spahis a lump sum (*filuriye*) were also having their rent modified in the eighteenth century. Relentless pressure was put on them, not only by the spahis but also particularly by the Ottoman state on its lands (*mukataa*s, *milikân*s),[19] to change their fixed cash payments into a tithe or other due characteristic of the military-fief (*timar*) system.[20]

These changes were pressed ahead during the century, not least because of the increased material demands of the ruling strata under the impact of the frequent wars with Austria. This process culminated in the nineteenth century. As a result of it the peasants became an alien labor force on the *çiftlik*s, and depending on the type of their enserfment, were required to surrender from one-fifth to one-half of their produce to the landowners (*ashâb*s, *alaka*s, *çiftlik sahib*s).[21]

At the same time as these burdens of the rayah were becoming more onerous, even greater changes were taking place in their obligations to the state. As a result of the general depopulation, particularly near the frontier, caused by the Great War, as soon as the Treaty of Karlowitz had been signed, the Sublime Porte, in an effort to entice back the rayah who had fled, exempted the Christian population of Bosnia from payment of the poll tax for two years and annulled all arrears of the poll and other taxes. It also decreed that in future the poll tax was to be levied at the lowest rate, a system that remained in effect until the end of Ottoman rule in Bosnia.[22]

Because of the vast material damage, numerous casualties and extreme impoverishment caused by the years of war, the entire population of Bosnia was freed in 1701 from paying the *bedel-i nezl*. Later eighteenth-century documents make it clear that the exemption continued in force throughout the century and that the Bosnians successfully resisted attempts by local and provincial authorities to reinstate the tribute.[23]

While these levies were eased or canceled as a result of the empire's eighteenth-century wars, other taxes and dues were raised or reintroduced for the same reason. As the borders of the province shrank and life became harder during the course of the Great War and, even more, the wars with Austria of 1716–1718 and 1737–1739,[24] the Bosnian valis' need for guard troops increased, and more and more often, from the beginning of the century on, they satisfied their material requirements by the collection of illegal *tekâlif-i şakka* payments.

Unlike the seventeenth century, when these tributes were first collected and were fairly limited, both their number and the revenue raised thereby rose steeply in the first decades of the succeeding century.[25] Although the central authorities, in response to the Bosnians' complaints, had often tried earlier to stop the collection of these tributes, they had eventually to legalize the practice in the province. A firman of 1720 recognized the right of the vali of Bosnia to exact special tributes from the population, both in wartime (*imdad-i hazariye*) and peacetime (*imdad-i seferiye*).[26] To eliminate arbitrariness and inequities in the way the tributes were imposed, a firman of 1731 fixed the annual sum of *imdad-i hazariye* from the whole province at 31,519.50 groş.[27]

While the amounts collected in the latter half of the century complied with the firman, they often exceeded it handsomely in the earlier years, particularly during periods of preparation for war and after the war of 1737–1739. In Herzegovina alone, for instance, the total of *imdad-i hazariye* and *seferiye* was set at 60,000 groş in 1734. A comparable amount must have been assessed on Bosnia, for a document of the same year refers to the resistance of the inhabitants of Sarajevo to collection of the *imdad-i seferiye*. In 1742 even higher amounts were set for the sanjaks of the province:—154,000 groş from Bosnia, 22,240 groş from Klis, 8,440 groş from Zvornik, and 64,992 groş from Herzegovina—a total of 249,672 groş from the whole eyalet.[28]

All the inhabitants of Bosnia occupying rayah land (*reaya emlâk ve erazi*), regardless of their social standing and whether or not formerly exempt from *avariz-i divaniye* and *tekâlif-i örfiye*, were required to pay the tribute levied by the vali. The guards of the province's fortresses were alone exempted by a special firman. When exactly the exemption was granted is not known, but a firman of 1783 cites existing precedent in extending immunity to the guards of the fortress of Kupreş in the sanjak of Klis.[29]

No less heavy, and perhaps even more onerous, than the financial burdens of the Bosnians in the eighteenth century was the compulsory labor they had to put in, repairing and building fortresses and redoubts (*palanka*s) and digging trenches (*hendek*s).[30] The periods of highest taxation coincided with the greatest demand for labor: before and after the wars with Austria, before and after conflict with the Venetians and Montenegrins, and after the great Muslim peasant revolt in Bosnia in the middle of the century, when several fortresses were seriously damaged and that of Zvornik was destroyed.[31] Contemporary military and financial records show that throughout the century the Ottomans continued a regular program of building and restoring strongholds in the province, especially in the frontier areas near Austria, Venice and Montenegro. As early as 1701, for instance, Çose Halil Pasha, the provincial governor, was ordered to undertake urgent repair and construction work on 28 fortresses and eight redoubts on the banks of the Sava and Una rivers (the frontier with the Austrian Empire) and to place all the fortresses and redoubts on the Venetian and Montenegrin borders on a war footing.[32] The work continued even after the Ottoman Empire concluded the Treaty of Passarowitz with Venice and Austria in 1718.[33] I 1734 Muşinzade Abdullah Pasha, the then vali, was ordered to visit every fortress and redoubt in the province personally to make an on-the-spot assessment of the priority and cost of the work that needed to be done to them. The pasha made his survey immediately, and informed the Sublime Porte that the most urgent repairs were needed by certain of the main frontier fortresses at an estimated cost of 91, 928 groş. Half of this sum was to be provided by the state, and the other half was to be raised from the local population in cash or corvée (*kulluk*).[34] The next major repair effort was undertaken following signature of the Treaty of Belgrade in 1739.[35] Work began in 1742 and was still going on when the Treaty of Sistova was concluded in 1791.[36]

Military construction and repair work thus went on continuously in Bosnia throughout the eighteenth century. Assigned special importance by the Ottoman state, the work required enormous material and physical expenditures. Financially straitened and under constant pressure from its foes within and without, the Ottoman state had no alternative but to place the major burden on the Bosnian populace. The official records for the years 1701–1798 demonstrate that, as the power of the state declined, so the exactions from the Bosnians grew in number and degree. Immediately after the Treaty of Karlowitz, when the population's poverty and helplessness was at its postwar height, the Ottoman treasury provided most of the financing needed for repair of the province's fortresses and redoubts, while the physical labor for it was supplied, on the sultan's orders, by the entire population of Bosnia, not only the rayah but even by the spahis and the commanders and men of the garrisons. For every two peasants on the job, a person of rank had to consent to take part in the construction work.

Documents from the early years of the century include a number of orders requiring Bosnia's spahis to go at once in person, or to send their deputies and military commanders (*alay beys*), to the fortress to which they had been assigned, and to join in the construction or repair work there together with their own rayah and the local rayah and garrison, under pain of forfeiting their property and income (*sipahilik, dirlik*) for failure to do so.[37] Since all too soon the spahis were required for the century's continual wars on the empire's frontiers, and in Russia, Persia and elsewhere, the Ottoman authorities had to modify this requirement by 1734. For some time thereafter, the burden of fortress and redoubt repair and construction was divided among the state, the men of the garrisons, and the rayah of the area where the military installation was situated. The central authorities assumed half the cost of the work, and the rest of the cost and the labor were provided by the garrisons and rayah.[38] By the latter half of the eighteenth century, the practice had been established of dividing the whole effort into three equal shares: one-third of the financial outlay came from the state, one-third from the garrisons, and one-third from the local peasantry. Many records from these years state: "The work is to be executed with maximum urgency in the manner customary in the marches [*krajina*]."[39]

In work on the fortifications, the rayah and the fortress guards generally had different tasks. The rayah usually did the heavy labor, cutting lumber and stone, transporting them with their own draft animals (horses or oxen), digging ditches, and burning lime. The garrison officers and men put up some of the money needed and would assist the craftsmen's skilled work. In emergencies, as when insufficient labor was available, men would be called in from surrounding districts and other garrisons. This happened quite often in the earlier years of the century. When expert skills were needed, specialized craftsmen would be hired at a fixed daily wage from other parts of the province, most often Herzegovina. In specially urgent cases, they might even be brought in from the more distant parts of Rumelia. The imperious and minatory tones in which the sultan's orders to mobilize skilled craftsmen were couched bear witness to the artisans' efforts to avoid the burden at all costs.

From the records that have come down it is hard to assess how many days' unpaid labor a year the rayah put in on work on the fortifications, but it is safe to conclude that it was an exceptionally heavy load. This can be deduced from the sluggish pace of work on some fortresses and, even more, from the Bosnians', and especially the Muslims', frequent complaints to the sultan in the first half of the century about local and provincial officials' violence and oppressiveness, which drove them more than once to open rebellion.

There were a considerable number of such outbreaks all over the eyalet during the first half of the century, outbreaks that grew in scale and intensity as a result of the continuous increase in the demands for tribute and the incidence of abuse. A firman of 1711 reveals that in 1699 a group of Christians and Muslims banded together to block roads to prevent the collection of the poll tax and to obstruct the enlistment of the masons (*duncers*) and other craftsmen to work on the fortresses of Mostar and Banja Luka. They twice attacked the courthouse (*mahkeme*) in Mostar, violating Muslim religious law and disrupting the officials' performance of their duties.[40] That same year there was a similar eruption in Banja Luka over work on the fortress there.[41] Ottoman sources mention disturbances in 1727, 1728 and 1732 in Mostar.[42]

An Ottoman document of 1739 describes rebellions in the cazas of Blagaj and Nevesinje. The long-disaffected local rayah joined forces with a certain Osman, a spahi from Počitelj in Blagaj caza, and some officers and men of the garrison of Postoljani in Nevesinje caza and attacked the two district courthouses in protest against the recruitment of craftsmen to work on the fortress in Sarajevo.[43]

Disturbances were reported all over the province during these years,[44] and finally coalesced into a general rebellion that affected the whole of Bosnia for more than a decade (1745–1757). Its immediate causes were the amount of corvée demanded, the levies imposed by the vali, and the abuses of local officials: combined, the burden had become intolerable. Most of the rebels were Muslim peasants, but this time they were also joined by many smaller spahis and lower Muslim clergy and even the cadi of Sarajevo himself, Abdurahman Muhremija.[45] The uprising amounted to a class war, pitting the lower levels of Ottoman society against the ruling strata (the cadis, *âyans*, *kapetans*, viziers, *mirimirans*), and in every respect resembled the peasant rebellions that occurred in many parts of Europe during the Middle Ages. How serious the revolt was is indicated clearly in a letter from the sultan himself to Mehmed Pasha Kukavica, the governor of Bosnia who stamped out the rebellion with ferocity, in which the Grand Turk refers to the "reconquest" (*fetih*) of the province.[46]

Even later in the century there were still outbreaks of local disorder, details of which are given in particular in the chronicle of Mula Mustafa Bašeskija.[47] He noted that in 1771 the inhabitants of Sarajevo revolted against the *imdad-i seferiye* and closed down the bazaar (*çarsı, čaršija*) in protest.[47] That same year some men of Zenica killed a tax collector (*serdengeçti aga*), [48] and the Muslim residents of Vlasenica rebelled against paying the tribute demanded of them.[49] Bašeskija reports that in 1773 a peasant from Visoko was strangled to death in the fortress of Sarajevo for evading payment of the *imdad-i seferiye*, and that early the next year force had to be used to exact this tribute from the people of Sarajevo.[50] His chronicle contains accounts of numerous similar occurrences.

The human and economic resources of Bosnia were exhausted by the Great War with the Holy League and the numerous wars of the eighteenth century. They shrank to the point where they could not meet the costs of two consequences of the hostilities: the need to restore the economy and prosperity of the province and its rulers, and the need for military construction work that the Sublime Porte considered essential for the defense of Bosnia's borders. The result was that the relationship between the various strata of Bosnian society as reflected in the level and extent of the obligations imposed on the population changed rapidly in the early part of the eighteenth century, and when these changes failed to raise the revenue required by the Ottoman administration, the Sublime Porte abrogated numerous privileges both of the Muslim peasantry and of those with higher social standing. The final outcome was to stir up Muslim opposition to Constantinople for the first time, and to spark revolts throughout Bosnia.[51]

## Notes

1. Avdo Sućeska, "Ajani [Âyans] (A Contribution to the Study of Local Authority in Our Lands in Turkish Times)," in *Naučno Društvo SR Bosne i Hercegovine* [The Society of Sciences of the S(ocialist) R(epublic of) Bosnia and Herzegovina] (Sarajevo, 1965), pp. 162–222.

2. Avdo Sućeska, "The Position of the Raya in Bosnia in the 18th Century," *Survey* (Sarajevo), III (1978), 209–216.

3. For somewhat greater detail on these tributes see Avdo Sućeska, "Die Entwicklung der Besteuerung durch die Avâriz-i Dîvanîye und die Tekâlîf-i Örfîye im Osmanischen Reich während des 17. und 18. Jh.," *Südost-Forschungen* (Munich), XXVII (1968).

4. See Halil Inalcık, "Osmanlilarda Raiyyet Rusumu" [Muslim Personal Taxes under the Ottomans], *Belleten* (Ankara), XXIII (1959), 575–608.

5. Muhamed Hadžijahić, "Sarajevska Muafnama" [The Tax-Exempt of Sarajevo], *Godišnjak Društva istoričara Bosne i Hercegovine* [Yearbook of the Society of Historians of Bosnia and Herzegovina] (Sarajevo), XIV (1964), 87–119; Avdo Sućeska, "Da li su sarajevski Jevreji bili mu'af?" [Were the Sarajevo Jews Tax-Exempt?], *Godišnjak Pravnog fakulteta u Sarajevu* [Yearbook of the Faculty of Law in Sarajevo] (Sarajevo), XXIII (1975), 191–204.

6. Başbakanlik Arşivi Istambul [Central Government Archives of Istanbul] (hereafter cited as BBAI), Mühimme Defteri [Major Records], No. 19 p. 154, doc. 325, and No. 73, p. 80.

7. *Kanuni* and *Kanunname* [laws and law codes] for the sanjaks of Bosnia, Herzegovina, Zvornik, Klis, Montenegro and Skadar (Sarajevo, 1957), pp. 11–15.

8. *Ibid.*

9. Milan Vasić, *Martolosi u jugoslavenskim zemljama pod turskom vladavinom* [The Martolos in the South Slav Lands under Turkish Rule] (Sarajevo, 1967), pp. 128–136.

10. Sućeska, "Da li su sarajevski Jevreji . . . ."

11. For greater detail on the development of *çiftliks*, see Avdo Sućeska, "O nastanku čiftluka u našim zemljama" [On the Emergence of *Çiftliks* in Our Lands], *Godišnjak Društva istoričara Bosne i Hercegovine*, XVI (1965).

12. Sućeska, "Die Entwicklung . . . ."

13. It is not know when, to what extent and in what amounts these tributes were collected; what is certain is that they were collected. This is evi-

dent from certain orders issued by the central authorities in 1686, during the Great War. BBAI, Mühimme Defteri, C—480/3.

14. BBAI, Mâliye Defteri [Financial Records], D—1163/202.

15. For somewhat greater detail, see Halil Inalcık, "Saray bosna şeriye sicilerine göre viyana bozgunundan sonraki harb yıllarinda bosna," *Tarif vesikalari* (Ankara), 9/II, pp. 178–187, and 11/II, pp. 372–384.

16. See, e.g., BBAI, Mâliye Defteri, D—305/1.

17. Cf. Ešref Kovačević, *Granice bosanskog pašaluka prema Austriji i Mletačkoj Republici po odredbama karlovačkog mira* [The Borders of the Bosnian Pashalik with Austria and the Republic of Venice under the Provisions of the Peace of Karlowitz] (Sarajevo, 1973).

18. Sućeska, "The Position of the Raya . . . ," pp. 209–216, 217–220.

19. On these kinds of tenure, see Avdo Sućeska, "Malikana (Doživotni zakup državnih dobara u osmanskoj državi)" [Malikana (Life Tenure of State Property in the Ottoman State)], *Prilozi za orijentalne filologije* [Contributions to Oriental Philology] (Sarajevo), VII–IX (1960).

20. Sućeska, "The Position of the Raya . . . ," p. 219.

21. For greater detail, see Avdo Sućeska, "Prvi pokušaj reguliranja agrarnih odnosa u Bosni i Hercegovini u XIX stoljeću" [The First Attempt to Regulate Agrarian Relations in Bosnia and Herzegovina in the 19th Century], *Godišnjak Pravnog fakulteta u Sarajevu,* XIV (1966).

22. BBAI, Mâliye Defteri, D—214/301–308; Hamid Hadžibegić, *Glavarina u osmanskoj državi* [The Poll Tax in the Ottoman State] (Sarajevo, 1966), p. 102.

24. *Istorija naroda Jugoslavije* [History of the Peoples of Yugoslavia] (Belgrade, 1960), II, 1232–1249.

25. Avdo Sućeska, "Novi podatci o nastanku i visini taksita u Bosni" [New Data on the Origin and Amount of Taxation in Bosnia], *Prilozi Instituta za istoriju Sarajeva* [Contributions of the Institute of History of Sarajevo] (Sarajevo), 10/11, 1974, pp. 135–145.

26. *Ibid.*, pp. 139–142.

27. *Ibid.*, pp. 143–144.

28. Avdo Sućeska, "Bune seljaka muslimana u Bosni u XVII i XVIII stoljeću" [Muslim Peasant Revolts in Bosnia in the 17th and 18th Centuries], *Zbornik radova* [Transactions (of the Institute of History)] (Belgrade), I (1976), 73.

29. BBAI, Mâliye Defteri, E—108.

30. On the construction of fortresses and redoubts in Bosnia and Herzegovina under the Ottomans, especially in the 18th century, see Hamdija Kruševljaković, *Stari bosanski gradovi: Naše starine* [Old Bosnian Castles: Our Antiquities], I (Sarajevo, 1953), 7–45; *idem* and Hamdija Kapidžić, *Stari hercegovački gradovi: Naše starine* [Old Herzegovinian

Castles: Our Antiquities], II (Sarajevo, 1954), 9–11.

31. BBAI, Măliye Defteri, 3609/353. On the recommendation of Mehmed Pasha, the sultan in 1757 decreed that the expense of rebuilding the fortress of Zvornik was to be borne by the inhabitants, above all the rayah, of the cazas of Zvornik, Tuzla, Gračanica, Biraç (Vlasenica), and Kladanj, that is, those areas in which the peasants had rebelled under the leadership of Abdurahman Muhremija and taken part in the destruction of the fortress in 1753. Under similar circumstances, Mehmed Pasha, the vali of Bosnia, had been removed from office and executed in 1706 for fraudulently converting to other uses state money entrusted to him by the Sublime Porte for repair of the fortress.

32. BBAI, Mâliye Defteri, 3609/353, 2945/260, 1483/260.

33. Further data on this work are to be found in the Mâliye and Mühimme Defteri from the first decades of the 18th century.

34. BBAI, Mâliye Defteri, 3609/321–359.

35. *Ibid.*

36. BBAI, Mâliye Defteri, D—374/3, D—386/2-6, D—394/3, D—395/1.

37. Further data are in the Mâliye and Mühimme Defteri for the first decades of the 18th century.

38. BBAI, Mâliye Defteri, 3609/321–359.

39. *Ibid.*, D—374/3, D—394/3, D—395/1, D—396/2-6. This was the case in theory, but in practice most of the burden fell on the rayah and the men of the garrisons because of the central authorities' shortage of funds for repair. Moreover, it was by no means unusual for those charged with the construction work simply to pocket the state funds allocated for it as well as what was raised from the rayah. An egregious example was that of Hasan, *kapetan* of Banja Luka, who in 1741 absconded from his lucrative office with 4,000 groş. *Ibid.*, A 71/6.

40. BBAI, Mühimme Defteri for 1711 (photocopies in the Academy of Science and Art of Bosnia-Herzegovina).

41. BBAI, Şikâyet Defteri [Grievance Records] for 1711 (photocopies in the Academy of Science and Art of Bosnia-Herzegovina).

42. *Ibid.* for these years (photocopies in the Academy of Science and Art of Bosnia-Herzegovina).

43. BBAI, Mühimme and Mâliye Defteri for 1729 (photocopies in the Academy of Science and Art of Bosnia-Herzegovina).

44. Much data are in the Mühimme, Şikâyet and Mâliye Defteri for the 1730s–1760s and in the chronicles of two Franciscan friars, Nikola Lašvanin and Bone Benić. See J. Jelenić, "Ljetopis Fra Nikole Lašvanina" [The Chronicle of Fra Nikola Lašvanin], *Glasnik Zemaljskog muzeja Sarajeva* [Herald of the Regional Museum of Sarajevo] (Sarajevo), 1914/1915; "Ljetopis franjevačkog samostana u Kr. Sutjesci" [Chronicle of the Franciscan Monastery

of Kr. Sutjeska], *Glasnik Zemaljskog muzeja Sarajeva*, XXXVII (1925) and XXXVIII (1926).

45. For greater detail, see Sućeska, "Bune seljaka muslimana . . . ," pp. 76–93.

46. *Sidžil kadije iz Tesnja iz polovine XVIII stoljeća* [The Register of the Cadis of Tesanj in the Mid 18th Century] (photocopy and Serbocroat translation in the Academy of Science and Art of Bosnia-Herzegovina).

47. Mula Mustafa Ševki Bašeskija, *Ljetopis (1746–1804)* [Chronicle 1746–1804)], trans. M. Mujezinović (Sarajevo, 1968), pp. 148–150.

48. *Ibid.*

49. *Ibid.*

50. *Ibid.*, p. 60.

51. Summary paragraph provided by the editors.

Paschalis M. Kitromilides

# War and Political Consciousness: Theoretical Implications of Eighteenth-Century Greek Historiography

Preoccupied with the problem of domestic political order, political thought in the early modern period paid only tangential attention to international relations and war as components of political life. Niccolò Machiavelli, for whom war was an integral part of political life and whose political thought therefore constitutes the first specifically modern contribution to the theory of international relations, was the only major theorist in his ordering of political priorities to break the exclusive precedence given to domestic over international politics, and to stress the essential identity and continuity between them. The characteristically modern nature of Machiavelli's thought consisted in this realistic appraisal of the interdependence of domestic politics and interstate relations. This distinguished him from the other exception to the neglect of war and international relations in early modern thought, the succession of just war theorists from Alberico Gentili to Hugo Grotius, who, however, in attempting to elaborate a normative "law of nations" based on a theory of just war, continued up to the end of the seventeenth century a very old medieval tradition of political discourse going back to Saint Augustine. The theory of just war itself, as a medieval vestige, was under attack by the exponents of Renaissance humanism like Desiderius Erasmus, who argued in *The Complaint of Peace* that it was absurd to prefer even the justest war to the most unjust peace.[1] In contrast to these arguments, Machiavelli discussed the problem of violence and war not as a question of morality and justice but as a necessary part of politics, given the nature of things, and thus he made it an integral part of his republican problematic.[2]

The great political theorists of the seventeenth century in turn, although they built largely on the theoretical foundations laid by

Machiavelli, departed from his framework as far as the centrality of war to political life was concerned. For both Thomas Hobbes and Benedict de Spinoza political society is the antithesis of war which therefore remains largely outside the purview of political thought. International relations, according to Hobbes, constituted the one area in the life of civilized humanity in which the original state of war persisted unabated,[3] but he did not occupy himself in any detail with the nature of international interaction and conflict in contrast to the obsessive attention he devoted to the dynamics of civil war. Thus, by remaining beyond the confines of the sovereign state, war fell also outside the problematic of political theory. John Locke, who tempered and made more palatable Hobbes's thought and transmitted it to the liberal tradition, did not go beyond his predecessor's conceptualization of international relations as an example of the state of nature. He simply allowed for a special branch of government, the federative power of the commonwealth, as the competent exponent of civil authority in external affairs and in relations with other commonwealths.[4]

In contrast to the relative paucity of early modern political theory on the issues of war and international relations, the eighteenth century witnessed an increasing recognition of the centrality of international relations and war to political life and thus to political thought.[5] The greatest political minds of the century shared in this reappraisal. Both the Baron de Montesquieu and Jean-Jacques Rousseau supplemented their main focus, which remained on domestic political order and legitimacy, with a serious appreciation of the international dimension of politics.[6] David Hume with his views on the problem of balance of power was the first major political thinker since Machiavelli to propose a systematic theory of international relations,[7] while Immanuel Kant reversed the traditional priorities of political philosophy by making the problem of war and peace his point of departure and considering the question of domestic political order in the framework of a theory of international relations.[8] Finally the generalized experience of war as an instrument of policy at the turn of the eighteenth and nineteenth centuries prepared the formulation of the great theory of modern war by Karl von Clausewitz, who returned to a study of Machiavelli's old equation of war with politics, taking into account the new conditions of warfare.[9]

It would be tempting to attempt a historical interpretation of the changing place of war in political thought by reference to the contextual circumstances stimulating the advent of each theory. Broadly speaking, one might suggest that, for as long as the consolidation of domestic order and state-building were the primary political reality in early modern history, international war as a subject of political thought remained in a condition of "underdevelopment." Once the tasks of domestic politics were accomplished, and a system of centralized sovereign states emerged from the chaos of seventeenth-century wars, thinking about that system, its workings, its rules, its balance, the possibilities of its improvement, became a legitimate concern of political theory. This can partly explain the increasing attention paid to international relations in eighteenth-century thought. Once this working hypothesis has been proposed however, an immediate methodological caveat must follow: the contextual interpretation can be no more than a point of departure in explorations in the history of ideas which, to be fully understood, must be studied in its own right by looking at its logic, arguments and symbols in order to capture its purposes. In this way the texts themselves, once taken seriously as historical projects, can be made to tell us something more substantive about the circumstances that gave them birth.

This second dimension of the history of ideas can be appreciated by looking at another aspect of the complex relationship between war and political thought as reflected in a process of ideological change which, over time, integrated the fact of international interaction and conflict into the parameters of political awareness. The question to be explored here is, if an expanding awareness of the facts of international life invited the great theorists to think systematically about them, how did perceptions of the same historical phenomena of war and of the character of international relations influence the emergence and growth of political self-consciousness, which developed at an accelerated pace during the eighteenth century among those European peoples not possessing sovereign states of their own? This is a difficult question of comparative history, but the dynamics of the problem just formulated could be grasped by looking at the evidence of a concrete case of ideological change illustrating the phenomenon of the politicization of historical consciousness under the impact of perceptions of international conflict. The present purpose is to attempt to present some evidence from Greek historical experience in the eighteenth century to bear on this general theoretical problem.

* * *

The eighteenth century is the great age of Neohellenic revival that culminated in the emergence of a revolutionary national consciousness that visualized the political freedom of the Greeks. That process was complex and multidimensional, but the focus now will be on only one limited aspect of it, examining in some detail the textual evidence that documents the interplay of perceptions of international conflict in the eighteenth century and the evolution of Greek historical consciousness during that period of social and cultural change. The international events that were most dramatically felt among the peoples of Southeastern Europe, including the Greeks, in the course of the eighteenth century were the Russo-Ottoman wars of 1711, 1735–1739, 1768–1774 and 1787–1792.[10] Attention will thus be on these wars and their impact on the historical self-definition and political aspirations of the awakening segments of the Greek nation—precisely those segments that produced and read the historical literature on those wars that is to be examined.

The new era inaugurated in Ottoman-Russian relations by the wars of Peter the Great against the Ottoman Empire since the closing years of the seventeenth century was reflected in Greek letters by the appearance of a literature of appeals and addresses to Peter voicing Greek hopes for redemption from Ottoman tyranny through his intervention in the east.[11] Peter's new war against the Ottomans, the first Russo-Turkish confrontation of the eighteenth century, was marked in 1711 by the publication of a proclamation composed by Petros Skordylis inciting the Greeks to fight with Peter's armies against their infidel oppressors.[12] This literature of hope inaugurated the stream of Russian propaganda that was channeled through Greek sources throughout the eighteenth century and was sustained among the popular masses by a millenarian tradition nurtured by Russian agents but couched in terms that meshed very effectively with older oracular beliefs about national redemption. Every new Russo-Ottoman confrontation in the course of the eighteenth century marked a new outpouring of such literature in the Greek language, thus registering the strides of an ideology that could be characterized as the "Russian expectation" in Greek political thought.[13]

Although Greek political, religious and cultural ties with Orthodox Russia were very old, dating back to the Christianization of the Russian Slavs by Byzantine missionaries in the tenth century, the hope that Greek redemption might come from the north was a new one and purely the product of the changing structure of international relations in the eighteenth century.[14] Until the turn of the seventeenth and eighteenth centuries, such hopes were focused on the west, especially on the Venetian republic which continued to hold an empire in the Levant and thus remained the major contender with Ottoman power in the east.[15] The expectations of the captive Greeks, systematically by Venetian propaganda through the seventeenth century abated were fueled by the monumental confrontations between Christendom, led by Venice, and Islam, such as the Cypriot War and the battle of Lepanto in 1570–1571, the protracted siege of Candia in Crete in 1649–1669, and the wars of the Holy League against the Ottoman Empire in 1684–1699. The hopes for western help came finally to an end upon the expulsion of Venetian power from the east in 1715 with the final fall of the Peloponnese to the Turks.[16] The ideological vacuum that was thus created by the disappearance of the hope for western help with the decline of Venice was promptly filled by the emergence of Russian power, which brought with it all the psychological force of traditional symbolism and religious affinity—in contrast to the religious antagonism always undermining earlier orientations toward Catholic Venice—sanctioning the aspirations of the Third Rome in the Greek east.[17]

Besides this propagandist and oracular literature, the Russo-Ottoman wars were reflected in Greek eighteenth-century historiography by a gradual reorientation from the traditional religious chronicles of the past toward contemporary international history—an intellectual phenomenon of great significance for the collective self-definition of the modern Greeks. Evidence of this historiographical reorientation emerged during the war of 1735–1739 with the publication of extensive biographies of Peter the Great, extolling the achievements of the regenerator of the Russian Empire. The works of westernized Greek authors with political connections with Russia, these biographies did belong on a certain level to the output of Russian propaganda in Southeastern Europe. At the same time however, these sources represented the first serious attempts in Greek intellectual life to come to grips with the important events of international relations in the broader world of which Greek society and the Ottoman state formed a part. The most renowned biography of Peter in Balkan culture was published in Italian by the Greek learned priest Antonios Katiphoros under the title *Vita di Pietro il Grande*. The work was reprinted six times between 1736 and 1792.[18] A Greek version appeared in 1737,[19] followed by translations into the languages of other Balkan nationalities.[20] Although Katiphoros had visited Russia at an earlier date, his book was far from an inconsequential work of political propaganda. In its two volumes the work conveyed a great deal of interesting information both about Peter's domestic policies of social and cultural change and about his foreign wars, which had proved not only that the terrifying Ottoman power was no longer invincible but also that it could be broken by the valor of Orthodox arms. In substance, Katiphoros's work could be considered a Greek harbinger of the political purposes of Voltaire's biography of Peter the Great[21] which attempted, through an account of Peter's reform and achievement, to project the paradigm of enlightened absolutism that ought to guide the European monarchs' policies of cultural change. Katiphoros's political message was clear, while the intellectual background of the author was indicative of the new cultural and political alignments taking shape in Greek society. In another work, published two years before the biography of Peter, Katiphoros had remarked that, "although in matters of faith every innovation or mutation would be dangerous and soul-destroying, precisely the opposite is the case in the sciences."[22] By thus affirming the separation of learning from religious belief and pleading for the pursuit of novelty in science, Katiphoros had enunciated one of the earlier instances of the will to Enlightenment in Greek thought. Such was the intellectual foundation of the political messages contained in the newfound awareness of contemporary history.

A new and articulate conception of the importance of contemporary secular history was characteristically projected in the preface of another biography of Peter which appeared the year immediately following the publication of Katiphoros's work. In his foreword the author, Athanasios Skiadas, who in 1742 published a Greek version of François Fénelon's *Télémaque*, articulated a completely utilitarian outlook on history. Acquaintance with the past and with the deeds of great men was worthwhile only on utilitarian grounds. Moral and religious edification, though deemed clearly desirable, was seen as only an incidental consequence of the lessons of historical study, not the exclusive objective of them as had been the case in the traditional conception of learning about the past exemplified in the religious chronicles of universal history. In the new framework history appeared important primarily because it taught how effectively to attain desirable ends in an individual's and in a nation's life.[23] The discovery of contemporary international history initiated by the biographies of Peter the Great was an integral part of this transition to secular purposes that was in the making among the segment of the Greek intelligentsia in closest contact with the West.

* * *

If the wars of Peter the Great provided an initial stimulus to the discovery of modern international relations in Greek culture, the repeated wars of Catherine II in the second half of the eighteenth century set the context of important developments in Greek historical and political thought. Following an already established pattern of Russian policy, Catherine's designs against the Ottoman state did not merely include assaults against the empire's northern territories but provided also for the incitement of the Sublime Porte's Christian subjects to revolt in order to divert Ottoman forces from the main fronts. This led to the 1770 rising in the Maina peninsula in the Peloponnese prompted by the appearance of a Russian fleet in the Mediterranean and by the promises given to the Greeks by the empress's agents, Counts Aleksey and Grigoriy Orlov. Although the Russian fleet scored a great victory against the Ottoman navy at Çeşme on the Anatolian coast opposite Chios, the rising of the Greeks was brutally put down by Ottoman forces; the Peloponnese was delivered to the ravages of Albanian bandits and the Greeks were abandoned by their Russian "friends" to their grim fate.[24] All this had a quite sobering impact on the credibility of the "Russian expectation" and planted some doubts in the minds of the exponents of the millenarian tradition.[25] The episode had critical consequences for the orientation of Greek political thought in the long run, but its immediate significance was most characteristically registered in the attempts of the most distinguished Greek intellectual figure of the time, Eugenios Voulgaris, to point at the possibilities immanent in the drama of war, revolt and agitation in Southeastern Europe for the collective future of his compatriots. In an historical essay Voulgaris presented the first systematic conceptualization of the Greek problem in the framework of a paradigm of international relations.

Eugenios Voulgaris had found refuge in the Russian court after his attempts at cultural and educational renovation in Greece during the 1740s and 1750s had been aborted by the vehement reaction of conservative intellectual circles. In Russia he embraced wholeheartedly the political theory of enlightened absolutism projected by Catherine II in her *Nakaz* or *Instruction for a New Code of Laws.* This text, in a Greek translation by Voulgaris, was meant to advertise among the translator's compatriots the programmatic purposes and the political philosophy of the Semiramis of the North.[26] The logic of Voulgaris's political argument involved fundamentally a rationalization of the traditional Russian expectation through an appeal to the model of enlightened absolutism. This model, as embodied in Catherine's policies, gave rational content to the mesmerism of the Third Rome and responded to the gropings for cultural and political change that animated enlightened Greek consciences. These gropings took shape under the pressures of international relations on political thought at the time. Voulgaris articulated the connection between the context of international relations and the content of political thought in a remark in his introduction to the Greek version of the *Nakaz* that the hopes of wretched Greece had been heightened ever since Catherine's fleets sailed from the north into the Aegean.[27]

The interaction between the analysis of international relations and political thought found its most fruitful expression in an important essay entitled "Reflections on the Present Critical State of the Ottoman Empire,"[28] apparently motivated by the Russo-Ottoman war of 1768–1774 and attributed to Voulgaris. The authenticity of the authorship can be accepted on the basis of the quality of its argument as well as on plausible internal evidence. The essay attempted to discuss, in terms of the eighteenth-century theory of balance of power, the role of the Ottoman Empire and Russia in the European state system. In a quite admirable manner, showing both great political realism and intimate knowledge of Ottoman society and government, the author refuted several misconceptions prevailing in contemporary European thought about the degeneracy and utter decay of Ottoman power. Despite their recent defeats, the author warned, the Turks were quick to learn from European civilization, and they could not long delay reconstituting their military might. In that eventuality, they would be the greatest threat to the European balance of power. The rise of Russian power in the eighteenth century was an important example that had not been lost on the Turks. Russian power on the contrary, Voulgaris suggested, knew its limits and had no intention of disrupting the international balance of power, but it rendered great services to it by weakening the Ottomans and keeping them under control.

Turning to an analysis of the Greek predicament in this context, Voulgaris referred bitterly to the several cruel disappointments experienced by the Greeks on account of the behavior of certain European powers which had remained indifferent to their plight or prevented would-be liberators from coming to their aid. The essay concluded by suggesting that the partition of the European provinces of the Ottoman Empire and the creation of an independent Greek principality of moderate extent would be conducive to the preservation of the international balance of power. Heartfelt concern for the fate of his compatriots, whom the then raging war—a reference to Catherine's first war with the Ottoman Empire—had exposed to mortal dangers, combined with his unwavering dedication to and faith in Russian policy, formed in this case too the essence of Voulgaris's argument.

The connection between international relations and political thought as expressed in a rationalized Russian expectation continued to be the key to Voulgaris's reflections on the Greek problem. His focus remained on Catherine's policies in the east through which he hoped to see the double achievement of national liberation and cultural reform in his homeland. His hopes and reflections at each turn of Russian policy were recorded in the semipropagandist pamphlets that he published during the turbulent decade of the 1770s. Amidst the news of the tragedy that followed the abortive rising in the Peloponnese in 1770, Voulgaris composed two appeals, one addressed to Catherine personally and another directed as a "supplication to all of Christian Europe." Both appeals entreated the Christian powers of Europe to come to the succor and rescue of the Greeks whose lamentable fate under the yoke of the Ottomans and their latest disaster at the hands of Albanian bandits were depicted in a shuddering account.[29] The war came to an end in 1774 with the conclusion of the treaty of Kuchuk Kainarji which greatly enhanced Russian power in the Balkans and sanctioned Russian intercession in the domestic affairs of the Ottoman Empire. In the same spirit that had inspired his earlier entreaties, Voulgaris celebrated the Russian victory by composing a hymn to the trophies of peace and a triumphant song in ancient Greek meters.[30] Celebration of Russian triumphs was an integral part of the psychology of the Russian expectation that Voulgaris wanted to implant in his compatriots. A complete identification with the Russian cause required not only supplications and pious hopes, but also a capacity for full empathy with the historical destinies of the great empire of a fellow Orthodox nation.

To the same end, Voulgaris translated into Greek two of Voltaire's narrative poems on the events of the war in the east. One of them, entitled "Voltaire's Epistle to the Empress of the Russians," epitomized in its verses the gist of Voulgaris's own political thought. The triumph that Catherine was expected to achieve was a double one: a victory over the tyrant residing in Byzantium, and conquest of the tyranny of superstition. This victory of the Russians would both vindicate the profound hatred of the Christians for their Ottoman oppressors and avenge the suffering the latter inflicted on Christendom. The real triumph, however, would only follow the annihilation of Ottoman tyranny by the resurrection of Greek civilization and virtue.[31] This would be the really miraculous effect of the benevolent intervention of Catherine's Russian armies in the Balkans. Characteristically, Voulgaris once again found in Voltaire the arguments and language he needed to convey his political message. Voltaire had supplied him with ammunition for his earlier campaign on behalf of philosophic and religious toleration. Now Voltaire's own expectations from Catherine's policies of enlightened absolutism proved useful to Voulgaris in his advocacy of his rationalized version of the Russian expectation. This position constituted the limit beyond which Voulgaris's political thought could not extend. In contrast to Voltaire, who was willing to give a chance to enlightened absolutism as represented by Catherine's policies and attempts to reform, but hated despotism as a form of government and had no faith in regimes that stifled liberty, Voulgaris could visualize no alternative political order. His hatred for despotism was consumed and exhausted in his loathing of Greece's Ottoman yoke. This was the motivation of Voulgaris's reflections on the dynamics of interstate relations and antagonisms that led him, for the first time in Greek thought, to a systematic appraisal of the possibilities of Greek freedom in the light of a theory of balance of power—the prevailing paradigm of international politics in his time.[32]

* * *

Voulgaris's commentaries on Catherine's first war against the Ottomans attempted to sustain the traditional Russian expectation by connecting it with the dynamics of contemporary power politics. The international perspective on the Greek problem likewise stimulated the efforts of other members of the Greek intelligentsia active in the communities of the Greek diaspora. A case in point was the publication of a six-volume *History of the Present War between Russia and the Ottoman Porte.*[33] The work appeared in the year 1770 in Venice under the name of the translator and editor, Spyridon Papadopoulos, who did not disclose the authorship of the original. The Italian source of the work can now be identified as a book of the Venetian publicist Domenico Caminer.[34] It had apeared in Venice earlier in the same year and its immediate Greek rendering was indicative of the intense interest provoked among educated Greeks by the war. This history was an account of the outbreak of hostilities between Russia and the Ottoman Empire, and the ensuing war in Eastern Europe. Many official documents of the belligerents were included in the text, and the translator enriched his version by including a selection of chapters from Voltaire on the religion and laws of Russia. Apparently these materials were taken from Voltaire's *History of the Russian Empire under Peter the Great.* Of particular interest to the Greek readers was the first chapter of the fourth volume which narrated the Russian expedition to the Aegean and the rising in the Peloponnese at the incitement of the Orlov brothers. The narrative is ideologically charged, stressing the element of religious war against the infidel, but it also betrays the translator's lively Greek conscience which led him to recognize in the valor of the contemporary Maniots a survival of the heroism of the ancients.

The awakened awareness of international conflict stimulated in addition an increased appreciation of the tasks of contemporary history. As events became more and more pressing with international wars raging all over Eastern Europe, not only was an intense need for information felt more directly because of the proximity of what was happening, but also the difficulties of the task were perceived to be greater. In the books' opening comments it was noted that events appeared unclear and that "the tendency and nature of things" were discernible only with great difficulty. Yet the importance of such a task as the narration of the wars of Orthodox Russia against the Ottoman Empire and their repercussions throughout Southeastern Europe was compelling enough to sustain the translator's effort to make knowledge about these events comprehensible and accessible to his compatriots. Accordingly it was claimed that use had been made of all relevant material that could make the work appealing to contemporaries by satisfying their curiosity and useful to future generations by providing them with safe knowledge of the crucial events that marked the author's time.[35] In his own prefatory note to the reader, the publisher in his turn stressed the importance of the knowledge contained in the book and emphasized that his motive in financing its publication was to be useful to the needs of his nation.[36]

The writing of contemporary history, emerging as it did out of the gropings for an understanding of international conflict, came to be considered as a pressing national necessity. In view of the importance of the task, the reliability of the knowledge that was to be conveyed by the accounts of contemporary history emerged as a serious preoccupation. Obviously, the problem was not simply epistemological. This became clear in the pages of the next work in eighteenth-century Greek writing on contemporary history which offered an account of the outbreak of Catherine's second war against the Ottoman Empire (1787–1792); this was a compilation of information from French and Italian sources about the events leading up to the declaration of war by the Russian and Habsburg emperors against the Sublime Porte in the years 1787 and 1788.[37] The relevance of knowledge of these events to the Greek nation was stressed by the compiler and translator, Agapios Loverdos, in his preface. He noted characteristically that all "foreign nations harbor the curiosity to learn what is happening in the domestic government of cities and in the campaigns of foreign wars." He therefore considered it proper to do his utmost to furnish his own Greek nation with such useful information—hence the selection of all that might be relevant to the interests of his Greek readers from the accounts of the war in Eastern Europe.[38] What the interests and preoccupations of the Greek readers of such works were in the last decade of the eighteenth century was clearly implied. An accurate account of the wars of the Russians and Austrians against the Ottomans had the utmost relevance to the emerging preoccupation with Greek liberation from the Ottoman yoke—especially at a time when Catherine's "Greek project" was rumored to be on the threshold of implementation.[39] It was by seizing opportunities arising out of such configurations in international relations that Greek hopes might be fulfilled.[40] The task of contemporary history extended beyond curiosity to deciphering concrete possibilities and to providing the basis for a calculus of national redemption. That was why knowledge of contemporary history and precise information about international relations and conflict were considered to be urgent national needs.

Furthermore the increasing awareness of the methological problems involved in such a crucial assignment as the writing of contemporary international history became a basis of distinction between ancient and modern history. Knowledge of ancient history, according to Agapios Loverdos, was undoubtedly useful because of its moral content. It was the foremost source of ethical lessons that pointed to the rules of "political science."[41] However, although morally sound, epistemologically such knowledge was suspect because of the subjective biases of ancient historians and the remoteness of the events they described—a remoteness that made critical scrutiny of their accounts practically impossible. Consequently, contemporary history was considered a cognitively safer field of judgment because

> we ourselves are witnesses and judges of events which we either watch or hear about while we are still alive, and we thus can easily examine them with precision and distinguish truth from falsehood, without having to rely on the opinions of others.[42]

Thus reflection on the epistemological nature of contemporary history affirmed the primacy of individual judgment over the authority of traditional wisdom in the determination of truth. This assessment offered one more avenue to the critical spirit of the age of the Enlightenment to come into its own in Greek culture. In the same light, another history of the Russo-Ottoman wars in the Crimea at the close of the eighteenth century pointed out in its preface that the study of the past and the investigation of the present exerted and cultivated the faculties of the human mind and gradually made men fit for civil social intercourse.[43] Thus the discovery of the dynamics of international conflict, the spirit of the Enlightenment and the yearning for life in a civil society appeared inextricably interwoven in an integral process of ideological transformation. The yearning to become fit for life in a civil society of their own, essentially conceived as contingent upon the intellectual and social maturity to which knowledge of contemporary history contributed, made plain the political relevance attributed by the Greeks to their acquaintance with the facts of international life.

* * *

The emergence of a historigraphy of contemporary international relations and war in eighteenth-century Greek culture was but one dimension of the advent of a secular conception of historical time under the impact of the Enlightenment. That process of intellectual change involved the secularization of modern Greek historical consciousness through its emancipation from the traditional Providential theory of history reflected in the chronicles of the shared past of all Christian peoples, which constituted the exclusive source of historical knowledge until the eighteenth century. A decisive factor in the process of intellectual emancipation was the Greek nation's heightened awareness of the international environment. This was clearly recorded in the historiography of contemporary international conflicts, the most representative specimens of which have just been surveyed. The eighteenth-century wars that were felt directly in the affairs of the Greek nation in the 1730s, the 1770s and the 1790s were registered in Greek intellectual history by the appearance of a literature of contemporary history that expanded along a synchronic dimension the scope of the nascent secular Greek historiography of that period. Since the middle of the eighteenth century this historiographical tradition had concentrated primarily on the classical age of ancient Greece in an effort to recreate diachronically the modern Greek ethnic genealogy and thus point up Greek national distinctiveness from the shared biblical lineage of all Christian peoples to which the Providential chronicles had fettered them.[44]

Writing on contemporary international history and war added to the process of secular historicization a sense of the modern world which gradually made the Greeks aware of the possibilities offered to them by the existing structure of international relations. All this gave them an initial feeling of their distinctiveness in modern international society and an intense and urgent awareness of their predicament under Ottoman rule. This was essentially a process of consciousness-raising which inevitably contributed toward the visualization of their political emancipation. The vision of freedom became the point at which the diverse intellectual influences composing the movement of the Neohellenic Enlightenment gradually converged over the three decades that followed the period whose historiographical output on international confrontations has been analyzed here. Chronologically the expanding awareness of war as a fact of international life can be seen to prepare very neatly over time the consolidation of the vision of Greek liberation during the culmination of the Enlightenment and its immediately subsequent phase (1789–1821). It must be added that developments in political consciousness during the ensuing period were influenced equally decisively by the impact of a new cycle of international conflicts, the wars of the French Revolution and Empire (1792–1815). In connection with the content of political orientations, it is significant to note that, as the earlier perceptions of the Russian offensives were inextricably attached to the political theory of enlightened absolutism, so the main political effect of the French Revolutionary wars among the Greeks was reflected in the advent of a militant republican theory whose foremost representative was Rhigas Velestinlis.

These ideological differentiations contributed powerfully to the political ferment that preceeded the Greek War of Independence. The new radicalism was integrally connected with an explicit repudiation of the earlier Russian expectation. The anti-Russian disposition, nurtured by repeatedly belied promises of Russian help, was gradually generalized in a desperate and proud attitude of self-reliance and self-help directed against all illusory hopes in foreign aid for the cause of Greek liberation. This was the message of Voulgaris's articulate young critic, Athanasios Psalidas[45]—himself an exponent of the Russian expectation in his early writings—and of the social radicalism of the satirical versification *Rossoangogallos*[46] and of the republican tract *Hellenic Nomarchy* (1806). These early commentaries on the role of the "foreign factor" in Greek politics and in the implementation of Greek national aspirations inaugurated a persistent theme of controversy and soul-searching that recurred throughout the subsequent phases of modern Greek political thought.

In conclusion it might be relevant to note that the Greek experience was perhaps the most pronounced in Southeastern European civilization, but was by no means unique. Parallel processes of intellectual change unfolded equally in the cultural history of other Balkan nations, such as the Serbs and the Rumanians. The wars and designs of Peter the Great were recorded in the works of Zaharije Orfelin and Dimitrie Cantemir, while the policies of Catherine II had ideological consequences in Rumanian political thought similar to those observable among the Greeks. The impact of international conflict was not felt only in the literature and historiography of the Southeastern European nations to whose national awakening it greatly contributed. Further north the effects of power politics were experienced by other Eastern European nations, such as the Poles upon whose homeland it inflicted the wounds of repeated partition. The traumatic pressures stemming from Poland's precarious international status, so acutely appreciated by Rousseau,[47] laid the psychological and historical foundation of one of the most heroic nationalist movements in nineteenth-century Europe. In this way the perception and experience of the effects of war provided an important stimulus to systematic theoretical projects in eighteenth-century political self-awareness and to the crystallization of political aspirations among the European nations that did not yet possess national states of their own. The responses elicited by the experience of war provided outlets for ideological expression to the process of nation-building in Eastern Europe and motivated the unredeemed nationalities of the region to claim their place in a world of nations zealous of their sovereignty, power and identity.

## Notes

1. Quentin Skinner, *The Foundations of Modern Political Thought* (Cambridge, 1978), I, 245.

2. The continuity between war and politics emerges clearly from Machiavelli's argument in *The Prince* and *The Discourses* (especially Bk. II) as well as from his considerations in *The Art of War*.

3. Thomas Hobbes, *Leviathan*, ed. C. B. Macpherson (Harmondsworth and New York, 1968), chap. 14, esp. pp. 187–188.

4. John Locke, *An Essay Concerning the True, Original Extent and End of Civil Government*, chap. XII, paras. 143–148.

5. For general surveys see Frank M. Russell, *Theories of International Relations* (New York, 1936), pp. 179–203, and more recently the chapter on Enlightenment in F. Parkinson, *The Philosophy of International Relations: A Study in the History of Thought* (Beverly Hills, 1977).

6. Mark Hulliung, *Montesquieu and the Old Regime* (Berkeley, 1976), pp. 173-211; Stanley Hoffmann, "Rousseau on War and Peace," in *The State of War* (New York, 1965), pp. 54–87.

7. See especially the famous essay "Of the Balance of Power" in David Hume, *Political Essays*, ed. Charles W. Hendel (Indianapolis, 1953), pp. 142–144.

8. Immanuel Kant, "Idea for a Universal History with a Cosmopolitan Purpose" and "Perpetual Peace: A Philosophical Sketch," in *Kant's Political Writings*, ed. Hans Reiss (Cambridge, 1970), pp. 41–53, 93–130.

9. For appraisals of Clausewitz's contribution see Michael Howard, "War

as an Instrument of Policy," in Herbert Butterfield and Martin Wright (eds.), *Diplomatic Investigations* (London, 1966), pp. 193–200; W. B. Gallie, *Philosophers of Peace and War* (Cambridge, 1978). On the moral implications of Clausewitz's argument see Michael Walzer, *Just and Unjust Wars* (New York, 1977), pp. 22–25.

10. For a general survey see L. S. Stavrianos, *The Balkans since 1453* (New York, 1958), pp. 178–197.

11. See Paul Cernovodeanu, "Pierre le Grand dans l'historiographie roumaine et balkanique du XVIIIe siècle," *Revue des études sud-est européennes*, XIII (1975), No. 1, 77–95, esp. 81. On the historical setting see B. H. Sumner, *Peter the Great and the Ottoman Empire* (Oxford, 1949).

12. Cernovodeanu, "Pierre le Grand."

13. The term is coined and elaborated in Paschalis M. Kitromilides, "Tradition, Enlightenment and Revolution: Ideological Change in Eighteenth and Nineteenth Century Greece" (doct. diss., Harvard University, 1978), pp. 167–194.

14. Cf. M. S. Anderson, *Europe in the Eighteenth Century* (London, 1961), pp. 152–193.

15. Frederic C. Lane, *Venice: A Maritime Republic* (Baltimore and London, 1973), pp. 407–411. Cf. Fernand Braudel, *The Mediterranean and the Mediterranean World in the Age of Philip II* (New York, 1973), II, 1068–1142.

16. On the reestablishment of Ottoman rule in the Morea see M. D. Sakellariou, *E Peloponnesos kata ten deuteran Tourkokratian, 1714–1821* [The Peloponnese during the Second Period of Turkish Rule, 1715–1821] (Athens, 1939).

17. Among the many sources that describe this transition in the political orientation of the subject Greeks, special mention should be made of the historical novel by Thanasis Petsalis, *Oi Mavrolykoi: Chronikon tis Tourkokratias, 1566–1799* [The Mavrolykoses: A Chronicle of the Era of Turkish Rule, 1566–1799] (Athens, 1947–1948), which recreates vividly and accurately the psychological and social climate of a whole era of Greek history.

18. Antonio Catiforo [Katiphoros], *Vita di Pietro il Grande* (Venice, 1736).

19. Translated by Alexandros Kagkellarios, a well-known translator of works of European scholarship. Several years later he brought out a Greek version of Charles Rollin's *Histoire ancienne* (Venice, 1750), 16 vols.

20. Cernovodeanu, "Pierre le Grand," pp. 84–90.

21. Cf. Voltaire, *Histoire de Russie sous Pierre le Grand* (1759–1763).

22. Antonios Katiphoros, *Grammatike Elleniki akribestate* [A Most Exact Greek Grammar] (Venice, 1734), p. vi.

23. Athanasios Skiadas, *Genos, ethos, kindynoi kai katorthomata Petrou*

*tou Protou* [Descent, Character, Risks and Achievements of Peter I] (Venice, 1737). The text of the preface is reprinted in Émile Legrand, *Bibliographie hellenique, XVIIIe siècle* (Paris, 1918), I, 256–259.

24. See generally A. Camariano Gioran, "La guerre russo-turque de 1768–1774 et les Grecs," *Revue des études sud-est européennes*, III (1965), 513–547. The older work by P. M. Kontogiannes, *Oi Ellenes kata ton proton epi Aikaterines B' rossotourkikon polemon, 1768–1774* [The Greeks during the First Russo-Turkish War of Catherine II, 1768–1774] (Athens, 1903), still retains its interest, as does the seminal study of Sakellariou, *E Peloponnesos*, pp. 146–206.

25. Anthanasios Komnenos Ypselantis, *Ta meta ten Alosin* [Matters Following the Fall] (Constantinople, 1870), p. 534.

26. Eugenios Voulgaris (trans.), *Eisegesis tis Autokratorikes Megaleiotetos Aikaterines B'* [Her Imperial Majesty Catherine II's Instruction] (Moscow, 1770). The standard English version of this important source of the theory of enlightened absolutism is W. F. Reddaway (ed.), *Documents of Catherine the Great* (Cambridge, 1931), pp. 216–309.

27. Voulgaris, *Eisegesis*, pp. xvii–xviii and more generally pp. xvii–xxiv on Greek hopes in Catherine's policies.

28. Eugenios Voulgaris, *Stochasmoi eis tous parontas krisimous kairous tou Othomanikou Kratous* [Reflections on the Present Critical Circumstances of the Ottoman State]. The work was published anonymously and reprinted in Corfu, 1894. Voulgaris's authorship was affirmed by K. Sathas, *Neoellenike philologia* [Modern Greek Literature] (Athens, 1868), p. 570, mentioning Leipzig as the original place of publication. Stephen Batalden, "Eugenios Voulgaris in Russia, 1771–1806: A Chapter in Greco-Slavic Ties of the Eighteenth Century" (PhD diss., University of Minnesota, 1975), pp. 66–69, 238, dates the first publication to St. Petersburg, 1772.

29. Eugenios Voulgaris, *Iketeria tou genous ton Graikon pros pasan ten Christianiken Europen* [Supplications of the Greek Nation to the Whole of Christian Europe] (St. Petersburg, 1771). The text is reproduced in Ph. Iliou, *Prosthekes sten ellenike bibliographia* [Additions to Greek Bibliography] (Athens, 1973), pp. 290–300.

30. Eugenios Voulgaris, *Epi te panendoxe eirene* [Upon the Most Glorious Peace] (St. Petersburg, 1774).

31. Eugenios Voulgaris (trans.), *Ouoltairou epistole pros ten Autokratorissan ton Rosson* [Voltaire's Letter to the Empress of the Russians] (St. Petersburg, c. 1771). The text is reprinted in Iliou, *Prosthekes*, pp. 303–307.

32. Cf. the essays on the balance of power by Herbert Butterfield and Martin Wright in *idem, Diplomatic Investigations*, pp. 132–148 and 148–175, respectively; and Edward V. Gulick, *Europe's Classical Balance of Power* (New York, 1967). For some classic views on the theory of balance of power

see Hume's essay (n. 7 above) and the selections from Lord Brougham, and Friedrich von Gentz and Richard Colden in M. G. Forsyth *et al.* (eds.), *The Theory of International Relations* (London, 1970), pp. 259–323.

33. Spyridon Papadopoulos (trans.), *Istoria tou parontos polemou anametaxy tes Rousias kai tes Othomanikes Portas* (Venice, 1770). The sixth volume appeared in 1773.

34. Domenico Caminer, *Storia della guerra presente tra la Russia e la Porta Ottomana* (Venice, 1770), Vols. I–VI. A new edition appeared in 1776 under the title *Storia dell'ultima guerra tra la Russia e la porta Ottomana*, Vols. I–IX, which also covered the conclusion of the peace treaties between the two powers. As far as I know, this is the first time the original of Papadopoulos's version has been identified. On Domenico Caminer (1731–1796), a prolific publicist in his time, see briefly Giannantonio Moschini, *Alla letteratura veneziana del secolu XVIII fine a nostri giorni*, IV (Venice, 1808), 121–122. Indicative of Caminer's interest in international affairs is a later work, *Storia della vita di Federigo II il Grande, rè di Prussia, elettore di Brandemburgo* (Venice, 1787), which did not, however, attract the interest of Greek translators.

35. Papdopoulos, *Istoria tou parontos polemou*, pp. 6–7.

36. *Ibid.*, pp. $2^r$–$3^v$.

37. Agapios Loverdos, *Istoria dyo eton 1787–1788* [History of the Two Years 1787–1788] (Venice, 1791). My attempts to identify an original of this work have led me to believe that it was probably an original compilation by the translator, as he claims on the title page. On the outbreak of this same war see also the pamphlet, *Aitiologia tou parontos polemou metaxy Rossias kai Tourkias* [Origin of the Present War between Russia and Turkey] (Venice, 1787), a collection of official documents on the declaration of the war. The publication of these works is indicative of the great interest the new conflict elicited among the Greeks.

38. Loverdos, *Istoria dyo eton 1787–1788*, pp. viii–ix.

39. On Catherine's "Greek project" the most recent thorough study is Edgar Hösch, "Das sogenannte 'griechische Projekt' Katharinas II," *Jahrbücher für Geschichte Osteuropas*, N.S., XII, No. 2 (July 1964), 168–206.

40. The new Russo-Ottoman war provoked another wave of Greek revolutionary activity. For brief surveys in English see R. C. Anderson, *Naval Wars in the Levant, 1559–1853* (Princeton, 1952), pp. 319–345; Norman E. Saul, *Russia and the Mediterranean, 1797–1807* (Chicago and London, 1970), pp. 11–14.

41. Loverdos, *Istoria dyo eton 1787–1788*, p. vi.

42. *Ibid.*, pp. vii–viii.

43. P. Lambanitziotis, *Istoria tes Tavrikes Chersonesou* [History of the Tauric Chersonese] (Vienna, 1792), preface.

44. On these intellectual changes see Kitromilides, "Tradition, Enlightenment and Revolution," pp. 72–116.

45. See Athanasios Psalidas, *Kalokinemata* [Auspicious Beginnings] (Vienna, 1795).

46. For the earliest record and commentary see William Martin-Leake, *Researches in Greece* (London, 1814), pp. 140–154. Leake's version of the title is *Russ-Anglo-Gaul.*

47. Cf. Jean-Jacques Rousseau, "Considérations sur le gouvernement de Pologne," in *The Political Writings of Jean Jacques Rousseau,* ed. C. E. Vaughan (New York, 1962), II, esp. pp. 510–513.

Illie Ceauşescu

# Military Aspects of the National Struggle of the Rumanian Principalities in the Eighteenth Century

The critical condition of the Ottoman state in the eighteenth century signaled a new phase in Europe's "Eastern Question." The policy of both the Habsburg and the Russian Empires to seek possession of the heritage of the "sick man of Europe" and their attempts to realize this policy created a new political situation in Southeastern Europe.[1] The peoples of the area in their turn tried to take advantage of the rivalry among the three empires to achieve their own emancipation. The emancipation movements in Moldavia and Wallachia, closely connected in the military as well as other fields with similar movements south of the Danube, formed an integral part of this widespread liberation effort.

The establishment of the Phanariot regimes in Moldavia in 1711 and in Wallachia in 1715 was the Sublime Porte's response to the challenge of the two principalities' striving to end their dependence and to the military actions of the Habsburg and Russian Empires, which threatened to deprive the Ottoman Empire of its chief granary, the strategically important Carpathian-Danubian region. Confronted by a demographic and fiscal crunch, the Phanariot rulers pursued a reform policy aimed at securing stability and increasing their tax base. They looked on the tax exemption of the special military categories of their populations as a sort of evasion of the fiscal system which sought to squeeze ever greater sums of money out of the taxpayers, both to satisfy the Sublime Porte's demands for tribute and to produce revenue for the hospodars and the boyar dignitaries. One objective of the Phanariots' fiscal reform was therefore to reduce the number of these tax-exempt military groups. At the same time, a concomitant of the Ottomans' strengthening their control over Moldavia and Wallachia by limiting the principalities' autonomy was also to bring about a substantial reduction of the military forces at the two states' command. Hospodar Constantin Mavrocordat thus had political as well as fiscal reasons for the measures he took to add a considerable number of the special military groups to the ranks of the taxpaying.[2]

The Rumanian generation of 1848, through the eyes of its most brilliant representative, Nicolae Bălcescu, considered these measures an abolition of the national army.[3] Yet the fact is that at no time during the Phanariot era did the Rumanian military forces cease to exist. The crisis in the Rumanians' "official" military structures—an undeniable reality of the eighteenth century—had its roots as far back as the sixteenth century. It was the result of the deterioration of the peasantry's material conditions and, as a consequence of Ottoman depredations, of the impossibility of reequipping the forces to meet the spread of firearms.[4] The military policy of the Phanariot rulers—with the exception of Hospodar Nicolae Mavrogheni of Wallachia (1786–1790), who fielded an army in service to the Ottomans—halted the development of the "official" forces. Military progress therefore had to take place outside the state framework and was closely related to the progress of the national liberation struggle.

Almost all the sociopolitical elements of Rumanian society, among whom national consciousness was developing strongly in tandem with changing social and economic conditions, were united around the goal of liberating Moldavia and Wallachia from Ottoman suzerainty. The great majority of the nobility, the inchoate bourgeoisie and the entire peasantry realized that the continuation of the Sublime Porte's overlordship was incompatible with their own interests. All these sectors of society rallied to the anti-Ottoman cause and demonstrated their political wishes by armed action.

At all levels of society there was action by military units that were the embryo of the modern Rumanian army. The content and form of their actions, however, bore the stamp of the socioeconomic structures of contemporary Rumanian society, preserving the patterns of an agrarian, feudal world where capitalist development was barely in bud.

The two fundamental classes in Moldavia and Wallachia were the peasantry and the great landowners. The former consisted of free peasants who owned land (*moşneni* in Wallachia, *răzeşi* in Moldavia) and landless peasants, who in turn were divided into serfs (*rumâni* in Wallachia, *vecini* in Moldavia) and contract laborers. Constantin Mavrocordat's reform abolishing bodily servitude in Wallachia in 1746 and Moldavia in 1749 classified all this great mass together as peasants (*clăcaşi*), legally free but owning no land and hence economically dependent on the landowner on whose estate they lived and to whom they owed the three customary forms of feudal due—labor, produce, money.

At the opposite pole of society, the nobility and high clergy (large landowners all) began in the last quarter of the eighteenth century to increase the obligations of the *clăcaşi*, especially in the form of labor, as they came to appreciate the benefits of the abolition of the Sublime Porte's monopoly on the cereal trade. Typical of this trend was the introduction of labor norms (*nart*) in Moldavia in 1776 and the demands of the nobility for more days of corvée. These demands were trimmed down and granted with reserve by the Phanariot rulers, whose main preoccupation was to preserve the taxability of the peasantry.

In addition to the two fundamental classes, the society of the two principalities comprised the small boyers, striving for social advancement; the maturing townspeople, who would become the bourgeoisie as capitalist relations, though hobbled by the Ottoman system, developed; and the workers in the few, transitory factories, who were the precursors of the future proletariat.

The special military categories of society were only a minute fraction of the population, for the Phanariot rulers were averse to tax exemption and to the consolidation of a Rumanian military force, as the Sublime Porte had charged them to be.

The volunteers who were to fight in special units alongside the Austrian and Russian armies when the latter reached Rumanian soil would be drawn from all these social sectors in circumstances that made of these units one of the major elements in the struggle for national emancipation.

These popular military forces went into action during the wars that the Ottoman, Habsburg and Romanov empires fought in the eighteenth century on the territory of Moldavia and Wallachia. The growing disproportion between the strength of the Rumanian Principalities' military forces and those of the Ottoman Empire left the Rumanians no alternative but to cooperate with the tsarist and Habsburg armies against the Turks. The Rumanians' cooperation with the two empires' armies does not imply, however, that the Rumanian national liberation movement was subordinate to the objectives of Vienna and St. Petersburg. In the political climate created by the presence of Austrian and Russian troops on the territories of Moldavia and Wallachia, the Rumanian volunteer units were the embodiment of the Rumanians' will to fight. Whether spontaneous or organized, these units were the ones that raised the banner of revolt against Ottoman oppression.

The purpose of the declaration of loyalty to the courts of Vienna and especially St. Petersburg was to protect the Rumanian Principalities against Ottoman reprisals by securing certain military "guarantees" from Austria and Russia. The appeals for protection by one or more Christian powers were always of a temporary or tactical nature dictated by historical circumstance. The ultimate objective of the Rumanians' social and political efforts was always independence.

The Russo-Ottoman war of 1711 in which Prince Dimitrie Cantemir of Moldavia joined in Peter the Great's campaign was both a beginning and an end. The Moldavian ruler took the field with the tsar at a moment when the signs were that the Sublime Porte was stepping up its abridgment of the Rumanian Principalities' autonomy.[5] Alliance with Russia seemed to be the only feasible way to counter the Ottoman threat. In Dimitrie Cantemir's view as well as that of Prince Şerban Cantacuzino of Wallachia (1678–1688), the struggle for liberation from Ottoman oppression went hand in hand with the need to establish an authoritarian regime in order to curb the great nobles' ambitions to set up a military oligarchy that would dominate the central government and assure their control over the state.

To forestall attempts by the boyars to secure the tsar's support for the establishment of a nobiliary polity, Cantemir concluded an alliance with Peter I at Lutsk on April 3, 1711. The agreement ruled out Russian intervention in Moldavian domestic affairs and consolidated the prince's authority by recognizing the Cantemirs' hereditary right to the princely throne. It also specified that the prince's sanction was final in matters of legislation in order to try to obviate the chance of future legal interference by the tsar. For Dimitrie Cantemir the treaty was a guarantee, even if not on the order he would have wished, that his country would not simply exchange one foreign master for another.

The diplomatic and political preparations for putting an end to Ottoman domination were closely linked with the military ones. Moldavia possessed a meager army in 1711, one inadequate to achieve the prince's purposes on its own. The tradition of calling the people to arms was so deep-seated and widely accepted, however, that Cantemir took it for granted that he could count on the "great host" in his plans, even though the bondage of the peasants and the development of new fighting techniques had rendered the general levy valueless by the beginning of the eighteenth century. The prince's call to arms was directed mainly at the peasantry and small boyars who had benefited from the covenant made during the rule of his father, Prince Constantin Cantemir (1685–1693). Ion Neculce in his *Chronicle of Moldavia* reported the response to the prince's summons: "The great (*mazili*) boyars began to reach the army after lengthy journeys. Very few failed to appear. . . . Likewise, from every corner of the land all his subjects who heard the call hastened to join the army. And on hearing the pay, not only serfs joined up but so too did cobblers, tailors, furriers and innkeepers. The boyars' servants left their masters and flocked to the colors."[6] The chronicler's account is borne out by a Russian document that also records the popular enthusiasm inspired by the prospect of being rid of Ottoman rule. "The Moldavians come to us all the time, very eager to help, and even the humblest peasants want to sign up for military service."[7] The glorious days of the great host, which had successfully opposed and stemmed Ottoman expansion, seemed to be coming back. Historical conditions had changed radically, however, and the realities of the battlefield now demanded military skills that only professional soldiers and trained civilians could possess and that the peasants and townspeople in Cantemir's army lacked. Nevertheless, the defeat on the River Prut at Stănileşti was not due to the shortcomings of the Moldavian troops but to other factors irrelevant here.

Cantemir's participation in the Russo-Ottoman war of 1711 was the last time a prince of Moldavia called out the ancient and by then outmoded military formation that had enabled the Rumanian Principalities to preserve their political autonomy even under Ottoman domination. At a certain stage in the development of feudal society, the levy outlived its historic and effective defensive function, but it bequeathed its popular character in a new form to the volunteer units that took shape during the Phanariot regime. Thus 1711 marked the end of a military era and the beginning of a new one.

The undoubted continuity between the two military formations should not be taken to mean that one immediately replaced the other. The Austro-Ottoman war of 1716–1718 and the Ottoman war with both Austria and Russia of 1736–1739 were a period of transition during which the people's and the boyars' attempts to organize popular bodies of troops matured.

The political convulsion of the establishment of the Phanariot regimes in Moldavia and Wallachia was assuaged by the help given to the Austrian army by the boyars and part of the populace to capture Nicolae Mavrocordat, who had inaugurated Phanariot rule in both principalities. A similar attempt on Mihai Racoviță, then hospodar of Moldavia, failed.[8]

The war of 1736–1739 foreshadowed the later tendency for separate Rumanian military forces to be formed alongside those maintained by the hospodars. It was also the first time that Austrian and Russian forces had fought as allies simultaneously on Rumanian soil. Each had fought many actions in the Danubian Principalities before, but always separately. Rumanian confessional identity with them favored the tsarist troops' quest for the heritage of the "sick man of Europe" over their Habsburg rivals' efforts. Russia frequently stressed this confessional community when giving the liberation of the Sublime Porte's Christian subjects as its reason for going to war. This propaganda found wide favor.

The arrival of Antioh Cantemir's two sons, Constantin and Dimitrie (Dumitrașcu), in Moldavia with the Russian army at the height of the Phanariot regime revived memories of their famous grandfather's fight. They came at the head of a unit of Moldavian fugitives from Ottoman and Phanariot exploitation who had fled over the Dniester into Russia. Their numbers were swollen by local Moldavian volunteers and some Rumanians from around Brașov in Transylvania.[9] Finally 3,000 strong, they took part in the capture of the important Moldavian stronghold of Hotin, and then marched into Iași, the capital, where they were welcomed ardently by the sympathetic population.

The Rumanian volunteers joined in the assault that drove the Ottoman forces out of Moldavia and in the defense of Iași against a combined offensive by Turkish and Tatar troops. Their activities were brought to an end by the Peace of Belgrade signed in 1739.

This war posed in microcosm the same problems that the Rumanian Principalities had to face in their later conflicts: the cumbersomeness of the administration set up by the occupation troops and the contradictory contribution of Rumanian sociopolitical forces to the struggle against the Turk. United only the goal of ending Ottoman domination, the forces remained divided by the social tension generated by the structure of Rumanian feudal society. The landowners always opposed any reduction of the "human inventory" on their estates by peasants joining the army. The war ultimately focused attention on the need to create an authentic national army. (An agreement between the Moldavian boyars and General Burkhard Münnich, the Russian commander, set its strength at 20,000 men.)[10] From the second half of the eighteenth century this project was to recur repeatedly in proposals for modernizing Rumanian society.

The Russo-Ottoman war of 1768–1774 marked Russia's definitive and ongoing involvement in the affairs of Southeast Europe. To achieve its policy objectives, the tsarist empire represented itself to the inhabitants of Moldavia and Wallachia as their protector against the Ottomans. Seeking all the support it could muster among both the establishments and the popular masses of Moldavia and Wallachia, Moscow encouraged all local initiatives that served its interests. The new evolving forces suited its aims to a tee.

For its part, in its efforts to realize its basic goal of liberation, winning independence and achieving national unity, the emancipation movement in Moldavia and Wallachia could not afford to forgo a military instrument. Yet of all the Phanariot rulers only Hospodar Constantin Ipsilanti of Wallachia (1802–1806) ever attempted to raise armed forces in support of an anti-Ottoman uprising he was planning. In this climate of official inertia, as long as army reorganization depended on the organs of state, the only times the military establishment ever helped the liberation movement were when hostilities were occurring on Rumanian territory. Then it would turn against the central authorities in Iaşi or Bucharest, paralyzing them and even destroying their ability to represent the Sublime Porte's interests. Russia's interest was to secure the Rumanians' military cooperation. It was the support offered by the Rumanians that solved the Russians' problems of manpower, intelligence, reconnaissance, supply, and security in their rear. Russia therefore readily encouraged the establishment of armed forces both in Moldavia and in Wallachia.

It was the war of 1768–1774 that made plain the coincidence of Rumanian and Russian interests in the revival of a national army. The war also saw a considerable enlargement of the social catchment area that supplied participants in the struggle against Ottoman rule. Alongside the units organized by the boyars, above all the

Cantacuzino family, a broad current of popular sympathy brought into the field large numbers of peasants and townspeople. The strength of this support was enough to prompt the Sublime Porte to have a mufti hand down a fetwa declaring all Rumanians over the age of 12 "traitors," giving anyone the right to rob or kill them. This legal pronouncement augmented the number of those who rallied to the anti-Ottoman cause, for now they were fighting for their lives.

For the peasant volunteers the fighting was also associated with a belief that it would lead to an improvement of their economic and social lot. This idea was put clearly in a petition from Moldavia's peasants to Gavril Callimachi, the metropolitan of Moldavia, in which they asserted that they had embarked on "the troubled and dangerous venture of war" in the hope of shedding "the heavy yoke of injustice that has been gnawing us to the bone."[11]

In the early stages of the war the 4,000 Rumanian volunteers played an important role in impeding the movement of Ottoman reinforcements to the garrisons in eastern Moldavia. Once the Russian army had entered Moldavia, the volunteers joined them in expelling the Ottoman forces form the principality. In October 1769 a mixed force of 800 Rumanians and 1,700 Russian soldiers conducted an offensive to free Galaţi and Bucharest. The enemy was taken completely by surprise when Galaţi was attacked on November 5 from the direction of Focşani to the west. The number of volunteers now swollen to 6,000 (including 2,000 Albanians) under the leadership of Pîrvu Cantacuzino, their impetus carried them into Wallachia all the way to Bucharest. In support of them the inhabitants of the Wallachian capital "all rose up, even the women, with sticks and bricks, shouting: 'The Russians, the Russians have come!'" They were not strong enough, however, to exploit the confusion they had thrown the Ottoman army into. An Ottoman pursuit force overtook the Russians and Rumanians at Comana Monastery nearby, and 600 of the 700 volunteers present fell in bitter fighting.

Rumanian volunteers took part in the three major battles of the Russian campaign of summer 1770—at Rîbîia Hill, Larga and Cahul. The contribution of the Wallachian units led by Răducanu Cantacuzino to the Russian victory at Cahul was expressly acknowledged by Count Peter Rumyantsev, the Russian field marshal.

The following year 400 volunteers from Oltenia distinguished themselves in the defense of Cerneţ and in raids across the Danube to harry the Turks. Other units were no less active in Giurgiu and Bucharest where the Ottoman counteroffensive was driven back.

In the conquest of Silistra across the Danube in 1773, a Rumanian regiment made up of Wallachians, Moldavians and Translyvanians (who thus demonstrated the essential unity of the Rumanians) under the command again of Pîrvu Cantacuzino was twice mentioned in Field Marshal Rumyantsev's reports for its bravery and heroism in combat. By the final year of the war the number of Rumanian volunteers had reached twelve thousand, three thousand of whom fought under Russian General Aleksandr V. Suvorov at the decisive battle of Cozluge.[12]

The action on the battlefield was matched by unceasing political activity, likewise aimed at the Rumanian Principalities' emancipation from Ottoman overlordship. A veritable barrage of memoranda was directed at the courts of Europe, entreating their backing for the liberation of Moldavia and Wallachia.[13]

Rumanian volunteer units were formed in support of the Habsburg and Russian armies at the very outset of the last eighteenth-century war to be fought on Rumanian territory (1787–1792). They contributed conspicuously to the Russian victories at Focşani, Rîmnic and Ismail. Captains Ion Udre and Pavel Vizirean and Second Lieutenants Hudache Popescu and Mihalache Arsenie all won recognition for their valor and initiative. Of 31 Ottoman colors captured at the battle of Rîmnic five were taken by Rumanian volunteers.

The volunteers were particularly active during this war in Oltenia. Units of them helped to take Tismana, Cozia, and Cîmpulung, monasteries that were real strongholds by virtue of their location, fortifications and stores. It was in this theater that a Rumanian unit called "the Brethren" earned high praise in 1790 for being "quick in war."[14]

The large number and readiness of the volunteers in Oltenia were due to the socioeconomic conditions there, the same factors that made its contribution to Tudor Vladimirescu's revolution in 1821 so important. The northern part of Oltenia, in the Getic foothills of the Transylvanian Alps, was where the stiffest resistance was offered to the boyars' depredations. As a result no latifundia had come into being there. Instead it remained an area inhabited by free peasants (*moşneni*) organized in strong village communities. Living close to the Wallachian frontier, the peasants evaded the controls on exports and carried on a lively trade in cattle and animal products across the Carpathians with Transylvania and other parts of the Habsburg Empire. This trade not only raised material conditions higher there than elsewhere in Wallachia but it also rendered Ottoman rule even more intolerable to the area's inhabitants. Ottoman monopolies limited their dealings and the Turks' arbitrariness and violence created a climate of insecurity hostile to economic enterprise. Little wonder, then, that many volunteer units and Vladimirescu himself came from Oltenia.

Although not properly within the time period of the present volume, the Russo-Turkish war of 1806–1812 cannot go unmentioned, for it was the culmination of the Rumanian volunteer movement, which symbolized the essentially popular will for national liberation all through the eighteenth century. It was in the ranks of these pandours that some of the leading cadres of the revolution of 1821 received their baptism of fire and that the modern Rumanian army, which was to be reestablished and reorganized after 1830, began to take shape.

The Rumanian national struggle was not confined to Moldavia and Wallachia in the eighteenth century. Much of it was also fought in Transylvania, whose Rumanian inhabitants had maintained their individuality, Orthodox rites, traditions and language through centuries of, first, Hungarian and then, after 1541, Ottoman suzerainty.[15] The principality was forced to accept Habsburg "protection" in 1686, and on December 4, 1691, Emperor Leopold I issued the *Diploma Leopoldinum* which recognized Transylvania as a separate, autonomous political entity. It subordinated it directly to the emperor and guaranteed that the principality's ancient Rumanian sociopolitical structures would be retained. After conclusion of the Peace of Satu-Mare (Szatmár) which in 1711 brought to an end the insurrection led by Prince Ferenc II Rákóczi, the court in Vienna, while subscribing to the provisions of the *Diploma Leopoldinum,* gradually curtailed the principality's autonomy, stripping the Transylvanian Diet and government of their prerogatives and turning the Transylvanian Court Chancellery in Vienna into the real seat of power.[16]

In Transylvania itself, serfdom was of the harshest, with the obligations imposed on the peasantry as oppressive as anywhere in Europe. The fact that three-quarters of the servile population was Rumanian only added to the national character of the peasants' social reaction. "The social fight of the Rumanian serfs undoubtedly had a national cause as well. Their struggle for emancipation was to become the popular motive for the emancipation fight of the entire Rumanian people."[17]

The mass of the dependent Transylvanian peasantry was divided into bondmen, adscripts endowed with a parcel of land (*sesie*), and landless serfs (*jeleri*), who were free to move on the expiration of the contract under which they were allowed to settle in a place.

The most significant and onerous of the serfs' dues was corvée (*robota*), which the Transylvanian Diet of 1714 set at four days a week for bondmen and three days a week for contract laborers. The nobility, dissatisfied with even this quota, tried to flout it, and resisted Maria Theresa's *Certa puncta* of 1747 and 1768, regulations that reduced the amount of unpaid labor due from the peasantry. One Transylvanian in 24 was a member of the numerous nobility, which was set on extracting the maximum profit from the dependent population of its estates. Social and simultaneously national upheaval was inevitable.

The anti-Habsburg insurrection led by the voivode of Transylvania, Ference II Rákóczi (1704–1711), gave the Rumanian peasantry its first eighteenth-century opportunity to manifest its desire for emancipation by fighting. Reduced to the status merely of a "tolerated" people in a land where they constituted a substantial majority of the population, the Rumanian peasants saw in Rákóczi's pledge to free the serfs who joined him the chance to escape their position of social inferiority. Their circumstances are what lent the uprising in Transylvania a markedly social character. The prime goal of those who joined Rákóczi was personal freedom, an ambition that underlined the contradiction between the nobility, which was hostile to the emancipation promised by the prince, and the peasantry. At the same time, the Rumanians were no less inspired to rise by the prospect of ridding Transylvania of Habsburg rule.

Serfs, freemen, soldiers or gentry, Rumanians took part in all the insurgent actions in Maramureş, Satu-Mare, Bihor, Chioar, Oaş. In the rebel army, which numbered 21,000 men in 1704, the Rumanians had their own units led by such men as Ştefan Sudriceanu, Marin Haţeganu and Vasile Ciudar. The Rumanian volunteers made decisive contributions to battles the insurgents fought in 1708 and 1709, especially at Arieş, Mureş, Odorhei and Chiurghiu. The unit led by Gligor Pintea, known as Pintea the Brave, who fell in combat near Baia Mare, won legendary fame for its exploits.[18]

The most serious Rumanian uprising in eighteenth-century Transylvania took place in 1784 under the leadership of Horea, Cloşca and Crişan. Popular opposition to fiscal, feudal and national oppression, fanned by Vienna's policy of encouraging Catholic proselytism, kept the principality in a constant ferment of unrest. Amid continual outbreaks of local resistance, the servile status of the peasants came to be identified more and more with the lack of rights of the entire Rumanian population. Finally, open, armed insurrection broke out in Zarand county, spread through the Mureş valley to the Arad area, inflamed the Strei valley, swept through the Haţag Country toward Turda and Cluj, and into the areas around Baia de Arieş, Mogoş, and Crăcui. Bands of rebels attacked the castles and mansions of the nobility, sacking them or putting them to the torch.

The peasant army was given a genuine military structure. At its head was Nicula Horea (the assumed name of Vasile Nicola Ursu) and his three deputies, Cloşca (Ioan Oargă), Crişan (Marcu Giurgiu) and Ioan Horea. They were assisted by captains of the first rank, appointed by the leaders of the uprising, and captains of the second rank, elected by the fighting men. Two or three appointed or elected corporals were at the command of each captain. In Zarand there was also a cavalry unit of 200 under the command of Crişan. The rebels supplied their own arms.[19]

The great 1784 uprising was both a social and a national convulsion. The insurgents' ultimatum issued in Deva on November 11 set forth their goal—abolition of the feudal order by distributing the estates of the nobility among the peasants. Horea's revolt thus differed from all the peasant uprisings of old and heralded the modern era because "it did not look back toward the past, as the old uprisings had usually done, but forward toward the future. It did not aim at improvement of feudal relations but at their overthrow."[20] Abolition of the feudal order was an expression of peasant radicalism that anticipated and even surpassed the goals of the bourgeois democratic revolutions.

After the Rákóczi insurrection Habsburg policy was to secure the empire's frontiers as inexpensively as possible to prevent the exodus of the Rumanians who, oppressed by serfdom and national discrimination, sought refuge with their fellow Rumanians over the Carpathian Mountains. This led in 1762 to the formation of Rumanian frontier guard regiments whose tasks included stemming such emigration. The regiments were established in Transylvania in service to the political, financial and military interests of the Habsburgs, whose preoccupation was to strengthen their control over the principality. The dynasty did not foresee the consequences.

The frontier guard regiments significantly increased the number of Rumanians freed from feudal obligations. Because service in them meant emancipation, the regiments had a strong attraction for a Rumanian peasantry overburdened by feudal services and dues. The regiments did much for the social advancement of the Rumanians. The guards' school opened in Năsăud in 1771, modeled on those existing elsewhere, helped to raise the Transylvanian Rumanians' cultural standards. The Rumanian regiment officers became part of Transylvania's Rumanian bourgeoisie which was in the forefront of the struggle for national liberation.

Drafted into distant theaters during Austria's wars with France, the Rumanian frontier guards distinguished themselves at such battles as Arcole and Rivoli. Service far from home gave the guards an unprecedented opportunity to expand their knowledge and enhance their sense of their own value. A distinct socioprofessional group gradually came into being, one that was aware of its social and national interests and joined the political struggle for the emancipation of the Rumanian population of which it was a part. The guards officers' complete identification with the ideals of the Rumanians' liberation struggle was evident in their subscription to the *Supplex libellus Valachorum* of 1791. This petitioned Vienna to recognize the Rumanian nobility as the fourth political "nation" of Transylvania, to grant the Orthodox and Uniate churches "accepted" status, to open the Diet and public office to Rumanians in proportion to their share of the principality's population, and to acknowlege the military status of the frontier guards.[21] The military patriots who thus demanded equality of rights for Transylvania's Rumanians were the progeny of these same people, and acquired their knowledge and awareness in service with the frontier guard regiments.

One other facet of the Rumanian struggle for emancipation continued throughout the eighteenth century in all three principalities. This was the popular and fundamental, if at times somewhat confused, social and national fight that took the form of outlawry. It was the expression of endemic popular resistance to oppression, be it native or alien.

In sum, the military manifestations of the Rumanians' national emancipation struggle in the eighteenth century permit the following conclusions. The effort was single-minded and involved all the territories inhabited by the Rumanians. Habsburg domination of Transylvania did not alter its homogeneous character; the effort merely took a different form there from in the other two principalities. On both sides of the Carpathians the national emancipation struggle was rooted deep and strong in the people, and in Moldavia and Wallachia found its most powerful expression in the armed actions of the volunteer units formed during the Ottoman Empire's wars with Austria and Russia. The military experience acquired in the century's wars was turned to best account during the Vladimirescu revolution of 1821 and in the reconstitition of the Rumanian army after 1830, when the projects for military reorganization first proposed during the eighteenth century finally took concrete form.

## Notes

1. Andrei Oţetea, *Contribution à la Question d'Orient* (Bucharest, 1930) contains a lucid account of the "Eastern Question." See also M. S. Anderson, *The Eastern Question, 1774–1923* (London and New York, 1966).

2. For the domestic policy of the Phanariot rulers, see Nicolae Iorga, "Le despotisme éclaté dans les Pays Roumains au XVIIIe siècle," *Bulletin of the International Committee for Historical Sciences*, II (1937), 101–115; Andrei Oţetea (ed.), *The History of the Romanian People* (New York, 1970), pp. 258–263.

3. Nicolae Bălcescu, *Scrieri militare alese* [Selected Military Writings] (Bucharest, 1952), p. 146.

4. Radu Rosetti, *Istoria artei militare a românilor pînă la mijlocul secolului al XVI-lea* [History of the Rumanians' Military Arts to the Mid 16th Century] (Bucharest, 1947), pp. 558–559.

5. For Dimitrie Cantemir's activities, see Dimitrie Cantemir, *Viaţa şi opere* [Life and Works] (Bucharest, 1958); Andrei Pippidi, "Politică şi istorie in proclamaţia lui Dimitrie Cantemir din 1711" [Politics and History in Dimitrie Cantemir's Proclamation of 1711], *Studii*, XXVI (1973), No. 5, 219–222.

6. Ion Neculce, *Letopiseţul Ţării Moldovei* [The Chronicle of Moldavia], ed. Iorgu Iordan (Bucharest, 1959), pp. 219–222.

7. A. Z. Mishlaveski, "War with Turkey in 1711," in *The History of Romania*, III (Bucharest, 1964), 217.

8. Andrei Pippidi, "Aux origines du régime phanariote en Valachie et en Moldavie," *Revue des études sud-est européennes*, XI (1973), No. 2, 353–355.

9. C. Şerban, "Relaţiile politice româno-ruse în timpul războiului ruso-turc din 1735–1739" [Rumanian-Russian Political Relations at the Time of the Russian-Turkish War of 1735–1739], *Analele rom.-sov.: Istorie*, X (1958), No. 4, 125; Damian P. Bogdan, "Legăturile serdarului Lupu Anastasă cu ruşii (1721–1752)" [Sirdar Lupu Anastasă's Links with the Russians

(1721–1752)], *Studii şi materiale de istorie medie* [Studies and Documents of Medieval History], II (1957), 34 -357.

10. Apostol Stan, *Renaşterea armatei naţionale* [The Rebirth of the National Army] (Craiova, 1979), p. 26.

11. Theodor Codrescu, *Uricariul* [The Chartulary], (Iaşi, 1857), IV, 373; Stan, *Renaşterea.*

12. For a detailed account see S. Vianu, "Din lupta poporului român pentru scuturarea jugului otoman şi cucerirea independenţei" [Of the Rumanian People's Struggle to Shake Off the Ottoman Yoke and Win Independence], *Studii,* VI (1953), No. 2; Stan, *Renaşterea.*

13. Vlad Georgescu, *Ideile politice şi iluminismul în Principatele române (1750–1831)* [Political Ideas and the Enlightenment in the Rumanian Principalities (1950–1831)] (Bucharest, 1972), p. 155.

14. Stan, *Renaşterea,* pp. 57–62. Nicolae Mavrogheni, hospodar of Wallachia (1786–1790), unwaveringly loyal to the Porte, formed an army that fought a number of victorious engagements against the Austrians. His devotion to his Ottoman masters did not save him when he was ordered beheaded.

15. For details see Ştefan Pascu, *Voievodatul Transilvaniei* [The Principality of Transylvania] (Cluj-Napoca, 1971–1973); Şerban Papacostea, "La fondation de la Valachie et de la Moldavie et les Roumains de Transylvanie: Une nouvelle source," *Revue roumaine d'histoire,* V (1979), 57.

16. *Istoria României* [The History of Rumania] (Bucharest), II (1962), 352–354.

17. David Prodan, *Răscoala lui Horea* [The Horea Uprising] (Bucharest, 1979), I, 57.

18. L. Gyémant, "Aspecte militare ale luptei sociale şi naţionale a românilor din Transilvania în secolul al XVIII-lea şi în prima jumătate a secolului al XIX-lea" [Military Aspects of the Social and National Struggle of the Rumanians of Transylvania in the 18th Century and the First Half of the 19th Century], in *Oastea cea mare* [The Great Host] (Bucharest, 1972), pp. 53–98.

19. *Ibid.*, pp. 76–77.

20. Prodan, *Răscoala,* II, 709.

21. David Prodan, *Supplex libellus Valachorum* (2nd ed.; Bucharest, 1967), p. 108.

Florin Constantiniu

# Tradition and Innovation in the Eighteenth-Century Military Structures of the Rumanian Lands

It is axiomatic these days that military structures have to be examined in close relation to overall economic and sociopolitical conditions. Whatever his philosophical viewpoint, no historian will quarrel with the principle enunciated by Friedrich Engels: "Nothing else depends so much on economic conditions as the army and the fleet. Equipment with armament, the effective strengths, the organization, the tactics and strategy depend, above all, on the stage reached by production and the means of communication at the moment in question."[1] An accurate appreciation and understanding of the double concept of war and society require exposition of the dialectical relationship between the three basic elements of the military (its organization, conception, and action) and the components of the socioeconomic system, namely, its infrastructure (the productive forces), its structure (the interrelationships of production) and its superstructure (the whole complex of ideas and institutions).

It is no easy task to examine this relationship in as large a region as Southeastern Europe, where the eighteenth century saw the beginnings of the transition from feudalism to capitalism, the repercussions of which are not yet over.[2] In this area of the continent the complexity of the process was compounded by interference in the development of local societies by certain external factors that either stimulated or delayed the process. In a period of dynamism the historian has to distinguish between the old and the new, the remnants of the past and the portents of the future, to weigh their roles and significance, and to reconstruct the impact of their influence and that of other outside factors. It is worth making a typological investigation of historical processes, and in the present case, this means examining the forms of transition from feudalism to capitalism, an exercise that underscores the unity in diversity of the great historical realities.[3]

In Central and Western Europe the eighteenth century up till the French Revolution was the century of "limited wars"[4] typical of societies with a predominantly agrarian structure where industry has at most reached the advanced handcraft stage. Industrial and political revolution (the French and American Revolutions), an expression of the development of new bourgeois relations, brought conscription (the new levy en masse) and total war to the west. This is well-explored territory where J. F. C. Fuller's work has become classic.[5]

In Southeastern Europe the disintegration of feudalism and the emergence of capitalism took quite different forms (hence the need for a typological approach) and gave the military structures features peculiarly their own. In this region, too, the ethnic diversity and the variety of economic and sociopolitical conditions have to be distinguished by types and subtypes. Furthermore, it is necessary to make a typological definition of Southeastern Europe's military structures, and to correlate them to the typology of the transition from feudalism to capitalism. From this will emerge a picture of the relationship between war and society in the eighteenth century in this great expanse of the European continent.

The military history of the Rumanian people in the eighteenth century indicates one typological approach to the relationship between contemporary war and society.[6] First, then, the basic elements of the Rumanian military reality at the time have to be examined.

During this period in all the Rumanian territories there flourished a society of clearly feudal agrarian character. The economic foundation of such a society is the relationship between the landowners and the peasant cultivators in the setting of the basic feudal unit, the large estate. The landowners' involvement in agricultural trade and the increase in the cultivation of cereals for the market, especially the foreign one, progressively altered conditions on the estates and resulted in the imposition of ever greater obligations on the peasantry, particularly the demand for corvée. Besides this development, the peasants were burdened by the oppressive fiscal demands of the state, and in Transylvania by systematic national discrimination and oppression.[7]

The eighteenth century also brought to the Rumanian countries major changes in their international status. The Treaty of Karlowitz of 1699 gave international recognition to the passage of Transylvania under Habsburg rule. In the other two principalities Ottoman domination was intensified by the establishment of the Phanariot regimes in Moldavia in 1711 and Wallachia in 1715. Under pressure from the growing intensity of the drive for national liberation and from the expansionist designs of the Russian and Habsburg Empires, the Phanariot regimes considerably reduced the autonomy of both principalities, but were unable to do away with it altogether. One deterrent was the memory of the great anti-Ottoman uprising led by Michael the Brave.[8]

## The Phanariot Regime and Its Military Consequences

The aims of the Phanariot hospodars, as representatives of Ottoman interests, were to strengthen Ottoman control over Moldavia and Wallachia, to meet the Sublime Porte's material demands, and to secure the stability of the mass of peasants, the countries' major source of income in their twofold capacity as creators of material goods and sources of tax revenue. The flight of peasants to escape fiscal and proprietary feudal exploitation[9] created a real demographic and fiscal crisis that the hospodars sought to cure by a policy of reform.[10] This set of fiscal, social, administrative, legal and military measures was intended to stabilize the two principalities' tax base by increasing the number of taxpayers and reducing the privileges and authority of the nobility, which was the mainstay of the struggle against Ottoman domination.

Just before the installation of the Phanariot regime, Prince Dimitrie Cantemir of Moldavia with the military support of Tsar Peter the Great had attempted to assert his country's independence within its former frontiers. His effort had wide popular backing and attracted large numbers of volunteers into his army.[11] In addition, bands of Rumanian volunteers under the leadership of such men as Captains Nicula, Cîrje, Abaza and Sirdar Donici of Orhei[12] joined the Russian army. The breadth of support for the prince's bid for independence justifies the assertion: "The war fought against the Turks was, as always, a popular one."[13]

The massive scale of this "treason" left the Ottomans in no doubt about the Rumanians' disloyalty. Deposing the two states' native princes, who kept secret contacts with the courts of Vienna and Moscow in the hope of some sort of joint anti-Ottoman action, was the Sublime Porte's first step toward strengthening its control over Moldavia and Wallachia, which were of considerable strategic and economic value to it.

Its second step in the same direction was intended to minimize the principalities' power, in particular, their military strength, which made free political and military action possible. After the princes' removal, the nobility remained the main political force able to challenge Ottoman supremacy programmatically and in practice. With popular support, should the latent and enduring anti-Ottoman sentiment of the population erupt again, the nobility could once more threaten Ottoman domination. To avert this danger, the Sublime Porte curtailed the privileges of the Rumanian nobility by taking measures to consolidate the hospodars' authority and to reduce the numbers of the military categories of the population.

These military and fiscal measures, particularly those taken in each principality by Constantin Mavrocordat, had a double purpose. On the one hand, they aimed to cut the number of tax-exempt and fiscally privileged in order to swell the number of taxpayers. On the other, this loyal servant of Constantinople attempted to bring the military potential of Moldavia and Wallachia down to a level where it would no longer constitute a menace to Ottoman preeminence. Substantial reduction of the privileged meant doing away with certain military castes, but Moldavia and Wallachia were never stripped of all their military forces, although their number became very small. These modest units perpetuated the institution of the army, which did not cease to exist for a moment. The functions of these reduced units were entirely internal: guarding the borders, especially against smuggling, enforcing order, and in service to the hospodars' courts, where their presence was supposed to add to the splendor of these rulers, who wished to be surrounded by pomp worthy of the "Byzantium after Byzantium" that they saw themselves to be.

Contemporary documents record a profusion of military formations—*vînători* (mountain troops), *roşii* (mounted troops), *joimiri* (Polish or Cossack mercenaries), uhlans, dragoons, *călăraşi* (cavalrymen), *dorobanţi* (infantry), *martalogi* (martolos), *saragele* (horse soldiers), *catane* (foot soldiers), pandours and so forth. The variety of terms, however, should not be taken as an indication that they had any real strength. The Phanariot regime sapped the military forces of Moldavia and Wallachia in order to increase the number of taxpayers, an essential step to fulfill the material demands of the Sublime Porte and to head off the threat to Ottoman domination by the existence of Rumanian military forces capable of large-scale action. In his work on Wallachia, F. G. Bauer, a Russian general of German extraction, remarked that the measures taken by Hospodars Nicolae and Constantin Mavrocordat deprived the principality of any effective means of resisting the Sublime Porte or retaliating against any violation of its autonomy.[14]

As the Ottoman Empire was required to make ever greater military efforts in its wars with Austria and Russia, efforts its anachronistic structure could barely cope with, outbursts of anarchy multiplied in the frontier areas of Southeastern Europe, a typical symptom of the serious crisis in the Turkish feudal system.[15] The Porte found itself obliged to accept increases in the effective strengths of the Rumanian armies, especially that of Wallachia, to serve Ottoman interests. During the Ottoman war with Austria and Russia of 1787–1792, for instance, Hospodar Nicolae Mavrogheni of Wallachia, one of the most loyal servants the Sublime Porte ever had on the princely thrones in Iaşi and Bucharest, organized an army of nearly 11,000 men.[16]

The unrest caused by the disloyalty of the pasha of Vidin, Osman Pasvanoğlu, one of the main opponents of the reformist trends of Sultan Selim III (1789–1807), obliged the princes of Wallachia to organize military forces to protect the country from the raids of rebel Turkish troops and their demands for money and supplies. Hospodar Alexandru Moruzi (1799–1801) recruited an army of which Rumanians formed only a very small part.[17] Most of its strength were Albanians, Serbs, Bulgars and Turks. His successor, Hospodar Mihai Suţu (1801–1802), faced the same danger but, concerned at the expense of its upkeep, he disbanded this army, and formed another, less costly one that turned out to be inferior in every respect.[18]

The small part taken by Rumanians in the military forces organized by Nicolae Mavrogheni, Alexandru Moruzi and Mihai Suţu requires explanation. As already noted, the major preoccupation of the Phanariot rulers was to increase the two principalities' fiscal potential to provide revenue for the Sublime Porte and themselves. The enlistment of local inhabitants, above all, peasants, reduced the number of taxpayers and hence the amount of taxes collected. The larger an army, the larger the military budget and the fewer the tax-payers. Under such circumstances, establishment of truly national military forces was out of the question.

### Military Initiatives of the Boyars

The hospodars were not the only ones to organize Rumanian military forces. One of the objectives of the Phanariots' reform policies was to curb the power of the boyars as a major force in the struggle for national emancipation. The hospodars' domestic meaures, particularly the abolition of bodily servitude and the elimination of tax exemptions, pitted the boyars even more sharply against them. Annulment of Constantin Mavrocordat's reforms thus became a key point in the political program of the great boyars.[19] The boyars were well aware that the Phanariot regime was an element of Ottoman domination, and that elimination of the former would mark the end of the latter. The restoration of native princes was therefore seen not only as a return to the *status quo ante* 1711 and 1715 but also as the recovery of independence, whether *de jure* or *de facto*. The suzerainty of the Sublime Porte was thus to be opposed by every means available, including political and military. The Ottoman Empire's wars on Rumanian territory with the Habsburg and Romanov empires offered opportunities for a wide range of action against the Porte. More than any other eighteenth-century outbreak, the Russo-Ottoman war of 1768-1774 gave the boyars the chance to assert themselves in matters of military organization and action.

The Cantacuzino family was without doubt the most prominent in the armed struggle against the Sublime Porte. The most remarkable representatives both of the family and of the current of anti-Ottoman sentiment were Pîrvu and Mihai Cantacuzino. The former had an important role in the liberation of Bucharest and in the subsequent battle at Comana, where he distinguished himself by his valor. "In this war, although they [the Rumanians] fought bravely so that 4,000 Turks fell in battle, victory nevertheless went to the Turks. . . . Pîrvu Cantacuzino with all his men perished in the fighting."[20] During the Sublime Porte's next war with Austria and Russia in 1787–1792, Pîrvu's nephew Ioan Cantacuzino, who had fought as a teenager in the previous conflict, became one of the leaders of the struggle for national emancipation. His actions are described in glowing terms in the works of Nicolae Bălcescu.[21]

In many documents that appeared between 1769 and 1821, the boyars argued again and again for restoration of a local army that would follow in a glorious tradition and defend the principalities' independence. One example from 1769, for instance, urged establishment of a force of 20,000 men with cavalry and artillery for Wallachia and a 12,000-man force for Moldavia.[22]

## Popular Military Initiatives in the Danubian Principalities

In the Middle Ages the defense of Rumanian independence was based on the entire population fighting invaders. From this came a tradition of popular war. The "great host," the mass levy of all men capable of bearing arms, proved an effective shield protecting the autonomy of the Rumanian territories. The gradual subjection of the peasantry, particularly during the sixteenth century, and the evolution of new techniques (infantry and artillery) in response to the development of firearms, however, weakened the mass basis and the combat effectiveness of the great host until it eventually fell into disuse.[23] The disappearance of the great host did not put an end to the fight against the Turk which flared up whenever the opportunity arose. The Ottoman wars with the Austrian and Russian Empires, which marked a new phase in the "Eastern question" in the eighteenth and early nineteenth centuries, offered the populations of Moldavia and Wallachia their chances to take up arms and demonstrate in the firmest way their will to end Ottoman domination and win their countries' independence.

The campaign of 1711 aroused broad popular enthusiasm for enlistment either in Prince Dimitrie Cantemir's army or in that of his ally, Tsar Peter I. In the war of 1735–1739 Constantin and Dimitrie Cantemir, the sons of Antioh Cantemir and grandsons of Moldavia's last native prince, Dimitrie Cantemir, arrived with the Russian forces, awakening memories of the fighting in 1711 and touching off volunteer enlistments in the Russian army. These volunteers fought during the summer of 1739 in the battles of Sobranets, Grozitsa and Stăuceni and at the capture of the fortress of Hotin.[24]

The Russo-Ottoman war of 1768–1774 brought increased evidence of popular readiness to take up arms. The national emancipation movement coalesced into a common struggle for independence by all the socio-political forces of Rumanian society. The boyars, who organized military units and penned demands for the rights of their countries, were joined spontaneously by the popular masses, whose numerous and often disorganized actions testified to their support for the struggle against the Ottomans. A telling example was the liberation of Bucharest in which the local inhabitants' military effort was decisive. There was broad popular support, too, for the Russian army fighting on Rumanian soil. The number of its Rumanian volunteers, who amounted to some 4,400 men at the outset, had tripled by the end of the hostilities. In smaller actions and in the great battles of the war, from Movila Rîibîiei and Larga to Cahul and Cozluge, the Rumanian volunteers acquitted themselves with great military distinction.[25] They added to the pages of the honor rolls in the next war, that of 1787–1792, when the heroism of such commanders as Ion Udre, Pavel Vizirean, Hudache Popescu and Mihalache Arsenie went down for posterity. General Aleksandr V. Suvorov, the Russian commander in chief, himself recorded the fact that at the battle of Rîmnic, in which the Grand Vizier's army was destroyed, five of the 31 colors captured were taken by Rumanian volunteers.[26] The popular alacrity to set up volunteer formations came to its peak in the Russo-Ottoman war of 1806–1812, in which the Oltenian pandours were especially conspicuous. This, however, was already a new century.

## Popular Military Initiatives in Transylvania

The establishment of Habsburg rule over Transylvania generated widespread sociopolitical unrest that culminated in the uprising led by Prince Ferenc II Rákóczi (1703–1711). The Rumanian populace joined the rebel forces because they saw in the promise to abolish serfdom for those who fought and in the anti-Habsburg nature of the insurrection a means to improve their economic and social status.

The Rumanian troops made their mark in the seizure of the fortress of Kálló on July 29, 1703, in the occupation of Baia Mare, and in the fighting in the western Carpathians in Oaş, Maramureş, Satu Mare, Şimleu, and the Haţeg. The feats of arms of Pintea the Brave, the legendary outlaw, and the action of the units headed by Ştefan Sudriceanu, Marcu Haţeganu, Vasile Ciulai, Nichita Balica, Vasile Negru and Bucur Cîmpian made a significant and often decisive contribution to a series of rebel victories. The participation of Rumanian units under Rumanian command "embodied a military organization that, by its many points of similarity, amounted to a continuation of the fighting experience of the new centuries that preceded Habsburg rule."[27]

The structure of the forces in the uprising of Horea, whose objective, as stated in the ultimatum issued in Deva on November 11, 1784, was complete abolition of the feudal regime, was based on a hierarchy of command. At their head was Horea as their supreme commander with three seconds in command, Cloşca, Crişan and Horea's son Ioan. Below them were captains whose subordinates were a number of appointed or elected corporals.[28] The suppression of the uprising stifled this popular organization's chance to make a really articulate stand.

### Imperial Military Initiatives in Transylvania

To defend the Habsburg Empire's southeastern frontiers and, in particular, to prevent the flight of the Rumanian population to Moldavia and Wallachia from the feudal exploitation and national oppression to which it was exposed in Transylvania, Vienna decided to set up a "military border" by organizing a few regiments of Rumanian and Szekler frontier guards.[29] Viewed by the peasants initially as another imposition, the recruitment of peasants to serve in these formations sometimes ran into violent opposition. Yet the creation of the first regiment at Orlat, of a second at Năsăud, and of a Rumanian battalion in the Banat had positive consequences for the Rumanian population as a whole. Through service in these units Rumanians were emancipated from serfdom, had their cultural standards raised through training, their horizons expanded by being stationed away from their homes, their sense of personal worth enhanced by their own feats of arms, and their national consciousness sharpened. The "military estate" (*militarus status*) of the "Rumanian nation" was one of the supplicants in the *Supplex libellus Valachorum* of 1791, the reform petition of the Transylvanian Rumanian's national emancipation movement.[30]

The eighteenth century was an era of transition from feudal organizational structures to modern ones. The feudal agrarian nature of Rumanian society still stood in the way of creating military forces equipped with the matériel produced by the industrial revolution that was taking hold elsewhere in Europe. The Ottoman domination of Moldavia and Wallachia obstructed the development of national armed forces there, while Habsburg rule over Transylvania resulted in the formation of Rumanian military units for Vienna's exclusive benefit. Besides initiatives from above to set up military units, the century saw a growth in iniatives from below. The role of the peasants under arms was both antifeudal and national in character. They had been enlisting in Rumanian frontier guard units for a generation before the Horea uprising.

The enrollment of Rumanian volunteers to fight alongside Austrian and Russian armies, considered by some historians as the decisive external factor in the formation of the Rumanian nation, was in fact a military demonstration of the national and political consciousness of the Rumanian people, whose transformation into a nation was already in progress. The wars between the Ottoman Empire and the Austrian and Russian Empires were not the cause of these manifestations, but rather the condition for their appearance. The three empires vied to dominate the Rumanians' territory, from which they tore sizable areas to include in their own realms.

The same is true of the frontier guard regiments, which are sometimes considered the key factor in shaping the Transylvanian Rumanians' national consciousness. The fact is that they were grafted onto a profound objective reality, the formative Rumanian nation, and only provided a propitious framework for the demonstration of national consciousness.[31]

The unity of the historical evolution of the Rumanian people is reflected in the unitary nature of the military formations of Moldavia, Wallachia and Transylvania which, despite the different frames of reference of Ottoman dominion and Habsburg rule, showed identical forms of popular military organization. The broadly national, popular character of eighteenth-century Rumanian military units was to be deepened and tempered in the heat of the revolutions of 1821 and 1848, which were themselves an expression of the historical unity of Rumanian society.

The eighteenth-century Rumanian armed forces thus display an original congeries of traditional and innovative elements that were the outcome of the specific developmental stages of Rumanian society. In Moldavia and Wallachia the traditional military structures had become anarchronistic and were thrown into crisis by the double pressure of socioeconomic transformation and the Ottoman imposition of the Phanariot regime. In setting up the frontier guard regiments in Transylvania, the Habsburg court created a foreign form with a Rumanian content. Neither the Austrian nor the Ottoman model provided any solution to the general crisis that beset the region.[32] Meanwhile, the peoples of Southeastern Europe, subjects of the Sublime Porte, were already involved in their struggle for national emancipation and evolving new forms of military organization that were compatible with their own traditions and conditions, and were suited to their political goal of liberation from Ottoman hegemony.[33] The eighteenth century was a time of ferment, but it was only late the following century that a truly modern military organization came into being.

## Notes

1. Friedrich Engels, *Opere militare alese* [Selected Military Works] (Bucharest, 1962), I, 12.

2. Cf. Eric Hobsbawm, "Du féodalisme au capitalisme," in Maurice Dobb and Paul M. Sweezy (eds.), *Du féodalisme au capitalisme: Problèmes de la transition* (Paris, 1977), II, 7.

3. Cf. Zbigniew Stankiewicz, "Some Remarks on the Typology of Transition from Feudalism to Capitalism in Agriculture," *Acta Poloniae historica*, XXVIII, 169–189.

4. Yves Gras, "Les guerres 'limitées' du XVIIIe siècle," *Revue historique de l'armée*, XXVI (1970), No. 1, 22–36; John F. C. Fuller, *La conduite de la guerre de 1789 à nos jours* (Paris, 1963), pp. 11–20.

5. *Ibid.*

6. The basic work on this topic is Apostol Stan, *Renaşterea armatei naţionale* [The Rebirth of the National Army] (Craiova, 1979). A useful survey is Dan Berindei, "The Romanian Armed Forces in the Eighteenth and Nineteenth Centuries," in Béla K. Király and Gunther E. Rothenberg (eds.), *War and Society in East Central Europe*, I: *Special Topics and Generalizations on the 18th and 19th Centuries* (New York, 1979), 215–223.

7. David Prodan, *Supplex libellus Valachorum* (Bucharest, 1967).

8. Florin Constantiniu, "De la Mihai Viteazul la fanarioţi: Consideraţii politice externe româneşti în secolul al XVII-lea" [From Michael the Brave to the Phanariots: Rumanian Foreign Policy Considerations in the 17th Century], *Studii şi materiale de istorie medie* [Studies and Sources of Medieval History], VIII (1975), 111.

9. G. Iscru, "Fuga, forma principală de luptă împotriva exploatării in

veacul al XVIII-lea în Ţara Românească" [Flight, the Major Form of Combat against Exploitation in 18th-Century Wallachia], *Studii* [Studies], XVIII (1965), No. 1, 124–146.

10. Florin Constantiniu and Şerban Papacostea, "Les réformes des premiers Phanariotes en Moldavie et en Valachie: Essai d'interpretation," *Balkan Studies*, XIII (1972), No. 1, 89–117.

11. Ion Neculce, *Letopiseţul Ţării Moldovei* [The Chronicle of Moldavia], ed. I. Iordan (Bucharest, 1975), p. 197.

12. *Istoria României* [The History of Rumania] (Bucharest, 1964), III, 217.

13. *Ibid.*, 216.

14. F. G. Bauer, *Mémoires historiques et géographiques sur la Valachie* (Frankfurt and Leipzig, 1778), p. 69.

15. For greater detail see A. F. Miller, *Mustapha Pasha Baïraktar* (Bucharest, 1975), pp. 25–34; Peter F. Sugar, *Southeastern Europe under Ottoman Rule, 1354–1804* (Seattle and London, 1977).

16. Stan, *Renaşterea*, p. 65.

17. R. Rosetti, "Arhiva senatorilor din Chişinău şi ocupaţia rusească de la 1806–1812" [The Senators' Archives in Kishinev and the Russian Occupation of 1806–1812], *An. Acad. Rom. Sect. Ist.*, 2nd series, XXXI (1908–1909), 367.

18. *Ibid.*, 369.

19. Cf. V. A. Urechia, *Istoria Românilor* [The History of the Rumanians], III, 329–331.

20. Mihai Cantacuzino, *Genealogia Cantacuzinilor* [The Genealogy of the Cantacuzinos], ed. Nicolae Iorga (Bucharest, 1902), p. 179. See also S. Vianu, "Din lupta poporului român pentru scuturarea jugului otoman şi cucerirea independenţei" [Of the Rumanian People's Struggle to Shake Off the Ottoman Yoke and Win Independence], *Studii*, VI (1953), No. 2, 73–75; Mircea Matei, "Despre poziţia claselor sociale din Moldova şi Ţara Românească faţă de războiul ruso-turc din 1768–1774" [On the Attitude of the Social Classes of Moldavia and Wallachia toward the Russo-Turkish War of 1768–1774], *Studii*, VI (1953), No. 3, 68–69 (unfortunately, though richly documented, the interpretation of both articles is rather schematic); L. Papoi, "Lupta de la Comana" [The Battle of Comana], in *File de istorie* [Pages from History] (Bucharest, 1978), pp. 211–217.

21. Nicolae Bălcescu, *Opere* [Works], ed. G. Zane (Bucharest, 1941), I, 137–149.

22. *Arhiva românească* [Rumanian Archives], I (1860), 209–210, 213–216; Berindei, "The Rumanian Armed Forces," p. 223.

23. N. Stoicescu, "Oastea cea mare in Ţara Românească şi Moldova sec. XIV–XVI" [The Great Host in Wallachia and Moldavia in the 14th–16th Centuries], in *Oastea cea mare* [The Great Host] (Bucharest, 1972), pp. 49–51.

24. C. Şerban, "Relaţiile politice româno-ruse în timpul războiului ruso-

turc din 1735–1739" [Rumanian-Russian Political Relations in the Time of the Russo-Turkish War of 1735–1739], *Analele rom. sov.: Istorie*, X (1956), No. 4, 126–127. It was rumored that Dimitrie Cantemir was to become hospodar of Moldavia.

25. Stan, *Renaşterea*, pp. 29–50.

26. *Ibid.*, pp. 56–62.

27. L Gyémant, "Aspecte militare ale luptei sociale şi naţionale ale românilor din Transilvania în secolul al XVIII-lea şi prima jumătate a secolului al XIX-lea" [Military Aspects of the Social and National Struggle of the Rumanians of Transylvania in the 18th Century and the First Half of the 19th Century], in *Oastea cea mare*, pp. 57–61.

28. *Ibid.*, pp. 74–75; and especially David Prodan, *Răscoala lui Horea* [The Horea Uprising] (Bucharest, 1979).

29. Carol Göllner, *Regimentele grănicereşti din Transilvania, 1768–1851* [The Border Regiments of Transylvania, 1768–1851] (Bucharest, 1973); Gunther E. Rothenberg, "The Habsburg Military Border System: Some Reconsiderations," in Király and Rothenberg, *War and Society*, I, 370–371, 380–387.

30. Prodan, *Supplex*, p. 237.

31. A. Ambruster, review of Mathias Bernath's *Habsburg und die Anfänge der rumänischen Nationalbildung*, in *Revue des études sud-est européennes*, XII (1974), No. 1, 159–162.

32. On Sultan Selim III's reforms, see Miller, *Mustapha Pasha*, pp. 73–95.

33. Cf. Vera Mutafchieva, *Kirdzhaliyski vreme* [The Time of Kirdzhaliy] (Sofia, 1977); Wayne S. Vucinich, "Serbian Military Tradition," in Király and Rothenberg, *War and Society*, I, pp. 297 ff.

Constantin Căzănişteanu

# The Consequences for the Rumanian Principalities of the Ottoman Wars with Austria and Russia

The critical condition of the Ottoman Empire, symbolized by its failure under the walls of Vienna in 1683, combined with the aggressive aspirations of the Habsburg and tsarist empires made the Rumanian lands the battlefield of three powers in the eighteenth century.

The Peace of Karlowitz of 1699, by recognizing Austria's rule over Transylvania, had brought the frontier of the Habsburg Empire to the Carpathian chain.[1] The following decade was one of respite for Moldavia and Wallachia, where the fiscal reforms of Prince Antioh Cantemir in Moldavia and Prince Constantin Brâncoveanu in Wallachia laid the groundwork for the demographic and economic recovery of the two principalities, which had suffered seriously from the military operations on their territory.[2] This period of tranquillity was short-lived. Fresh from his victory at Poltava in 1709 over Charles XII of Sweden, who had taken refuge in Bender on Ottoman territory, Tsar Peter I seized the opportunity not only to take the king's place as arbiter of Northeastern Europe but also to launch Russia's drive toward the former Byzantine capital of Constantinople to make it once more an emperor's city.[3]

The tsar's campaign in Moldavia in 1711 was the opening salvo of a series of wars to be fought on Rumanian territory as the Habsburg and Russian Empires strove for possession of at least part, if not all, of the Ottoman heritage in Europe. Moldavia and Wallachia were the theater of action of five wars: the Russo-Ottoman war of 1711, the Austro-Ottoman war of 1716–1718, the Russo-Austro-Ottoman war of 1735–1739, the Russo-Ottoman war of 1768–1774, and the Russo-Austro-Ottoman war of 1787–1792.[4] These conflicts have been discussed in depth in many works of European history from that of Albert Sorel[5] to recent studies by Mathew S. Anderson[6] and Peter F. Sugar.[7] Suffice it to remark now that, in view of the scale of the crisis in the Ottoman military system and the serious defeats suffered by the Turkish armies, the Sublime Porte got away lightly with only the loss of the banate of Timişoara and the Bukovina. (Oltenia, which it ceded to Austria by the Treaty of Passarowitz of 1718, was ceded back by the Treaty of Belgrade in 1739.) The fact that all three territories were Rumanian goes to show one of the impacts of these wars on Rumanian society.

During the war of 1711 Prince Dimitrie Cantemir of Moldavia fought alongside Peter I, with whom he had signed the Treaty of Lutsk recognizing the principality's frontiers. This precipitated the installation of the Phanariot regime in Moldavia, and three years later in Wallachia.[8] The intensification of the national emancipation movement, typified by Prince Dimitrie's action, and its two neighbors' attempts to acquire the two strategically important principalities, which were also its granary, determined the Sublime Porte to supplant the native princes with Phanariot rulers who would strengthen its control over both territories. The formal perservation of the territories' autonomy enabled the Sublime Porte to keep up the appearance of an administrative status quo, giving the impression that no substantial change in their status was taking place. Behind the screen, however, an iron Ottoman hand intended to turn the two principalities into vilayets. This was to be achieved by whittling away the autonomy that Moldavia and Wallachia enjoyed under the terms of their acts of allegiance to the Ottoman state. The custom of the countries was for the boyars to elect their princes, though this had become a rare event by the end of the seventeenth century. Now it ceased altogether, except for a solitary instance in 1730 when Constantin Mavrocordat was elected to succeed his father Nicolae as hospodar of Wallachia, an election that was overturned by the Porte. Instead of native princes raised to the throne by factions of boyars and invested by the sultan, hospodars were appointed by the Porte, without consulting the countries' political groupings, from among the great Greek families of the Phanar district of Constantinople.

In the two Rumanian capitals, Iaşi and Bucharest, now virtually outposts of the Ottoman Empire, the Phanariot rulers had a double function to perform. They were to keep an eye on international political developments by organizing in their neighbors' capitals a network of informers who would report back on the policies of European cabinets, which were being drawn increasingly into discussing plans for dividing up the Ottoman Empire's European provinces. This information the Phanariot regimes were supposed to analyze and pass on to the Sublime Porte.

Of far greater significance to the two principalities was their Phanariot rulers' second function. Acting as the Porte's proxies, as representatives of Ottoman interests, the hospodars were to keep Moldavia and Wallachia in a state of subjection and exploit their economic resources to the utmost.

The Phanariots had perforce to find ways and means to fulfill this task. Installed at a moment when Ottoman domination over the two principalities was in crisis, the hospodars were faced with resistance expressed in a variety of forms from almost all the sociopolitical forces in Rumanian society as well as with the devastation caused by the succession of wars fought on Rumanian territory. In spite of their demographic and economic potential, Moldavia and Wallachia, drained by Ottoman spoliation and the calamities of war, were less able to meet the demands for money, cereal and cattle than ever before. These demands came in an endless stream. The gap between socioeconomic reality and the rapidly increasing material exactions of the Sublime Porte generated a state of permanent unrest among the rural population. The peasants became fugitives to escape the merciless extraction of tribute, the clashes between the boyars and the hospodars, and the multiplication of spontaneous or organized movements to overthrow the Ottoman-Phanariot regime. The Sublime Porte and its Phanariot agents resorted to exceptional means to deal with the situation. The autonomy of both principalities was subtantially curtailed and the Porte's control tightened.

The Phanariot century (1711–1821) was above all the period of Moldavia's and Wallachia's most onerous material obligations to the Sublime Porte. With payments of tribute and other financial levies as well as the satisfaction of such requirements as supplying produce, timber for the Ottoman fleet, and manpower for constructing fortifications, the period was the culmination of five centuries of Ottoman domination and exploitation of the Rumanian lands.[9] The curtailment of the two principalities' autonomy went hand in hand with a reduction of their military forces. The Porte's measures to weaken their military potential were determined by both fiscal considerations (the need to increase the number of taxpayers) and political ones (the need to nullify any military threat). The Moldavian and Wallachian armies were not actually dissolved, as claimed by some authors, but had their strength greatly reduced.

The installation of the Phanariot regime was thus one of the first consequences of the wars fought on Rumanian territory, though the national liberation movement may have contributed equally to the creation of this new political form of Ottoman dominion.

The presence of foreign armies on Rumanian soil during the wars and the longer or shorter periods of foreign occupation placed a heavy burden on the populations and economies of both principalities and aroused a widespread sense of insecurity. The periods of occupation were numerous. After the war of 1716–1718, Oltenia was under Austrian occupation until 1739; during the war of 1735–1739, Moldavia was occupied by the Russians from the beginning of September through October 1739; during the war of 1768–1774, Moldavia was under Russian occupation from September 1769 to October 1774 and Muntenia from November 1769 to July 1774; the campaign of 1787–1792 brought Muntenia under Austrian occupation from November 1789 to July 1791, and Moldavia from 1787 to August 1792, interrupted by a few weeks of Ottoman occupation in July and August 1788 and Russian occupation between October 1788 and January 1792. During the same four years Moldavia was practically evenly divided between the Austrians and Russians. Through this same era of turmoil the Ottoman garrisons in the military enclaves around the fortresses of Turnu, Giurgiu, Brăila, Bender and Hotin were heavily reinforced. These enclaves (*raias*) were Rumanian territory under direct Ottoman administration. The Rumanians' already crushing burden of obligations was further increased by extraordinary levies and additional labor services during periods of occupation and active hostilities.

No precise figures are available to gauge the magnitude of the demands made on the principalities' revenues, or even to make a reasonable estimate. It is known only that during the war of 1787–1792 the Austrians collected an annual revenue of 420,782.13 piasters from their half of occupied Moldavia in 1790 and again in 1791. Besides requisitions, services and loot, the Austrian occupation forces extracted 5,079,148 piasters from twelve counties of Wallachia between November 1, 1789, and August 31, 1791. The whole state's net revenue at that time was only 1,200,000 florins a year, yet the Austrians managed to squeeze 1,127,445.37 piasters out of Oltenia alone in the same period.[10] These would be substantial sums at any time, but they represent only a minor part of the exorbitant total cost to the Rumanian principalities of the wars waged on their territories. This economic drain was at its worst when all three empires were locked in combat for control of the principalities.

Contemporary logistics were still so primitive that armies in combat had to rely for their supplies on forage from the population of the area where they were fighting. These armies were not only consumers of local produce but also carriers of germs. With the sanitary conditions of the time, outbreaks of great epidemics were commonplace. Applying Le Roy Ladurie's theory of the microbial unity of the world, historical research has been studying the military role in the spread of epidemics with growing interest. As pathogenic agents, the foreign armies on Rumanian soil were instrumental in causing epidemics that decimated the populations of Moldavia and Wallachia in the eighteenth century.

Each new war brought ever more virulent outbreaks mostly of the plague. Each time it was the Russian, Austrian or Ottoman troops who were the major disseminators of the terrifying scourge. In those days the safest prophylactic measure was to take refuge in a more elevated area that the infection had not reached. The thousands and thousands who died and the mass flight of those who were spared added considerably to the depopulation of the Rumanian lands (even if only temporarily in some places), the number of abandoned villages, and the depth of the despair sensed by visitors. Not even approximate figures exist for the loss of life occasioned by the epidemics, which were one of the grimmest and costliest consequences of the century's wars. This makes the few figures that are available all the more valuable and indicative. In 1718, for instance, 18,088 persons died in Braşov and the Bîrsa area.[11] So severe was the plague that swept through all the Rumanian lands in the war of 1735–1739 that there was some question of canceling the Leipzig fair. In Bucharest alone it took 10,000 lives between March 1 and October 1, 1738, and in three years felled 33,300 citizens and 236 clergy.[12] In Transylvania at the same time it spread to 501 communes in 23 districts, infecting 48,254 persons, of whom 41,622 died and only 6,632 recovered.[13] In 1769–1774 there was an extremely virulent outbreak, spread once again by foreign troops. Within two months some 2,000–3,000 inhabitants of Botoşani died, reducing its population to just 800. Half the residents and half the soldiers billeted in Iaşi succumbed to the disease. Orraeus, a Finnish physician in service with the Russians in Iaşi, left a moving account of the fate of those, mostly the poorest, who contracted the dread infection.

> To avoid suspicion the poor Moldavians who had relatives with the plague would surreptitiously carry them off into the forests nearby. There they would lay them out in a shady spot on a bed of grass and clothing. They would leave a pitcher of water and some food near at hand, and leave the poor devils to their fate. If they had friends to take pity on them, these would visit them from time to time and bring them what they needed, particularly water. Those who were a little stronger would gather brushwood for themselves and make a fire. When they died, grave diggers would bury them on the spot, but quite often they were simply left to rot and be torn to pieces by dogs, consumed by maggots, and devoured by wild beasts.[14]

The war of 1787–1792 left the same dismal trail in its wake. "After the soldiers had retreated across its [Wallachia's] frontiers, there came the plague, spread by them and fed by the decay of their [dead]. It spread like deadly wildfire as soon as they had gone."[15] It took a fearsome toll: leaving "up to 10,000 victims in Bucharest and up to 3,000 in Craiova, the disease spread from these two major centers to all the towns and even the villages in the country."[16]

Nor was the plague the only pestilence brought to the Rumanian lands by the foreign armies; they also caused epidemics of typhus, known at that time by the significant name of war fever,[17] and venereal diseases, which first appeared in the principalities after the passage of foreign invaders toward the end of the seventeenth century.[18] In the second half of the eighteenth century there was an alarming increase in the incidence of syphilis as well as other venereal diseases, mainly due to the movement of Austrian troops and to an Imperial decree that banished all Vienna's prostitutes to the remote provinces of the Habsburg Empire.

In addition to the loss of life, the outbreaks of plague seriously injured the Rumanian principalities' trade, both domestic and foreign. The enforcement of Austria's rigorous and mostly ineffectual quarantine regulations paralyzed the commercial life of Transylvania's frontier districts, whose economic wellbeing was dependent on unimpeded trade with the transcarpathian principalities. It was significant that Transylvania's quarantine authorities made an exception for imports of wool from Wallachia even when the border was closed because of plague.[19] Interruption of this trade would have brought southern Transylvania's cloth mills to a virtual standstill. A recommendation of 1799 from the Transylvanian Court Chancellery suggested easing the quarantine regulations because of "the close connection of the Grand Principality of Transylvania with the neighboring provinces of Muntenia and Moldavia and the much needed imports of certain raw materials required in large quantities by the Grand Principality of Transylvania. Cattle-raising is the main pursuit of the majority of the inhabitants, especially those living near the frontier, who have been taking their herds to pasture in Muntenia and Wallachia since time immemorial."[20]

Foreign troop movements also spread animal diseases through the Rumanian lands. In his account of the withdrawal of the Russian troops under the command of General Burkhard Münnich in 1740, the Moldavian chronicler Ion Neculce recorded that the countryside had been laid waste and "the few cattle left were dying. . . . The cattle and sheep had the pox which was playing havoc with them."[21]

The series of calamities brought on by the Ottoman Empire's wars with Austria and Russia was crowned by the widespread destruction of property and loss of life caused by the fighting. The movement of Austrian, Russian and Ottoman troops and the battles they fought were accompanied by arson, loss of goods and civilian massacre. Epidemics, veterinary disease, requisitioning, looting and famine, combined all too often with natural disasters like floods, droughts, locust swarms, earthquakes and fires, pushed a disastrous situation to the point of the unendurable. *The Chronicle of Moldavia*, attributed to Nicolae Muste, contained a telling description of Moldavia in 1716–1718 when every possible scourge had befallen the country: "Germans and soldiers entered the country, occupied and sacked it." The chronicler continued: "After the occupation, a great famine occurred, such that a measure of cornmeal cost up to 10 lei. Many souls died, many others fled abroad. After the famine came the plague—wailing and lamentation on every hand. Afterwards the cattle were struck by diseases, leaving some families without a single head, and this cattle fever raged all over the country. On top of it all there was a terrible fire that ravaged even the prince's court."[22]

Areas of wasteland lined the routes of the warring armies. A comparison of Moldavia's population increase between 1591 and 1772 shows that it was greatest in the areas farthest removed from the usual routes of access taken by invading foreign armies. The population of Bacău increaseed 697 percent over this period, Tecuci by 151 percent, Cîrligătura by 160 percent, Cernăuţi by 491 percent, and Roman by 153 percent. In contrast, areas directly affected by the foreign incursions showed a much lower rate of population growth during these years (that of Covurlui increased only 42 percent, Iaşi 38 percent, Orhei and Fălciu only 54 percent each) or even a net loss. The population of the Vaslui area, for instance, dropped 12 percent between 1591 and 1772.[23]

In some cases entire villages lying on major access routes moved and resettled in more secluded areas, away from the lines of movement of the Russian, Austrian and Ottoman armies. They were thus spared some of the sacking and violence and a great deal of the corvée exacted by the foreign forces. A deed of November 12, 1780, defining the boundaries of the estates of Pardeşti, Slăvileşti and Vlăduleani, for instance, noted: "Osica village (from Romanaţi county), which used to lie south of the river Olteţ, moved east across the river Olt after the uprising [of 1768–1774] onto the Vlăduleani estate where it is known as Prundul Vacilor."[24] This relocation was a direct result of the Russo-Ottoman war of 1768–1774.

Eighteenth-century foreign visitors to the Rumanian lands commented unanimously on the exceptional fertility of the soil and the sparsity of the population in relation to what the land could support. In his description of the Danube plain written in 1702 the Englishman E. Chishull observed that, despite the verdure,"these places are almost uninhabited and left fallow."[25] In 1780 the Pole W. Chrzanowski wrote: "The great expanses of excellent land make one regret that agriculture is so utterly neglected."[26] Another English traveler, John Jackson, reported in 1797 that, after crossing the Danube into Muntenia from Ruse, he saw no cultivated land all the way to Călugăreni, some 25 miles of riding. Thereafter his road passed through a "beautiful region, but little cultivated, however, in spite of the fact that it appeared uncommonly fruitful."[27] Other contemporary writers recorded exactly the same impressions.

No less unanimity was shown in ascribing Rumanian society's lack of progress to the effect of continual war.[28] A native eyewitness of the impact of the fighting wrote: "These past few centuries have given us a pitiful view of our country's land: they have seen it turned into a wasteland by war, scoured by retreating troops, and overrun with tears."[29] The historian Constantin Erbiceanu noted that in the eighteenth century "the Rumanians' land was the scene of a large number of devastating wars that caused the stagnation of development, the degeneration of morals, and grievous conditions for society. . . . These were hard times of ordeal when everything was in short supply and almost everything had to be begun again from scratch."[30] Erbiceanu goes on to describe the objectives of the three empires contending on Rumanian territory: "We all feel that the explanations given [by the Ottoman, Russian and Habsburg Empires] are meant solely to conceal the following historical truth: they were all fighting for us, or to put it more clearly, were fighting on our land, each intent on occupying us, annexing us, enslaving us."[31] Ioan Christian Struve, an attaché at the Russian embassy in Constantinople, wrote in 1793: "From time to time a new war breaks out and leaves behind only a wasteland, and that's the way this calamitous century is ending."[32]

The climate of instability and the repeated destruction of goods by war in the eighteenth century robbed Rumanian society of one of the basic conditions for the development of capitalist relations: security of production and exchange. Neither the immediate producer (the peasant) nor the organizer of production on estate land (the boyar or the abbot) nor the owner of factories nor even the merchants enjoyed the atmosphere of safety essential to stimulate production and exchange. Circumstances militated against the accumulation of capital. The increasing ruthlessness of Ottoman exploitation and requisitioning by occupying armies drained the financial resources of the two principalities.[33]

The harm done by the wars was not limited to the economic and demographic sectors. As the terrain on which the Ottoman, Habsburg and Russian Empires fought their wars, the Rumanian countries found themselves in the unhappy position of having to pay for Ottoman defeats with sacrifices from their own body politic. Under the 1718 Treaty of Passarowitz the Sublime Porte ceded the Banat and Oltenia to Austria. Austria's neutrality in 1775 had to be recompensed by the cession of the Bukovina to it. Moldavia thus had torn from it a densely populated region that had constituted the nucleus around which the state had formed and contained numerous memorials of a glorious past in the form of monuments and valuable works of art. The Sublime Porte made these transfers of Rumanian territory (the banate of Timişoara had been a pashalik since 1552) in flagrant violation of the mutually binding terms of the capitulations proclaimed by Constantinople to secure acceptance of Ottoman suzerainty over the Rumanian principalities. These affirmed the territorial integrity of the two states and gave the Sublime Porte no right to surrender any part of them to any other power. The territorial mutilations of the eighteenth century raised another obstacle to the achievement of the Rumanian people's unity but could not stifle the yearning for it.

Other considerations must also be weighed in a dialectical approach to understanding the consequences of the eighteenth century's wars for the Rumanian lands. While it may be an exaggeration to claim that, as consumers of cereal products, the foreign armies on Rumanian territory played a role similar to that of the towns in Western Europe, there is no doubt that here and in neighboring countries the armies' presence stimulated grain production.[34] An eloquent indication of this is offered by a princely injunction issued on January 26, 1790. This urged all the peasants to start their year's work on the land that month or "in due course" so that "the crops are good, for besides the food that will be yielded by tilling the land well, they will make good earnings from selling their crops to the numerous imperial troops to be found in the country, who will pay for everything in cash." All those who made timely efforts "to till and plow the land properly for their own benefit and good" would also "derive profit and advantage from their toil."[35] Increased consumption required additional areas of land to be brought under cultivation. Once this had occurred, the great estates had to start looking elsewhere for outlets for their produce to replace their military customers when hostilities were over.

The armies of the Habsburg and tsarist empires, which included numerous German officers and, after the outbreak of the French Revolution, French aristocrats as well, were agents of westernization among the upper segments of Rumanian society. Both in disseminating western culture, including the thinking of the Enlightenment and revolutionary ideas, and in introducing elements of the western way of life, the armies contributed to the intensification of Rumanian society's contacts with Europe at large. The Rumanians' assimilation of facets of western material and intellectual culture through contact with the Austrian and Russian armies, however, was tempered by its own native standards. Acceptance was not automatic; it was integrated into a process of adaptation of European cultures that had been going on for a long time and accorded with the level of development that Rumanian society had attained at any given historical moment.[36]

The wars fought on Rumanian territory gave the Rumanians the opportunity to assert themselves by military action of their own. The intensification of the struggle for national liberation and the decline of Ottoman military power, underscored by the Turks' defeats on Rumanian territory, led to the formation of unofficial Rumanian military forces whose objective was to drive out the Ottoman troops and end Ottoman supremacy.[37] During every war fought in Moldavia or Wallachia detachments of Rumanian volunteers fought shoulder to shoulder with the Austrian and Russian armies. Whether organized by the nobility or the peasantry, these detachments were the military expression of the Rumanian people's aspiration to independence. In the course of these wars the Rumanian units made a major contribution to victory in many battles and clashes. Their presence on the battlefield was the clearest proof that the Rumanians did not intend to be passive onlookers in the solution of the Eastern Queston but were emphasizing their political and military identity by action. These volunteer detachments were the real embryo of the future, nineteenth-century, modernized Rumanian army.

The military failures of the Sublime Porte in the eighteenth century impressed on the Rumanian consciousness Dimitrie Cantemir's concisely formulated belief in the "decline" of the Ottoman Empire. The conviction that Ottoman domination of Southeastern Europe was on the point of collapse turned Rumanian political thought to new ways of organizing Rumanian society once it was free of the Sublime Porte's overlordship. The needs that would result from the new political status of Moldavia and Wallachia together with the experience gained from the activities of the volunteer detachments lent major significance to military matters in the reform projects drafted in these years.

In sum, it is fair to say on balance that the Ottoman Empire's wars with Austria and Russia in the eighteenth century had a harmful impact on the development of Rumanian society. The periods of crippling occupation, the displacements of population, the devastation due to looting and violence, the crushing extra burdens imposed on the peasantry, the ravages of epidemics, and the general stagnation in all spheres of endeavor occasioned by the wars held back the transition from feudalism to capitalism. The wars intensified foreign domination of Rumanian territory and resulted in territorial mutilation. Yet the presence of the combatants on Rumanian soil led to an increase in grain production and facilitated Rumanian society's contact with the trends of Central and Western European thought. In a comprehensive and eloquent description of the wars and the ensuing periods of occupation, the great historian Nicolae Iorga pointed out that their importance extends beyond the purely political and military framework into areas of far greater interest. The eighteenth-century wars and occupations, Iorga noted, "brought in their wake new habits, other ways of governing, other administrative procedures, other fashions, other entertainments and other vices. In addition, western ideas, coming directly from the West or through the intermediary of St. Petersburg, . . . invaded with the foreign armies and remained after the departure of the latter. On the other hand, the occupations entailed heavy burdens and great suffering that soon dispelled certain illusions about Christians' impartiality, justice, mercy and love of mankind."[38]

The Russo-Austro-Ottoman wars on Rumanian soil in the eighteenth century brought the crisis of the Ottoman Empire to the fore and created the crucial framework for the emergence of Rumanian sociopolitical forces that would keep up the pressure for national emancipation.

## Notes

1. On Austrian expansion after 1683 see Hugo Hantsch, *Geschichte Österreichs, 1648-1918* (3rd ed.; Vienna, 1962); Hanns L. Mikoletzky, *Österreich—das grosse 18. Jahrhundert* (Vienna, 1967).

2. Şerban Papacostea, "Contribuţie la problema relaţiilor agrare în Ţara Românească în prima jumătate a secolului al XVIII-lea"[ Contributions to the Problems of Agrarian Relations in Wallachia in the First Half of the 18th Century], *Studii şi materiale de istorie medie* [Studies and Materials in Medieval History], II (1959), 255–260.

3. Cf. Georg von Rauch, "Politische Voraussetzungen für west-ostliche Kultur-Beziehungen im 18. Jahrhundert," in Erna Lesky *et al.* (eds.), *Die Aufklärung in Ost- und Südosteuropa* (Cologne and Vienna, 1972), pp. 10–13.

4. A. D. Xenopol, *Războaiele dintre rusi şi turci* [The Wars between the Russians and the Turks] (Bucharest), Vol. I (1880).

5. *La Question d'Orient au XVIIIe siècle* (Paris, 1889).

6. *The Eastern Question, 1774–1923* (London and New York, 1966).

7. *Southeastern Europe under Ottoman Rule, 1354–1804* (Seattle and

London, 1977).

8. Andrei Oţetea (ed.), *The History of the Romanian People* (New York, 1972), pp. 251, 254.

9. Mihai Berza, "Haraciul Moldavei şi Ţării Româneşti în sec. XV-XIX" [The Tribute of Moldavia and Wallachia in the 15th-19th Centuries], *Studii şi materiale de istorie medie*, II (1957), pp. 7-47; *idem*, "Variaţiile exploatării Ţării Româneşti de către Poarta Otomană în sec. XVI-XVIII" [The Variations in the Ottoman Porte's Exploitation of Wallachia in the 16th-18th Centuries], *Studii* [Studies], XI (1958), No. 2, 59-71.

10. Mihail Popescu, "Războiul ruso-austro-turc din 1787-1792 şi ocupaţia Principatelor Române" [The Russo-Austro-Turkish War of 1787-1792 and the Occupation of the Rumanian Principalities], *Convorbiri literare* [Literary Colloquies], 1930, pp. 450, 456-458.

11. Al. Lenghel, "Contribuţii la epidemia de ciumă din anul 1786 în sudul Ardealului" [Contributions to the Plague Epidemic of 1786 in Southern Transylvania], *Clujul Medical* [Medical (Journal of) Cluj], 1932, No. 12 (December), p. 3.

12. Ionescu Gion, *Istoria Bucureştilor* [The History of Bucharest] (Bucharest, 1899), p. 639.

13. Pompei Gh. Samarian, *Ciuma* [The Plague] (Bucharest, 1932), p. 84.

14. Nicolae Iorga, *Istoria românilor prin călători* [The History of the Rumanians through Travelers] (2nd ed.; Bucharest, 1928), I, 264.

15. Samarian, *Ciuma*, p. 139.

16. A. D. Xenopol, *Istoria Românilor din Dacia Traiană* [The History of the Rumanians of Trajan's Dacia] (Iaşi, 1894), Vol. IX.

17. *Contribuţii la istoria medicinei în Republica Populară Română* [Contributions to the History of Medicine in the Rumanian People's Republic] (Bucharest, 1956), p. 160.

18. V. Gomoiu, *Din istoria medicinei şi a învăţămintelor medicale* [On the History of Medicine and Medical Training] (Bucharest, 1923), p. 148.

19. Gheorghe Brătescu, "Despre rosturile sociale şi economice ale vechilor carantine din ţările române" [On the Social and Economic Role of the Old Quarantines in the Rumanian Lands], in *Din istoria luptei antiepidemice din România* [From the History of the Struggle against Epidemic in Rumania] (Bucharest, 1972), p. 246.

20. I. Moga, "Politica economică şi comerţul Transilvaniei în veacul al XVIII-lea" [Austrian Economic Policy and Transylvania's Trade in the 18th Century], *Analele Institului de istorie naţională* [Analele Institutului de istorie naţională [Annals of the Institute of National History] (Cluj), VII (1936-1938), 144.

21. Pompei Gh. Samarian, *Medicina şi farmacia în trecutul românesc, 1382-1775* [Medicine and Pharmacy in the Rumanian Past, 1382-1775] (Călăraşi, 1928), p. 281.

22. Mihail Kogălniceanu, *Cronicele României sau letopiseţele Moldovei şi Valachiei* [The Chronicles of Rumania or the Annals of Moldavia and

Wallachia] (2nd ed.; Bucharest, 1874), II, 69.

23. I. A. Kotenko *et al.*, "Tendința de creștere a populației din Moldova în epoca feudală" [Moldavia's Population Growth Trends in the Feudal Era], *Probleme de istorie* [Problems of History], 1967, No. 3, pp. 115–117.

24. N. Gh. Dinculescu, *Contribuțiuni la miscările de populație* [Contributions to Population Movements] (1915), p. 74.

25. According to General F. Bauer, Wallachia could have fed a population five or six times greater than it did. Bauer, *Mémoires historiques et géographiques sur la Valachie* (Frankfurt and Leipzig, 1778), pp. 19–20

26. *Buletinul Societății de Geografie* [The Bulletin of the Geography Society], XVI (1922), 198.

27. P. P. Panaitescu, *Călători poloni în țările române* [Polish Travelers in the Rumanian Lands] (Bucharest, 1930), p. 235.

28. C. J. Karadja, "O călălorie prin Muntenia în anul 1797" [A Journey through Muntenia in 1797], *Viața Românească* [Rumanian Life], XV (1923), No. 10–11, 160–162.

29. Ion Bianu and Nerva Hodoș, *Bibliografia românească veche, 1508–1830* [Old Rumanian Bibliography, 1508–1830], II: *1716–1808* (Bucharest, 1910), 407.

30. Constantin Erbiceanu, *Istoria Mitropoliei Moldovei și a Suceavei și a catedralei mitropolitane din Iași* [History of the Sees of Moldavia and Suceava and the Metropolitan Cathedral of Iași] (Iași, 1888), p. lxiii.

31. Constantin Erbiceanu, *Cronicarii greci care au scris despre români în epoca fanariotă* [The Greek Chroniclers Who Wrote about the Rumanians in the Phanariot Era] (Bucharest, 1890), p. xxii.

32. Gheorghe G. Bezviconi, *Călători rusi în Moldova și Muntenia* [Russian Travelers in Moldavia and Muntenia] (Bucharest, 1947), p. 142.

33. Andrei Oțetea, "Constrîngerea economică a clăcașilor la începutul secolului al XIX-lea" [Economic Constraints on the Serfs at the Beginning of the 18th Century], in *Studii și referate privind istoria României* [Studies and Papers Concerning the History of Rumania] (Bucharest, 1954), II, 10.

34. Béla K. Király, *Hungary in the Late Eighteenth Century* (New York and London, 1969), p. 9.

35. V. A. Urechiă, *Istoria românilor* [The History of the Rumanians] (Bucharest, 1893), III, 427–428.

36. Alexandru Duțu, *Coordonate ale culturii românești în secolul XVIII* [Coordinates of Rumanian Culture in the 18th Century] (Bucharest, 1968), *passim.*

37. Cf. Apostol Stan, *Renașterea armatei naționale* [The Rebirth of the National Army] (Craiova, 1979).

38. Nicolae Iorga, *Ceva despre ocupațiunea austriacă* [Something on the Austrian Occupation] (Bucharest, 1911), p. 1.

Radu Florescu

# Contemporary Western Reaction to the Battle of Stănileşti

The Russian victory at Poltava on July 8, 1709 not only stirred renewed hopes of liberation among the oppressed peoples of the Balkan Peninsula but also triggered the first spark of interest in the "Eastern Question" by a few journals read by a small and enlightened public in England, the Netherlands and France.[1] The presence of Charles XII, a refugee at Bender on the Moldavian border, projected the affairs of the Rumanian Principalities for the first time into the headlines of a few contemporary periodicals. During 1710–1711, Bender became a Pandora's box, where diplomats, generals, travelers and couriers scurried to and fro on secret missions on behalf of the Swedish king.[2] The granting of political asylum to his enemy in a town so dangerously close to the frontiers of Russia worried Peter the Great, and he instructed his ambassador, Count Peter Tolstoy, to have Charles XII removed from Ottoman territory. Despite British and Dutch mediating efforts, the Turks refused, imprisoned Count Tolstoy in the Seven Towers in Constantinople and declared war on Peter in November 1710. There followed no less than five propagandistic proclamations, undoubtedly inspired by the tsar's Balkan adviser, Sava Raguzinskiy of Dubrovnik, addressed to the Serbs, the Montenegrins, the Greeks, the Moldavians and the Wallachians, declaring that the tsar, in the name of Orthodoxy, was coming to liberate them from Ottoman oppression. There can be no question that Peter was counting on the aid of Princes Constantin Brâncoveanu of Wallachia (1688–1714) and Dimitrie Cantemir of Moldavia (November 1710–July 1711) who had pledged their military support.[3] Of the two, only Dimitrie Cantemir was committed on paper by the 16 clauses of the secret Treaty of Lutsk signed in April, which guaranted hereditary succession in his family.[4]

In this age of instant satellite electronic communications, it is difficult to conceive the enormous difficulties, delays and distortions facing the transmission of news by a handful of informants attempting by messenger to reach the editors of the more important papers from such an obscure theater of war as Moldavia, which few had even heard of. It should be remembered that neither the Russians, nor the Austrians nor the Turks had regular postal service with that area, and that diplomatic couriers were few and far between, as were travelers who happened to be sojourning to that part of the world in the year 1711. There were undoubtedly brilliant and ambitious men stationed in the two crucial capitals. Charles de Ferriol, marquis d'Argental, representing Louis XIV; Lord Paget and Sir Robert Sutton, envoys of Queen Anne,[5] Jacob Colyer, the ambassador of the Netherlands; Count Stanisław Poniatowski, representing the king of Sweden, were all posted in Constantinople. In Moscow France had Jean-Casimir de Baluze and Britain had Whitworth. These capitals, however, were hundreds of miles distant from Moldavia.[6] It irked some Western representatives that Peter allowed only the representatives of his immediate allies, Poland, Denmark and Saxony, to accompany him on his campaign. Bender, where Poniatowski often traveled, was deemed such an important vantage point that a British representative, Captain James Jeffereys, secretary to the British ambassador in Poland, John Robinson, was sent there for the duration of the campaign, but couriers carrying dispatches from this "enemy" center were denied the most direct routes to the West through Poland.[7] It might thus take as long as two months for their dispatches to be printed in Paris, London, Stockholm or the Hague.

The fact that Russia and its allies controlled most of the obvious routes constituted one obvious source of difficulty. The waging of two major wars during this period—the War of the Spanish Succession, which involved France against Austria, Britain and the United Provinces, and the Great Northern War, pitting Russian and its allies against Sweden for control of the Baltic—impeded the transmission of news. Each power inevitably viewed the Russo-Ottoman war from its own narrow, political, diplomatic or military interests. Neutral observers who might have contributed toward furthering historical truth were scarce, and rumors were arranged in a manner consistent with national interests. A final problem facing unprejudiced reporting was the overawing image that the tsar's personality projected almost everywhere after Poltava, coupled with a rather negative view of Ottoman military capacities after the Treaty of Karlowitz. The tendency to hero worship affected the vision of many Western diplomats and ultimately found its way into the writings of the day.

At the time of the battle of Stănileşti, journalism as it is known today was a new art that had begun in Holland with the *Leyden Gazette*, printed in two columns in French two or three times a week. Although the Dutch press had a reputation for independence, most newspapers at the beginning of the eighteenth century in such states as France, Spain and Russia (where Peter established the *St. Petersburg Zeitung*) were rigidly controlled by the respective monarchs and their censors. The situation of the press was particularly dismal in France during the last inglorious days of the reign of the Sun King. Few newpapers had survived, and those few that reported foreign news like the *Gazette de France*, founded by Théophraste Renaudot, and the *Mercure galant*, bore the imprimatur of the chancellery of foreign affairs and, for Eastern Europe particularly, that of the powerful French ambassador in Constantinople, de Ferriol. Muget's *Journal historique sur la matière des temps*, published in Verdun, far from the capital, was usually better informed than the Parisian press, and some of the most impartial discriminating and methodical accounts of the war came from the pen of its correspondent. Any diplomat interested in actual information on the Prut campaign was better advised to travel to the Netherlands or England and read the four-page biweekly *Mercure politique et historique*, edited by Henrie von Balderon, or the *Lettres historiques*, printed by Adrian Moetjens, both in the Hague, the prestigious *Gazette d'Amsterdam*, or the *London Gazette* or *The Daily Courant*, which reported news of Eastern European battles regularly after Poltava.[8]

For simplicity's sake, reporting on the Prut campaign can be divided into three phases: early troop movements by both armies and the action of the Rumanian princes; the march of the Russian army down the River Prut and Ottoman strategy leading to the ill-fated battle of Stănileşti; and commentators' explanations for the Russian defeat.

News of the Sublime Porte's declaration of war reached the West in December with one month's delay—though the actual document of the Ottoman proclamation of war couched in the mystical terms of a Muslim jihad reached Vienna only in January 1711. The Grand Vizier, Teberdar Mehmed Pasha, known as Baltacı Mehmed (Mehmed the Halberdier), had advanced his army from Adrianople along the traditional Balkan military route through the Dobruja, and intended to cross the Danube at Isaccea by means of a pontoon bridge once the high waters of winter had receded (*Gazette d'Amsterdam*).[9]

Characteristic of the tendency of Western periodicals to underestimate the total strength of the Ottoman force, the *Mercure galant* mentioned the presence only of 42,000 janissaries and as many Tatars.[10] It is now known from Ion Neculce, an actual eyewitness in the Moldavian ranks, that the total number of the Turkish army together with its contingents from Arabia, Persia and Egypt as well as its Tatar allies may have reached 200,000 men and that they had numerous pieces of artillery and bombards at their disposal.[11]

First tidings of Russian military moves were contained in a letter of February 1711 to the *Gazette d'Amsterdam* to the effect that General Janus von Eberstadt had been assigned to lead a cavalry detachment with orders to attack Bender and prevent the Turks from crossing the Danube.[12] The *Mercure galant* reported similar news from Warsaw in a July issue, which stated that Count Johann Bernard von Weisbach had been dispatched with 25,000 men to Moldavia to prevent an Ottoman crossing of the Danube, clearly the prime objective of Russia's strategists.[13]

There can be no question that the Russians' plan of campaign had reckoned on the active collaboration of both Rumanian princes, though the West seems to have been very slow to receive the news of Cantemir going over to them.[14] Both the *Gazette de France* and the *Gazette d'Amsteram* professed to know as a fact that Nicolae Mavrocordat had been dethroned because of his pro-Russian proclivities (a mistake) and that "a Greek" variously called "Dimitranski" or "Dimitraneski" (in actual fact the Rumanian Dimitrie Cantemir) had been named prince in his stead through the intervention of the Crimean khan's representative in Constantinople, Ismail Effendi. The *Mercure galant* as late as March further described Cantemir as "being thoroughly in Sweden's pocket."[15] Readers of the two gazettes were similary informed that in accordance with treaty stipulations the Turks expected 40,000 Wallachians and 15,000 Moldavians to collaborate with the Grand Vizier, who also expecting from them the horses, oxen, grain and other provisions needed to supply the Ottoman army.[16] Reports such as these continued to circulate in the West until June and prompted the dispatch, so readers were told, of Brigadier General Gabriil Ivanovich Krotopotov to Iaşi.[17]

Not for another month, until July, did Jeffereys's more accurate dispatches from Bender and Sutton's from Constantinople reach the foreign secretary in London, Henry St. John, the future Lord Bolingbroke. Then the English world learned that it was Cantemir himself who had precipitated Russia's action. Fearful lest loyal Turkish merchants had wind of his duplicity and might have him deposed, he had sent urgent appeals to the tsar to guarantee his throne. The Russian advance guard reached the Moldavian capital in May. Later Cantemir rode out to meet the tsar at Zarancea on the Prut, and in June the two returned to the Moldavian capital, where lavish celebrations were held in an atmosphere of euphoria and optimism.[18]

The news of Cantemir's volte-face, which had an incalculable impact and changed the whole course of the campaign, reached the *Gazette de France* only on July 14. The journal stated without mentioning its source: "Information has it that after Field Marshal [Boris] Sheremetev had advanced to the vicinity of Jassy with half his army, the Hospodar of Moldavia finally decided to ally himself with the Russians. He ordered all the Turks within the capital to be butchered, a fate that also befell the Turks in Bırlad, Vaslui and other cities. After sending Field Marshal Sheremetev all the provisions he could gather from neighboring villages, Cantemir placed himself at the head of 20,000 men and joined the armies of the Tsar"—a gross piece of exaggeration.[19] The same journal reported the tsar's arrival in Iaşi—but only in August through an informant in Hamburg and thus two months after the event and a month after the battle of Stănileşti had been fought. Sutton, the English ambassador in Constantinople, undoubtedly possessed more accurate information when he wrote to his superiors that the Moldavian prince could at most raise 4,000 men.[20] Even after this most of the newspapers persisted in the erroneous report that the Russian army and its Moldavian ally were heading straight toward Isaccea on the Danube.

The West was completely in the dark until several months after the end of the campaign about the diplomatic and military activities of Prince Brâncoveanu. The assumption was that the Wallachian would be faithful to his Ottoman suzerain; only the presence of one of his emissaries, George Castriota, at Iaşi and the defection to the Russians of Hetman Toma Cantacuzino and his cavalry raised a few eyebrows among the more observant.[21] A portentous note that aroused some consternation in Paris and London in August was the news that Brâncoveanu had sought political asylum on Habsburg territory.[22]

Brâncoveanu's decision to play a waiting game, Toma Cantacuzino's defection, and the Ottoman crossing of the Danube were all factors that necessitated a change of strategy in the impending campaign.[23] At a council of war in June attended by all the Russian military commanders and the tsar's Balkan advisers (Vice Chancellor Peter Shafirov, Cantemir and Cantacuzino), the fateful plans were drawn up to divide the Russian force and proceed along the right bank of the River Prut as far Fălciu, below which the Turks were not expected to be able to cross because of the marshy terrain. A crucial part of the operation hinged on the success of General Karl Ewald von Rönne and Toma Cantacuzino, who with a force of eight cavalry regiments (some 12,000 men) were to invest and capture the fortress of Brăila, destroy the Turkish bridge at Isaccea to prevent an Ottoman retreat, and join the main body of the Russian force before the decisive battle was fought.

The earliest detailed account of the military operations which led to the battle of Stănileşti is contained in a lengthy but fairly accurate report written by an anonymous veteran of the campaign under the title *A Journal of the Army of H. M. the Tsar from the 3rd of June to the 28th of July.*[24] It was offered to the readers of the *Mercure historique et politique* in the Hague, and is thus the first authentic historical source for the study of that battle. It had been decided to divide the main Russian army into three separate contingents. One advance cavalry force of 7,000 men, with 500 Moldavians who knew the terain well, was charged with securing Fălciu and preventing a Turkish crossing of the Prut.[25] At two hours' distance would follow the main Russian army with Field Marshal Count Boris Sheremetev, the tsar, his consort Catherine, Shafirov, Cantemir—roughly 15,000 men. Behind them would come the rearguard with the artillery and bombards under the command of General Anikita I. Repnin.

Suprised by a superior Ottoman force at Gura Sărăţii on July 17, and realizing that the Turks and their Tatar allies had already crossed the Prut, General Janus von Eberstadt received permission from Peter to withdraw during the night in an attempt to reach the main Russian force at the mouth of the Pruteţ River.[26] In spite of a sally by some 4,000 Russians and 2,000 Moldavians in support, Janus's army was worsted by an overwhelming Ottoman force the following day (July 18) at Berezeni. When the remains of his force had reached the tsar's camp, orders were given for the whole Russian army to withdraw to the village of Stănileşti which was then fortified *en carré.*[27]

The Turks and their Swedish and Tatar allies thereupon surrounded the village and cut all communications with the outside. In spite of brave efforts made by General Wiedemann to break through the Ottoman ring, the accuracy of the fire of the Russian cannoneers and bombardiers, and the successful repulse of a janissary attack on his eastern flank, the tsar was only too conscious of the weakness of his position because of lack of ammunition and food supplies.[28] Following a council of war, Peter decided to send Vice Chancellor Shafirov and Field Marshal Sheremetev's son to the vizier's camp to seek an armistice. The Turks demanded the surrender of Azov, the Russian fleet, all the territory that Russia had gained since 1700, free passage for Charles XII back to Sweden, and the extradition of Cantemir and Raguzinskiy both of whom the Turks considered traitors.[29] The Russians accepted the terms which permitted the tsar and his army to leave for Iaşi and Poland.[30] Honor was saved by the tsar's refusal to hand over Cantemir, who was smuggled out in a barrel. It was rumored that the tsar had given lavish baksheesh to the grand vizier to obtain the generous terms contained in the Treaty of Fălciu. The only successful aspect of the whole campaign was the capture of Brăila by von Rönne, though the city had to be handed back to the Turks in accordance with the terms of the treaty.[31]

It was a humiliating setback for the tsar's role as emancipator of the Balkan Christians, and there was a sense of deep disillusionment among the leaders of the Orthodox Christians who had welcomed the Russian offensive. Western observers were so certain of a Russian victory that the mere rumor of "a battle near the Dniester" elicited a spate of so-called "news" that either predicted a great Russian victory or spoke of it as a realized fact, even though no one knew the precise circumstances of the battle until October. Thus the *Gazette de France* stated emphatically on July 29 that it had learned from Breslau "that the Turks were totally defeated by the Russians in a battle that lasted from July 22 to 24 and that the Grand Vizier was suing for peace."[32] When finally news was confirmed in Vienna at the beginning of August that the Russians had indeed lost the battle, though the Habsburg court was not too displeased, the Russian defeat hit the editors of the Western periodicals and journals like a bolt from the blue. There was at first disbelief, stupefaction and consternation. The news was all the more difficult to digest or explain away since all the gazettes had predicted a Russian victory, a prediction which in the pitiful words of one commentator "had prepared us for an entirely different result." More surprising are the exaggerated comments of experienced diplomats like Sutton, who greeted the news in one of his dispatches "as one of the most surprising and extraordinary events which has ever occurred."[33] In Constantinople the Turks celebrated the event with salvos of cannon fire.

The French newspaper that published the first details of the Russian debacle was the *Gazette de France* in an issue dated August 30. It based its information on a letter written by General Golovkin from the Russian camp on the Prut to Prince Yakov Dolgoruky, Peter's prime minister. The general admitted, "Although the Russian army proceeded with great speed, it was not able to reach its assigned destination [Fălciu] in time. The Turks overtook it and attacked unexpectedly from all sides. After several engagements lasting three days, the Russians lacking ammunition and provisions were unable to advance or to retreat."[34]

Once the cat was out of the bag, the journals had to find a suitable scapegoat to save face—it would never do to lay the onus of responsibility on their hero, the tsar, whose stature had been built up progressively in the course of the campaign. It was all the fault of his so-called allies, who had betrayed Peter the Great at the last moment: the Tatars, the Serbs, the Montenegrins, and especially Princes Dimitrie Cantemir of Wallachia and Constantin Brąncoveanu of Wallachia.

The argument against Cantemir ran somewhat as follows. The prince had in the first instance been hopelessly imprudent in summoning the Russians when he knew the wretched, impoverished conditions of his province which had been devastated by plagues of locusts, crop failures and unprecedented drought. At the time of the Russian entry into Iaşi, the Moldavian prince apparently knew that he had provisions for only three days in the storehouses of his capital and that the resources of his state were incapable of sustaining a large army. He had moreover deceived the Russians by exaggerating the principality's capacity to raise men in return for the Russian silver that had been spirited away. He had passed on erroneous intelligence to the effect that the main bulk of the Ottoman army would be sent to Azov and had underestimated the numbers of Turkish troops to be deployed on the Danube (50,000 men). It was also alleged that Cantemir was at least in part responsible for the numerous delays that had held up the Russian army and, most seriously, that his selfish desire to secure his throne had fatally vitiated the course of the whole campaign. For reasons such as these, stated the *Gazette de France* in September, "the Hospodar of Moldavia has contributed greatly to the Turkish victory."[35]

Most of these allegations have been disproved over the years by scholarly analysis of genuine historical documents and impartial contemporary narratives. Far from delaying the Russians, Cantemir, who was impetuous by nature, had consistently goaded them on; the prince's Moldavians had fought with courage and intervened successfully at several crucial junctures of the campaign. The tsar's confidence in the Moldavians was so great that he had asked Hetman Neculce to try to smuggle him out of the camp at Stănileşti—a request the wily Moldavian politely declined. Apparently, the Moldavian prince had also warned the Russian high command well in advance of the adverse economic conditions prevailing in Moldavia, one reason why he had supported the offensive on Brăila where supplies had been gathered by Brąncoveanu. Besides, the scorched and desolate condition of the fields between the Dniester and the Prut ought to have given ample warning to the Russians. There can hardly be more eloquent proof of the tsar's satisfaction with his Moldavian ally than that he richly rewarded him on his retirement to Russia with properties at Kharkov and the means to pursue a brilliant scholarly career.

More persistent and serious were the allegations against Brąncoveanu whom some Western journals labeled "traitor."[36] This was due to the fact that, militarily speaking, Wallachia had a far more powerful army of 40,000 men and incomparably richer resources than Moldavia. Brąncoveanu, so ran the argument, had negotiated with the tsar for several years, had been decorated with the Order of St. Andrew, had continued to feign collaboration by sending his envoy Castriota to Iaşi, and had mobilized his army close to the Moldavian border at Urlaţi in return for substantial sums of money from the Russian court. Yet he had consistently maintained channels of communication with the vizier, had disbanded his forces after pocketing the Russians' silver rubles, and had sent provisions destined for the Russians to the Ottoman camp. He had also prevented 15,000 Serbs and Montenegrins from crossing the Danube in support of the tsar.

In its official version of the events of 1711, the *St. Petersburg Zeitung* formally accused Brąncoveanu of being a "traitor." The English, Dutch and French press went along with this interpretation, stating that the tsar made no greater error than to pin his faith on the prince. It would have been asking much of contemporary Western journalists and diplomats to understand the impossible predicament in which Brąncoveanu was placed by Wallachia's exposed geographic position and partial occupation by the Turks. No one could have known that through his representative in Constantinople he was far better informed than any Western ambassador on the true strength of the Turks and the comparative weakness of Russia. No correspondents really knew Brąncoveanu the statesman, a man who pondered every action he took and preferred to maintain a wait-and-see attitude until a Russian army had actually reached the Danube. His appreciation of circumstances proved correct, though it was small consolation and the Russian defeat represented a great personal disappointment. Nevertheless, he continued to correspnd with the tsar until his deposition in 1714 when his whole family was executed.

Only a minority of polemists were willing to place the blame for the Russian defeat squarely where it belonged.[37] One article in the *Gazette de France* dated September 5, 1711, makes mention of natural factors: two years of locust plagues, a severe drought, crop failures, and the torrid climate of Moldavia to which the Russian soldiers were unaccustomed, as well as the losses caused by dysentery which felled a great many soldiers unused to the produce and diet of Moldavia. Diplomats in St. Petersburg, such as Whitworth and his secretary, Weisbrod, focused attention on the tsar's unpreparedness, his underestimation of the Ottoman forces, the overconfidence of the Russian army after Poltava, and its belittlement of the Turks. The lack of accurate information about Ottoman troop movements, the slowness of the Russian advance, tactical and organizational problems within the general staff, the constant division between the tsar's Russian generals and the Germans who had the support of Cantemir, and the splitting of the small Russian force failed to be mentioned as contributing to the Russian defeat. It was however, noted by Sutton, who was a Russophile, that the Russian army still remained intact as a fighting force and that the Russians had suffered far more casualties from malnutrition and disease than from Ottoman fire.

Were all the contemporary commentaries about the campaign on the Prut that were written in western capitals during 1711 and the years immediately following gathered together, they would constitute a hefty tome. From a strictly Rumanian point of view such a book, no matter how biased, would have some interest as the first instance of journalistic reporting from the Rumanian lands, projecting the principalities of Moldavia and Wallachia onto the European scene in the context of the Russo-Ottoman conflict. As an exercise in journalism centering on the Eastern Question, the information provided would bear all the flaws already noted and thus contribute to the deformation of historical truth, serving the ends of generations of romantic biographers such as Voltaire whose mission it was to extol the virtues of the tsar and find scapegoats like Cantemir for Peter's failures. It took over a century for the first eyewitness accounts to be published: the memoirs of Field Marshal Sheremetev, those of Peter Henry Bruce, a British volunteer in Peter's army, the accounts of travelers such as Aubry de la Mottraye, Marsan de Brassey, Ernest de Fabrice and others, which had the essential merit of piecing the facts together. The eyewitnesses on the Rumanian side, such as Ion Neculce, Nicolae Costin (who had fought with Charles XII) and others had to await the great compilations of Nicolae Iorga and Eudoxiu de Hurmuzaki to become available to the historian. In Rumania the task of interpreting such material can be said only to have begun; it has yet to gain acceptance in the wider field of Western scholarship.

## Notes

1. The Russian victory at Poltava was reported in several English newspapers: in *The Daily Courant* on December 29, 1708, and in the *London Gazette* on the same date and on January 3, 1709.

2. For Charles XII's stay at Bender see Ernest de Fabrice, *Anecdotes du séjour du roi de Suède à Bender* (Hamburg, 1760).

3. Among the best studies on Dimitrie Cantemir are I. Minea, *Despre Dimitrie Cantemir, omul, scriitorul, domnitorul*[ On Dimitrie Cantemir, the Man, the Writer, the Prince] (Iaşi, 1926); P. P. Panaitescu, *Dimitrie Cantemir, viaţa şi opera* [Dimitrie Cantemir, Life and Works] (Bucharest, 1958); Scarlat Callimachi, *Demetrius Cantemir* (Bucharest, 1966); A. Duţu and P. Cernovodeanu, *Cantemir, Historian of South East European and Oriental Civilization* (Bucharest, 1973); G. Tocilescu, *Operele lui Dimitrie Cantemir* [The Works of Dimitrie Cantemir] (Bucharest, 1901). On Constantin Brâncoveanu see Nicolae Iorga, *Viaţa şi domnia lui Constantin Vodă Brâncoveanu* [The Life and Reign of Prince Constantin Brâncoveanu] (Bucharest, 1914); Ionescu Gion, *Ludovicu XIV şi Constantin Brâncoveanu:*

Studiu asupra politicei franceze în Europa resăritenă [Louis XIV and Constantin Brâncoveanu: A Study about French Policy in a Resurgent Europe] (Bucharest, 1884); Constantin Șerban, *Constantin Brîncoveanu* (Bucharest, 1969).

4. Among other provisions the Treaty of Lutsk guaranteed Moldavian autonomy under Russia's protection. *Istoria Romîniei* [History of Rumania], III (Bucharest, 1964), 215.

5. An excellent monograph on Anglo-Rumanian relations that covers the period is Ludovic Demeny and Paul Cernovodeanu, *Relațiile politice ale Angliei cu Moldova, Țara Românească și Transilvania în secolele XVI–XVIII* [England's Political Relations with Moldavia, Wallachia and Transylvania in the 16th–18th Centuries] (Bucharest, 1974), pp. 256–270. On Sutton see A. N. Kurat, *The Despatches of Sir Robert Sutton, Ambassador at Constantinople, 1710–1714* (London, 1953).

6. This is why the historian has occasionally to depend on travelers' reports. Among the more interesting travelers during the period of conflict was Aubry de la Mottraye, an Englishman of French origin, who published *Travels through Europe, Asia and into Part of Africa,* Vol. I (London, 1723).

7. Jeffereys's invaluable reports are in Ernst Carlson, *Kapten Jeffereys bref till engelske regeringen fran Bender och Adrianopel 1711–1714 fran Stralsund 1714–15* [Captain Jeffereys's Despatches to the English Government from Bender and Edirne (1711–1714) [and] from Stralsund (1714–15)] (Stockholm 1897).

8. Another English newspaper that published occasional reports from Eastern Europe was *Post Boy*. A good study of English coverage of another crisis in Russian history is Theodore Mackie, *Prince Mazeppa, Hetman of Ukraine, in Contemporary British Publications, 1687–1709* (Chicago, 1967). See also L. Baidaff, "Petru cel Mare la Prut (1711): Documente contemporane" [Peter the Great on the Prut (1711): Contemporary Documents], *Revista istorică: Dari de seamă, documente, notițe* [History Review: Reports, Documents, Notes], XIII, No. 4–6 (April–June 1927), 97–116.

9. *Gazette d'Amsterdam*, March 20, 1711.

10. *Mercure galant*, January 1711, p. 301–2. The report was received from a correspondent in Danzig.

11. Ion Neculce, *Letopisețul Țării Moldovei* [The Chronicle of Moldavia], ed. I. Iordan (Bucharest, 1959), p. 217.

12. *Gazette d'Amsterdam*, February 3, 1711.

13. *Mercure galant*, July 18, 1711, p. 64–7. This information was confirmed by the reports of Capt. Jeffereys, who calculated the total strength of the Russian contingents as they crossed the Dniester at Rascov at no more than 30,000 men. Carlson, *Kapten Jeffereys*, p. 6, doc. 2.

14. In an agreement with Peter the Great, Brâncoveanu had promised to

send an army of 30,000 men to his aid as well as 20,000 Serbian volunteers, perhaps one reason for the small number of Russian troops. Demeny and Cernovodeanu, *Relaţiile politice ale Angliei*, p. 255.

15. *Gazette de France*, June 20, 1711; *Gazette d'Amersterdam*, January 27, 1711. The March 1711 issue of *Mercure galant* described Cantemir as a "descendant of Tartars and a good Swede"—wrong on both counts.

16. *Gazette de France*, June 20, 1711; *Gazette d'Amsterdam*, July 10, 1711.

17. *Lettres historiques* (The Hague), August 1711, XL, 131–5.

18. *Gazette d'Amsterdam*, August 4, 1711, reported: "Moldavia and Wallachia have submitted to H. M. the Tsar. The Emperor has given the Hospodar of Wallachia a considerable sum of money to raise an army in his country, which he has promptly done: 30,000 men have enlisted up to the present, and in three weeks he will have least as many again. At present each soldier receives five gold ducats. Their pay is three écus a month. The Moldavian Hospodar in turn has raised 20,000 Transylvanians and 10,000 Hungarians and Croats." This was a gross exaggeration of the actual numbers but emphasizes the international character of the anti-Ottoman war. A good study of the impact of Cantemir's proclamation of 1711 is Andrei Pippidi, "Politica şi istorie în proclamaţia lui Dimitrie Cantemir din 1711" [Politics and History in Dimitrie Cantemir's Proclamation of 1711], *Studii* [Studies], XXVI (1973), No. 5, 923–940.

19. This information appeared in *Gazette d'Amsterdam*, July 14, 1711, based on a report from Warsaw dated June 30.

20. Kurat, *Despatches of Sir Robert Sutton*, p. 55, doc. 17.

21. "The Hospodar of Wallachia sent Cavalry General the Count de Cantacuzino to meet the Tsar." *Gazette d'Amsterdam*, August 14, 1711. Cantacuzino's defection was first mentioned in a dispatch from Sutton to Lord Dartmouth dated July 6/17, 1711. Kurat, *Despatches of Sir Robert Sutton*, p. 56, doc. 17. See also *Gazette de France*, August 22, 1711; *Mercure historique et politique* (The Hague), September 1711.

22. "The Voivode of Wallachia has asked the Court of Vienna's permission to seek asylum in Transylvania, should circumstances require it. The Austrian government deemed it inappropriate to grant such a request because it might provoke a rupture of relations with Turkey." *Gazette d'Amsterdam*, July 31, 1711. A supplement to the same issue added: "While Vienna has officially refused the request of the Wallachian Hospodar to seek asylum on Transylvanian soil, he has secretly been told that, since he had always been on friendly terms with the Austrian Court, he will be able to enter Transylvania should he feel threatened by the Turks. The Court of Vienna has sent the necessary instructions to General Stainville, Governor of that province, for such an eventuality."

23. The Turks had sent Tatar auxiliaries across the Dniester to harass Russian communications with the Ukraine. Carlson, *Kapten Jeffereys*, pp. 7–8, doc. 3.

24. The pamphlet was offered in *Mercure historique et politique*, October 1711, LI, 381–6. It gave a fairly accurate account of the progress of the campaign on the Prut. Cf. Peter Henry Bruce, *Memoirs of a British Officer in the Service of Prussia, Russia and Great Britain* (Dublin, 1783), and Field Marshal Sheremetev's memoirs published in St. Petersburg in 1898. The latter have been translated into Rumanian by Constantin Şerban: "Jurnalul feldmareşalului B. P. Şeremetev despre campania de la Prut (1711)" [Field Marshal B. P. Sheremetev's Journal about the Prut Campaign (1711)], in *Relaţii romăno-ruse în trecut: Studii şi conferinţe* [Rumanian-Russian Relations in the Past: Studies and Lectures] (Bucharest, 1957), p. 77. See also Neculce, *Letopiseţul;* Dimitrie Cantemir, *Opere* [Works], Vol. III-IV: *Istoria Imperiului otoman* [The History of the Ottoman Empire], trans. I. Hodoş (Bucharest, 1876); S. Callimachi, "Un document inedit din anul 1711 privitor la colaborarea militară romîno-rusă" [An Unpublished Document of 1711 Concerning Rumanian-Russian Military Cooperation], *Studii*, III (1950), No. 3, 178–179.

25. Neculce, *Letopiseţul*, pp. 234–235.

26. Bruce, *Memoirs*, pp. 47–48; Carlson, *Kapten Jeffereys*, pp. 9–10.

27. A. N. Kurat, *Prut seferi ve barısı 1123* [The Prut Campaign and the Peace of 1711], II (Ankara, 1953), 785.

28. Neculce, *Letopiseţul*, pp. 238–239; Cantemir, *Istoria Imperiului otoman*, III, 37–42.

29. The peace terms are discussed in Panaitescu, *Dimitrie Cantemir*, p. 116.

30. Kurat, *Prut seferi*, p. 78. The Russian forces' withdrawal is recalled in Sheremetev's memoirs. Şerban, "Jurnalul," p. 95.

31. The capture of Brăila is mentioned in Sutton's dispatches to Whitworth of August 10/21, 1711, and September 1/12, 1711. Kurat, *Despatches of Sir Robert Sutton*, p. 65, doc. 20, and p. 75, doc. 23. See also Constantin Şerban, "Un episod al campaniei de la Prut, cucerirea Brăilei (1711)" [An Episode in the Prut Campaign, the Conquest of Brăila (1711)], *Studii şi materiale de istorie medie* [Studies and Materials in Medieval History], II (1975), 449–456.

32. *Gazette de France*, August 29, 1711, based on news from a correspondent in Hamburg dated August 14. News of Peter the Great's defeat was not confirmed in Western Europe till September.

33. Kurat, *Despatches of Sir Robert Sutton*, p. 59, doc. 18 (dated July 25/August 5, 1711).

34. Gen. Golovkin's letter appeared in *Gazette de France* and was dated August 20, 1711. *Mercure galant* mentioned that a Russian army of 16,000

men had been all but destroyed.

35. *Gazette de France*, September 5, 1711. Western European attitudes toward Cantemir were ambivalent. Sutton had harsh words; Whitworth was more *nuancé* (see Whitworth's dispatch to Henry St. John of October 2/13, 1711). The British ambassador in Russia blamed Shafirov and Raguzinskiy for the tsar's decision to advance deep into Moldavian territory. As has been correctly pointed out, had Peter held Cantemir responsible for his defeat, he would hardly have granted him political asylum or recompensed him with property in Russia. Neculce, *Letopisețul*, pp. 253–255; Panaitescu, *Dimitrie Cantemir*, pp. 127–128.

36. Sutton places most of the onus for Peter's defeat on Brâncoveanu's putative defection. Kurat, *Despatches of Sir Robert Sutton*, p. 75, doc. 17. So did *Mercure historique et politique*, October 1711, and several other newspapers and journals. None of them showed any understanding of the Wallachian prince's difficult situation or of the grave consequences to which he would be exposed in case of a Russian defeat. As it turned out, Brâncoveanu was deposed and he and his family were all executed by the Turks.

37. Whitworth's secretary Weisbrod, who remained in Moscow throughout the campaign, was far more to the point in blaming the Russian defeat on the small number of Russian troops involved, Peter's underestimation of Ottoman strength, shortage of food and supplies, the intense summer heat, and the dysentery the Russian troops suffered from eating local produce. Demeny and Cernovodeanu, *Relațiile politice ale Angliei*, p. 269.

C.W. Bracewell

# Uskoks in Venetian Dalmatia before the Venetian-Ottoman War of 1714–1718

The Republic of Venice would have been hard pressed to pay a large enough army of mercenaries to fight its land battles in the Turkish wars of the seventeenth and eighteenth centuries. Instead, particularly in Dalmatia, it relied on the local population and on Christians on the Ottoman side of the border to provide the troops it needed. The republic's territorial gains in Dalmatia in the seventeenth century were due largely to the efforts of the Uskoks, refugees from the Ottoman hinterland who flocked into Venetian territory under their own leaders to the benefit of the Lion of St. Mark. But in the war of 1714–1718, unlike the campaigns of the preceding century, the majority of the Uskoks remained passive. This war marked the end of the Uskok phenomenon in Dalmatia. An explanation can be sought in the changes that took place in their military organization and socioeconomic condition as they became a part of Venice's border system.

As the Ottoman border pushed into Dalmatia in the fifteenth century, refugees fled from the Ottoman-held territories to settle on Habsburg or Venetian lands, which were then used as a base for incursions across the frontier. These Uskoks carried on a continual petty guerrilla of raids across the border, directed against both Muslim and Christian subjects of the Grand Turk, pillaging livestock, taking captives, and laying waste to the countryside. Both the Habsburgs and the Venetians incorporated the Uskoks into their systems of border defense.

The Dalmation Uskoks of the seventeenth and eighteenth centuries are known under a variety of names. To the Venetions of this period the term Uskok was reserved for the Uskoks of Senj, whose depredations were still fresh in their memory.[1] The Venetians had no one term to describe the Uskoks who defended their borders. The word they used to denote the peasant and nomadic stockherding population of the hinterland, living outside the confines of the coastal cities and their immediate environs, was Morlach. During the Candian War of 1645–1666 and the Morean War of 1684–1699, when these people flooded into Venetian Dalmatia to take up arms against the Ottomans, the Venetians often used Morlach for the concept of "Uskok."[2] Those along the Makarska littoral they usually called *haiduchi* (haiduks). The Ottomans, in correspondence with the Venetians, use the term Uskok for them.[3] And to the people from whose collective consciousness came the epics celebrating the deeds of these warriors against the Turk they were Uskoks as well.

Since the sixteenth century the militia (*cernide*) had been the main military organization of Venice's *Acquisto vecchio* (old acquisitions) in Dalmatia—the islands, coastal cities, and a narrow strip of coastland from Novigrad to Split.[4] The system required the entire male peasant population between 18 and 50 years of age to serve in the militia, which concentrated on local defense, and to perform corvée for state needs. The first traces of the incorporation of the Uskoks into this system date from the Candian War.[5] During the Morean War this military system was again extended to cope with the influx of large numbers of Uskoks onto Venetian territory and the inland and southward expansion of the borders of Venetian Dalmatia. However, the colonialistic socioeconomic system that had developed in the *Acquisto vecchio* since the Middle Ages was not introduced into these newly acquired lands (*Nuovo acquisto*). Instead the republic proclaimed these territories the property of the state and apportioned them out in individual grants, settling Uskok families there and offering the land as an inducement to further immigration from Ottoman territory. The settlers held the land in permanent possession, with the right of inheritance in the male line, on condition of military service, the payment of a tithe to the state, and performance of corvée for the state. At the same time Venice established a military hierarchy that controlled not only the military but also the civil administration of the area. In this way the republic was able to settle the war-devastated border, forming a military frontier that provided not only a cheap and efficient system of defense and administration, but also a source of income for the state.[6]

The organization of the Venetian border paralleled the border defense system that existed on the Ottoman side of the frontier. Not only was the military-fief system similar, but the Venetians also adopted the same terminology—the titles of *serdaro* or *sardar* (high military commander, from Turkish *serdar*) and *carambassa* (junior military commander, from Turkish *haram başi* [bandit chief]), and even the term *Craina* (from Serbocroat *krajina* [borderland])—for the military frontier as a whole. Interestingly, some Uskok officials on the Venetial marches had held corresponding positions on the other side of the border, not only as popularly chosen leaders but as officials appointed by the Ottomans.[7]

These Uskoks were accustomed to independent guerrilla warfare, fighting in small bands under leaders elected from their own ranks or in certain cases chosen from members of a particular family. Military leadership in these bands was based on demonstrated qualities of skill and heroism. The Venetians accepted and institutionalized this system of small bands, allowing the Uskoks wide autonomy in warfare and in choice of leadership in the Candian War and in the first years of the Morean War. By the outbreak of war in 1714, however, the Venetian authorities had curtailed their independence by regulating their actions and controlling their leaders.

In the constantly turbulent Venetian-Ottoman frontier region, raiding was a way of life on both sides of the border. During times of war, particularly with news of Turkish defeats, the Uskoks stepped up their activities. Groups of men penetrated Ottoman territory, often to a distance of several days' march. Should they encounter enemy troops they would engage them in battle, but they usually did not seek out direct confrontation, preferring ambushes and surprise attacks. These incursions were inspired equally by hatred of their Ottoman rulers and the desire to drive them out, and the Uskoks' desire for plunder. Pavao Šilobadović's chronicle of the numerous small actions on the Makarska littoral between 1662 and 1686 gives a vivid picture of this sort of warfare. "Our troops went to Vrgorac, 400 heroes, plundered, did much damage, fired as many houses as they could, brought back ten people and killed six." "The Zadvarje heroes, 45 people, on their faith as haiduks, plundered what livestock they found in Lukovac, in Šovića and in Gorica and drove them this way across Blato and into Slivno. When they were in Luka, at Budalić's house, the Turks met them there, seized their booty, killed four and took one alive."[8]

Proveditor Domenico Mocenigo's disapproving assessment of the Uskoks as a fighting force in 1684 sums up their guerrilla qualities from the viewpoint of a conventional military leader: "These are coarse and fierce people, incapable of regular military discipline, devoted only to raids and to pillaging, fit for nothing save assaulting people from ambush; suddenly, in great numbers, surprising some area or undefended place and sacking it; and they act inasmuch as they have hopes of certain booty; but should they meet with opposition or conflict, they abandon the undertaking and flee the danger in precipitous escape. They do not want to endure the discomforts of a campaign for more than a few days, nor to be far from their hovels or their herds."[9]

Inasmuch as these Uskok raids did a great deal of damage and drove the enemy back from the border, the Venetians supported them. They reaped a benefit not only from the losses inflicted on the Ottomans but also from the booty the Uskoks brought back, imposing a tax of ten percent on all captives and other plunder.[10] The Venetians encouraged the Uskoks' raids particularly in order to increase immigration onto Venetian territory. The Uskoks would bring entire villages across the border intimidating them with the threat of attack or enticing them with promises of land. This shift of population deprived the Ottomans of a defensive belt of settlement, resettled empty areas on the Venetian side, and provided an increased pool for Uskok recruits.[11]

But, as Mocenigo's remarks indicate, the Venetians did not fully approve of the Uskok methods of warfare. The Uskok guerrilla incursions were not the most efficient means of achieving Venice's military objectives, and had some serious drawbacks. Large Uskok actions, which could involve all the able-bodied men of a district and last more than a week, left the border undefended.[12] Furthermore, the indiscriminate nature of Uskok attacks alienated the Christian subjects of the sultan, hindering Venice's attempts to win them over.[13]

The Venetian authorities tried to limit Uskok independence of action and to introduce control and discipline into their activities. From the beginning of the Morean War the Venetians insisted that any plans to raid Ottoman territory had to be reported in advance and receive approval from the Venetian military commanders. No actions were to take place without the knowledge of the Uskok leaders, and they in turn were responsible for securing permission from the proveditor general, the highest Venetian dignitary in Dalmatia.[14]

A 1690 decree (*terminazione*) to Knin was explicit in this respect: "Under pain of death, let no one dare to enter onto enemy territory in bands of greater or smaller numbers if there exists no general permit for this from the Proveditor General and if the *governatore* and sirdars have not been informed in advance as well." All plunder from unauthorized raids was confiscated by the state.[15]

At the same time as the Venetian authorities were curtailing independent raiding, they were redirecting Uskok energies into regular military operations. Uskok troops, assembled by their leaders, supplemented the mercenaries and other regular forces in all the major Venetian campaigns in Dalmatia in the Morean War. In these operations they fought alongside the regular troops, but in their own bands under their own leaders.[16]

Uskok troops who supplemented the regulars did not at first receive any pay for their participation, though in the case of a successful operation they might be granted a reward. In one such case in 1684 the Uskoks refused the reward, asking instead for regular monthly pay and provisions. This was refused them.[17] In the course of the war, however, they did begin to receive some regular remuneration, for, as Proveditor Valier found in 1685, "it is impossible to keep them in the field for a long time with only hard tack and a few casks of wine."[18] Uskok reinforcements still were less expensive to keep than regulars.[19] In contrast to the rank and file, the Uskok sirdars did receive regular pay for raising troops, as well as rewards for successful actions, though the amounts varied.

Uskoks were also recruited into units of the regular army, where they served with pay equal to that of the other troops. These Uskok forces were organized in two ways: either mingled in units with the regulars or, more usually, raised as separate units, serving under the Uskok leader who had mustered them and who was given the pay of an army officer.

For most of the Morean War Uskok bands continued marauding through Ottoman territory, in spite of Venetian attempts to control them and subject them to military discipline. By the end of the war, however, the main Uskok leaders were deeply involved in raising troops for the regular army, bringing Uskok actions more into line with those of the regular troops, and reducing the degree of the Uskoks' irregular activity.

Before the beginning of the eighteenth century, the republic encouraged a certain amount of autonomy in local administration based on the authority of local leaders. This local autonomy was chaneled through the assemblies (*lighe* or *zborovi*), an institution of customary law that had developed in the *Acquisto vecchio*. The assemblies were made up of heads of household or village headmen who met to discuss matters of common interest and fulfilled a legislative, judicial and police function. Although formal assemblies had become almost defunct in the *Acquisto vecchio*, after the Candian War the Venetians began to introduce the concept into areas where there were concentrations of Uskoks.[20] As the *Craina* took shape during the Morean War, the assemblies were made a part of its administrative system, eliminating the need for an expensive civil bureaucracy. These Uskok assemblies were responsible for maintaining order, for deciding minor disputes, and for seizing bandits, abductors of women, debtors, those who tried to defraud the state of the tithe, and other malefactors. They were also expected to carry out the decrees of the Venetian authorities. Permission for Uskok bands to make incursions into enemy territory was strictly controlled through the assemblies.[21] The authority and activity of the assemblies were carefully regulated by the Venetians. The proveditor set the date and location for meetings, and required that a representative should be present to supervise and report back on all assembly decisions and actions. All leaders of the Uskoks were required to attend on pain of a fine.[22]

As long as the assemblies did not overstep the limits of their authority, they were encouraged by the Venetians, especially in consideration of the fact that assembly decisions were firmly respected by the Uskoks. But the Uskoks espoused the assemblies too enthusiastically, for by 1685 the proveditor general was complaining that the assemblies had "taken more authority than belongs to subjects, and more than can be tolerated".[23] When the Uskoks began to use the assemblies to express dissent and dissatisfaction with the system, "convoking seditious unions not only without permission but in contempt of orders," as Marin Zane complained in 1704, the Venetians dissolved them.[24]

The administrative hierarchy set up by the Venetian authorities included representatives of the Uskoks, the Dalmation urban patriciate and the Venetians. The immediate leaders of the Uskoks, chosen from their ranks, were the *carambasse* and sirdars. These men dealt with local civil affairs, minor judicial matters and military actions, and provided the link between the people and the Venetian government. Over the *carambasse* and sirdars in each administrative district the Venetians appointed *governatori, colonnelli* or *soprain-tendenti* (officers of varying rank not necessarily equivalent to the same rank in the regular army)[25] from prominent Uskoks, Dalmation patricians or Venetian nobles, who were in turn subordinate to the proveditor general.

The Uskok *carambasse* functioned as village headmen and military leaders. In military actions each *carambassa* led a band of anywhere from a handful of men to over 100. As the organization of the *Craina* developed, the *carambasse* were assigned administrative duties by the Venetians. In a decree issued by the Venetian authorities in the course of the Morean War, the *carambasse* were made responsible for collecting the tithe and various fines, seeing that the land was worked properly, keeping order at assemblies, and enforcing assembly decisions. *Carambasse* seldom received a regular salary, except in certain cases as a reward for service, though as an incentive to carry out their administrative duties they were given a percentage of all tithes and fines they collected. The selection of *carambasse* was usually independent of Venetian control, and indeed in the first few years of the Morean War the Venetians stressed the necessity of having the *carambasse* chosen from Uskok ranks. Gradually it became the custom for their election to be confirmed by the proveditor, and in some cases for them to be directly appointed by the proveditor on the recommendation of the sirdars.

The sirdar, the next higher rank, headed a *serdarija,* an administrative unit of 15 to 25 villages, and commanded the *carambasse* and Uskoks of the area. The sirdar was the military commander, administrator and judge for his district, and was expected to report all important matters to the Venetian authorities.[26] The Uskoks in turn expected their elected sirdars to represent their interests in dealings with the Venetians and relay back their responses.

At first, following the migration of a fresh group of Uskoks into Dalmatia, new sirdars were elected according to the Uskoks' customs. The *carambasse* would select a leader by popular acclaim from their own number. In some cases sirdars were traditionally chosen from the members of a single prominent family, but the selection was generally based on fighting record and leadership abilities. As the groups of Uskoks became established in the *Craina* during the Morean War, the proveditor began to arrogate to himself the right to appoint the sirdars. By the beginning of the eighteenth century sirdars were routinely named by the proveditor general and confirmed by the Venetian senate. Not only did the Uskoks lose their role in the selection process, but their commander might not even be chosen from among their own number, but brought in from another area entirely.[27]

The Venetians extended the custom of keeping the office of sirdar in certain families into a general principle, regularly appointing sirdars' sons to official positions, and in many cases going so far as to name minors to the post of sirdar and designating a relative to fill the post until the child reached his majority.[28]

The *governatori, colonnelli* and *sopraintendenti* were originally appointed by the proveditor, but by the beginning of the eighteenth century these posts had often become hereditary. These officials were not intended to represent the Uskoks; rather, each had the "precise and particular duty of holding them in obedience, order and submission, all the other leaders and heads of these same people recognizing him as their superior, respecting and obeying him."[29] In addition to their administrative duties, they gradually took over some of the military functions of the Uskok sirdars and *carambasse*, initiating and directing military actions and raising troops from among the Uskoks for the regular army.

While the Uskoks still chose their immediate leaders themselves, the latter by virtue of their position were not quite like the rank and file. They wielded more authority, were accorded greater respect, and enjoyed certain material advantages. In negotiating the conditions under which they would settle in Venetian territory, Uskok groups frequently requested certain special privileges for their leaders: pay, land, status, and so on. Nonetheless, these leaders were a part of Uskok society. They lived among the other Uskoks, were in constant consultation with other leaders, and constantly had to reaffirm their claim to leadership by their actions.

As the Uskok leaders became a part of the Venetian *Craina* system, a distinct stratification developed in Uskok society, separating the leaders from the rank and file. An appointment to the post of sirdar or any of the superior offices in the *Craina* organization brought the holder prestige and the opportunity for enrichment. The Venetians rewarded loyal service with payments, land grants, and other material benefits. The Venetian practice of making *Craina* offices hereditary led to the accumulation of great wealth in certain favored Uskok families, whose names become associated with the areas that they administered. The Mitrović, Janković and Smiljanić families in Ravni Kotari and Bukovica, the Sinobad family in Knin, the Nakić family in Drniš, the Nonković family in the Neretva valley were all Uskok families distinguished by their power and wealth in the *Craina* system. The financial transactions of these families attest to the considerable sums of money they commanded. Zaviša Janković, for example, paid 8,000 silver ducats to buy half of the island of Olib in 1701.[30]

These prominent leaders increased their incomes by shifting the sphere of their military activities to the regular army, raising units from among the Uskoks and assuming command of them, and then receiving the rank and pay of army officer.[31] Their children, too, entered the regular army as officers. The troops recruited from among the Uskoks and commanded by these leaders were not small guerrilla bands fighting in areas directly across the border, but a part of the regular army and subject to the same regulations and discipline. They were involved in military operations all over Dalmatia and were even sent to fight for Venice abroad. By the end of the Morean War many prominent Uskok leaders were no longer involved in the classical form of Uskok warfare.

This upper echelon moved farther and farther away from the ranks of the Uskoks, becoming assimilated into the ranks of the urban patricians. They would move into the coastal cities, away from the Uskok settlements in the *Acquisto nuovo*, and establish family ties with the patricians.[32] In addition to land, wealth and military positions, many received noble titles from the Venetians.[33]

These changes in the structure and leadership of Uskok society occurred wherever Uskok groups were assimilated into the Venetian *Craina* system, following a similar pattern all along the border. The process did not take place simultaneously throughout the area—rather, it developed as the *Craina* expanded. By the outbreak of war in 1714, most of the Uskok leadership was in Venetian hands, its independence being progressively curtailed as its selection was increasingly controlled by the Venetians. The republic rewarded loyalty by appointments and punished troublemakers by removing them. The sirdars, once the Uskoks' representatives, now beholden to the Venetians for their positions and power, more and more became loyal servants of the Serene Republic.

In contrast to the lands and wealth that service to Venice brought the great Uskok families, by the beginning of the eighteenth century the average household had very little. The obligations owed to the state in return for the use of the land further burdened their situation.

It is difficult to generalize about the amount of land distributed to the average Uskok family between the beginning of the Morean War and the War of 1714–1718. Certainly there were variations from area to area, depending on the nature of the land and the density of the population. Land was parceled out to the Uskoks as they settled on Venetian territory and as new lands were conquered, the size of the allotment being determined by the number of people in the family. The *carambasse* and sirdars usually received larger allotments. As more immigrants flooded into an area, the original grants were often trimmed to make room for the new settlers. The average lot granted to the Uskoks around Sinj during the Morean War was 2 *campi* a head.[34] In Trogir's *Acquisto nuovo* the average holding in 1711 was about the same. In contrast, Sirdar Stjepan Čudin had a property of 76 *campi* in the same area.[35]

Though their holdings might not have been large, by 1714 most of the homeless, landless refugees who had crossed into Dalmatia held some land. Many of them had formerly been stockherders, but the Venetians strove to ensure that the land they dealt out to the immigrants would be put under cultivation, hoping to remedy Dalmatia's chronic shortage of grain. This was constantly echoed in their instructions to the sirdars and *carambasse* and to the assemblies, and indeed, by the early eighteenth century a large part of the population of the *Acquisto nuovo* was engaged in agriculture.

In return for use of the land the state exacted a tithe (*decima*) and corvée. In principle these were for the benefit of the state and were to be used in maintaining the *Craina.* The corvée consisted of personal labor (*fazioni personali*) and the use of the settlers' livestock (*fazioni reali*) in such tasks as building and maintaining roads and fortifications. The tithe, a 1/10 tax on income derived from the use of the land, was introduced in the *Acquisto nuovo* at the beginning of the Morean War. Originally it was payable only on plowed land, but by the end of the war it had been extended to all income from the land (hay, wine, and so on). The Uskoks strongly resisted paying the tithe when it was introduced, and were often able to ignore it with impunity during the turbulent years of the war.[36] In this early period the taxpayer was responsible for transporting his tithe to the state warehouses in Zadar, Skradin, and Šibenik. By 1690 in the Trogir district collection of the tithe was being farmed out. The tax farmer paid a sum to the state for the privilege, and then collected the tithe himself.[37] Tax-farming was also introduced in other areas of the *Craina*. The local leaders were required to assist in the collection of the tithe, whether it was done directly by the state or by a tax-farmer, and received a percentage as a reward. During the Morean War the tithe was paid in kind, as had been the corresponding taxes under the Turks, but by the early years of the eighteenth century it was required to be paid in cash. Other fees and obligations were also introduced, including the duty of keeping horses for military use, and the payment of grazing and milling fees. The collection of the fees was farmed out under the same system as the tithe.[38]

All these obligations were open to abuse by those responsible for enforcing them (the sirdars, and other officers of the border) and many did not hesitate to take advantage of the opportunities the system offered. Some sirdars and higher officers in the *Craina* with large landholdings exploited the corvée to their own benefit, forcing the people of the area to work their land without compensation.[39] Those who acquired the right to collect the tithe or other fees naturally extracted as much as possible in order to increase their profits—sometimes trying to collect the tax even where it was not owed.[40] An observer writing in 1740 was appalled at the injustices inflicted on the population by *Craina* officials in the name of obligations to the state.[41] This was only the culmination of a process begun a half century earlier.

The growing Venetian control over military and social organization, the inequitable system of land distribution, and the burdensome obligations to state and officials all contributed to Uskok dissatisfaction with the situation in the *Acquisto nuovo*. This dissatisfaction was expressed in various ways. There were cases of emigration to Austrian territory, expressly because of the tithe.[42] The Uskoks evaded or resisted the obligations due the state. Protests over the extent of the obligations and their leaders' arbitrary acts multiplied. In the Zadar area, protest and resistance eventually broke into rebellion. In the course of the Candian War Ravni Kotari, Zadar's hinterland, was liberated from the Turks and Uskoks flooded into the Zadar area, as well as into the coastal villages devastated by the hostilities. During the war the Uskoks elected their own village headmen and sirdars, who were confirmed by the proveditor. After the war the Uskoks who had settled on Venetian territory continued to live as they had under the Turks. Many worked land on the Ottoman side of the border, paying to the owners an agreed sum in kind roughly equivalent to the tithe.[43] When news of the defeat of the Ottoman army before Vienna in 1683 reached Dalmatia, the Uskoks around Zadar took up arms against the Turk under their own leaders. In 1684 the Venetians divided these Uskoks into four groups, placing them under the command of two Uskok sirdars, Stojan Janković and Smoljan Smiljanić, and two Zadar patricians, Simon Bortolazzi and Francesco Possedaria.[44] A month later, Bortolazzi, at his own request, was placed in command of the Uskoks of Vrana. The *carambasse* protested, asking that they be allowed to choose a leader from their own ranks, as they had been accustomed to doing under the Ottomans.[45] In a second protest they complained that Bortolazzi "neither wanted to call together the leaders, nor consult with them" as was the custom.[46] In 1686 more complaints were heard about Bortolazzi and Janković. They took the Uskoks' goods, had innocent men killed, and Janković forced the Uskok villagers to plow and sow large tracts of his own land.[47] In 1692 Bortolazzi was murdered by villagers from Biograd, Pakoštane and Vrana, who had agreed to rid themselves of him at a clandestine assembly. Venice took severe measures against the conspirators—the villages were placed under interdict and two of the murderers were drawn and quartered.[48]

In 1704 open rebellion broke out in Zadar over the extent of obligations imposed on the people of the area. The leaders convened an assembly to air their numerous complaints. Uskoks were required to pay for damages done to Ottoman territory by stockherders; the tithe had to be paid in cash, and not only on the fields, but on all other produce; the tithe collectors were ruthless; the corvée was excessive, and villagers were forced to billet cavalry. The assembly tried to rouse the whole *Craina*, issuing a call to the population of Skradin, Drniš, Knin, and Šibenik. The rebels attacked the tithe collectors and those who refused to join the rebellion, burning their houses and seizing their belongings. Seventy village leaders, followed by 7,000 armed rebels, advanced on Zadar and called out the *colonnello* of the Uskoks and the three Uskok sirdars. The rebels presented their demands, "point by point, raising their hands and demanding support from the crowd in roaring voices."[49] When Possedaria proposed that the Uskoks should choose elders to deliver their demands to the proveditor, they refused, replying that the three sirdars were their representatives, and that it was their duty to deliver the demands. Otherwise, the Uskoks would no longer recognize them as their leaders. The sirdars carried the news of the uprising to the proveditor in Split, though not as representatives of the Uskoks, but as worried Venetian officials. The uprising was quickly suppressed before it could spread to other parts of the border. The three main instigators fled to Austrian Lika.[50]

Though open rebellion was the exception rather than the rule, the same general conditions that led to the uprising in the Zadar area existed throughout the *Craina* and contributed to widespread dissatisfaction with the Venetian regime.

When the war of 1714–1718 broke out, Venice issued its usual appeals to the Christian population of the Ottoman territories to join the republic in battle. As in the Candian and Morean wars, Venice relied on the Uskoks to protect its borders and provide the bulk of its fighting strength. But in this war, the Uskok bands ignored the Venetian call to arms and played only a minor military role. The guerrilla incursions into enemy territory on which their military reputations had originally been based all but disappeared. Even the conquest of Imotski and the the news of the fall of Belgrade to the Austrians in 1717 failed to produce the enthusiasm and military fervor that the news of the defeat of the Turks before Vienna had aroused only a generation before. Uskoks participated in the important military campaigns of the war, but as regular troops, in units that had been raised by members of the leading Uskok families, organized and directed by Venetian commanders, not as guerrilla bands. In these operations the Uskoks demonstrated a mercenary quality, fighting half heartedly, and then only after persistent efforts by their leaders and the Venetians to secure their cooperation. Proveditor Angelo Emo complained in 1715 that the Uskoks had demanded payment for fighting in the army, writing that they "will not serve one day under the flag without bread."[51] Even immigration onto Venetian territory nearly ceased, and those few inhabitants who chose to leave the Ottoman border area, already depleted by earlier wars and emigration, and to settle in Venetian (and not Austrian) territory, provided few new Uskok recruits.

The development of the Venetian *Craina* led to the end of the Uskok guerrilla warfare in Dalmatia. By the outbreak of the hostilities in 1714 all Uskok military activity on the *Acquisto nuovo* had been subordinated to Venetian control, and the Uskoks no longer acted as an independent force. While prominent Uskok leaders were still able to raise the Uskoks on the strength of their names and reputations, these troops fought as regulars in the Venetian army, and their targets and their methods of warfare were dictated not by Uskok perceptions, but by the interests of the Venetian high command. The Uskok leaders, wealthy and powerful, pledged their allegiance to Venice, upon whose favor their fortunes now depended, rather than to the Uskoks. The great majority of the Uskoks, separated from their leaders by a social and economic gulf, dissatisfied with their situation in Venetian Dalmatia, saw little point in fighting for Venice unless assured of material recompense. Ironically, it appears that it was precisely the organization of the Venetian *Craina*, brought into being in order to take advantage of the military opportunities offered by the influx of Uskoks, that led to the eventual suffocation of Uskok warfare in Dalmatia.

## Notes

1. See Piero Valier's *relazione* of 1680 in *Commissiones et relationes Venetae*, VII ("Monumenta spectantia historiam Slavorum meridionalium," Vol. LI) (Zagreb, 1977), 62.

2. On the Venetian use of the word Morlach, see G. Novak, "Morlaci (Vlasi) gledani s mletačke strane" [Morlachs (Vlachs) from the Venetian Point of View], *Zbornik za narodni život i običaje* [Papers on Popular Life and Customs], XLV (1971), 579–603. In the 17th and 18th centuries the Venetians used Morlach for the entire peasant population of the hinterland, regardless of any national or religious differences. In the period under discussion, then, the term meant primarily Orthodox but also Catholic Uskoks. Some modern writers have used Morlach and Uskok as synonyms, but this practice is misleading as there were some groups acting as Uskoks in parts of Venetian Dalmatia whom the Venetians never called Morlachs. Furthermore, the use of Morlach tends to create confusion with the ethnic concept of Vlach.

3. B. Desnica, *Istorija Kotarskih uskoka* [History of Local Uskoks] ("Zbornik za istoriju, jezik in književnost srpskog naroda" [Papers on the History, Language and Literature of the Serbian People], Vol. XIII) (Belgrade, 1950–51), I, 285, 323, 335.

4. The term *Acquisto vecchio* (old acquisition) refers to the areas of Dalmatia in Venetian possession after the peace treaty of 1669, which, except for Klis and a few other small areas, the republic had held before the Candian War. *Acquisto nuovo* (new acquisition) refers to those territories gained by the end of the Morean War in 1699.

5. For the origins of *Craina* see L. Jelić, "Lički sandžakat i postanje mletačke krajine početkom kandijskog rata, 1645–48 godine" [The Sanjakate of Lika and the Origin of the Venetian March at the Beginning of the Candian War, 1645–48], *Narodni koledar za 1898* [National Almanac for 1898] (Zadar, 1898), pp. 78–115. The Herzegovinian and Montenegrin haiduks (or Uskoks) played a similar role in the Venetian expansion around Boka Kotorska. See G. Stanojević, *Jugoslovenske zemlje u mletačko-turskim ratovima* [The South Slav Lands during the Venetian-Turkish Wars] (Belgrade, 1970). Events there, however, are outside the present scope.

6. The Venetian authorities appear never to have issued comprehensive legislation defining the organization of the frontier system. Its legal basis, administration and territorial divisions were established piecemeal in a series of *terminazioni* issued by the proveditor general with each expansion of the border. Zadar Historical Archive, Papers of G. Cornaro, Proveditor General (1686–89), I. 540 (Zadar, 1689), 542 (Šibenik, 1689), 545 (Trogir, 1689). A. Molino's *terminazione* for Knin (1690) is summarized in I. Grgić, "Postanak i početno uredjenje vojne krajine kninskog kotara pod Venecijom" [Origin and Initial Arrangements of the Military Border of the District of Knin under Venice], *Starine JAZU* [The Past: Y(ugoslov) A(cademy of) S(ciences and) A(rts)], LII (1962), 260–262.

7. Jelić, "Lički sandžakat," pp. 95–99; T. Macan, "Iz povijesti donjeg Poneretavlja potkraj XVII i na početku XVIII stoljeća" [From the Records of the Lower Neretva Valley at the End of the 17th and Beginning of the 18th Century], *Historijski zbornik* [Historical Papers], XXI–XXIII (1968–69), 200.

8. S. Zlatović, "Kronika O. Pavla Šilobadović o četovanju u Primorju, 1662–86" [Father Pavao Šilobadović's Chronicle of the Guerrilla on the Coast, 1662–86], *Starine JAZU*, XXI (1889), 110, 115.

9. Desnica, *Istorija*, II, 19.

10. *Ibid.*, 52, 112, 114.

11. Grgić, "Postanak," pp. 257–259; Macan, "Iz povijesti," pp. 205–208.

12. Desnica, *Istorija*, III, 222–223.

13. *Ibid.*, I, 319–320, 333–334.

14. *Ibid.*, II, 7, 173, 221–222, 322–324; also Molino's *terminazione* (*v.* n. 6).

15. Grgić, "Postanak," p. 262.

16. Gligor Stanojević, *Dalmacija u doba morejskog rata*[ Dalmatia at the Time of the Morean War] (Belgrade, 1962), pp. 61–78.

17. Desnica, *Istorija*, II, 15–16.

18. *Ibid.*, p. 90.

19. *Ibid.*, p. 61.

20. I. Grgić, "O ligama i osobama" [About Assemblies and People], *Zadarska revija* [Zadar Review], III, No. 3 (1954), 1–15.

21. *Ibid.*, pp. 6–7, 12–13; Desnica, *Istorija*, II, 7, 322–324.

22. See, for example, *ibid.*, II, 222–223.
23. Grgić, "Postanak," p. 251.
24. Desnica, *Istorija*, II, 388.
25. Grgić, "Postanak," pp. 252–253.
26. Desnica, *Istorija*, II, 270–271, where in 1690 A. Molino set out the sirdars' duties in detail. The sirdars were instructed to run local administration "according to the customs and ancient institutions of the country."
27. Jovan Sinobad, for example, was appointed to head the Knin-Vrlika sirdarship in 1692 even though he was from Bukovica. *Ibid.*, p. 266. The Venetians did take care to select leaders of the same religion as the local Uskoks.
28. *Ibid.*, 369–370, 371, 403, for the process by which Ilija, Zaviša Janković's young son, was made sirdar of Gornji Kotari.
29. *Ibid.*, 376.
30. *Ibid.*, 366.
31. An example is in *ibid.* 354—a proposal from four leaders of the Zadar *craina* to recruit cavalry units from among the Uskoks, and requesting pay as cavalry captains in addition to what they were already receiving.
32. *Ibid.*, 147.
33. *Ibid.*, 325, 392.
34. J. Soldo, "Zemljoposjed porodice Lovrić iz Sinja u XVIII st." [Landholdings of the Lovrić Family of Sinj in the 18th Century], *Radovi JAZU u Zadru* [Transactions of the Y(ugoslav) A(cademy of) S(iences and) A(rts) in Zadar], XIX (1972), 296. A *campo padovano* equals 0.9 acre (3,656 square meters).
35. V. Omašić, "Katastik trogirskoga dijela 'nove stečevine' iz 1711 godine" [The Land Register of the Trogir Area of the 'Nuovo Acquisto' from 1711], *Izdanje Historijskog arhiva u Splitu* [Publications of the Historical Archives in Split], VII (1974), 226, 228–229.
36. Desnica, *Istorija*, II, 226, 228–229.
37. Zadar Historical Archive, Papers of A. Molino, Proveditor General (1689–92), II, 417.
38. Desnica, *Istorija*, II, 380.
39. *Ibid.*, 172, 318.
40. *Ibid.*, 134–135, 358, 361–362.
41. J. Tomić, "Memorijal Frančeska Borelli" [The Francesco Borelli Memorandum], *Spomenik SAN* [S(erbian) A(cademy of) S(ciences) Memorial], XLVII, 73.
42. Desnica, *Istorija*, II, 263.
43. S. M. Traljić, "Tursko-mletačko susjedstvo" [Turkish-Venetian Proximity], *Radovi JAZU u Zadru*, IV–V, 411.
44. Desnica, *Istorija*, I, 336–337.
45. *Ibid.*, II, 44–45.

46. *Ibid.*, 45–46.
47. *Ibid.*, 134–135.
48. *Ibid.*, 274, 275–278.
49. *Ibid.*, 381.
50. *Ibid.*, 379–384, 386–387, 388–389.
51. G. Stanojević, "Dalmacija za vreme mletačko-turskog rata 1714–1718 godine" [Dalmatia during the Venetian-Turkish War of 1714–1718], *Istorijski glasnik* [Historical Herald], Nos. 1–4, 1962, pp. 11–49. For the war as a whole, see A. Bernardy, *L'ultima guerra turco-veneziana, 1714–1718* (Florence, 1902).

# VI

# The Cossacks and Warfare

Philip Longworth

# Transformations in Cossackdom: Technological and Organizational Aspects of Military Change, 1650–1850[1]

Tracing the technological and organizational aspects of Cossack history is a peculiarly difficult task for the historian. Despite the wide measure of similarity in the nature and development of the various Cossack communities from the mid seventeenth to the early nineteenth century, there were also significant variations due to uneven population growths, different strategic locations and other factors. These make generalizations dangerous and comparisons hazardous. There are also problems with sources. Literacy levels, even among the Cossack elite, were low. Furthermore, since the communities tried jealously to protect their traditions and their ways of life against encroachments by the imperial Russian government, even as late as the early nineteenth century the Ministry of War, according to Prince Vyazemskiy, could place no reliance on the reported number of Cossacks liable for service.[2] Such factors make for a scarcity of hard evidence. Finally, difficulty arises from the fact that Cossack weaponry was not standardized during this period, and that their institutions were rudimentary and largely informal.

Notwithstanding the difficulties, however, it is possible to outline the salient characteristics and trends by relating scattered fragments of evidence (whether emanating from the Cossacks themselves, from Russian governmental records, memoir material, or the observations of travelers passing through the Cossack lands) and what is known of the general context and surrounding circumstances.

Some intriguing paradoxes emerge: Cossack forces throughout the period reflected the technologically "backward," nonindustrial nature of their societies, yet they continued to serve certain military purposes extremely well; although capable of bringing the Cossack hosts under its full control, the modernizing, militaristic Russian state was slow to do so; and it proved to be strangely loath to introduce modern armaments to the Cossack forces and impose rational organization on them.

The present purpose is to explain these paradoxes in the course of describing the characteristics of the Cossacks' technology, more particularly of their arms and equipment, and of their military organization, and the changes to which they were subjected. First to be considered are their technology and the implications of its backwardness; then the question of military organization, although the two areas are interlinked.

Like all technologically backward societies, the Cossack communities imported most of their weaponry. Furthermore, since arms of up-to-date design tended to be scarce, they continued to use weapons of antique design or manufacture alongside the new throughout the period under consideration. Cossack armaments therefore constituted a miscellany of the modern and the ancient, which both reflects the peculiar nature of their military activity and illustrates the uneven impact of "progress" in the history of such frontier regions, in East Central Europe no less than elsewhere.

The proportions of modern to antiquated weapons in use in any one community is virtually impossible to establish for any given moment in time. The appearance of new weapons and the origins of some older models can be traced with some accuracy, however. From the very beginnings of their recorded existence, the Cossack communities used weapons and weapon designs that derived from their parent cultures, notably Tatar, Russian and Ukrainian, or which had been borrowed from neighboring societies through trans-frontier trade and culture contacts.[3] Hence the seven-foot, iron-tipped lances, the Tatar-type sabers and even the bows and arrows used along with more modern weapons such as carbines and pistols by the Don Cossacks in the eighteenth century;[4] the long bow still employed by the Ural Cossacks at that time,[5] the design of which corresponded closely to that of their neighbors, the Kazakhs;[6] the Turkish, Caucasian and Persian weapons, especially cold arms, used by Cossacks throughout the period; and the unwieldy ten-foot lances, Turkish and Circassian sabers, poniards and even spears carried along with carbines and pistols by the Black Sea Cossacks at the beginning of the nineteenth century.[7]

The Cossacks were always dependent on outside sources for military matériel, more particularly firearms, cannon and ammunition. War booty was one important means of acquiring these (thirty cannon were taken from the Turks in 1646, for example),[8] though an essentially uncertain one, and by the middle of the seventeenth century the Russian government had become the major source of supply for these items as well as such others as grain, cloth, banners and Bibles.

This dependence reflected the communities' economic backwardness. Societies that began to develop agriculture only toward the end of the seventeenth century (as the Don Cossacks) or during the eighteenth (as the Zaporozhe Cossacks) lacked the prerequisites for any sort of industrial enterprise beyond the artisan's workshop (and artisans were few even in the Don capital, Cherkassk, at the end of the eighteenth century),[9] still less the capacity to cast cannon and manufacture firearms. It is true that the necessary raw materials, notably coal and iron deposits, were present in or near some Cossack territories, but they were not exploited, a fact that may well explain why, outside the Ukraine, Cossack horses went unshod and why most of their riders never used spurs or bit. Some of the requisite metalworking skills were probably available. The case of two Cossacks arrested on the Don in 1749 for forging coins suggests as much.[10] Furthermore, the Russian government apparently assumed that the Don Cossacks were capable of maintaining their artillery and even of repairing and recasting faulty cannon.[11] On the other hand, evidence from the 1760s indicates that in fact they could repair only the wooden gun carriages, not the guns themselves; when charged in 1769 with the construction of gun carriages, they had to engage non-Cossack craftsmen to carry out the tasks.[12] The Zaporozhe Cossacks could manufacture gunpowder, but it was of poor quality, and they tended to meet their requirements in exceess of official supplies by purchases from the Ukraine and Poland.[13]

Throughout the period, then, the Russian imperial government supplied the Cossacks with the bulk of their ammunition requirements (powder, lead and iron), varying the quantities in accordance with the incidence and location of wars in which the Cossacks' services were required. Thus in 1706, during the Great Northern War, the Don Cossacks received nearly half a ton of powder and almost two of lead, as well as three hundredweight of iron;[14] in 1737, during an offensive against the Turks and Tatars in the south, the supplies included three and three-quarter tons of artillery powder and nearly two and half tons of lead.[15] The state was cautious, however, in furnishing the Cossacks with artillery itself.

The Zaporozhe Cossacks had accumulated an assortment of cannon and mortars over the decades, and the Don Cossacks also possessed some guns of their own. However, precise evidence on the subject is scanty. In 1673, when 1,200 cannonballs were supplied to them for use in campaign against the Turks, it was reported that there were forty-eight guns of various calibers at Cherkassk.[16] It is known that by the 1730s the Don Cossacks' artillery was considered inadequate to defend the territory, for in 1738 they were allotted sixty-seven guns together with ball shot, some of them to be stationed at vulnerable settlements at the mouth of the River Khoper, the remainder to be used in action against the Turk. In sending these guns, however, the imperial government demanded the return of some falconets to its gun-park in Azov. In 1740, presumably the same sixty-seven guns were still at Cherkassk and the Cossacks were permitted to keep them, provided they maintained them in good condition. They were ordered to surrender twelve bronze cannon to the nearby imperial fort of St. Anna, however, and the Don hetman was enjoined to have all his host's guns inspected and to report which were needed and which were not.[17] It seems safe to conclude, then, that the technological backwardness of the Cossack communities forced them into dependence on the Russian government for artillery, and then to cede control of it to the state.

Such artillery as the Don Cossacks were suffered to retain appears to have been obsolescent by the standards prevailing in Northern and Central Europe, for as early as 1766 the imperial government deliberated long and hard whether the host's old artillery should be exchanged for new. The upshot was an order to cast twenty-four bronze cannon for them in the Moscow arsenal.[18] Nevertheless in the years that followed a further deterioration set in both in the guns themselves and in the Don Cossacks' capacity to use them. Six out of thirty bronze three-pounders, used as horse artillery rather than for settlement defense, were found to be faulty; furthermore, Cossacks were found to be unable to use the serviceable ones efficiently and had to be retrained for the purpose.[19]

During the eighteenth century, then, the imperial government monopolized the supply of artillery, and it exercised its monopoly with caution. This caution was fed by fear that the Cossacks might some day turn these weapons against the state. However, more mundane cost-benefit considerations also prompted the state to limit and control the supply of heavy or up-to-date weapons to the Cossacks. So long as the hosts were engaged in combat against frontier peoples exclusively, they had little need for such weapons. The technology of frontier warfare, after all, saw little change until the nineteenth century. Cold arms and antiquated firearms were adequate for sporadic skirmishes against Nogais, Kazakhs, Bashkirs, or the tribesmen of the Caucasus.[20]

The case altered, however, when Cossacks had to confront better-equipped Ottoman forces or were required to participate in actions against modernized Western armies, or when British agents began to run more up-to-date arms to the warrior tribes of the Caucasus in the 1830s.[21] On the other hand, since the regular imperial forces came to play the principal fighting roles in such encounters, the modernization of the Cossacks' weaponry was not perceived to be as pressing a consideration as might otherwise have been the case.

The question of the standard of the individual Cossack's arms when he turned out for service with the imperial armies was more serious. Simple shortages of arms was one cause of the problem; the lack of standardization consequent upon the Cossacks providing their own equipment was another. An inspection of Ural Cossack servicemen carried out in 1745 revealed that only one man in twenty had a saber.[22] Toward the end of the century their arms were reported to be of good quality, but they were not standard.[23] Furthermore, Cossacks themselves often valued their weapons as much for their decorative and ancestral associations as for their efficiency. This cultural factor in itself served to reinforce the technological lag in armaments, but population growth was another, perhaps more important, internal factor tending to lower the standard of the individual Cossack's equipment. For all the unrealiability of statistics already referred to, it seems that the Cossack population of the Don increased by a factor of about seven during the eighteenth century from some 30,000 to approximately 200,000 males.[24] The provision of weapons did not keep pace, and a growing proportion of Cossacks became unable to afford the expense of fitting themselves out for service—so much so that the state was finally persuaded to intervene both by providing efficient weapons and ultimately by taking indirect steps to ensure that the rank and file were able to afford to buy satisfactory arms for themselves by attempting to stem their creeping impoverishment.

So many Don Cossacks called out in 1737 to serve under Field Marshal Count Burkhard Münnich against the Turks were found to lack firearms altogether that the imperial government had to provide them with 3,133 carbines from its arsenals at Reval and Riga. The carbines were of Swedish manufacture, however, and probably dated from the time of the Great Northern War fought twenty and more years before.[25] A register of firearms drawn up on the Don in 1812 confirmed a continuing, indeed accentuated, deterioration. Cossacks reporting for service that year carried weapons of various calibers, even including matchlocks, which persuaded the Don hetman to buy in a quantity of standard firearms from the state factory at Tula.[26] Large numbers of them were found to be too poor to equip themselves for service at all, even though price controls had been imposed on the sale of firearms.[27]

The trend continued. As late as the Crimean War, Cossack firearms were found to be even worse than the generally poor muskets carried by the Caucasian Line regulars. Indeed, most of them had to be assembled from an assortment of parts of various manufacture, some dating back fifty years or more. The fact that some such weapons sold at only one-seventh the price of a new musket gives an indication of their probable efficiency. Many were probably dangerous to use; others did not work at all.[28]

So far as armaments are concerned, then, Cossack history presents a pattern of relative backwardness or obsolescence which tended to deepen toward the east, and to deepen also with the passage of time. Yet although the Cossack communities had no capacity to manufacture their own armaments and used an ever-increasing proportion of obsolescent and even antiquated weapons, there was one sector, more especially in the first half of the period, in which the Cossacks were more advanced technologically than any of their neighbors—the building of light marine craft. Indeed, by contrast to the pattern of technological loan from north to south and from west to east that is apparent in the field of land warfare, in the naval sphere, where timber rather than metal was the basic material for construction, a pattern is discernible of technological loan from south to north—from more primitive societies to more sophisticated ones. Furthermore, this generalization holds good not only for the Cossack territories but also for the rest of East Central Europe.

It is exemplified by the Cossack *chaika* (seagull), a small but highly effective vessel employed by the Zaporozhe Cossacks and described in some detail by Pierre Chevalier in the seventeenth century.[29] About sixty feet in length and twelve in beam and draft, the *chaika* stood very low in the water and had to be buoyed up with bundles of reeds. Though equipped with sail, in action it was propelled by oars. Steered by rudders in the prow and stern, it carried up to sixty men and two guns. Reflecting both the traditional designs in use throughout the Mediterranean world and a good deal of ingenious improvisation, such craft were highly maneuverable, could enter shallows where larger ships would run aground, and could cross the Black Sea to Turkish Anatolia in less than forty hours. A flotilla of such boats proved ideal for seaborne raiding and was capable of sinking sizable, more cumbrous ships, as happened on Stenka Razin's Caspian campaign in the 1670s.

Contemporaries compared such craft to the vessels used by the notorious Senj Uskoks[30] who preyed on shipping in the Adriatic in the sixteenth and early seventeenth centuries, and presented very serious problems for the much-vaunted Venetian war galleys that policed the sea.[31] It is hardly surprising, then, that such craft came to be regarded as the best available for certain kinds of waterborne operations, notably on rivers and in shallow seas such as the Baltic. In 1628 Imperial General Prince Albrecht von Wallenstein had recruited Uskoks as the best experts to build a fleet for use against the Danes,[32] and in 1660 the Muscovite state armory employed Cossack craftsmen to construct flotillas of such "seagoing" vessels both near Voronezh in the south and near Dorogobuzh in the west.[33] The adoption by Russia of marine technology from the south continued into the eighteenth century, despite the increasing employment of Dutch, English, Swedish, Danish and Venetian masters.[34] Peter the Great engaged the Dalmatian Greek, Botsis, for the construction of his Baltic galley fleet;[35] Don Cossacks were again employed to build 110 boats for the Ottoman campaign of 1737,[36] and the double sloops or *scheers* much used in that war also reflected Cossack style in that they were of shallow draft and were propelled by soldiers rather than by gangs of specialist oarsmen.[37] Thereafter, however, although the ex-Zaporozhe Black Sea Cossacks were still using *chaiky* in the 1790s,[38] the style fell out of favor for all but small-scale frontier engagements.

Cossack military organization in the seventeenth century was primitive. True, the Ukrainians had a skeletal military structure in that Cossacks were grouped territorially in "regiments," but these served civil, administrative functions as much as military ones.[39] On the Zaporozhe Sich Cossacks were divided among "barracks" *(kureni)*, each containing between two hundred and five hundred men and boys. Elsewhere the grouping was by settlement and there was no identifiable structure to the Cossack forces. In short, though all the Cossack hosts possessed rudimentary hierarchies of elected commanders—campaign hetmans, "elders," captains *(esauly)*, lieutenants *(sotniky)*, and a field secretary *(pokhodnyi pisar')*, they had barely emerged from the war-band stage in terms of organization.

Even when the concept of the regiment emerged, as it did on the Don in the eighteenth century, it was not associated with any notion of a standard complement. A regiment might consist of five hundred or seven hundred men, and even the Cossack "hundred" belied its name. Furthermore, mobilizations continued to be carried out on an *ad hoc* basis and, to judge by the remuneration of Don Cossack officers on campaign in the first quarter of the century, distinction between ranks was small.[40]

It must be borne in mind, however, that the Russian army had itself only recently undergone a change from a "feudal" structure to a structure modeled on regular, Western lines. It was Tsar Aleksey Mikhailovich (1645–1676) who laid the foundations of a permanent standing army organized and trained "according to the rules of military science."[41] Yet "new formation troops" constituted only one-fifth of his army's strength in the middle of the century; and amorphous crowds of Cossacks constituted the bulk of the estimated 106,000 regulars available at that time.[42] The modernization of the Russian army, that is, its regularization, professionalization, equipment with modern arms, and training in up-to-date and principally German methods, was not completed until early in the eighteenth century.[43] It was only subsequently that the Cossack forces experienced any significant degree of regularization, and then the change was fitful in implementation and uneven in its effects, reflecting muddle both on the part of central government and of the host administrations.

The transformation came soonest and most completely in the Ukraine with the effective abolition of the Cossack system obtaining there. Registration was discontinued in 1699, and so was the hetmanate itself in 1734, though it was subsequently revived for Kiril, the brother of Tsarina Elizabeth's favorite Aleksey Razumovskiy.

The territorial regimental system in the Slobodskaia Ukraina, modeled on that of the Ukraine proper, was also transformed early in the eighteenth century and the Cossacks eventually formed into regular hussar regiments. The Zaporozhe, Don, Ural and remaining Cossack hosts, though never fully absorbed into the imperial system, experienced significant changes in military organization designed to fit them better to the specific purposes for which the state required them.

The developments took place against a background of wars in which Cossacks had to campaign ever farther away from home and for increasing lengths of time. In these circumstances the state wanted greater reliability, and hence better organization, from the Cossack contingents, not merely numbers as before. It was by these criteria that the Ukrainian Cossacks[44] came to be reckoned to be virtually useless by the 1730s. As General Manstein recalled, the 22,000 Ukrainians who had participated in the Ottoman War of 1736–1737 had been no good "for anything but to augment the number of . . . troops. . . . In the last campaign they scarce did any other service than that of bringing wagons of provisions to the army."[45] By contrast, the Don Cossacks and those of other hosts continued to be valued both for their flexibility on campaign[46] and as reservoirs from which to recruit the necessary manpower for the new Cossack communities to police the Russian Empire's extending frontiers (for instance, the Orenburg, Astrakhan and Mozdok Cossacks). Nevertheless, their organizational norms were changed quite significantly. Complements were to become, at least in theory, fixed; officers came to be appointed rather than elected; the ranking system was aligned with that of the imperial Russian cavalry; pay was more highly differentiated,[47] and controls were established over promotions, retirements and terms of service. Each of these aspects merits some attention.

As late as 1735 there was no fixed complement for the Don Cossack forces, whose wartime strength was in the region of twelve to fifteen thousand men.[48] A government mobilization order issued to them that year was couched in the vaguest terms, the host authorities being enjoined simply to raise "as many Cossacks as possible from the upriver settlements" to serve under General Count von Weissbach, commander of the Ukrainian Division.[49] By contrast, in March 1763, when Hetman Yefremov of the Don received orders to call Cossacks to the colors to serve the following year at Smolensk and on the Courland frontier, they were quite specific about numbers and organization: eight regiments, each five hundred strong, were to be raised.[50] Furthermore, regiments were grouped into divisions.[51] The size of a regiment remained stable until 1802 when it was raised to 578 men.[52] By 1805 the Don host had a wartime obligation to raise seventy-two regiments, each of five squadrons, in addition to three guards regiments, each one thousand men strong.[53] By that time the Black Sea Cossacks could mobilize ten regiments each of cavalry and infantry, the Ural host ten cavalry regiments, and the Terek, Bug and Orenburg Cossacks between one and four regiments apiece, although the Siberian Cossacks and some of the smaller communities were still obliged to furnish only a stipulated number of men.[54]

Officer establishments were introduced during the eighteenth century, and measures were taken by the imperial government to control the appointment of officers, their promotion and retirement. The contrast between the terms on which the Volga Cossack host and the Black Sea Cossack host were set up in 1734 and the 1790s, respectively, is instructive in this respect. The thousand Don Cossacks sent to form the Volga community were allowed to elect their officers (elders) other than the hetman himself, and in order to prevent the proliferation of elders, as was happening on the Don, rank conferred on the elected elders was not considered permanent.[55] By contrast, when the Black Sea host was formed only local headmen were to be elected by the rank and file. The colonels and other senior officers, like the hetman himself, were to be appointed and the ranks were permanent.[56] In 1738, as part of the process by which the state sought to control the Cossack communities by buying the loyalty of their elites with priviliges, Hetman Danilo Yefremov of the Don and two elders of the host were commissioned brigadiers in the imperial army.[57] By the middle of the century it had become customary to grant Don hetmans general rank, while campaign hetmans came to be appointed majors general. The alignment of Cossack ranks with ranks in the imperial army continued to creep downwards through the hierarchy until in 1798 Tsar Paul I recognized all Cossack officers as officers within the imperial system, and consequently members of the Russian nobility. Thus "elders" became majors, *esauly* captains, *sotniki* lieutenants, and *khorunzhie* (standard-bearers) cornets, and were paid the same rates as regular officers whenever they served sixty miles or more beyond the borders of the territory of their host. By 1800 a standard regimental establishment of a colonel, two majors, five captains (squadron commanders), five lieutenants and five cornets had been laid down;[58] and by 1802 the total Don Cossack officer establishment (those, that is, who were available for active service) consisted of fiteen generals, 177 staff officers (majors and colonels) and 902 junior officers.[59] In that year an establishment of ten noncommissioned officers was fixed for each regiment.[60]

Nevertheless, these changes had been prompted as much by political as by military considerations. Parities with the regular officer corps did not necessarily reflect parity in military competence, and the authorities knew it. Hence their initial reluctance to grant equivalent imperial ranks to Cossacks as a matter of routine, and their continued fear that the quality of the Cossack officer corps, such as it was, might become diluted. Its caution is exemplified by a case in 1764 when, in granting permission to the newly promoted Major General Krasnoschchekov to appoint an aide *(esaul)*, the state insisted that the officer should not be referred to as adjutant, the regular army designation, until he had satisfactorily completed a period of probation.[61] The same year the government demanded lists of Cossack officers, scrutinized lists of those retired from duty, questioned the reasons for such retirements, and ordered the hetman to grant no more without the College of the War's sanction.[62] It also took measures to prevent the practice that had grown up by which the sons of Cossacks officers were promoted virtually automatically to the ranks that their fathers held.[63] Nevertheless, the measures were apparently of little effect. Certainly the inclusion of children in the lists in order that they should have gained commissioned rank by the time they actually began to serve, a practice that had been widespread in the regular officer corps in the middle of the eighteenth century, was still "a frequent abuse" on the Don early in the nineteenth century.[64] Stricter control over promotions to commissioned rank, stressing "capacity for service and worth," backed up by demotions, was introduced shortly after Paul's death in 1801, and thenceforth colonels were appointed by the crown rather than by the host authorities.[65]

As for the terms of service, Cossacks were liable from the age of fifteen to fifty, and had to provide their clothing, arms and mounts at their own expense.[66] Despite the injunction made as early as 1763 that no "hired men" should be included in the numbers raised on the

Don,[67] the practice continued, however. It was not actually banned in the Black Sea (later Kuban) Cossack host until 1820. Elsewhere the regulations on substitution varied, and continued to be evaded or ignored.

The question of substitution was intimately bound up with the problem of maintaining minimum standards in the arms and equipment of the Cossack units. The ability of these units to carry out even their limited active-service roles as scouts and skirmishers was already being questioned on these grounds before the Napoleonic Wars, and the matter presumbably became more pressing when in 1801 the Military Commission decided that "when need arises, the cavalry may immediately be supplemented by Cossacks and other irregular forces."[68] Yet with the cost of equipment (clothing, carbine, saber, pistol, lance, mount and saddle) rising above 200 rubles,[69] the numbers of men prepared to serve as substitutes or who could not afford to serve at all continued to increase. Indeed, increasing poverty among the Cossack rank and file soon threatened to reduce the numbers available for service to a point where the fixed complements of service units could not be met, and the matter then became one of very sharp concern to the imperial Russian authorities.

At first they tried to rectify the problem by resorting to interventionist economic measures designed both to protect the Cossack rank and file and to stop the elite arrogating further economic privileges to themselves. In particular, the state began to question the basis on which the host authorities distributed land, for land was the basis of the individual Cossack's ability to arm and equip himself for service. However, it was not until 1819 that a special commission, including a representative of the Justice Department and one from the War Department, was set up and given a wide brief to reform the administration of the Don host.[70] The outcome was a radical reform program implemented in 1835.

The host's conduct of business was indeed found to be so disorderly that the host chancery was abolished altogether[71] and the host hetman, now appointed from St. Petersburg and answerable to the Ministry of War, was given the powers of a provincial governor. Measures were also introduced to ensure that Cossacks liable for service were capable of meeting their obligation, to enforce strict fulfillment of complements, to stop the proliferation of officers, and to guarantee their competence under threat of compulsory retirement.[72]

Finally, to ensure that the rules of service were adhered to, the first printed order book for the Don forces was issued in 1836.[73] One measure of the success of these reforms is that between 1819 and 1842 the number of Cossack servicemen, including noncommissioned officers, almost doubled from 70,810 to 134,742 while the number of officers was held stable at under 2,700.[74]

By the early 1850s all the ten Cossack hosts then in existence had fixed establishments for both peacetime and wartime service. The Don Cossacks furnished thirty-four cavalry regiments and four and a half artillery batteries in peacetime, fifty-eight regiments in war.[75] Establishments had also been laid down for the recently formed Caucasian Line Cossacks: twelve regiments of cavalry and nine of infantry *(plastuny)*, plus three horse artillery batteries. Each regiment, made up of six squadrons or companies 140 men strong, was supported by a population of between 12,000 and 15,000, and every officer and man was allotted a landholding reckoned sufficient for his maintenance (at least eighty acres per Cossack and from 540 to 1,620 per officer depending on his rank).[76] The affairs and obligations of the other hosts[77] were also strictly defined with some variations according to population, land availability, proximity to the frontier and, to some extent, local tradition; service liabilities were fixed; and Cossacks now wore uniforms.[78]

By the end of the period under consideration a significant degree of regularization and regimentation had at last been enforced. The inchoate mobilization and command systems characteristic of the early eighteenth century had gradually been replaced by more rational and effective forms replicating many features associated with the regular imperial army; and an officer establishment had been created, and subjected to the central government's control. The question arises, however, why regularization came so late and so slowly; and why the transformation was as incomplete as it was.

Several explanations suggest themselves. Firstly, insofar as organization is a function of population size, there was little need for any very formal or highly structured organization of the Cossack communities so long as their numbers remained comparatively low. The fact that the Ukraine and Zaporozhe, where the Cossack population was significantly denser than in the other communities, possessed rather more sophisticated and hierarchical systems than the rest bears out this point. Furthermore, the defense of sparsely populated frontier zones and the raiding and ambush tactics that characterized frontier warfare throughout the period under review required only a very simple and informal military structure. Hence, so long as the state valued Cossacks primarily as frontier troops confronting technologically primitive, often nomadic enemies, it had no need to change their primitive organizational systems. With the Russian occupation of the Crimea and the northern Caucasus, the Don Cossacks were no longer required for that purpose. However, as the Russian Empire's frontiers were extended toward the Caucasus, Central Asia and China, more frontier settlements and more Cossacks were needed, so that the Cossack system retained its value. Indeed, it continued to be regarded as the model for frontier defense—as witness Prince Potemkin's schemes to create new quasi-Cossack hosts to police the Russian Empire's northern borders, and the actual formation of new Cossack communities (such as the Transbaikal and Seven Rivers hosts) in the nineteenth century. Count Aleksey Arakcheyev's notorious military colonies were also inspired, at least in part, by the Cossack example.

The drive to regularize the Cossacks, then, was largely motivated by the state's need for Cossack units to fight alongside its regular forces. On the other hand, the experience of Yemelian Pugachev's rising and the ferment over regularization that had preceded it among the Don, Volga and Ural Cossacks restrained the state from pushing any program of regularization too fast. Furthermore, the effectiveness of such reforms as were instituted before 1835 was inhibited by a certain lethargy in the executive arm of the state and by the influence that the more prominent members of the Cossack elite were able to wield in St. Petersburg, particularly through friendships they had made with key officers in the War Department. This evidently helped them to ignore those rules laid down for them that conflicted with their interests and yet go unpunished. It is curious to note in this connection that, whereas up to 1775 the state sought to control the Cossack rank and file in alliance with the Cossack elite whose emergence it had done so much to encourage, by the turn of the century the thrust of its reforms was directed toward controlling that same elite establishment in order to safeguard the economic position, and hence the military viability, of the Cossack masses.

The state's fluctuating conception of the Cossacks' military role also helps to account for its caution, indeed dilatoriness, in reforming and reorganizing the Cossack hosts. Cossacks were valued as auxiliary troops as well as permanent frontier guards and occasionally, as at the turn of the century, also as a useful supplement to the regular line cavalry. However, despite the reforms of the early nineteenth century Cossacks played only restricted and often low-grade roles in the Caucasian and Crimean wars. During this period the state was content to ensure minimum standards in organization and armaments to enable Cossack units to fulfil such restricted wartime functions. From the middle of the century, with the advent of modern, industrial methods of waging war, the Cossack hosts had clearly outlived their traditional wartime purposes. However, they had by then acquired a new role as a gendarmerie, used to suppress the state's enemies within the Russian Empire rather than combating frontier peoples and fighting the state's enemies abroad.

## Notes

1. This essay supplements its companion, "Transformations in Cossackdom," in Béla K. Király and Gunther Rothenberg (eds.), *War and Society in East Central Europe*, I (New York, 1979), 393–407.

2. Heber's journal in [Amelia Heber], *The Life of Reginald Heber* (London, 1830), I, 237.

3. Characteristic Cossack tactics also reflected such borrowings (as well as available resources and the nature of the terrain)—e.g., the cavalry attack in extended line *(lava)* intended to envelop the enemy's flanks; the ambush or feigned retreat; or the triangular wagon-fort *(tabor)* for defense against attack on the open steppe. See G. Levasseur, sieur de Beauplan, *Description d'Ukraine* (Rouen, 1650); E. A. Razin, *Istoriya voyennogo iskusstva* [History of the Art of War] (Moscow, 1961), III, 295–297; *Sbornik oblastnogo voyska donskogo statisticheskago komiteta* [Handbook of Provincial Forces of the Don Statistical Committee] (Novocherkassk, 1915), XIII, 71–72; I. Bykadorov, "Boy kazachey konnitsy" [Cossack Cavalry Combat], *Kazachi Dumy* [Cossack Thought] (Sofia), IX (1923), 1–11 and X (1923), 2–9.

4. G. Georgi, *Opisanie vsekh obitayuschchikh v rossiyskom gosudarstve narodov* [Description of All the Inhabitants of the Russian National State] (St. Petersburg, 1799), IV, 206.

5. See I. G. Rozner, *Yaik pered burey* [The Ural before the Storm] (Moscow, 1966), citing Pallas.

6. See G. I. Semenyuk, "Oruzhie, voyennaya organizatsiya i voyennoe iskusstvo Kazakhov v XVII–XIX vv." [Arms, Military Organization and the Art of War of the Cossacks in the 17th–19th Centuries], in V. I. Shunkov *et al.* (eds.), *Voprosy voyennoy istorii Rossii* [Issues in the Military History of Russia] (Moscow, 1969), 263–272.

7. Heber, *Life*, I, 253, 676.

8. N. A. Smirnov, *Rossiya i Turtsiya v XVI*–XVII vv. [Russia and Turkey in the 16th–17th Centuries] (Moscow, 1946), II, 96.

9. Georgi, *Opisanie*, IV, 211.

10. A. A. Lishin (comp.) *Akty otnosyashchiesya k istorii voyska donskogo* [Acts Bearing on the History of the Army of the Don] (Novocherkassk, 1891–1894), II, i, 555–556.

11. *Ibid.*, 239–240.

12. *Ibid.*, III, 79–80, 151–152.

13. Georgi, *Opisanie*, IV, 371.

14. Lishin, *Akty*, I, 251–258.

15. *Ibid.*, II, i, 156–158.

16. Smirnov, *Rossiya i Turtsiya*, II, 46, 112.

17. Orders of June 8, 1738, August 28, 1738, and May 14, 1740 (O.S.). Lishin, *Akty*, II, i, 195, 200, 239–240.

18. *Ibid.*, III, 284.

19. *Sbornik*, XIII, 75–78.

20. See, for example, the account of Leo Tolstoy, who lived among the Terek Cossacks for some months in the early 1850s, in his novel *The Cossacks.*

21. Among these was James Stanislaus Bell who gave an account of his experiences in the Caucasus in *Residence in Circassia* (London, 1840).

22. Philip Longworth, *The Cossacks* (New York, 1970), p. 180.

23. Georgi, *Opisanie*, IV, 222–228.

24. Longworth, *The Cossacks*, pp. 177–178.

25. Lishin, *Akty*.

26. P. Krasnov, "Donskoy kazachiy polk sto let nazad" [The Don Cossack Regiment 100 Years Ago] *Voyennyy sbornik* [Military Papers], CCXXV, 68–69.

27. Longworth, *The Cossacks*, p. 239; Bruce W. Menning, "The Emergence of a Military-Administrative Elite in the Don Cossack Land, 1708–1836," in D. K. Rowney and W. M. Pintner (eds.), *Russian Officialdom from the 17th to the 20th Century* (Chapel Hill, N.C., 1980), Chap. 6.

28. Menning, "The Emergence," quoting V. G. Fedorov, *Vooruzhenie russkoy armii v krymskuyu kampaniyu* [The Armaments of the Russian Army in the Crimean Campaign] (St. Petersburg, 1904).

29. Pierre Chevalier, *A Discourse on the Original Country . . . of the Cossacks* (London, 1672); Levasseur, *Description.* For a convenient summary, see Razin, *Istoriya*, II, 299–300.

30. J. Fiedler, *Die Relationen der Botschafter Venedigs über Deutschland und Österreich im 17. Jahrhundert* (Vienna, 1866–1867), I, 92–93.

31. See *inter alia* A. Tenenti, *Piracy and the Decline of Venice* (London, 1966).

32. J. V. Polisensky, *The Thirty Years War* (London, 1974), p. 176.

33. Moscow, Central State Archives of Ancient Acts, Oruzheynaya palata, opis' 1659–61, Nos. 416, 488.

34. See, for example, the references to Eleazar Isbrandt, Andreus Manter and others at the Voronezh shipyards in 1698 in N. Ustrialov, *Istoriya tsarstvovaniya Petra Velikogo* [History of the Reign of Peter the Great] (St. Petersburg, 1858), II, 509 ff.

35. B. H. Sumner, *Peter the Great and the Ottoman Empire* (Oxford, 1949), p. 19.

36. Lishin, *Akty*, II, i, 155, 158–159.

37. Christof H. von Manstein, *Memoirs of Russia* (London, 1770), pp. 144, 161, 415–416; Sumner, *Peter the Great*, p. 26.

38. V. A. Golubitskiy, *Chernomorskoe kazachestvo* [The Black Sea Cossacks] (Kiev, 1956), p. 167.

39. J.-B. Scherer, *Annales de la Petite Russie* (Paris, 1788), I, 76–78.

40. Lishin, *Akty*, II, i, 2–4 (March 20, 1725). They were apparently higher in Zaporozhe, however, where the hetman received 600 rubles, judges, the field secretary and *esauly*, 300 apiece, the *oboznyi* 100, and the chief gunner and drum major 15. A total of 5,520 rubles was divided among all the other men. Georgi, *Opisanie*, IV, 367. From 1779 Don Cossack colonels on active service received 300 rubles a month, captains and lieutenants 50, the field secretary 30, and the ordinary troopers one ruble each. Krasnov, "Donskoy kazachiy polk," 59.

41. Major General Rusinow's manuscript (18th century) on the foundation of the regular Russian army, quoted by L. G. Beskrovnyy, *Russkaya armiya i flot v XVIII veke* [The Russian Army and Navy in the 18th Century] (Moscow, 1958), p. 7.

42. P. O. Bobrovskiy, *Perekhod Rossii k regulyarnoy armii* [Russia's Transition to a Regular Army] (St. Petersburg, 1885), pp. 75–76. Of the irregulars 50,000 came from the Ukraine, 16,000 from Slobodskaya Ukraina, 15,000 from Zaporozhe, and 20,000 from the Don.

43. Beskrovnyy, *Russkaya armiya i flot*, pp. 3–6.

44. These then consisted of some 20,000 tax-exempt servicemen supported by a considerable number of auxiliaries. In addition, Ukrainian volunteers manned three cavalry regiments, a fusilier company, a hussar squadron and artillery units. Georgi, *Opisanie*, IV, 332–334.

45. Manstein, *Memoirs*, p. 17.

46. In 1790 they were even used dismounted to help storm the Ottoman citadel of Ismail. Philip Longworth, *The Art of Victory* (New York, 1966), pp. 167 ff.

47. Some anomalies persisted. For example, Ural Cossack officers continued to be elected, and distinctions of rank reflected in fishing rights rather than pay. Georgi, *Opisanie*, IV, 222–228.

48. Manstein, *Memoirs*, pp. 20–21. The host had experienced a sharp

drop in population as a result of the Bulavin revolt of 1707-1708.

49. Lishin, *Akty*, II, i, 119-120.

50. *Ibid.*, III, 6-7.

51. Beskrovnyy, *Russkaya armiya i flot*, p. 65.

52. A. Kirillov in *Sbornik oblastnogo voyska donskogo*, XIII (1915), 67-69.

53. Heber, *Life*, I, 238.

54. L. G. Beskrovnyy, *Russkaya armiya i flot v XIX veke* [The Russian Army and Navy in the 19th Century] (Moscow, 1973), p. 32. For estimates of mobilized strength just before this, see Georgi, *Opisanie*, IV, 212-214 (Terek), 222-228 (Ural), 220-221 (Orenburg), 217-219 (Volga), 215 (Mozdok), 378-379 (Black Sea), 229-232 (Siberian), 217-219 (Astrakhan).

55. Lishin, *Akty*, II, i, 75-78.

56. See Golubitskiy, *Chernomorskoe kazachestvo;* I. I. Dmitrenko, *Sbornik istoricheskikh materialov po istoriei kubanskogo kazach'iago voyska* [Collected Historical Materials on the History of the Kuban Cossack Army] (St. Petersburg, 1896).

57. Menning, "Emergence."

58. Krasnov, "Donskoy kazachiy polk," 58-59.

59. Heber, *Life*, I, 99.

60. Kirillov, *loc. cit.*

61. Lishin, *Akty*, III, 2.

62. Catherine II to the Don, November 9, 1764. *Ibid.*, III, 23-25.

63. E.g. in 1775. Menning, "Emergence."

64. Heber, *Life*, I, 236.

65. *Ibid.*, 99.

66. Georgi, *Opisanie*, IV, 200, 204, 205, 208; S. Plescheef, *Survey of the Russian Empire* (London, 1792), p. 323.

67. Lishin, *Akty*, II, 6-7.

68. Quoted by Beskrovnyy, *Russkaya armiya i flot v XIX veke*, p. 32.

69. By 1830 it was almost 300 rubles. Golubitskiy, *Chernomorskoe kazachestvo*, pp. 171-172.

70. Lishin, *Akty*, III, 262-265.

71. A comptroller had been seconded from the central government late in the eighteenth century, but without sufficient effect.

72. Order to the Imperial Senate, May 26, 1835. Lishin, *Akty*, III, 265-266.

73. M. G. Vlasov, *Polkovoe instruktsiya dlya donskago voyska* [Regimental Instructions for the Don Army], 1836.

74. See Table VI-I in Menning, "Emergence." The fact *per se* suggests that the officer corps was becoming professionalized.

75. Beskrovnyy, *Russkaya armiya i flot v XIX veke*, p. 33.

76. [F. von Gille], *Lettres sur le Caucase et la Crimée* (Paris, 1859), pp. 22–23, 209–210, 212.

77. The Siberian, Black Sea/Kuban, Ural, Orenburg, Transbaikal, Astrakhan, Dunai, and, finally, the tiny (fewer than 1,000 men) Azov Cossack Hosts. Beskrovnyy, *Russkaya armiya i flot v XIX veke,* p. 33.

78. Some confusion exists about when precisely uniforms were introduced. Heber (*Life,* I, 253) observed that in 1806 the Black Sea Cossacks dressed "without any regard to uniformity," but (*Life,* I, 99, 233) some Don Cossack units and ranks were uniformed, albeit at their own expense or the private expense of their commanders. Krasnov insists that only officers and Cossacks close to the hetman wore uniforms at this time. The uniform appearance may have been due to a combination of traditional cut and the use of standard cloth supplied to the Host by the government. *Sbornik oblastnogo voyska donskogo,* XIII, 87. I am indebted to Professor Menning for these last two references.

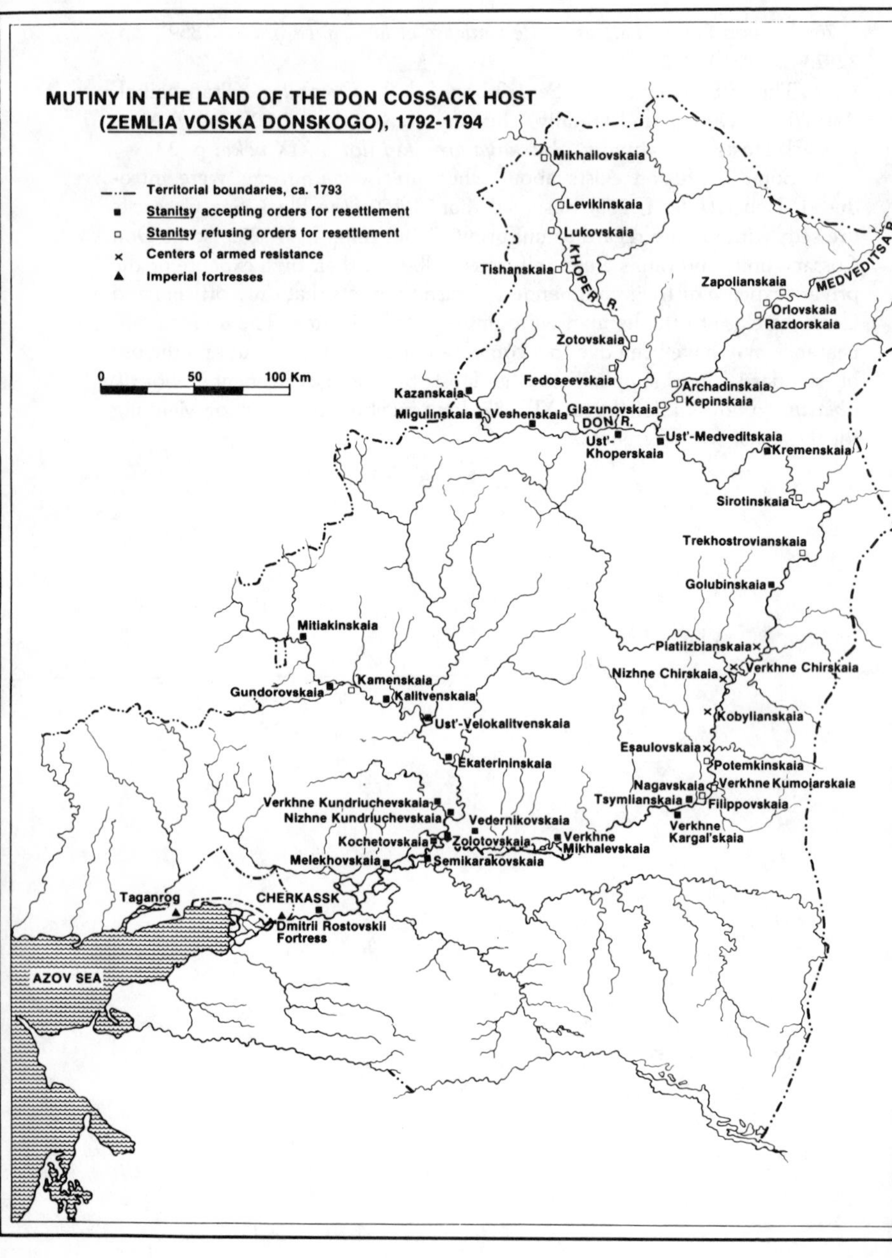
MUTINY IN THE LAND OF THE DON COSSACK HOST
(ZEMLIA VOISKA DONSKOGO), 1792-1794
Territorial boundaries, ca. 1793
Stanitsy accepting orders for resettlement
Stanitsy refusing orders for resettlement
Centers of armed resistance
Imperial fortresses
0
50
100 Km
Mikhailovskaia
Levikinskaia
Lukovskaia
Tishanskaia
KHOPER R.
MEDVEDITSA R.
Zapolianskaia
Orlovskaia
Razdorskaia
Zotovskaia
Fedoseevskaia
Archadinskaia
Kepinskaia
Kazanskaia
Migulinskaia
Veshenskaia
Glazunovskaia
DON R.
Ust'-Khoperskaia
Ust'-Medveditskaia
Kremenskaia
Sirotinskaia
Trekhostrovianskaia
Golubinskaia
Mitiakinskaia
Piatiizbianskaia
Nizhne Chirskaia
Verkhne Chirskaia
Kamenskaia
Gundorovskaia
Kalitvenskaia
Kobylianskaia
Ust'-Velokalitvenskaia
Esaulovskaia
Ekaterininskaia
Potemkinskaia
Nagavskaia
Verkhne Kumoiarskaia
Tsymlianskaia
Filippovskaia
Verkhne Kundriuchevskaia
Nizhne Kundriuchevskaia
Vedernikovskaia
Verkhne Kargal'skaia
Kochetovskaia
Zolotovskaia
Verkhne Mikhalevskaia
Melekhovskaia
Semikarakovskaia
Taganrog
CHERKASSK
Dmitrii Rostovskii Fortress
AZOV SEA

Bruce W. Menning

# Cossacks against Colonization: Mutiny on the Don, 1792–1794

Between 1792 and 1794, Don Cossack rebels once again raised the standard of revolt in the homeland of Stenka Razin and Yemelian Pugachev. What originally began as a disturbance among Don regiments on the Caucasian Line eventually flamed into a serious mutiny encompassing at various times and in varying degrees of intensity fifty Cossack settlements along the Don River and its chief tributaries. Imperial Russian authorities were able to quell what culminated in the so-called Esaulovskaya mutiny only with the dispatch of nearly 10,000 troops from nearby provinces and the foothills of the Caucasus. For the first time since the reign of Peter the Great and the ill-fated rising of another Don rebel, Kondratiy Bulavin, the Land of the Don Cossack Host *(Zemlya voyska Donskogo)* witnessed punitive military expeditions, mass reprisals, courts-martial, and subsequent beatings, mutilations, executions, and exile.[1]

Tsarist officials determined from the very beginning that the events of 1792–1794 were to remain only locally significant. Mindful of earlier precedents, they were eager to avoid provoking further disturbances by granting untoward public attention to imperial Russia's mutinous Cossacks. Therefore, except for select public punishments intended to serve as object lessons for the Cossacks themselves, most facets of the insurrection remained confidential, suitable only for *in camera* discussion or for executive action on the part of the field commanders directly concerned. Once quiet returned to the Don, more than seventy years passed before the Don Statistical Committee published related documents and the first in-

The author wishes to thank Edward C. Thaden and Herbert L. Oerter for commenting on an earlier version of this paper and to acknowledge indebtedness to the International Research and Exchanges Board and the Miami University Faculty Research Committee for supporting the underlying research.

complete version of the insurrection.[2] In 1897, E. D. Felitsyn added more detail to the mosaic after he stumbled upon thirty pertinent documents in a forgotten fortress archive.[3] Thanks to this and the forays of others into archival materials, prerevolutionary historians of the neighboring Kuban region were able to write credible accounts of the affair as an introductory chapter in the formation of the Kuban Cossack host.[4] More recently, local Soviet historians, anxious perhaps to secure a place in the revolutionary sun for their native region (Rostovskaya oblast), have devoted considerable attention to the mutiny of 1792–1794.[5] However, their efforts have elicited only passing interest from their colleagues. After all, the disturbance remained isolated, a local curiosity that failed to ignite a widescale jacquerie in the hallowed tradition of Razin and Pugachev.[6]

It is for other reasons that the events of 1792–1794 merit attention. They afford useful insight into some of the stresses associated with the transformation of the Cossacks from a semiautonomous society of warrior frontiersmen into a special military class *(voyennoye sosloviye)* designed to meet the needs of the imperial Russian state. In addition, the mutiny illuminates the kind of grievances, including arbitrary military orders, the violation of historic rights and privileges, and the question of colonization, capable of moving the Cossacks to insurrection. Indeed, varying reactions to these and related issues demonstrate how the Cossacks, both officers and rank and file, viewed the Don host's position within the changing imperial military order. Finally, and perhaps most importantly, the course of the mutiny provides a rare glimpse into the governing activities of local officials confronted with a serious crisis. Unlike the rebellion of Pugachev, which precipitated widescale breakdowns in local government, the Esaulovskaya revolt proved that local Cossack officials were capable of containing and defusing an explosive situation.

* * *

The Don Cossack mutiny of 1792–1794 had its immediate origins in imperial Russian military endeavors aimed at pacifying and settling recently acquired territory in the foothills of the Caucasus. Prior to the conclusion of the Russo-Ottoman War of 1787–1791 in December 1791,[7] Catherine II instructed I. V. Gudovich, her commander in chief in the Caucasus and the Kuban, to submit comprehensive plans for the improvement and strengthening of Russian defenses along the Caucasian frontier. At the time these defenses consisted of the Caucasian Line, a string of several small forts and some seventeen hastily constructed redoubts extending from the shore of the Sea of Azov along the right bank of the Kuban River to the headwaters of the Terek River, then down the Terek to the Caspian Sea in the region of the fortress at Kizlyar.[8] To render this temporary line proof against the incursions of various hostile mountain peoples, that is, to make it a genuine "cordon line," General Gudovich on January 16, 1792, submitted a twofold recommendation to the imperial Military College. First, he proposed the systematic rebuilding and troop reinforcement of all fortified strongpoints along the line. Second, he recommended construction of an entirely new supplementary line to replace an interior segment of the existing series of redoubts between Ust'-Laba on the upper Kuban and Belaya Mecheta on the upper Terek. This new line was to consist of twelve fortified Cossack settlements *(stanitsy)* whose settlers would be drawn from several different Cossack groups, including the personnel of at least three Don Cossack regiments then completing a three-year term of temporary duty on the line.[9]

On February 28, 1792, Catherine approved—apparently with the concurrence of the Military College—a modified version of General Gudovich's proposal. As expected, she ordered the allocation of sufficient funds, supplies, and military manpower to implement the first part of the project. Unexpectedly, however, and probably for the sake of expediency, the tsarina allowed the burden of colonizing the new segment of the line to fall completely on the shoulders of the Don Cossacks. The other two Cossack groups originally scheduled for resettlement, the Volga and Khoper Cossacks, were released on the grounds that since 1777–1778 they had already been heavily committed to various other Caucasian colonization projects.[10] Besides, three Don regiments, those of the commanders Andrey Pozdeyev, Ivan Koshkin, and Gavrila Lukovkin, were already on the scene, awaiting homeward rotation after having completed nearly three years' service on the line.[11] Their replacements, the regiments of Mikhail Davidov, Petr Rebrikov, and Aleksey Pozdeyev, were only then being mustered for service from the lists of eligible Cossacks in the Land of the Don Host. To facilitate settlement with all possible speed, Catherine simply decreed that all six regiments—both the relieved and the relievers—take up permanent residence on the new segment of the Caucasian Line. General Gudovich received instructions to aid the Cossacks in the task of constructing new dwellings and fortifying their settlements by loaning them manpower and equipment from reinforced regular army units in the general area. Until the arrival of the participants' families signaled completion of the project, each Cossack colonist was to receive provisions, military pay, and forage. To help ease the burden of resettlement, the tsarina granted twenty rubles to each Cossack and 500 rubles to each settlement, the latter sum for the construction of church buildings.[12] Gudovich named Major General Savel'ev, commander of the Mozdok Cossack Regiment, to supervise Don Cossack resettlement. Neither the tsarina nor Gudovich seemed to have expected any difficulties. They did not even bother to inform local Don Cossack officials of the project.

To be fair with Catherine and her military advisers, there seemed little reason to expect resistance to the Caucasian resettlement order. Since 1756 the Don Host had rendered faithful military service through three major foreign wars, one against Prussia and two against the Ottoman Empire. In addition, the Cossacks had served well through a longer undeclared war that raged between them and their age-old enemies of the steppe, the Crimean and Nogai Tatars.[13] True, during the troubled years of the Pugachev rebellion, some Cossacks had wavered in their loyalty to the throne, but the majority had repeatedly resisted the appeals of their Don brothers to join the crusade against the tsarina.[14] More important, in 1775, Grigoriy A. Potemkin, vice president of the Military College and commander in chief of all light cavalry and irregular hosts, had installed a new local administration, the Host Civilian Government *(Voyskovoye Grazhdanskoye Pravitel'stvo)*, to reduce the combined military and civil power of the host hetman and to make the institutions of the Don host more responsive to the military and political requirements of St. Petersburg. Both the collegial nature of the Host Civilian Government and its formal separation of civilian and military functions promised to prevent any recurrence of an earlier situation in which a single Cossack family, the Yefremovs, strove to become "God and Tsar" in the territory.[15]

To complement changes in structure and procedure, Potemkin took steps to assure the continued loyalty of the Don Cossack elders, those officers who bore primary responsibility for local civil and military administration. The elders *(voyskovye starshiny)* were Cossack notables who had risen within the host to positions of prominence for a variety of reasons, including personal ability, meritorious service, wealth, and family connections. Since the last quarter of the seventeenth century, tsarist policy had aimed at transforming them and their descendants into docile collaborators successively of Muscovite and imperial Russian rule among the Cossacks. In exchange for loyal service, the elders received favors, honors, money, offices, and significantly, access on a selective basis to the status of Russian nobility. In 1775 Potemkin wisely proposed to reduce bickering among the elders and to broaden the base of imperial support within the host by uniformly ennobling all elders. Catherine agreed to the proposal in legislation that equated elder rank with staff rank (senior to captain but junior to second major) in the regular army. In accordance with the Table of Ranks promulgated by Peter the Great in 1722, the possession of staff officer rank automatically conferred hereditary nobility.[16] As a final measure, Potemkin engineered the appointment of A. I. Ilovaiskiy to the post of host hetman. An officer of proven loyalty and high local standing, Ilovaiskiy had distinguished himself in the campaign against Pugachev. By 1792 Ilovaiskiy had risen to the rank of lieutenant general and was in his seventeenth year as hetman of the Don host. Although Potemkin had died during the previous year, there was little reason to doubt the capacity of Ilovaiskiy or that of his chief deputies, Major General Dmitrii Martynov and Major General Amvrosiy Lukovkin, to implement a direct order to settle six Don Cossack regiments on the Caucasian Line.[17]

Tradition was also largely on the side of those who expected the Cossacks to discharge the colonization order without undue difficulty. From the time of Peter the Great, the imperial government had repeatedly, and for the most part successfully, summoned the Cossacks to participate in various resettlement projects. In 1724–1725, 500 Don families had obeyed a decree to resettle on the banks of the Sulak River where they reinforced the Grebensk host and helped form the Agrakhan host. During the 1730s and 1740s, more than 1,000 families had responded to orders calling for resettlement along the Tsaritsyn Fortress Line, where they came to form the Volga Cossack host.[18] Only during the period between 1770 and 1774, when

Cossacks actively resisted assignment to permanent garrison duty at the Azov and Taganrog fortresses, did imperial orders fall on insubordinate ears.

Against the overall record of success, that single instance of insubordination provided a most instructive precedent for imperial Russia's military colonizers of the future. On September 9, 1769, the Military College had published orders for the recruitment of two Don Cossack regiments (about 1,000 men) to settle on the territory of the Azov and Taganrog fortresses, both of which had only recently been forcibly reclaimed from the Turks.[19] When only five Cossacks volunteered for duty, the Military College instructed Hetman Stepan Yefremov of the Don host to begin the arbitrary assignment of available Cossacks to fortress duty. This procedure completely ignored the long-standing tradition according to which the Cossacks met within their own *stanitsa* assemblies to determine candidates for resettlement either by calling for volunteers or by casting lots *(po zhrebiyu)*. Almost immediately rumors began to circulate among the Cossacks that they were under imminent threat of being registered "as regulars" *(v regulyarstvo)*, that is, being transformed into regular soldiers and thereby losing their ancient rights and privileges as free Cossacks. Despite repeated threats and the removal of Hetman Yefremov from office, the resettlement order went largely unheeded until the tsarina rescinded it in 1774. By that time the growing threat of mutiny and the danger of Pugachev had rendered enforcing the order an unwarranted and unwise risk.[20]

Another consideration of importance to the colonization project of 1792 was the human factor, something well understood by both Lieutenant General Ilovaiskiy and Major General Savel'ev. After having completed a legitimate term of active service, Cossacks in the regiments of Andrey Pozdeyev, Koshkin, and Lukovkin would be anxious to return to their families and homes in the Don. To order the regiments to settle permanently in the foothills of the Caucasus would be to court the appearance of grave disaffection among the Cossacks. In April 1792, after having been finally informed of the tsarina's resettlement order, Hetman Ilovaiskiy requested that General Gudovich petition Catherine directly to relieve the regiments of the resettlement burden. Ilovaiskiy's request fell on deaf ears. The officer in direct charge of the operation, Major General Savel'ev, was so filled with misgiving that he refused to publish the resettlement order. Instead, without affording the Cossacks any kind of explanation, he ordered the three regiments to deploy by small parties into designated areas where they were to begin work on the construction of dwellings and fortifications.[21]

Savel'ev's tactics failed to deceive the Cossacks. Rumors of impending colonization had already begun to circulate among the regiments, and the officer's refusal to publish the order only created consternation and confusion. From the beginning most of the Cossacks openly refused to begin construction work. When they sent representatives to query Savel'ev about the specific nature of his orders, he supplied evasive answers. When he placed the Cossacks on military alert and began seizing their horses in a misguided attempt to forestall desertion, the Cossacks believed the rumors and their suspicions confirmed. With the reins of authority rapidly slipping from his hands, Savel'ev attempted to coerce the Cossacks into obeying orders by calling out the Pozdeyev regiment's horse artillery against the recalcitrants.[22]

Summoning the horse artillery produced exactly the opposite of expected results. Rather than subduing the Cossacks, the threat of force increased their resolution to seek additional information about the resettlement order. Under the leadership of H. I. Belogorokhov, a rank-and-file Cossack already known as an inveterate troublemaker, the Cossacks decided to disregard any orders related to resettlement until they could verify those orders as having come directly from the tsarina. Apparently they believed that the abrupt change in their future had resulted not from any imperial decree but from an arbitrary decision of Hetman Ilovaiskiy. Accordingly, Belogorokhov and his chief supporters, Foka Sukhorukov, Trofim Shtukarev, Savva Sadchikov, Ivan Podlivalin, and Dmitriy Popov, proposed that the regiments send a three-man delegation to Cherkassk, the Don Cossack capital, to request that the hetman show them a copy of the resettlement order signed by the hand of the empress.[23] On May 22, 1792, the delegation—under Foka Sukhorukov—arrived in the capital, and the hetman convinced its members that the order had indeed come from the tsarina and that it was the Cossacks' duty to execute her orders faithfully. Therefore the delegates should return to their regiments, and meanwhile the hetman would personally petition Catherine to rescind the resettlement order.[24]

Before the hetman could keep his promise, insubordination on the Caucasian Line gave way to mass desertion. Without waiting for the return of their delegates from Cherkassk, 788 Cossacks lost patience, seized their regimental colors, and set out independently across the open steppe for the Cossack capital where they intended to discover for themselves who had issued orders for resettlement. On May 30 they arrived on the south bank of a flood-swollen Don River opposite Cherkassk. After a brief parley *(krug)*, during which the Cossacks swore an oath to shed blood if necessary to resist resettlement, they commandeered a number of boats to cross the river.

On the other side the boisterous fugitives stormed into the small square before the hetman's residence and loudly demanded an audience with General Ilovaiskiy. After some delay, the hetman appeared, only to be met with shouts that he reveal whose command "was leaving them on the line." In an attempt to pacify the mob, Ilovaiskiy ordered the host clerk *(d'yak)*, Fedor Melent'ev, who was standing on the steps of the hetman's residence, to descend and read aloud a copy of the tsarina's order. When Melent'ev began reading, the Cossacks interrupted him to assert that they had not yet eaten anything that day. At this point they abruptly dispersed to find food. When they reappeared a short time later, Melent'ev again began reading the order. He had scarcely finished when the Cossacks, with shouts of "You are deceiving us," fell upon him and began to pummel him. Fortunately, Melent'ev was able to beat a safe, if not dignified, retreat by taking refuge under the steps of the hetman's residence. With his unexpected guests becoming more ungovernable with every passing minute, General Ilovaiskiy took immediate steps to forestall violence by assuring the Cossacks that they would not have to return to line duty. Then he repeated his earlier promise to Sukhorukov's delegation that he would travel immediately to St. Petersburg to petition the tsarina to rescind the resettlement order. Meanwhile he asked that the Cossacks return to their home *stanitsy*. To preclude their being mistaken for deserters upon return home, he ordered the Host Civilian Government to issue them written certificates *(bilety)* that they had satisfactorily completed their required line service. The Cossacks agreed to these concessions, and on June 3, 1792, Hetman Ilovaiskiy set out for the imperial capital.[25]

The mutinous Cossacks had barely begun to disperse to their home *stanitsy* when the Host Civilian Government abruptly changed its heretofore indulgent policy. With no warning, Major General Dmitriy Martynov, acting hetman in the absence of Ilovaiskiy, issued orders for all fugitives from line service to return to their regiments without delay. Compliance with this order would merit each of the deserters both a pardon and exemption from colonization. At last it appeared that local authorities had recovered sufficiently from their surprise and fearful paralysis to pursue a more resolute course.

The Host Civilian Government's new resolve stemmed not from any local change of heart but from pressure of an imperial military nature. By this time General Gudovich had informed the president of the Military College, Count N. I. Saltykov, of what had occurred on the Caucasian Line. With some sense of alarm and haste, Saltykov ordered the Host Civilian Government to secure the deserters' return to line service. The arrival of this order caused the curious countermanding of General Ilovaiskiy's earlier instructions. It also provoked response from Major General Prince A. P. Shcherbatov, a chance witness to events in the Cossack capital. Shcherbatov, commander of the Kuban Corps, and two of his light infantry battalions were temporarily bivouacked at nearby St. Dmitriy Rostovskiy fortress (present-day Rostov-na-Donu) on their way south to duty in the Kuban steppe. Though no equal to the Cossack General Martynov in seniority, Shcherbatov reinforced Saltykov's orders by constantly pressuring the acting hetman to take decisive measures against the mutinous Cossacks. Meanwhile the officious prince dispatched a steady stream of correspondence to both Count Saltykov and General Gudovich, keeping the two informed of the various sins committed by Martynov and his associates in their continuing efforts both to implement orders and avert a local crisis.[26]

Under the relentless pressure of Saltykov and Shcherbatov, General Martynov dispatched senior Cossack officers to the various *stanitsy* to supervise the return of the deserters to their regiments. At first not all the officers were successful: the Cossacks of at least six settlements refused to listen either to the orders of the host or to the entreaties of the officers. Gradually, however, most of the deserters thought better of resistance and responded to the enticements associated with return to the Caucasian Line. Only a small group of malcontents, including Belogorokhov, Sukhorukov, Podlivanov, and Sadchikov, out of distrust deliberately chose to ignore the Host Civilian Government. At the end of June 1792 they sent one of their leaders, Nikita Belogorokhov, to St. Petersburg where he was to petition the imperial government for a clarification of their affairs. The rest, under the leadership of Foka Sukhorukov, began riding through the *stanitsy* along the middle reaches of the Don to secure additional adherents to their anticolonization cause. Their number swollen to about 200, they eventually reached the vicinity of Pyatiizbyanskaya *stanitsa* where they were overtaken and made prisoners by a large detachment of loyal Cossacks under the command of a Cossack elder, army Lieutenant Colonel Grigoriy Sychev. According to instructions from the Military College, the Host Civilian Government sent the ringleaders in chains to St. Petersburg where they joined the hapless Belogorokhov who was already in prison awaiting trial.[27]

During late 1792 and early 1793, a special commission of the Military Court convened to consider the cases of the half-dozen most prominent mutineers. After reviewing the events and the roles of various participants in them, the commission pronounced sentence. As ringleaders in the mutiny, Nikita Belogorokhov and Foka Sukhorukov were sentenced respectively to fifty and thirty lashes with the knout. Four Cossacks of lesser guilt, Shtukarev, Sadchikov, Podlivanov, and Popov, were sentenced to be whipped and then ordered to military service outside of normal rotation. In accordance with strict instructions, the sentences were carried out on August 12, 1793, at the St. Dmitriy Rostovskiy fortress before the assembled representatives of every Don Cossack *stanitsa*. Both Belogorokhov and Sukhorukov expired before the end of the day. In addition to these major punishments, the Host Civilian Government imposed lighter punishments on nearly 400 other Cossacks who had taken part in the mutiny.[28]

* * *

Ever since the publication of Catherine's original order on resettlement, members of the Host Civilian Government and officials of the Military College had failed to agree on matters either of substance or procedure. Throughout late 1792 and early 1793, Hetman Ilovaiskiy had used the Caucasian Line mutiny as an excuse not to comply with the imperial decree of February 28, 1792. By late summer 1793, with Belogorokhov and Sukhorukov laid to rest, Catherine and Count Saltykov both grew increasingly impatient with the delaying tactics of the Cossack hetman. Finally, in late August 1793, Ilovaiskiy received a direct order from the tsarina to begin implementing her decree on resettlement. The only changes mandated occurred in the important area of procedure where the empress was now willing to allow the candidates for colonization to be determined "according to ancient Don custom." This meant that the Cossacks themselves, either by calling for volunteers or by casting lots, were to select those whose fortune it was to migrate to the Caucasian Line.[29]

To the continuing credit of Ilovaiskiy's administration, both he and the Host Civilian Government chose to rely—at least at first—on persuasion rather than force to accomplish what had already become a most distasteful task. In mid September 1793, the hetman dispatched a small group of handpicked officers, the *chinovnik* agents of local government, to circulate among the Cossack *stanitsy*. Their mission included familiarizing the Cossacks with the contents of the revised resettlement order, persuading each *stanitsa* to compile a list of candidates for colonization, and returning unscathed with those lists to Cherkassk. The *chinovniki* were enjoined to act with great discretion and not to interfere in any matters falling within the substantive jurisdiction of the *stanitsy*.[30]

Special instructions for discretion proceeded from two considerations: the obvious problem of the immediate past and the particularly inopportune moment at which Catherine chose to press for the implementation of her colonization decree. At the time, records indicated that there were 28,314 Cossacks of military age within the Don host. Yet, because of important military commitments to such problem areas as the Crimea and Poland, nearly two-thirds of this number were away on active duty with their regiments outside the territory of the Don host. Of the 9,025 Cossacks of military age actually at home in their *stanitsy*, only 5,032 possessed the health, military equipment, and two war-horses required of every colonist. To recruit—even voluntarily—3,000 heads of household from this reduced manpower pool would impose a severe hardship on nearly every Cossack settlement.[31] It was not without reason that Ilovaiskiy approached the problem of colonization with such great circumspection. No change in procedure could obscure the fact that slightly more than one-half of all qualified Cossacks and their families then in Don residence would soon be departing their homeland for the foothills of the Caucasus.

In view of this situation, it was no surprise that during the fall of 1793 the visits of General Ilovaiskiy's *chinovniki* moved many Cossacks once again to the brink of mutiny and beyond. Only the inhabitants of Cherkassk and the *stanitsy* located along the Donets River willingly heard the resettlement decree and compiled lists of colonists for the Host Civilian Government. Even then the officer charged with responsibility for the area, Elder Ivan Miller, encountered stiff opposition in two of the *stanitsy*, Kalitvenskaya and Kamenskaya, where Cossacks at first steadfastly opposed obeying the order. The remainder of Miller's counterparts fared much worse. Elder Aleksey Makarov, charged with securing compliance in fourteen settlements along the lower Don River, confronted such hostility that he gave up and returned to Cherkassk after having visited only four *stanitsy*. His replacement, Colonel Stepan Leonov, weathered a series of stormy meetings and was unable to report obedience to orders in Semikarakovskaya, Kochetovskaya, Vedernikovskaya, and Verkhne-Mikhalevskaya. Farther upstream along the Don, Elder Il'ya Kumshatskiy reported that only one of his allotted eleven settlements would even accept the resettlement decree for reading. On the banks of the Khoper, Elders Petr Kul'bakov and Matvey Grevtsov informed the Host Civilian Government that sixteen settlements refused to accept the decree. Along the Medveditsa ten out of eleven *stanitsy* followed suit, and the story was nearly the same along the Buzuluk. As the reports continued to flow into Cherkassk, there was no escaping the conclusion that the situation was growing disturbingly grave. On October 13, 1793, the Host Civilian Government grudgingly informed Count Saltykov and the Military College that no fewer than fifty Cossack settlements were now in a state of open mutiny by refusing to obey an imperial command.[32]

General Ilovaiskiy had anticipated just this state of affairs. In the event that persuasion failed to achieve positive results, he was reluctantly prepared to resort either to force or to the threat of force. Already during the closing days of September, he had ordered loyal officials in various *stanitsy* to arrest anyone guilty of plotting against the implementation of imperial orders. At the same time, to strengthen the forces of loyal military power at his disposal, Ilovaiskiy requested that Prince Shcherbatov detain his two light infantry battalions in the area for an unspecified length of time. On October 10, Count Saltykov reinforced the hetman's request by ordering Shcherbatov to prepare for the immediate deployment of his troops should the Cossacks threaten armed uprising. Meanwhile General Gudovich hastily began the movement of reinforcements to the Don from neighboring provinces and the Kuban Steppe. By the beginning of January 1794 Ilovaiskiy and Shcherbatov would have nearly 10,000 troops at their disposal.[33]

Despite his willingness to countenance forcible suppression of the Cossack mutiny, General Ilovaiskiy decided to embark on one last attempt at persuasion. Both the reports of his *chinovniki* and the sketchy accounts of his informers revealed that sentiment in the majority of the mutinous *stanitsy* was seriously divided between loyal *(blagonamerennye)* Cossacks who counseled obedience to orders and genuine rebels who advocated resistance at all costs. Between these two poles stood the majority of the Cossacks whose opinion was subject to change with varying circumstances and under varying pressures. Indeed, as debate enveloped various *stanitsy*, elective offices might change hands several times before one faction emerged victorious. Such had been the case, for example, in Nagavskaya and Glazunovskaya, where the loyal Cossacks finally assumed the ascendancy after several weeks' bitter wrangling with the opponents of colonization. Ilovaiskiy sought advantage in similar developing situations by accelerating the process governing, or if need be, tipping the scales in favor of, the emerging loyalist Cossacks.[34]

For maximum effect the hetman proposed openly marshaling his military forces for action while simultaneously dispatching his *chinovniki* to circulate once more among the mutinous *stanitsy*. The officers alternately cajoled, threatened, and ordered the Cossacks to observe their loyalty oaths and thus avoid the fate of Belogorokhov and Sukhorukov. Gradually the efforts of Ilovaiskiy and his officers bore fruit: between December 5, 1793, and January 2, 1794, forty-one settlements responded to orders by submitting lists of colonizers to the Host Civilian Government.[35] On January 9, Guards Lieutenant Colonel Pankrat'ev, personal informer to Count Saltykov, reported to the president of the Military College that four additional settlements had reentered the loyalist fold.[36] Thanks largely to the skill and understanding of the hetman and a few Cossack officers, only five *stanitsy* now remained in a state of mutiny.

* * *

By alternately coaxing and threatening the Cossacks, the Host Civilian Government and its agents managed to secure lists of colonists from all but the most recalcitrant *stanitsy*. By the end of the second week of January 1794 there were only five settlements that had failed to comply with resettlement instructions: Esaulovskaya, Kobylyanskaya, Nizhne-Chirskaya, Verkhne-Chirskaya, and Pyatiizbyanskaya. Why these *stanitsy* held out after the others had capitulated remains unclear. They were among the most populous of the Cossack settlements, and therefore probably had been ordered to provide more settlers. They also constituted a well-known stronghold of Old Believer sentiment. Apparently during earlier periods when the Cossacks had come under pressure to secure religious conformity within their settlements, colonization had served as a convenient pretext for ridding the host of dissenters. By the 1790s, though, religious toleration was an established policy among the Cossacks. Perhaps a mixture of rumors and memories rekindled fears that the Old Believers might become prime candidates for the new colonization drive.[37]

For whatever reason the majority of the population of these five settlements refused to comply with the ukase on colonization. During October and November 1793, opponents to Ilovaiskiy and the Host Civilian Government gained the upper hand and turned loyalists out of *stanitsa* offices, replacing them with hetmans and clerks in sympathy with the mutineers. Under the leadership of Captain *(Esaul)* Ivan Rubtsov, representatives from the five *stanitsy* gathered to establish communication and assure one another of mutual support in the event of trouble. None of the settlements was to permit free entry to any of the *chinovnik* emissaries who attempted to counsel obedience to the imperial decree. In fact, the mutineers declared that Ilovaiskiy's agents would be subject to beating and forcible expulsion from the settlements. Although there was some talk of the need to arm themselves, the Cossacks did not become openly bellicose until the end of December 1793.[38]

What seems to have incited the mutineers to consider taking offensive action against legitimate authority was an exchange of correspondence between them and the Don hetman. On December 22 the mutineers had sent a written communication to Ilovaiskiy requesting that he again personally petition the tsarina to rescind the resettlement order. The hetman, apparently at the end of his patience, answered the mutineers by labeling them "monsters" and "state rebels" in the tradition of Razin and Pugachev.[39] Ilovaiskiy concluded the stream of invective by urging the mutineers to obey the imperial will.

Ilovaiskiy's harsh words probably helped spur the Cossacks into beginning active preparation for the conduct of military operations. They took steps to initiate the fortification of their *stanitsy* and began gathering various types of military supplies, including quantities of gunpowder and lead. Despite some resolve to begin military activity, the mutineers failed to reach agreement over their exact course of action. Some favored a campaign into the upper Don area to enlist additional support, while others spoke of an immediate march on Cherkassk to conduct a surprise attack on the Cossack capital. In the end they agreed simply to post guards and mount round-the-clock patrols of the surrounding steppe to prevent surprise attack by government forces. Should an attack come, the mutineers continued to assure one another of mutual support.[40]

By the end of January 1794 the five mutinous settlements represented a growing source of concern for both Hetman Ilovaiskiy and Prince Shcherbatov. The longer the *stanitsy* held out against the government, the greater the possibility they might attract support from other settlements. The mutineers themselves spoke of having "like-minded" allies not in five, but in thirty-eight *stanitsy*. To make matters worse, Ilovaiskiy was not entirely sure that the earlier process by which he had converted to his side forty-five *stanitsy* was irreversible. Surely the situation could not be allowed to persist until spring, when the hetman could legitimately expect an increase in the level of antigovernment activity. Then too, another concern was the resurgence within the Don Land of the earlier phenomenon of desertion. Rumors of impending trouble had reached the ears of Cossacks on active duty with their regiments in Kuban and the Crimea, and small numbers of deserters had already begun to appear in the region of Cherkassk.[41] To delay quelling the mutiny might mean confronting still more difficulty in the coming months.

As early as January 19 Prince Shcherbatov concluded that the mutiny could be suppressed only by force of arms. However, it was not until February 20 that the commander of the Kuban Corps had sufficiently concentrated the additional troops now under his command to assure a coordinated assault on all the mutinous settlements. The attack itself—an envelopment from all sides—occurred during the early morning hours of February 26. Shcherbatov's battalions took Esaulovskaya *stanitsa*, the headquarters of the mutiny, while the detachments of his subordinates occupied Pyatiizbyanskaya and Verkhne-Chirskaya. Since the Cossacks laid down their weapons and surrendered upon the approach of the regulars, there was no bloodshed. Only outside Nizhne-Chirskaya and Kobylyanskaya was there difficulty when approximately 1,000 Cossacks attempted to block entrance to their settlements. Again, since the Cossacks did not resort to their weapons, there was no bloodshed.[42]

The real bloodshed occurred when the imperial government imposed punishment upon the Cossacks for their mutinous acts. Again a special commission of the Military Court convened to hear the cases of the reluctant colonists. This time, however, in view of the tsarina's desire to try all parties to the mutiny—something in excess of 5,000 Cossacks—the commission held its proceedings in Nizhne-Chirskaya *stanitsa* in the Land of the Don Cossack Host. The sentences handed down by the commission held little surprise. As expected, Ivan Rubtsov, the ringleader of the Esaulovskaya mutiny, was to die under the knout. A total of 146 of his most enthusiastic supporters were scheduled to receive varying degrees of corporal punishment and then undergo periods of exile in Siberia ranging up to twelve years. Nearly 5,000 other Cossacks were sentenced to be whipped for refusing to hear the imperial decree on resettlement.[43]

The original source of discontent, the resettlement decree, was modified by the Military College to reduce the number of participating families from 3,000 to 1,000. In a gesture aimed at limiting the extent of discontent while simultaneously fulfilling the letter of the law, the Military College further ruled that the colonists be drawn primarily from the five recalcitrant *stanitsy*. Thus the majority of the Cossack communities were excused from the burden of resettlement. Eventually 644 families were relocated from the middle reaches of the Don to the foothills of the Caucasus.[44] Ironically, more were not drafted into the effort because settlement areas along the Caucasian Line were inadequately prepared to accept additional families without imposing undue hardship on them. Despite General Gudovich's fulminations against the Cossacks, he lacked the resources to assign regular troops to facilitate the task of resettlement without jeopardizing completion of other crucial construction projects. An added irony was that subsequent reports to the Military College noted that most of the colonists adjusted with remarkable ease to their new surroundings.[45]

* * *

The mutiny of 1792–1794 indicated that the process of transforming the Don Cossack host into a reliable military instrument remained essentially incomplete. In some ways, very limited to be sure, the Cossacks still resembled the proverbial two-edged cutting sword of the past. One edge, the light cavalryman and the frontier colonist, was useful, while the other, the mutineer and armed rebel, remained a threat to the empire. Don Cossack institutions, while significantly altered by Potemkin and patterned more closely on the general Russian model, failed to assure St. Petersburg full compliance with military orders. Nor did any combination of institutional change, closer supervision, and the more systematic granting of awards and punishments necessarily guarantee the blind obedience of local Cossack officials to orders. In fact, the host elders, whether out of fear or concern for their fellow Cossacks, chose to retain considerable flexibility in the way they transmitted the imperial will to the rank and file. True, the elders probably prevented the mutiny from erupting into a more serious antigovernment rising, but their conduct sometimes had reflected less than a total commitment to the empress and the Military College.

In view of these considerations, transforming the Cossacks into a true military class remained a prime objective of imperial Russian policy in the south steppe. In the Land of the Don Cossack Host, the largest of the Cossack groupings, this policy portended more of what had occurred in the past, more military subordination and more institutional and personnel changes. By the beginning of the nineteenth century, a restructured organization, the Host Chancery, replaced Potemkin's Host Civilian Government. In time the new government and its hetman, M. I. Platov, came to represent the imposition of a more highly structured military bureaucracy than the Cossacks had ever witnessed. The mutiny of 1792–1794 also paved the way for changes in *stanitsa* government, the last bastion of self-government with the exception of Orthodox Church administration.[46] Finally, there was the issue of the elders who had come to form the backbone of a local military-administrative elite among the Cossacks. They needed to be more closely identified with the high command and more isolated in a physical and psychological sense from the rank and file, twin objectives that time and additional reform legislation were to accomplish during the first four decades of the nineteenth century.[47]

Occasional mutinies and other uncertainties did not deter St. Petersburg from its pursuit of that elusive ideal, the perfect military colonist. That quest would continue among the Cossack hosts and gradually extend to the peasant soldiery. The tragedy was that imperial authorities never stopped equating colonists with automata.

## Notes

1. A concise description of the mutiny appears in S. G. Svatikov, *Rossiya i Don* [Russia and the Don] (Vienna, 1924), pp. 234–238, while the most comprehensive account is A. P. Pronshtein, *Zemlya donskaya v XVIII veke* [The Don Territory in the 18th Century] (Rostov-na-Donu, 1961), pp. 323–350. The appropriate archival material is in the Tsentral'nyy gosudarstvennyy voyenno-istoricheskiy arkhiv (hereafter cited as TsGVIA), *fond* 41 (N. I. Saltykov), *opis'* 1/199, *delo* 331 ("Pobeg s Kubani trekh donskikh polkov" [The Flight from the Kuban of Three Don Regiments]).

2. Andronik Savel'ev (comp.), *Trekhsoletie voyska donskogo, 1570–1870 g.* [Three Centuries of the Army of the Don, 1570–1870] (Novocherkassk, 1870), pp. 98–103; "Akty o pereselenii s Dona semeynykh kazakov" [Reports on the Migration of Cossack Families from the Don], *Trudy oblastnogo voyska donskogo statisticheskogo komiteta* [Works of the Local Forces of the Don Statistical Committee] (Novocherkassk, 1867), I, 1–56.

3. E. D. Felitsyn, "Pobeg s Kubani trekh donskikh polkov v 1792 godu, bunt na Donu i poselenie stanits, voshedshikh v sostav kubanskogo konnogo polka" [The Flight of Three Don Regiments from the Kuban in 1792, Mutiny on the Don, and the Settlement of Communities Joining the Kuban Cavalry], *Kubanskiy sbornik* [Kuban Papers], IV (1897), 3–62.

4. F. A. Shcherbina, *Istoriya kubanskogo kazachiago voyska* [History of the Kuban Cossack Army] (Yekaterinodar), I (1910), 655–700; A. Lamonov, "Istoricheskiy ocherk o zaselenii stanitsy kavkazskoy, kubanskogo kazachiago voyska i zhizni yeya s 1794 po 1914 god" [Historical Study of the Settlement of the Caucasian Communities, the Kuban Cossack Army, and Their Life from 1794 to 1914], *Kubanskiy sbornik*, XIX (1914), 451–471.

5. The most recent example is V. A. Zolotov and A. P. Pronshtein, *Za zemlyu, za volyu: Iz istorii narodnykh dvizhenii na Donu* [For Land, for Freedom: From the History of the National Movements on the Don] (Rostov-na-Donu, 1974), pp. 126–143.

6. This observation is based in part on an afternoon's discussion on December 28, 1974, with members of the History Faculty (Feudal Period) of Moscow State University.

7. Dates are given throughout according to the Julian calendar then in use in the Russian Empire. During the 18th century the calendar was 12 days behind the Gregorian calendar.

8. A map and description of the Caucasian Line appear in *Voyennaya Entsiklopediya* [The Military Encyclopedia] (1911–1915), Vol. XI, *s.v.* "Kavkazskaya liniya."

9. For a detailed account of General Gudovich's proposal, see Felitsyn, "Pobeg s Kubani," pp. 4–6.

10. Catherine's order is reprinted in I. I. Dmitrenko (ed.), *Sbornik istoricheskikh materialov po istorii kubanskogo kazachiago voyska* [Collected Historical Materials on the History of the Kuban Cossack Army] (St. Petersburg, 1896), I, 162–163.

11. Normal line service was for periods of three years. Until well after the era of the Napoleonic Wars, Don Cossack regiments bore no specific designation other than the names of their commanders. The first names of the commanders cited here were gleaned from a service list in TsGVIA, *fond* VUA, No. 11776, folios 301–307.

12. Felitsyn, "Pobeg s Kubani," p. 6.

13. Pronshtein, *Zemlya donskaya*, pp. 122–124.

14. See, for example, A. P. Pronshtein (comp.), *Don i nizhneye povolzh'e v period krest'yanskoy voyny, 1773–1775 godov* [The Don and the Lower Volga Area during the Peasant War of 1773–1775] (Rostove-na-Donu, 1961), p. 36.

15. Problems of pre-1775 Don Cossack government are discussed at length in M. M. Postnikova-Loseva, "Iz istorii donskogo kazachestva XVIII v. (Formirovaniye dvoryanskogo klassa na Donu v XVIII v.)" [From the History of the Don Cossacks of the 18th Century (Formation of the Noble Class on the Don in the 18th Century)] (Candidate thesis, Moscow State University, 1944), chaps. 3 and 4.

16. A concise description of the appearance of the Don nobility is L. M. Savelov, *Donskoye dvoryanstvo* [The Don Nobility] (Moscow), I (1905), 9–13, and II (1914), 5–10. The process of ennoblement and its impact on Don society are discussed at length in Bruce W. Menning, "The Emergence of a Military-Administrative Elite in the Don Cossack Land," in Walter Pintner and Don K. Rowney (eds.), *Russian Officialdom from the Seventeenth to the Twentieth Century* (Chapel Hill, N.C., 1980), Chap. 6.

17. TsGIVA, *fond* 52 (G. A. Potemkin-Tavricheskiy), *op.* 194, *d.* 93, *chast'* 1, folio 38. See also Marc Raeff, "The Style of Russia's Imperial Policy and Prince G. A. Potemkin," in Gerald N. Grob (ed.), *Statesmen and Statecraft in the Modern West: Essays in Honor of Dwight E. Lee and H. Donaldson Jordan* (Barre, Mass., 1967), pp. 8–9.

18. On the question of colonization, see, for example, L. B. Zasedateleva, *Terskiye kazaki (seredina XVI-nachalo XX v.): Istoriko-etnograficheskiye ocherki* [The Terek Cossacks (Mid 16th to the End of the 19th Century): Historical-Ethnographic Notes] (Moscow, 1974), pp. 197–200.

19. *Polnoe sobranie zakonov Rossiyskoy imperii* [The Complete Code of Laws of the Russian Empire], First Series (St. Petersburg, 1830–1839), Vol. XVIII, No. 13351, and Vol. XIX, No. 13376.

20. Savel'ev, *Trekhsoletiye*, p. 98.

21. M. S. Frenkin, "Donskoye kazachestvo v posledney chetverti XVIII v.

(Period voyskovogo grazhdanskogo pravitel'stva 1775–1796 gg.)" [The Don Cossacks in the Last Quarter of the 18th Century (Period of the Host Civilian Government, 1775–1796)] (Candidate thesis, Moscow State University, 1938), pp. 286–287.

22. Felitsyn, "Pobeg s Kubani," p. 8.
23. Lamonov, "Istoricheskiy ocherk," pp. 452–453.
24. Felitsyn, "Pobeg s Kubani," pp. 8–9.
25. This story is entertainingly related in Shcherbina, *Istoriya*, I, 665–667.
26. *Ibid.*, 667–668.
27. Frenkin, "Donskoye kazachestvo," pp. 291–293.
28. Dmitrenko, *Sbornik istoricheskikh materialov*, I, 177–178.
29. "Akty o pereselenii," p. 36.
30. Felitsyn, "Pobeg s Kubani," pp. 25–26.
31. Pronshtein, *Zemlya donskaya*, p. 330.
32. Shcherbina, *Istoriya*, I, 687–691.
33. TsGIVA, *f.* 41, *op.* 1/199, *d.* 331, *ch.* 1, folios 63–64.
34. *Ibid.*, 65.
35. *Ibid.*, 17–19.
36. *Ibid.*, 21–22.
37. See, for example, M. Bylov, "Raskol v voronezhskoy yeparkhii pri Yepiskope Tikhone I (Svyatitelya) (1763–1767 gg.)" [Dissent in the Voronezh Eparchy under Bishop Tikhon I (Prelate) (1763–1767)], *Voronezhskiye yeparkhial'nye vedomosti* [Voronezh Diocesan Gazette], No. 2 (1890), pp. 61–63.
38. Felitsyn, "Pobeg s Kubani," pp. 29–30.
39. TsGIVA, *f.* 41, *op.* 1/199, *d.* 331, *ch.* 1, folios 166–167.
40. Pronshtein, *Zemlya donskaya*, pp. 340–341.
41. TsGIVA, *f.* 41, *op.* 1/199, *d.* 331, *ch.* 1, folios 207–212.
42. Pronshtein, *Zemlya donskaya*, pp. 343–346.
43. P. Yudin, "K istorii Pugachevshchiny" [Toward a History of the Pugachev Revolt], *Russkiy arkhiv* [Russian Archive], 1896, No. 2, pp. 182–184.
44. Dmitrenko, *Sbornik istoricheskikh materialov*, I, 197–200.
45. Lamonov, "Istoricheskiy ocherk," pp. 460–463.
46. A summary of this development appears in Svatikov, *Rossiya i Don*, pp. 251–263.
47. Menning, "The Emergence of a Military-Administrative Elite," pp. 192–193.

Avigdor Levy

# Formalization of Cossack Service under Ottoman Rule

In the traditional Ottoman state, service in the regular armed forces was reserved for Muslims only. The state did, however, employ some of its non-Muslim subjects in a variety of auxiliary military services. The most enduring and familiar were those forces known as Martolos, recruited from Serbs, Greeks, Orthodox and Catholic Albanians and other hardy mountain peoples of the Balkans. These units performed various services, such as guard duty along the frontiers, strategic roads and waterways, and the protection of bridges and mountain passes. The Martolos and similar units operated in Ottoman service from the fifteenth century, and possibly earlier, until well into the nineteenth century.[1] The Ottoman navy also relied heavily on the services of Greek sailors, but the Greeks were primarily engaged in noncombatant seafaring duties.[2] In the modern era the first non-Muslims to be officially admitted to the regular Ottoman armed forces were recruited from the Cossack (Turkish *Kazak*) population of the Dobrudja and the lower Danube basin.

The history of the Dobrudja and Danube Cossacks is shrouded in uncertainty. What appears clear is that from the beginning of the eighteenth century the sparsely populated Danube delta and the Dobrudja increasingly served as a haven for refugees, Cossacks and others, fleeing the expansion and centralizing policies of the Russian state. Many of these fugitives arrived as individuals or in small bands, but the organized settlement of two large groups, which absorbed many of the other Russian and Ukrainian elements, gave this population its Cossack characteristics.

The first large-scale settlement was that of a group of Don Cossacks, followers of their leader Nekrasov. Several thousand Nekrasovites, as they became known, in 1708 settled under Ottoman protection in the Kuban. In the 1720s the Ottoman government resettled them in the Danube delta around Tulcea. From there they gradually spread also to the environments of Babadag, Măcin, Hîrşova and Silistra.[3] The Nekrasovites, who were schismatic Old Believers, were known in the Dobrudja also as "Russians," "Great Russians," or "Lipovans." Living primarily by fishing and agriculture, the number of Nekrasovites was maintained and even augmented by the continual arrival of more fugitive Old Believers. Although divided among themselves on religious issues, they tended to congregate in a few large villages, which in time became prosperous. These included Sarichioi and Jurilovca on Lake Razelm; Slava Rusă near Babadag; Camena near Măcin; Ghindăreşti near Hîrşova; and Tataritsa near Silistra. Nekrasovites also lived in the town of Tulcea.[4]

The second large group to find shelter in the Dobrudja were Zaporozhe Cossacks. In 1775 the Ottoman government allowed them to settle in the Danube delta in a number of villages including Chilia Veche and Caraorman. The Zaporozhians spread up the river basin and into the Dobrudja itself. Unlike the Nekrasovites, they were Orthodox and lived in small communities in a large number of villages together with other ethnic groups. The Zaporozhians were known also as "Little Russians," "Ukrainians," or simply "Cossacks." They engaged in the same occupations as the longer-established and more prosperous Nekrasovites and competed with them. Consequently an intense hostility, occasionally erupting in major armed conflicts, existed between the two groups.[5] In 1850 a traveler counted in the Dobrudja villages 747 Nekrasovite and 1,092 Zaporozhian families.[6] The Treaty of Berlin of 1878 ceded to Rumania northern Dobrudja where most of the Cossack communities were located. In 1880 a total of 8,250 Nekrasovites and 4,555 Zaporozhians were counted in this area.[7] After Rumania had also acquired southern Dobrudja in 1913, the Cossack population of the entire area was estimated in 1918 at about 18,500 Nekrasovites and 21,500 Zaporozhians.[8] It appears that during the nineteenth century the two groups together made up about ten percent of the total population of the Dobrudja.[9]

The Ottoman authorities allowed the Cossacks to settle in the Dobrudja on condition that they perform guard duty and that in wartime they furnish the army with men and animals.[10] The Cossacks thus became part of the empire's irregular auxiliary forces. The Dobrudja Cossacks fought against the Russians in the wars of 1787–1792 and 1806–1812. In the latter conflict, some of them went over to the Russians, [11] but it appears that the majority continued to serve the Ottomans faithfully. In 1817 several hundred of them were recruited to serve in the reformed Ottoman Danube flotilla and in 1821 they took part in suppressing the Greek uprising in Moldavia.[12]

In addition to the Dobrudja and Danube, Cossack communities were independently established in two locations in Anatolia. Zaporozhe Cossacks were settled near the mouth of the Kizil River on the Black Sea coast. A community of Nekrasovites was first established near Anapa, on the northeast coast of the Black Sea. When this area was ceded to Russia as its Black Sea Province by the Treaty of Adrianople in 1829, they were resettled by the Ottomans in western Anatolia near Bursa. Very little is known about these two communities other than that they enjoyed communal autonomy and had certain military obligations to the Ottoman authorities.[13]

The induction of the Dobrudja Cossacks into the regular Ottoman army was primarily due to the personal experience and efforts of Benderli Mehmed Selim Sırrı Paşa. Born in Bender about 1773, Benderli Mehmed was a military man who gained considerable renown during the Russo-Ottoman war of 1806–1812. Following the war he carried out a number of military assignments in support of the centralizing policies of Sultan Mahmud II. In September 1819 he was rewarded by being appointed governor of the province of Silistra. He served in that capacity for five years until September 1824 when he was summoned to the capital to assume the highest appointed office in the realm, that of grand vizier.[14] As governor of Silistra, and possibly even earlier, Benderli Mehmed had come to appreciate the martial qualities of the Dobrudja Cossacks.

Meanwhile the uprising that had broken out in Greece in 1821 cut off the Ottoman navy from its traditional sources of recruits in the Aegean islands and coastal districts. To offset these losses and to achieve a modernization and expansion of the navy, the Ottoman government in 1824 launched a massive drive to recruit sailors from other areas. As part of this effort, five hundred Cossacks from the Dobrudja were enrolled on the grand vizier's initiative in the Ottoman navy. Their numbers included a priest and dragomans, and they arrived in Istanbul in February 1824. Their monthly pay was good: their leader and priest each received one hundred kuruş, standard-bearers and dragomans fifty, and the men twenty-five kuruş each. The imperial arsenal issued each man a musket and a saber, a fact suggesting that they were enlisted as combatants.[15] Four years later the traveler Adolphus Slade met sixty of these Cossacks aboard the battleship "Selimiye." Among the 1,400 members of the crew they were "remarkable by their fair hair and sheep-skin caps . . .. They were tall, stout, quiet men, and lived apart from the others. . . . They ate olives, bread, and rice, twice a day with apparent content . . . . Two of them only spoke Turkish."[16]

In 1826 the sultan embarked on a general reorganization and modernization of the Ottoman army. The recruitment and training of new infantry regiments was pressed that summer in Istanbul and many provinces. Financial difficulties, however, delayed the establishment of modern cavalry units. Finally, again at the urging of Grand Vizier Benderli Mehmed, the sultan agreed that the first modern cavalry regiment in the empire would be recruited and stationed in the province of Silistra. Ottoman sources ascribe this decision to three factors. First, horses and fodder were readily available in the province, making the project more economically feasible. Second, excellent horsemen were found among the heterogeneous population of the Dobrudja. And finally, the province of Silistra was considered one of the most sensitive on the empire's military frontier.[17]

Since the formation of the first mounted regiment was put in the charge of the new governor of Silistra, Ahmed Pasha, the government consulted him first on the subject, and sent him a draft of the proposal for the organization of the new cavalry. Ahmed Pasha studied the proposal, made his own recommendations, and returned the documents to Istanbul where they were approved by the grand vizier's council and, finally, by the sultan. As a result the regulation setting up the first cavalry regiment became law only on November 16, 1826.[18]

The Silistra cavalry regiment was recruited from three ethnic groups. The first two were Muslims—Tatar and Turkish tribesmen settled by the Ottomans in the Dobrudja to strengthen their Danube frontier; the third group consisted of Christian Cossacks. Unlike provincial infantry regiments founded in other areas where the officer cadres had been sent out from Istanbul, the officers of the Silistra cavalry were recruited locally. The regiment's first colonel was Mehmed Emin Aga, a former city notable *(âyan)* of Mangalia, a small town on the Black Sea. The Tatar tribesmen made up the right wing of the regiment. The post of major of the right wing was therefore assigned to one of their chiefs *(mirzas)*. The left wing was made up of Turks and Cossacks in equal numbers. The ranks of major and adjutant major of that wing were occupied by Turks. The troop companies, however, consisted of only one ethnic group, either Turks or Cossacks. Troop officers were therefore members of their respective groups. The Turkish troops were assigned imams and the Cossacks priests *(rahibs)*. The Cossack companies were also granted a certain amount of administrative autonomy within the left wing under a special officer called chief cossack *(kazak başı)*, who himself was a Muslim. The first to hold this rank was a certain Ali Koç Aga. A regimental clerk was jointly appointed by the provincial governor and the colonel. In addition, matters of financial administration were supervised by a commissary officer responsible to the superintendant of the army in Istanbul.

In spite of the peculiarities of the Silistra-based unit, its organization was intended to serve as a model for setting up other cavalry regiments. The regiment's complement was set at 1,323 officers and men, of whom 329 were Cossacks (see Table I). The regiment consisted of two wings of six troops apiece. Each troop had a complement of 109 officers and men. In peacetime the troopers were required to serve on active duty only four months a year in rotation, so that at all times there would be at least four cavalry companies present at Silistra. Only the colonel, the two majors and the chief cossack were full-time staff officers and received regular pay and rations throughout the year. All other officers and men received full pay, considerably less than that of equal ranks in the regular infantry, only when on active duty (see Table I). When they returned to their villages, they continued to draw half pay but no rations. Only the colonel and the majors received full army rations; all other men received only bread and meat, although by way of compensation their bread ration was three, instead of the usual two, loaves a day.

The Cossacks received the same pay as their Muslim peers in the regiment, except that the priests were allotted only 24 kuruş a month, compared with 30 kuruş for the imams. The Cossack captains received the same pay but only half as much meat, barley and straw rations as their Muslim counterparts. Furthermore, Cossacks were barred from promotion beyond the rank of captain, and so could not hope to command mixed formations. Even the chief bugler of the left wing was always a Muslim. The troops were organized exactly like infantry companies with the sole difference that each troop had one extra sergeant. A notable departure of a nonmilitary nature was the reduction in the ratio of clergy. Saddlers and farriers were not assigned to the regiment on a regular basis. Leather and iron

*Table I*

*ORGANIZATION OF THE SILISTRA CAVALRY REGIMENT BY THE REGULATION OF NOVEMBER 16, 1826*

| Rank | No. of Men | Monthly Salary* per person in kuruş | | Daily Rations** per person Bread | Meat | Barley | Straw |
|---|---|---|---|---|---|---|---|
| *Regimental Officers* | | | | | | | |
| Colonel *(Binbaşı)* | 1 | 750 | (750) | 8 | 800 | 8 | 16 |
| Clerk *(Kâtib)* | 1 | 150 | (150) | — | — | — | — |
| *Officers and Men of the Right Wing Tatars—Six Troops* | | | | | | | |
| Major *(Kolağası)* | 1 | 250 | (400) | 4 | 400 | 6 | 12 |
| Adjutant Major *(Kolağası Mülâzimi)* | 1 | 125 | (250) | 3 | 100 | 2 | 4 |
| Captain *(Yüzbaşı)* | 6 | 100 | (180) | 3 | 200 | 4 | 8 |
| Lieutenant *(Yüzbaşı Mülâzimi)* | 12 | 70 | (120) | 3 | 100 | 2 | 4 |
| Standard-Bearer *(Sancaktar)* | 6 | 50 | (100) | 3 | 100 | 2 | 4 |
| Sergeant *(Çavuş)* | 12 | 50 | (60) | 3 | 100 | 2 | 4 |
| Corporal *(Onbaşı)* | 60 | 20 | (30) | 3 | 100 | 2 | 4 |
| Trooper *(Nefer)* | 540 | 15 | (20) | 3 | 100 | 2 | 4 |
| Imam | 4 | 30 | (60) | 3 | 100 | 2 | 4 |
| Water-Bearer *(Saka)* | 6 | 25 | (20) | 3 | 100 | 2 | 4 |
| Chief Bugler *(Borazan Başı)* | 1 | 60 | (60) | 3 | 100 | 2 | 4 |
| Bugler *(Borazan)* | 12 | 30 | (20) | 3 | 100 | 2 | 4 |
| *Officers and Men of the Left Wing Turks—Three Troops* | | | | | | | |
| Major *(Kolağası)* | 1 | 250 | (400) | 4 | 400 | 6 | 12 |
| Adjutant Major *(Kolağası Mülâzimi)* | 1 | 125 | (250) | 3 | 100 | 2 | 4 |
| Captain *(Yüzbaşı)* | 3 | 100 | (180) | 3 | 200 | 4 | 8 |
| Lieutenant *(Yüzbaşı Mülâzimi)* | 6 | 70 | (120) | 3 | 100 | 2 | 4 |
| Standard-Bearer *(Sancaktar)* | 3 | 50 | (100) | 3 | 100 | 2 | 4 |

*Table I, cont.*

| Rank | No. of Men | Monthly Salary* per person in kuruş | | Daily Rations** per person Bread | Meat | Barley | Straw |
|---|---|---|---|---|---|---|---|
| Sergeant *(Çavuş)* | 6 | 50 | (60) | 3 | 100 | 2 | 4 |
| Corporal *(Onbaşı)* | 30 | 20 | (30) | 3 | 100 | 2 | 4 |
| Trooper *(Nefer)* | 270 | 15 | (20) | 3 | 100 | 2 | 4 |
| Imam | 2 | 30 | (60) | 3 | 100 | 2 | 4 |
| Water-Bearer *(Saka)* | 3 | 25 | (20) | 3 | 100 | 2 | 4 |
| Chief Bugler *(Borazan Başı)* | 1 | 60 | (60) | 3 | 100 | 2 | 4 |
| Bugler *(Borazan)* | 6 | 30 | (20) | 3 | 100 | 2 | 4 |
| *Cossacks—Three Troops* | | | | | | | |
| Chief Cossack *(Kazak Başı)**** | 1 | 150 | (—) | 6 | 200 | 4 | 8 |
| Captain *(Yüzbası)* | 3 | 100 | (180) | 3 | 100 | 2 | 4 |
| Lieutenant *(Yüzbaşı Mülâzimi)* | 6 | 70 | (120) | 3 | 100 | 2 | 4 |
| Standard-Bearer *(Sancaktar)* | 3 | 50 | (100) | 3 | 100 | 2 | 4 |
| Sergeant *Çavuş)* | 6 | 50 | (60) | 3 | 100 | 2 | 4 |
| Corporal *(Onbaşı)* | 30 | 20 | (30) | 3 | 100 | 2 | 4 |
| Trooper *(Nefer)* | 270 | 15 | (20) | 3 | 100 | 2 | 4 |
| Water-Bearer *(Saka)* | 3 | 25 | (20) | 3 | 100 | 2 | 4 |
| Priest *(Rahib)* | 2 | 25 | (—) | 3 | 100 | 2 | 4 |
| Bugler *(Borazan)* | 6 | 30 | (20) | 3 | 100 | 2 | 4 |

* Salary paid to members of the Silistra regiment when on active duty. The numbers in parantheses indicate the salaries of men serving in regular infantry regiments and holding equal rank.

* Daily rations were measured as follows: bread by loaves; meat in dirhems (silver pieces); barley and straw in okes (2.8 pounds).

*** The chief cossack was the only Muslim in this subdivision.

work was done by outside craftsmen whose expenses were met by the commissary officer in Silistra.

The enlisted men had to be between the ages of fifteen and thirty, healthy, fit for military service, and unmarried. A special exception was made in the case of the Tatars, among whom 150 men out of the total 661 could be married. Each ethnic group had to maintain the full complement assigned as its share in the regiment. Upon the death or retirement of a trooper, the leaders of the Tatar tribes or Cossack communities were required to find replacements. The governor was to exercise the same responsibility in regard to the Turkish personnel. A fixed number of men were to be recruited from each village or community, which had also to supply a mount and one complete set of riding gear for every man. For every horse the government made a one-time payment of 150 kuruş. Thereafter the village or community was to supply the same number of men and horses without further compensation.

While the trooper was on reserve at home, the village was responsible for maintaining his horse fit for duty. Every tour of duty had to take place at Silistra where special barracks were built, or on various guard functions assigned by the provincial governor. In wartime the whole regiment had to be mobilized in readiness for any assignment ordered by Istanbul. Upon completion of their tours of duty, the men had to turn in their weapons, and also their uniforms in clean and good condition. A tag with the man's name was attached to the uniform, and it was to be kept in a special warehouse for his next tour of duty. This last arrangement proved unworkable, so in June 1827, at the request of Ahmed Pasha, governor of Silistra, and with the approval of army headquarters, this practice was changed. Thenceforth the troopers had to turn in only their weapons and were allowed to take their uniforms home.[19] The cavalry's uniforms were similar to those of the infantry. Each man was given a vest and short jacket, a pair of oriental breeches and a sash. The notable difference were the black leather riding boots with spurs. Since under normal conditions the men of this regiment served only four months a year, they were to be issued new uniforms only once every other year. The troopers were armed with a carbine, pistols and a broad crooked falchion.[20]

The organization of the Silistra regiment was completed within several months. In November 1827 two hundred troopers were brought to Istanbul to be instructed in the new cavalry drill, and on the thirteenth of that month they were reviewed by the sultan at

Davud Pasha barracks.[21] However, since infantry regulations had been changed during the previous summer, the cavalry, too, now had to undergo modifications to conform to the new infantry organization. Instead of one regiment of 1,325 troopers, Silistra now was required to provide two battalions *(taburs)* of 884 troopers each. This was accomplished by breaking up the original regiment and enrolling some 450 additional men. Apparently there had been some difficulties in recruiting Tatars, for their ratio in the new organization was reduced while that of the Turks was increased. The proportion of Cossacks remained the same, but now they had to provide more officers and men, 436 instead of 329. One battalion now consisted of Turks only and was commanded by a Turkish officer. The other was made up of Tatars and Cossacks in equal numbers and was commanded by a Tatar.[22]

Under the new regulations, which went into effect in March 1828, the number of Cossack priests was reduced from two to one. The marked distinction of the reorganization was a further gradation of ranks in closer accord with the contemporary French system (see Table II). Each battalion consisted of six enlarged troops. The pay and Turkish titles of the two senior grades remained the same, that is *binbaşı* and *kolağası,* but they were now understood to be equivalent in rank to the French major and adjutant major, respectively. As of 1830, following Western practice, a cavalry battalion *(tabur)* was redesignated a regiment and called in Turkish an *alay.* Its strength and organization remained exactly the same as before: 884 officers and men divided into six troops. Its commanding officer, however, was now raised to the rank of colonel, renamed in Turkish *miralay.*[23]

The Silistra cavalry fought in the war of 1828–1829 against Russia, but some of the Cossacks deserted to the enemy during the early stages of the 1828 campaign. As a result the Cossack troops were transferred from the European front to Istanbul and later to Anatolia. Apparently desertion affected only a few, for Cossacks continued to serve in the Silistra cavalry. In fact, following the war the two regiments were placed on a regular full-time footing, and the pay and conditions of service were brought up to par with the regular guards cavalry[24] (see Table II).

The Silistra regiments served as a model for the establishment of a regular cavalry regiment in Istanbul in February 1827.[25] In 1830 the Istanbul-based cavalry was transferred to the Corps of the Imperial Guards *(Asâkir-i Hassa-yı Şahane).* Throughout the 1830s the two Silistra regiments served as the principal regular cavalry attached to

*Table II*

*ORGANIZATION OF A SILISTRA CAVALRY BATTALION (TABUR)/REGIMENT (ALAY) BY THE REGULATION OF MARCH 16, 1828*

| *Rank* | *No. of Men* | *Monthly Salary per Man in Kuruş (1828)* | *(1830)** |
|---|---|---|---|
| Major *(Binbaşı)*/Colonel *(Miralay)* | 1 | 750 | 1200 |
| Adjutant Major *(Kil Ağa)* | 2 | 250 | 400 |
| Clerk *(Kâtib)* | 2 | 150 | 200 |
| Imam | 2 | 30 | 75 |
| Standard-Bearer *(Sancaktar)* | 3 | 50 | 90 |
| Sergent of Buglers *(Çavuşu-Boru)* | 1 | 60 | 60 |
| Water-Bearer *(Sakkâ)* | 3 | 25 | 25 |
| Captain *(Yüzbası)* | 6 | 100 | 200 |
| Subcaptain *(Yüzbası Vekili)* | 6 | 85** | 150 |
| First Lieutenant *(Mülâzim-i Evvel)* | 6 | 70 | 120 |
| Sub First Lieutenant *(Mülâzim-i Evvel Vekili)* | 6 | 60** | 100 |
| Second Lieutenant *(Mülâzim-i Sâni)* | 6 | 70 | 120 |
| Sub Second Lieutenant *(Mülâzim-i Sani Vekili)* | 6 | 60** | 100 |
| Sergeant *(Çavuş)* | 24 | 50 | 50 |
| Lance Sergeant *(Çavuş Vekili)* | 24 | 35** | 40 |
| Corporal *(Onbaşı)* | 48 | 20 | 36 |

*Table II, cont.*

| Rank | No. of Men | Monthly Salary per Man in Kuruş (1828) | (1830)* |
|---|---|---|---|
| Lance Corporal *(Onbaşı Vekili)* | 48 | 17.5** | 30 |
| Bugler *(Borazan)* | 12 | 30 | 30 |
| Farrier *(Nalband)* | 6 | 40** | 60 |
| Trooper *(Nefer)* | 672 | 15 | 24 |
| TOTAL | 884 | | |

The battalion including Cossack troopers listed also the following:

| | | | |
|---|---|---|---|
| Chief Cossack *(Kazak Başı)* | 1 | 150 | — |
| Priest *(Rähib)* | 1 | 25 | — |

Each troop had the following organization:

| | |
|---|---|
| Captain | 1 |
| Sub Captain | 1 |
| First Lieutenant | 1 |
| Sub First Lieutenant | 1 |
| Second Lieutenant | 1 |
| Sub Second Lieutenant | 1 |
| Sergeants | 4 |
| Lance Sergeants | 4 |
| Corporals | 8 |
| Lance Corporals | 8 |
| Buglers | 2 |
| Farriers | 1 |
| Troopers | 112 |
| TOTAL | 145 |

* Salary increases by the regulation of July 4, 1830

** New rank

the troops of the line *(Asâkir-i Mansûre)*.[26] The governors of Silistra continued to be responsible for maintaining the full complement of this force from the Turkish, Tatar and Cossack communities that provided the original recruits.[27]

At some point in the early 1840s, possibly in connection with the military reorganization of 1843, the Nekrasovites of the Bursa district were also enrolled in a regular cavalry regiment.[28] During the Crimean War the Cossack contingents fought against the Russians on the Asiatic front.[29] Abdolonyme Ubicini, a generally reliable source, in 1876 listed among the regular Ottoman forces two Cossack regiments of four squadrons each with a total complement of 1,040 officers and men.[30] These units were attached to the First Army Corps (Imperial Guards) with headquarters in Istanbul.[31] Although the Cossacks might have lent their name to these units, a memorandum by Foreign Minister Fuad Pasha of May 1867 indicates that they were actually "mixed regiments . . . consisting of Muslims and Christians."[32]

By the Treaty of Berlin of 1878 the Ottoman Empire ceded the Dobrudja to Rumania and Bulgaria. The available statistical evidence suggests that the Cossack communities generally remained where they were, thus passing out of the Ottoman orbit. For this as well as other reasons it is likely that the Cossack regiments were disbanded during the early years of Sultan Abdülhamid II's reign (1876–1909).[33]

As of the 1840s small numbers of non-Muslim subjects of the sultan were enrolled in the regular Ottoman armed forces, but their admission differed from that of the Cossacks in two important aspects. First, they were recruited as individuals and not as a group serving in their own distinctive units under their own officers. Second except in the navy they generally served in noncombatant positions, such as army doctors and engineers.[34] The experience of the Cossack contingents remains therefore unique in Ottoman annals. Their contribution, however, to the modernization of the Ottoman navy and army at a critical juncture was considerable and totally disproportionate to the small size of the Cossack communities.

## Notes

*A note on transliteration:* Ottoman Turkish names and terms are transliterated by using present-day Turkish spelling. In words of Arabic origin the final b and d are preserved *(kâtib,* not *katip;* Mahmud, not Mahmut).

1. Robert Anheger, "Martolos", *Islâm Ansiklopedisi* (henceforth abbreviated as *IA*), VII, 341–44; Paul Fesch, *Constantinople aux derniers jours d'Abdul-Hamid* (Paris, 1907), pp. 250–256 ff.

2. Hamilton Gibb and Harold Bowen, *Islamic Society and the West,* I, Pt. 1 (Oxford, 1950), 104–107.

3. St. Romansky, *Carte ethnographique de la nouvelle Dobroudja roumaine* (Sofia, 1915), pp. 27–28; Philip Longworth, *The Cossacks* (New York, 1970), p. 164.

4. J. J. Nacian, *La Dobroudja économique et sociale* (Paris, 1886), pp. 50–51; Eugène Pittard, *La Roumanie* (Paris, 1917), pp. 264–268; St. Romansky, "Le caractére ethnique de la Dobroudja", in A. Ichirkov *et al., La Dobroudja* (Sofia, 1918), pp. 190–192; Müstecib Ülküsal, *Dobruca ve Türkler* [Dobrudja and the Turks] (Ankara, 1966), p. 33.

5. Romansky, "Caractère ethnique", pp. 191–192; Longworth, *The Cossacks,* p. 228; W.E.D. Allen, *The Ukraine: A History* (New York, 1963), pp. 229, 259–260.

6. Nicolae Iorga, "La population de la Dobrogea vers la moitié du XIXe siècle d'après un manuscrit récemment découvert," in N. Iorga *et al., La Dobrogea roumaine* (Bucarest, 1919), p. 169; Aurel Decei, "Dobruca", *IA,* III, 641.

7. N. P. Comnène, *La Dobrogea: Essai historique, etc.* (Paris, 1918), p. 135.

8. Romansky, "Caractère ethnique," p. 190.

9. Cf. Comnène, *La Dobrogea,* p. 135.

10. Nacian, *La Dobroudja,* pp. 47–50.

11. Allen, *The Ukraine,* p. 260; Longworth, *The Cossacks,* pp. 368–369, n. 6.

12. Mehmed Ataullah Şanizade, *Tarih-i Şanizade* [Şanizade's History] (Istanbul, 1290–1291 [1873–1874]), III, 22–25; Longworth, *The Cossacks,* pp. 368–369, n. 6.

13. Abdolonyme Ubicini and Abel Jean Baptiste Pavet de Courteille, *État présent de l'Empire ottoman* (Paris, 1876), pp. 34–36. This source estimates the total number of the Cossack population in the Ottoman Empire in 1876 at 30,000–35,000, but it excludes from this figure the Nekrasovites of the Dobrudja who are separately estimated at 18,000–20,000 souls. The Zaporozhians of the Dobrudja are estimated at 1,000–1,200 families. If we deduct this last figure from the total, the estimate for the two Anatolian Cossack communities would be 24,000–30,000 persons. Of the two the Zaporozhian community is described as "more numerous" and "older."

14. Mehmed Süreyya, *Sicill-i Osmani* (Istanbul, 1308–1311 [1890–1893]), III, 60–61.

15. Mehmed Esad, "Tarih-i Esad" [Esad's History], I, (MS, Süleymaniye Library, Istanbul, Esad Efendi Collection, Y 2084), 296b–297a; Ahmed Cevdet, *Tarih-i Cevdet,* [Cevdet's History], XII (Istanbul, 1301 [1883]), 122.

16. Adolphus Slade, *Records of Travels in Turkey, Greece, etc.* (Philadelphia, 1833), I, 97.

17. Ahmed Lutfi, *Tarih-i Lutfi* [Lutfi's History] (Istanbul, 1290–1328 [1873–1910]), I, 195.

18. The text of this regulation and related documents of later dates are found in *Başbakanlık Arşivi* [Prime Minister's Archives], Istanbul (henceforth abbreviated ast BBA), *Kanunname-i Askerî Defterleri* [Registers of Military Regulations] (henceforth abbreviated as *KAD*), I, 26–36. Some details are found also in Lutfi, *Tarih-i Lutfi,* I, 196. The description that follows is based primarily on the official documents.

19. BBA, *KAD,* I, 36.

20. In addition to the sources cited above, descriptions of uniforms and arms are found in: Archives de la Guerre (henceforth abbreviated as AG), Paris, MR 1619, No. 39; Charles MacFarlane, *Constantinople in 1828* (London, 1829), p. 351.

21. BBA, *KAD,* I, 71; Hızır Ilyas, *Vekâyı-ı Letâif-i Enderun* (Istanbul, 1276 [1859]), p. 419.

22. BBA, *KAD,* I, 71–73; *Maliyeden Müdevver Defterleri* [Registers of Financial Records] (henceforth abbreviated as *MMD*), Register No. 9002, p. 107.

23. BBA, *MMD,* 9002, 39, 42 n.; *Takvîm-i Vekâyı* No. 1 (25 Cemâzıelevvel 1247 [November 2, 1831]).

24. BBA, *KAD,* I, 74–75; *MMD,* 9002, 39, 160; Lutfi, *Tarih-i Lutfi,* I, 306; Georg Wilhelm von Valentini, *Traité sur la guerre contre les Turcs* (Berlin, 1830), pp. 224–225; Édouard Engelhardt, *La Turquie et le Tanzimat* (Paris, 1882–1884), I, 89.

25. BBA, *KAD,* I, 45–52.

26. In addition, Ottoman cavalry at that period included four regiments of guards, twelve regiments of reformed feudal *(timarlı)* troopers and irregular horsemen (BBA, *MMD,* pp. 117–118, 163–64; *Cevdet-Askeri,* No. 673).

27. AG, MR 1619, Nos. 58–60; Topkapı Saray Archives, Istanbul, No. E-119.

28. Ubicini and de Courteille, *État présent,* p. 36.

29. W.E.D. Allen and Paul Muratoff, *Caucasian Battlefields* (Cambridge, 1953), p. 95 and note.

30. Ubicini and de Courteille, *État présent,* p. 179.

31. *Ibid.,* pp. 180–181.

32. "Il existe . . . dans l'armée Ottomane deux régiments de Cosaques mixtes, c'est-à-dire composés de musulmans et de chrétiens." *Ibid.,* p. 252. Fuad

Pasha mentions this fact to disprove the often repeated claim that Muslim prejudice precluded Ottoman Christians from military service.

33. Capt. M.C.P. Ward, *Handbook of the Turkish Army* (London, 1900) does not mention the Cossack regiments. Also, Fesch, *Constantinople*, which has a separate chapter (pp. 247–266) dedicated to the subject "Les Chrétiens et le service militaire," does not refer to Cossack military service during the reign of Abdülhamid.

34. In addition to Fesch, a discussion of this question is found in Roderic H. Davison, *Reform in the Ottoman Empire, 1856–1876* (Princeton, 1963), pp. 95–96 ff.

Philip Longworth

# Conclusions

The autonomous warrior societies of East Central Europe constitute one of the most curious phenomena of the region's history, yet one that has attracted little sustained attention from historians. Nests of bandits and freebooters, centers of innumerable popular insurrections, sources for mercenary recruitment, these communities also conducted guerrilla wars on their own accounts, defended the frontiers of empires, and provided contingents to fight in the Austrian, Ottoman, Russian and Venetian armies. Involved in virtually all the wars that afflicted the steppe zone and the Balkans from the fifteenth to the nineteenth century, the nature of warfare and societal change in East Central Europe cannot adequately be understood without them.

During the eighteenth century most of these communities, which had so long been a cause as well as a reflection of instability in the frontier zone, were effectively subjected and absorbed into the military systems of the great states of the region.[1] Some of the complexities of this process have been described and analyzed in the preceding essays, each of which deals with a hitherto neglected episode or aspect of the subject.

In concentrating on Cossacks and the Venetian Uskoks, the essays lay no claim to be a comprehensive treatment of all frontier societies in the region and all their related phenomena. Such an exhaustive exploration is obviously beyond the scope of these few pages. Nor is it entirely necessary. The processes by which the Habsburg and Russian military frontier systems were built up have already been described in recent literature;[2] the activities of other groups (notably the haiduks of Bulgaria) have also received well-documented attention[3]—and there is no need to recapitulate the details here. On the other hand, all this together amounts to no more than a partial clearing of an historiographical area much of which is still obscure.

The reasons for this are not difficult to find. As pointed out in the first essay, there are problems with the sources. Marginal societies of the kind under discussion, which were egalitarian in sentiment, largely illiterate in composition, primitively organized, and suspicious of the great bureaucratic states that sought to control them, left little direct evidence to posterity. This obviously inhibits the reconstruction of their history from their own point of view. Furthermore, the disordered state of the Turkish archives has put a brake on research into the warrior societies of Ottoman Europe. Yet there are other reasons for the neglect of the subject and, indeed, for its obfuscation. The reasons are ideological, and they help to account for the unsatisfactory state of so much East Central European historiography in general. Soviet historians, for example, have understandably tended to emphasize the Cossacks' role in raising and sustaining peasant revolts, producing voluminous and admirable work, which, however, reflects a neglect of other relevant aspects. It is on this account that Professor Menning's original contribution on a little-known Don Cossack rebellion against forced colonization is particularly welcome.

More serious than the sins of omission, however, are the sins of commission, and in particular those deriving from political nationalism. Many historians, themselves in the forefront of the nationalist movements of the nineteenth and twentieth centuries, have tended to distort the past not merely by constricting the treatment of these warrior communities within the framework of exclusively national pasts, but by representing them as the standard-bearers of continuing national feeling through centuries of alien rule. This has resulted in the distortion of much of the history of East Central Europe and particularly of the phenomena under discussion here. Serb and Croat scholars have vied with each other to claim the Uskoks exclusively to themselves.[4] Greeks have tended to idealize the klephts, Bulgarians the haiduks; some Ukrainian historians still present the rebellious Ukrainian Cossacks of the seventeenth and early eighteenth centuries as ardent nationalists;[5] all of them strain the available historical evidence in making their cases.

Armed uprisings ran like an unbroken thread through the history of such groups during the eighteenth century as in earlier times. Whether they were led by some local warlord such as Ferenc Rákóczi or Ivan Mazepa, or by leaders that emerged from the masses, such as Kondratiy Bulavin or Yemelian Pugachev, these insurrections generally reflected a reaction to encroachments by organized states on the liberties of their communities. Sometimes, too, they reflected the opportunism of some ambitious prince. All of them were inspired by long-standing cultural and social traditions, but they were not nationalist uprisings in the modern sense[6]—any more than were Bruce Menning's Cossacks protesting over compulsory resettlement or C.W. Bracewell's Uskoks rebelling over the corvée.

When the ideal of freedom proved unattainable, there were occasions when entire groups crossed frontiers to seek the protection of another power. This may account for some of those Uskoks who crossed from the Ottoman into the Venetian sphere. It certainly accounts for the presence of Cossack communities in the Ottoman Empire—refugees from the Bulavin rising of 1708 (Nekrasovites) and from successive destructions of the Zaporozhe Sich. Some of these were organized for service within the Ottoman system. How far, in each case, the traditional cultures and military traditions of such groups were modified by their new environments remains, as yet, largely a matter for conjecture—although the Cossacks under Turkish rule were still recognizably *sui generis* well into the twentieth century.

The persistence of culture and traditions is also reflected in the fighting characteristics of all these groups. The Uskoks' raiding methods, as described by Dr. Bracewell, represent a continuity of mode that dates back at least to the sixteenth century. The same applies in large measure to the Cossacks. The difficulties which the imperial states of the region found in coping with such traditional, technologically primitive methods of warfare should not on that account seem surprising, however. After all, the effectiveness of time-honored guerrilla tactics (given support of the people and knowledge of the terrain) against highly organized armies deploying sophisticated weaponry has been demonstrated on several occasions even in our own times. Furthermore, as emerges from all the essays in this section, the states themselves appreciated the uses to which such warriors could be put as colonizers and military auxiliaries, and this tended to mitigate the force of the suppressive actions. It was partly for this reason, partly for reasons of economy, that the states used privileges as well as force as means of controlling these essentially unstable, sometimes anarchic elements.

Initially, the Venetians not only accorded favors to newly arrived Uskok war bands but allowed them great latitude in military action. By the beginning of the eighteenth century, however, the clampdown had begun. It was a similar story on the Austrian Military Border and in the Cossack lands, although the process of harnessing these frontier communities proceeded at a very uneven rate. In some respects the Venetians were in advance of their Austrian neighbors in organizing frontier peoples into their defensive system and integrating them into society at large. This was rendered possible by the existence of an ordered and structured society in Dalmatia prior to the Uskoks' arrival. On the Don, by contrast, the Cossacks themselves constituted society and newcomers tended to be absorbed into it. But the fact that these Uskoks tended to be displaced peasants rather than transhumant shepherds no doubt facilitated the process of their absorption. Land implied fixity of abode, hence easier control, and the Venetian practice of granting land to individual families, rather than to entire communities, as a heritable possession in return for service tended to weaken ties with the war band and strengthen loyalty to the state.

The granting of land was a major inducement held out by all the states in question to these frontier groups. Even when, as in the case of the Cossacks, the warrior communities already possessed land, the state took pains to create a legal fiction (as Russia did in the eighteenth century) that they owed their lands to the crown. A related and more effective means of control was for the state to buy off the elite or even to encourage its emergence—a device that was also marked throughout the region. By encouraging elitist tendencies, the states were able to erode the natural democratic forms of these primitive societies; and by absorbing the elites into the regular officer corps, they were able to hasten the process of regularization. To this extent the organization of the Venetian *Craina* will be familiar to readers of Part III of the first volume in this series. But there were differences too. The Don, Ural, and Black Sea Cossack hosts retained their own distinct although controlled, administrations, and continued to provide distinct units which retained some of the traditions, however emasculated, of the old days of independent Cossackdom. The Uskoks, by contrast, lost all corporate identity, though their legends lingered on. The various groups of the Austrian Military Frontier and the Ukrainian Cossacks (other than those who moved into the Ottoman orbit and those who formed the Black Sea host) represent intermediate stages in this process.

For all their differences, then, such groups belong to a common social and military genus. If the genus is difficult to define precisely in a way that takes account of all groups in all periods this is partly attributable to semantic confusion. This relates not only to Dr.

Bracewell's Uskoks, Morlachs and haiduks (not to mention komitaji and Martolos), but to the term *kazak* as well.[7] Such semantic uncertainties, together with the ideological historiographical tendencies already mentioned and the misconceptions generated by too narrow a focusing on particular states and institutions, have tended to make the subject seem more elusive than in fact it is. As these essays show, military exigencies placed similar strains on the social fabric of all these free warlike formations from the extreme east to the extreme west of the region. All of them experienced broadly similar transformations between the late seventeenth and the early nineteenth century in reaction to the demands placed on them and the favors accorded to them by states that were struggling to control their frontiers and to fight their wars more effectively.

Much more work needs to be done before the interplay between society and warfare in the great frontier zones of East Central Europe can be fully understood. The frontier societies themselves are not the only relevant focus of inquiry in this connection. But they are a potentially rewarding one, and these essays have at least filled some gaps in our knowledge and improved our understanding on this problematical but important area. They have also indicated some avenues for further research. It is to be hoped that at least some of these avenues will soon be explored.

## Notes

1. The continued survival of some of the more amorphous of them, notably clephts, komitaji and haiduks, reflects the progressive decline of the Ottoman state as an effective controlling force.

2. See Gunther E. Rothenberg, *The Austrian Military Border in Croatia* (Urbana, Ill., 1960); *idem, The Military Border in Croatia* (Chicago, 1966); *idem*, "The Habsburg Military Border System," in *idem* and Béla K. Király (eds.), *War and Society in East Central Europe*, I (New York, 1979), 361–392; Philip Longworth, *The Cossacks* (New York, 1969); *idem*, "Transformations in Cossackdom," in Rothenberg and Király, *War and Society*, I, 393–407; and the associated bibliographies.

3. Bistra Cvetkova, *Haydutstvoto v bĭgarskite zemi prez 15*–18 v. [The Haiduks in the Bulgarian Lands in the 15th–18th Centuries] (Sofia, 1971).

4. See Philip Longworth, "The Senj Uskoks Reconsidered," *Slavonic and East European Review*, LVII, No. 3, 348–368.

5. The Mazepa rebellion of 1709 has often been interpreted in these terms. In a paper presented to the first conference on "War and Society," however,

Professor Orest Subtelny suggested that rather than seeking independence for the Ukraine the Cossack leadership was motivated by a perceived need to find a protector more effective than the Russians seemed to be.

6. An altercation between Professor Rudnytsky and myself on the subject of late seventeenth- and early eighteenth-century nationalism, with particular reference to the Ukrainian Cossacks *(Slavic Review,* XXXIII, No. 2 (June 1974, 411–416*)*, may be of interest in this connection. In it Rudnytsky tacitly accepts some of my arguments and ignores others while persisting in an attempt to demonstrate the existence of a specifically "national" feeling among the Ukrainian population at that time and in overemphasizing the distinctiveness of Ukrainian institutions. The Velychko chronicle which he cites undoubtedly reflects local patriotism, but is no evidence of widespread national feeling. Nor can a "national" dimension be attributed to Bohdan Khmel'nytsky's rising and its aftermath on the ground that Cossacks "maintained the Ukraine as a distinct political entity" by opposing Tatars, Poles and Russians. In fact they were never able to oppose any of these enemies without support from one of the others and (as the chaotic *Ruina* period showed) various factions among the Cossacks sided with those powers rather than combining together to resist them. The Ukrainians were no more a "nation" than the Transylvanians of those times, and the persistent, exclusive attempts to trace the roots of modern nationalisms to that period serve to distract attention from the importance of such societies as frontier societies.

7. Longworth, *The Cossacks*, pp. 342–344.

# VII

# Military Emigration from Central and Eastern Europe to France in the Seventeenth and Eighteenth Centuries

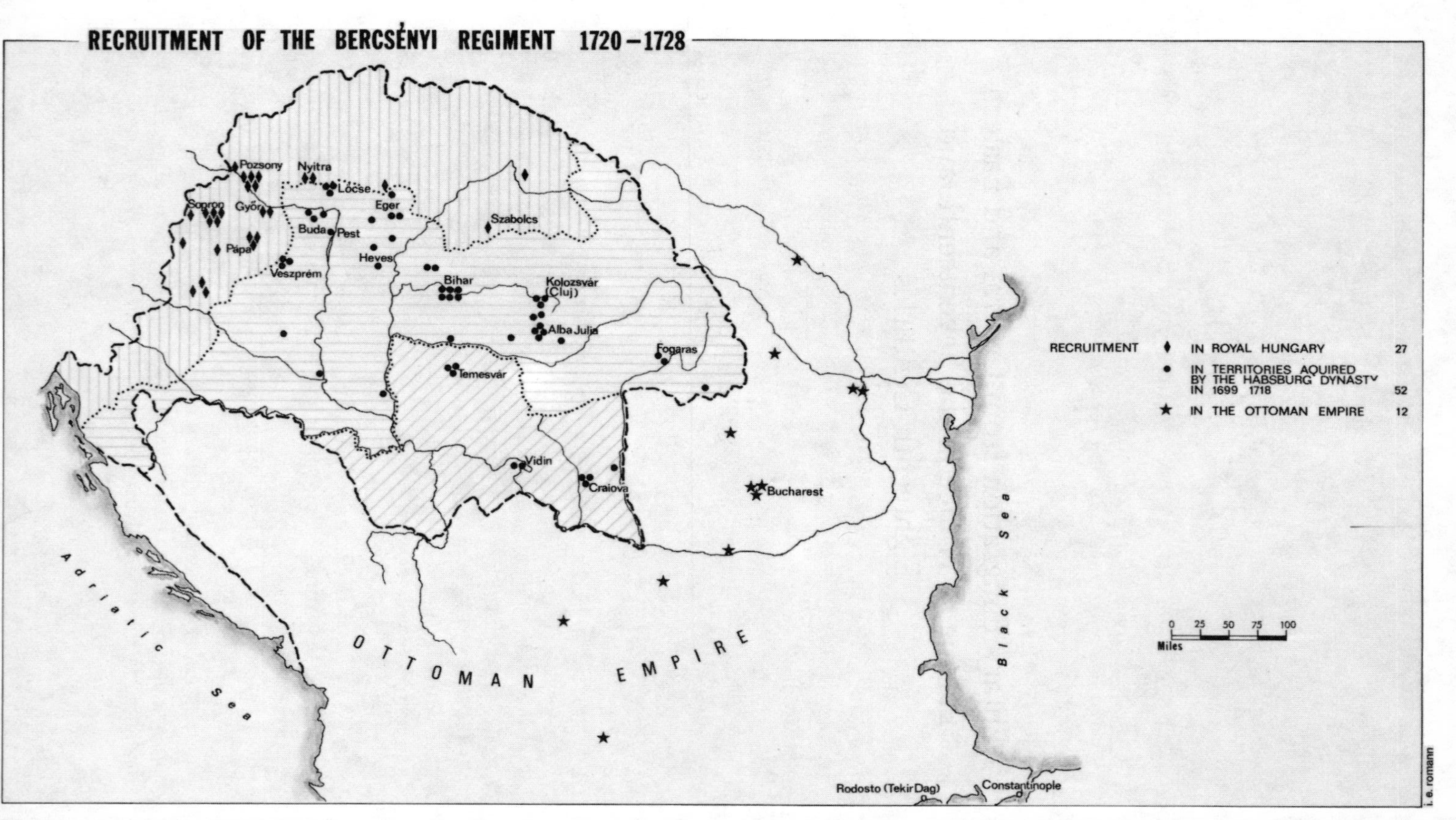
RECRUITMENT OF THE BERCSÉNYI REGIMENT 1720–1728
Pozsony
Nyitra
Löcse
Sopron
Győr
Eger
Buda
Pest
Szabolcs
Pápa
Heves
Veszprém
Bihar
Kolozsvár (Cluj)
Alba Julia
Fogaras
Temesvár
Vidin
Craiova
Bucharest
Adriatic Sea
OTTOMAN EMPIRE
Black Sea
Rodosto (Tekir Dag)
Constantinople
RECRUITMENT
IN ROYAL HUNGARY 27
IN TERRITORIES AQUIRED BY THE HABSBURG DYNASTY IN 1699 1718 52
IN THE OTTOMAN EMPIRE 12
0 25 50 75 100
Miles
i. e. romann

André Corvisier

# Military Emigration From Central and Eastern Europe to France in the Seventeenth and Eighteenth Centuries

Migrations have often been linked to wars as both causes and effects. Within the general context it is possible to single out for closer examination migrations composed uniquely of soldiers. These movements remained discernible even after states' defense became associated with national consciousness, and military service had been made compulsory. Throughout history armies have included foreigners in their ranks, not only refugees from religious, political or social persecution, but also professional soldiers—labeled somewhat hastily and with perjorative connotations as mercenaries—as well as volunteers for a national or supranational cause. These movements were particularly noticeable among the nations of Western Europe, but were there similar movements between the nations of Eastern Europe and those of the West?

To avoid undue confusion and to place the present study within recognizable geographic bounds, the line between Eastern and Western Europe is here taken to mean the historical frontier that for five centuries divided Europe into two zones of sovereignty: the eastern borders of the Holy Roman Empire, a line running from the Baltic Sea to the Adriatic. To the west, Pomerania, Brandenburg, Silesia, Moravia, Austria, Styria, Carinthia. Of course, the eastern limits of the Empire were not unchanging. In the north they followed the political frontier with Poland; to the south they constituted the line of resistance to Ottoman conquest, beyond which only a few bastions held on, remnants of the Christian states of Central Europe, notably the kingdom of Hungary, considerably reduced in size after the defeat of Mohács in 1526.

It is probable that few Christians from the West took service with the Turks or even with the Poles or Russians. Those who did were generally either officers or military engineers. The movement in the opposite direction, from east to west, was probably more numerous. Negligible in the case of Russians serving in Western armies, it was much more substantial for Poles and for the Christian subjects of the sultan or the inhabitants of territories reconquered from the Turks.

Starting in the fifteenth century, the Venetians used the services of Dalmations, "Slavonians," and Albanians and Greeks—the latter known as stradiots. The stradiots came principally from the Peloponnese and the Ionian and Aegean islands, and formed a national unit fighting in the manner of their homeland. With the advent of the Italian Wars some of them moved on to the armies of other Western states. France saw its first stradiots under King Louis XII. The few East European soldiers who served in the armies of Western Europe during the sixteenth and early seventeenth centuries were mainly infantry, known as fantassins. The seventeenth century wars between the Holy Roman and Ottoman Empires wrought considerable changes to the art of war in Central Europe. The vast distances of the Great Hungarian Plain, devoid of obstacles other than dust and mud, depopulated and lacking food and fodder, enhanced the role of mounted troops, especially the most mobile of them, light cavalry adapted to long-distance raids. The Hungarians furnished the model for these troops with the hussars. Out of his Hungarian subjects, whose number grew after the Ottoman defeat before Vienna in 1683, the Emperor organized hussar regiments. These were used not only against the Turks, but a number were also sent to the west against the French army.

The armies of Western Europe were quick to recognize the importance of raising similar light cavalry regiments. The men of these units, under whatever flag they served, were soon wearing uniforms previously unseen in Western Europe with the characteristic galllooned tunic worn over the left shoulder, tall shako, and light boots *à la housarde* which remained a tradition in Western European armies until 1814.

Western armies' recruitment in Eastern Europe was not limited to hussar regiments, however. Before the French Revolution Eastern Europeans were found in both infantry and cavalry formations. Though the Revolution saw a temporary halt in this practice, the Napoleonic empire revived it, using troops from annexed territories such as the Illyrian Provinces or from vassal states such as Poland.

After 1814 the Habsburg Monarchy appears to have monopolized Eastern recruitment which noticeably diminished elsewhere. However, starting in 1832, the Foreign Legion revived the tradition of foreign service in France. It received the influx of political refugees after the failure of the nineteenth-century nationalist revolutions: Poles after 1831 and 1863, Hungarians after 1849. The number of these East Europeans serving in the French army thereafter varied according to political conditions and events in their homelands.

France thus offers an example of relative continuity from the sixteenth century to the present day. Two essential types of movement of Central and Eastern European soldiers toward the west can be readily distinguished: ethnic group transfers and individual moves during periods of unrest.

The quality of the surviving administrative archives of the French army dating from Louis XIV and his war minister, the Marquis de Louvois, makes France an informative focus for sociological study, but so vast is the field that it would be impossible to encompass its whole scope in a single paper. The imperial period has already been the subject of numerous studies, mainly of an institutional or military character. Investigation of the Foreign Legion is impeded by the frequent deception of recruits in revealing their backgrounds. The period that has been least studied because of its relative remoteness and difficulty is the earliest period, which, however, best typifies the phenomenon of military migration from East to West, that is, the seventeenth and eighteenth centuries. The present paper is largely based on a study undertaken in a research seminar under the author's direction at the Sorbonne, "Armées et sociétés en Europe du XVI^e^ au XIX^e^ siècles," and is limited to considerations of the conditions surrounding Eastern recruitment in France, the national background of the migrants, and experiences.

## The Circumstances of Eastern Recruitment in France

The French kings and the polities that succeeded them, with the exception of the Revolution, all sought to recruit soldiers outside their borders. Even before the period of large-scale national migrations, the recruitment of soldiers abroad was considered important. The reasons for this were clearly expressed in a memoir of 1780 that restated a number of traditional arguments.[1] The political reasons had already been expressed on September 29, 1711, by the Marquis de Chamlay, Louis XIV's chief of staff, in a "speech on the coming discharges": "As a political necessity the foreign regiments must be maintained, not strictly for their military value, but to strengthen links with the nations of their origin."[2]

One aim of French recruiting policy was thus to maintain cliental relationships with the aristocrats of these nations. The anonymous author of the 1780 memoir stressed the political nature of these links: "The maintenance of foreign troops enlarges the political relations of a state with the nations that furnish them, enhances its influence over them, increases its commerce because of their needs or through their industry, and lastly inspires for this same state a feeling of attachment that adds to its preponderance in a general system."

To this reason can be added a second political argument. To welcome these refugees, primarily officers exiled from their nations by civil unrest or for personal or family reasons, meant that in case of their repatriation they would have reason to show their indebtedness to the country that had received them and often continued to pay them a pension. This political argument is less cogent for ordinary soldiers than for officers. The French army, however, like all armies of the period, did not hesitate—especially during a war—to accept deserters from other armies with open arms.

There is moreover a third argument of more strictly military nature. It was best expressed by Marshal General Maurice de Saxe in a letter of January 24, 1748, to Marshal Maurice de Noailles: "To us a German's worth is equivalent to three men: he replaced one of ours, he takes one from the enemy, and he serves in the ranks."[3]

It should be noted that, if this argument was fully valid in the case of German soldiers, it did not invariably apply to troops originating in Eastern Europe. The Hungarians opposed to the Habsburgs were more useful to France when they remained in Hungary, constantly on the verge of revolt with the aid of French subsidies, than when they were transplanted to the West.

A last argument of a more technical nature has also to be considered. As already noted, it was necessary to find a weapon to counter the excellent Austrian light cavalry. The Hungarians, formed into hussar regiments, fulfilled this need.

On the basis of these considerations two forms of recruitment were employed. There was recruitment organized by the Ministry of War which sent missions to Poland or, with the sultan's permission, to the Ottoman Empire. These missions, composed of foreign officers serving France, were dispatched to enlist entire units. There was also recruitment organized by French troops, during periods of peace mostly in Alsace, and during hostilities throughout the theater of operations in Germany. This enlistment consisted mainly of accepting all deserters who offered to join the French colors.

The major opposition to these practices obviously came from the Habsburg Empire. Until 1755 the Habsburgs and Bourbons were at war. The Eastern recruiting of the French army was directed against the House of Austria and was realized at least partially to the Habsburgs' detriment. French recruiters had therefore either to bypass the physical obstacle of the Austrian monarchy or else to infiltrate across it. Austria could be bypassed either to the north, with Polish recruitment, or to the south, with recruitment of Hungarian refugees in the Ottoman Empire.

Polish recruiting was commonest during the Thirty Years' War among the troops who fought in the Holy Roman Empire, but at that time it was largely indistinguishable from German recruiting. It was only in 1747 that first attempts were made to regroup the Polish contingents within the French army into a specific regiment. When Louis XV married Maria Leszczyńska, he purchased a French regiment from the Marquis de Monteils to offer as a present to his father-in-law, Stanislaus Leszczyński. It became known as the King Stanislaus Regiment. In 1747 Stanislaus returned the regiment to his son-in-law and it was renamed the Royal Poland Cavalry. This regiment, however, was completely French, the only Polish element being its name.

By contrast, a foot regiment raised in 1747, the Royal Poland Infantry, was composed of Germans. Its colonel, Pierre Grégoire, Count d'Orlick, was the son of a Lithuanian who served in turn the Cossacks, King Charles XII of Sweden, and finally Louis XV. He gathered within its ranks a certain number of Polish officers and soldiers, but mostly Germans. When he died in 1760, the regiment was incorporated into France's Royal Swedish Regiment.[4] Generally speaking, however, Polish recruiting remained individual, Poles serving chiefly in German regiments.

Recruiting in the Ottoman Empire retraced the steps of Venice and of the few soldiers of Balkan origin who were recruited into the French army during the seventeenth century. It does not appear that the French expeditionary corps that fought in Crete from 1767 to 1769 brought back many Greeks, or that the Christian refugees who reached Corsica in 1676 from the Maina Peninsula in the Peloponnese were attracted by French service. However, there is evidence of a number of Dalmation or Greek soldiers in the Royal Italian Regiment and a few in the Royal Roussillon.

On entering the war against the Austrian Habsburgs in 1635, Louis XIII took three Hungarian cavalry regiments into his pay. The regiments (La Meilleraye, d'Epernon and Sirot) were the property of their officers, virtual entrepreneurs, as was the custom in the Empire. They were organized out of the bands of Hungarians and Croats who had been ravaging Alsace, Lorraine and Wallonia since the death of King Gustavus II of Sweden in 1632. In 1641 they were reorganized into the Raab Croat Regiment and the Croat Regiment of Wumberg.

The majority of these regiments disappeared with the death of Louis XIII in 1643. By that time, however, there were in France enough soldiers of Croat origin—or presumed to be—to organize a new Croat regiment. This unit, known as the Ralthazard Regiment, lasted longer than its predecessors, fighting under French colors against Spain until the Peace of the Pyrenees in 1659. A noteworthy exception to its service occurred from 1650 to 1653 when its commander led it in revolt against the king. Reduced to a single company after discharges in 1661, it was not disbanded. Tradition dictated its participation in the expedition sent by Louis XIV to aid in the relief of Vienna from the Ottoman threat of 1664. In 1667 it became the Royal Cravatte Regiment, the word Cravatte being a French derivation from *Croat* that eventually gave its name to the article of clothing. Paradoxically, it was at the point when this unit assumed the name Cravatte that it virtually ceased to recruit Croat cavalrymen.[5]

Only in 1692 did the French army acquire hussar regiments. The first unit was formed by a certain M. de Kroneberg out of deserters from the Austrian army. In 1701 a second regiment was sent to France by the Elector of Bavaria. Louis XV had three hussar regiments grouped together in 1716 as the De Rattsky Regiment.[6]

It was not until 1720 that the king made a real effort to organize Hungarian recruitment. The opportunity came after Louis XV granted aid to Ferenc II Rákóczi, the prince who raised Translyvania and much of Hungary in insurrection against the Emperor. After the insurgents and Vienna concluded the Peace of Szatmár in 1711, Rákóczi had sought refuge in France. He stayed for a period in Paris at the Hôtel de Transylvanie where he maintained a small court of émigrés. In 1717 Rákóczi left for Turkey and established himself along with a certain number of refugees at Rodosto on the north shore of the Sea of Marmara to the west of Constantinople. A relative of one his closest lieutenants, Ladislas-Ignace de Bercsényi, who remained in France, suggested to the French government the idea of raising a hussar regiment from among Rákóczi's followers. Sultan Ahmed III gave his consent. Bercsényi requested from Louis XV authorization to travel to Constantinople, accompanied by a captain and three lieutenants whom Rattsky placed at his disposal, to take the recruits in charge. In addition, he wanted an order given to the Marquis de Bonnac, the French ambassador to the Sublime Porte, to help recruit the men and arrange their transportation. Bercsényi also requested a letter of credit for Constantinople.

His wishes were apparently granted. The recruits were to assemble in Marseilles because it was not possible to transport them in a single group. From there they were to be sent to Hagenau or Colmar in Alsace where they would be provided with mounts and equipment. As his lieutenant colonel Bercsényi selected a French officer, a Monsieur Bonnaire, who stayed on in Marseilles. He chose as his major a M. Kisfaludy, a member of the Hungarian gentry, and proposed as captains some Hungarian officers who had already proved their mettle in French service.[7]

It was thus a full-scale recruiting mission that Bercsényi led to Rodosto where it achieved a fair measure of success. Because of an outbreak of the plague in Marseilles, however, the regiment had finally to assemble in the Montpellier region. Its initial task was distinctly pacific—helping to establish a *cordon sanitaire* against the epidemic that threatened the French Midi.

The regiment was composed mostly of Hungarians, Transylvanians and Wallachians. It appears that Bercsényi then returned to Rodosto to raise new recruits on the Hungarian frontier. In 1756 his age prevented him from going back again in person, in his stead he sent a Baron de Tott, a former page of Rákóczi. Throughout this period the Ottoman lands continued to attract Hungarian refugees, but recruiting in Eastern Europe was very costly. The recruiting officers complained of shortage of funds, and the number of men they enlisted dropped to a few dozens.[8] Louis XV continued to maintain four or five hussar regiments but with their strength reduced to some 200 to 400 men.

Another interesting attempt to recruit in the East was made by Maurice de Saxe in 1743. The ongoing War of the Austrian Succession had again demonstrated the excellence of the Austrian light cavalry, veterans of the wars with the Turks. In response the Western armies themselves outfitted light cavalry units. De Saxe had the idea of forming a mixed corps of six brigades of 160 men each. Each was to consist of a company of uhlans armed with lances and a company of carabineers known as Pacolets. The idea soon ran into problems. In Poland the uhlans were recruited from the gentry and the Pacolets from the peasantry, and it was in Poland and Central Europe that Maurice de Saxe had hoped to raise the units, counting on the aid of his half-brother Augustus, Elector of Saxony and king of Poland.

Maurice next thought of forming a Turkish or Tatar regiment. On February 15, 1747, he wrote to Count Heinrich von Brühl, Augustus's powerful first minister: "I take the liberty to request a favor of Your Excellency. It is to send to me six *tovaritch* Tatars, but genuine Mohammedan Tatars. I will turn them into uhlan officers for my regiment."[9] Maurice de Saxe also had the notion of organizing a uhlan company entirely of Negroes.

The order authorizing the formation of the De Saxe Volunteer Regiment is dated March 30, 1743. The assembly point was Hagenau. A recruiting center was established first at Chocim and then at Usatin near the Ottoman border. About a hundred Polish Tatars of the Lipko clan were recruited in the region to the south of Kamieniec Podolski, together with Poles, Bosnians (among them Basbac, the first Moslem officer in the French army, who eventually attained the rank of lieutenant colonel), and Kalmuks. This recruitment ceased on Maurice de Saxe's death in 1750. His regiment was transformed into a regular dragoon regiment and renamed the Schomberg Dragoons. Despite his efforts, Maurice de Saxe attracted only a small number of Eastern Europeans into French service.

To these examples can be added one of lesser consequence, the Beniowski Volunteers. This short-lived unit (1771–1774), organized by the Polish-Hungarian adventurer Baron Móric Benyovszky (Beniowski) during his travels, included a handful of Poles and Hungarians.

The most durable experiment in the direct recruitment of Eastern European soldiers remained the hussars, but the hussar regiments later restricted their enlistments to Hungarian deserters from the German armies (especially the Austrian) and to prisoners of war.

It was usual during the seventeenth and eighteenth centuries for armies to try to hire their soldiers, especially their foriegn troops. Numerous French agents operated in the Holy Roman Empire. They in turn relied on the *clientèles* that the French king maintained in the smaller German states. These agents would circulate fliers extolling the advantages of French military service. The "king's money," the bounty paid on enlistment, was relatively high, as the French had to compete with the recruiting agents of other European sovereigns, especially the Prussian, English and Dutch. During wartime when deserters showed up with their horses, the price was correspondingly higher; if not the recruiting agents might have to accept a man with a horse of inferior quality that would often have to be replaced later.

In 1742 the king paid recruiters 200 Tours livres for each able mounted hussar ready to serve. It was not enough. The same year Bercsényi wrote: "To be truthful, it is easy to find men and even some hussar deserters who come in on horseback, but the majority of their mounts are worthless. We are forced to rehorse them well and arm them, give them equipment and uniforms. Besides this, it is necessary to give each man forty écus when he joins up."[10]

The French were able to count on the good reputation enjoyed by French service in Europe. The foreign regiments in the French army, notably the German ones, served as reception units for the Eastern Europeans. The Hungarians, Transylvanians, Wallachians and Croats found compatriots in the hussar regiments, and at least for the first half of the eighteenth century, the language of command was Hungarian. When Hungarian recruiting dwindled, there still remained a few subordinate officers to translate orders into that language. Central and Eastern Europeans were also to be found in the German regiments of the French army. In the French army the pay for the German regiments was higher than for other units; discipline was stricter, but apparently less so than in the armies of some German states.

The French army did not generally allow certain privileges that were important to soldiers from Central and Eastern Europe and were to be found in the Austrian army. Married men, for instance, were frowned upon, but an exception was made for the foreign regiments in French service. A certain number of wives were authorized to accompany their husbands. During the Seven Years' War they were granted an allowance of one sou a day.[11] The customs of Hungarian service were likewise respected. As the Hungarians were used for deep raids, they suffered heavy losses. In compensation it was accepted that they could engage in looting. The Hungarian regulations governing plunder and the auction of it were followed, although these practices were forbidden in other French regiments.[12]

Increasing difficulty in recruiting Hungarians meant that the hussar regiments filled with Germans and Frenchmen, especially German speakers from Alsace and Lorraine. Louis XV tried in vain to bar his subjects from serving in these foreign regiments, and sought to continue at least to enlist Hungarian captains. He endeavored to develop the hussar regiments beyond the potential levels of Hungarian recruiting, however. Marshal Victor-François de Broglie thus confessed to Bercsényi in 1742: "It would he advisable to mix some French officers into the hussar regiments. This could only have good results by familiarizing them with your service."[13] To no avail Bercsényi protested against this practice by invoking the king's primary goal of "employing Hungarians in preference to other nations," and adding a little sardonically: "I know that the French are good at all trades, but in twenty years of command I have yet to be aware of this need."[14]

The same trend affected the De Saxe Volunteer Regiment. After 1749 the Treffa Company signed on about forty, probably Breton-speaking recruits from Brittany. Their ignorance of French and the war commissioners' ignorance of Polish facilitated the fraud. The names of these men were rendered in a sort of Polish transcription, so that, for instance, an entry for Mischoo was probably really Michaud.[15]

Throughout the eighteenth century recruiting was carried on among prisoners of war, especially those of foreign origin. Some Hungarians passed in this manner from the Austrian army to the French army. Subsequently the situation changed. War became institutionalized in Western Europe during the eighteenth century. Belligerents adopted the practice of exchanging their prisoners. Nor did they always wait for war to be declared to sign agreements known as concordats which called for prisoner exchanges during the next conflict. This humanitarian procedure ended the poaching of prisoners of war. In practice, however, these conventions were not always honored. In 1745, War Commissioner Cornillon was obliged to repatriate eight exchanged soldiers. Two of them stated that they had joined the Bercsényi Regiment to landau. Cornillon wrote: "I will send them to Landau, and the drum major of the Vibraye Regiment, ordered to take the six others back, will say that these two were sick."[16]

The high point in the recruitng of deserters appears to have occurred during the beginning of the War of the Austrian Succession. Near bankruptcy, Empress Maria Theresa had difficulty paying her troops. On April 18, 1743, M. D'Espagnac wrote to Eckendorff: "The number of deserters arriving is uncountable."[17] A letter addressed to Marshal François Franquetot de Coigny on October 24, 1744, noted: "A large number of Austrian deserters arriving at Huningue are asking to enter the king's service."[18]

The Austrian obstacle to French recruitment of Hungarians became more consequential in 1755 when France and Austria became allies. There could no longer be any question of the two states stealing each other's soldiers. The French king was able to secure facilities from his new allies for recruiting within the Empire, but it was no longer possible to undertake direct recruiting in Hungary, even on a clandestine basis.[19]

French recruiting of Central and Eastern European soldiers became fortuitious and intermittent. The king succeeded in gaining the allegiance of those families of gentry living in France, but it was difficult to replace old or dead soldiers, especially as losses were high. It does not seem that the rate of desertions was any higher than in other units of the French army, but raiding caused more casualties among the hussars and light cavalry. These troops could not be trained quickly;[20] the result of haphazard recruiting was to reduce the quality and value of the regiments. By about 1760 these units were largely composed of old men and shiftless veterans who had served in numerous armies. The routes by which these men came into the ranks followed three essential patterns.

The first route was through the Mediterranean. It comprised the men brought through Rodosto or some other place in the Ottoman Empire. The French recruiters also signed up refugees or men they sought out on the borders of the Habsburg Monarchy. They were brought to France by ship, a trip made hazardous by the frequency of war between England and France. It was Baron de Tott who noted that English "corsairs" continually harassed the French ships to take their passengers off to England "where, by means of the misery to which they are reduced, these men are forced to accept service with the enemy."[21]

The second route was that of the groups of hussars who had crossed from an eastern army to the French army. In 1710 a considerable number of hussars crossed together from Spain to France.[22] When the king of Sardinia disbanded some of his regiments in 1736, about a hundred hussars found themselves freed for reassignment. They were given the choice of being incorporated into a dragoon regiment or having the right to go wherever they pleased. Thirty of them delegated one of their French officers to seek French service as hussars. Unfortunately for them, this moment coincided with the end of the War of the Polish Succession and the French king was also disbanding regiments. He had no need of them.[23] There is no doubt, however, that hussars frequently preferred to move from army to army.

The third route was through Germany. This was often a source of disappointment as it included deserters from the Austrian army or prisoners of war. Frequent desertions occurred en route when they learned of more advantageous conditions offered in another army.

Table I gives an idea of the relative importance of troops recruited by the first and third routes at the period of the Rodosto center's greatest activity. There is no doubt that the German route was used more than the Mediterranean.

It remains to try to evaluate the number of migrants the miltary service brought from Central and Eastern Europe to France. Officers will be considered separately from men. The muster rolls of various Hungarian regiments furnish an idea of the proportions. Table II compares the number of Hungarian captains in several regiments with the total number of captains.

The ratio of hussar captains of Hungarian origin appears to have remained at a satisfactory level until the end of the war of the Austrian Succession. Thereafter it steadily diminished—more so than the table indicates since by the end of the *Ancien Régime* many Hungarian officers were second-generation immigrants perfectly integrated into French society. There is no exact figure for the total number of captains of Eastern or Central European origin in the French army, but adding together Hungarians, Poles, Croats, etc., their number can be estimated at about fifty in 1749. At that time the French army had some 3,000 captains on the active list, of whom about 700 were foreigners. Thus captains from east of the Empire comprised seven percent of the foreign contingent and 1.6 percent of the whole French officer corps.

*Table I*

*RECRUITING CENTERS OF THE BERCSÉNYI HUSSARS, 1720–1728**

| Years | Rodosto | Constantinople | Bucharest | Vidin | Haguenau | Sélestat | Other France | Total |
|---|---|---|---|---|---|---|---|---|
| 1720 | 45 | 4 | 1 | 1 | — | — | — | 51 |
| 1721 | 15 | 4 | — | — | — | — | — | 19 |
| 1722 | — | — | — | — | 4 | — | — | 4 |
| 1723 | — | — | — | — | 6 | — | — | 6 |
| 1724 | — | — | — | — | — | 13 | — | 13 |
| 1725 | — | — | — | — | — | 30 | — | 30 |
| 1726 | — | — | — | — | 6 | 3 | — | 9 |
| 1727 | — | — | — | — | — | — | 1 | 1 |
| 1728 | — | — | — | — | — | 18 | 2 | 20 |
| Total | 60 | 8 | 1 | 1 | 16 | 64 | 3 | 153 |
| | | 70 | | | | 83 | | 153 |

*From the muster rolls of the Bercsényi Regiment, Archives de la Guerre, Paris, 3 Yc 313.

*Table II*

*PROPORTION OF HUNGARIANS AMONG CAPTAINS OF HUSSARS**

| Years | Rattsky, later Lynden, Regiment | Ferrary Regiment | Polleretsky Regiment | Bercsényi Regiment | Esterházy, later David, then Turpin, Regiment | Esterházy Regiment (formed in 1764) | Total | |
|---|---|---|---|---|---|---|---|---|
| | | | | | | | Ratio | Percentage |
| 1722 | — | — | — | 3/4 | — | — | 3/4 | 75% |
| 1724 | — | — | — | 3/4 | — | — | 3/4 | 75% |
| 1729 | 4/4 | — | — | 3/4 | — | — | 7/8 | 87% |
| 1737 | 6/8 | — | — | 6/8 | 4/4 | — | 16/20 | 80% |
| 1749 | 3/4 | 2/4 | 4/4 | 8/8 | 4/4 | — | 21/24 | 87% |
| 1763/4 | — | — | — | 9/12 | 8/12 | 4/8 | 21/32 | 65% |
| 1772 | — | — | — | 5/8 | 5/8 | 4/8 | 14/24 | 58% |
| 1776 | — | — | — | 4/4 | 0/4 | 3/4 | 7/12 | 58% |

*André Corvisier, *Les contrôles des troupes de l'Ancien Régime*, III (Paris, 1970), 257–268.

*Table III*

*PROPORTION OF HUSSARS FROM CENTRAL AND EASTERN EUROPE**

| *Years* | | *Rattsky later Lynden, Regiment* | *Ferrary Regiment* | *Polleretsky Regiment* | *Bercsényi Regiment* | *Esterházy, later David, then Turpin & Chamborant Regiment* | *Esterházy Regiment (formed in 1764)* |
|---|---|---|---|---|---|---|---|
| | *a* | 19.8% | — | — | 60.1% | 67.4% | — |
| 1737 | *b* | 21.1% | — | — | 60.6% | 70.0% | — |
| | *c* | 23.1% | — | — | 72.7% | 73.6% | — |
| | *a* | — | — | — | — | 11.2% | — |
| 1744 | *b* | — | — | — | — | 11.2% | — |
| | *c* | — | — | — | — | 13.2% | — |
| | *a* | — | 29.4% | — | — | — | — |
| 1747 | *b* | — | 36.4% | — | — | — | — |
| | *c* | — | 39.7% | — | — | — | — |
| | *a* | — | 11.4% | 45.9% | 66.8% | 61.7% | — |
| 1749 | *b* | — | 11.4% | 53.4% | 71.2% | 64.4% | — |
| | *c* | — | 11.8% | 54.9% | 75.7% | 65.5% | — |
| | *a* | — | — | 5.6% | 78.2% | — | — |
| 1757 | *b* | — | — | 7.0% | 78.6% | — | — |
| | *c* | — | — | 7.2% | 79.5% | — | — |
| 1763 | *c* | — | — | — | — | four men | — |
| | *a* | — | — | — | — | — | 2.5% |
| 1764 | *b* | — | — | — | — | — | 2.8% |
| | *c* | — | — | — | — | — | 3.1% |
| 1772 | *c* | — | — | — | — | four men | 1.5% |
| 1776 | *c* | — | — | — | — | one man | 1.5% |

*According to the muster roles of the regiments named, Archives de la Guerre, Paris, 3 Yc 311; 8 Yc 13 & 14, 3 Yc 312, 313 & 314; 8 Yc 2, 4 & 3; 8 Yc 12, 9, 23, 6 & 5; 8 Yc 10.

It is even more difficult to assess the number of ordinary soldiers of Eastern origan. As in the case of the captains, only their proportion within the hussar regiments will be considered. Table III shows the percentage in each regiment of (*a*) men recognized as Hungarian, (*b*) Hungarians and Transylvanian troops, and (*c*) men originating in the countries of Eastern and Central Europe. A degree of inaccuracy is introduced by the fact the same place of origin is sometimes included in Hungary, sometimes in Transylvania—a commentary on the recruits' perception of their origins.

This table shows changes due to various circumstances: regiments decimated by battle, perhaps desertions, and probably withdrawals from one regiment to form another. Such was the case of the David Regiment in 1744 which the Count de Turpin-Crisse remanned with Hungarian troops freed from the regiments disbanded at the Peace of Aix-la-Chapelle. Furthermore, Hungarian recruiting collapsed after the Seven Years' War as a result of the Franco-Austrian alliance.

Two methods have been used to try to reach a rough estimate of the ratio of Central and Eastern European soldiers to the whole of the French army. The first was based on the author's earlier study of the soldiers listed in the muster rolls for 1716. The global figure for this group reached nearly 40,000 men. Of these only 36 were Hungarians or natives of Transylvania, 21 were Poles, three Muscovites, 13 subjects of the sultan, and six Dalmations, for a total of 79, or 0.2 percent of total strength. It should be noted, however, that in 1716 the number of French troops was reduced by the major demobilization that marked the end of the wars of Louis XIV. These discharges affected the hussar regiments more deeply than others, reducing their number from three to one. It is thus possible that the proportion had been higher during the wars.[24]

The other method consists of random samples from the registers of the Invalides. To the author's analyses of 1,157 admissions to the Paris disabled veterans' home in 1715–1716 and 1,057 admissions in 1762–1763 (that is, one-fifth and one-tenth of the totals, respectively),[25] have been added the results of two other studies undertaken during the Sorbonne seminar. Robert Chaboche studied the admissions from 1674 to 1690 (about 9,200 men), and Jean-Pierre Bois produced figures for admissions in 1767–1769 and 1785–1786. On the basis of these somewhat disparate figures, it is nevertheless possible to sketch a possible long-term evolution (see Table IV).

The number of Eastern and Central Europeans admitted to the Invalides appears relatively high. Though it was just of the king to reward those who had come such a distance to serve him, admission to the Invalides caused problems for these men, who were ill-suited to the institutional life of the home. Moreover, it seems that after the Seven Years' War they were admitted at a later age then their French comrades, so that it warrants grouping the figures for 1762–1763 and those for 1767–1769 together.

*Table IV*

*PROPORTION OF CENTRAL AND EASTERN EUROPEAN VETERANS ADMITTED TO THE INVALIDES*

| *Periods* | *East Europeans As Percentage of Foreign-Born Admissions* | *East Europeans As Percentage of Whole Intake* | *Foreign-Born Admissions As Percentage of Whole Intake* |
|---|---|---|---|
| 1674–1690 (men admitted before 1649) | 4.6% | 0.83% | 17.4% |
| 1674–1690 (total men) | — | 0.71% | — |
| 1715–1716 | 1.3% | 0.30% | 23.3% |
| 1762–1763 | 1.0% | 0.16% | 16.0% |
| 1767–1769 | 14.7% | 0.62% | 4.2% |
| Total of 1762–1763 and 1767–1769 | 1.8% | 0.26% | 14.2% |
| 1785–1786 | 1.5% | 0.01% | 4.6% |

From these figures a long-term trend is apparent. The percentage of Eastern and Central Europeans was high during the Thirty Years' War, and remained steady during the eighteenth century at about 1.5 percent of the foreigners admitted. Their percentage relative to the all those admitted to the Invalides steadily decreased, however, notably between 1690 and 1715, and was negligible just before the Revolution. After 1715 it roughly paralleled the drop in the number of foreign soldiers admitted to the home.

The government's attitude toward foreign soldiers does not seem to have changed. With relaxation of the requirement that admissions should be of the Catholic faith, the Hôtel des Invalides may even have been open to foreign Protestants. This change was the result of the same circumstances that slowed and complicated recruiting for the hussar regiments, and numerous sources from the second half of the eighteenth century attest to it. Foreign recruitment became progressively more difficult in a Europe where national feelings were awakening. Besides, even if the king still favored foreign recruiting, the French people no longer viewed this influx as genially as before. Hostility toward mercenaries, who were preying on the civilian population considerably less than than a century earlier, was not born with the Revolution. It had already surfaced in France during the final years of the *Ancien Régime*.

## The Origins and Character of the Migrants

It is relatively easy to trace the origins of officers from Eastern Europe because they were members of families whose migrations had been caused by political or religious stimuli and who benefited from the king's favor. Many had settled in France during the eighteenth century and raised families. Some achieved distinction; biographical dictionaries have recorded their social and regional origins. Among the most prestigious families were the Rattskys, Bercsényis, Esterhazys; with the Revolution many disappeared. This was in particular the case with those families linked to the Bourbons and the court, who fled the country, often out of fear of the xenophobia directed against foreign aristocrats.

It is more difficult to find information on the common soldiers. These belonged to the category that Voltaire so unjustly stigmatized in *Candide:* "A million regimented assassins running from one end of Europe to another practicing murder and brigandage with discipline to earn their bread because they lack a more honest profession." These quasi-vagrants were kept under careful scrutiny by the military administration because they were costly and prone to desert.

The muster rolls, begun in 1716, give a bare-bones description of the common soldier: family name, first name, place of birth, age, height, date of enlistment, rank, date of severance from his unit by death, discharge, or desertion. Indications of parents and profession do not figure in the rolls of foreign regiments, but they can be found for those foreigners who chanced to serve in a French regiment. This information is not always illuminating, however. What is one to make of such an entry as "Jacob Houssart, called Jacob, from Quingueche in Hungary, aged 37 years, signed on July 15, 1715, country of the same name," found in the rolls of the King's Regiment of Infantry for 1736?[26] The name Houssart is probably not a patronymic, but already a surname indicating this man's association with a hussar regiment. How is it possible to identify with certainty the location of Quingueche, even knowing the name of the county of which it was part?

There is better information about the men admitted to the Invalides. From the very creation of the institution in 1674, those admitted were carefully registered. As well as the aforementioned information, there are further personal details: their marital status, religion, service status, and the end of their term in France either by death or return home. Despite its precision, this information is largely unverifiable, and it has to be borne in mind that numerous soldiers lied about either place of birth or age.

A major study is under way examining the entire group of foreign soldiers who served in the French army between 1716 and 1786. Only such a study will elicit the maxium of information about the common soldiers and their travels from regiment to regiment, but it has only just begun. For the time being, samplings have yielded some indicative results.

Among the most consistent items of information in the muster rolls is place of origin. For the first men admitted to the Invalides, this datum was limited to general categories: Polish, Hungarian, Dalmatian, etc. Soon to the place of birth was added the administrative authority to which this locality was subject. With this it becomes possible to draft a recruiting map, at least for certain units.

It is a task, however, beset with difficulties. The first has to do with the rendering of foreign names by the records officers, majors and *aide-majors* who could not always speak the recruit's language. Patronymics were often distorted to conform phonetically with German or French orthography. Place-names were often given in their German, Hungarian, Romanian, Polish or Croation forms. Sometimes this was done correctly, when the records officer knew the name in one of those languages; more often incorrectly when the name was unfamiliar. Many names were recorded incompletely: Neu, Nagy, Sankt, Szent, Saint were frequently omitted, causing confusion.

It was the native French officers who made the most mistakes. Veszprém for example, one sees spelt *Besprun*. It is also essential to correlate carefully different language forms of the same place: to remember that Pressburg, Pozsony and Bratislava, for instance, are one and the same city; so, too, Kolozsvár, Klausenburg and Cluj; Ofen and Buda; Raab and Györ, and so forth.

The indication of the jurisdiction under which a soldier's place of origin fell is not always of much value. Frequently the entry is either vague or false. Many a Hungarian recruit did not understand the exact meaning of the word jurisdiction. The officer who enrolled him did not always know the term *comitat* (county) or have a list of the names of them. As already noted, "Transylvania" and "Hungary" was often put down without it being possible to know whether this was the recruit's term or the records officer's. Confusion was especially common over the states within the Ottoman Empire. Finally, it is not always certain that the place named in the rolls was the place of birth; it is possible that in some cases it was the recruit's last home before entering the army. When all this is said and done, however, it is still possible to construct if not a detailed map of recruitment areas, at least a general impression of the geographic origins of the men that is not entirely without interest.

The geographic origins of the men should indicate which of them were directly recruited in the Ottoman Empire and which were subjects of the Holy Roman Empire recruited after deserting, but this is difficult, for regions of sovereignty changed during the wars between the Emperor and sultan between 1664 and 1734. An attempt has been made, however, to group the recruits as coming from four regions:

1) Royal Hungary, basically reduced until 1683 to a strip of territory just east of Austria and to the Carpathian area of present-day Slovakia.
2) The part of Hungary freed from Ottoman rule by the Treaty of Karlowitz in 1699, that is, most of the Great Hungarian Plain, and Transylvania.
3) The territories the Habsburgs acquired from the Ottoman Empire by the Treaty of Passarowitz in 1718, that is, the banate of Temesvár, Oltenia (Wallachia west of the River Olt), Srem, northern Bosnia, and the northern half of Serbia including Belgrade. All except the banate of Temesvár were ceded back to the Ottoman Empire by the Treaty of Belgrade in 1739.
4) The countries never subject to Habsburg rule till the 1770s.

Tables V and VI, which trace the places of origin of newcomers to the Bercsényi between 1720 and 1737 show that recruitment among the nations remaining under Ottoman rule was marginal. Most of the recruits seem to have been subjects of the Emperor at the time of their enlistment. They came to the French army particularly through Rodosto in 1720–1722, and chiefly through desertion after that date.

The large number of recruits drawn from Royal Hungary in 1720–1721 is significant. Most of them appear to have come from the area conquered by Imperial troops between 1683 and 1699. Between their departure from their place of origin and their arrival in Rodosto, these men probably led an adventurous existence. It is

*Table V*

*REGIONAL ORIGINS OF RECRUITS OF THE BERCSÉNYI REGIMENT*

| | 1720/21 | | 1722/31 | | 1732/36 | | 1737 | | Total | |
|---|---|---|---|---|---|---|---|---|---|---|
| *Countries of Eastern and Central Europe* | | | | | | | | | | |
| Hungary / Transylvania | 124 | 79.5% | 7 | 5.5% | 77 | 60.4% | 45 | 47.3% | 253 | 50.0% |
| Other Countries | 29 | 18.5% | 5 | 3.9% | 9 | 7.3% | 9 | 9.5% | 52 | 10.3% |
| Total | 153 | 98.0% | 12 | 9.4% | 86 | 67.7% | 54 | 56.8% | 305 | 60.3% |
| *Countries of Western Europe* | | | | | | | | | | |
| Holy Roman Empire | 1 | 0.7% | 31 | 24.4% | 27 | 21.2% | 35 | 36.8% | 94 | 18.6% |
| France | 2 | 1.3% | 71 | 55.9% | 14 | 11.1% | 5 | 5.3% | 92 | 18.2% |
| Other Countries | — | — | 13 | 10.3% | — | — | 1 | 1.1% | 14 | 2.9% |
| Total | 3 | 2.0% | 115 | 90.6% | 41 | 32.3% | 41 | 43.2% | 200 | 39.7% |
| Grand Total | 156 | 100% | 127 | 100% | 127 | 100% | 95 | 100% | 505 | 100% |

likely that the majority of them fought with Prince Ferenc II Rákóczi and withdrew into the Ottoman Empire when his insurrection collapsed. A number may also have fought alongside the Turks during the Austro-Ottoman war of 1716–1718. Whatever their circumstances, return to their homeland appeared to them either impossible or inadvisable. Most would have enlisted in Rodosto, although some must have been signed up in Bucharest or Vidin. News of the recruitment of hussars in Rodosto would have attracted others to the town.

The fortuitous and limited scope of recruitment in Rodosto is readily apparent. Between 1722 and 1731 it came to a virtual standstill, and the Bercsényi Regiment filled with Germans and German-speaking Frenchmen. A serious effort was made during the War of the Polish Succession to restore the regiment's Hungarian makeup, but it is possible that recruiting deserters was primarily relied on. The Turpin Regiment in 1749 and Ferray Regiment in 1747 saw a drop in recruitment in Royal Hungary. Balkan recruitment seems not to have gotten off the ground.

It is difficult to establish what proportion of the soldiers came from towns and what proportion came from the county, and whether to consider as townsmen all those coming from county seats, communities that may scarcely have had the character of towns by Western European standards. Yet the proportion of these townsmen among the recruits was larger than the ratio of town dwellers in the population at large.[27] Perhaps this is a reflection of the same phenomenon as gave rise in Western Europe to the hyperbole that all soldiers were recruited from the "dregs of the cities." To the

*Table VI*

*REGIONAL ORIGINS OF THE BERCSÉNYI HUSSARS: DETAIL*

| | *1720* | *1721* | *1722* | *1723* | *1724* | *1725* | *1726* | *1727* | *1728* | *1729* | *1730* | *1731* | *1732* | *1733* | *1734* | *1735* | *1736* | *1737* |
|---|---|---|---|---|---|---|---|---|---|---|---|---|---|---|---|---|---|---|
| Hungary | 71 | 20 | 1 | — | 1 | 1 | — | — | 1 | — | 1 | 1 | 6 | 13 | 27 | 19 | 12 | 45 |
| Transylvania | 18 | 15 | — | — | — | — | — | — | — | — | 1 | — | — | — | — | — | — | — |
| Wallachia | 4 | 17 | — | 1 | — | — | — | — | — | — | — | — | — | — | — | — | — | — |
| Moldavia | 1 | — | — | — | — | — | — | — | — | — | — | — | — | — | — | — | — | — |
| Poland | — | 1 | — | — | 1 | — | — | — | 1 | 1 | 1 | — | 1 | 1 | — | — | 2 | 6 |
| Russia | — | 3 | — | — | — | — | — | — | — | — | — | — | — | — | — | — | — | — |
| Bulgaria | 1 | 2 | — | — | — | — | — | — | — | — | — | — | — | — | — | — | — | — |
| Slavonia | — | — | — | — | — | — | — | — | — | — | — | — | — | — | — | — | — | 1 |
| Turkey | — | — | — | — | — | — | — | — | — | — | — | — | — | — | 5 | — | — | 2 |
| *Total Eastern Europe* | 95 | 58 | 1 | 1 | 2 | 1 | — | — | 2 | 1 | 3 | 1 | 7 | 14 | 32 | 19 | 13 | 54 |
| Holy Roman Empire | — | 1 | 2 | 3 | 5 | 5 | — | 1 | 4 | 5 | 3 | 3 | 5 | 8 | 8 | 2 | 3 | 35 |
| France | 1 | 1 | 2 | 4 | 4 | 21 | 8 | 1 | 8 | 4 | 10 | 9 | 5 | 2 | 6 | — | 1 | 5 |
| Other Western European Countries | — | — | — | — | — | 1 | — | 2 | 9 | 1 | — | — | — | — | — | — | — | 1 |
| *Total All Countries* | 96 | 60 | 5 | 8 | 11 | 28 | 8 | 4 | 23 | 11 | 16 | 13 | 18 | 24 | 46 | 21 | 17 | 95 |

extent that the places of origin cited were theoretically places of birth, should the list of townsmen also include countrymen who had moved to the town before they joined up? Was the rural exodus of the same magnitude in the eighteenth century in the Danubian plain as in Western Europe?

The religion is known only of those who entered the Invalides.[28] In theory, only Catholics or Protestants who undertook to convert were admissible. It is not surprising then that few Protestants are found in the registers of the Invalides, especially after the revocation of the Edict of Nantes in 1685. The eight cases (out of 65) where the entrant's religion is not mentioned may have been due either to a certain tolerance or simple oversight of the clerk. It is unlikely that France's Catholic faith deterred foreign Protestants from French service; in the foreign regiments of the French army Protestantism was tolerated.

Age is often shown approximately in the records. Recruits tended to round out their ages. Thus in the Bercsényi Regiment in 1722 only one soldier was listed as 29 and only one as 31, while the age of 23 recruits is given as 30. A scale of corrected ages can be constructed by taking for the number of men aged 30 the average of the number of men aged 28 and the number aged 32. This gives 12 + 9 = 21 ÷ 2, or about ten men aged 30. If 10 is correct, then the figure of 23 men aged 30 is an overstatement of about 130 percent, approximately equal to that observed for the totals in the French army in 1716. Despite this, one can obtain a fair picture of age grouping when treating large enough samples (see Table VII).

The age on enlistment appears high. For Bercsényi's hussars the average was 30 years 5 months, which supports the idea that a number of the men had already served in other armies. This is even more likely for 63 of the men admitted to the Invalides between 1674 and 1690. Their age on enlistment can be determined by subtracting their number of years' service from their age on admission. According to their service records, which may not have been accurate, the average age on enlistment into a French regiment was 33 years 9 months for the 45 Poles, 35 years 11 months for the eight Croats, and 38 years 4 months for the ten Hungarians. Even if these ages are inflated by the omission of some period of French service, the impression remains that when they enlisted they were generally veterans.

Men under 26 were the most likely to be enlisting in the military for the first time. They were relatively few, however, accounting for only 22.7 percent of those who enlisted in the Bercsényi Regiment in

*Table VII*

*AGE ON ENTERING FRENCH SERVICE*

| *Age* | *Admissions to the Invalides, 1674–1690* *Poles* | | *Hungarians* | | *Croats* | | Bercsényi Regiment Enlistments, 1720/1 | |
|---|---|---|---|---|---|---|---|---|
| 16 to 20 | 3 | 6.8% | 1 | 10% | 1 | 12.5% | 6 | 4.0% |
| 21 to 25 | 4 | 9.1% | 1 | 10% | — | — | 28 | 18.7% |
| 26 to 30 | 12 | 27.3% | 2 | 20% | 1 | 12.5% | 50 | 33.3% |
| 31 to 35 | 8 | 18.2% | 1 | 10% | 1 | 12.5% | 29 | 19.3% |
| 36 to 40 | 8 | 18.2% | 1 | 10% | 3 | 37.5% | 28 | 18.7% |
| 41 to 45 | 5 | 11.3% | 1 | 10% | 2 | 25.0% | 7 | 4.7% |
| over 45 | 4 | 9.1% | 3 | 30% | — | — | 2 | 1.3% |

1720–21. They were even fewer among those admitted to the Invalides from 1674 to 1690: 15.9 percent of the Poles, 20 percent of the Hungarians, and 12.5 percent of the Croats. It should be remembered, however, that the service records at the Invalides may be incomplete because they show only the period in the French army.

Some examples of enlistment of very old men are striking. A hussar in the Bercsényi Regiment signed up at age 60, and a Pole entered French service at 51—at least if the records are to be believed. As astonishing as these are, they are not isolated cases. It is to be wondered what sort of service these oldsters could perform in the light cavalry: instructors, weapons maintenance, perhaps interpreters? If it is remembered that in the seventeenth and eighteenth centuries a man of 45 would seem quite old, then the men in question must either have lied about their advanced age or have been valued for the richness of their experience.

Finally there is the matter of height. Here, too, calculations can only be approximate, as during the eighteenth century men were generally measured with their shoes on. In the nineteenth century the hussar's image was small, lean and spry. What about the eighteenth century? Cavalrymen were generally chosen a little taller than fantassins: five *pieds* four *pouces* (1.732 meters or 5 feet 8¼ inches), for the former compared with five *pieds* two *pouces* (1.678 meters or 5 feet 6 inches) for the latter.[29] Bercsényi's hussars in 1729 were not very tall: the average was 5 *pieds* 1.8 *pouces* (1.674 meters or 5 feet 6 inches). In the David Regiment, heights varied from 5 *pieds* (1.624

meters or 5 feet 4 inches) to 5 *pieds* 5½ *pouces* (1.827 meters or 6 feet). The colonel reserved the tallest man for his own company. The average height in his unit was 5 *pieds* 2.9 *pouces* (1.703 meters or 5 feet 7 inches), and two men reached 5 *pieds* 7 *pouces* (1.813 meters or 5 feet 11½ inches). These heights *with their shoes on* are not tall to modern eyes, but in the eighteenth century they were considered big. Tall in comparison with the average Frenchman, these hussars were still rather shorter than other cavalrymen.

## The Foreigners' Service Experience in France

The regimental muster rolls and especially the registers of the Invalides afford a glimpse of the service careers of France's foreign recruits.

It is known that French soldiers changed regiments fairly frequently even at the risk of losing seniority. They would make the change either at the end of their term of enlistment or after obtaining leave from their captain. As the latter was rarely granted, many preferred to desert rather than wait for the chance of receiving permision. They would go from one regiment to another, either because they were unhappy in their first regiment or because they were greedy to receive another enlistment bounty. Certain men reenlisted several times over.

Foreign troops serving France followed the same practice. When a foreigner transferred from a French "foreign" to a regular regiment, despite the obstacles and regardless of the lower pay in the latter, he was often attracted by the comparatively easier discipline of the French unit. This implies, however, that he had become relatively at home with the French language and customs. Was this practice widespread? Unfortunately the only complete records are those of the foreigners admitted to the Invalides, that is, a small minority comprising the best soldiers.

Sixty-three East Europeans admitted to the Invalides entered service in France between 1635 and 1680. Twenty joined up during the wars of 1635 to 1659, eleven during the armed peace of 1659 to 1671, fourteen during the Dutch War of 1672 to 1678 and the two years thereafter, and eighteen at dates unknown. This group was composed of 43 Poles, 10 Hungarians, eight Croats, and two of unspecified but probably Polish origin. Table VIII shows a limited but not insignificant tendency for East European soldiers to leave

France's Polish and Italian regiments in preference for its German and especially Swiss regiments. This constituted a certain degree of westernization of these men (who would have needed to cope adequately with a Western European language) or at least a narrowing of the French army's normal recruitment zones (see Table VIII).

About three-fourths of these men had served in the infantry, a fact that tends to modify the traditional idea that soldiers from Eastern Europe served mainly in the cavalry.

These men admitted to the Invalides had generally completed many years in service to France. The average was 21 years 3 months for the Poles, 15 years for Hungarians (who on average entered French service at a later age), and 21 years 7 months for the Croats. The actual length of service varied from one to 49 years (see Table IX).

Wounds were the main reason for the East Europeans' admission to the Invalides. This was the case for 44.4 percent of the Poles, 60 percent of the Hungarians and 40 percent of the Croats. Sickness accounted respectively for 18.1 percent of the Poles, 15 percent of the Hungarians, and 35 percent of the Croats. Finally, old age accounted for 37.5 percent, 25 percent, and 40 percent respectively. (In some cases, they were admitted for more than one cause.)

Taking into account the limitations imposed by the narrowness of the sample, some tentative conclusions can nevertheless be drawn. It appears as if the experience of the Hungarians significantly differed from that of the Poles and Croats: wounds were more frequently the cause of their admission. Does this reflect more daring soldiering?

What can be learned from the muster rolls of the Bercsényi Regiment made fifty years later? They show that, like other units, only a minority of its veterans were admitted to the Invalides. Comparison of the rolls of 1722 and 1729 indicates that 48.4 percent of the men who enlisted in 1720 and 24.1 percent of those who enlisted in 1721 were still serving in 1729. One gains the impression that the best men enlisted in 1720: 50.5 percent of the Hungarians and 20 percent of the Transylvanians serving then were still there in 1729. Of the fifteen men from Transylvania enlisted in 1721, only one remained in 1729, and of 21 Wallachians enlisted in 1720 and 1721, only one was still on the rolls in 1729.

Examination of the reasons for leaving the regiment between 1729 and 1737 allows a number of observations to be made (see Table X). This table permits comparison of the service records of soldiers of various origins. The twenty soldiers from Central and Eastern

*Table VIII*

*REGIMENTS SERVED IN BY MEN ADMITTED TO THE INVALIDES BETWEEN 1674 AND 1690*

| *Regiments* | *Poles Regiment* | | *Hungarians Regiment* | | *Croats Regiment* | | *Total Regiment* | |
|---|---|---|---|---|---|---|---|---|
| | *First* | *Last* | *First* | *Last* | *First* | *Last* | *First* | *Last* |
| Polish | 2 | — | — | — | — | — | 2 | — |
| Italian | 1 | — | — | — | 3 | 2 | 4 | 2 |
| Irish | 1 | — | — | — | — | — | 1 | — |
| Catalan | — | — | — | — | 1 | — | 1 | — |
| German | 17 | 18 | 5 | 5 | — | 2 | 22 | 25 |
| Swiss | 13 | 19 | 5 | 5 | 1 | 2 | 19 | 26 |
| French | 7 | 8 | — | — | 2 | 2 | 9 | 10 |
| Not Known | 4 | — | — | — | 1 | — | 5 | — |
| Total | 45 | 45 | 10 | 10 | 8 | 8 | 63 | 63 |

*Table IX*

*LENGTH OF SERVICE IN FRANCE OF MEN ADMITTED TO THE INVALIDES FROM 1670 TO 1690*

| *Time Served* | *Number of Men* | | |
|---|---|---|---|
| | *Poles* | *Hungarians* | *Croats* |
| Under 6 years | 5 | 2 | — |
| 6 to 10 years | 8 | 1 | 3 |
| 11 to 15 years | 4 | 2 | — |
| 16 to 20 years | 3 | 2 | 1 |
| 21 to 25 years | 8 | 2 | — |
| 26 to 30 years | 4 | 1 | 3 |
| 31 to 35 years | 4 | — | — |
| 36 to 40 years | 6 | — | 1 |
| 41 to 45 years | 1 | — | — |
| Over 45 years | 1 | — | — |
| Average | 21 years 3 mths. | 15 years | 21 years 7 mths. |

*Table X*

*LENGTH OF SERVICE AND REASONS FOR LEAVING THE BERCSÉNY REGIMENT, 1729–1737**

| *Country of Origin* | *Authorized Discharge* | | *Death* | | *Desertion* | | *Admitted to the Invalides* | |
|---|---|---|---|---|---|---|---|---|
| | *No. of men* | *Average length of service* | *No. of men* | *Average length of service* | *No. of men* | *Average length of service* | *No. of men* | *Average length of service* |
| Hungary and Transylvania | 5 | 5 yrs. (a few mths. to 11 yrs.) | 5 | 9 yrs. 9 mths. (6 to 12 yrs.) | 4 | 9 yrs. 4 mths. (9 to 10 yrs.) | 1 | 8 years |
| Other Eastern Europe states | 4 | 2 yrs. (1 to 5 yrs.) | 1 | 10 years | — | — | — | — |
| Holy Roman Empire | 8 | 2 yrs. 11 mths. (a few mths. to 9 yrs.) | 2 | 5 years | 10 | 2 yrs. 7 mths. (a few mths. to 5 yrs.) | — | — |
| France | 18 | 5 yrs. 2 mths. (a few mths. to 8 yrs.) | 3 | 2 yrs. 10 mths. (a few mths. to 5 yrs.) | 6 | 3 yrs. 7 mths. (1 to 5 yrs. | 1 | 3 yrs. |

*Archives de la Guerre, Paris, 3 Yc 312.

Europe served longer on average than the twenty from the Empire and the 18 Frenchmen. Among the first group only four deserted, compared with ten of those from the Holy Roman Empire and six of their French comrades. One East European entered the Invalides. The East Europeans' length of service was greater than the Germans', even among the deserters. There can be no question of using such a limited group to draw general conclusions about the comparative military virtues of the men of these different nations. When Hungarians were lacking for the hussar regiments, the recruiters naturally took whomever they could.

What happened to these men after their discharge? It is impossible to say except for those admitted to the Invalides. The average age of admission of the 63 men already studied was 55 years for the Poles, 53 years 4 months for the Hungarians, 57 years 6 months for the Croats. According to the home's registers, the youngest was 20 and the oldest 82.

The men were not uniformly happy in the Invalides. The strict discipline, the obligation for all to attend Mass, nostalgia for their regiment or homeland made a number of them leave, including 34 percent of those whose religion was not recorded, compared with 26 percent of the declared Catholics. Maybe a fair number of the former were Protestants.

Those who left were given 15 Tours livres and a uniform, or 18 livres, to return to their homes. Some left after only a few days, others stayed a little longer, but in no case more than two and a half years. Twenty Poles left after an average stay of eleven months, three Croats after a year, and five Hungarians after six months. Despite their age, three of the Hungarians and two of the Poles asked to return to active service. If the records are correct, one of them was 77, and he later returned to the Invalides to die at age 86.[30]

Again there are indications of differences in the Hungarians' reaction to the Invalides in comparison with the Poles' and Croats'. The former found it harder to adapt to conditions there. The remainder of the 63 men died at the Invalides—23 Poles, two Hungarians and two Croats—after stays varying from one to seventeen years. On average, after leaving the regiment the Poles stayed for 6 years 2 months, the Hungarians 4 years 11 months, and the Croats, who were admitted particularly late, 1 year 3 months. The average age at death was 62 years 7 months for the Poles, 63 years for the Hungarians and 65 years for the Croats.

Only three of these East European veterans were listed as married, one in Alsace, the others in Lorraine; two of them left the Invalides, the third returned to active duty. As the Invalides registers list only 18 unmarried men, there remain 42 whose marital status is unknown. It does not appear as if this was always due to a clerk's negligence, as 18 (53 percent) of these men left the home compared with only eight (44 percent) of the bachelors. Married men were not favored at the Invalides because, since women were not admitted, they had to leave their wives.

It is extremely difficult to say if many of these soldiers from Central and Eastern Europe established families in France. During this period usage soon gallicized foreign names, and it is not always easy to trace Slavic or Magyar roots in names that look French. The ending *-niak* soon came to be written *-gnac*, for instance. Yet it was undoubtedly difficult for these men to blend into the general population, except perhaps in France's German-speaking provinces.

Two of the East European veterans were absorbed into French society. The first, André Roze, known as Iaroslav, born at "Myaouslaff" in Poland, aged 60, married in Alsace and retired there.[31] The second was Jean Lomiński, a Pole, who was given special licence by War Minister Louvois to retire to Arras where he would receive his soldier's pay from the Invalides. This was an exceptional favor.[32] A third, Georges Marel, a 52-year-old Pole from Kraków, married in France, then rejoined the colors, and returned to the Invalides after seven years to die there at age 72.[33]

These three Poles entered French service in 1658, 1650, and 1656, respectively. The Poles' absorption into French society was facilitated in 1738 by a royal decree granting French nationality to all the Poles living in France then. Stanislaus Leszczyński's presence in France at that time probably encouraged a number of Poles in French service to settle there. The main Polish migration to France, however, did not occur before the Revolution but rather in the nineteenth and twentieth centuries. The sources give no information about Hungarians or Croats settling in France except for a few important families who furnished officers.[34]

From a study that is only just beginning, and from a few random samples from it, it is difficult to obtain results other than conjecture or hypothesis. Yet these indications are of some value.

Provisionally, then, it appears reasonable to assume that military migration from Eastern and Central Europe to France during the seventeenth and eighteenth centuries involved fewer than 5,000 persons. An extraordinary congeries of individual adventures led them from their homelands to France, which they often reached at a relatively advanced age. Perhaps because of their origins or because they found themselves particularly isolated by virtue of their background—more so than other foreigners—these men were less affected by the scourge of desertion that eroded the armies of Europe in those days. The number of these men whom the king of France allowed into the Invalides was proportionally higher than their strength within the army.

It is possible to note some differences of conduct among them according to their national origins. The Hungarians seem to have adapted least well to France. They remained closely attached to their regiment if it was a hussar unit, which they saw as a creation of their homeland. Croats and, above all, Poles appear to have blended into the French population with greater ease than the Hungarians. This was especially so for the latter even well before King Stanislaus Leszczyński retired to France. Perhaps the French government gave them more help?

In any case, through all the upheavals caused by the conquests and fall of Napoleon, as well as later by the revolutions in Poland and Hungary, the tradition endured in France of foreigners in the French army. Whenever there was need, France would reconstitute the necessary military structures to receive these foreigners. And among the Central and East Europeans, too, the tradition of service to France was never entirely lost.

## Notes

1. Archives de la Guerre, Paris, Mémoires et reconnaissances, 1722, No. 10, 1780, Anon.
2. *Ibid.*, 1777, No. 4, September 29, 1711.
3. Quoted in *Ibid.*, 1722, No. 10.
4. Susane, *Histoire de la cavalerie française* (Paris, 1874), II, 107–116: *Histoire de l'infanterie française* (Paris, 1853), VIII, 339.
5. Susane, *Histoire de la cavalerie française*, II, 75–85.
6. *Ibid.*, III, 297.
7. Archives de la Guerre, Paris, A[1] 2770, items 12 & 13, June 20, 1720. See also E. Fieffé, *Histoire des troupes étrangères au service de la France* (Paris, 1854) [now rather dated]; J. Mathorez, *Les étrangers en France* (Paris, 1919), I, 266–288.
8. Archives de la Guerre, Paris, A[1] 3407, No. 22, Letter from Bercsényi to the minister, Lunéville, April 10, 1756.
9. *Ibid.*, A[1] 3200. See also André Corvisier, "Les soldats noirs du Maréchal de Saxe," *Revue Française d'Histoire d'Outre-Mer*, Vol. LV (1968).
10. Archives de la Guerre, Paris, A[1] 2969, No. 20, January 28, 1742.
11. *Ibid.*, A[1] 3611, No. 115, December 21, 1762.
12. *Ibid.*, A[1] 3069, No. 65, September, 24, 1744.
13. *Ibid.*, A[1] 2969, No. 32, January 1, 1742.
14. *Ibid., No. 32 bis, February 5, 1742.*
15. *Archives de la Guerre, Paris, 7 Yc 278 and 7 Yc 40, Muster rolls of the De Saxe Volunteer Regiment.*
16. *Ibid.* A[1] 3123, No. 60, Usingen, April 9, 1745.

17. *Ibid.*, $A^1$ 3000, No. 187.

18. *Ibid.*, $A^1$ 3069, No. 116.

19. *Ibid.*, $A^1$ 3407, No. 350, December 28, 1756.

20. *Ibid.*, $A^1$ 3394, No. 65, 1748, Plan for the discharge of hussar units.

21. *Ibid.*, $A^1$ 3407, No. 30, Coded letter from M. de Tott to the minister Constantinople, May 15, 1756.

22. *Ibid.*, 3 Yc 311, Muster roll of the Rattsky Regiment, 1729.

23. *Ibid.*, $A^1$ 3072, No. 25, Letter from M. de Senneterre to the Minister, Turin, December 20, 1736.

24. André Corvisier, *L'armée française de la fin du XVIIe siècle au ministère de Choiseul: Le soldat* (Paris, 1964), I 655, Table.

25. *Ibid.*, 806–807.

26. Muster roll of the King's Regiment, 2nd Battalion, Le Camus Co., 1 Yc 813.

27. Corvisier, *L'armée française*, I, 655.

28. Archives de la Guerre, Paris, Admission registers of the Invalides, Nos. 6–10.

29. Moheau affirmed that in France he found no more than one man in 30 between the ages of 16 and 40 years whose real height was five *pieds* (1.624 meters or 5 feet 4 inches) or more. Moheau, *Recherches et considérations sur la population de la France (1778)*. One *pied* (French foot) = 0.3248 meter; one *pouce* (French inch) = 0.02707 meter.

30. Invalides, Register 10, No. 3318.

31. *Ibid.*, Register 6, No. 834.

32. *Ibid.*, Register 10, No. 4388.

33. *Ibid.*, No. 4392.

34. Parish registers occasionally record cases of abjuration by Hungarian Protestant soldiers and of their marriages in very unexpected parts of France. The Orléans City Archives record the abjuration of five Hungarian prisoners of war in 1706. Mathorez, *Les étrangers en France*, I, 284–285.

# Appendix

## The Impact of *Devşirme* on Greek Society

Vasiliki Papoulia

# The Impact of *Devşirme* on Greek Society*

Although there has been some satisfactory research concerning the institution of the *devşirme* additional work dealing with this Ottoman practice is still needed. One very important difficulty encountered by the researcher is the dearth of statistical data, but he faces also a methodological and, indeed, a logical difficulty. Most of those who wrote about the influence of the *devşirme* on the Christian population really discussed only the negative aspect of this influence. Yet to determine the true extent of this influence it is important to find out what the situation of the Christian population would have been if such an institution had not existed. To state simpy that it totally silenced the *reaya* is inconclusive. The great historian Leopold von Ranke had such a statement in mind when he wrote that the first heroic song of Christos Melionis rang out in the mountains only after the abolition of this heavy tithe of blood.[1] On the other hand, one could maintain that this oppressive measure rendered the Turkish rule so hateful that it led eventually to the uprisings of the Christians. It is quite possible that the *devşirme* was both stultifying and incendiary. In other words, this institution could have played a restraining role for as long as it lasted while creating conditions which were so traumatic that they brought about the uprising even after its disappearance.[2] One is forced, therefore, to hypothesize with regard to the impact of this institution. The ground is much firmer when some aspects related to the function of this institution are studied: for example, the number of the recruited children; the resistance of the population; the reasons for the abolition of the *devşirme;* the frequency of recruitment; the phenomenon of the alienation from the ethnic milieu of a segment of the population; the

*Although *devşirme* no longer existed during the period covered by this volume, its lasting effect on relations between the Ottoman Turks and the Balkan nations was so profound that the inclusion of this essay seems fitting. *Editors.*

Islamization which is related to the alienation, in spite of the fact that the available data are restricted. We are, therefore, confronted with a peculiar situation. As far as the impact of the *devşirme* as a whole is concerned, we are, on the one hand, not bound so much by statistical data, but we must be very careful because of the resulting general methodological difficulty which is, after all, present in every aspect of scientific research and especially in history. On the other hand, as far as the particular aspects of the institution are concerned, we do not have such methodological reservations, but we deal with insufficient data. We are therefore obliged to consider both sides of the problem and thus arrive, both indirectly and directly, at the essence.

Before presenting my views on the *devşirme*, I would like to mention those of Arnold Toynbee. According to him, nomadic states collapse due to their unsatisfactory adaptation to life *in partibus agricolarum*. There is, however, the exception of the Ottoman Empire which was able to flourish for over 300 years. Toynbee tried to find an explanation for this exception in the successful substitution of an essential element of the nomadic life, the nonhuman actor, the secondary animals, by humans. These animals played a very important role in the nomadic life because, although they were not productive, they assisted the nomads in their work: for example, they protected the herds and kept them in obedience. The same function was performed by the *Kapı kulları* the slaves of the Porte. The sultans recruited Christian children who fell into their hands either by capture, by purchase or by tithe of blood. In Ottoman Society the nomadic life is represented by three elements: the sultan and his military caste (the feudal cavalry); the enslaved population—the rayah (the herd); and the *Kapı kulları* including the *Iç Oğlan*, the *Acemi Oğlans*, the janissaries, the spahis of the Porte, etc. Here in a rather figurative sense, we have an adaptation of the nomadic life to a settled environment. I cannot discuss here the explanatory value of Toynbee's theory. I have done this in an article, "Uber die Knabelese im osmanischen Reich: Bemerkungen zur Theorie Arnold Toynbees," *Byzantina*, III (1971), 389–407. I just want to point out that it lacks specific explanatory value because it is too general and therefore it applies to all repressive societies in which the ruling class kept a part of the population in obedience, in subjection, by means of specialized forces which play the role of watchdogs. Nevertheless, Toynbee's picture is valuable because it enables us to capture an essential dimension of the whole phenomenon. However, in order to grasp better this essence we must complete the picture presented by Toynbee with results of a different level of research.

In my view,[3] the creation of all the slave guards in the Islamic world constitute an attempt by the Islamic nomadic societies to adapt to the new conditions that they faced during the transitory stage between the collapse of the tribal society, the old foundation of the ruling order, and the establishment of permanent settlements. These guards constituted a sort of artificial tribal grouping affiliation (a fake adoption) by the soveriegn who did not possess those social elements from which a sovereign could draw support. The Islamic factor is an important one because only in the Islamic world do we encounter the phenomonen of military slavery to a highly developed degree. The elevation of elements of alien ethnic origin to a special imperial bodyguard, devoted to the sovereign and having special privileges as a result of its direct dependence on him, was possible only on the basis of Islamic law which declares: "Those who submit to the true faith become brothers through Islam." This principle permitted the overcoming of the narrow-minded solidarity of the *aşabiyyah*. The result was the very peculiar phenomenon of the creation of new bonds of social solidarity on the basis of an artificial kinship between the sovereign and his slaves. This bodyguard had the task of protecting the sovereign from internal and external enemies. In order to fulfill this task it was subjected to very rigorous and special training, the janissary education famous in Ottoman society. This training made possible the spiritual transformation of Christian children into ardent fighters for the glory of the sultan and their newly acquired Islamic faith. Besides these two main factors, Islamic law and nomadic tradition, that made the *devşirme* possible, there is a third important one, the absolute character of the dynastic power. It functioned as a leveling instrument on the social status of all subjects and created the necessary institutional frame for the elevation of these slaves to the status of the ruling class for more than three centuries, discriminating to the detriment of the native Muslim element. It must be noted that no native Muslim rose above the rank of sanjakbey for a considerable time span.

Although Toynbee's and my interpretations are based on differing approaches, they converge on significant points. First, in both analyses an integrative process of new elements into Ottoman society appears and, second, this integration is seen as the result of a complete alienation of its new members from their origins.[4] Toynbee's concept differs from mine because he sees these children as substitutes for secondary animals, while I feel that they were degraded to the level of animals, as shown by their dog-like devotion to the sultan in time of peace and their wild behavior when in revolt, reminiscent both of the blind devotion of domestic animals and their occasional feral outbursts. Contemporary texts also allude to this behavior pattern. It is interesting to note that this type of alienation corresponds from the point of view of philosophical anthropology to the alienation of the Middle Ages when the alienated man was regarded not as a thing *(res)* as in the ancient Mediterranean societies (characteristic of commercial societies), but as a semi-animal, semi-human being, according to Friedrich Tomberg in his work, *Polis und Nationalstaat.* He was still considered semi-human because he still deserved respect as a Christian who can win the kingdom of God in the next world (he had a soul), and as a semi-animal because he was treated as one in the present world by the powers which required his services.[5] In the same manner a janissary was a human because he could attain the Moslem paradise, but in life he was at the disposal of his master who had the power to kill him without justification, load him down with all burdens of everyday life and with all the tasks necessary for the preservation of order in the *reaya* society as well as with the defense of the sovereign from every enemy. That this task raised the slaves to a ruling class does not change the essence of their situation, the alienation of the man. Tomberg does not mention it, nor does Toynbee allude to this dimension of the *devşirme* system. This institution is a representative example of the alienation of the man's personality, of his inner transformation into an instrument in the hands of a militant political power.[6] This sort of alienation corresponds to the semi-nomadic, semi-agrarian Ottoman society.

To what extent was this inner transformation of the children and young boys complete? This question is hard to answer given the paucity of relevant sources. This dearth of information is, of course, another expression of the alienation of these children. Nevertheless we do learn from certain sources that it was not rare for these young men to attempt to preserve their faith and some recollection of their homeland and their families. For instance, Stephan Gerlach writes: "They gather together and one tells another of his native land and of what he heard in church or learned in school there, and they agree among themselves that Muhammad is no prophet and that the Turkish religion is false. If there is one among them who has some little book or can teach them in some other manner something of God's world, they hear him as diligently as if he were their preacher."[7]

The Greek scholar Janus Kaskaris, who visited Constantinople in 1491, found among the janissaries many who not only remembered their former religion and their native land but also favored their former coreligionists. The renegade Hersek, the sultan's relative by marriage, told him that he regretted having left the religion of his fathers and that he prayed at night before the cross which he kept carefully concealed.[8]

It is possible that the characterization of Gerlach with regard to two renegades that they were "neither Christian nor Turk" also holds true for several others of these Christian children. We also know that the patron of the janissary corps was Hacci Bektaş, the founder of the Bektaşi Order, which, like all Islamic orders, had many syncretic elements as a result of the symbiosis of the Turks and Christians in Asia Minor and in the Balkans. The lack of family ties—the Greeks named them *apatores* and *amitores* (fatherless and motherless)—had as a result that the janissary corps took on the characteristics of a brotherhood, of a *Männerbund*, with strong solidarity bonds. The discrepancy between the external peaceful appearance of the janissaries giving the impression of monks (after the vivid description of Busbeck in his *De re militari*[9]) and their dreadful activities not only against enemies but also against the Christian and Turkish population in time of war or revolt is an expression of their peculiar situation. They are the *pessimum hominum genus*, the *diaboli aulici* of the Greeks.[10]

The consciousness that they had been born of Christian parents naturally bred in them feelings of guilt resulting in a strong aversion to their fellow countrymen. One might say that it was this guilt that drove them to such outbursts of fanaticism—the other side of alienation. For the essence of alienation is the individual's confusion between himself and his controlling environment

The cultural *niveau* of a society is in direct correlation to its ability to understand and to feel events that affect its existence. The higher this *niveau*, the deeper the tragedy is felt. It is easy, therefore, to understand the dramatic tone of the relevant Greek texts that have survived. For the parents this complete transformation of the children with its familiar consequences meant the total loss, as fatal as death. In the Tübingen manuscript written by Andre Argyros and John Tholoites and given in 1585 to Martin Crusius, these feelings are vividly described: "You undertand, then, my lords and Christian gentlemen, what sorrow the Greeks bear, the fathers and the mothers who are separated from their children at the prime of life. Think ye of the heart-rending sorrow! How many mothers scratch out their cheeks! How many fathers beat their breast with stones! What grief these Christians experience on account of their children who are separated from them while alive, and how many mothers say, 'It would have been better to see them dead and buried in our church, rather than to have them taken alive in order to become Turks and abjure our faith. Better that you had died.'"[11]

It seems that this sentiment was often expressed because Gerlach cites the case of a women from Panormos in Asia Minor who had two handsome sons and daily begged God to take them away because she would soon have to give up one of them.[12] The distress expressed here was motivated not only by religious considerations, which are easy to understand during that particular period, but also by the low opinion which the Byzantines held about the barbarians.[13]

It is obvious that the population strongly resented the recruitment of their children and that this measure could be carried out only by force. Those who refused to surrender their sons—the healthiest, the handsomest and the most intelligent—were on the spot put to death by hanging.[14] Nevertheless we have examples of armed resistance. In 1565 a revolt took place in Epirus and Albania. The inhabitants killed the recruiting officers and the revolt was put down only after the sultan sent five hundred janissaries in support of the local sanjak-bey.[15] We are better informed, thanks to the historic archives of Yerroia, about the uprising in Naousa in 1705 where the inhabitants killed the *Silahdar* Ahmed Çelebi and his assistants and fled to the mountains as rebels. Some of them were later arrested and put to death.[16]

Since there was no possibility of escaping recruitment the population resorted to several subterfuges.[17] Some left their villages and fled to certain cities which enjoyed exemption from the child levy or migrated to Venetian-held territories. The result was a depopulation of the countryside. Others had their children marry at an early age. Many exchanged their children with those of their Muslim neighbors who hoped that their son would thus attain a successful career, or purchased uncircumcised boys from poor Muslims. Often they sent their children to hide in the mountains or in the homes of Turkish officials who, according to Nicephorus Angelus, were friendly towards the Greeks.[18] The same writer states that at times the children ran away on their own initiative, but when they heard that the authorities had arrested their parents and were torturing them to death, returned and gave themselves up. La Guilletière cites the case of a young Athenian who returned from hiding in order to save his father's life and then chose to die himself rather than abjure his faith.[19] According to the evidence in Turkish sources, some parents even succeeded in abducting their children after they had been recruited. The most successful way of escaping recruitment was through bribery. That the latter was very widespread is evident from the large amounts of money confiscated by the sultan from corrupt recruiting officials. Finally, in their desperation the parents even appealed to the Pope and the Western powers for help.[20] Of course, the reactions of the population were not always the same. As it is shown from the writings of Trevisano, Crusius and Gerlach, parents in times of great need wished that their children were among the chosen—since they usually took the best-looking, healthiest, and most intelligent—sometimes bringing themselves their children to those who came to collect them in order to get rid of the burden of supporting them. Hoping that their children would thus have a better opportunity.[21] These cases, however, must be the exceptions and not the rule, since it is contrary to human nature for parents to part happily with their children forever.

The methods that were used for the child recruitment as well as its results regarding the loss of a vital segment of the population constitute the elements which define it within the frame of political theory as a *de facto* state of war. The fact also that the Greek term *paidomazoma*[22] does not appear—to be exact—before the seventeenth century, and that the sources speak of *piasimo* (seizure) *aichmalotos paidon* (capture) and *arpage paidon* (grabbing of children)[26] indicates that the children lost through the *devşirme* were understood as casualties of war.[23] Of course, the question arises whether, according to Islamic law, it is possible to regard the *devşirme* as a form of the state of war, although the Ottoman historians during the empire's golden age attempted to interpret this measure as a consequence of conquest by force *be'anwa.* It is true that the Greeks and the other peoples of the Balkan peninsula did not as a rule surrender without resistance, and therefore the fate of the conquered had to be determined according to the principles of the Koran regarding the *Ahl-al-Qitâb:* i.e. either to be exterminated or be compelled to convert to Islam or to enter the status of protection, of *aman*, by paying the taxes and particularly the *cizye* (poll-tax). The fact that the Ottomans, in the case of voluntary surrender, conceded certain privileges one of which was exemption from this heavy burden, indicates that its measure was understood as a penalization for the resistance of the population and the *devşirme* was an expression of the perpetuation of the state of war between the conqueror and the conquered.[24] We cannot, unfortunately, discuss here in detail the subtleties of Islamic law regarding the state of war, but the sole existence of the institution of *devşirme* is sufficient to postulate the perpetuation of a state of war. I can only mention here that we cannot view *devşirme* as being in accordance with the holy law.[25]

In conclusion, in order to determine the number of Greek casualties in this peculiar case of a society at war, we need adequate statistics which we unfortunately lack.[26] Of course, a very important element in determining the number of losses is the exact date of the beginning of child-levy. It is evident that the earlier it started, the greater the losses. Another important point concerns the frequency of recruitment and the number of children recruited. Unfortunately the sources do not present a clear picture regarding these matters. Nevertheless we can arrive, directly or indirectly, at certain conclusions and determine certain stages in the process. As far as the beginning of the institution is concerned, there is no reason to doubt the testimony of the historians of the empire's golden age, Idris and Saadeddin, that *devşirme* was introduced during the reign of Orhan, about 1330. It is, however, certain that recruitment was not frequent until the time of Murad II who reorganized the janissary corps and established periodic recruitment every five years.[27] But this was not a regular procedure. Recruitment could take place every four, three or two years, and at times even annually, according to the needs of the sultan. The biggest losses in children coincided with the peak of Ottoman expansion in the fifteenth and sixteenth centuries under Selim I and Süleyman the Magnificent. A decline in the numbers occurred during the reign of Selim II when the sons of janissaries were permitted to join the janissary corps. At a diminishing rate the recruitment of Christian children continued in later centuries to meet the needs of the Porte for slaves. From the seventeenth century the levy of children continued to lose its importance until it slowly disappeared. Occasional recruitments took place until the rebellion of 1705 and perhaps also later. Finally, though a final consideration of the total losses is impossible, there is no doubt that this heavy burden was one of the hardest tribulations of the Christian population.

A general estimation of the influence of the institution within the framework of the Greek society results in the conclusion that this influence was mainly defined by the perpetuation of the state of war mentioned above and had its impact not only on the demographical level, but also on the psychological, because it sharpened, to a great degree, the hostile relations between the conqueror and the conquered. Certainly it cannot be coincidental that the evolution of the Ottoman society is characterized by a deep antithesis that led to the creation of fighting gangs in mountainous regions whose members eventually became the liberation armies of the Christian population. To what extent there existed a direct relation between the two phenomena, of the instutiton of *devşirme* and the revolutionary movements, is not easy to define nor the degree of this negative demographic influence be assessed because without doubt this institution was a bleeding for the Greek, and more generally, for the Christian community of the Ottoman Empire. In a text from the beginning of the seventeenth century, the *threnos* of Metropolitan Matthaios Myreon, we can find an allusion to a revolutionary attitude. On the one hand, he scorns the Greeks for expecting their liberation for pseudo-prophecies and the Great Powers, and on the other hand, he enumerates the evils of the Turkish domination, among them the *devşirme.*[28] Clearer is the relationship between revolutionary attitudes and the existence of this institution, which was felt as a calamity, in the petition of Janus Lascaris to the Emperor Charles V.[29] It can be said that a connecting link in this evoution was the revolt of the inhabitants of Naousa in 1705, at which time they killed the Turks who were entrusted with the levy of the children.

The appearance of outlaw bands in the mountains was, in part, a result of the repressive character of the Turkish domination. These groups formed a kind of "subculture" that arose from the reaction to it. This subculture meant a regression from the social point of view, a regression to patriarchical patterns of social action, but it led through revolutionary activity to a new political organization. It seems as if a state of permanent war passed from the conquered to the conquerors. Nevertheless, we cannot postulate a direct causal relation between the two pheomonena. *Devşirme* and revolutionary gangs were parallel phenomena but on different levels. We understand this better if we remember that these slave guards were sort of artificial tribes which the sovereign needed after the dissolution of the original social order as a result of his domain's growth. Robbery, as a way to solve the economic problem and as a way to escape from a humiliating *reaya* existence as a cultivator of the great domains of the Turkish landowners and *tımarlı,* belongs to the same level of social activity, to a partiarchical conception of life. Naturally it would be a simplification if we wanted to maintain that this characteristic concerns the whole social structure of the Ottoman Empire. It is a phenomenon that appears in some regions. It is an expression of the "segmentary" nature of the Turkish Empire in the sense that E. Durkheim gives to the term, as we pointed out in another context speaking about professional differentiation and the social mobility in the Ottoman society. It is perhaps owing to this segmentary nature of Ottoman society that one cannot strictly speak of a direct connection between these related phenomena.

## Notes

1. Leopold von Ranke, *Die Osmanen und die spanische Monarchie im sechzehnten und siebzehnten Jahrhundert,* 4. Aufl. Berlin 1877, p. 69–70; G.F. Herzberg, *Geschichte der Byzantiner und des Osmanischen Reiches bis gegen Ende des sechzehnten Jahrhunderts,* Berlin 1883, p. 121 agrees with Ranke: "Nun erst Konnte wieder von einem Aufblühen der physischen wie der moralischen Volkskraft die Rede sein, seitdem nicht mehr die besten jügendlichen Kräfte der Nation ihr für immer entfremdet wurden. Wie aber die Dinge in Griechenland einmal lagen, wirkte die Abstellung des Knaben-Zins hier zuerst am fühlbarsten zurück auf den Aufschwung des Klephtenthums. Ein grosser Historiker macht mit gewohntem Scharfblicke darauf aufmerksam, dass der erste Klephte, den die Lieder der Neugriechen preisen, noch in dem siebzehnten Jahrhundert seine wilde Laufbahn eröffnet." Here it is clear that Herzberg finds, as Ranke does, a close relationship between the abolition of the *devşirme* and the revolutionary activity of the enslaved Greeks.

2. This is demonstrated by the various petitions that are mainly directed to the influential men of that time, begging them to free them from the Turkish yoke (see n. 20 below). The "Digisis synoptiki" (Brief Accounts) of Ioannis Axagioles in *Karolos o E'tis Germanias kai i pros apeleftherosin prospathia* (Charles V of Germany and Attempts toward Liberation), edited by

G. Zoras. Proceedings of the School of Philosophy, Athens University, 2 (1954) pp. 420–472 describes the lamentation of parents who take refuge in monasteries and beg God with tears in their eyes to deliver them from the Turkish yoke. In a song of Epirus (P. Aravantinos, *Syllogi dimodon asmaton tis Epirou* (Society of the Popular Songs of Epirus) Athens, 1880, p. 3) the sultan is anathematized for this evil deed. "Damn you king and damn you again for the evil you have done, the evil you are doing. You push aside the old men, the elders, and the clergy. You gather all the young ones and make them janissaries. Cry you mothers for the young, sisters for the brothers, and I cry and despair, last year they took my son, this year my brother."

3. Cf. B. Papoulia, *Ursprung und Wesen der "Knabenlese" im Osmanischen Reich*, München 1963 (:Südosteuropäische Arbeiten 59), where the older bibliography and all the known sources concerning the *devşirme* can be found.

4. The term alienation is used here in a broad sense to include the economic as well as the moral and spiritual dependency and exploitation of the people. Regarding the stages of this alienation cf. my work mentioned above regarding Toynbee (pp. 404–407).

5. Friedrich Tomberg: *Polis und Nationalstaat Eine vergleichende Überbau Analyse im Anschluss an Aristoteles.* Darmstadt und Neuwied; Sammlung Luchterhand, 93), p. 184.

6. Leopold von Ranke describes very characteristically this development as a result of complete seclusion and severe collective life, a principle that was once proposed by a German philosopher allowing a new will to appear in the place of the old: "Die hier erzogenen, ihrer ersten Jugend, ihrer Eltern, ihrer Heimat vergessend, kennen kein Vaterland als das Serai, keinen Herrn und Vater als den Grossherrn, keinen Willen als den seinen, keine Hoffnung als auf seine Gunst; sie kennen kein Leben als in strenger Zucht und in unbedingtem Gehorsam, keine Beschäftigung als den Krieg zu seinem Dienst, für sich keinen Zweck als etwa im Leben Beute, im Tode das Paradies, das der Kampf dür den Islam eröffnet." Was der Philosoph zur Bildung von Sittlichkeit, Religion und Gemeinschaft in der Idee vorgeschlagen hat, ist hier, Jahrhunderte vor ihm zur Entwicklung eines zugleich sklavischen und doch kriegerischen Sinnes in Ausführung gebracht. *Die Osmanen und die spanische Monarchie*, p. 12.

7. Stephan Gerlach, *Tage-Buch der von . . . Kaysern Maximiliano und Rudolpho an die ottomanische Pforte . . . abgefertigten Gesandtschaft herfür gegeben durch Samuel Gerlach* (Frankfurt/M, 1674), p. 3. See also Denys A. Zakythinos, *The Making of Modern Greece. From Byzantium to Independence* (Oxford: 1976), pp. 26–30.

8. E. Legrand, *Bibliographie hellénique*, p. clvi; Sathas, *Tourkokratoumeni Ellas* [Turkish-Occupied Greece], (Athens, 1868), p. 85. The same information is also given by Bartholomeo Georgewitz, *De Turcarum*

*moribus epitome*, p. 100. See also A. E. Vakalopoulos, *Istoria tou Neou Ellenismou* [History of Neo-Hellenism], $B^1$, *Tourkokratia 1453–1669* II:(Thessaloniki, 1964), p. 55, n. 2.

9. Cf. Augerius Gislenius Busbequius, *De legationis Turcicae epistolae quatuor . . . eiusdem de re militari contra Turcam instituenda consilium* (Hanover, 1605), p. 15 (text of the English translation, p. 87): "These janissaries generally came to me in pairs. When they were admitted to my dining room they first made a bow and then came quickly up to me, all but running and touched my dress or hand, as if they intended to kiss it. After this they would thrust into my hand a nosegay of hyacinth or narcissus; then they would run back to the door almost as quickly as they came, taking care not to turn their backs, for this, according to their code, would be a serious breach of etiquette. After reaching the door, they would stand respectfully with their arms crossed, and their eyes bent on the ground, looking more like monks than warriors. On receiving a few small coins (which was what they wanted) they bowed again, thanked me in loud tones and went off blessing me for my kindness. To tell you the truth, if I had not been told beforehand that they they were janissaries, I should, without hesitation, have taken them for members of some order of Turkish monks or brethren of some Moslem College. Yet there are the famous janissaries, whose approach inspires terror everywhere."

10. Martin Crusius, S. Cabasilas, *Turcograeciae libri octo* (ed.) (Basiliae 1584), Annotations, p. 193.

11. K. Dyobuniotes, *Anakoinosis* . . . [Communication . . .] (Athens, Proceedings of the Academy of Athens, No. 11, 1936), p. 275.

12. Gerlach, *Tagebuch*, p. 257.

13. S. Bryonis, "Isidore Glabas and the Turkish Devshirme," *Spéculum* XXXI (1956) 433–444.

14. Cf. K. Vasdravelle, *Istorikon archion Verroias* [Historical Archives of Verroia] (Thessaloniki, 1942), pp. 10–12, where orders to the Beylerbey of Rumeli, dated March 29, 1601, can be found that include the following: "You must also know that the *bubasirides* that will be sent will have by my permission the right to enforce, when necessary, the provisions of the holy feta according to which parent of the infidel or anyone else, resists the surrender of his janissary son, is to be hanged at his front door, his blood regarded of no value."

15. Cf. J. W. Zinkeisen, *Geschichte des Osmanischen Reiches in Europa*, III (Hamburg, 1955), 220–221; E. Charrière, *Négotiation de la France dans le Levant*, II, (Paris, 1850), p. 802, also B. Papoulia, *Ursprung und Wesen den Kanben leve Istorikon Arhion Verrias* (Historical Archives of Verria), p. 109. n. 3.

16. Ch J. K. Basdrabelles, p. 45 ff. *Armatoloi Kai Klephteseis tin Makedo-*

*nian* [Armatoles and Klephts in Macedonia] (Makedonike Bibliothese, (Thessaloniki, 1948), pp. 13 ff., 54 ff., 70 ff.

17. The case of Giovan Antonio Menavino, author of *Trattato de costumi et vita de Turchi* (Firenze, 1548), is an interesting one. He managed to escape after 10 years of service as *iç Oĝlan*, and to return to this home in Vultri, Italy. He had been captured by Turkish pirates at the age of twelve. His escape and return had a meaning only because his family lived outside of the Ottoman realm. Such an escape was not possible for the Greek and other Christian youths of the Balkans, as shown in the related documents. Cf. Ahmet Refik, *Devşirme usulü Acemi Oğlanlar* (Edebiyat- Fakultesi Meĝmû asî, 5, 1927) p. 10.

18. Nichephoros Angelos, *Enchiridium de statu hodiernorum Graecorum . . . cum versione latine . . .* (Lipsiae, 1666), p. 62.

19. La Guilletière, *Athènes ancienne et nouvelle*, (Paris, 3rd ed., 1676), This incident is confirmed by J.B. Babin, *Relation de l' état présent de la ville d'Athènes*, (Lyon, 1674), pp. 56 f.

20. For the petition of the Greeks of Asia Minor addressed to the Grand Master of the Knights Hospitalers of Rhodes, Jacques de Milly (1451–61), see F. Miklosich J. Mîler, *Acta et diplomata medaevi sacra et profana* (Vienna, 1860–1890). The English translation from Sp. Vryonis, Jr. *The Decline of Medieval Hellenism in Asia Minor and the Process of Islamization from the Eleventh through the Fifteenth Century* (Berkeley and Los Angeles, 1971) p. 442. We have also another petition of the inhabitants of Himara from the year 1581, addressed to the Pope: "Holiest father, if you could convince him and save us and the children of Greece, that are taken every day and are turned into Turks, if you could only do this, God may bless you. Amen" A. Theiner F. Miklosich, *Monumenta spectantia ad unionem ecclesiarum*, (Vienna, 1872), p. 59. Cf. the other sources concerning the reaction of the Greek population in Papoulia, *Ursprung und Wesen, pp. 109*–111.

21. *Ibid.*, p. 112 n. 11.

22. As "Paidomazoma", "jannitsaromazoma", (*Ibid.* p. 59 note 49, p. 80 note 12, p. 94 and 94 note 14, p. 109 note 3).

23. As "piasmos paidon", "arpaqi paidon", "dekatismos paidon", "syllogi paidon," "poniron ethos." (*Ibid.*, p. 49 n. 16, p. 80 ns. 11 and 12.)

24. H.A.R. Gibb—H. Bowen, *Islamic Society and the West*, Vol. I Pt. 2 (London — New York — Toronto, 1957), p. 223, sees the *paidomazoma* as "penalization on this score for the sins of their fathers."

25. Papoulia, *Ursprung und Wesen p.p.* 47–54.

26. There have been some efforts to calculate the population losses resulting from the *devşirme.* Joseph v. Hammer (*Geschichte des Osmanischen Reiches*, I (Pest, 1934), 98) expressed the opinion that the recruited children must have been 500,000 while K. Paparregopoulos *(Istoria tou*

*hellenikou ethnous)* [History of the Greek People], vol. 5, Pt. 1, p. 15 raised the number to one million. As A. Vakalopoulos *(op. cit.*, p. 59) pointed out these numbers are not based on real evidence. The losses of the Greeks were heavy in the early period of occupation but with time they succeeded to restrict them. From Giovio (Jovius Paulus), *Turcicarum rerum commentarius* (Paris, 1538), p. 94, and Ch. Richer, *Des Coustumes et manières de vivre des Turcs* (Paris, 1542), we learn that the janissaries of their time spoke mostly a Slavonic dialect.

27. A. E. Vakalopoulos, "Provlimata tis istorias tou paidmazomatos" [Problems Concerning the History of the Child-Levy], *Hellinika,* XIII (1954), pp. 274–293.

28. E. Legrand, *Bibliothèque grecque vulgaire,* II (Paris, 1881), 313, 321 and 322.

29. B. Knös, *Un ambassadeur de l'hellénisme -Janus Lascaris- et la tradition grécobyzantine dans l'humanisme français* (Uppsala-Paris, 1945), p. 191.

# Toponymic Index

Many communities are known by a variety of names, according to the language of the speaker referring to them. As a result of the massive redrafting of the map of Eastern Europe and the rise of nationalism, many towns and districts cited in the foregoing pages appear under different names in today's atlases. The list below shows to the left the name used in the text and to the right the name that appears on late-twentieth-century English-language maps.

| | |
|---|---|
| Adrianople | Edirne |
| Akerman | Belgorod Dnestrovskiy |
| Árva | Orava |
| Avretalan | Koprivshtitsa |
| Bender | Bendery |
| Breslau | Wrocław |
| Brixen | Bressanone |
| Candia | Iráklion |
| Cernăuţi | Chernovtsy |
| Cherkassk | Novocherkassk |
| Cherson | Sevastopol |
| Chocim | Khotin |
| Cozluge | Kostlidzhi |
| Danzig | Gdańsk |
| Domstadtl | Domašov |
| Glatz | Kłodzko |
| Gross Jägersdorf | Mezhdurechye |
| Gyulafehérvár | Alba Iulia |
| Hotin | Khotin |
| Işkodra | Shkodër |
| Ismail | Izmail |
| Jassy | Iaşi |
| Josefstadt | Josefov |
| Kamieniec Podolsk | Kamenets Podol'skiy |

| | |
|---|---|
| Karlowitz | Sremski Karlovci |
| Königgrätz | Hradec Králové |
| Kuchuk Kainarji | Kaynardzha |
| Küçük Kaynarca | Kaynardzha |
| Kunersdorf | Kunovice |
| Lepanto | Návpaktos |
| Lerin | Flórina |
| Leuthen | Lutynia |
| Liegnitz | Legnica |
| Morea | Peloponnese/Pelopónnisos |
| Nagyszombat | Trnava |
| Neisse | Nysa |
| Nisch | Niš |
| Olmütz | Olomouc |
| Orhei | Orgeev |
| Otlukköy | Panagyurishte |
| Passarowitz | Požarevac |
| Philadelphia | Alaşehir |
| Podgorica | Titograd |
| Pozsega | Požega |
| Ragusa | Dubrovnik |
| Reval | Tallin |
| Rodosto | Tekirdağ |
| Salonika | Thessaloníki |
| Schweidnitz | Świdnica |
| Scutari | Shkodër *or* Skadar |
| Seres | Sérrai |
| Sistova | Svishtov |
| Targowica | Novo Arkhangelsk |
| Temesvár | Timişoara |
| Tenedos | Bozca Ada |
| Theresienstadt | Terezin |
| Tighina | Bendery |
| Trent | Trento |
| Tsaritsyn | Volgograd |
| Veles | Titov Veles |
| Voden | Édhessa *or* Edessa |
| Warasdin | Varaždin |
| Wilno | Vilnius |
| Zorndorf | Sarbinowo |

# Contributors

Allmayer-Beck, Johann Christian—Director, Military History Museum, Vienna

Barker, Thomas—Professor of History, SUNY at Albany, Albany, New York

Bracewell, C. Wendy—Ph.D. Candidate, Department of History, Stanford University, California

Căzănişteanu, Constantin—Professor of History, Military History Institute, Bucharest

Ceauşescu, Ilie—Major General, Professor of Military History, Academy of Social and Political Sciences, Bucharest

Constantiniu, Florin—Doctor of History, Nicolae Iorga Institute of History, Bucharest

Corvisier, André—Professor of Modern History, Sorbonne, Paris

Cvetkova, Bistra—Professor of History, University of Sofia

Davies, Norman—Professor of History, School of Slavonic and East European Studies, University of London

Duffy, Christopher J.—Department of War Studies and International Affairs, British Commission for Military History, Royal Military Academy, Sandhurst

Florescu, Radu—Professor of History, Boston College, Boston, Massachusetts

Gierowski, Józef Andrzej—Professor of History, Jagiełłonian University, Kraców

Ingrao, Charles W.—Assistant Professor of History, Purdue University, Lafayette, Indiana

(The late), Kann, Robert A.—Visiting Professor of History, Universty of Vienna, Professor Emeritus of History, Rutgers University, New Jersey

Király, Béla K.—Professor of History, Brooklyn College, Graduate School and University Center, City University of New York, New York

Kitromilides, Paschalis—Research Associate, Center for European Studies, Harvard University, Cambridge, Massachusetts

Kowecki-Jerzy—Professor of History, Institute of History, Polish Academy of Sciences, Warsaw
Levy, Avigdor—Professor of History, Department of Near Eastern and Judaic Studies, Brandeis University, Waltham, Massachusetts
Longworth, Philip—Professor of History, McGill University, Montreal
Menning, Bruce W.—Associate Professor of History, Miami University, Oxford, Ohio
Papoulia, Vasiliki—Professor of Balkan History, Aristotelian University of Thessaloniki
Rauchensteiner, Manfried—Military History Museum, Vienna
Ratajczyk, Leonard—Colonel, Associate Professor of History, Military Historical Institute, Warsaw
Roider, Karl A., Jr.—Assistant Professor of History, Louisiana State University, Baton Rouge, Louisiana
Rostworowski, Emanuel—Professor of History, Institute of History, Polish Academy of Sciences, Warsaw
Rothenberg, Gunther E.—Professor of History, Purdue University, Lafayette, Indiana
Shanahan, William O.—Professor of History, Hunter College, Graduate School and University Center, City University of New York
Stone, Daniel Z.—Associate Professor of History, University of Winnipeg, Canada
Sućeska, Avdo—Professor, Faculty of Law, University of Sarajevo, Yugoslavia
Sugar, Peter F.—Professor of History, University of Washington, Seattle, Washington
Vucinich, Wayne S.—Robert and Florence McDonnell Professor of East European History, Stanford University, Stanford, California
Zgórniak, Marian—Professor of History, Jagiełłonian University, Kraców

# BROOKLYN COLLEGE STUDIES ON SOCIETY IN CHANGE

Distributed by Columbia University Press (Except No. 5)

Editor-in-Chief Béla K. Király

No. 1
*Tolerance and Movements of Religious Dissent in Eastern Europe.* Edited by Béla K. Király, 1975. Second Printing, 1977.

No. 2
*The Habsburg Empire in World War I.* Edited by R.A. Kann, B.K. Király, P.S. Fichtner, 1976. Second Printing, 1978.

No. 3
*The Mutual Effects of the Islamic and the Judeo-Christian Worlds: The East European Pattern.* Edited by A. Ascher, T. Halasi-Kun, B.K. Király, 1979.

No. 4
*Before Watergate: Problems of Corruption in American Society.* Edited by A.S. Eisenstadt, A. Hoogenboom, H.L. Trefousse, 1979.

No. 5
*East Central European Perceptions of Early America.* Edited by B.K. Király and G. Barany. Lisse, The Netherlands: Peter de Ridder Press, 1977. Distributed by Humanities Press.

No. 6
*The Hungarian Revolution of 1956 in Retrospect.* Edited by B.K. Király and Paul Jonas. Second Printing, 1980.

No. 7
Rita S. Miller. *Brooklyn U.S.A.: Fourth Largest City in America,* 1979.

No. 8
János Décsy. *Prime Minister Gyula Andrássy's Influence on Habsburg Foreign Policy.* 1979.

No. 9
Robert F. Horowitz. *The Great Impeacher: A Political Biography of James M. Ashley.* 1979.